THE RHETORIC OF THE HUMAN SCIENCES

The Rhetoric of the Human Sciences

LANGUAGE AND ARGUMENT

IN SCHOLARSHIP AND

PUBLIC AFFAIRS

EDITED BY JOHN S. NELSON,

ALLAN MEGILL, & DONALD N. McCLOSKEY

THE UNIVERSITY OF WISCONSIN PRESS

The University of Wisconsin Press
114 North Murray Street
Madison, Wisconsin 53715

3 Henrietta Street
London WC2E 8LU, England

10   9   8   7   6   5   4   3   2

Printed in the United States of America

Library of Congress Cataloging-in-Publication Data
The Rhetoric of the human sciences.
  (Rhetoric of the human sciences)
  Includes bibliographies and index.
  1. Rhetoric. 2. Learning and scholarship.
3. Research. I. Nelson, John S., 1950–   .
II. Megill, Allan. III. McCloskey, Donald N.
IV. Series.
P301.R465   1987   808   86-34030
ISBN 0-299-11020-6
ISBN 0-299-11024-9 (pbk.)

FOR SPRIE

CONTENTS

vii

PREFACE

This book results from the 1984 University of Iowa Humanities Symposium on the Rhetoric of the Human Sciences. Its essays explore an emerging field of interdisciplinary research on rhetoric of inquiry, a new field that stems from increased attention to language and argument in scholarship and public affairs. It examines how scholars communicate among themselves and with people outside the academy, and it investigates the interaction of communication with inquiry. Thus it tries to improve the conduct and content—as much as the communication—of research.

Rhetoric of inquiry studies what Abraham Kaplan has called "logics in use." But it does not combine them into some general "reconstructed logic." Instead it works within projects of research, to give them greater awareness of their practices and assumptions, and across fields of inquiry, to put them in better communication. It does not replace logic of inquiry as an authority over research in substantive fields; nor can it become an academic discipline in its own right. It seeks merely to increase self-reflection in every inquiry, and already it proceeds as a part of current research in several fields. Yet it remains a dialogue among diverse disciplines because comparison enhances the capacity of each field for self-criticism. In short, rhetoric of inquiry explores how reason is rhetorical and how recognizing that fact should alter research.

Rhetoric of inquiry turns away from modernism and foundationalism in the philosophy of science. It rejects the notion that there can be a single and autonomous set of rules for inquiry—rules standing apart from actual practices. As the name implies, it differs from other postmodern accounts of science in appreciating the importance of *rhetoric*—the quality of speaking and writing, the interplay of media and messages, the judgment of evidence and arguments. Rhetoric of inquiry takes special interest in the accounts that scholars give of their own research, so it is fitting that we introduce the book and its field by telling of the symposium that encouraged them.

The symposium bridged conversations begun recently in many disciplines in order to enrich them and extend them to other fields. Thus its essays compose an early report on the rhetorical turn in scholarship. The book's twenty-two chapters represent most of the academic disciplines in the humanities and social sciences—and several beyond. We asked the authors to write about the rhetorical strategies of their disciplines, explaining what they could contribute to rhetoric of inquiry or what it could learn from them. Most of the essays do all these things, focusing on one field and making some of its rhetorical challenges evident to both specialists and outsiders.

On March 28–31, 1984, the essays were presented at the Old Capitol on the main campus of the University of Iowa; over the ensuing months, they were revised and edited for the book. But the story of the symposium starts four years earlier, when Donald McCloskey and Alan Nagel founded the University of Iowa Rhetoric Seminar. Since then, members of the faculty of the University of Iowa and neighboring institutions have met every two weeks to discuss original papers on questions of rhetoric in research. In the second year of the Rhetoric Seminar, McCloskey proposed that it hold a national conference on what another member, John Nelson, was calling rhetoric of inquiry. Allan Megill joined these two in seeking seed money from the Iowa Humanities Task Force.

A Task Force grant brought Keith Baker, Stephen Graubard, Renato Rosaldo, and Stephen Toulmin to the University's Oakdale campus, where they joined University of Iowa faculty in planning the symposium. Nelson became the principal director of the project, aided by Megill and McCloskey. Jay Semel and Mary Jane McLaughlin of the Iowa Division of Sponsored Programs helped to seek additional funds. The symposium would not have happened without help from many members of the Iowa administration, and the secretarial staffs of the departments of history and political science were also very helpful. The aid of Karen Stewart, administrative assistant in political science, proved particularly indispensable.

Lively discussions during the symposium improved the papers. Thus we thank participants from the University of Iowa: Mitchell Ash, Samuel L. Becker, Lane Davis, Bruce E. Gronbeck, Nancy L. Harper, Linda K. Kerber, Howard Laster, Thomas E. Lewis, Alan F. Nagel, Alan B. Spitzer, Albert E. Stone, and Geoffrey C. Waite. And we thank scholars who traveled to Iowa City: Christina Bicchieri (Barnard), William E. Connolly (Johns Hopkins), Constantine W. Curris (Northern Iowa), Edward Davenport (CUNY), James F. Davidson (Tulane), Clifford Geertz (Institute for Advanced Study), Robert Hollinger (Iowa State), Thomas S. Kuhn (MIT), Larry E. Shiner (Sangamon State), Herbert W. Simons (Temple), Richard F. Somer (Hamilton), and Ira L. Strauber (Grinnell).

All but four of the papers originally prepared for the symposium have been redrafted for this volume. The exceptions appear elsewhere: "Rhetoric and the Writing of History" by Dominick La Capra (Cornell);

"Telling Likely Stories: The Rhetoric of the New Psychology, 1880–1920" by David E. Leary (New Hampshire); "The Literary Character of Economics" by Donald N. McCloskey; and "The 'Objectivity' Question and the Professional Culture of American Historiography" by Peter Novick (Chicago). A short version of the opening remarks of University of Iowa President James O. Freedman has been published in the *New York Times*. Parts of the essay by McCloskey and Megill have appeared in *History and Theory*, and they are reprinted here with the permission of the publisher.

The book begins with an account of the renewal of interest in rhetoric and its significance for inquiries of all kinds. The editors explain the origins and purposes of rhetoric of inquiry. Michael Leff identifies the decisive shifts in rhetoric connected with its recent revival. Then Richard Rorty addresses some rhetorical dimensions of his recent attempt to replace epistemology with hermeneutics in understanding scientific inquiry.

The next ten essays address individual disciplines, ranging from the most naturalistic to the most institutional. Philip Davis and Reuben Hersh examine both rhetorical mathematics and mathematical rhetoric to show that even the citadel of abstraction, rigor, and precision is thoroughly rhetorical. John Campbell portrays Darwin as a self-conscious rhetorician of science whose success was constrained by his rhetorical circumstances. Renato Rosaldo explores objectivity in anthropological fieldwork, showing how styles of rhetoric become epistemic standards for inquiry. Misia Landau highlights the influence on paleoanthropology of narratives about human expulsion and liberation from nature, arguing that better inferences about human evolution depend on better stories about it.

Charles Bazerman analyzes the publication manuals of the American Psychological Association, showing how its rules for professional rhetoric consolidate and carry forward the behaviorism of twentieth-century psychology. Donal Carlston explains what the social psychology of cognition can teach us about the importance of rhetoric to inquiry—and how psychologists should apply these lessons to their own research. Arjo Klamer identifies appeals by which economists persuade each another, concentrating on metaphors of rationality in the theories of economists. Richard Brown unifies recent projects in sociology, generating a rhetorical conception of reason and tracing how it figures in sociological research. Finding much the same situation in political science, John Nelson displays that discipline's intertwining of stories about its conduct of inquiry with stories about its subject of inquiry. Donald McCloskey and Allan Megill call attention to the rhetorical character of historiography, which the official rhetoric of the discipline tends to discount.

The next two essays draw from recent theories of literary interpretation to identify what the humanities can contribute to rhetoric of inquiry. Gerald Bruns explores the conception of language advanced in the hermeneutical tradition of Wilhelm Dilthey, Martin Heidegger, and Hans-Georg Gadamer. Paul Hernadi portrays interpretation as three dialectically related moments of understanding, overstanding, and standing in for the subject, suggesting a radical alteration of recent theories and practices of inquiry in the human sciences.

Then the focus of the book shifts to how scholars communicate with larger publics. Religion, law, and women's studies maintain especially strong ties to constituencies beyond the academy. David Klemm argues that theology in our century proceeds paradoxically but properly to offer "arguments that are not arguments." James Boyd White contends that the law is less a system of rules than a branch of rhetoric—which in turn is the main art for founding, keeping, and changing communities. Jean Bethke Elshtain discerns two grand stories of feminism running through most recent studies of women, and she urges that their conflict be transcended in a more open narrative. Charles Anderson and Michael Shapiro survey rhetorical relationships between scholars and the politics of advanced industrial societies. Anderson defends the American heritage of liberal and pragmatic standards for inquiry and communication in public affairs; Shapiro pursues a deconstructivist strategy of "snickering" at the oppressive moves that characterize much political argument in our times.

These days the study of rhetoric makes its main academic home in communication studies. Speaking from the traditionally low position of rhetoric as a house of ill-repute, Michael McGee and John Lyne ask the other essayists, "What Are Nice Folks Like You Doing in a Place Like This?" Exposing the rhetorical nexus of expertise and power, they welcome the interdisciplinary interest in rhetoric of inquiry but caution against altogether abandoning logic of inquiry. John Nelson concludes the book with general reflections on rhetoric of inquiry, bringing together the concerns of the previous essays to assess relationships among the poetics, rhetorics, ethics, and politics of research.

The Iowa Symposium joined two enterprises usually kept distinct: a research conference for scholars on the frontiers of an emerging field and a public forum for considering issues important to a broad audience inside and outside the academy. A grant from the National Endowment for the Humanities financed activities tied to the first mission; a grant from the Iowa Humanities Board supported the second; and the University of Iowa Vice President for Educational Development and Research, Duane Spriestersbach, paid the remaining bills. We deeply appreciate the help. Of course, neither the positions taken at the symposium nor those presented in this book represent the views of these three institutions. We also thank Jane Barry and Katy Neckerman for invaluable editorial assistance in transforming the symposium papers into this book.

The symposium drew scholars from more than half the states in the Union. It also attracted a good audience from outside the academy. Later the symposium was heard by many more people through weekly broadcasts from an Iowa affiliate of National Public Radio. It has inspired a number of other conferences and panels on rhetoric of inquiry. At the University of Iowa, it has led to a continuing Project on Rhetoric of Inquiry. And through the efforts of Gordon Lester-Massman at the University of Wisconsin Press, it has led to the series of books on the Rhetoric of the Human Sciences in which the essays now appear.

In covering the symposium for the *Chronicle of Higher Education*, Ellen K. Coughlin wrote that "elements of rhetoric . . . are so thoroughly ingrained in scholarly research as to affect every step of the enterprise—how sources are used, how data are interpreted, how findings are communicated." The essays here explore this thesis from many angles, with many rhetorics. But far more remain; and we hope that the book will encourage readers to examine for themselves the rhetorical dimensions of scholarship.

THE RHETORIC OF THE HUMAN SCIENCES

1 RHETORIC OF INQUIRY

JOHN S. NELSON

ALLAN MEGILL

DONALD N. McCLOSKEY

Scholarship uses argument, and argument uses rhetoric. The "rhetoric" is not mere ornament or manipulation or trickery. It is rhetoric in the ancient sense of persuasive discourse. In matters from mathematical proof to literary criticism, scholars write rhetorically.

Only occasionally do they reflect on that fact. The most common occasion is the manifesto, which seeks to expose the rhetoric of an earlier line of scholarship, demonstrating how the tone, figures of speech, and other devices of style to be discarded have lied or misled us. Yet even writers attacking an earlier rhetoric customarily pay no attention to their own. Modern scholars usually deny their rhetoric. Wearing masks of scientific methodology first donned in the seventeenth century, they have forgotten about the rhetorical faces underneath. Their simple repetition of official rhetoric against rhetoric serves mainly to dampen anxieties about how things really happen in the lab or library. Of late, the propaganda of governments and advertising agencies has devalued rhetoric still more.

Since the 1950s, however, and especially in the last few years, rhetoric has revived. Literary critics, theorists of communication, and teachers of public speaking never wholly abandoned Cicero, Quintilian, and company. Now the rhetorically minded seem prescient in their steadfastness, for the masks of methodology are wearing thin. Many people grow weary of claims that experimental technique, documentary interpretation, or regression analysis can avoid "subjectivity." Many scholars doubt that science opposes or replaces art, that "ought" ought not be derived from "is," or that any method ensures un-

3

John S. Nelson, Allan Megill, and Donald N. McCloskey

problematical results. Thus scientists and humanists alike appear again in the classical guise of rhetors: good people skilled at persuasion and the inquiry needed to support it.

I

One way to see beneath the masks of methodology is to look at how scholars really do converse. In anthropology, history, law, political science, sociology, architecture, medicine, economics, biology, physics, psychology, and mathematics, scholars have recently begun to attend to actual argumentation. The attention reforms their inquiry and helps them talk intelligently about it. They can recognize how mathematical inquiry connects to social and literary inquiry, and how all connect to politics.

To emphasize the rhetoric of scholars is to replace simple acceptance of their reports with insightful scrutiny of their reasons. Treating each other's claims as arguments rather than findings, scholars no longer need implausible doctrines of objectivism to defend their contributions to knowledge. At a practical level, to stress rhetoric is to discount claims to neutrality in measuring, say, the costs and benefits of a subway system. Detailed attention to rhetoric can reveal underlying issues and better ways to consider them responsibly. At a theoretical level, to take rhetoric seriously is to dispute the spectator story of inquiry. To be sure, challenges to the received view of science are not unique to rhetoric. The spectator theory has suffered attacks for two centuries, though only recently has it lost decisive ground. The professed neutrality of social engineering has never been supported universally, though only recently has it attracted widespread scorn. Rhetoric of inquiry shows how such views fail to explain or to improve the words and deeds of scholars. It also fosters more effective thinking, speaking, and acting by their students and by audiences outside the academy.

Rhetoric of inquiry rests on two assertions. It maintains that argument is more unified than is commonly understood, and far more unified than the fragmentation of academic fields might imply. Every scientist or scholar, regardless of field, relies on common devices of rhetoric: on metaphors, invocations of authority, and appeals to audiences—themselves creatures of rhetoric. But rhetoric of inquiry also insists that argument is more diverse than is commonly understood, and far more diverse than the official philosophies of science or art allow. Every field is defined by its own special devices and patterns of rhetoric—by existence theorems, arguments from invisible hands, and appeals to textual probabilities or archives—themselves textures of rhetoric.

Rhetoric of inquiry does not deny that there are things to discuss in the methodological midlands that intellectuals now cultivate so intensively. But it does connect discussions of methodology to concrete inquiries in various contexts, and especially to the languages of their conduct. Thus it encourages methodology to become comparative, situating itself in actual researches and exploring their mutual implications for better inquiry. Accordingly, rhetoric of inquiry does not seek to be a subject unto itself or an authority over other investigations. Fields properly divide into separate conversations with distinct dialects. Nonetheless, they share the grammar of our civilization more than they know. Rhetoric of inquiry makes us more widely aware of this, making the arts and sciences more intelligible to themselves and to others.

Without much effort, and with no central orchestration, rhetoric of inquiry is emerging in most departments of the intellect. Philosophers who practice it are startled to find, for instance, that it is arising in economics also; students of communication are surprised to see it in psychology; nonmathematicians are amazed that mathematicians do it at all. Their varied practices are parts of a single project. A lawyer cannot directly help physicists to run experiments in particle accelerators, but physicists can learn that their arguments follow courtroom forms and—like legal arguments—depend on precedent. An anthropologist cannot help economists measure the elasticity of cocoa supply, but economists can learn that observations are subtle forms of participation, and that supply curves are symbols which shape economic inferences. These are parts of a common rhetoric of scholarly inquiry. It creates languages for talking about what we have in common and for understanding why we do not—and cannot—have everything in common. Rhetoric of inquiry is a way of conversing about intellectual conversation—and improving its quality.

Rhetoric, like most important matters, has a long history. It begins with the sophists of the fifth and fourth centuries, wise men whose name in common usage has become a tag for deviousness. The sophists aroused an enemy, *philosophia*, whose champions nearly stifled *rhetoreia* at its origin. Socrates was a sophist—though his student, Plato, would have none of that, and portrayed rhetors as blowhards careless of Knowledge and Truth. Aristotle, Plato's student, appreciated rhetoric; and rhetoricians use his *Rhetoric* still. He nonetheless widened the rift between philosophy (determined by truthspeaking dialecticians) and mere persuasion (left to courtroom hacks). The Romans for a time

John S. Nelson, Allan Megill, and Donald N. McCloskey

took a broader view. Three centuries after Plato, Cicero propounded a scheme to unify philosophy and rhetoric. A century later, Quintilian contended in *Institutio Oratoria* (I: 11) that philosophical matters "are truly part of our subject, and properly pertain to the art of oratory."

The Ciceronian view that rhetoric is the whole of argument survived the death of classical civilization, to reemerge at its rebirth. But under the onslaught of a Method claiming neutrality and universality, rhetoric fell precipitously from favor in the seventeenth century. Henceforth it was redefined as suitable only for the underside of public life, for turning a crowd this way or that. Those who acted and spoke in public would cultivate it—but did so at the price of soiling themselves, inviting suspicion by trying to persuade. The ancient fear of rhetoric, as a powerful weapon, gave way to scorn.

The private person, it was said increasingly from the seventeenth century on, could ignore rhetoric. Individuals could see directly the results of their experiments and feel directly the experiences of their souls, letting the wordiness of discourse take care of itself. Science and even poetry came to be viewed as essentially solitary undertakings, with achievements spilling out by natural cause or ineffable inspiration, as though inquiry and language were individual accomplishments. By the eighteenth century, communication among scientists began to shift away from the sometimes vituperative arguments of earlier science toward the stilted rhetorics of reportage in present day journals of science. Late in the century, even poetry took an intensely personal turn, exchanging private for public subjects. Romance and science both devalued the social character of inquiry.

Philosophy reflects these changes. We suffer from seventeenth-century dichotomies of subject and object, which gave fresh force to opposing truth and rationality on the one side to conversation and rhetoric on the other. Solitary spectation came to be contrasted with talk. Talk is of course social, admitting many reasons. The older, rhetorical style bids the listener well and offers gentle arguments; the newer, scientismic way makes the reader subject to hierarchies of proof or method that intimidate and exclude most people—even if we grant that, in principle, the subject may aspire to personal expertise. Those who really *know* benefit from privileged and usually undiscussable observations, compelling because scientific techniques certify that the findings must mirror nature. Capable of opinion only, the humble subject must submit to the rigors of Method in order to ascend the heights of Truth. This opposition spurns rhetoric and substitutes conviction for persuasion. Alternately we might say that authoritarian rhetorics of compelling proof and convincing demonstration usurp the office of sweet reason. *Convincere* means "to defeat thoroughly," but *suadere* shares a root with *suavis*, Latin for "sweet." As Cicero enjoined (*De Oratore*, I: 31: 138), "the first duty of the orator is to speak in a manner suitable to persuading."

Philosophically, then, the denigration of rhetoric has its modern origin in René Descartes. The larger history of the denigration is complex, but recent foes of rhetoric are Cartesian in a broad sense, committed to the idea of Method. The revival of rhetoric has therefore taken an anti-Cartesian form. There is irony in this, since Descartes's own rhetoric was as self-conscious as it was successful. Exploring his "Experiments in Philosophical Genre," Amelie Oksenberg Rorty observed that "despite his austere recommendations about the methods of discovery and demonstration, he hardly ever followed those methods, hardly ever wrote in the same genre twice." Indeed, he "found himself using the very modes he intended to attack."[1] As Cicero said of Plato, Descartes was the best rhetorician when making merry of rhetoricians.

II

The twentieth century has seen a weakening of the Cartesian base (and Kantian superstructure) of philosophy. In the English-speaking world, countermovements remain in the minority; but even here, their recent momentum is impressive. And their diversity should open many eyes. Even a brief survey must mention more than two handfuls of philosophers. In various ways, they all point toward rhetoric of inquiry.

Friedrich Nietzsche, for instance, assaulted directly the dichotomy of subject and object. "The objective," he wrote, "is only a false concept of a genus and an antithesis *within* the subjective."[2] He reviled the positivist view that "there are only *facts*." On the contrary, facts are "precisely what there is not, only interpretations. We cannot establish any fact 'in itself': perhaps it is folly to want to do such a thing."[3]

Martin Heidegger made Nietzsche's attack systematic, perhaps too much so. *Being and Time* undermines oppositions between subject and object by rejecting the notion of subjects as spectators, standing in isolation from objects.[4] It substitutes *Dasein*, an existence that is "always already" constituted by the situation within which it acts. *Dasein* is not the modern "subject" (whose very mention implies an object) but a "Being-in-the-world." Humans are not to be addressed apart from their worlds, as though the world were separate from the self. Only in interaction within the world do they create identities, and only in this creation of identities does the world of human beings take shape.

Neither Nietzsche nor Heidegger developed the rhetorical implications of this attack on Descartes and his successors. In fact, some aspects of their styles continue the Cartesian bias against rhetoric. Speaking thus as Zarathustra, Nietzsche delivered tablets of a new law, rather than presenting reasons for a new persuasion. Speaking as a German professor of philosophy, Heidegger pronounced Truth *ex cathedra*, rather than arguing for interpretations in context. Still, other aspects of their styles and substantive claims remain favorable to rhetoric. This holds not only for their criticisms of earlier philosophers but also for their views of action in everyday life. In overthrowing "the fact in itself," for example, Nietzsche and Heidegger disputed the notion that facts speak for themselves. Rhetoric of inquiry is needed precisely because facts themselves are mute. Whatever the facts, *we* do the speaking—whether through them or for them.

To admit these rhetorical dimensions of inquiry has seemed dangerous to modernists, who crave certainty. Some oppose rhetoric with shouts of "Relativism!" But as Stanley Cavell and Richard Rorty argue, though to different ends, epistemology is more cause than cure of this philosophical disease. It would be better to stop requiring an ever larger number of certainties and to start accepting the partial assurances of human speech. For inquiry as for business, accepting uncertainty can lead to riches. It pluralizes science; and it chides philosophy of science separated from the histories, sociologies, aesthetics, and rhetorics of real sciences in actual practice. This is the best part of what Nietzsche intended in celebrating *Leben*, and it is the main implication of Heidegger's argument that practice is constitutive of human beings. It returns the attention of scholars to that most practical of human pursuits, rhetoric. Conference maketh a ready scholar.

John Dewey's attack on the Cartesian quest for certainty is comparable to Heidegger's, although in many respects the two philosophers could hardly be more different. Heidegger performed briefly (and disastrously) in politics, but was generally hostile to it. Dewey, by contrast, displayed a central and participatory concern with politics. He celebrated American democracy and its public rhetoric, though rejecting the false certainties of left and right. Philosophically and politically, he provided a rhetorical way of relating scholarship to politics.

Ludwig Wittgenstein was another who wanted to free scholarship from philosophers, or at least from philosophers who wished to separate it from practical life. From the start of Wittgenstein's sparring with philosophy, he manifested a preoccupation with the corruption of ordinary language. To be sure, he tried first to assimilate language to the alleged certainties of logic and mathematics. But he later renounced this craving for certainty in favor of a practical and rhetorical emphasis on human languages as games among speakers, listeners, and actors. The metaphor of the game encourages attention to the back and forth, the give and take, of real argument.

Another major contribution of Wittgenstein to rhetoric of inquiry is his deconstruction of philosophical criteria for criticism and truth. Stanley Cavell has extended that work in detail, with sensitivity to its rhetorical and political implications. Especially in *The Claim of Reason*, he shows that standards of judgment reflect everyday life.[5] They are properly applied and refined *within* the worlds of inquiry, not at a philosophical distance. The standards are not simple, because they stem from the welter of everyday events and perspectives. Yet Cavell's account implies that it is precisely through rhetoric that we come to understand every human activity, including scholarship.

Hans-Georg Gadamer's contribution to the revitalization of rhetoric is to add a dialogic dimension that is missing, or at best undeveloped, in Nietzsche and Heidegger. Gadamer emphasizes the communitarian side of interpretation, as Cavell emphasizes the ties of reason to community. The similarity is especially notable considering that these two come from mutually hostile communities of philosophy. Gadamer flirts with the possibility of redefining argument and epistemology as hermeneutics, the study of understanding. A similarly hermeneutical perspective has been urged by Richard Rorty. At the end of *Philosophy and the Mirror of Nature*, he claims "that there is no point in trying to find a general synoptic way of 'analyzing' the 'functions knowledge has in universal contexts of practical life,' and that cultural anthropology (in a large sense which includes intellectual history) is all we need."[6] Rorty has detailed his vision of a cultural anthropology of knowledge in ways that agree closely with the rhetorical tradition. Above all, he promotes a philosophy that would edify through persuasive contributions to "the conversation of mankind."[7]

For Rorty, inquiry that avoids trying to mirror nature escapes "seeing the attainment of truth as a matter of necessity,"[8] whether logical or empirical. The rejection of necessitarian truth and coercive argument is now shared by many philosophers, among them John Searle, Hilary Putnam, and Nelson Goodman. Even Robert Nozick, in many ways a polar opposite of Rorty, has written eloquently on behalf of less dictatorial and more persuasive styles of academic discourse. His *Philosophical Explanations* begins by decrying the coercive terminology of recent philosophical argument.[9] After a subtle inquiry into how he is

John S. Nelson, Allan Megill, and Donald N. McCloskey

actually persuaded when reading philosophical texts, he proposes revisions in the presentation of philosophy. These impart priority to persuasion over logical demonstration, implying both a new rhetoric and new openness to rhetoric by its old foes.

Yet another stylistic (and political) facet of rhetorical consciousness is exemplified by Jürgen Habermas, the target of Rorty's complaint about analysis in terms of "universal contexts of practical life." Instead of dissolving philosophy into hermeneutics or rhetoric, Habermas has been trying to incorporate rhetorical principles into philosophy. His indictment of "distorted" communication produces a pointedly political version of rhetoric of inquiry. His version is also among the more self-conscious. His *Theory of Communicative Action* brings a wide range of recent projects in social theory under the rubric of communication.[10]

Habermas can be said to seek a rapprochement of rhetoric and philosophy. The writings of Michel Foucault and Jacques Derrida are more aggressive. It may be misleading even to call them philosophers, though it is equally misleading to call them historians, culture critics, or other common name—good or bad. Their heritage is plain enough: they are children of Nietzsche and Heidegger. After devastating criticisms of the modern legacy in scholarship, they turn to language. Derrida's notorious assertion that "there is nothing outside the text" is, among other things, a reminder of the rhetorical constitution of reality. The relentless unlogic of his deconstructions unravels what lies behind demonstrative arguments, if anything at all can be said to "lie behind" them. Like Derrida, Foucault displayed striking sensitivity to rhetoric in politics and inquiry. He drove even more directly toward rhetoric. Always he insisted that we uncover the machinations of power within claims to white-coated objectivity in science or society. It is not necessary to accept everything that either of these corrosive theorists has said in order to learn from them. What they most obviously teach are the rhetorics of myths and stories. Time and again, these wild men of contemporary "discourse" have provoked starts of recognition by discovering residues of oppressive myths within scholarship itself. Repeatedly, they have urged us to reach beyond questioning past tales to compose new stories of our own.

The restoration of storytelling to scholarship is also a major theme of Alasdair MacIntyre's *After Virtue*.[11] There he condemns as impossible and incomprehensible the modern project of a single social science pursuing lawlike generalizations tested empirically. In its place, he defends the dependence of actual social sciences on ethics—and the dependence of ethics in turn on social ''roles,'' in something close to the theatrical sense. Any view that provides for the virtues in human living must focus on life's dramatic or narrative structure. MacIntyre's stories of modern morality and scholarship show that "relativism" is a result of modern philosophy and politics, not a reason for retaining them in their antirhetorical form. As in Rorty and Cavell, rhetoric is the cure, not the disease.

Even taken together, these writers are nothing like a school—unless common enemies make a school. What they share is a sensitivity to language taken beyond language alone into the practices of living in our times, plus a conviction that the conduct of inquiry is as communal as its consequences. Thus we see in their work anticipations of the concerns that constitute rhetoric of inquiry.

III

The vision of a single, certain, natural, and rational order haunts us still and may never disappear entirely. But it is fading in recent practices of science and scholarship. An important project of the late twentieth century, only partly acknowledged, has been to deconstruct Enlightenment rationalism and its culture of authoritarian liberation. As a result, the study of rhetoric is slowly returning to the center of our self-awareness.

Literary critics such as I. A. Richards and William Empson struggled to keep rhetoric from becoming completely peripheral. Still, the related drives to create sciences of society and to ascertain the fundaments of inquiry have in the last hundred years eclipsed most of the scholar's rhetorical needs and resources. Popular myths have presented scientists as individual machines of awesome logic occasionally informed by flashes of inspiration. Scholarly conceptions concede increases in the scale and significance of institutions in science but otherwise have been much the same. What place might there be for communal arts of persuasion in technical halls of science where logical rigor and unaccountable genius reign supreme?

Steps toward transforming logic of inquiry into rhetoric of inquiry are especially evident in the work of Chaim Perelman, Stephen Toulmin, and Thomas Kuhn. Indeed, the transformation is evident more widely in the history, philosophy, and sociology of science. As we have already suggested, one sign of the growing awareness of rhetoric is greater attention to actual argumentation. The catalysts were two books published in 1958, *The New Rhetoric* by Chaim Perelman and Lucie Olbrechts-Tyteca,[12] and *The Uses of Argument* by Stephen Toulmin.[13] Perelman and Toulmin are philosophers: Perelman was

John S. Nelson, Allan Megill, and Donald N. McCloskey

trained in law; Toulmin in analytical philosophy of a British sort. Yet much of their inspiration and most of their impact so far lies outside professional philosophy. Many of their notions derive from argument in law and other speechmaking, and the first audience for their books was the peculiarly American discipline of communication studies, which has been much enriched by their work.

Perelman came to rhetoric as a student concerned with the nature of justice. This led him to ask how we reason about values, which in turn led him to casemaking in law. The need for a new rhetoric emphasizing reasoned persuasion was forced on him by the contrast between law and more formalized inquiry. Toulmin's initial concern was also ethical. In *An Examination of the Place of Reason in Ethics,* he explored how moral reasoning actually occurs, as distinct from deriving principles a priori from postulates.[14] Turning then to logic, he looked for a way to focus on "practical" rather than on "theoretical" reasoning; and he too found it in law. *The Uses of Argument* treats logic as a "generalized jurisprudence" concerned with "the sort of *case* we present in defense of our claims."[15]

The European inspiration for a rhetoric of inquiry, then, was law; the American inspiration was politics. Since its formal beginnings around World War I, the study of speech communication has focused on political speech. Political rhetoric flourished in the nineteenth century, when American democracy was creating its rhetorical traditions. The American concern with politics is evident in Thomas S. Kuhn's *Structure of Scientific Revolutions.*[16] Its dominant metaphor of revolution is political. The history of modern science reveals patterns of change dramatically different from the picture implied by extant logics of inquiry, and better suited to a rhetoric. It therefore challenges philosophy to account for the actual operation of scientific communities—their professional devices of communication and socialization, their political structures, their reliance on aesthetics, their rhetorical dependence on persuasion.

Perelman and Toulmin are drawn to law because of its self-conscious tradition of argument constrained by alterable standards. Kuhn's attraction to politics seems to stem from its interplay of order, authority, communication, and change. Both law and politics put a premium on narrative, putting in context the timeless generalizations pursued by philosophers of science. Both fields are notable for their concern with actual conduct and practical action. And both appreciate, as Dewey did, that persuasion is necessary for action. Like the pragmatists before them, the new rhetoricians treat inquiry as action—and law and politics are assuredly arenas of action.

Further glimmerings of a rhetoric of inquiry appear in the work of other dissenters from received views in the philosophy of science, such as Norwood Russell Hanson, Imre Lakatos, and Paul Feyerabend. They joined Kuhn and Toulmin in challenging the rhetorical insensitivity of epistemology. At about the same time, circa 1970, the study of science itself underwent a revolution. Bernard Barber, Robert Merton, and others developed a sociology of science; the history of science attained maturity and an unprecedented popularity; and Peter Berger and Thomas Luckmann revitalized the sociology of knowledge in *The Social Construction of Reality*.[17] This work is being extended into a variety of projects in the anthropology, history, and sociology of science, including the "strong programme" of the Edinburgh School. Philosophers of science such as Max Black, Mary Hesse, and Earl MacCormac began about the same time to turn epistemology toward the rhetoric of thinking—which is to say, the rhetoric of models and metaphors. And now scholars in virtually every field are looking beyond official methodologies, to address how their research is really done.

All these precursors of rhetoric of inquiry have opposed the overemphasis on formal logic in the philosophies of "ideal language." The programs of Gottlob Frege, Bertrand Russell, and Rudolf Carnap pivoted on developing a grammar separate from and superior to substantive inquiry. The goal was to yield a single methodology for all fields—that is, a unified science. Such programs were loosely tied to an idealized (and erroneous) view of physics, taken as the height of Science. But this narrow logic of inquiry and its attempt at a neutral language of observation failed decisively, in its own terms. For example, Carl Hempel's covering-law account of historical explanation strikes most practicing historians as unilluminating and implausible. No one follows it literally. Yet scholars who are insecure about the status of their disciplines, or who simply lack ideas, have *tried* to follow such prescriptions. Especially in the social sciences, the attempt has caused immense confusion and wasted effort. What researchers actually find reasonable fits ill or not at all with what a formal logic of inquiry implies to be their duty.

The old program evades such difficulties by distinguishing between "perfect" and "imperfect" sciences, attributing all incompatibilities between the proposed methodology and actual practices to the immaturity of the practices. The imperfection is seen as a failure to resemble some pure form compatible with a simple logic. The rhetoricians start instead with the substantive arguments. They might be said to replace models from mathematics and physics (though misapprehended) with models from law, politics, and literature. Rhetoric of inquiry regards

John S. Nelson, Allan Megill, and Donald N. McCloskey

any field of human discourse as a reasonable starting point for a study of inquiry.

This means that rhetoric of inquiry begins with texts. It is literary. Because literary critics never entirely abandoned rhetorical ways of reading texts, the specifically rhetorical turn of literary theory enjoys many contributors. Still, Kenneth Burke and Wayne Booth deserve special notice for spreading rhetorical consciousness beyond literary studies, and the same may be said of Hayden White in history. Their work converges with the interest of speech communication in the epistemic status of rhetoric.

Burke led a reunion of rhetoric with poetics, which he defines as the serious business of acting with symbols. In regarding *Language as Symbolic Action*, he has pursued *The Philosophy of Literary Form* into such areas as *Attitudes Toward History, A Grammar of Motives, A Rhetoric of Motives, The Rhetoric of Religion*, and *Terms for Order*.[18] White has extended Burke's rhetorical mix of politics and poetics into historical and social inquiry. In *Metahistory*[19] and many essays since, he has joined Burke, Northrop Frye, Roman Jakobson, Stephen Pepper, and others in attending to how scholars "prefigure their phenomenal fields." He explores the rhetoric of tropes, ideologies, genres, and stories. Booth, too, uses Burke to connect diverse realms—of philosophy, art, literature, music, politics, and psychology. But Booth's rhetoric emphasizes the more traditional dimension of argument. Against modern dogmatisms and relativisms, he defends a rhetoric of "good reasons" that aims to encourage thinking about when we should and should not change our minds. In his literary theory and in books directed at wider audiences, such as *Now Don't Try to Reason with Me* and *Modern Dogma and the Rhetoric of Assent*,[20] he has advocated a pluralism rendered coherent by rhetoric.

In speech communication, Booth's books have contributed both to the theory of argument as a presentation of "good reasons" rather than logical proofs and to the study of "rhetoric as epistemic." The latter phrase was introduced in 1967, in a seminal and still controversial essay by Robert L. Scott.[21] Since then, speech communication has studied the rhetorics of science and of other special fields. It recognizes the need we identified at the outset for a binocular view of the unity and diversity of scholarship. Rhetorical studies are beginning to spread onto the scholarly sites themselves, fulfilling another need: locating rhetoric of inquiry out in the field.

Two barriers sometimes frustrate efforts at rhetoric of inquiry. One is the philosophical tendency to contrast rhetoric and rationality, taking rhetoric to endorse radical relativism (or mere nihilism). The other is the failure to examine rhetoric within actual practices, academic or otherwise. The best response, given in this book, is to do rhetoric of inquiry, showing that it works. That is the usual way of overturning established methods and jargon-laden expertise. It would involve directing attention away from Methodology toward specific pieces of scholarly inquiry and communication. To borrow Toulmin's terms, it would include shifting attention away from the abstract and allegedly universal standards of Reason and toward the "warrants" and "backings" of particular reasonings. It means stressing the importance of the audience in humanistic and scientific speech: the warrants and backings must be shared with audiences if an argument is to have power. And it entails focusing on the figurative and even the mythic parts of inquiry. In short, it requires that we study concrete communities of inquiry instead of abstract logics.

IV

There is a lot to be studied, and the questions are many. What does the rhetoric of a piece of scholarship imply for its uses? Why do genres of scholarship differ from one field to another? How do narratives matter? What roles do metaphors play in scientific persuasion? How have rhetorical conventions affected particular fields? How does their rhetoric affect their public reception? What do theories of rhetoric imply for the conduct of research? What does rhetoric imply for relations among the humanities, social sciences, natural sciences, and professions? How might recent theories of rhetoric revise our conceptions of rationality? What are the connections among rhetoric, epistemology, ethics, logics, myths, poetics, politics, psychology, sociology, and other aspects of inquiry? How might increased awareness of rhetoric reform education in the disciplines?

Rhetoric of inquiry is especially valuable for the human sciences, the systematic studies of humankind. Rhetoric is generally recognized as part of the humanities. Its renaissance started there, and it promises important revisions at home. But the social sciences have less awareness of rhetoric than do the humanities, and would benefit more from increased rhetorical self-consciousness. The humanities already regard human acts and products as events for understanding, criticism, and celebration; the social sciences now regard them as objects for explanation, prediction, and control. The role of rhetoric has been played down in the humanities, but it has been downright ignored in

John S. Nelson, Allan Megill, and Donald N. McCloskey

the social sciences. In consequence, the social sciences float in warm seas of unexamined rhetoric.

But rhetoric of inquiry can also bring down needless walls between the human sciences. Its lessons come often from comparing different inquiries, encouraging scholars to learn from their colleagues—whereas Methodology tells them to learn exclusively from Plato, Descartes, Hempel, or Popper. Rhetoric acknowledges, too, the capacity of every field to encompass diverse and changing rhetorics. Discovering the sciences and the professions to be no less (but differently) rhetorical than the humanities may lead scholars to abandon the ramparts of Method.

The main challenge is to integrate rhetoric of inquiry into the normal business of scholarship. Caught up in abstraction, logicians of inquiry often fail to address actual practice. Rhetoricians of inquiry must not make the same mistake: they must not seek an abstracted and autonomous field. Their work must arise from practice. It must learn from many projects, and alter many. And it must reach beyond academic life.

There are places for specialists in rhetoric of inquiry, but not just in a single discipline, such as literary theory or communication studies. Such a concentration would produce outside authorities, obliged to speak from afar and tempted to instruct from above. Rhetoricians of inquiry must be able to talk with the persuasiveness of insiders. Experts on literature and communication have much to teach others about historical comparisons and theoretical principles important in rhetoric of inquiry. But there also need to be economic critics of economics and anthropological critics of anthropology, in the style of poetic critics of poetry—a new race of Coleridges and Eliots.

The literary criticism of a field requires showing how it departs from its official norms of research. Such critics can discern in detail what is obvious in outline: that scholars call on different reasons that are persuasive at different points. They can examine how inquiries should be sensitized to their own rhetorics. These rhetoricians can take advantage of the tendency of rhetoric to merge the field of study with the practices studied. "Rhetoric" covers at once what is communicated, how it is communicated, what happens when it is communicated, how to communicate it better, and what communication is in general. Rhetoric of inquiry enlarges these meanings to encompass the interdependence of inquiry and communication, and to encourage connecting all the skeins of rhetoric into a commitment for better inquiry to inform action.

Rhetoric of inquiry reflects a renewed concern for the quality of speaking and writing in scholarship. It emphasizes the interaction of style and substance. But mostly it tries to improve the conduct of inquiry, inside and outside the academy, by learning from its diversity. As immanent epistemology, within particular fields, rhetoric of inquiry shows what we are really doing and how to criticize it. As comparative epistemology, across different fields, rhetoric of inquiry shows what others are doing and how to learn from it. Rhetoric of inquiry explores how reason is rhetorical.

NOTES

1. Amelie Oksenberg Rorty, "Experiments in Philosophical Genre," *Critical Inquiry* 9 (1983): 548.
2. Friedrich Nietzsche, *Werke: Kritische Gesamtausgabe,* part 8, vol. 2: 17.
3. Ibid., 1: 323.
4. Martin Heidegger, *Being and Time,* trans. John Macquarrie and Edward Robinson (New York: Harper and Row, 1962).
5. Stanley Cavell, *The Claim of Reason* (New York: Oxford University Press, 1979).
6. Richard Rorty, *Philosophy and the Mirror of Nature* (Princeton: Princeton University Press, 1979), p. 391.
7. Ibid., p. 389.
8. Ibid., p. 376.
9. Robert Nozick, *Philosophical Explanations* (Cambridge: Harvard University Press, 1981).
10. Jürgen Habermas, *The Theory of Communicative Action, Volume One: Reason and the Rationalization of Society,* trans. Thomas McCarthy (Boston: Beacon Press, 1984). This work was originally published in German in 1981.
11. Alasdair MacIntyre, *After Virtue* (Notre Dame, Ind.: University of Notre Dame Press, 1981).
12. Chaim Perelman and Lucie Olbrechts-Tyteca, *The New Rhetoric: A Treatise on Argumentation,* trans. John Wilkinson and Purcell Weaver (Notre Dame, Ind.: University of Notre Dame Press, 1969). This book was originally published in French in 1958.
13. Stephen Toulmin, *The Uses of Argument* (Cambridge: Cambridge University Press, 1958).
14. Stephen Toulmin, *An Examination of the Place of Reason in Ethics* (Cambridge: Cambridge University Press, 1970).
15. Toulmin, *The Uses of Argument,* p. 7.
16. Thomas S. Kuhn, *The Structure of Scientific Revolutions,* 2d ed. (Chicago: University of Chicago Press, 1970).

John S. Nelson, Allan Megill, and Donald N. McCloskey

17. Peter L. Berger and Thomas Luckmann, *The Social Constuction of Reality* (Garden City, N.Y.: Doubleday, 1966).

18. Kenneth Burke, *Language as Symbolic Action* (Berkeley: University of California Press, 1937); idem, *A Grammar of Motives* (Berkeley: University of California Press, 1945); idem, *A Rhetoric of Motives* (Berkeley, University of California Press, 1966); idem, *Attitudes Toward History* (Berkeley: University of California Press, 1950); idem, *The Rhetoric of Religion* (Berkeley: University of California Press, 1961); idem, *Terms for Order,* ed. Stanley Edgar Hyman (Bloomington: Indiana University Press, 1964).

19. Hayden White, *Metahistory: The Historical Imagination in Nineteenth-Century Europe* (Baltimore: John Hopkins University Press, 1973).

20. Wayne C. Booth, *Now Don't Try to Reason with Me: Essays and Ironies for a Credulous Age* (Chicago: University of Chicago Press, 1970); idem, *Modern Dogma and the Rhetoric of Assent* (Chicago: University of Chicago Press, 1974).

21. Robert L. Scott, "On Viewing Rhetoric as Epistemic," *Central States Speech Journal* 18 (1967): 9–17.

2 MODERN SOPHISTIC AND THE UNITY OF RHETORIC

MICHAEL C. LEFF

The study of rhetoric occupies an equivocal place within the Western intellectual tradition. Its history is long and continuous, but it co-exists with an equally persistent strain of antirhetorical thought. No other humanistic pursuit so firmly entrenched in classical precedent has suffered such potent attack or such prolonged disdain. Moreover, cyclic changes in the status of rhetoric dramatically punctuate this pattern of general tension. At times the discipline surfaces against the friction of the antirhetorical current and serves as an organizing force in education and culture. More often it succumbs to this friction; its ideals are denounced, its elements fragmented and distorted. Yet however attenuated its form, the rhetorical tradition survives to mingle with and trickle through the mainstream of thought. It becomes an anomalous element within the cultural medium. And so it remains available for periodic rediscovery, for direction into a channel of its own, and for use as a corrective to the prevailing drift of mainstream ideology.

This volume is one among many signs that we are entering another period of renewed interest in rhetoric. This revival, like its historic predecessors, owes much of its impulse to reaction against the dominant tendencies in the intellectual environment. The contemporary turn toward rhetoric often displays less enthusiasm for rhetoric per se than for its use as a weapon against the decaying but still powerful empire of foundationalist thought.[1] Consequently, argument normally centers on the way in which a rhetorical perspective might correct errors in various departments of learning or the way in which it might improve the whole enterprise. I wish to reverse this focus. Since I am merely a rhetorician and not actually a human scientist, I am less concerned about how the intrusion of rhetoric into the human sciences is likely to affect the human sciences than about how it is likely to affect the study

Michael C. Leff

of rhetoric. The attempt to align these two areas marks a significant expansion of and departure from traditional conceptions of rhetoric. Certain dangers are implicit in this innovation, for it threatens to revive rhetoric at the cost of destroying its integrity. At the same time, however, the rhetorical tradition itself suggests a means for coping with these dangers and for incorporating new interests within its ancient frame. In what follows, I intend to sketch the dimensions of this issue and suggest how the merger of the two rhetorics might be accomplished.

The first problem, of course, is to find a concrete method for comparing the old rhetoric with its new variant. This is a complicated matter, since traditional rhetoric assumes many different forms. But there is a standard, well-established basis for the attack against rhetoric. I will briefly examine it and attempt to show that the contemporary approach has a special feature that blunts this attack. My hypothesis is that anything that blocks a traditional attack against rhetoric must itself represent a departure from the rhetorical tradition. In this way I hope to clear the ground and establish a basis for the comparison that follows. Moreover, the complaints about rhetoric are not without foundation, and it is always wise to consider them before plunging forward.

At base, academic antipathy toward the study of rhetoric arises from the fear that, in pursing this subject, intellectuals might chart a course for their own destruction. To some degree the fear has sociological origins. Intellectuals, like the members of all other subcultures, define themselves largely through negation. They conceive of themselves as different from other, ordinary people, and the differences surface most clearly in respect to the way they talk and think. The study of rhetoric, however, totters unsteadily between intellectual inquiry and the mundane transactions of common life. Its objective, at least according to one classic formulation, is to comprehend the way people ordinarily talk and think, and to treat this matter seriously poses a threat to the identity and solidarity of the intellectual class.

But something more is at stake here than the emblems of the academic subculture. In this instance the surface-level marks of status reflect much more profound distinctions that reach to the core of the humane studies. The classic model of civic rhetoric affects our attitudes not only about language, but about the rules by which we conduct and evaluate the study of human behavior. In fact, the model converts rules into strategies and seems to undermine the boundary conditions of knowledge and argument that define conventional notions of intellectual inquiry. This problem weighs heavily on even the most ardent enthusiasts for rhetoric. As Cicero observes, the orator must adapt to the language of the crowd precisely because he has to adapt to its imperfect understanding.[2] Rhetoric, then, threatens to reduce all judgments to the question of immediate persuasive effect. It is, to borrow a figure Max Black uses in another context, as though we are playing a game of chess in which any move is legal, provided we can persuade our opponent to accept it.[3] The logician may have the power to stipulate which forms of inference are legitimate in the game of logic, but the rhetorician has no control over the oratorical contest. The rules are negotiated every time it is played, and no one can stipulate what will work in a given case. Thus, rhetoric appears to be radically unsystematic; and worse yet, if left to its own devices, it threatens to undermine the basic criteria for reason and morality in the mainstream Western tradition.

This problem undergirds the tension between rhetoric and philosophy, between the active and contemplative lives, that has become a commonplace in humanist literature. The responses to it are extensive and sometimes very subtle, but they are not entirely relevant in the present context. The purpose of this volume, consistent with a general movement in recent rhetorical scholarship,[4] is to reconstruct the relationship between rhetoric and the special sciences of man. The older humanistic tradition firmly roots the art of rhetoric in the business of the general public. In fact, the rhetoricians of classical antiquity, the period in which rhetoric most nearly achieved a distinct and autonomous status, define the subject of their art as the civil issue. This type of issue embraces the topics of general public debate, including such matters as justice, political policy, prudential conduct, and the like. And it specifically excludes discourse in the technical and theoretical sciences.[5] Clearly, then, the contemporary shift to the rhetoric of the human sciences blurs the sharp classical distinction between public and technical discourse and thus alters the terms of the old conflict between rhetoric and philosophy. It is one thing to develop a rationale for discourse based on what works in addressing the mob. But it is quite another matter to rely on the arguments of expert, scrupulously credentialed practitioners of, for example, economic science, especially since their work is already filtered through the referee system of professional journals.

I do not mean to say that the old tension has completely evaporated. Contrary to the ideals of positivists and strict rationalists, students of the rhetoric of the human sciences freely acknowledge that scientists are human beings and approach their work within the structure of their own human interests. They also hold that scientific discourse bears a resemblance to the processes involved in ordinary public argument. Nevertheless, the points of affinity are generic and remote, and the dis-

Michael C. Leff

course of the human sciences is not likely to be confused with populist rhetoric. Both John Maynard Keynes and Huey Long, for example, present discourses on economic policy, but whatever our standards of style and argument, it is difficult to assign their works to the same rhetorical category. Foundationalists, of course, might contend that the rhetorical standard would contaminate economics by introducing fuzzy standards into what should be a precise science. Nevertheless, local contamination hardly strikes the same terror in our Westernized hearts as the wholesale degeneration of ethics and reason that philosophers extrapolate as the consequence of rhetorics built on the oratorical model. All sorts of tacit constraints operate to eliminate irrationality from academic argument; and even if they did not, academics would believe they did anyway. Thus Donald McCloskey's defense of the rhetoric of economics ends on the reassuring note that economists have nothing to fear in abandoning strict methodological dogma in favor of a study of their own ordinary practices. Study of these practices, after all, demonstrates that economists behave as economists in an intelligent and intellectually honest fashion.[6] Human scientists, then, prove to argue just like ordinary people, except that they are thoroughly trained in and honestly committed to the subject of their arguments. The exception is crucial, since it blocks the charge of vicious relativism fundamental to the traditional critique of rhetoric, even as it protects the social emblems of academic subgroups.

Foundationalists may discover some means of overcoming this exception and reviving the old rhetoric of antirhetoric. More likely they will have to invent a new strategy to protect their territory. That remains to be seen, since they have yet to mount a sustained counterattack against the rhetorical invasion of the human sciences.[7] If and when they do, a fascinating debate is certain to follow, and it is tempting to speculate about its content and likely outcome. But that matter is for someone else to pursue. My present interest is not the fate of the human sciences, important as that is, but the fate of rhetoric. And the very feature that protects the new rhetoric of the human sciences from traditional antirhetoric also marks an important change in the basic conception of the art. Most notably, it extends rhetoric well beyond its original domain into the realm of technical academic discourse. Moreover, evaluation of the impact is not entirely speculative, since, in the literature of speech communication, the expansive view has been pushed so long and so hard that it is now orthodoxy.[8] If this effort has dislodged a stodgy conservatism from one obscure corner of the academic world, it has also stretched the conception of rhetoric to the point that it has lost virtually all meaning. It has also occasioned a notable change in the way people in the field communicate with one an-other. The literary and "rhetorical" style of the older generation has given way to a much more analytic and technical kind of discourse, a style that often assumes characteristics of sociological or philosophical prose. With the central interest in the conduct of public argument re-moved, both the style and the content of the scholarship have verged in the direction of other and more intensely specialized academic fields. Ironically, then, strong advocates of the revival of rhetoric, even as they urge a rejuvenated study of the public dimension in discourse, adopt the interests and modes of expression of the disciplines they would somehow have rhetoric organize.

The problems of speech communication are largely *sui generis,* and it would be foolish to generalize on the basis of what has happened there. Nevertheless, the difficulties involved in expanding the old rhetoric are sufficiently great to discomfort anyone seriously interested in the rhet-oric of the human sciences. As I understand it, the key issue consists in the relationship between the rhetorical *perspective* and the kind of *ac-tivity* it seeks to describe. The terms here are crucial, since there is an implicit contrast with the foundationalist emphasis on objects and methods. For foundationalists, both members of this pair are static and knowable, and they are capable of being separated without disrupting the system. Hence, a shift from one kind of object to another causes no problem. The terms "perspective" and "activity," on the other hand, indicate interaction between elements that are not fixed and that con-stantly interact with each other. Form and content resist separation, and a shift from one field of activity to another affects the entire enter-prise. Consequently, the extension of a rhetorical model from one re-gion of activity to another cannot occur in the same straightforward manner as the application of a foundationalist methodology to a yet un-studied class of objects.[9] The extension of rhetoric into the human sci-ences, then, must be approached with great caution. We need to understand the perspective involved in this project, and its relation to traditional perspectives; and we need to grapple with the problem of how interest in new forms of activity influences the perspectives avail-able to the rhetorician. I deal with these matters seriatim.

John Nelson aptly uses the term "sophistic" to characterize the stance now current among students of the rhetoric of the human sci-ences.[10] As contrasted with modernism, the most obvious feature of this approach is its rejection of global generalizations, grand theories, and synthetic methodologies. Sophistic gives priority to the unity of concrete experience as it is filtered through our interests rather than to the theoretical coherence of the varieties of experience as they are or-

Michael C. Leff

dered according to an abstract, rational calculus. Sophistic implies a pluralism in which methods of inquiry and argument are adapted to the particular subject under investigation. It seeks to solve situated problems rather than to formulate abstract theoretical principles. Explanation replaces prediction as the standard for verifying arguments. And such verification depends upon agreement within the community of those concerned about the subject, not upon a process of matching evidence against a disinterested criterion of proof. All abstract categories are treated with suspicion. This does not mean that they are avoided, for such categories may aid in the effort to understand some particular situation.[11] But the understanding they yield is not complete or final. One category system may offer a useful way of organizing the available data, though another system may produce an equally plausible but different account of the same data. Furthermore, we can always discover data that do not conform with a categorical scheme; and if examined with sufficient care and a certain sophistic turn of thought, these anomalies inevitably subvert the entire scheme. Categories, in short, are temporary, motile structures; and they assume importance only as they come into contact with the specifics of a case at hand. They can be transferred from one situation to another, but this is a delicate business requiring insight derived from analogy rather than the iron rules of methodology. Finally, sophistic collapses the modernist dichotomy between theory and practice. In this view theorizing does not occur in a purely rational corner of the psyche. Rather, it is a product of the way that we encounter and filter the phenomena of the world, and it is enmeshed in the texture of our ordinary experience. In short, the construction of theory is itself a form of practice and is not categorically distinct from our other forms of activity.

The sources of this doctrine are various, but the label "sophistic" seems appropriate. Its general characteristics closely parallel the tradition that originated with the old Greek sophists and was carried foward through the works of Isocrates, Cicero, and the Italian humanists. Nevertheless, in this field a comparison of abstract, general principles is obviously incomplete. The philosophy of action advocated by both ancient and modern sophists has little meaning until it engages specific activities. Sophistic is a field-dependent approach that relies on concrete models. Thus, the coherence of the program requires the generation of a model that encompasses the unity of form and content, of perspective and action, in respect to some domain of practice. Once established, the model becomes the referent for something that abstract language cannot capture, and the model can be extended by analogy to other domains of action.

The ancient sophists found their model in the activity of the orator, and the model was well suited to the general goals of their program. The orator had to command knowledge of all matters relevant to civic affairs, had to combine this knowledge with a command of language, and had to adapt both language and content in the specific act of making a persuasive message. Hence his task involved an obvious and practical union of form and content. Furthermore, the orator confronted diverse and shifting situations where success depended on adjustment to specific circumstances, and thus no set of static rules could enclose his activity.

The open-ended character of practice in this domain militated against its reduction to an abstract general theory. So long as rhetoric remained faithful to practice, it could not give a coherent theoretical account of itself.[12] Thus sophistic veered away from a conception of the art as an ordered set of principles and stressed its function as the development of certain human capacities. The goal was to achieve the flexibility needed to make a coherent rhetorical response in particular situations. This was not a matter of teaching someone how to make a speech; it was a process of promoting skill in speaking. And the skill required had to emerge organically from particular experiences. Consequently, sophistic education proceeded along rather concrete lines. Some theory was useful, but only as a place to begin, and once learned, theoretical principles became important mainly as points of reference that the mature orator would transcend and violate in response to the problem at hand. More important were practice in composition and the study of works that instanced rhetorical excellence. The latter exercise fell under the heading of imitation, but the term was deceptive. The objective was not to copy what someone else did, but to spark what we might call a concrete abstraction; the student was trained to recognize principles embedded in a particular text that had potential application to other situations.

In sum, the whole sophistic program had an integrity about it. It advocated a practical, concrete approach to human relations; it embodied that approach in the concrete activity of oratorical performance, and it evolved a system of education based in concrete learning experiences. It was surely no accident that sophistic and rhetoric emerged at the same point in history, since the coherence of sophistic antitheory depended on its interactive relationship with the art of oratory. It was crucial, moreover, for the art to retain its status as a type of performance. When conceived as a theoretical art, rhetoric became self-reflexive and thus obscured its link with the model activity that provided direct access to and control from the world of practical experience. This stress

Michael C. Leff

on performance betokened a thoroughly antimodernist attitude, and it was most clearly articulated by Quintilian when he came to classify rhetoric among the forms of art. Rhetoric, he maintained, had an affinity with the theoretical and productive arts, but it was first and foremost a performing art, more akin to dance than to either metaphysics or sculpture.[13]

Taken strictly on its own terms, the old sophistic could retain vitality only if the orator played a significant role in civic life and if that role was conceived in broad, humanistic terms. Fulfillment of the first of these conditions depended on the prevailing social and political institutions. In later antiquity, when these institutions changed, the scope of the orator's work narrowed, and sophism began to redefine itself. The rhetorical schools remained intact, and the sophistic concept of the orator retained currency; but the political conditions eroded the connection between the older system and the actual practice of the art. Oratory became largely a vehicle for the display of virtuosity, and the schools taught an increasingly schematic version of the art.[14] At the same time, the monism of Christianity and mystical pagan philosophy worked against the grain of the oratorical ideal and its commitment to civic culture. Yet—and here we have striking evidence of the conservatism of Western education—a distorted but recognizable form of the sophistic program survived until the final collapse of Roman cultural institutions. Thereafter the elements of classical rhetorical lore, cut loose from their institutional moorings, were scattered across a variety of medieval academic endeavors. Within the encyclopedic tradition and to a certain extent within the medieval schools, rhetoric maintained a separate identity, but its boundaries were hedged within a disciplinary matrix that gave priority to politics, logic, or theology.[15] Rhetoric did not disappear during the Middle Ages, but it was fragmented and distorted in a way that effectively disguised the sophistic center from which it had originated.

The renaissance humanists attempted to reverse these medieval developments. In the process, they effected what Hannah Barbara Gerl has called a "paradigm shift," for the elevation of eloquence implied a sharp break with medieval traditions and an attempt to reconstitute the grounds of human knowledge.[16] Eloquence for the humanists, as for the ancient sophists, was not mere embellishment but an expression and source of truth as experienced in the arena of human action. The consensus of the community, the conditions of civic life, and the language of the public again became vehicles for the conduct of serious thought. Moreover, the humanists instituted sweeping educational reforms that drove the curriculum toward an integrated and practical program in the language arts. Both the goals and the methods of this endeavor reflected important aspects of the sophistic inheritance.

Nevertheless, the renaissance humanists were sophists only in a rather loose sense of the term. This was true for a number of reasons; one of them, a matter that has not received due consideration, rested in the model activity on which they chose to center their vision of the active life. The humanists were as clear in this regard as the sophistic rhetoricians of antiquity. Thanks to the influence of Cicero and Quintilian, and perhaps the social and political conditions of the Italian city states, the orator was still accorded great status.[17] But for most humanists, the poet stood on equal if not superior ground. True enough, renaissance thought blurred the distinction between oratory and poetry; poets normally were classified as orators who made important and concrete contributions to political life. Still, under any circumstances, it was difficult to treat poetry as a practical, situationally grounded activity on the same order as forensic oratory. For Isocrates, Cicero, and Quintilian, the aesthetic dimension of language represented a weapon, a resource in the arsenal of persuasive discourse. The humanists paid more attention to the aesthetic, were more inclined to value it for its own sake. Thus, renaissance sophistic was more literary (in the modern sense of the term) than the classical sophistic that inspired it. Its focus gravitated toward eloquence per se without fixing so intently on eloquence as manifested in law courts and political assemblies. It was, in short, less clearly anchored in a definite activity.

Moreover, the renaissance intellectual context forced the unified field of sophistic to operate against the pull of already well-established canons of abstract thought. Greek sophistic had originated before education was institutionalized and before the divisions of learning were solidified. Aspects of learned culture, still in solution and not yet sedimented, glided naturally into the frame of a practical activity. Even as late as the mid-fourth century B.C., Isocrates passed from theory to practice and from *logos* as speech to *logos* as thought with little apparent strain.[18] Subsequent attempts to recover this unified vision encountered the resistance of layers of academic tradition. Cicero revived this perspective only with great effort. And the measure of success he achieved depended on a number of special circumstances—that is, that he was not a professional educator, that he had no compunctions about sacrificing academic rhetoric to his ideal of oratorical performance, and that he lived in a society that still was evolving its own high culture. By contrast, renaissance sophistic arose against the all too solid background of the scholastic enterprise. Reform of learning entailed tearing down and, to a certain extent, encompassing what was already there.

Michael C. Leff

And so the new rhetorical orientation had to assimilate some of the purposes and principles of grammar and logic, and it had to compete with the precise methods of scholastic philosophy and pedagogy. These points of stress further stretched the fabric of a program already weakened by the lack of a clearly defined referent for action in the world. There existed a constant pressure for more methodical and more rigorous accounts of humanist doctrine. Gradually academic humanism became abstract and systematic. By the mid-sixteenth century, this process culminated in Ramistic method; under the guise of Ciceronian humanism, Ramus divided the language arts into a series of sterile, self-contained, and brittle categories, categories as confining as those of scholasticism but rooted in far shallower ground.[19]

The trajectory of academic humanism, then, rose from grounded practice to abstract method. This ascent was futile and self-defeating, for the presuppositions of the movement were unable to absorb or sustain a systematic category scheme. As rhetoric became more theoretical, it was forced to adhere to standards of philosophic rigor it could not achieve. It was thus reduced to theoretical incoherence or empty linguistic formalism. Left stuttering between these unhappy consequences, rhetoric was open to devastating attacks from both sides of the modernist dichotomy. For objectivists, rhetoric was too soft, too tainted with emotive and linguistic distortions to aid in the search for genuine truth. For subjectivists, rhetoric was too hard, too cumbered with formalist contrivance to permit spontaneous expression of genuine feeling. Trapped between the rock of scientific rationalism and the soft spot of romantic poetics, rhetoric virtually disappeared from the circle of learned disciplines.[20]

Current efforts to open a space between objectivism and subjectivism encourage another revival of the sophistic rhetorical tradition. Like the renaissance humanists, modern thinkers can describe general features of the sophistic program that underscore defects in the dominant modes of thought and provide avenues for their correction. Furthermore, though the issue has yet to receive systematic treatment, modern sophism implies an educational reform that would emphasize the study of concrete practice in place of generalized methodology.[21] Nevertheless, the sophistic middle ground, precisely because it is not all one thing or the other, remains treacherous and unstable. In attempting to hold to it, modern sophists appear to face all of the problems that plagued their renaissance predecessors, and some of these problems now assume an even more emphatic form.

In the first place, modern sophistic rhetoric must also struggle against entrenched concepts and institutions that threaten to destroy or contaminate it. The bureaucratization of knowledge in the modern university compounds this problem. Renaissance intellectuals could still rally the humanities around the Ciceronian notion of civic education. That program includes the study of law, politics, history, literature, dialectical logic, and moral philosophy. The scope of studies is ambitious, but perhaps manageable. And except in the case of law and logic, renaissance thought does not reserve these departments of knowledge to specialized departments in the academy; they are still viewed as elements of general learning available to the general public, connected with public affairs, and directly relevant to the work of a practicing orator. Contemporary higher education, however, proliferates and dismantles these studies, dividing them into a massive array of special sciences and further subdividing them into even narrower specializations. Proficiency in any of these areas requires intensive training, and it seems hopeless that anyone could command them all. Moreover, each discipline generates a technical language alien to the discourse of the generally educated public. The differentiation of these languages is so intense that an expert in one subfield is often unable to make sense out of literature in another subfield of the same discipline. I suppose that everyone reading this essay has experienced this frustration and understands how severely it limits the sense of general community within the human sciences. Is it possible to translate this Babel of Tongues into a common idiom? Is it possible to unearth the buried treasures of knowledge locked within so many arcane pursuits and bring them to public view? Perhaps it is, but the magnitude of the project staggers the imagination and goads us toward simpler expedients.

One temptation is to search for a general rhetoric that encompasses all the special rhetorics implicit in the divisions of the human sciences. But the range of these sciences is so broad that this rhetoric could only accommodate general patterns of discourse without reference to their content, thus violating one of the cardinal principles of sophistic. Worse yet, effort in this direction might encourage attempts to generate a normative rhetoric that would regulate work across the human sciences. This, of course, involves a generalized rhetorical method and invites again the disaster that renaissance scholars visited on themselves. The effort is doomed to failure, and a good thing too. If it succeeded, we would push the foundationalist bully off the academic block at the cost of permitting an even less disciplined rhetorical bully to terrorize our work.

So, then, where are we to locate rhetoric in the new sophistic project? The obvious answer is everywhere and nowhere. Rhetoric is not a separate discipline, but a part of every discipline. This is comfortably pluralistic. We no longer talk of rhetoric, but of rhetorics (as in the rhetoric of economics, the rhetoric of anthropology, etc., or to cut the distinctions along a different angle, the rhetoric of Marxist economics, the rhetoric of Keynesian economics, etc.). This view of rhetoric as a dimension in rather than a type of discourse introduces an important and probably necessary refinement in the sophistic program. The seemingly impossible task of finding a single model domain for rhetorical activity is avoided, since we can generate many models. The specificity here also reduces the temptation to separate form from content, a problem that haunted renaissance humanists who committed themselves to a generalized concept of eloquence. Where the domain of interest is limited to any one of the human sciences, we are less likely to drift away from questions of substance, less likely to separate what is said from how it is said and what is argued from how it is argued. Consequently, increasing the number of rhetorical models assures us that each model is anchored in a definite, concrete kind of activity.

Or does it? We must understand what kind of activity we are studying and under what circumstances it is conducted. And these issues bring the differences between the old sophists and the new into clear relief. By the standards of the old sophistic, the human sciences, as they are now practiced, do not engage in civic or public business. Discourse in these sciences is indeed tailored to meet the needs of an audience, but the audience does not consist of the general public; it is an audience of specialists. Clearly there is rhetorical activity occurring in the human sciences, but in what sense can we regard it as public rather than technical? This is a crucial question, and if the neo-sophists cannot answer it satisfactorily, their entire project is in jeopardy. Lacking a model that provides entry into the world of civic action, the rhetoric of the human sciences would leave human scientists isolated in the web of their own technical practice.

The current literature suggests two approaches to this problem. One is to argue that when we eliminate the false pretensions of foundationalist methodology and examine the discourse of human scientists on its own terms, such discourses do not appear radically different from those used in ordinary public argument. The second is to advocate a reform in the style of academic writing so as to make it accessible to the general public. From the perspective of traditional rhetoric, I do not believe that either approach is completely satisfactory. But both have merit and should help move us toward a solution.

I have sketched a response to the first of these positions earlier in this paper, but the matter now demands more careful attention. I believe that the position is seriously flawed because it unwittingly accepts the terms of a questionable foundationalist dichotomy even as it attempts to overturn it. That dichotomy is the simple and radical separation of scientific from ordinary discourse. The foundationalist ideal posits an enormous gap between the two and denies value to any discourse that does not measure up to the scientific standard. This leads to an unrealistically rigid criterion, and so it is easy to deconstruct the work of foundationalists by exposing the rhetorical elements lurking within it. Staunch behaviorists, for example, often rely on metaphor to carry important points; and economists routinely deploy the flexible strategies of oratorical argument when their methodology demands syllogistic entailments. Hence, the temptation is almost irresistible to reverse the terms of the dichotomy and generalize the result. The argument proceeds in this way: scientists are not and cannot be disembodied thinking machines; they adapt their arguments to their audiences and sometimes make blatant use of rhetorical appeals; consequently, scientific discourse is really ordinary rhetoric.

To accept this reversal is to let our enemy do his worst. It perpetuates the false dichotomy that is the cause of the whole problem. In fact, there is no categorical distinction between the scientific and the rhetorical. Rhetoric enters into every kind of discourse, even the most scientific. That fact is sufficient to overturn the claims of those who demand a bloodless, neutral ideal for language. But the fact that rhetoric is present in all discourse does not mean that all discourse is essentially the same, or that all discourse uses the same kind of rhetoric. In the gap between an ideally rational language and ordinary talk, we can recognize various types of discourse that cluster together by virtue of common themes, strategies, and styles. No type is absolutely different from any other type, but the differences are sufficient to mark out basic genres. In fact, if we take the operation of the rhetorical dimension in discourse seriously, we can hardly avoid this conclusion. Different settings, subjects, and audiences require different forms of address. Each occasion for discourse raises certain unique problems, and so no two are precisely the same; and there are no rules that guarantee success even in a narrowly conceived genre. Nevertheless, discourse occurs in institutional settings, and the communities that establish and work within these institutions develop expectations and norms about how deliberation ought to proceed. These differ considerably from one institution to the next. Thus along the continuum of discursive practices, we can locate one identifiable cluster belonging to the human sciences and another belonging to the forum of public debate. If we are foolish enough to judge both against a rigid foundationalist ideal, they may appear essentially the same, since both are closer to each other than to a nonhuman voice of pure reason. A more realistic perspective, however, leads to the conclusion that popular oratory and scientific discourse are characteristically different, not because one employs rhetoric and the other does not, but because they use rather different rhetorics.

Institutions, however, are the products of human makers and are always open to reform. Hence we come to the second approach to our problem, an approach that would reduce the distance between the human sciences and civic activity by changing the norms of discourse in the human sciences. Advocates of this position acknowledge that the human sciences now employ types of discourse that are far removed from public practice and filled with arcane terminology, obscure references, and abstruse discussions of methodology. But, they add, these problems reflect the pretensions that follow from foundationalist dogma. These pretensions can be removed; and once human scientists cease chasing after impossible goals and recognize the affinity between their work and the business of the public, they can alter their prose in a more humane direction. This would lead to a more self-conscious awareness of the audience and would promote a better, less artificial, and more accessible rhetoric.

So far as it goes, this argument seems beyond objection. Much of the technicality of academic prose is gratuitous; it erects artificial barriers among the human sciences and between the human sciences as a whole and the public interest. Reforms that reduce these barriers are obviously beneficial. Nevertheless, I do not believe it possible, or even desirable, to remove all the essential distinctions between the way in which academics communicate with one another and the ways in which they, and other citizens, communicate with the general public. For the reasons I have just outlined above, sophistic antitheory leads to the conclusion that these two forms of communication follow different models of activity. The character of discourse must change in respect to the audience addressed, and the technical audience of the human sciences is not the same as the general audience of citizens.

The use of technical vocabulary illustrates this point clearly. The proliferation of jargon for its own sake is never desirable, but groups that work together often develop a special lexicon for good and practical reasons. A technical vocabulary allows for convenience and precision that no other mechanism can supply. This benefit applies even to my own pseudo-discipline of rhetoric. Rhetoricians generate complex, technical lexicons to describe various strategies of argument and configurations of style. This sometimes encourages the worst kind of pedantry and a confusion between the tools for studying a subject and the subject itself. Nevertheless, even those most skeptical about this paraphernalia make frequent use of it. From the sophistic perspective, of course, the lexicon tells us nothing essential about rhetoric. It can never be complete; and its elements defy arrangement in a static, logically ordered set of categories. In fact, when used properly, the lexicon changes almost every time that it is applied to a particular case. Still, it is very convenient to have such inventories available. They can help alert us to what is happening in a particular case by reference to a loose catalogue of features that we would normally expect to find, and they certainly make it easier for specialists to communicate with each other. It is far more efficient to say, "Cicero uses prosopopoeia" than to say, "Cicero addresses an audience that is not present as though it were present"—more efficient, of course, only when the writer or speaker can assume that the audience knows the technical term. But there are many instances in which this assumption is perfectly safe; and in these instances, not to use the term is to encumber the discourse, to fail to adapt to the audience, and thus to practice bad rhetoric.

Such productive use of a technical vocabulary is more than a matter of diction. In the first place, special vocabularies often enable strategies of argument that are otherwise impossible. More important, the vocabulary is one sign of a special sense of community residing within a particular audience. Where a common lexicon exists, we can also anticipate common knowledge of certain texts, of basic information and forms of argument, and the like. Taken together, these elements of common knowledge distinguish those who possess them from the general public. And these distinctions prompt forms of discourse that are rhetorically appropriate within a particular field but wholly inappropriate in other contexts.

In sum, the principles of sophistic allow us to classify the language of orators and of human scientists under the generic heading of rhetoric. Both groups practice persuasive reasoning, and both have access to a common reservoir of rhetorical techniques. Yet these same principles call attention to crucial differences that divide academic and public rhetoric into separate species. Sophistic proceeds from the study of actual practice, and practice in the two domains varies in ways that are hardly trivial. They differ typically in complexity of reasoning, use of evidence, frequency and types of images, syntactic constructions, vocabulary, assumptions about the audience's knowledge, and almost every other category relevant to classification of types of rhetoric. Those who doubt these distinctions should compare the text of a congressional debate with the prose of an academic journal. The distinctions are exaggerated by modernist presuppositions, but the main lines of division appear intractable.[22] Apparently, then, the inherent conditions surrounding academic discourse require deviation from the practices of public deliberation. Rhetorical models for technical fields and for the public sphere do not correspond, and attempts to map one directly onto the other are bound to produce considerable distortion.

At this point someone might object that my own argument rests upon a false dichotomy. The sharp distinction between the rhetoric of the human sciences and public rhetoric presumes that the business of human scientists is entirely confined to technical audiences. This is plainly not true. Human scientists often address the public, sometimes quite eloquently, and to stipulate that these efforts fall outside the business of the human sciences is to adopt a more than foundationalist rigidity. But note that my position does not involve absolute distinctions; it argues for a unified rhetorical field that displays certain clusters of rhetorical activity. The typical practices of human scientists come well within the orbit of the technical cluster; other practices fall between the technical and the public range: and still others are clearly public. As I have persistently argued, rhetoric cannot achieve abstract theoretical coherence, and so it must rely on models specific to relatively well defined spheres of activity. Consequently, rhetorical practices in the middle zone of the continuum present special problems and should be approached by analogical extensions of models from one of the two more stable zones, or better yet by the juxtaposition of models of both types. But when the discourse of human scientists clearly falls within the characteristics of the public cluster, their discourse becomes part of and responsive to a public rhetorical model. Human scientists then become, in Cicero's broad sense of the term, orators. This does not mean that they cease to be human scientists, but it does mean that they adopt a rhetorical model drawn from another region of typical activity. It also means that oratory is part of the business of the human sciences, since they operate within the larger context of public life. Nevertheless, what marks out a human science and distinguishes it from other activities is its technical, not its public, rhetoric. Hence, the extension of the human sciences into the public domain does not eradicate the distinction between technical and public models for rhetorical discourse. It simply creates a split reference in the human sciences.

Viewed from this perspective, the main problem in the new sophistic appears as the obverse of the main problem in its older variants. Traditional humanists struggle to control the anarchistic tendencies of public rhetoric by discovering philosophical controls capable of narrowing its open texture without destroying it. Modern sophists struggle against the constrictive tendencies of technical rhetoric by finding a means of opening it to public rhetoric without destroying its integrity. Fortunately, however, the symmetry of oppositions here is not total. In the humanist tradition, the split reference between the philosophical and rhetorical ideals hardens into a dilemma, since the two assume distinct goals (truth as opposed to persuasion) and attach themselves to different forms of experience (contemplation as opposed to action). The split reference in modern sophistic does not entail such bald confrontations. A general concept of rhetorical practice unifies the technical and public domains. In both, the goal of discourse is persuasion; and the tension between contemplation and action is reduced considerably, since persuasion about theoretical issues becomes a kind of activity in its own right. The conditions for effecting persuasion in the two domains are typically different, and thus they generate specifically different models of rhetorical practice. A model for one cannot be forced on the other. But unlike the schismatic relationship between the rhetorical and philosophical ideals, models from the technical and public domains exist in an analogic, not an antagonistic, relationship. Features identified in one region bear a generic resemblance to features contained within the other, and with sufficient care and attention to detail, the two frames of reference can interact in a way that deepens perception in both.

The greatest obstacle to this productive interaction consists in the categorical, unqualified effort to collapse the scientific into the rhetorical. That project begins with concepts that are too general and promises to end with results that are too specific. Its almost certain outcome is to solidify research within the practices of many different human sciences. The abstract credo of sophistic rhetoric is too amorphous and fragile to bind the study of such practices together and resist their fragmentation into isolated modules. Moreover, without reference to a concrete model in the public domain, special rhetorics invariably turn inward and lose contact with the larger context of public action. Ironically, then, a unified, general conception of rhetoric seems likely to destroy the unity of rhetoric. Sophistic rhetoric sacrifices theoretical coherence for the power of coherent practical action. It seeks to arm us in the effort to encompass and explain particular situations, and so it retains a useful identity only by reference to common situations and problems. This leads us back to the one realm of practical action common to all of us, the domain of public affairs. The modern specialization of knowledge is so vast and cuts so deep that no one can hope to overturn its results and restore the unified structure of the old humanist culture. But it does not need to be overturned, merely placed in a proper context. This is, I believe, the authentic goal of sophistic rhet-

Michael C. Leff

oric; and to achieve it, we must learn to split our references to the world of action and to balance in harmonious tension the perspectives of both the old and the new sophistic.

NOTES

1. I borrow the term "foundationalism" from John Nelson's essay "Political Theory as Political Rhetoric," in *What Should Political Theory Be Now?* (Albany: State University of New York Press, 1983), pp. 169–240. The term refers to the common characteristics of philosophic positions such as positivism and strict rationalism.

2. *De Oratore*, I:108. See Jerrold E. Siegel, *Rhetoric and Philosophy in Renaissance Humanism: The Union of Eloquence and Wisdom from Petrarch to Valla* (Princeton: Princeton University Press, 1968), for an analysis of this issue in Cicero and the renaissance humanists.

3. Max Black, *Models and Metaphors: Studies in Language and Philosophy* (Ithaca: Cornell University Press, 1962), pp. 41–42.

4. Much of the impulse for this movement arises from Chaim Perelman's effort to revive rhetoric as an intellectual discipline and apply its perspective to scholarly as well as public discourse. The most complete statement of this program is Chaim Perelman and Lucie Olbrechts-Tyteca, *The New Rhetoric: A Treatise on Argumentation*, trans. John Wilkinson and Purcell Weaver (Notre Dame, Ind.: University of Notre Dame Press, 1969). The work was originally published in French in 1958.

5. See Michael C. Leff, "The Material of the Art in the Latin Handbooks of the Fourth Century A.D.," in Brian Vickers, ed., *Rhetoric Re-Valued* (Binghampton, N.Y.: Center for Medieval and Early Renaissance Studies, 1982), p. 72.

6. Donald McCloskey, "The Rhetoric of Economics," *Journal of Economic Literature* 21 (1983): 508–15.

7. To my knowledge, the most notable effort in this direction is the comment by Paul Osker Kristeller at the end of his *Renaissance Thought and Its Sources* (New York: Columbia University Press, 1979), pp. 257–59.

8. See Michael C. Leff, "In Search of Ariadne's Thread: A Review of Recent Literature on Rhetorical Theory," *Central States Speech Journal* 29 (1978): 73–91.

9. See Perelman and Olbrechts-Tyteca, *The New Rhetoric*, pp. 509–14.

10. Nelson, "Political Theory as Political Rhetoric," pp. 176–93.

11. Ibid., p. 185.

12. This is one basis for Plato's indictment of rhetoric in his dialogue *Gorgias*. That dialogue perceptively locates essential features of sophistic rhetoric and recognizes clearly the threat they pose to the author's own philosophical program. Ironically, then, it is one of the best available sources for reconstructing the thought of the ancient sophists.

13. *Institutio Oratoria*, II: xviii: 1–4.

14. These characteristics describe what is generally known as the "second sophistic" movement, the dominant approach to rhetoric in late antiquity. See George Kennedy, *The Art of Persuasion in the Roman World* (Princeton: Princeton University Press, 1972), pp. 553–613.

15. See Richard McKeon, "Rhetoric in the Middle Ages," *Speculum* 17 (1942): 1–32.

16. Hannah Barbara Gerl, "Inventio und Dispositio: Zum Paradigmenwechsel von der Scholastik zum Humanismus," paper presented at the Fourth Biennial Meeting of the International Society for the History of Rhetoric, Florence, June 1983.

17. Our knowledge of the role that oratory played in renaissance culture is still rather vague. Recent scholarship indicates that it was more broadly used and more important than previously thought. See Kristeller, *Renaissance Thought*, pp. 248–9.

18. See, for example, *Nicocles*, 5–9.

19. This whole complex matter is analyzed in Walter J. Ong's excellent book, *Ramus, Method and the Decay of Dialogue* (Cambridge: Harvard University Press, 1958).

20. This paragraph broadly follows Walter J. Ong, *Rhetoric, Romance, and Technology: Studies of the Interaction of Expression and Culture* (Ithaca: Cornell University Press, 1971), pp. 6–9.

21. McCloskey, "Rhetoric of Economics," p. 513, indicates the relevance of this approach to the teaching of economics. His reference to Polanyi's concept of tacit knowledge seems especially significant.

22. I would cite the career of Cicero as a case in point. He is a quintessentially premodern man, a consummate rhetorician, and a thinker devoted to bridging the gap between the theoretical and the practical. Yet his *De Re Publica* uses a rhetoric of a different complexion and configuration than the rhetoric of his *Pro Murena*, a forensic oration incorporating reference to political theory. If, as is often asserted, Cicero writes rhetorical philosophy, his works demonstrate that philosophical and popular rhetoric adhere to measurably different models.

3 SCIENCE AS SOLIDARITY

RICHARD RORTY

In our culture, the notions of "science," "rationality," "objectivity," and "truth" are bound up with one another. Science is thought of as offering "hard," "objective" truth: truth as correspondence to reality, the only sort of truth worthy of the name. Humanists like philosophers, theologians, historians, and literary critics have to worry about whether they are being "scientific"—whether they are entitled to think of their conclusions, no matter how carefully argued, as worthy of the term "true." We tend to identify seeking "objective truth" with "using reason," and so we think of the natural sciences as paradigms of rationality. We also think of rationality as a matter of following procedures laid down in advance, of being "methodical." So we tend to use "methodical," "rational," "scientific," and "objective" as synonyms.

Worries about "cognitive status" and "objectivity" are characteristic of a secularized culture in which the scientist replaces the priest. The scientist is now seen as the person who keeps humanity in touch with something beyond itself. As the universe was depersonalized, beauty (and, in time, even moral goodness) came to be thought of as "subjective." So truth is now thought of as the only point at which human beings are responsible to something nonhuman. A commitment to "rationality" and to "method" is thought to be a recognition of this responsibility. The scientist becomes a moral exemplar, one who selflessly exposes himself again and again to the hardness of fact.

One result of this way of thinking is that any academic discipline which wants a place at the trough, but is unable to offer the predictions and the technology provided by the natural sciences, must either pretend to imitate science or find some way of obtaining "cognitive status" without the necessity of discovering facts. Practitioners of these disciplines must either affiliate themselves with this quasi-priestly order by using terms like "behavioral sciences" or else find something other than "fact" to be concerned with. People in the humanities typically choose the latter strategy. They either describe themselves as con-

38

cerned with "value" as opposed to facts, or as developing and inculcating habits of "critical reflection."

Neither sort of rhetoric is very satisfactory. No matter how much humanists talk about "objective values," the phrase always sounds vaguely confused. It gives with one hand what it takes back with the other. The distinction between the objective and the subjective was designed to parallel that between fact and value, so an objective value sounds as vaguely mythological as a winged horse. Talk about the humanists' special skill at critical reflection fares no better. Nobody really believes that philosophers or literary critics are better at critical thinking, or at taking big broad views of things, than theoretical physicists or microbiologists. So society tends to ignore both these kinds of rhetoric. It treats humanities as on a par with the arts, and thinks of both as providing pleasure rather than truth. Both are, to be sure, thought of as providing "high" rather than "low" pleasures. But an elevated and spiritual sort of pleasure is still a long way from the grasp of a truth.

These distinctions between hard facts and soft values, truth and pleasure, and objectivity and subjectivity are awkward and clumsy instruments. They are not suited to dividing up culture; they create more difficulties than they resolve. It would be best to find another vocabulary, to start afresh. But in order to do so, we first have to find a new way of describing the natural sciences. It is not a question of debunking or downgrading the natural scientist, but simply of ceasing to see him as a priest. We need to stop thinking of science as the place where the human mind confronts the world, and of the scientist as exhibiting proper humility in the face of superhuman forces. We need a way of explaining why scientists are, and deserve to be, moral exemplars which does not depend on a distinction between objective fact and something softer, squishier, and more dubious.

To get such a way of thinking, we can start by distinguishing two senses of the term "rationality." In one sense, the one I have already discussed, to be rational is to be methodical: that is, to have criteria for success laid down in advance. We think of poets and painters as using some faculty other than "reason" in their work because, by their own confession, they are not sure of what they want to do before they have done it. They make up new standards of achievement as they go along. By contrast, we think of judges as knowing in advance what criteria a brief will have to satisfy in order to invoke a favorable decision, and of business people as setting well-defined goals and being judged by their success in achieving them. Law and business are good examples of rationality, but the scientist, knowing in advance what would count as disconfirming his hypothesis and prepared to abandon that hypothesis as a result of the unfavorable outcome of a single experiment, seems a truly heroic example. Further, we seem to have a clear criterion for the success of a scientific theory—namely, its ability to predict, and thereby to enable us to control some portion of the world. If to be rational means to be able to lay down criteria in advance, then it is plausible to take natural science as the paradigm of rationality.

The trouble is that in this sense of "rational" the humanities are never going to qualify as rational activities. If the humanities are concerned with ends rather than means, then there is no way to evaluate their success in terms of antecedently specified criteria. If we already knew what criteria we wanted to satisfy, we would not worry about whether we were pursuing the right ends. If we thought we knew the goals of culture and society in advance, we would have no use for the humanities—as totalitarian societies in fact do not. It is characteristic of democratic and pluralistic societies to continually redefine their goals. But if to be rational means to satisfy criteria, then this process of redefinition is bound to be nonrational. So if the humanities are to be viewed as rational activities, rationality will have to be thought of as something other than the satisfaction of criteria which are statable in advance.

Another meaning for "rational" is, in fact, available. In this sense, the word means something like "sane" or "reasonable" rather than "methodical." It names a set of moral virtues: tolerance, respect for the opinions of those around one, willingness to listen, reliance on persuasion rather than force. These are the virtues which members of a civilized society must possess if the society is to endure. In this sense of "rational," the word means something more like "civilized" than like "methodical." When so construed, the distinction between the rational and the irrational has nothing in particular to do with the difference between the arts and the sciences. On this construction, to be rational is simply to discuss any topic—religious, literary, or scientific— in a way which eschews dogmatism, defensiveness, and righteous indignation.

There is no problem about whether, in this latter, weaker, sense, the humanities are "rational disciplines." Usually humanists display the moral virtues in question. Sometimes they don't, but then sometimes scientists don't either. Yet these moral virtues are felt to be not enough. Both humanists and the public hanker after rationality in the first, stronger sense of the term: a sense which is associated with objective truth, correspondence to reality, and method, and criteria.

We should not try to satisfy this hankering, but rather try to eradicate it. No matter what one's opinion of the secularization of culture, it was a mistake to try to make the natural scientist into a new sort of priest, a link between the human and the nonhuman. So was the idea that some sorts of truths are "objective" whereas others are merely "subjective" or "relative"—the attempt to divide up the set of true sentences into "genuine knowledge" and "mere opinion," or into the "factual" and "judgmental." So was the idea that the scientist has a special method which, if only the humanists would apply it to ultimate values, would give us the same kind of self-confidence about the moral ends as we now have about technological means. I think that we should content ourselves with the second, "weaker" conception of rationality, and avoid the first, "stronger" conception. We should avoid the idea that there is some special virtue in knowing in advance what criteria you are going to satisfy, in having standards by which to measure progress.

One can make these issues somewhat more concrete by taking up the current controversy among philosophers about the "rationality of science." For some twenty years, ever since the publication of Thomas Kuhn's book *The Structure of Scientific Revolutions*, philosophers have been debating whether science is rational. Attacks on Kuhn for being an "irrationalist" are now as frequent and as urgent as were, in the thirties and forties, attacks on the logical positivists for saying that moral judgments were "meaningless." We are constantly being warned of the danger of "relativism," which will beset us if we give up our attachment to objectivity, and to the idea of rationality as obedience to criteria.

Whereas Kuhn's enemies routinely accuse him of reducing science to "mob psychology," and pride themselves on having (by a new theory of meaning, or reference, or verisimilitude) vindicated the "rationality of science," his pragmatist friends (such as myself) routinely congratulate him on having softened the distinction between science and nonscience. It is fairly easy for Kuhn to show that the enemies are attacking a straw man. But it is harder for him to save himself from his friends. For he has said that "there is no theory-independent way to reconstruct phrases like 'really there.'"[1] He has asked whether it really helps "to imagine that there is some one full, objective, true account of nature and that the proper measure of scientific achievement is the extent to which it brings us closer to that ultimate goal."[2] We pragmatists quote these passages incessantly in the course of our effort to enlist Kuhn in our campaign to drop the objective-subjective distinction altogether.

What I am calling "pragmatism" might also be called "left-wing Kuhnianism." It has been also rather endearingly called (by one of its critics, Clark Glymour) the "new fuzziness," because it is an attempt to blur just those distinctions between the objective and the subjective and between fact and value which the criterial conception of rationality has developed. We fuzzies would like to substitute the idea of "un-

Richard Rorty

forced agreement" for that of "objectivity." We should like to put all of culture on an epistemological level—or, to put it another way, we would like to get rid of the idea of "epistemological level" or "cognitive status." We would like to disabuse social scientists and humanists of the idea that there is something called "scientific status" which is a desirable goal. On our view, "truth" is a univocal term. It applies equally to the judgments of lawyers, anthropologists, physicists, philologists, and literary critics. There is no point in assigning degrees of "objectivity" or "hardness" to such disciplines. For the presence of unforced agreement in all of them gives us everything in the way of "objective truth" which one could possibly want: namely, intersubjective agreement.

As soon as one says that objectivity is intersubjectivity, one is likely to be accused of being a relativist. That is the epithet traditionally applied to pragmatists. But this epithet is ambiguous. It can name any of three different views. The first is the silly and self-refuting view that every belief is as good as every other. The second is the wrong-headed view that "true" is an equivocal term, having as many meanings as there are contexts of justification. The third is the ethnocentric view that there is nothing to be said about either truth or rationality apart from descriptions of the familiar procedures of justification which a given society—*ours*—uses in one or another area of inquiry. The pragmatist does hold this third, ethnocentric, view. But he does not hold the first or the second.

But "relativism" is not an appropriate term to describe this sort of ethnocentrism. For we pragmatists are not holding a positive theory which says that something is relative to something else. Instead, we are making the purely *negative* point that we would be better off without the traditional distinctions between knowledge and opinion, construed as the distinction between truth as correspondence to reality and truth as a commendatory term for well-justified belief. Our opponents call this negative claim "relativistic" because they cannot imagine that anybody would seriously deny that truth has an intrinsic nature. So when we say that there is nothing to be said about truth save that each of us will commend as true those beliefs which he or she finds good to believe, the realist is inclined to interpret this as one more positive theory about the nature of truth: a theory according to which truth is simply the contemporary opinion of a chosen individual or group. Such a theory would, of course, be self-refuting. But we pragmatists do not have a theory of truth, much less a relativistic one. As partisans of solidarity, our account of the value of cooperative human inquiry has only an ethical base, not an epistemological or meta-physical one.

To say that we must be ethnocentric may sound suspicious, but this will only happen if we identify ethnocentrism with pig-headed refusal to talk to representatives of other communities. In my sense of ethno-centrism, to be ethnocentric is simply to work by our own lights. The defense of ethnocentrism is simply that there are no other lights to work by. Beliefs suggested by another individual or another culture must be tested by trying to weave them together with beliefs which we already have. We *can* so test them, because everything which we can identify as a human being or as a culture will be something which shares an enormous number of beliefs with us. (If it did not, we would simply not be able to recognize that it was speaking a language, and thus that it had any beliefs at all.)

This way of thinking runs counter to the attempt, familiar since the eighteenth century, to think of political liberalism as based on a con-ception of the nature of man. To most thinkers of the Enlightenment, it seemed clear that the access to Nature which physical science had provided should now be followed by the establishment of social, politi-cal, and economic institutions which were "in accordance with Nature." Ever since, liberal social thought has centered on social re-form as made possible by objective knowledge of what human beings are like—not knowledge of what Greeks or Frenchmen or Chinese are like, but of humanity as such. This tradition dreams of a universal human community which will exhibit a nonparochial solidarity be-cause it is the expression of an ahistorical human nature.

Philosophers who belong to this tradition, who wish to ground soli-darity in objectivity, have to construe truth as correspondence to real-ity. So they must construct an epistemology which had room for a kind of justification which is not merely social but natural, springing from human nature itself, and made possible by a link between that part of nature and the rest of nature. By contrast, we pragmatists, who wish to reduce objectivity to solidarity, do not require either a metaphysics or an epistemology. We do not need an account of a relation between be-liefs and objects called "correspondence," nor an account of human cognitive abilities which ensures that our species is capable of entering into that relation. We see the gap between truth and justification not as something to be bridged by isolating a natural and transcultural sort of rationality which can be used to criticize certain cultures and praise others, but simply as the gap between the actual good and the possible better. From a pragmatist point of view, to say that what is rational for

Richard Rorty

us now to believe may not be *true* is simply to say that somebody may come up with a better idea.

On this pragmatist view of rationality as civility, inquiry is a matter of continually reweaving a web of beliefs rather than the application of criteria to cases. Criteria change in just the way other beliefs change, and there is no touchstone which can preserve any criterion from possible revision. That is why the pragmatist is not frightened by the specter of "cultural relativism." Our interchange with other communities and cultures is not to be thought of as a clash between irreconcilable systems of thought, deductively inferred from incompatible first premises. Alternative cultures should not be thought of on the model of alternative geometries—as irreconcilable because they have axiomatic structures and contradictory axioms. Such geometries are *designed* to be irreconcilable. Individual and cultural webs of belief are not so designed, and do not have axiomatic structures.

Cultures can, indeed, protect themselves by institutionalizing knowledge-claims and making people suffer who do not hold certain beliefs. But such institutional backups take the form of bureaucrats and policemen, not of "rules of language" or "criteria of rationality." The criterial conception of rationality has suggested that every distinct culture comes equipped with certain unchallengeable axioms, "necessary truths," and that these form barriers to communication between cultures. So it has seemed as if there could be no conversation between cultures but only subjugation by force. On the pragmatic conception of rationality, there are no such barriers. The distinction between different cultures differs only in degree from the distinction between theories held by members of a single culture. The Tasmanian aborigines and the British colonies, for example, had trouble in communicating, but this trouble was different only in extent from the difficulties in communication experienced by Gladstone and Disraeli. The trouble in all such cases is just the difficulty of explaining why other people disagree with us, and of reweaving our beliefs so as to fit the fact of disagreement together with the other beliefs we hold. The same pragmatist (and, more specifically, Quinean) arguments which dispose of the positivist's distinction between analytic and synthetic truths dispose of the anthropologists' distinction between the intercultural and the intracultural.

Another reason for describing us as "relativistic" is that we pragmatists drop the idea that inquiry is destined to converge to a single point—that Truth is "out there" waiting for human beings to arrive at it. This idea seems to us an unfortunate attempt to carry a religious conception over into a culture. All that is worth preserving of the claim that rational inquiry will converge to a single point is the claim that we must be able to explain why past false views were held in the past, and thus explain how we go about reeducating our benighted ancestors. To say that we think we are heading in the right direction is just to say, with Kuhn, that we can, by hindsight, tell the story of the past as a story of progress.

But the fact that we can trace such a direction and tell such a story does not mean that we have gotten closer to a goal which is out there waiting for us. We cannot, I think, imagine a moment at which the human race could settle back and say, "Well, now that we've finally arrived at the Truth we can relax." Paul Feyerabend is right in suggesting that we should discard the metaphor of inquiry, and human activity generally, as converging rather than proliferating, becoming more unified rather than more diverse. On the contrary, we should relish the thought that the sciences as well as the arts will *always* provide a spectacle of fierce competition between alternative theories, movements, and schools. The end of human activity is not rest, but rather richer and better human activity. We should think of human progress as making it possible for human beings to do more interesting things and be more interesting people, not as heading toward a place which has somehow been prepared for us in advance. To drop the criterial conception of rationality in favor of the pragmatist conception would be to give up the idea of Truth as something to which we were responsible. Instead we should think of "true" as a word which applies to those beliefs upon which we are able to agree, as roughly synonymous with "justified." To say that beliefs can be agreed upon without being true is, once again, merely to say that somebody might come up with a better idea.

Another way of characterizing this line of thought is to say that pragmatists would like to drop the idea that human beings are responsible to a nonhuman power. We hope for a culture in which questions about the "objectivity of value" or the "rationality of science" would seem equally unintelligible. Pragmatists would like to replace the desire for objectivity—the desire to be in touch with a reality which is more than some community with which we identify ourselves—with the desire for solidarity with that community. They think that the habits of relying on persuasion rather than force, of respect for the opinions of colleagues, of curiosity and eagerness for new data and ideas, are the *only* virtues which scientists have. They do not think that there is an intellectual virtue called "rationality" over and above these moral virtues.

On this view there is no reason to praise scientists for being more "objective" or "logical" or "methodical" or "devoted to truth" than other people. But there is plenty of reason to praise the institutions they have developed and within which they work, and to use these as models for the rest of culture. For these institutions give concreteness and detail to the idea of "unforced agreement." Reference to such institutions fleshes out the idea of "a free and open encounter"—the sort of encounter in which truth cannot fail to win. On this view, to say that truth will win in such an encounter is not to make a metaphysical claim about the connection between human reason and the nature of things. It is merely to say that the best way to find out what to believe is to listen to as many suggestions and arguments as you can.

My rejection of traditional notions of rationality can be summed up by saying that the only sense in which science is exemplary is that it is a model of human solidarity. We should think of the institutions and practices which make up various scientific communities as providing suggestions about the way in which the rest of culture might organize itself. When we say that our legislatures are "unrepresentative" or "dominated by special interests," or that the art world is dominated by "fashion," we are contrasting these areas of culture with areas which seem to be in better order. The natural sciences strike us as being such areas. But, on this view, we shall not explain this better order by thinking of the scientists as having a "method" which the rest of us would do well to imitate, nor as benefiting from the desirable hardness of their subjects compared with the undesirable softness of other subjects. If we say that sociology or literary criticism "is not a science," we shall mean merely that the amount of agreement among sociologists or literary critics on what counts as significant work, work which needs following up, is less than among, say, microbiologists.

Pragmatists will not attempt to explain this latter phenomenon by saying that societies or literary texts are squishier than molecules, or than the human sciences cannot be as "value-free" as the natural sciences, or that the sociologists and critics have not yet found their paradigms. Nor will they assume that "a science" is necessarily something which we want sociology to be. One consequence of their view is the suggestion that perhaps "the human sciences" *should* look quite different from the natural sciences. This suggestion is not based on epistemological or metaphysical considerations which show that inquiry into societies must be different from inquiry into things. Instead, it is based on the observation that natural scientists are interested primarily in predicting and controlling the behavior of things, and that prediction and control may not be what we want from our sociologists and our literary critics.

Despite the encouragement he has given it, however, Kuhn draws back from this pragmatist position. He does so when he asks for an explanation of "why science works." The request for such an explanation binds him together with his opponents and separates him from his left-wing friends. Anti-Kuhnians tend to unite in support of the claim that "merely psychological or sociological reasons" will not explain why natural science is so good at predicting. Kuhn joins them when he says that he shares "Hume's itch"—the desire for "an explanation of the viability of the whole language game that involves 'induction' and underpins the form of life we live."[3]

Pragmatists think that one will suffer from Hume's itch only if one has been scratching oneself with what has sometimes been called "Hume's fork"—the distinction between "relations of ideas" and "matters of fact." This distinction survives in contemporary philosophy as the distinction between "questions of language" and "questions of fact." We pragmatists think that philosophers of language such as Wittgenstein, Quine, Goodman, Davidson, and others have shown us how to get along without these distinctions. Once one has lived without them for a while, one learns to live without those between knowledge and opinion, or between subjective and objective, as well. The purposes served by the latter distinctions come to be served by the unproblematic sociological distinction between areas in which unforced agreement is relatively infrequent and areas in which it is relatively frequent. So we do not itch for an explanation of the success of recent Western science any more than for the success of recent Western politics. That is why we fuzzies applaud Kuhn when he says that "one does not know what a person who denies the rationality of learning from experience is trying to say," but are aghast when he goes on to ask *why* "we have no rational alternatives to learning from experience."[4]

On the pragmatist view, the contrast between "relations of ideas" and "matters of fact" is a special case of the bad seventeenth-century contrasts between being "in us" and being "out there," between subject and object, between our beliefs and what those beliefs (moral, scientific, theological, etc.) are trying to get right. Pragmatists avoid this latter contrast by instead contrasting our beliefs with proposed alternative beliefs. They recommend that we worry only about the choice between two hypotheses, rather than about whether there is something which "makes" either true. To take this stance would rid us of questions about the objectivity of value, the rationality of science, and the causes of the viability of our language games. All such theoretical questions would be replaced with practical questions about whether we ought to keep our present values, theories, and practices or try to replace them with others. Given such a replacement, there would be nothing to be responsible to except ourselves.

Richard Rorty

This may sound like solipsistic fantasy, but the pragmatist regards it as an alternative account of the nature of intellectual and moral responsibility. He is suggesting that instead of invoking anything like the idea-fact, or language-fact, or mind-world, or subject-object distinctions to explicate our intuition that there is something out there to be responsible to, we just drop that intuition. We should drop it in favor of the thought that we might be better than we presently are—in the sense of being better scientific theorists, or citizens, or friends. The backup for this intuition would be the actual or imagined existence of other human beings who were already better (utopian fantasies, or actual experience, of superior individuals or societies). On this account, to be responsible is a matter of what Peirce called "contrite fallibilism" rather than of respect for something beyond. The desire for "objectivity" boils down to a desire to acquire beliefs which will eventually receive unforced agreement in the course of a free and open encounter with people holding other beliefs.

Pragmatists interpret the goal of inquiry (in any sphere of culture) as the attainment of an appropriate mixture of unforced agreement with tolerant disagreement (where what counts as appropriate is determined, within that sphere, by trial and error). Such a reinterpretation of our sense of responsibility would, if carried through, gradually make unintelligible the subject-object model of inquiry, the child-parent model of moral obligation, and the correspondence theory of truth. A world in which those models, and that theory, no longer had any intuitive appeal would be a pragmatist's paradise.

When Dewey urged that we try to create such a paradise, he was said to be irresponsible. For, it was said, he left us bereft of weapons to use against our enemies; he gave us nothing with which to "answer the Nazis." When we new fuzzies try to revive Dewey's repudiation of criteriology, we are said to be "relativistic." We must, people say, believe that every coherent view is as good as every other, since we have no "outside" touchstone for choice among such views. We are said to leave the general public defenseless against the witch doctor, the defender of creationism, or anyone else who is clever and patient enough to deduce a consistent and wide-ranging set of theorems from his "alternative first principles."

Nobody is convinced when we fuzzies say that we can be just as morally indignant as the next philosopher. We are suspected of being contritely fallibilist when righteous fury is called for. Even when we actually display appropriate emotions we get nowhere, for we are told that we have no *right* to these emotions. When we suggest that one of the few things we know (or need to know) about truth is that it is what wins in a free and open encounter, we are told that we have defined "true" as "satisfies the standards of our community." But we pragmatists do not hold this relativist view. We do not infer from "there is no way to step outside communities to a neutral standpoint" that "there is no rational way to justify liberal communities over totalitarian communities." For that inference involves just the notion of "rationality" as a set of ahistorical principles which pragmatists abjure. What we in fact infer is that there is no way to beat totalitarians in argument by appealing to shared common premises, and no point in pretending that a common human nature makes the totalitarians unconsciously hold such premises.

The claim that we fuzzies have no right to be furious at moral evil, no right to commend our views as true unless we simultaneously refute ourselves by claiming that there are objects out there which *make* those views true, begs all the theoretical questions. But it gets to the practical and moral heart of the matter. This is the question of whether notions like "unforced agreement" and "free and open encounter"—descriptions of social situations—can take the place in our moral lives of notions like "the world," "the will of God," "the moral law," "what our beliefs are trying to represent accurately," and "what makes our beliefs true." All the philosophical presuppositions which make Hume's fork seem inevitable are ways of suggesting that human communities must justify their existence by striving to attain a nonhuman goal. To suggest that we can forget about Hume's fork, forget about being responsible to what is "out there," is to suggest that human communities can only justify their existence by comparisons with other actual and possible human communities.

I can make this contrast a bit more concrete by asking whether free and open encounters, and the kind of community which permits and encourages such encounters, are for the sake of truth and goodness, or whether "the quest for truth and goodness" is simply the quest for that kind of community. Is the sort of community which is exemplified by groups of scientific inquirers and by democratic political institutions a means to an end, or is the formation of such communities the only goal we need? Dewey thought that it was the only goal we needed, and I think he was right. But whether he was or not, this question is the one to which the debates about Kuhn's "irrationalism" and the new fuzzies' "relativism" will eventually boil down.

Dewey was accused of blowing up the optimism and flexibility of a parochial and jejune way of life (the American) into a philosophical system. So he did, but his reply was that *any* philosophical system is going to be an attempt to express the ideals of *some* community's way of life.

Richard Rorty

He was quite ready to admit that the virtue of his philosophy was, indeed, nothing more than the virtue of the way of life which it commended. On his view, philosophy does not justify affiliation with a community in the light of something ahistorical called "reason" or "transcultural principles." It simply expatiates on the special advantages of that community over other communities. Dewey's best argument for doing philosophy this way is also the best argument we partisans of solidarity have against partisans of objectivity: it is Nietzsche's argument that the traditional Western metaphysico-epistemological way of firming up our habits is not working anymore.

What would it be like to be less fuzzy and parochial than this? I suggest that it would be to become less genial, tolerant, open-minded, and fallibilist than we are now. In the nontrivial, pejorative, sense of "ethnocentric," the sense in which we congratulate ourselves on being less ethnocentric now than our ancestors were three hundred years ago, the way to avoid ethnocentrism is precisely to abandon the sort of thing we fuzzies are blamed for abandoning. It is to have only the most tenuous and cursory formulations of criteria for changing our beliefs, only the loosest and most flexible standards. Suppose that for the last three hundred years we had been using an explicit algorithm for determining how just a society was, and how good a physical theory was. Would we have developed either parliamentary democracy or relativity physics? Suppose that we had the sort of "weapons" against the fascists of which Dewey was said to deprive us—firm, unrevisable, moral principles which were not merely "ours" but "universal" and "objective." How could we avoid having these weapons turn in our hands and bash all the genial tolerance out of our own heads?

Imagine, to use another example, that a few years from now you open your copy of the *New York Times* and read that the philosophers, in convention assembled, have unanimously agreed that values are objective, science rational, truth a matter of correspondence to reality, and so on. Recent breakthroughs in semantics and meta-ethics, the report goes on, have caused the last remaining noncognitivists in ethics to recant. Similar breakthroughs in philosophy of science have led Kuhn formally to abjure his claim that there is no theory-independent way to reconstruct statements about what is "really there." All the new fuzzies have repudiated all their former views. By way of making amends for the intellectual confusion which the philosophical profession has recently caused, the philosophers have adopted a short, crisp, set of standards of rationality and morality. Next year the convention is expected to adopt the report of the committee charged with formulating a standard of aesthetic taste.

Surely the public reaction to this would not be "Saved!" but rather "Who on earth do these philosophers think they *are*?" It is one of the best things about the form of intellectal life we Western liberals lead that this *would* be our reaction. No matter how much we moan about the disorder and confusion of the current philosophical scene, about the treason of the clerks, we do not really want things any other way. What prevents us from relaxing and enjoying the new fuzziness is perhaps no more than cultural lag, the fact that the rhetoric of the Enlightenment praised the emerging natural sciences in a vocabulary which was left over from a less liberal and tolerant era. This rhetoric enshrined all the old philosophical oppositions between mind and world, appearance and reality, subject and object, truth and pleasure. Dewey thought that it was the continued prevalence of such oppositions which prevented us from seeing that modern science was a new and promising invention, a way of life which had not existed before and which ought to be encouraged and imitated, something which required a new rhetoric rather than justification by an old one.

Suppose that Dewey was right about this, and that eventually we learn to find the fuzziness which results from breaking down such oppositions spiritually comforting rather than morally offensive. What would the rhetoric of the culture, and in particular of the humanities, sound like? Presumably it would be more Kuhnian, in the sense that it would mention particular concrete achievements—paradigms—more, and "method" less. There would be less talk about rigor and more about originality. The image of the great scientist would not be of somebody who got it right but of somebody who made it new. The new rhetoric would draw more on the vocabulary of Romantic poetry and socialist politics, and less on that of Greek metaphysics, religious morality, or Enlightenment scientism. A scientist would rely on a sense of solidarity with the rest of her profession, rather than a picture of herself as battling through the veils of illusion, guided by the light of reason.

If all this happened, the term "science," and thus the oppositions between the humanities, the arts, and the sciences, might gradually fade away. Once "science" was deprived of an honorific sense, we might not need it for taxonomy. We might feel no more need for a term which groups together paleontology, physics, anthropology, and psychology than we do for one which groups together engineering, law, social work, and medicine. The people now called "scientists" would no longer think of themselves as a member of a quasi-priestly order, nor would the public think of themselves as in the care of such an order.

In this situation, "the humanities" would no longer think of themselves as such, nor would they share a common rhetoric. Each of the disciplines which now fall under that rubric would worry as little about its method or cognitive status as do mathematics, civil engineering, and sculpture. It would worry as little about its philosophical foundations. For terms which denoted disciplines would not be thought to divide "subject-matters," chunks of the world which had "interfaces" with each other. Rather, they would be thought to denote communities whose boundaries were as fluid as the interests of their members. In this heyday of the fuzzy, there would be as little reason to be self-conscious about the nature and status of one's discipline as, in the ideal democratic community, about the nature and status of one's race or sex. For one's ultimate loyalty would be to the larger community which permitted and encouraged this kind of freedom and insouciance. This community would serve no higher end than its own preservation and self-improvement, the preservation and enhancement of civilization. It would identify rationality with that effort, rather than with the desire for objectivity. So it would feel no need for a foundation more solid than reciprocal loyalty.

NOTES

1. Thomas S. Kuhn, *The Structure of Scientific Revolutions*, 2d ed. (Chicago: University of Chicago Press, 1970), p. 206.

2. Ibid., p. 171.

3. Thomas S. Kuhn, "Rationality and Theory Choice," *Journal of Philosophy*, 80 (1983): 570.

4. Ibid., pp. 569–70.

4 RHETORIC AND MATHEMATICS

PHILIP J. DAVIS

REUBEN HERSH

If rhetoric is the art of persuasion, then mathematics may seem to be its antithesis. This is believed, not because mathematics does not persuade, but rather because it seemingly needs no art to perform its persuasion. The matter does it all; the manner need only let the matter speak for itself.

In Euclid we find only bare statements of the "common notions" (the "axioms" or "postulates") followed by a rigorous and unmerciful chain of theorem, proof, theorem, proof. Indeed, in the high school geometry in which Euclid was force-fed to uncounted millions of schoolchildren, "proof" was reduced to a formal scheme in which two adjacent columns, "statements" on the left and "reasons" on the right, led inexorably from the "given" to the "to prove," from hypotheses to conclusion.

From the definitions and the axioms, the theorem is inescapable. Anyone who understands its statement will agree to its truth; to fail to agree would be to declare oneself incompetent before class and teacher.

"Mathematical certainty" is a byword for a level of certainty to which other subjects can only aspire. As a consequence, the level of advancement of a science has come to be judged by the extent to which it is mathematical. First come astronomy, mechanics, and the rest of theoretical physics. Of the biological sciences, genetics is top dog, because it has theorems and calculations. Among the so-called social sciences, economics is the most mathematical and offers its practitioners the best job market, as well as the possibility of a Nobel prize.

Mathematization is offered as the only way for a field of study to attain the rank of a science. Mathematization means formalization, casting the field of study into the axiomatic mode and thereby, it is supposed, purging it of the taint of rhetoric, of the lawyerly tricks used

53

Philip J. Davis and Reuben Hersh

by those who are unable to let facts and logic speak for themselves. For those who want to challenge this dogma, to assert the claim of rhetoric as a necessary and valid aspect of any human endeavor, mathematics appears as the dragon which must be slain.

Now, the purpose of the present article is to undermine these claims for mathematization. We say "undermine," not "refute" or "destroy," for we are well aware that the claims for mathematization are not made without reason. But their validity is limited. As skeptical a look should be cast upon mathematical theories as upon theories stated in "ordinary language."

Our goal is to show that mathematics is not really the antithesis of rhetoric, but rather that rhetoric may sometimes be mathematical, and that mathematics may sometimes be rhetorical. Our first task will be to point out (what is already generally admitted) that mathematical language, mathematical trappings, are used as a rhetorical device in various fields of endeavor, and especially in the so-called behavior sciences. Our second and major task will be to show that within the practice of mathematics itself, among the professional mathematicians, continual and essential use is made of rhetorical modes of argument and persuasion, in addition to purely formal or logical procedures.

Part 1: Mathematics as Rhetoric

It is generally believed that there are two branches of mathematics: pure and applied. We wish to point out that there are three: pure mathematics, applied mathematics, and rhetorical mathematics.

Pure mathematics is number theory, or geometry, or algebra, or analysis. It is what mathematicians do to please themselves, or each other. When they are pleased with the way something comes out, they are likely to say that it is elegant, or deep. What does that mean? Well, "deep" means difficult, nonobvious, requiring excavation of many layers beneath the surface. And "elegant" means surprising, unexpected, accomplishing much with comparatively little labor, by means of an ingenious device or a penetrating insight.

Applied mathematics, our second category, is what mathematicians do to accomplish the tasks set by the rest of society. It is numerical weather prediction, or statistical quality control of electric light bulb manufacture, or plotting of the trajectory of a rocket to Saturn. More and more often, these days, the tasks are set and paid for by the military and involve the preparation of the premature end of life on this planet.

Finally, there is rhetorical mathematics. What is that? It is what is neither pure nor applied. Not pure, because nothing of mathematical interest is done, no new mathematical ideas are brought forward, no mathematical difficulties are overcome; and not applied, because no real-world consequences are produced. No practical results issue from rhetorical mathematics—except publications, reports, and grant proposals. The word "rhetoric" means many things. One of its invidious meanings is empty verbiage or pretentious obfuscation. Mathematics can be rhetoric in this sense of the term. We call it rhetorical mathematics.

For example, you might develop a "mathematical model" for international conflict. The model might be just a list of axioms: an axiomatic model. Or it might be a collection of strategies with an associated payoff matrix: a game-theoretic model. Or again, maybe a collection of "state variables" to specify the international military-political situation, together with a set of equations relating the values of the state variables today to their values tomorrow. Program this into your computer, and you've got a simulation model.

It doesn't really matter which way you do it. You can calculate, publish, readjust your model (or throw it out and start again from scratch), calculate again, and publish again.

Why is this activity not applied mathematics? The standard picture of applied mathematics, which can be found in the first few pages of many textbooks, breaks down the work of the applied mathematician into three phases, which can be represented schematically in an arrow diagram (figure 4.1). The upper level is theory; the lower level is physical reality. The mathematical study of real-world problems (as distinct from problems in pure mathematics) begins by construction of a mathematical model. This means the representation of quantities of physical interest by mathematical variables (most often numerical, but sometimes nonnumerical: for instance, geometrical or logical) and the derivation from physical experience of relations among these variables (most often algebraic and differential equations and inequalities).

The second step, mathematical analysis, may in some cases be _solving the equation,_ obtaining an explicit formula for some variable, such as temperature, population size, or position of a planet. In other cases an explicit solution may not be attainable, but some approximate or qualitative conclusions can be obtained by mathematical reasoning; for example, the planet will remain within a certain distance of the sun; or, the population will at first increase rapidly and then level off

Philip J. Davis and Reuben Hersh

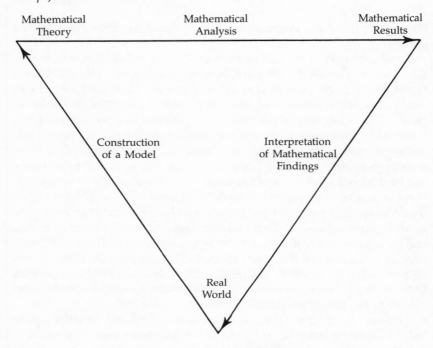

Figure 4.1.   Applied mathematics

and approach a certain limiting value; or, the temperature depends smoothly and monotonically on the diffusivity of the medium.

In addition to strict mathematical reasoning, step 2 may involve ad hoc simplifications, such as replacing some variables by constants, or dropping some "small" terms from the equations. Such steps may sometimes be justified by physical reasoning; sometimes they may merely be tentative trials, whose validity remains to be decided by the final result. Step 2 nowadays most often involves a machine computation. The act of setting up a computer program to analyze a real-world problem requires as a preliminary the introduction of variables and relations to model the problem in question. The machine computation may sometimes serve as a labor-saving substitute for thought and human analysis. But most often a certain amount of thought prior to computing is essential if the computation is not to be in one way or another misguided and useless.

The third step, interpretation in real-world terms of the mathematical or computational results, may take several forms. It may be a *prediction* that the system of interest will behave in a certain way. It may be an *explanation,* showing that certain causes could have (or could not have) certain effects. In either case, the value of the whole modeling and analyzing procedure remains undetermined until the interpretation, the final result of step 3, is tested against observation or experiment, against real-world data. The merit or validity of a model depends first of all, on, the inherent reasonableness or plausibility of the assumptions involved in step 1; second, on the tractability of the model, the possibility of carrying out in step 2 mathematical operations leading to conclusions of some novelty and interest; and finally, in step 3, on the goodness-of-fit of the results, on the degree to which the theoretical results conform to the real-world data.

This "Schaum's outline" of scientific methodology is intended to give criteria by which one may evaluate the claims for applications of mathematics in one or another field of study. The three-step paradigm is conventional and perhaps simplistic. Any particular piece of research may be limited to only one step of the three. Or all three steps may be iterated several times, as a model is gradually refined and corrected. Again, it may sometimes be impossible or inconvenient to make a clear-cut demarcation between one step and the next.

Granted all this, there are certain criteria by which the mathematician judges whether an "application" of mathematics is genuine or bogus:

> Does the depth of the real-world problem justify the complexity of the mathematical model?
> Are any genuine mathematical reasonings or nontrivial calculations carried out which require the resources of the mathematical model being proposed?
> Are the coefficients or parameters in the equations capable of being determined in a meaningful and reasonably accurate way?
> Are the conclusions capable of being tested against real-world data? Do any nonobvious practical conclusions follow from the analysis?

The introduction of mathematical methods into economics, psychology, and other branches of the so-called behavioral sciences has always been accompanied by controversy. The opponents of mathematization may have had good grounds for their resistance. But their arguments could be discounted by raising the suspicion that they did not understand the mathematical methods they were challenging. For this reason it is important to state publicly that among professional mathematicians the skepticism about behavioral-science mathematics

Philip J. Davis and Reuben Hersh

is much stronger than it is among nonmathematical behavioral scientists.

This skepticism is rarely stated in print. Unlike philosophers and literary critics, mathematicians dislike controversy. They are not used to it and will usually keep their mouths shut to avoid it. (A famous instance was Gauss's suppression of his own discovery of non-Euclidean geometry, for fear of a clamor from the "Boeotians.")

An additional reason why we mathematicians seldom state in print our skepticism about behavioral-science mathematics is this: we know that *some* of it must be worthwhile. So we cannot condemn *all* of it. As a practical matter, it would be a dreary undertaking to separate the wheat from the chaff. As a consequence we say nothing, but behind the back of the speaker on mathematical psychodynamics, we raise our eyebrows at each other and shrug.

Perhaps the knowledge that mathematicians share the opinion will strengthen the resolve of those who wish to oppose rhetorical mathematics. If they need advice or encouragement from a professional mathematician, they need go no farther than the mathematics department on their own campus. They should look for the best mathematician they can find. It does not matter whether this person is pure or applied; what matters is that he has high mathematical standards.

We can restate our negative definition of rhetorical mathematics in positive terms. Rhetorical mathematics is a form of academic gamesmanship. It depends above all on the high prestige accorded to mathematics by twentieth-century North America. Rhetorical mathematics presents itself as applied mathematics. But it is easy to tell them apart. Applied mathematics sooner or later leads to an experiment or a measurement. Either initially or ultimately, work in applied mathematics leads back to the phenomenon being modeled. Rhetorical mathematics is often incapable in principle of being tested against reality. For instance, the model may contain numerical parameters that are obviously incapable of measurement (e.g., a model of international conflict, with coefficients equal to the "aggressiveness" of the major powers).

An amusing example is brought to light in Neal Koblitz's essay "Mathematics as Propaganda."[1] He quotes from *Political Order in Changing Societies*, a definitive work on problems of developing countries by the very influential Samuel Huntington. On page 55 of the book are found three equations relating certain social and political concepts:

$$\frac{social\ mobilization}{economic\ development} = social\ frustration \left(\frac{a}{b} = c\right)$$

$$\frac{social\ frustration}{mobility\ opportunities} = political\ participation \left(\frac{c}{d} = e\right)$$

$$\frac{political\ participation}{political\ institutionalization} = political\ instability \left(\frac{e}{f} = g\right)$$

As Koblitz remarks, "Huntington never bothers to inform the reader in what sense these are equations. It is doubtful that any of the terms (a)–(g) can be measured and assigned a single numerical value. What are the units of measurement? Will Huntington allow us to operate with these equations using the well-known techniques of ninth grade algebra? If so, we could infer, for instance, that

$$a = bc = bdc = bdfg,$$

i.e., that 'social mobilization is equal to economic development times mobility opportunities times political institutionalization times political instability!'"

Part 2: Rhetoric in Mathematics

We turn now from rhetorical mathematics to mathematical rhetoric. We want to look at mathematical utterances or writings (the talk or writing of mathematicians in the pursuit of their work as mathematicians) and see what rhetorical aspects we can identify.

On the basis of the customary definition of rhetoric as natural discourse which serves to convince, rhetoric in mathematics would simply be common language put to the purpose of convincing us that something or other about mathematics is the case. What might we want to argue rhetorically? Certainly we would want to argue the utility of mathematics in its many applications. The philosophy of mathematics is also built up by rhetorical argumentation. But the *truth* of mathematics—moving down one level from a discussion of the truth to the truth itself—is considered to be established by means which are the antithesis of rhetoric. The claim made in the classroom, in the textbook, and in a good deal of philosophical writing is that mathematical truth is established by a unique mode of argumentation, which consists of pass-

Philip J. Davis and Reuben Hersh

ing from hypothesis to conclusion by means of a sequence of small logical steps, each of which is in principle mechanizable. T. O. Sloane has written ("Rhetoric," *Encyclopaedia Britannica*), "All utterance, except perhaps the mathematical formula, is aimed at influencing a particular audience at a particular time and place." Mathematical utterances, it would seem, stand apart. But the small measure of doubt which Professor Sloane has allowed himself can be enlarged greatly. Mathematical proof has its rhetorical moments and its rhetorical elements.

Suppose you were to eavesdrop on a college mathematics class which is sufficiently advanced that the instructor sets considerable store by mathematical proof. Imagine that you have broken into the lecture in the middle of such a proof. In theory, you should be hearing the presentation of those small logical transformations which are to lead inexorably from hypothesis to conclusion. Part of what you hear will indeed be such a litany. But other phrases will undoubtedly intervene: "It is easy to show that . . .", "By an obvious generalization . . .", "a long, but elementary computation, which I leave to the student, will verify that . . ."

These phrases are not proof: they are rhetoric in the service of proof. A hilarious compendium of rhetorical devices, used as proof substitutes, has recently been circulating among graduate students in mathematics and computer science. We quote a few lines from this work, which was compiled by Dana Angluin of the Yale Computer Science Department.

How to Prove it

Proof by example:
　The author gives only the case $n = 2$ and suggests that it contains most of the ideas of the general proof.
Proof by intimidation:
　"trivial"
Proof by eminent authority:
　"I saw Karp in the elevator and he said . . ."
Proof by cumbersome notation:
　Best done with access to at least four alphabets and special symbols.
And so on for a total of twenty-four categories.

The objection may be raised that all these rhetorical handwavings, desk-poundings, appeals to intuition, to pictures, to meta-arguments, to the lack of counterevidence, to the results of papers which have not yet appeared, reflect only the laziness of the lecturer or author. Somewhere behind each theorem which appears in the mathematical literature, there must stand a sequence of logical transformations moving from hypothesis to conclusion, absolutely comprehensible, certified as such by the authorities in the field, verifiable as such by even the novice, and accepted by the whole mathematical community. This impression is absolutely false. Yet it is commonly held by people outside the mathematics profession. Mathematics students sometimes carry this picture in their minds until they are themselves involved in research; at this point they experience a sudden and unexpected shock when they realize that the real world of mathematics is far from the ideal world.

In the real world of mathematics, a mathematical paper does two things. It testifies that the author has convinced herself and a circle of friends that certain "results" are true. And it presents a part of the evidence on which this conviction is based.

It presents part, not all, because certain "routine" calculations are deemed unworthy of print. Readers are expected to reproduce them for themselves. More important, certain "heuristic" reasonings, including perhaps the motivation which led in the first place to undertaking the investigation, are deemed "inessential" or "irrelevant" for purposes of publication. Knowing this unstated background motivation is what it takes to be a qualified reader of the article.

But how does one acquire this background? Almost always, by word of mouth from some other member of the intended audience, some other person already initiated into the particular area of research in question.

And what does it mean for a mathematician to have convinced himself that certain results are true? In other words, what constitutes a mathematical proof as recognized by a practicing mathematician? Disturbing and shocking as it may be, the truth is that *no explicit answer can be given*. One can only point at what is actually done in each branch of mathematics. All proofs are incomplete, from the viewpoint of formal logic. How do we decide which of these incomplete proofs are wrong, and which are correct, in the sense that they are convincing and acceptable to qualified professionals?

This can be answered only by mastering the mathematical theory in question. The answer involves knowing the difference between a serious difficulty and a routine argument. A mathematician who is a certified expert in algebraic number theory might be quite unable to tell a correct from an incorrect proof in nonstandard analysis.

Philip J. Davis and Reuben Hersh

All that one can say is that part of being a qualified expert in, say, algebraic number theory is knowing which are the crucial points in an argument where skepticism should be focused; which are the "delicate" points, as against the routine points, in an argument; which are the plausible-seeming arguments that are known to be fallacious.

A mathematics research article (or reference work or treatise) is *never* written out in complete logical detail. If it were, no one would want or be able to read it. Its logical completeness would not make it more comprehensible; rather, it would make it incomprehensible, except perhaps to computing machines. (We return to the computing machine angle below.)

If it is not completeness in the sense of formal logic, then in actual practice what does guarantee correctness of mathematical proofs? Well, there is the referee, or referees, whose approval is a necessary condition for publication. Do the referees fill in and check all the logical details of every argument? Not at all. After all, they are busy people, and refereeing is done free, as a service to the profession, on top of all their other duties. It would be difficult to obtain any broad picture of what referees actually do, since this is an activity which is private and semi-anonymous (the referee's identity is known only to the editors). Certainly there is a tremendous variation in referees. Some read every line and check every calculation; they refuse to referee any paper they cannot check in this way. It is our impression that only a small percentage of the papers published in mathematical journals receive this kind of refereeing.

For one thing, only another mathematician whose interests and training are very close to the author's would be willing and able to do this kind of checking. Such a referee would likely be favorably prejudiced toward the submitted article and thus might be a poor judge of its interest and importance for the mathematical community at large. Someone more detached from the author's special interest might be more objective, but probably less intensive in reading. A well-known American probabilist once described the refereeing process as follows: "You look for the most delicate part of the argument, check that carefully, and if that's correct, you figure the whole thing is probably right."

Undoubtedly, other factors will also influence the referee's judgment. Do the methods and result "fit in," seem reasonable, in the referee's general context or picture of the field? Is the author known to be established and reliable, or is the author an unknown, or worse still, someone known to be unoriginal or liable to error?

If an article appears in print, it is hard to be sure what that means, in terms of anyone but the author's having thoroughly understood its contents. It might help if one knew at first hand the editorial and refereeing policies of the journal in question. An editor has been quoted to us to this effect: "By choosing the referee in one way or another, I can guarantee that any particular article will be either accepted or rejected."

Once an article is published, it might be thought that it is subject to the scrutiny of the whole mathematical community. Far from it. Most published mathematical articles attract very few readers and are forgotten within a few months, except by their authors and perhaps the author's graduate students.

There are, of course, articles which are widely read and influential. "Widely read" must be understood in a relative sense; in most mathematical specialties, the total of active practitioners (publishers of research articles) is only a few hundred or so. The results that appear in an influential article will be read by dozens of scores of people and will be presented in seminars across the country and around the world. There is a premium, a reward, waiting for the student or mathematician who can find a serious error in such a paper. There is also an incentive to find extensions, generalizations, applications, alternative proofs, connections with other results.

If a mathematical result attracts widespread attention and survives continued scrutiny and analysis, it enters what might be called the tried and tested part of mathematics.

Does it then have guaranteed certainty? Of course not. The geometry of Euclid was studied intensively for two thousand years, yet it had major logical gaps which were first detected in the 1880s. How could we ever be sure that we are not also blind to some flaw in our reasoning?

Aha, someone may answer, we could be sure if we would only take the trouble, however troublesome it might be, to code our mathematical proofs in some appropriate computer language, insist that proofs be restricted to logical steps whose conditions could be incorporated into a computer program, and thereby make our proofs verifiable by machine.

As a matter of fact, this idea has actually been tried. One of the most arduous efforts in this direction was carried out in the 1970s by the Dutch mathematician N. G. de Bruijn and his associates. They developed a special computer language, AUTOMATH, with an associated Automath program. Their goal was to automate the process of checking the correctness of mathematical proofs. After years of intensive experimentation, the Automath project has been virtually abandoned. There are several reasons for this:

Philip J. Davis and Reuben Hersh

1. The formalized counterpart of normal proof material is difficult to write down and can be very lengthy.
2. Even if these translations into Automath were available in great abundance, how would one verify that they were correct, that the Automath program is itself correct, that the machine program has been correctly written, that it all has been run correctly?
3. Mathematicians and computer scientists are not really interested in doing this kind of thing.

The Automath approach represents an unrealizable dream. At the turn of the century, one might have said that a proof is that which is verifiable in an absolutely mechanical fashion. Now that a much more thoroughgoing mechanization is possible, there has been a reversal, and one hears it said that computerizability is not the hallmark of a proper proof. At the same time, the accepted practice of the mathematical community has hardly changed, except for the enlargement of the computer component.

We can show the difficulties of this "formalism" at an elementary level by looking at an attempt to present a complete, rigorous proof of a very simple theorem. Even for a very tiny piece of mathematics, the task of giving an absolutely air-tight formal proof turns out to be amazingly complicated. Professedly rigorous proofs usually have holes that are covered over by intuition. Consider the example displayed in table 4.1. This table is reproduced, with a few changes, from an excellent undergraduate textbook. It is used there to illustrate the workings of axiomatic systems, in preparation for developing the theory of non-Euclidean geometry. It is comparable to the proofs that are given in advanced works, but it is much less complex, and the individual steps are spelled out in much more detail. Table 4.1 shows three axioms, which have to do with committees and their members, and one theorem: "Every person is a member of at least two committees." This theorem does indeed follow from the axioms. This may be seen with the help of the diagram in Figure 4.2 But the point of the example is to give a completely rigorous proof. This purportedly rigorous proof is presented in 10 steps in the bottom half of table 4.1.

Without disputing the conclusion—namely, that it follows from axioms 1, 2, and 3 that every person is a member of at least two committees—let us examine the claim that the written material located between the symbols "Proof" and "Q.E.D." constitutes a proof. There is no formal definition of what an acceptable proof is. There is an informal idea that a proof is a sequence of statements written in an unambiguous and strictly formal language which proceeds from the axioms to the conclusion by means of allowed and formalized logical transformations.

TABLE 4.1.
A Simple Example of a Deductive System

The primitive terms are "person" and "collection."

Definitions: A "committee" is a collection of one or more persons. A person in a committee is called a "member" of that committee. Two committees are equal if every member of the first is a member of the second and vice versa. Two committees having no members in common are called "disjoint" committees.

Axioms: 1. Every person is a member of at least one committee.
       2. For every pair of persons there is one and only one committee of which both are members.
       3. For every committee there is one and only one disjoint committee.

Theorem: Every person is a member of at least two committees.

Proof:

Statement	Reason
1. Let p be a person.	Hypothesis; naming
2. p is a member of some committee C.	Axiom 1; naming
3. Let D be the committee which is disjoint from C.	Axiom 3; naming
4. Let r be a member of D.	Definition of "committee"; naming
5. r is not a member of C.	Definition of "disjoint"
6. There is a committee E of which p and r are members.	Axiom 2; naming
7. C and E are not equal.	Definition of "equal"; 5 and 6
8. p is a member both of C and E.	2 and 6
9. p is a member of at least two committees.	7 and 8
10. Therefore every person is a member of at least two committees.	Generalization Q.E.D.

Note: Reproduced, with a few changes, courtesy of the author, from Richard J. Trudeau, *The Non-Euclidian Revolution* (Cambridge: Birkhäuser Boston, 1987).

Philip J. Davis and Reuben Hersh

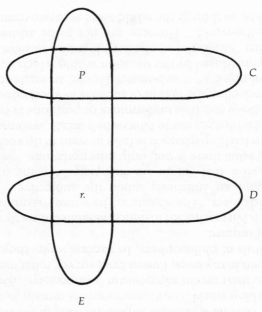

Figure 4.2. Committee membership

As we read through the proof, we find that there is one step that is more troublesome than the others. This is step 7. We pause there, and our mind has to grind a bit before going on. Why are C and E not equal? Spell out the reasons a bit more. They are not equal because r is a member of E by line (6) but not a member of C by line (5); therefore, by the definition of the equality of committees, C and E are not equal. This argument requires that we keep in the forefront of our mind three facts and then verify, mentally, that the situation implies nonequality. This conclusion is deduced from the definition, which speaks only of equality. Thus, in our mind, we have to juggle simultaneously a few more facts: what equality means and how we can proceed to get nonequality out of it. In order to make clear what is going on, the author attaches to his exposition a symbolic diagram (figure 4.2), which he says is not really a part of the proof. The picture (which is *not* part of the "proof") supplies the conviction and clarity which are not adequately achieved by the "real proof." This leaves us with a very peculiar situation: the proof does not convince; what *does* convince is not the proof.

In all human-human interfaces or human-machine interfaces, there is always the problem of verifying that what is asserted to be so is, in fact, so. For example, we assert that we have added two integers properly, or entered such and such data into the computer properly, or the computer asserts that it has carried out such and such a process properly. The passage from the assertion to the acceptance must proceed ultimately by extra-logical criteria.

This problem confronts us constantly. We find in the "reason" column of the above proof two mysterious words: "naming" and "generalization." There is no explanation of how "naming" and "generalization" are used in the proof. Now, if there is nothing worth discussing about these ideas in their application to the proof, why did the author bother mentioning them? Both are, in fact, difficult concepts, and philosophers have dedicated whole books to them. If they are important in the present context, how do we verify that the naming process or the generalization process has been carried out properly?

Look at "generalization." In step 1, a typical person is selected and named. Since it is a typical person, it is not specified which person it is. The idea is that if one reasons about a typical person, and uses only the characteristics which that person shares with all other persons, then one's deductions will apply to all persons (line [10]). Should it not be verified, then, as part of the proof, that only those characteristics have been used? What are the formal criteria for so doing? By raising such questions, one can force the proof into deeper and deeper levels of justification. What stands in the reason column now, the single word "generalization," is pure rhetoric.

A rather different point is this. Suppose we have set up certain abstract axioms. How do we know that there exists a system which satisfies these axioms? If there is no such system, then we are not really talking about anything at all. If there is such a system, its existence might be made known to us by display: "such and such, with such and such definitions, is an instance of a system that fulfills axioms 1–3." Would we then merely glance at this statement and agree with a nod of the head, or does the statement require formal verification that a purported model of a system is, indeed, a model? Again we have been driven into a deeper level of verification.

The way out of these difficulties is to give up the needless and useless goal of total rigor or complete formalization. Instead, we recognize that mathematical argument is addressed to a human audience, which possesses a background knowledge enabling it to understand the intentions of the speaker or author.

In stating that mathematical argument is not mechanical or formal, we have also stated implicitly what it is—namely, a human interchange based on shared meanings, not all of which are verbal or formulaic.

Philip J. Davis and Reuben Hersh

Closure

Let us conclude. The myth of totally rigorous, totally formalized mathematics is indeed a myth. Mathematics in real life is a form of social interaction where "proof" is a complex of the formal and the informal, of calculations and casual comments, of convincing argument and appeals to the imagination and the intuition.

The competent professional knows what are the crucial points of his argument—the points where the audience should focus its skepticism. Those are the points where he will take care to supply sufficient detail. The rest of the proof will be abbreviated. This is not a matter of the author's laziness. On the contrary, to make a proof too detailed would be more damaging to its readability than to make it too brief. Complete mathematical proof does not mean reduction to a computer program. Complete proof simply means proof in sufficient detail to convince the intended audience—a group of professionals with training and mode of thought comparable to that of the author. Consequently, our confidence in the correctness of our results is not absolute, nor is it fundamentally different in kind from our confidence in our judgments of the realities of ordinary daily life.

REFERENCES

Berlinski, David, *On Systems Analysis*. Cambridge: MIT Press, 1976.
Davis, Philip J., and Reuben Hersh, *The Mathematical Experience*. Cambridge: Birkhäuser, 1981.
de Bruijn, N. G., "A Survey of the Project Automath." In J. P. Seldin and J. R. Hindley, eds., *Essays on Combinatory Logic, Lambda Calculus, and Formalism*. New York: Academic Press, 1980.
Koblitz, Neal, "Mathematics as Propaganda." In Lynn Arthur Steen, ed., *Mathematics Tomorrow*, pp. 111–20. New York: Springer-Verlag, 1981.

5 CHARLES DARWIN

RHETORICIAN OF SCIENCE

JOHN ANGUS CAMPBELL

To claim that Charles Darwin was a "rhetorician" may seem to confuse the provinces of rhetoric and science. Their juxtaposition, however, is not only warranted; it is also inescapable. Even scientific discourse must be persuasive to rescue insight from indifference, misunderstanding, contempt, or rejection. Aristarchus was not believed when he argued that the earth moved around the sun, and although Mendel discovered the laws of inheritance, he failed to convince his scientific peers.[1] To claim that Darwin was a rhetorician, therefore, is not to dismiss his science, but to draw attention to his accommodation of his message to the professional and lay audiences whose support was necessary for its acceptance. Commonly overlooked in studies of Darwin is that he persuaded his peers and the wider community by using plain English words and plain English thoughts.[2]

Prior to Darwin, no evolutionist, whether popularizer or professional scientist, enjoyed both a popular and a professional following.[3] (Some enjoyed neither.) To understand why Darwin was persuasive with the reading public as well as with a key minority of his professional peers requires an examination of Darwin as a rhetorician of science.

I

That *The Origin of Species* was a popular book should hardly be surprising. *The Origin* is rhetorical from the ground up. The brevity of Darwin's classic work—indeed, its appearance as an "abstract"—is evidence of its rhetorical character. That *The Origin* made its appearance as a single compact volume, accessible to a general au-

John Angus Campbell

dience, was the result of a remarkable circumstance. In June 1858 Darwin was in the second year of writing *Natural Selection,* a book on transmutation which he had been planning since 1837. On the sixteenth of that month Darwin was startled to receive from the young naturalist Alfred Russel Wallace the sketch of a theory virtually identical to his own. In the wake of the Wallace letter, Darwin put aside his mammoth text, then two-thirds complete, and in nine months produced the work on which his fame rests.[4] Darwin received Wallace's letter on June eighteen, 1858.[5] He began *The Origin* on July 20, and by March 22 the book was written. *The Origin* went on sale on November 24, 1859.[6]

The ethos of its author is further proof that *The Origin* is rhetorical. Darwin directly appeals to the reader's sympathy: "my health is far from strong. . . . This Abstract . . . must necessarily be imperfect. I cannot here give references and authorities for my several statements; and I must trust to the reader reposing some confidence in my accuracy."[7] As Darwin's son Francis observed, "The reader feels like a friend who is being talked to by a courteous gentleman, not like a pupil being lectured by a professor. The tone of . . . *The Origin* is charming, and almost pathetic."[8]

The rhetorical character of *The Origin* is further established by its everyday language. Darwin's very title, *On the Origin of Species by Means of Natural Selection, or, The Preservation of Favoured Races in the Struggle for Life,* is colloquial. The themes of "origin," "selection," "preservation," "race," "struggle," and "life" underscore the intimacy, not the distance, between the author and the everyday world. Further, Darwin's exposition is as down to earth as his title. C. C. Gillispie's list of Darwin's commonplaces could be easily duplicated by any reader:

> So ordinary is the language that it almost seems as if we could be in the midst of reading a lay sermon on self-help in nature. All the proverbs on profit and loss are there, from pulpit and from counting house—On many a mickle making a muckle: 'Natural selection acts only by the preservation and accumulation of small inherited modifications, each profitable to the preserved being'; On the race being to the swift: 'The less fleet ones would be rigidly destroyed'; On progress through competition: 'Rejecting those that are bad, preserving and adding up all that are good; silently and insensibly working, whenever and wherever opportunity offers, at the improvement of each organic being'; . . . . On saving time: 'I could give many examples of how anxious bees are to save time'; . . . On the compensation that all

is, nevertheless, for the best: 'When we reflect on this struggle, we may console ourselves with the full belief, that the war of nature is not incessant, that no fear is felt, the death is generally prompt, and that the healthy and the happy survive and multiply.'[9]

Further evidence that *The Origin* is rhetorical is seen in Darwin's deference to English natural theology. Everyone knows that theological objections were raised against *The Origin*. What might surprise the modern reader is the theological defense within it. In the first edition, Darwin's flyleaf contained two citations from works in the tradition of English natural theology, one from William Whewell's *Bridgewater Treatise* and one from Francis Bacon's *Advancement of Learning*. In the second edition the first two citations were reinforced by a third from Bishop Butler's *Analogy of Revealed Religion*. In the first edition, the famous final line, which begins, "There is grandeur in this view of life," continues, "with its several powers, having been originally breathed into a few forms or into one." Starting in the second edition, the line has been changed to read "breathed by the Creator into a few forms or into one." In the fourth edition of the work, the reader finds the following postscript at the end of the table of contents: "An admirable . . . Review of this work including an able discussion on the Theological bearing of the belief in the descent of species, has now been . . . published by Professor Asa Gray, M.D., Fisher Professor of Natural History in Harvard University."[10] The reader of *The Origin* would not know that Darwin himself was responsible for financing the publication of Gray's essays in pamphlet form (originally they appeared as unsigned essays in the *Atlantic Monthly*), and until 1867 he would have no way of knowing that Darwin did not believe in the argument they contained.[11] Although Darwin privately expressed his difference with Gray in a letter in the fall of 1860, it was not until 1867 that he publicly rejected Gray's argument in the conclusion to his two-volume *Variation in Plants and Animals Under Domestication*.[12] No mention of this refutation was ever made in the subsequent two editions of *The Origin* (1869, 1872). Indeed, throughout the body of his book, whether the reader examines Darwin's case for the common ancestry of the horse, hemionus, quagga, and zebra or his account of how natural selection could have formed the eye, Darwin urges his views as more in keeping with proper respect to the ways of Providence than the views of his opponents.[13]

The rhetorical character of *The Origin* is also seen in Darwin's appeal to common sense. In language reminiscent of Scottish Commonsense Philosophy, Darwin urged that we can trust a theory which explains so many large classes of facts because this "is a method used in judging in the common events of life."[14]

II

In light of the manifest rhetorical features which would have recommended *The Origin* to a general audience, an obvious question suggests itself. Why did the clearly popular character of Darwin's writing not impede the reception of his ideas among his scientific peers? One reason Darwin's literary language did not pose the kind of obstacle to professional acceptance it would today is, as Susan Gliserman has noted, that all science was so plainly literary in Darwin's day: "I have considered the literary structure of the science writers as no difference from that of Tennyson's poems."[15] Yet, as Darwin's imagistic language was an issue, even by the standards of his own time, something more than Darwin's conformity with accepted literary conventions seems to have been involved in his generating both professional support and popular appeal.

A reputation for eloquence can be a dangerous thing. Although the art of rhetoric may make a speech or book striking, if its artistry is detected, that very fact may be advanced as reason for rejecting it. If it seems unlikely that anyone in real life could claim, "I am no orator as Brutus is," and then deliver an eloquent address without the audience's getting suspicious, it is well to recall the example of Thomas Henry Huxley. It was the no-nonsense Huxley who coined the term "agnosticism" and who characterized Comte's religion of humanity as "Catholicism *minus* Christianty."[16] Both Darwin and Huxley enjoyed solid reputations as scientists, both were unusually gifted writers, yet neither man's literary skills ever compromised his reputation for fact and dusty sobriety. Like Huxley, Darwin minimized his literary gifts. He also minimized his formidable theoretical power. Darwin's dismissal of his own colorful language and deemphasizing of the hard, sustained theoretical work behind his theory are connected.

Darwin introduced the major theoretical work of modern biology by minimizing the importance of his own speculative powers; he used provocative images throughout his exposition, yet he explained away his originality by insisting that his ideas were the result of "facts" and his metaphors mere expressions of convenience.

The thesis I am arguing is that Darwin was able to make his rhetoric seem unimportant or at best incidental to his scientific point and to persuade his professional peers because his narrative was governed by the conventions of Baconian induction and quasi-positivist standards of proof. Examination of the discrepancies between Darwin's public and private attitudes toward his method, language, and achievement offers a rare glimpse of a process which, in successful science at least, is infrequently observed: the production of the Mark Anthony effect, in which rhetoric is freely employed and effectively masked.

One of the most striking discrepancies between Darwin's public and private attitudes toward the conventions of proper scientific theory is the contrast between his declared and his actual path to discovery. In the opening paragraph of *The Origin* we read the following account:

> When on board H.M.S. 'Beagle,' as naturalist, I was much struck with certain facts in the distribution of the inhabitants of South America, and in the geological relations of the present to the past inhabitants of that continent. These facts seemed to me to throw some light on the origin of species—that mystery of mysteries as it has been called by one of our greatest philosophers. On my return home, it occurred to me, in 1837, that something might perhaps be made out on this question by patiently accumulating and reflecting on all sorts of facts which could possibly have any bearing on it. After five years work I allowed myself to speculate on the subject, and drew up some short notes; these I enlarged in 1844 into a sketch of the conclusions, which then seemed to be probable: from that period to the present day I have steadily pursued the same object. I hope that I may be excused for entering on these personal details, as I give them to show that I have not been hasty in coming to a decision.[17]

In his *Autobiography* Darwin similarly affirms: "I worked on true Baconian principles, and without any theory collected facts on a wholesale scale." Of his famous insight on reading Malthus, Darwin records: "Here, then, I had at last got a theory by which to work."[18]

What one finds when one examines Darwin's private notebooks, however, is irreconcilable with Darwin's public statements about his research method. One of the closest students of these notebooks, Howard Gruber, says of Darwin's public comments on method: "Insofar as he said anything publicly on the subject of method, Darwin presented himself in ways that are not supported by the evidence of the notebooks." In response to Darwin's granddaughter, Nora Barlow, who affirmed that in the earlier days there was a closer fit between her grandfather's theorizing and observations, Gruber observed that "it seems to me that even in these early notebooks, . . . he delighted in far-ranging speculations and saw himself as creating ideas of the same grandeur and cosmic scale as the 'early astronomers' to whom he likened himself."[19] Of the specific citations we have noted from *The Origin* and the *Autobiography,* Gruber comments:

> Taken together, these statements give an extremely misleading picture. Darwin certainly began the notebooks with a definite theory, and when he gave it up it was for what he thought was a better theory. True, when he gave up his second theory he remained in a theoretical limbo for some months. But even then he was always trying to solve theoretical problems. . . . he almost *never* collected facts without some theoretical end in view. It was not simply from observations but from hard theoretical work that he was so well prepared to grasp the significance of Malthus' essay.[20]

Occasionally in his correspondence, Darwin would similarly present himself as a firm inductionist. In a letter to Herbert Spencer's American disciple John Fiske, Darwin diplomatically avoided discussing Fiske's books by affirming: "my mind is so fixed by the inductive method, that I cannot appreciate deductive reasoning. I must begin with a good body of facts and not from principle (in which I always suspect a fallacy), and then as much deduction as you please."[21] But in letters to his associates, Darwin expressed himself quite differently. In a letter written in June 1860 to his long-time friend Charles Lyell, Darwin bemoaned a paper by Hopkins, who would not accept the argument of *The Origin* on the ground that the mere explanatory value of a theory did not prove its correctness: "on his standard of proof, natural science would never progress, for without the making of theories, I am convinced there would be no observations."[22] In a letter written in 1861 to his colleague Henry Fawcett, Darwin criticized strict inductionists in these words: "About 30 years ago there was much talk that geologists ought only to observe and not theorise; and I well remember some one saying that at this rate a man might as well go into a gravel pit and count the pebbles and describe the colours. How odd it is that anyone should not see that all observation must be for or against some view if it is to be of any service!"[23]

Given that Darwin not only understood the importance of theory, but began his own research with a conclusion that transmutation had occurred, and held to that conclusion even when he could not factually support it, how are we to account for the discrepancy between Darwin's private and public statements on method? The discrepancy, I believe, is explained by the view that Darwin was using a methodological convention important to his colleagues, though irrelevant to his science, to give a traditional warrant to a controversial thesis and hence make it persuasive.

That Darwin's public account of his method was rhetorically motivated is supported by the esteem in which Baconian induction was held by all English philosophers of science in the mid-nineteenth century. John Herschel, William Whewell, and John Stuart Mill disagreed about many particulars, but on one thing they were resolved—true science was inductive. In analyzing the place of induction in mid-century philosophy or science, David Hull makes the wry observation: "It would be nice to be able to set out at this point the meaning which the disputants attached to this word, but I cannot. Everyone meant something different by it, and in the works of a single man, one is likely to find many different uses of the word."[24] In short, by Darwin's time "Baconian Induction" had become what Bacon would have called an "Idol of the Theatre."

As Charles Bazerman points out in his paper on the history of the American Psychological Association's stylesheet, professional conventions dictate the form of scientific discourse.[25] In Darwin's time, no less than in our own, data certified by the appropriate method are far more likely to be accepted than argument about fundamentals. Even M. T. Ghiselin, who along with Gavin DeBeer holds that Darwin was true to the canons of the hypothetical-deductive method, describes Darwin's introductory paragraph to *The Origin* as a "dialectical maneuver" and observes that "Darwin, like other scientists of his day, gave much lip service to 'induction,' and such hypocrisy has long obscured the real nature of scientific discovery." Ghiselin's way of avoiding misunderstanding Darwin is "to abandon the study of words and to derive our understanding from concepts." In Ghiselin's view, "The structure of Darwin's systems explains his success and failure alike. When the process through which his discovery was generated has been understood, there is no reason whatever to treat his perfectly ingenuous accounts of the discovery as mistaken, contradictory, or hypocritical."[26]

I concur with Ghiselin's assessment of the importance of understanding "Darwin's systems." I reluctantly differ with his judgment that once this is done Darwin's statements on method emerge as "perfectly ingenuous." The testimony of Darwin's notebooks argues strongly that Darwin thought long and hard, not only about nature, but about persuasion, and that he went to great lengths, including not developing his views on the evolution of man, to minimize the shock of novelty *The Origin* would occasion.[27] No one serious about making a revolution can lightly ignore accepted professional standards. How far

John Angus Campbell

one goes in deferring to standards irrelevant or hostile to one's actual research procedures determines the personal dimension in science. Some writers, like René Descartes or Noam Chomsky, may storm the citadel of convention directly. The fact is, however, that frontal assault was not Darwin's style, and thus a certain disingenuousness was necessary for Darwin to be persuasive. Edward Manier puts the issue of Darwin's rhetorical strategy succinctly: "the early drafts of the theory do not conform to the 'hypothetico-deductive model' of scientific explanation, although they indicate Darwin's intent to represent his views as *if* they did conform to that model."[28]

To appreciate how much rhetorical ingenuity went into the composition of *The Origin*, one has only to contrast the reassuring inductivist style of *The Origin* with the rapid sequence of topics, inferences, and reflections on strategies of persuasion one finds in Darwin's notebooks. There is ample science in Darwin's notebooks and much of it is outstanding science. But the story-line is not the same as that in *The Origin*. In the notebooks, we see the young Darwin, even before he solved the technical problem of speciation, thinking of ways to solve the problem of persuasive exposition. In the "C" notebook Darwin reminds himself to point out to his audience the moral responsibility of the scientist as epochal truth-bearer:

> Mention persecution of early Astronomers,—then add chief good of individual scientific men is to push their science a few years in advance only of their age . . . . must remember that if they *believe* & not openly avow their belief they do as much to retard as those whose opinion they believe have endeavored to advance the cause of truth.[29]

The same notebook illustrates the intermingling of his scientific insight with his theological and strategic reflections:

> Study Bell on Expression & the Zoonomia, for if the former shows that a man grinning is to expose his canine teeth ((this may be made a capital argument. if man does move muscles for uncovering canines)) no doubt a habit gained by formerly being a baboon with great canine teeth.—((Blend this argument with his having canine teeth at all.—)) . . . Hensleigh says the love of the deity & thought of him / or eternity / only difference between mind of man & animals.—yet how faint in a Fuegian or Australian! Why not gradation.—no greater difficulty for Deity to choose. when perfect enough for Heaven or bad enough for Hell.—(Glimpses bursting on mind & giving rise to the wildest

imagination & superstition.—York Minster story of storm of
snow after his brother's murder.—good anecdote.[30]

In the "M" notebook Darwin's awareness of the rhetorical dimension
of his task is registered in his reflection on how best to make his underlying philosophy: "To avoid stating how far I believe in materialism, say
only that emotions, instincts, degrees of talent, which are hereditary
are so because brain of child resembles parent stock."[31] The "M" notebook also makes clear that from the first Darwin speculated freely on
both science and philosophy and did not begin by amassing facts and
postponing thought: "Origin of Man now proved.—Metaphysics must
flourish.—He who understands baboon would do more toward metaphysics than Locke."[32] When one contrasts the breadth and exuber-
ance of Darwin's early reflections, which freely move backward and
forward through philosophy, theology, rhetoric, psychology, and numerous branches of natural science, and encompass ethics and aesthetics, with the chastened tone and narrow range of topics addressed in
The Origin, one is little short of awed by the massive restraint and carefully premeditated adaptation of his public argument.

Darwin's care to redescribe his path to discovery so that it appeared
to conform with conventional standards of Baconian inductionism is
not the only way in which he adapted his ideas to his scientific peers.
Darwin was rhetorical both in his concern with persuasion and in the
heavily metaphorical character of his thought. His images lent his ideas
popular appeal, but since they drew attention to themselves as images,
explaining them away posed a distinct rhetorical challenge. As of his
method, so of his metaphors. Darwin argued that his language con-
formed to accepted professional standards.

The highly imagistic character of Darwin's language was a center of
controversy from the very first. Ghiselin's recommendation that Darwin's language simply be set aside indicates that the problem of how to
interpret it is still an open question. C. C. Gillispie has long held that
Darwin expressed himself in a needlessly misleading manner, and
even Howard Gruber, who does not appear to share Ghiselin's view of
the cogency of Darwin's approach to method, cautions that making too
much of the social roots of Darwin's language is "unDarwinian."[33] It is
at least curious that so many distinguished interpreters of Darwin, who
do not necessarily agree on other points, concur in deemphasizing the
importance of his language for an understanding of his achievement.
The thesis is worth considering that Darwin used metaphorical language to make his scientific point and that the very connotations we are
warned not to take seriously were instrumental in his ability to per-

John Angus Campbell

suade both his professional peers and the general public. To determine what importance to attach to Darwin's language, let us contrast his public statements concerning language with the testimony of his private papers.

Starting with the third edition of *The Origin*, Darwin responded to the criticism of his imagistic language by pointing out that certain of his metaphors were in fact metaphors:

> In the literal sense of the word, no doubt, natural selection is a misnomer; but who ever objected to chemists speaking of the elective affinities of the various elements?—and yet an acid cannot strictly be said to elect the base with which it will in preference combine.
>
> It has been said that I speak of natural selection as an active power or Deity; but who objects to an author speaking of the attraction of gravity as ruling the movements of the planets? Everyone knows what is meant and is implied by such metaphorical expressions; and they are almost necessary for brevity. So again it is difficult to avoid personifying the word Nature; but I mean by Nature, only the aggregate action and product of many natural laws, and by laws the sequence of events as ascertained by us. With a little familiarity such superficial objections will be forgotten.[34]

Darwin's public account of his metaphors creates the impression that his images could be replaced by literal statements if time were not a factor. But Darwin's philosophy of language, as well as his use of language generally, shows that rhetoric is essential, not incidental, to his case.

Darwin's minimizing of metaphor manifests his seeming deference to the linguistic standards of Comtean positivism. In August 1838 Darwin read David Brewster's review of the first two volumes of Comte's *Philosophie Positive*.[35] Brewster's review convinced Darwin of Comte's thesis that, like humankind in general, each science goes through the stages of myth and metaphysics before reaching a final positive stage. After reading Brewster's review, Darwin took as his own the mission of bringing biology out of the metaphysical stage.[36] A significant point of difference between Darwin and Comte, revealed by Darwin's notebooks and underscored by his published writing, however, concerns the language proper to science. Comte's philosophy of language was thoroughly nominalist. Both in his theory of language and in his use of language, Darwin was a realist. Comte, for example, would ban from chemistry such expressions as "elective affinities" and ban "attraction" from the language of astronomy. In the above quotation from the *The Origin,* although he retains the offensive terms from astronomy and chemistry, Darwin's definition of "nature" and "natural law" are solidly in line with Comtean linguistic standards.[37]

Darwin's difference with Comte on the language proper to science in fact was radical. First, in keeping with the realism of Scottish Commonsense Philosophy, Darwin saw nature itself as expressive. Human language, in the Scottish Commonsense view, was a continuation of the natural expressiveness of all sentient life.[38] Having accepted this position, Darwin did not have the horror of anthropomorphism that was endemic to positivism, with its demand for a language appropriate to a Cartesian billiard-ball universe. Second, and as a corollary, Darwin saw the aim of scientific language as persuasive communication and not conceptual precision.[39]

Darwin's philosophy of language is as important to his *scientific* achievement as to his popular success because it, rather than the inductivist-positivist theory of language to which he publicly deferred, helps explain his success in estabishing a novel research paradigm. We can see the distance between Darwin's public quasi-positivist account of his metaphors and the actual use he made of figurative language by examining his key terms, "natural selection" and "struggle for existence." In a crucial section of his chapter on "Natural Selection," Darwin dramatically contrasts man's puny powers with the powers of nature: "Man can act only on external and visible characters: nature cares nothing for appearances. . . . She can act on every internal organ, on every shade of constitutional difference, on the whole machinery of life." In the next paragraph, Darwin says, "It may metaphorically be said that natural selection is daily and hourly scrutinising, throughout the world, every variation, even the slightest; rejecting that which is bad, preserving and adding up all that is good; silently and insensibly working, whenever and wherever opportunity offers."[40]

There is a marked discrepancy in these passages between Darwin's claim that he is merely adopting a way of speaking and his inability to speak any other way. Since in Darwin's own terms nature's selection is invisible and insensible, his metaphor is a matter of necessity and not of convenience. In this passage Darwin uses rhetorical language simultaneously to propose a new paradigm for science and to create a new popular understanding of humanity's relation to nature. The key element is the tension between Darwin's image of the human selector (the breeder), whose operations are known to the audience, and the operations of nature, whose ways are unknown. The image of the selector is persuasive precisely because it brilliantly exploits a technological sym-

John Angus Campbell

bol and thus competes with the idea of miracle in a concretely believable way. Miracles were more credible to Darwin's contemporaries than
the obvious a fortiori argument, popularly advanced by Robert Chambers and Herbert Spencer, that since natural law governed every other
department of science, it *must* govern biology as well. A common expression in the science of Darwin's time was "the laws of creation."[41]
Darwin, we may surmise, was persuasive because he took the "confused notion" of "creation" by "law" and gave it a decisive naturalistic
turn.[42] In comparison with Milton's "The grassie Clods now calv'd,
now half appeer'd the Tawnie Lion, pawing to get free His hinder
parts," Darwin's "natural selection" was equally concrete yet provided
a more believable illusion because the reader knew how domestic varieties came into being.[43] The image of nature forming species, much as
the cattle-breeder or the pigeon-fancier formed varieties, is a naturalistic image that for scientist and general reader is truer to experience
than is miracle. For the scientist in particular, "natural selection"
heuristically embodies a richer research program than the one embodied in the notion of "laws of creation." When we appreciate that Darwin
had originally hoped to explain variation, and could not, we begin to
understand why it is the rhetorical tradition of the Scottish Commonsense Philosophers, and not the positivist tradition of August Comte,
that accounts for his language.

"Natural selection" does not explain how an imperceptible variation
internal to the organism could be selected. Nor does it allow us to predict the kind of internal variations we would expect to find in organisms in a particular environment. What natural selection does is clear
a semantic space that a natural law might fill. Indeed, Edward Manier
describes the semantic-rhetorical function of natural selection precisely
when he describes it as a "place-holding allusion."[44] Natural selection
is not incompatible with any known law, and it is not supernaturalistic,
because although Darwin magnifies nature's powers, his concept of
"nature," like the breeder, acts only on variations when they happen to
occur.

The nonpositivist character of Darwin's term is underscored when
we consider its ancestry. In his sketch of 1842, and again in his draft of
1844, Darwin had asked the reader to imagine "a being more sagacious
than man, (not an omniscient creator)."[45] Although "natural selection"
is less anthropomorphic than the "being more sagacious than man,"
the function of the image remains identical. Rather than asking the
reader to imagine "a being," Darwin simply has the reader project
what is known of the operations of the domestic breeder onto nature.
Although Darwin's image does not explain variation, or even how im-

perceptible unspecified internal variations could be of use to the organism, it does provide science with a heuristically rich "as if" to guide research.

What we have seen as true of "natural selection" holds equally for Darwin's other centrally important term, "struggle for existence." In both cases, the affective connotations of the terms seem to have been at least as important as their literal meanings. When we see the variety of terms Darwin considered, the self-consciously rhetorical character of Darwin's choice of "struggle for existence" becomes clear. In *Natural Selection*, the book Darwin abandoned when he received the Wallace letter, the section which corresponds to chapter 3 of *The Origin*, "The Struggle for Existence," had once been entitled "War of Nature." An early topic sentence had read, "The elder De Candolle in an eloquent passage has declared that all nature is at war."[46] Manier notes that Darwin at one time considered using Lyell's expression "equilibrium in the number of species." Indeed, Darwin affirmed that Lyell's expression was "more correct" than his own. Significantly, however, Darwin rejected Lyell's expression on the ground that it conveyed "far too much quiescence." By Darwin's own account, accuracy was not his criterion. He chose "struggle for existence" because it occupied a desirable semantic space mid-way between "war" and "equilibrium."[47] In *The Origin*, Darwin distinguished three uses of the term "struggle." He indicated that we could speak of organisms as "truly" engaged in struggle where two animals were in competition with one another for the same scarce resource and if one obtained more of the resource, that animal would increase its life expectancy or prospects of leaving progeny, while its adversary would not. Second, the "less proper" meaning of struggle would describe a situation in which an organism confronted a limited environment, as in the case of a plant in time of drought. Darwin recognized that it would be "more proper" in such an instance to say that the plant was "dependent" upon moisture than to say that it was struggling to survive. Finally, Darwin used "far fetched" to characterize a struggle in which a parasite so increased in power that it threatened its host's existence and, ultimately, its own. Darwin noted that the three meanings "pass" or "graduate" into each other.[48] As Manier observes of these three meanings:

> it is necessary to consider the possibility that each meaning
> influenced his understanding of the other two. The domain of
> events referred to by the terms 'war' or 'conflict,' for example,
> may be significantly redescribed if the same term ('struggle') is
> used to designate it and two other domains (those more

John Angus Campbell

commonly designated by 'dependence' and 'chance') as well. The result is not the expression 'too much quiescence' but rather an elaborate qualification of the 'strict meaning' of 'struggle' within the context of Darwin's theory. Darwin's use of this metaphor may have been poetic as well as scientific. He was willing to risk the ambiguity resulting from the inter-connection of a variety of related but distinct meanings in a single, compressed metaphoric representation.[49]

Darwin's invocation of quasi-positivistic disclaimers for his use of metaphoric terms can be reconciled neither with his adherence to Scottish Commonsense linguistic philosophy nor with the functions of his key terms "natural selection" and "struggle for existence" in *The Origin*. His public insistence that his images were for convenience was an apparent attempt to defer to scientific conventions too professionally entrenched to challenge. Darwin's distinct genius for giving old terms new meanings in order to present persuasively a novel vision of nature was central to his scientific and popular success, even though the linguistic-rhetorical theory which informed his choice of language could not have been made explicit without damage to his credibility.

A final aspect of Darwin's adaptation to his professional audience concerns his endeavor to convince his peers that in natural selection he had identified the specific mechanism by which evolution occurs. Clearly, since Erasmus Darwin, Jean Baptiste Lamarck, Etienne Geoffroy Saint-Hilaire, Robert Chambers, and Herbert Spencer all had argued the general case for evolution, Darwin's unique scientific contribution was his theory of natural selection. In presenting his theory, he was careful to use language that would communicate to his peers the unique explanatory power he believed natural selection possessed. Following the theoretical language popularized by John Herschel, Darwin spoke of natural selection as the *vera causa* of organic change.[50]

As has been often remarked, the irony of Darwin's achievement is that he succeeded in popularizing all forms of evolutionism but his own.[51] Even Huxley, wholehearted as he was in advancing science through championship of Darwin, did not believe natural selection to be the sole cause of evolution. Whereas Darwin insisted that "natura non facit saltum," Huxley was willing to allow an occasional leap, particularly when Lord Kelvin insisted that data from physics denied that the earth was as old as Darwin needed it to be. Although personally, as Michael Ruse puts it, Darwin "miserably dug in his heels and refused to defer to the physicists," he concluded in private and in a letter to the

Athenaeum that the specific theory one adopted was less important than the choice between evolution of whatever kind and special creation.[52]

From a rhetorical standpoint, the irony of Darwin's achievement is only partial. However scientifically important natural selection is for contemporary science, in historical and rhetorical perspective, Darwin's discovery was only an incident in the development of a general argument he already believed in on other grounds. In the spring of 1838, before he had read Malthus, Darwin observed in his notebook that there was scarcely any novelty in his theory of transmutation and that the whole object of his prospective book was proof. Dov Ospovat concluded his examination of the pre- and post-Malthus Darwin by underscoring the early emphasis on the general argument: "Darwin was fond of the theory of natural selection, but his greatest concern was to establish the doctrine of descent."[53] Darwin's use of the theoretically fashionable expression *vera causa* was not entirely lost on his professional peers and no doubt made his ideas seem all the more impressive to the general reader. His brilliant evolutionary reinterpretation of the known facts and theories of mid-century science persuaded a significant number of his peers and no doubt many of his lay contemporaries that some naturalistic *vera causa* could account for organic change.[54] We err when we think that Darwin's underlying intent was to offer an original scientific theory. Darwin's initial intent was to make evolutionism persuasive.

III

Charles Darwin was a brilliant scientist, but neither an iconoclast nor a martyr. Shortly after his return to England, probably as a result of reviewing the data on geographical distribution from the *Beagle* voyage, Darwin became a convinced transmutationist. As his was a bold and original mind, Darwin at once proceeded to draw out the various implications of his discovery. As Darwin's notebooks demonstrate, theological, aesthetic, and moral theorizing, as well as sustained reflection on how best to persuade, were integral to his thought from the first. After formulating and abandoning two theories of transmutation, Darwin at last recognized in Malthus the principle long implicit in his own thought. His personal identification with the professional scientific community of his time made him anxious that advocacy of evolutionism not damage his scientific reputation. Darwin found in the language of Baconian inductivism and positivism the pro-

John Angus Campbell

tective coloration he needed for his unorthodox conclusions. Indeed, Darwin was so persuasive in redescribing his path to discovery and his philosophy of language that he even convinced himself. Various letters and the statement in his *Autobiography* that only with Malthus did he at last have a theory all indicate that as he grew older Darwin began to remember his path to discovery not as it had been, but as Baconian and positivist method held that it should have been.[55]

Darwin's disavowal of his own rhetoric was not without cost. Consequent to his denial of his philosophy of language, Darwin lost his ability to delight in what he beheld. In later life he complained, "My mind seems to have become a kind of machine for grinding general laws out of large collections of facts, but why this should have caused the atrophy of that part of the brain alone, on which the higher tastes depend, I cannot conceive."[56]

At the beginning of this essay I affirmed the propriety of juxtaposing rhetoric and science. For Darwin, the consequence of denying his own rhetoric was poignant. For us, affirming Darwin as a rhetorician of science underscores rhetoric as the bridge uniting science with culture and, far from denying the integrity of Darwin's vision, restores the motive which gave it life.

NOTES

1. Giorgio de Santillana, *The Origins of Scientific Thought* (New York: Mentor Books, 1961), pp. 248–50; Loren Eiseley, *Darwin's Century* (New York: Anchor Books, 1961), pp. 205–7.

2. Paul N. Campbell, "Poetic-Rhetorical, Philosophic, and Scientific Discourse," *Philosophy and Rhetoric* 6 (1973): 1–3. Dov Ospovat observes in *The Development of Darwin's Theory* (Cambridge: Cambridge University Press, 1981), p. 229, "that the formation and transformation of Darwin's theory represent not so much the results of an interaction between the creative scientist and nature as between the scientist and socially constructed conceptions of nature."

3. Michael Ruse, *The Darwinian Revolution* (Chicago: University of Chicago Press, 1979), pp. 94–131.

4. R. C. Stauffer, ed., *Charles Darwin's Natural Selection* (Cambridge: Cambridge University Press, 1975), pp. 8–10.

5. For a critical discussion of the date on which Darwin received the Wallace letter, see John Landon Brooks, *Just Before the Origin* (New York: Columbia University Press, 1984), pp. 229–57.

6. November 24 is the traditional date. For discussion of November 26 as the true date see Morse Peckham, *The Origin of Species by Charles Darwin:*

A Variorum Text (Philadelphia: University of Pennsylvania Press, 1959), p. 18.

7. Charles Darwin, *On the Origin of Species: A Facsimile of the First Edition with an Introduction by Ernst Mayr* (New York: Atheneum, 1967), pp. 1–2.

8. Francis Darwin, ed., *Charles Darwin's Autobiography,* with introductory essay by Gaylord Simpson (New York: Collier Books, 1950), p. 115.

9. Charles Coulston Gillispie, *The Edge of Objectivity* (Princeton: Princeton University Press, 1960), pp. 303–4.

10. Peckham, *Origin of Species,* pp. [ii], 759, 57.

11. A. Hunter DuPree, *Asa Gray 1810–1888* (Cambridge: Harvard University Press, 1959), pp. 298–301.

12. Sir Francis Darwin, ed., *More Letters of Charles Darwin* vol. 1 (London: John Murray, 1903), p. 146; see also pp. 190–94; Charles Darwin, *Variation in Plants and Animals Under Domestication,* vol. 2 (New York: D. Appleton & Co., 1896), pp. 248–49.

13. Darwin, *The Origin,* 1st ed., pp. 167, 188–89. For other examples of the same kind, see, for instance, pp. 243–44, 484, and Peckham, *Origin of Species,* pp. 748, 753.

14. Peckham, *Origin of Species,* p. 748, 6th ed.

15. Susan Gliserman, "Early Victorian Science Writers and Tennyson's 'In Memoriam': A Study in Cultural Exchange," Pt. 2, *Victorian Studies* 18 (1975): 456.

16. Cited in William Irvine, *Apes, Angels and Victorians* (New York: Meridian Books, 1964), pp. 249–50.

17. Darwin, *The Origin,* 1st ed., p. 1.

18. Nora Barlow, ed., *The Autobiography of Charles Darwin: 1809–1882* (London: Collins, St. James Place, 1958), p. 120.

19. Howard Gruber, *Darwin on Man: A Psychological Study of Scientific Creativity: Together with Darwin's Early and Unpublished Notebooks,* transcribed and annotated by Paul Barrett, foreword by Jean Piaget (New York: E. P. Dutton), p. 123.

20. Ibid., p. 173.

21. Francis Darwin, ed., *Life and Letters of Charles Darwin,* vol. 2 (New York: D. Appleton, 1896), p. 371.

22. Francis Darwin, ed., *More Letters of Charles Darwin,* vol. 1 (New York: D. Appleton, 1903), p. 195.

23. Ibid.

24. David Hull, *Darwin and His Critics* (Cambridge: Harvard University Press, 1973), p. 4.

25. Charles Bazerman, "Codifying the Social Scientific Style: The APA *Publication Manual* as a Behaviorist Rhetoric," in this volume.

26. Michael T. Ghiselin, *The Triumph of the Darwinian Method* (Berkeley and Los Angeles: University of California Press, 1969), pp. 35, 75.

27. Gruber, *Darwin on Man,* pp. 23–24.

28. Edward Manier, *The Young Darwin and His Cultural Circle* (Boston: D. Reidel, 1978), p. 195.

29. Gruber, *Darwin on Man*, p. 450 (C123).

30. Ibid., p. 454 (C243).

31. Ibid., p. 276 (M57).

32. Ibid., p. 281 (M84).

33. Gillispie as cited in Manier, *The Young Darwin*, p. 19; Gruber, *Darwin on Man*, p. 12.

34. Peckham, *Origin of Species*, p. 165, 3d ed.

35. Manier, *The Young Darwin*, p. 40.

36. Gruber, *Darwin on Man*, p. 278 (M69-M73).

37. Manier, *The Young Darwin*, pp. 39-40.

38. Ibid., p. 199.

39. Ibid., pp. 61–64, 149, 150, 154–56, 158, 161.

40. Peckham, *Origin of Species*, pp. 168–69, 2d ed.

41. Ruse, *Darwinian Revolution*, pp. 152–57, 99, 100; Charles Coulston Gillispie, *Genesis and Geology* (New York: Harper & Row, 1951), pp. 146–50.

42. Chaim Perelman, and Lucie Olbrechts-Tyteca, *The New Rhetoric: A Treatise on Argumentation* (Notre Dame, Ind.: University of Notre Dame Press, 1969), pp. 79, 132–35, 450.

43. John Milton, *The Complete Poetry and Selected Prose*, vol. 7: *Paradise Lost*, introduction by Cleanth Brooks (New York: Modern Library, 1950), p. 260.

44. Manier, *The Young Darwin*, p. 174.

45. Ibid., 174–75; Charles Darwin and Alfred Russel Wallace, *Evolution by Natural Selection*, with a foreword by Sir Gavin DeBeer (Cambridge: Cambridge University Press, 1958), pp. 45, 114, 115.

46. Stauffer, *Darwin's Natural Selection*, pp. 175, 569. Darwin attributes the phrase "All nature . . . is at war" to the elder De Candolle rather than to Hobbes as Manier affirms. See Manier, *The Young Darwin*, p. 181.

47. Manier, *The Young Darwin*, p. 181.

48. *The Origin*, pp. 62–63, 1st ed.

49. Manier, *The Young Darwin*, p. 13.

50. Darwin, *The Origin*, e.g., pp. 159, 482, 1st ed. For the role of *vera causa* in the dispute, see Hull, *Darwin and His Critics*, pp. 27, 45, 109, 115, 163, 180, 355.

51. Ruse, *Darwinian Revolution*, pp. 205–6.

52. Ibid., pp. 222–25; Ospovat, *Development of Darwin's Theory*, p. 89.

53. Ospovat, *Development of Darwin's Theory*, pp. 87, 88.

54. Ibid., pp. 210–35.

55. See nn. 18, 21, 22.

56. *Autobiography*, p. 139.

WHERE OBJECTIVITY LIES

THE RHETORIC OF

ANTHROPOLOGY

RENATO ROSALDO

One foggy night a number of years ago, I found myself driving with a physicist along the mountainous stretch of Route 17 between Santa Cruz and San Jose. Being a little anxious about the weather and having nothing better to do, we tried to talk about our respective fields. He began by asking me, as only a physicist could, what anthropologists had discovered.

"Discovered?" I asked, pretending not to know what he meant and hoping something would come to me.

"Yes," he said, "like the properties or laws of other cultures."

"Oh," I mumbled, my heart sinking, "you mean something like $E = mc^2$."

"Yes," he said.

"There's one thing," I suddenly heard myself saying, "that we know for sure. We all know a good description when we see one. We haven't discovered any laws of culture, but we do think there are classic ethnographies, really telling descriptions of other cultures, like the Trobriand Islanders, the Tikopia, and the Nuer."

What a relief! Probably I burbled on about Tom Kuhn's notion of exemplars: classic experiments that physicists learn in the process of mastering their trade.[1] Though such experiments cannot be reduced to rules or recipes, they are vehicles through which young physicists learn to recognize and produce a good piece of work. Similarly, perusal of classic ethnographies rather than a set of methodological procedures teaches young anthropologists what a good description of other lifeways looks like.

Considering the discipline's folk belief in an ethnographic canon, it is peculiar that apprentice anthropologists, as a matter of course, do not study rhetoric with a view to learning how the sacred texts were made. They could, for example, not unlike young artists or physicists, imitate exemplary ethnographic modes of composition and argumentation. In a manner both literary and conceptual, they could study, as I shall in a moment, narrative point of view, tone, and mode. In studying point of view, they could, for example, ask whether analyses of exploitation depict the system as a whole. Or do they instead assume the position of the oppressor? Alternatively, though in fact less frequently, analysts can adopt the perspective of the oppressed. Playing subversively on a masculine idiom, analyses of narrative viewpoint attend to the differences between how the arrow and the target experience a bull's-eye. Matters of tone, in contrast, involve characterizing distinctive moods and asking whether particular human subjects are just going through the motions or are actually caught up by intense emotions. Mode, finally, requires assessments as to whether people are joking, teasing, insulting, playing, pontificating, pleading, whining, speaking in earnest, or simultaneously assuming more than one of these postures.

Indeed, the human sciences have, in the manner of Monsieur Jourdain, only recently noticed that their work is written.[2] Even today a course on methodology routinely includes a battery of techniques for the collection and manipulation of data, but precious little about how to write field notes and record interviews, and certainly nothing about how in the end to write articles or books. How can one write about other people's lives in a way that preserves differences without losing sight of similarities; that displays both structural constraints and more improvised struggles; that moves between lucid distance and telling closeness?[3] These kinds of questions about how to represent other forms of life rarely enter discussions of method in anthropology. It is as if one imagined that photographs told the unadorned real truth without ever noticing how they are constructed—framed and taken from particular angles, at certain distances, and with different depths of field.

The relative silence about writing in discussions of method seems especially conspicuous in anthropology, where the book-length ethnography has been so enshrined as a form of knowledge that we speak, often rather unreflectingly (and sometimes desperately, as on the road to San Jose), about classics or well-described cultures. Such lists usually begin with Bronislaw Malinowski's work on the Trobriand Islanders, Raymond Firth's on the Tikopia, and E. E. Evans-Pritchard's on the Nuer. The notion of classic ethnographies assumes a discipline-wide consensus about great works (canonized, one might add, more for their descriptive veracity than their compelling narrative).

Arguably, the rhetoric of ethnography, like that of the human sciences in general, requires study in two modes, which one can call the
appreciative and the critical. The appreciative mode reads texts in their
own terms and attempts to evaluate them in relation to their own goals.
This approach introduces the admirable caution of trying to understand what somebody else is saying before engaging in argument. In
this vein one can argue that ethnography *is* what ethnographers *do*.
One should therefore begin with exemplary works and through close
readings discover what they *do* say rather than imposing rules
about what they *ought* to say, as the philosopher Carl Hempel did to the
historians.[4]

The critical mode, on the other hand, begins with a project for the
discipline and assesses works, methods, and theories in relation to desired forms of analysis. The admirable quality that this approach introduces is that of giving direction to future studies rather than rehearsing
past achievements. This approach sets goals and considers means of
achieving them. It looks wherever it can (both within the discipline and
beyond its bounds) for the resources needed to pursue the project.

In my view the appreciative and the critical modes need to be combined in studying the rhetoric of the human sciences. The former mode
taken by itself provides significant exemplars that can orient vanguard
work, play a pedagogical role, and guard against reinventing the
wheel. Yet it can prove less effective in defining projects that look into
the future. The latter mode in isolation, on the other hand, fails to recognize that the state of the art rather than an imagined final goal constitutes the point of departure for current projects. One measures
progress in the human sciences in relation to current knowledge (better than before) and not in teleological terms (the ultimate truth). Thus
in what follows I shall attempt to tack back and forth between the appreciative and the critical modes of inquiry.

Let me begin by advancing a version of the anthropological project
along with a criterion for assessing the validity of ethnographic descriptions. Anthropologists aspire to describe other cultures in ways
that render them familiar (or at any rate intelligible and humanly plausible) without losing sight of their differences. Good descriptions neither bring other people so close that they become just like ourselves nor
so distance them (in the name of objectivity) that they become objectified and dehumanized. Anthropology's project thus is viewed as the
study of human possibilities. Its activist trajectory calls for culture-specific analyses oriented toward the actual workings of particular societies rather than toward the metropolitan Eurocentric designs of
planning agencies. Its contemplative conception affirms that the actual

Renato Rosaldo

variety of human cultures far exceeds that imagined within the confines of any single tradition. Ethnography can expand our imaginations by teaching us how other cultures conceive and confront such fundamental life issues as labor, love, cooperation, conflict, play, birth, and death.

One plausible criterion, among others, for descriptive adequacy could be a thought experiment: how valid would we find ethnographic discourse if it were applied to ourselves? Perhaps I should begin by taking this question one step further and asking about the validity of other people's actual (rather than hypothetical) characterizations of ourselves.

All anthropologists surely have been moved, if not shaken, by the astute ethnographic observations that their subjects of research have made about American or European culture. The most dramatic experience of this kind in my fieldwork suggests a dialogic potential, one of critical reflection and reciprocal perceptions, as yet rarely realized in the official rhetoric of anthropology.

When I was residing in the late 1960s as an ethnographer among the Ilongots of northern Luzon, Philippines, I was struggling against a diffusely overwhelming reaction to one of their central cultural practices: headhunting.[5] Despite my indoctrination in cultural relativism, headhunting seemed utterly alien and morally reprehensible. At the time I wanted simply to bracket my moral perception in order to carry out the ethnographic project of understanding the practice in its own terms.

Early answers to my questions suggested that headhunting had ended with the last Japanese beheaded in June 1945. These beheadings, Ilongots said, aided the American army. When asked about more recent headhunting episodes, they indignantly replied, "How could you think such a thing of us? I helped carry you across a stream. I fed you. I've cared for you. How could you think such a thing?" I could not but agree.

After about a year of fieldwork there, Tukbaw and I were flying in a small plane when he pointed down below and said, "That's where we raided." He had gone headhunting here more recently than I had dared imagine. Soon everyone began to tell me their headhunting stories. Within a few weeks I realized that every man in the settlement had taken a head. I was shocked and disoriented because my companions had indeed been kind and generous. How could such caring hosts also be brutal killers?

Some months later I was classified 1–A for the draft. My companions immediately told me not to fight in Viet Nam and offered to conceal me in their homes. Though it corresponded to my sentiments, their offer could not have surprised me more. Unthinkingly I had supposed that headhunters would see my reluctance to serve in the armed forces as a form of cowardice. Instead they told me that soldiers are men who sell their bodies. Pointedly they interrogated me: "How can a man do as soldiers do and command his brothers to move into the line of fire?"

This act, ordering one's own men to risk their lives, was utterly beyond their moral comprehension. My own cultural world suddenly appeared grotesque. Yet their earnest incomprehension significantly narrowed the moral chasm between us, for their ethnographic observation about modern war was both aggressive and caring. They condemned my society's soldiering at the same time that they urged me not to sell my body.

Through such encounters the possibility for reciprocal critical perceptions opened between the Ilongots and myself. This encounter suggests that we ethnographers should be open to asking not only how our descriptions of others would read if applied to ourselves, but also how we can learn from other people's descriptions of ourselves. In this case I was repositioned through an Ilongot account of one of my culture's central institutions. I could no longer speak about headhunting as one of the clean addressing the dirty, the innocent addressing the guilty. My loss of innocence enabled me and the Ilongots to face each other on more nearly equal ground, as members of flawed societies.[6] We both lost positions of purity from which to condemn the other without at the same time having to condone what we found morally reprehensible in ourselves and in the other. Neither war nor headhunting, in deeply serious ways, has been the same for me since.

That their telling question ignored state authority and hierarchical chains of command mattered little. Their off-centered observation, though offering raw material for caricature, was critical rather than parodic or satirical. Satire and parody, of course, tend to be modes of speaking assumed by marginal members of the society being caricatured. My position, that of a person neither an Ilongot nor about to marry one, barely allowed such rhetorical liberties between us. Such cross-cultural observations, nonetheless, do lend themselves, as shall become clear in a moment, to being understood as humor.

Consider once again the question of how ethnographic descriptions would look if applied to ourselves. The available literature in fact indicates that a divide between serious conception and laughing reception can separate the author's intentions from the reader's responses. Human subjects have often reacted with bemused puzzlement over the ways they have been depicted in anthropological writings. It suggests, in other words, that ethnographies written in accord with disciplinary norms, though humorless in intent, can be read by their subjects as parodic. The record of such readings indicates that anthropologists could profit from defamiliarizing their discipline's most taken-for-granted rhetorical strategies. This excursion in analyses at once rhetorical and conceptual can be most productive if it leads to a shift in anthropological norms that encourages practitioners both to read the past and to write the future with more critical and humane representations of other forms of life.

The problem of validity in ethnographic discourse has reached crisis proportions over the past fifteen years, among other places in Chicano responses to anthropological depictions of themselves. The most balanced yet most devastating assessment of these issues has been put forth by Americo Paredes. He begins rather gently by saying, "I find the Mexicans and Chicanos pictured in the usual ethnographies somewhat unreal."[7] He goes on to suggest, in the following manner, that the people studied find ethnographic accounts written about them more parodic than telling: "It is not so much a sense of outrage, that would betray wounded egos, as a feeling of puzzlement, that *this* is given as a picture of the communities they have grown up in. Many of them are more likely to laugh at it all than feel indignant" (his emphasis).[8] His critique of the somewhat unreal picture put forth in ethnographies about Chicanos continues with a stunning item-by-item enumeration of such errors as mistranslations, taking jokes seriously, missing double meanings, and accepting as the literal truth an apocryphal story about brutal initiation rites in youth gangs. To top it off, a team of anthropological researchers in south Texas failed even to notice the emergence during their research period of a locally powerful political movement called the Raza Unida Party.

Paredes's diagnosis is that most ethnographic writing on Mexicans and Chicanos has failed to grasp significant variations in the tone of cultural events. In an ethnography he sees as representative, Paredes says, for example, that Chicanos portrayed "are not only literal-minded, they never crack a joke."[9] He argues that ethnographers who attempt to interpret Chicano culture should recognize not only the larger context, but also matters of mode: "whether a gathering is a wake, a beer bust, or a street-corner confabulation."[10] Knowledge about the cultural framing of events could aid the ethnographer in distinguishing earnest from joking speech. Even when using technical concepts, the analysis should not lose sight of whether the speech is serious (to be taken literally) or deadpan (to be read as farce).

Lest there be any confusion, I am saying neither that the native is always right nor that Paredes as native-ethnographer could never be wrong. Instead my claim is that we should take the criticisms of our subjects in much the same way that we take those of our colleagues. Their criticisms simply should be listened to and taken into account, to be accepted, rejected, or modified, as we reformulate our analyses. At issue is not the real truth versus the ethnographic lie. After all, the pragmatic concerns of everyday life can diverge from those of disciplined inquiry. Technical and everyday vocabularies differ in large measure because the projects they reflect and create are oriented to different purposes. In addition, natives can be just as insightful, sociologically correct, axe-grinding, self-interested, or mistaken as ethnographers. In this case Paredes has called attention to how straight ethnography can easily be read by natives as parodic, "somewhat unreal" and more "to laugh at" than "feel indignant" about. His response, among other things, calls for a reassessment of ethnographers' rhetorical habits.

The difficulties of using ethnographic discourse for self-description should have long been apparent to anthropologists, who, for the most part, have read the classic, if heavy-handed, paper "Body Ritual Among the Nacirema" by Horace Miner. In that paper a particular distanced normalizing mode of ethnographic discourse became parodic (not unlike certain anthropological writings on Chicanos) when applied to Americans ("Nacirema" spelled backward, of course, is "American"). In the following passage, for example, Miner says:

> The daily body ritual performed by everyone includes a mouth-rite. Despite the fact that these people are so punctilious about care of the mouth, this rite involves a practice which strikes the uninitiated stranger as revolting. It was reported to me that the ritual consists of inserting a small bundle of hog hairs into the mouth, along with certain magical powders, and then moving the bundle in a highly formalized series of gestures.[11]

His essay thus defamiliarizes both through the narrator's position as uninitiated stranger and through the distanced idiom that transforms everyday practices into more elevated ritual and magical acts.

Clearly there is a gap between the technical idiom of ethnography and the language of everyday life.[12] Miner's description employs terms used by a certain group of professionals rather than the words most Americans, the people described, would normally use in talking about their life experiences. Both kinds of language, of course, have their place. My project is to juxtapose the two with a view to showing the debilitating consequences of restricting unduly the range of legitimate technical rhetoric.

Renato Rosaldo

In Miner's case the discrepancy between what we all know about brushing our teeth and the ethnographer's distanced discourse is precisely what makes the article parodic. Here jarring discordance enters less in terms made explicit in the text (despite what text-positivists may think) than in the disjunction between textualized technical concepts and the reader's tacit everyday life knowledge (held prior to and independent of reading about the Nacirema) that Miner is simply talking about people brushing their teeth in the morning.

It is curious in retrospect that Miner's article was taken simply as a joke rather than as a scathing critique of ethnographic discourse. Who could continue to feel comfortable describing other people in terms that sound ludicrous when applied to ourselves? In certain cases the detached observer's objectivity arguably resides more in a manner of speaking than in apt characterizations of other people's use and experience of their social forms. How can one widen the range of possible descriptive idioms so that they can prove appropriate to other people's and our own experiences?

Lest it appear that no actual ethnography has ever been written in the manner of Miner's ritual mouth-washing, one should probably cite an actual case. Otherwise the reader could regard the particular rhetoric of anthropology under discussion as merely a straw man rather than as the dominant, most legitimate, and most frequently deployed assemblage of discursive practices in the discipline. Consider, for example, the following passage from A. R. Radcliffe-Brown's classic ethnography, *The Andaman Islanders:*

> When two friends or relatives meet after having been separated,
> the social relation between them that has been interrupted is
> about to be renewed. This social relation implies or depends
> upon the existence of a specific bond of solidarity between them.
> The weeping rite (together with the subsequent exchange of
> presents) is the affirmation of this bond. The rite, which, it must
> be remembered, is obligatory, compels the two participants to act
> as though they felt certain emotions, and thereby does, to some
> extent, produce these emotions in them.[13]

This passage, we should keep in mind, describes the tears of greeting between long-separated old friends. Nonetheless, the ethnographer manifests skepticism as to whether or not people actually feel anything under the circumstances: they "act as though they felt certain emotions." Indeed an obligatory ritual is required to do the job and "to some extent, produce these emotions in them." Yet the status of Radcliffe-Brown's term "obligatory" remains obscure. Does it mean that when he witnessed weeping greeters they always turned out to be long-lost intimates? How could he have observed greetings without tears between long-lost intimates? Or did people simply tell the ethnographer that when long-lost intimates greet one another, they weep? It is curious that obligation as a cultural construct carries such analytical weight yet remains simply asserted rather than explored in conceptual terms.

Radcliffe-Brown's detached, dehumanizing descriptive idiom, of course, could potentially offer analytical insight not available through more everyday concepts. Certainly Thorstein Veblen and Erving Goffman, for example, used distanced normalizing descriptions with a deliberately satirical intent to jolt their readers into thinking afresh about their everyday lives. The problem resides less in the use of such descriptions than in an unreflective attachment to them as the sole vehicle for literal objective truth. Thus Radcliffe-Brown, following the descriptive norms of natural history and legitimating their extension to professional ethnography, so detached himself from his human subjects that his account lends itself to being read as unwittingly parodic, even absurd. Surely tearful greetings between long-lost intimates, however defamiliarized in discourse, must be deeply familiar in the lived experience of most readers.

Nonetheless, most anthropological readers of Radcliffe-Brown probably take his account at face value. When, for example, I told a colleague about my analysis of Radcliffe-Brown's depiction of Andaman weeping rites, she correctly followed the code for ethnographic readers and replied, "Yes, but for them, unlike for us, the rites are obligatory." Such are the costs of ignoring rhetoric and following rarely examined habits of reading and writing. Why, one wonders, does this kind of discourse sound earnest when applied to the Andaman Islanders and parodic when applied to ourselves? Could an ethnographer write a parodic account of the Andaman Islanders? Would the Andaman Islanders find Radcliffe-Brown's account parodic? It does seem curious that ethnography is so uniform in its tone that its characters, to the extent that it has any beyond the group noun ("the Andaman Islanders"), rarely laugh and enjoy themselves.

The detached objectivity of the dominant legitimate form of ethnographic discourse can work against the anthropological project of understanding other cultures by familiarizing yet preserving differences. In what follows I shall review a series of ethnographic instances with a view to indicating how ethnographic discourse can fail to apprehend the realities it attempts to describe and analyze. This critique will end by suggesting positive changes—experiments with point of

Renato Rosaldo

view, tone, and mode—that can improve our apprehension of other people's life experiences.

One arena for judging the adequacy of ethnographic accounts could be anthropological writings on death and mourning. Indeed the discourse on death, compared with that on other topics, appears particularly distanced and normalizing. Yet it has the virtue of being relatively well represented in the literature (unlike such similarly emotion-laden significant topics as love, adulterous passion, and spontaneous fun). The problems of rhetoric and analysis that emerge so clearly with reference to mourning and bereavement also obtain, with appropriate modifications, for a number of other topics as well.

That the topic of death has proven refractory for ethnographic analysis probably comes as no surprise. Most intensive ethnographic studies have been conducted by relatively young people who have not yet experienced devastating losses. Furthermore, such researchers usually come from upper-middle-class Anglo-American professional backgrounds where people (unlike policemen and crop-dusters) often shield themselves by not talking about death and other people's bereavement. Such ethnographers probably have grown up with the notion, itself a version of the stiff upper lip, that outsiders should not talk to the chief mourners about how they experience their grief.

My sketch of reactions to death and bereavement in upper-middle-class Anglo-American culture represents a central tendency, more a statistical probability than a monolithic certainty. Since readers can judge the representativeness of anecdotes about their own culture, a brief example from a local newspaper, a source as familiar as it is rarely used in academic writing, can probably suffice to fill in the sketch. The *San Jose Mercury News* on January 17, 1984, carried a story about how parents react to their children's death. The reporter pointed out that most upper-middle-class people strive to live out the illusion of being in control of their lives. Death, the brute fact of human mortality, threatens their sense of being in control. In this context one of the parents featured, Pamela Mang, whose daughter Jessica died of cancer, said: "One of the most profound insights I got out of Jessica's illness was that the way most of us live in the American culture is to try to protect ourselves from disasters and difficulties, and that we miss a lot of life because of that." She went on to describe how friends could not cope with her bereavement:

> Oh, God, you just want to get it out, to talk about it, because somehow getting it out into the air makes it something of a size that is manageable, that you can handle. There is a lot of love and

sympathy from friends in the beginning, but they have a lot of fear in them and they begin to withdraw as the illness settles down into just a horrible daily grind. You represent to them the living proof that cancer can just come right in and strike the all-American family.

Pamela Mang's statement is indicative of the difficulties most ethnographers without personal experience of loss could have in confronting the bereavement of other people, whether next-door neighbors or far-away members of other cultures. Young ethnographers in particular are unlikely to have learned much about loss and could find it awkward, in doing field research, to interview the chief mourners about their experiences. Such matters, culturally speaking, are not to be talked about. It thus is no accident that normalizing, distanced ethnographic discourse has found extensive application in studies of mourning.

Most ethnographic writing on death collapses funerary ritual with mourning and discusses only the former while pretending to analyze the latter.[14] Indeed, even discussions of funerary ritual usually employ it as a vehicle for the analysis of social structure rather than—perhaps in order to avoid—discussing bereavement as a humanly significant experience. Thus one finds what can be called "they vary with" statements as central organizing tropes in the analyses. Representative of such statements are the following (italics added):

The number as well as the scale of the funerary rites *vary with* the age, sex, and status of the deceased.[15]

Any death plunges a Kwaio community into the shock of collective bereavement. How deep the shock, how dramatic the subsequent events, *depend on* the age and identity of the decedent, and the circumstances of the death. We shall first look at these *axes of variation*, then turn to their outcomes.[16]

The role of the living in the rituals *varies according to* sex as well as degree of relationship to the deceased.[17]

These different methods of tying and restraining the bereaved are *indices of* the socially expected reactions to grief on the part of *various categories of person* and are therefore of particular value in elucidating certain general aspects of these roles.[18]

Funerary ritual evidently has proven an elegant arena for studies in concomitant variation (a methodology pioneered by Emile Durkheim) that have repeatedly demonstrated how social structural factors determine visible differences in mortuary scale and elaboration.

Most descriptions of death stand at a peculiar distance from the obviously intense emotions expressed. There are a number of strategies for normalizing what from the point of view of the bereaved husband or mother cannot be other than a unique and devastating loss. In certain cases ethnographers relate intense expressions of bereavement to expectations and conventions, as in the following (my italics):

> A man *will be expected* to display great grief at the death of a young son.[19]

> Another indication of the same imbalance in the parent-child relationship is to be seen in the occurrence of suicide attempts, which are a *standardized method* of demonstrating grief at the loss of a relative.[20]

> Only the chief mourners among the women—the mother, sisters, and the widows of the deceased—*are expected* to express their grief more violently, by loud sobbing and an occasional high pitched wail (called *tigi*) which is the *conventional expression* of deep sorrow.[21]

Why does ethnographic discourse promote skepticism, a distanced agnosticism about the authenticity of heart-rending expressions of emotion when a father loses a son, a bereaved person attempts suicide, or a woman sobs and wails violently? Surely nobody in that culture, or in any culture, would be surprised to find a father distraught over the loss of a son.

It is difficult to imagine, for example, a San Francisco ethnographer actually following the above formulas and telling a bereaved father that his son followed the expected, standardized, conventional method of committing suicide by jumping off the Golden Gate Bridge. On the other hand, the ethnographer could use such formulas to discuss Bay Area suicide in general rather than somebody's son's suicide in particular. The latter could be a telling and humane enterprise. Yet the problem remains that unreflective talk about culturally expected expressions of grief easily slips, for both readers and writers of ethnography, into skepticism about the reality of the emotions expressed. These canonical writings substitute the term "conventional" for Radcliffe-Brown's key term, "obligatory." It is all too easy to mistake the force of conventional forms of life for the merely conventional, as if sobs and high-pitched wails were the same kind of culturally preferred gestures as those used in brushing teeth.

Neither one's ability to anticipate other people's reactions nor the fact that people express their grief in culturally specific ways should be conflated (as in the cited passages above) with the notion that the devastatingly bereaved are merely conforming to conventional expectations. Even eye-witness reports cast in the normalizing ethnographic idiom trivialize the events they describe by reducing the force of intense emotions to spectacle. Their accounts visualize people's actions from the outside and fail to provide the participants' reflections on their own experiences. They normalize by presenting generalized recipes for ritual action rather than attempting to grasp the particular content of bereavement.[22]

The dominant mode of discourse appears, among other places, with particular clarity in Jack Goody's book *Death, Property and the Ancestors*. A chapter entitled "The Day of Death: Mourning the Dead," for example, begins with the response of the close kin of the deceased and provides a recipe drawn in a composite manner from a number of observations and descriptions:

> While the xylophones are playing, the lineage "wives" and
> "sisters" of the dead man walk and run about the area in front of
> the house, crying lamentations and holding their hands behind
> the nape of the neck in the accepted attitude of grief. . . . From
> time to time, one of the immediate mourners breaks into a trot,
> even a run, and a bystander either intercepts or chases after the
> bereaved and quietens him by seizing his wrist.[23]

The analyst has positioned himself as a spectator who looks on from the outside. Do the women experience their lamentations and gestures as an accepted attitude of grief in the manner portrayed by their ethnographer? What about the experience of the bereaved person being restrained? In the latter case the ethnographer simply remains silent, though this chapter, subtitled "Mourning the Dead," purports to describe the process of mourning. Only a detached observer witnessing, or at any rate representing, devastating loss in the most external manner could write such an account.

The ethnography immediately goes on to discuss not the bereaved, but the structural determinants that govern who can play the role of restraining the chief mourners from injuring or killing themselves. Within a paragraph the reader is presented with the following table giving a mechanical index of degrees of bereavement:

Man's funeral
Father . . . . Tied by hide

Renato Rosaldo

Mother	Tied by hide
Wife	Tied by hide
Brother	Tied by fiber
Sister	Tied by fiber
Son	String tied around the ankle
Daughter	String tied around the ankle[24]

Put into words, the table simply says that a dead man's parents and wife can be tied by hide, his siblings can be tied by fiber, and his children can be tied with string around the ankle. (One can only wonder at the objectifying impulse behind casting such a readily verbalized statement in tabular form.) The ethnography continues in this manner: "Before analyzing these categories of bereaved in greater detail, note should be taken of some other ways in which mourners are visually differentiated."[25] The ethnographer's position as uninvolved spectator has become yet more evident. The spectacle itself, seen from the outside, is largely visual: "ways in which mourners are visually differentiated." The violent upheaval of grief, its wailing and attempts at self-injury and suicide, have become normalized both in descriptive narrative and analytical presentations.

This mode of ethnographic discourse makes it difficult to show how social forms can be both imposed by convention *and* used more spontaneously to express feelings. In relying exclusively on such an idiom, ethnographers can represent other lives *as if* they doubted even the most visible agonies of the bereaved, including, for instance, a father mourning a son or a husband grieving his wife who died in childbirth. Claude Lévi-Strauss, for example, places normalizing rhetoric in its most general theoretical garb in the following passage:

> Men do not act, as members of a group, in accordance with what each feels as an individual; each man feels as a function of the way in which he is permitted or obliged to act. Customs are given as external norms before giving rise to internal sentiments, and these non-sentient norms determine the sentiments of individuals as well as the circumstances in which they may, or must, be displayed.[26]

Lest the reader wonder how fully Lévi-Strauss intends to dismiss the explanatory import, indeed the reality, of emotions or sentiments, he continues as follows:

> Moreover, if institutions and customs drew their vitality from being continually refreshed and invigorated by individual sentiments, like those in which they originated, they ought to

conceal an affective richness, continually replenished, which would be their positive content. We know that this is not the case, and that the constancy which they exhibit usually results from a conventional attitude.[27]

Lévi-Strauss finds such customs so devoid of affect that he can assert that emotions are experienced, not in the performance, but in the violation of conventional acts: "Emotion is indeed aroused, but when the custom, in itself indifferent, is violated."[28] What would the mourners, "crying lamentations and holding their hands behind the nape of the neck," reply to this assertion that they felt nothing at all and were simply conforming to indifferent custom?[29] The normative rhetoric of objective ethnographic description in this case both stimulates and appears to provide evidence supporting abstract theoretical statements that are neither humane nor accurate. In attempting to apprehend the complexities of other cultures, disciplined inquiry can ill afford to build its theories on such a slim rhetorical foundation.

What, one wonders, can supplement normalizing distanced discourse in ethnographic writing? A positive critique, after all, should attempt to develop alternative modes of doing ethnographic writing rather than simply multiplying negative examples. Other rhetorical modes, of course, are possible and have been used. In this paper, for example, I have used, among others, moral indignation, satire, and critique. For present illustrative purposes, however, I shall consider two among the myriad possible ways of writing ethnography. First, a more personal, particularizing, experiential rhetoric can offer another way of representing other forms of life. This mode, I should add, already appears in ethnographies, though with a status so secondary as to be relegated, for the most part, literally to the margins: prefaces, introductions, afterwords, footnotes, and italicized or small-print case histories. Second, normalized discourse deployed in more oblique, off-centered, or satirical ways, rather than in its usual monolithic, authoritative mode, can render its subjects in surprisingly multi-dimensional ways. In what follows I consider three instances of the first mode and one of the second with a view to developing a more varied array of rhetorical instruments for the analysis of other lifeways.

To begin, Godfrey Wilson has produced a rather different account of mourning: "That some at least of those who attend a Nyakyusa burial are moved by grief it is easy to establish."[30] In speaking about dancing, he begins by describing it as spectacle but goes on to remark that although "there are no very apparent signs of grief," the onlookers say that the dancers "are mourning the dead."[31] He cites an old man, for example, who describes the experience of dancing as mourning: "We dance because there is war in our hearts.—A passion of grief and fear exasperates us."[32] The reader can both envision dance as spectacle and apprehend the sense in which dancing can be a form of mourning. Wilson achieved this shift simply by recording spontaneous as well as more conventional expressions of emotion and by asking people to talk about their experience of the dance.

In another case Clifford Geertz has described the mood of a Javanese funeral as "a calm, undemonstrative, almost languid letting go, a brief ritualized relinquishment of a relationship no longer possible."[33] After a brief normalizing description ("the men begin to cut wooden grave markers and to dig a grave"),[34] he describes a particular case, a boy's death, where one thing after another went wrong. The cutting of wooden grave markers, just cited as recipe, becomes transformed in this manner:

> After a half hour or so, a few of the abangans began to chip half-heartedly away at pieces of wood to make grave markers and a few women began to construct small flower offerings for want of anything better to do; but it was clear that the ritual was arrested and that no one quite knew what to do next. Tension slowly rose.[35]

Always at risk in living through the anguish of loss, normalizing cultural patterns were shredded by confusion between divergent religious and political practices that made a mockery of routine. Delving into the particulars of this agonizing event rather than the generalities of a composite construction revealed the severe limits of collapsing mourning with ritual and ritual with routine.

In yet another instance Loring Danforth begins with an account that moves from spectacle to rather more intimate portraits of mourners. Early in the account one envisions what people do in this vivid though external manner:

> Soon the graveyard was alive with activity, and a forest of candles burned at the foot of each grave. About ten women, all dressed in shades of black, brown, or blue, busied themselves lighting lamps and sweeping around the graves. Several women began hauling water in large buckets from the faucet in the church courtyard nearby.[36]

Though a particular rather than a composite account (notice, for example, the past tense rather than the normalizing ethnographic present), this smacks of visual spectacle complete with candlelight and dresses of various colors. The mood is one of almost bucolic calm and routine.

Yet as the account proceeds, the analysis shifts so that the reader soon learns the particular histories of the mourners. Thus the following passage:

> The death of Irini's twenty-year-old daughter Eleni was generally acknowledged to have been the most tragic the village of Potamia had experienced in many years. Eleni died almost five years earlier, in August 1974. She had been a very attractive young woman, tall, with long black hair. . . . One month before she was to begin her first teaching job, Eleni was struck by a car and killed in a hit-and-run accident in the city of Thessaloniki.[37]

The reader then hears verbatim laments, learns how the mother never left her house for a full year following her daughter's death, discovers the friendship that developed with another bereaved mother, and witnesses the daughter's exhumation as the participants, by then known in certain biographical particulars, find themselves overcome with emotion. The ethnographer provides a sense of the emotions experienced by the actors through their words, their gestures, and their biographies. One begins to approach the content of mourning.

Now another anecdote seems in order, but this time, in the spirit of moving between appreciation and criticism, the story concerns my surprise at how earnest ethnographic rhetoric, applied to ourselves, can be both revealing and parodic. It all began in the summer of 1983 when I spent a couple of weeks at a family cottage on the shore of Lake Huron in Western Ontario. The family owning the cottage were by the next fall to become my in-laws, hence my ambiguous (Victor Turner would have called it liminal) position as an outsider on the way in. Much as one would expect (unless one was, as I was, too much in the thick of things), the parents-in-law-to-be treated the groom-to-be with reserve and suspicion.

My peculiar position, literally surrounded as I was by future in-laws, nourished a project that began to unfold over a two-week period in barely conscious daydreams. I started to turn the daily family breakfast into a ritual described in normalizing ethnographic discourse. The morning of our departure I began telling, with feelings mixed between malice and tenderness, my in-laws-to-be the ethnography of their family breakfast while we all were still eating.

My dense description, as told that morning, started with the reigning partriarch, who every morning, as if off on the hunt, shouts from the kitchen, "How many people would like a poached egg?" Women and children take turns saying yes or no. In the meantime (while the patriarch hunts), the women talk among themselves and designate one among them the toast-maker. As the eggs near readiness the reigning patriarch calls out to the designated toast-maker, "The eggs are about ready. Is there enough toast?" "Yes," comes the deferential reply, "the last two pieces are about to pop up." The patriarch then enters, as if just in front the hunt, bearing a plate of poached eggs before him. Throughout the course of the meal, the women and children, including the designated toast-maker, perform the obligatory ritual praise song, saying, "These sure are great eggs, Dad."

The reception of this ethnographic vignette about (and with which I interrupted) the family breakfast startled me because its telling was greeted with such amusement. Instead of seeming thin and earnest, as I had anticipated, my description was received as revealing and parodic. The reception of my tale, as has become evident in retrospect, was conditioned by the family's enjoyment of witty, teasing banter colored by hues of tender malice. All the participants, including the singers of the praise song, the designated toast-maker, and even the reigning patriarch, laughed and laughed, saying they had learned something. They said that the microethnography contained a recognizable measure of insight and truth.

My ethnographic discourse, in other words, not only transformed a particular experience (say, a fun meal together) into a generic family breakfast, but it also transformed a relatively spontaneous event into a caricatured analysis of routinized hierarchy organized along lines of gender and generation. The descriptive idiom deployed in the microethnography shifted jaggedly between terms ordinarily used by the family (mainly in such direct quotations as "These sure are great eggs, Dad") and those never used by them (such as "reigning patriarch," "designated toast-maker," and "obligatory ritual praise song"). The technical concepts displayed both tender hostility toward the future father-in-law (the reigning patriarch) and hesitant sympathy with the future sisters-in-law (the designated toast-maker and the singers of the praise song). One could, of course, have told a different story. On the one hand, there is the tale of how this breakfast differed from all others. On the other hand, the narrator could assume the father's point of view by describing how the "family provider" distributed his gifts to the "starving horde."

The ethnographic account turned out to have been a timely intervention that altered without destroying mealtime practices. The participants—the father approaching retirement and his daughters well along in their careers—had at the time been in the process of changing certain aspects of their relations. The insight I only half-consciously offered was that family breakfast routines, by then closer to empty ritual than they had been when the children were growing up, themselves embodied certain of the relations of gender and hierarchy that were being altered. My normalizing account inserted itself into this process by helping my in-laws-to-be see more clearly yet another arena for change.

The analysis was not an eternally objective statement, but an objectifying intervention that made the system under that description obsolete. The breakfast routine will doubtless change in certain respects and not others. The ritual praise songs honoring the well-poached eggs and their maker, for example, will probably continue to be sung, though in a different key and with tongue in cheek. In this case to defamiliarize was to transform everyday taken-for-granted reality.

The discourse deployed to describe the family breakfast formally resembled Radcliffe-Brown's, but the objectifications were so differently situated that the former could be called transformative and the latter dehumanizing. My account turned out to be parodic in large part because of the peculiar distance—that of an outsider becoming an in-law—at which I was analyst-narrator found myself positioned. This difference between transformative and dehumanizing objectifications thus resides more in how the analyst is positioned within a field of social interaction than in the distanced, normalizing text read as a field of intrinsic meaning. How rhetorical forms of discourse are read depends not only on their formal linguistic properties, but also on how narrators are positioned.

This paper has ended where its composition actually started. It was in fact the startling experience of having an earnest narration greeted with gales of laughter that made me wonder why a way of talking that sounded so serious when applied to absent Andaman Islanders could be so funny when applied to present Canadians. This question revolved around a pair of closely related difficulties. It is difficult to use distanced discourse to write an intentionally parodic account of such markedly distinctive customary lifeways as those of the Andaman Islanders. At the same time, this idiom so readily lends itself to parody, when applied to ourselves, that serious rather than satirical self-description becomes difficult to achieve. This paradox—a single rhetoric's being either parodic or serious depending in large measure on whether it is applied to Self or to Other—was the point of departure for this project.

In time I came to see that anthropology as a discipline has authorized normalizing accounts of so-called primitives to be read as earnest, objective descriptions of their forms of life. Ethnography beckons us to grow so accustomed to distanced normalizing discourse that it seems natural. Its authority has become so well established, so much taken for granted, that it appears within the norms of the discipline not as one rhetorical mode of representation among others, but as the one and only legitimate form for telling the literal truth about other people's lifeways. Yet no single rhetoric, whatever current fashions may dictate, has a monopoly on objectivity.

As a corrective to such literal-mindedness, I have taken this rhetorical mode, one that defamiliarizes the everyday world, and made it itself appear strange. This analysis has indicated how short is the distance between objective characterization and objectifying caricature. A discipline that grants detachment, or at least distance, exclusive rights to objective truth condemns itself to being at least as likely to reveal where objectivity lies as where it tells the truth. Ethnographies written in the present tense and cast in an idiom of generality usually gain their authority by contrast with more particular personal narratives and case histories. Yet the latter forms, using the past tense and talking about particulars as they do, can depict the experience of mourning in ways more difficult to achieve through normalizing discourse. If people suffer through their bereavement, it hardly appears objective to represent their experiences as if they were merely conforming with conventions by going through the expected motions.

In the end, of course, there is no single recipe for writing enthnographies of fine insight and imagination. Indeed Ilongot observations on modern warfare and mine on the family breakfast suggest that off-centered normalizing rhetoric can at times yield forceful accounts. Certainly standing current fashion on its head by substituting tales of specific cases for distanced normalizing discourse will not yield a solution to the vexed problem of representing other lives. Instead an increased disciplinary tolerance for diverse legitimate rhetorical forms could allow for reading and writing any particular text against other possible versions. Allowing forms of writing that have been marginalized or banned altogether to gain legitimacy could enable the discipline to approximate people's lives from a number of angles of vision. Such a tactic could enable us better to advance the ethnographic project of apprehending the range of human possibilities in their fullest complexity.

NOTES

I am grateful for the critical comments that I have received on this paper from Don McCloskey, Susan McCoin, Mary Louise Pratt, and Kathy Weston. Clifford Geertz, as a discussant, gave a particularly thoughtful critical appraisal of it.

1. Thomas S. Kuhn, *The Structure of Scientific Revolutions,* 2d ed. (Chicago: University of Chicago Press, 1970), pp. 43–51, 187–98.

2. The essays in this collection, of course, indicate that a number of people in different disciplines now have come to similar realizations. Other works that I have found especially helpful in studying the rhetoric of the human sciences include: Richard H. Brown *A Poetic for Sociology: Toward a Logic of Discovery for the Human Sciences* (Cambridge: Cambridge University Press, 1977); Robert H. Canary and Henry Kosicki, eds., *The Writing of History: Literary Form and Historical Understanding* (Madison: University of Wisconsin Press, 1978); W. B. Gallie, *Philosophy and the Historical Understanding* (London: Chatto and Windus, 1964); J. H. Hexter, "The Rhetoric of History," in David L. Sills, ed., *International Encyclopedia of the Social Sciences* (New York: Macmillan, 1968), 6: 368–94; Dominick LaCapra, *Rethinking Intellectual History: Texts, Contexts, Language* (Ithaca: Cornell University Press, 1983); Donald N. McCloskey, "The Rhetoric of Economics," *Journal of Economic Literature* 21 (1983): 481–517; Mary Louise Pratt, "Conventions of Representation: Where Discourse and Ideology Meet," in Heidi Byrnes, ed., *Georgetown University Round Table in Languages and Linguistics 1982* (Washington, D.C.: Georgetown University Press, 1982), pp. 139–55; idem, " 'Scratches on the Face of the Country,' or What Mr. Barrow Saw in the Land of the Bushmen," *Critical Inquiry* (forthcoming); idem, " 'Under Our Very Eyes': Ethnography and Travel Writing," in George Marcus and James Clifford, eds., *Writing Cultures* (Berkeley: University of California Press, 1986); Hayden White, *Metahistory: The Historical Imagination in Nineteenth-Century Europe* (Baltimore: Johns Hopkins University Press, 1973). Within anthropology I have learned particularly from the following: James Boon, *Other Tribes, Other Scribes: Symbolic Anthropology in the Comparative Study of Cultures, Histories, Religions, and Texts* (Cambridge: Cambridge University Press, 1982); James Clifford, "On Ethnographic Authority," *Representations* 1:2 (1983): 118–46; Vincent Crapanzano, "On the Writing of Ethnography," *Dialectical Anthropology* 2 (1977): 69–73; Clifford Geertz, "Slide Show: Evans-Pritchard's African Transparencies," *Raritan* 3:2 (1983): 62–80; George Marcus and Dick Cushman, "Ethnographies as Texts," in *Annual Review of Anthropology,* vol. 11 (Palo Alto: Annual Reviews, 1982), pp. 25–69.

3. The first project, that of seeing cultural differences without losing sight of human similarities, has been most influentially articulated by Clifford Geertz, "Thick Description: Toward an Interpretive Theory of Culture," in *The*

Renato Rosaldo

Intepretation of Cultures (New York: Basic Books, 1973), pp. 3–30, esp. p. 14. The second, that social analysis should include both structure and agency, can be found, among other places, in the following: Richard J. Bernstein, *The Restructuring of Social and Political Theory* (Philadelphia: University of Pennsylvania Press, 1978); Pierre Bourdieu, *Outline of a Theory of Practice* (Cambridge: Cambridge University Press, 1977); Anthony Giddens, *Central Problems in Social Theory: Action, Structure and Contradiction in Social Analysis* (Berkeley: University of California Press, 1979); Raymond Williams, *Marxism and Literature* (Oxford: Oxford University Press, 1977). The third, that of moving between closeness and distance, has been discussed in the following: Clifford Geertz, " 'From the Native's Point of View': On the Nature of Anthropological Understanding," in *Local Knowledge: Further Essays in Interpretive Anthropology* (New York: Basic Books, 1983), pp. 55–70, esp. 56–58; Renato Rosaldo, "Grief and a Headhunter's Rage: On the Cultural Force of Emotions," in Edward M. Bruner, ed., *Text, Play, and Story: The Construction and Reconstruction of Self and Society* (Washington, D.C.: American Ethnological Society, 1984), pp. 178–95; T. J. Scheff, *Catharsis in Healing, Ritual, and Drama* (Berkeley: University of California Press, 1979); Max Weber, "Politics as a Vocation," in H. H. Gerth and C. Wright Mills, eds., *From Max Weber: Essays in Sociology* (Oxford: Oxford University Press, 1946), pp. 77–128, esp. pp. 115–16.

4. For a series of replies to Hempel, see William Dray, *Laws and Explanations in History* (Oxford: Oxford University Press, 1957); Hexter, "The Rhetoric of History"; Louis Mink, "The Autonomy of Historical Understanding," *History and Theory* 5 (1965): 24–47.

5. For further information on the Ilongots see Michelle Rosaldo, *Knowledge and Passion: Ilongot Notions of Self and Social Life* (Cambridge: Cambridge University Press, 1980); Renato Rosaldo, *Ilongot Headhunting, 1883–1974: A Study in Society and History* (Stanford: Stanford University Press, 1980). For outsiders' perceptions of Ilongot headhunting, see Renato Rosaldo, "The Rhetoric of Control: Ilongots Viewed as Natural Bandits and Wild Indians," in Barbara A. Babcock, ed., *The Reversible World: Symbolic Inversion in Art and Society* (Ithaca: Cornell University Press, 1978), pp. 240–57.

6. Perhaps I should add that the American army strategy of taking lowland highways and driving the Japanese into the hills where they would starve to death or surrender decimated the Ilongots. One-third of their population died in June 1945. For a largely Ilongot perspective on this period, see R. Rosaldo, *Ilongot Headhunting, 1883–1974*, pp. 120–34.

7. Americo Paredes, "On Ethnographic Work Among Minority Groups: A Folklorist's Perspective," in Ricardo Romo and Raymund Paredes, eds., *New Directions in Chicano Scholarship* (La Jolla: Chicano Studies Monograph Series, 1978), p. 2.

8. Ibid., p. 2.

9. Ibid., p. 5.

10. Ibid., p. 28.

11. Horace Miner, "Body Ritual Among the Nacirema," *American Anthropologist* 58 (1956): 503–7.

12. My distinction between everyday and technical language is borrowed from Clifford Geertz, who expressed this distinction in the terms "experience-near" and "experience-distant" (which he in turn borrowed from the psychoanalyst Heinz Kohut). In his words: "An experience-near concept is, roughly, one that someone—a patient, a subject, in our case an informant—might himself naturally and effortlessly use to define what he or his fellows see, feel, think, imagine, and so on, and which he would readily understand when similarly applied by others. An experience-distant concept is one that specialists of one sort of another—an analyst, an experimenter, an ethnographer, even a priest or an ideologist—employ to forward their scientific, philosophical, or practical aims. 'Love' is an experience-near concept, 'object-cathexis' is an experience-distant one." See Geertz, " 'From the Native's Point of View,' " p. 57.

13. A. R. Radcliffe-Brown, *The Andaman Islanders* (New York: Free Press of Glencoe, 1964), p. 241.

14. See R. Rosaldo, "Grief and a Headhunter's Rage."

15. S. F. Nadel, *Nupe Religion* (New York: Schocken, 1970), pp. 122–23.

16. Roger Keesing, *Kwaio Religion* (New York: Columbia University Press, 1982), p. 143.

17. Jane C. Goodale, *Tiwi Wives* (Seattle: University of Washington Press, 1971), p. 241.

18. Jack Goody, *Death, Property and the Ancestors* (Stanford: Stanford University Press, 1962), p. 87.

19. Ibid., p. 91.

20. Ibid.

21. Nadel, *Nupe Religion*, p. 125.

22. See Renato Rosaldo, "The Story of Tukbaw: 'They Listen as He Orates,' " in F. E. Reynolds and Donald Capps, eds., *The Biographical Process: Studies in the History and Psychology of Religion* (The Hague: Mouton, 1976), pp. 121–51; idem, "Beyond the Rules of the Game," in Edward Bruner and Victor Turner, eds., *The Language of Experience* (Urbana: University of Illinois Press, 1984).

23. Goody, *Death, Property and the Ancestors*, p. 87.

24. Ibid.

25. Ibid., p. 88.

26. Claude Lévi-Strauss, *Totemism*, trans. Rodney Needham (Boston: Beacon Press, 1963), p. 70.

27. Ibid.

28. Ibid.

29. In this context it probably comes as no surprise that most anthropologists, including Lévi-Strauss, write about incest (despite widespread publicity on its occurrence in the United States) as if it never happened.

30. Godfrey Wilson, "Nyakyusa Conventions of Burial," *Bantu Studies* 13 (1939): 22.

31. Ibid., p. 12.

32. Ibid., p. 13.

33. Clifford Geertz, "Ritual and Social Change: A Javanese Example," in *The Interpretation of Cultures*, p. 153.

34. Ibid., p. 154.

35. Ibid., p. 156.

36. Loring Danforth, *The Death Rituals of Greece* (Princeton: Princeton University Press, 1982), p. 11.

37. Ibid., p. 13.

7 PARADISE LOST

THE THEME OF TERRESTRIALITY

IN HUMAN EVOLUTION

MISIA LANDAU

I might as well begin with a confession. I have never studied Milton's poem, despite the allusion or, you might say, illusion in my title. Nor am I the first to suggest an analogy between the Fall and the Descent of man from the trees. In his *Cartoon History of the Universe,* Larry Gonick not only draws the connection but manages to capture the central hominid dilemma in a single balloon: "What do we do with our hands?" asks a tottering ramapithecine. Rather than redraw old parallels, I would like to look at a broader archetype, familiar even to those who have not read Milton, Darwin, or Gonick. That is, the myth of the turning point.

To speak of turning points is already to say something still more general. To speak of turning points is to say something about beginnings and ends. It was, of course, Aristotle who first drew attention to this obvious fact. Telling a story does not consist simply in adding episodes to one another. It consists in creating relations between events, in constructing what Paul Ricoeur has called "meaningful totalities" or configurations. Elsewhere I have described theories of human evolution in terms of a nine-part narrative structure.[1] Following Aristotle, however, we can see them simply as stories consisting of a beginning, middle, and end. Basically, the course of human evolution can be viewed as a passage between two equilibria:

ARBOREALITY——X——TERRESTRIALITY
(successful life in the trees)—(successful life on the ground)

Given this formal and admittedly oversimplified description, we might expect, first, that arboreality and terrestriality will be dialec-

111

Misia Landau

tically defined and, second, that the middle ground between them will be viewed as a transitional phase or turning point. I would not be bothering with all this if I did not believe that, more or less, this is what we find.

Not that there is no controversy surrounding the descent to the ground. Paleoanthropologists still do not agree about how, when, and why it occurred. But to listen to them is to hear that, however it happened, coming to the ground was a "departure," a "decisive step" in human evolution. Take, for example, the following passage from a classic paper on human evolution by the early twentieth-century geologist Joseph Barrell: "How was this step taken which transferred the habitat and transformed the quadrumanous arboreal man-ape into a bipedal terrestrial ape-man standing nearly erect and facing the dangers of the ground?"[2]

No wonder so much attention is paid to this question, for, as Barrell describes it, all of human evolution seems to follow on the heels of our descending ancestors. And yet there is nothing inherently transitional about the descent to the ground, however momentous the occasion. Nor, I might add, is it inherently a departure or step (at least not in the intended metaphorical sense). It only acquires such value in relation to our overall conception of the course of human evolution. Indeed, this was the point of my brief lesson in narrative. The problem, as Frank Kermode observes, is that once an event is conceived of as a transition or turning point, it assumes a paradigmatic aspect.[3] It becomes associated with moments of transition found in other narratives and may be reconstructed according to principles governing these other narratives.

Let us return for a moment to Barrell's description of the descent to the ground as a kind of "step" or "departure." To begin with, I want to point out the perfect symmetry of his sentence. Right down to their hyphens, the quadrumanous arboreal man-ape and the bipedal terrestrial ape-man are depicted in opposition. Not only ancestors but also environments form dialectical pairs: the "transference" of the habitat corresponds to the "transformation" of the ape-man. That organism and environment are symmetrically related is a truism in evolutionary biology. "Le milieu fit son oeuvre" in the words of H. F. Osborn, a well-known early twentieth-century paleontologist. Depending on how you read it, Osborn's motto could sound like a French pun on Burke's maxim that, in drama, "the scene is a fit container for the act." Indeed, both Osborn and G. Elliot Smith, another early twentieth-century authority on human evolution, frequently refer to the environment as a "theater," "stage," and "backdrop" for the "great drama of human evolution."

These might, of course, be figures of speech, metaphors for the biological concept of adaptation. Behind these words, Osborn and Smith, and also Barrell, could be referring to the scientific principle of natural selection which describes a biological relationship between organism and environment. Yet of the three, only Barrell was a Darwinian. Osborn and Smith were orthogenists. So though all see symmetry between organism and environment, they do so from quite different biological perspectives: whereas Osborn and Smith emphasize internal organic factors operating in definite directions, Barrell sees evolution as the result of a "series of fortunate physical events, conditioned in the internal nature of sun and earth, rather than the byproduct of mere life activities as expressed in orthogenesis."[4] Given such profound theoretical differences—indeed, they appear to describe different planets—it may seem odd that Barrell and Osborn are commonly credited with telling very similar stories of human evolution. For example, both attribute the descent to the ground to a change in climate. And yet, though they speak in similar narrative terms, biologically they use a very different logic: whereas Barrell uses a change in climate to call into play natural selection, Osborn uses it to evoke the latent energy of our prehuman ancestors.

Now, there is a tendency to view the history of paleoanthropology as a series of debates over sequence. Brain first or bipedalism? Events, like fossils, are treated as movable objects—observed, reconstructed, and arranged in some order that is more or less real and true. What I am getting at here is a different view of paleoanthropological activity: one that might be called semiotic. Assuming that fossils and events mean different things to different people, it looks not at fossils and events but, instead, at the sets of relations by which they are given their various shapes. It looks not at the descent to the ground but at the sets of relations by which it is defined as a turning point.

As I have shown, these relations are defined in part biologically, but they are also defined nonbiologically, by what I have been referring to as principles of narrative symmetry: (1) the tendency to define past events dialectically, and (2) the tendency to define organisms and environments in terms of corresponding attributes, again, as reflections of each other. Indeed, I would argue that it is the priority of such narrative terms which gives us a sense that, despite significant theoretical ambiguity, paleoanthropologists have been telling the same kind of story. Not that our ancestors did not come to the ground, for there is good reason to believe they did, one way or another. My point is simply that, in depicting this almost unimaginable event, we have borrowed terms from other sources. We have recreated old turning points.

Judging by the metaphors paleoanthropologists use, the Fall is only one such prototype. "The birth of humanity," "the emancipation of the forelimb," "the road to hominization"—to scientists these may sound like embarrassing clichés, mere phrases. And yet to hear one is to hear an entire story. They are like narrative holograms, carrying within a single image a beginning, middle, and ending. I turn, then, to two archetypal turning points commonly found in theories of human evolution, expressed metaphorically above as "birth" and "emancipation," and in the headings below as "expulsion" and "escape."

Expulsion

Gonick's cartoon notwithstanding, the descent to the ground is usually portrayed as a rather serious crisis in human evolution. Whether imagined as a form of exile (as in the biblical account) or a kind of birth (in this sense an expulsion from a secure womblike existence), there is a sense in many theories that the descent to the ground signifies a dangerous move: from an environment that is relatively safe and prosperous into one that is hostile and life-threatening. Not only is this reflected in the metaphors paleoanthropologists use; it is also reflected in the scientific descriptions they give of the arboreal and terrestrial realms. Emphasizing the abundance of fruit and the refuge found in forests, Barrell portrays the prehominid dilemma as follows:

> Did a climatic change in the Tertiary period acting on a species of large brained and progressive anthropoid apes isolated from the regions of continued forest compel them to adapt themselves to a terrestrial life or die? Did the gradual dwindling leading even to the extermination of forests . . . produce a rigorous natural selection which transformed an ape largely arboreal and frugivorous in habits into a powerful terrestrial, bipedal primate, largely carnivorous in habit, banding together in the struggle for existence and by that means achieving success in chase and war? The gradual elimination first of the food of the forests, lastly of the refuge of the trees, through increasing semi-aridity, would have been a compelling cause as mandatory as the semi-aridity which compelled the emergence of vertebrates from the water, transforming fishes into amphibians, the first vertebrate rulers of the land.[5]

Like Barrell's previous quotation, this one is noteworthy, not least for its symmetry. Here Barrell compares the difference between land and trees to the difference between water and land. Again ape and ape-man differ symmetrically and to a corresponding degree. Indeed, Barrell compares the transformation of ape into ape-man to the transformation of fish into amphibian. (Treating the differentiation of ape and human as an event equivalent to the emergence of a new Class or even Kingdom—that is, judging by its ultimate consequences—is in fact a common habit in the study of human evolution.)

Though difficult to see, there is yet another distinction lurking in Barrell's text: between the natural/familiar and the unnatural/alien. This distinction is embedded not so much in the way the terrestrial realm is depicted, in contrast to the arboreal, as a dangerous place, as in the way humans are portrayed in that realm: at odds and out of place, forced to adapt by unusual means. This view of man as somehow ill-suited to his terrestrial environment is, in fact, central to Darwin's conception of human evolution.[6] For though Darwin is vague about the actual appearance of our early ancestors,

> we should, however, bear in mind that an animal possessing
> great size, strength, and ferocity, and which, like the gorilla,
> could defend itself from all enemies, would not perhaps have
> become social: and this would most effectually have checked the
> acquirement of the higher mental qualities, such as sympathy
> and the love of his fellows. Hence it might have been an immense
> advantage to man to have sprung from some comparatively weak
> creature.[7]

Thus Darwin shows in terms of natural selection how the weak might inherit the earth. That they do so largely by means of their intelligence has led several Darwinian critics to draw parallels to the biblical account[8], as though this act of disobedience, the acquisition of knowledge, was the cause of man's moral downfall (and it is the case that man's moral character is blackened regularly in the book). But a more profound resemblance between Darwin's account and the Edenic paradigm has to do with the almost perfect symmetry which exists between its parts. Like the world of the Bible, Darwin's world is so carefully conceived, and the relations between its parts are so thoroughly drawn, that events appear not merely as a succession but instead as an interconnection of parts all mutually implied and conditioned in the whole. (Perhaps this is why *The Descent of Man* can be made to tell more than one story.)

It is in light of his overall conception of human evolution as a dialectical process leading from a position of physical weakness to mental strength that Darwin reconstructs our arboreal origins. Discussing the "small strength and speed of man, his want of natural weapons" and also such rudiments as Darwin's point and man's weak sense of smell, Darwin concludes that his ancestors must have lived in a "warm, forest-clad land," where they would not have been exposed to special danger "even if far more helpless." Conceiving of human ancestors as poorly designed terrestrial creatures, Darwin furthermore explains the origins of bipedalism: "They would thus have been better able to defend themselves with stones or clubs, to attack their prey, or otherwise to obtain food."[9] Note here how, in contrast to the safety of the arboreal realm, defense from predators becomes a motivating factor.

Linking tool-use and bipedalism as a response to the dangers of terrestrial life, Darwin foreshadows a common theoretical practice among twentieth-century paleoanthropologists. Raymond Dart, John Robinson, and Sherwood Washburn all view tool-use as a critical factor in the emergence of the first bipedal hominids. Even those who assign tool-use to a later stage often see bipedalism as an adaptation to the dangers of terrestrial life. For example, Oakley and Howells see bipedalism as an adaptation for spotting predators. For Leakey, upright posture is a way of keeping a bearing on the trees. Piveteau goes one step further. Like the first Amphibia who, according to Alfred Romer, were forced to move overland from one pond to the next in arid environments, our ancestors became bipedal, Piveteau argues, not simply to spot the dwindling forests but to stay in them.

Assuming, as these theories do, that coming to the ground was a dangerous step from the point of view of predation, the question arises: why specifically bipedalism and not some other adaptation? Because our ancestors were physically weak and defenceless, and relied on tools instead of natural weapons for self-protection. The problem with Darwin's explanation—indeed any explanation invoking pre-adaptation[10]—is that it is almost unavoidably teleological. For even if predator pressure were a necessary and (for argument's sake) sufficient condition of bipedalism, a nonteleological description of the origins of bipedalism would still require an adequate description of its antecedent state independent of predator pressure (or, for that matter, any other motivating condition).[11] The problem is that we simply do not have an adequate description of the antecedents of bipedalism. Given the recent debate over the locomotor behavior of *Australopithecus afarensis*,[12] some might say that we do not have an adequate description of bipedalism itself, at least not its initial state. But assuming with Lovejoy that the first australopithecines were essentially human-type bipeds, we still draw a blank about antecedents. Try what we will, only prehominid fossils can tell us how our prehominid ancestors moved. And though the Miocene hominoid fossil record looks good from the neck up, it is still poor with regard to postcranials.

So it remains: without some idea of the anatomical, behavioral, and ecological antecedents of bipedalism, there is very little we can say about how it developed. This has not, of course, stopped paleoanthropologists from trying. The problem is that given so little fossil material to work with, they are forced to reconstruct both the antecedents of bipedalism and the conditions of its development on the basis of end products (which are themselves ambiguous). Consequently, there is a tendency in theories of hominid evolution to define origins in terms of endings and to place the burden of explanation on the dialectical relationship between them. In short, there is a tendency to depend on narrative principles as well as biological principles to explain the origins of bipedalism.[13] Whether predator pressure did or did not shape bipedalism, the real danger is this: that in focusing on the current utility of having our hands free and eyes elevated for self-defense, we may have exaggerated the extent to which bipedalism originally evolved as an adaptation to a dangerous and alien terrestrial environment and, thus, the extent to which the terrestrial realm (in contrast to the arboreal realm) was dangerous and alien. Whether this tendency to focus on the hostile aspects of the terrestrial realm in contrast to the arboreal also has its roots in some symbolic vision of forests as womblike or of man as somehow out of place in a cosmological sense, I am not sure (though I bet it does). The point is, this vision of hominid origins as the result of a shift between two worlds is, in form if nothing else, the restatement of the old mythic formula of expulsion.

Escape

This brings me to the second archetype—escape. Like expulsion, this view of the descent to the ground also involves a shift between antithetical worlds. But rather than a casting-out into a terrestrial world of danger, here the descent to the ground signifies a kind of breaking-away into a terrestrial world of adventure and promise. Like expulsion, this breaking-away can occur for a variety of reasons, in a variety of ways. But whether they were closed out by an ever-shrinking forest or lured by opportunity on the ground, the feeling here is that in making the move our ancestors took an evolutionarily wise, if nonetheless challenging, step.

Not surprisingly, these theories tend to be especially teleological. Facing as they do the problem of defining antecedents on the basis of

Misia Landau

descendants, they confront yet another danger: the idea of purpose. Indeed, for Osborn the descent to the ground was literally a "decision" forced upon our ancestors by a great wave of aridity in Oligocene times. This wave of aridity caused a "cleavage" between lowland forests and elevated plateaus, which in turn

> profoundly affected the whole mammalian world of this region; not only the horses, rhinoceroses, tapirs, and even-toed animals like the progenitors of the deer, the cattle, and the camel families had to make their choice between forest regions and the plains. . . . It is not at all probable that the Primates . . . were exempt from this compelling and fateful decision. Why was it postponed by the progressive progenitors of man when adopted by all the progressive elements in the remaining mammalian world?[14]

Osborn answers his own rhetorical question.

> An alert race cannot develop in a forest—a forested country can never be a center of radiation for man. Nor can the higher type of man develop in a lowland river-bottom country with plentiful food and luxuriant vegetation. It is upon the plateaus and relatively level uplands that life is most exacting and response to stimulus most beneficial. . . . In brief, while the anthropoid apes were luxuriating in the forested lowlands of Asia and Europe, the Dawn Men were evolving in the invigorating atmosphere of the relatively dry uplands.[15]

The idea that by leaving the trees, our ancestors escaped evolutionary stagnation can also be found in the writings of Arthur Keith.[16] But nowhere is the link between terrestriality and evolutionary progress better illustrated by Dart's description of the South African veldt as a kind of evolutionary testing ground. The discovery of australopithecines in the region of the veldt, Dart argued, was proof that these hominids

> had evolved an intelligence (to find and subsist upon new types of food and to avoid the dangers and enemies of the open plain) as well as a bodily structure (for sudden and swift bipedal movement, to elude capture) far in advance of that of the slothful, semi-arboreal, quadrupedal anthropoids. They had thus attained a degree of physical and psychical advancement that sundered them irrevocably from their tropical cousins.[17]

"It is my opinion," Dart continues,

that we have in Australopithecus a troglodytic anthropoid which, in addition to, and probably because of, its increased intelligence and its skill in using its hands as hands and its feet as feet, had become sufficiently weaned from its frugivorous tropical diet to vary its table with the fruits of the chase. Today the limestone cliffs are riddled with bees' and birds' nests. Small rodents, turtles, lizards, and other reptiles are plentiful. The Thabaseek "river" pools are filled with rushes drooping with birds' nests, and provide fish, amphibian and reptilian life in profusion. Wild game of the water and the veldt, though not so abundant today, previously existed there in great numbers.[18]

Truly a carnivore's paradise!

Compared with Barrell's bleak terrestrial landscape, Dart's terrestrial realm does appear a different world. Whereas for Barrell the terrestrial realm with its predators and lack of fruit is life-threatening, for Dart it is, with its dropping rushes and fruits of the chase, life-supporting. (Indeed, for Osborn and Dart, life in the trees is the dead end.) Similarly, Dart and Osborn's first hominids appear quite a different breed from Darwin's weak and defenseless semihuman progenitor: they were the fearless hunters, not the feeble hunted.

Still, these two conceptions have much in common. Though arboreal and terrestrial may be described in different terms, nevertheless they are still formulated as an antithesis. This is especially graphic in Osborn's conception of a physical "cleavage" between plateau and lowland as a result of continental elevation. This cleavage in turn corresponds to the split between humans and apes. Similarly, Dart talks about how, by crossing the veldt barrier, the australopithecines become "sundered" from the apes, their tropical cousins. Again, this illustrates the point I have been making about symmetry between organism and environment. Indeed, this tendency to describe the environment in terms of the organic qualities it ellicits—in particular the mental qualities—is especially pronounced in these accounts. "Invigorating," "challenging," "exhilarating," "elevated"—all these are terms used by Osborn and Dart to describe the terrestrial realm. So tight is the symmetry between environment and organism that Osborn actually describes the mind in terms of environmental characteristics: "man has a bipedal, dextrous, wide roaming psychology; the ape has a quadrupedal, brachiating, tree-living psychology."[19]

Yet behind this image of the progressive frontier and the restless human intellect lies an even more powerful idea: that humans are "more evolved" than apes—that apes are the barely evolved, even de-

Misia Landau

generate, descendants of the common ancestor. This image of the ape as somehow confined or arrested in an evolutionary sense is perhaps the greatest popular misconception about human evolution.[20] Nor is it confined to the popular imagination. Indeed we have seen it recently in the pages of *Science,* in C. Owen Lovejoy's theory of human origins.[21]

Briefly, Lovejoy's theory is as follows. Because apes raise so few offspring in the course of a lifetime, their numbers have fallen to dangerously low levels. Like their late Miocene ancestors, they face a "demographic dilemma." Hominids, in contrast, managed to avoid this by developing what Lovejoy calls a "breakthrough adaptation": that is, shortened birth interval. They did this, according to Lovejoy, by shifting their reproductive and feeding strategies, specifically by developing monogamous pair bonding and provisioning by males of females and offspring. Thus freed from having to earn a living, hominid females stayed home and had more babies, thereby shortening the birth interval. Males, faced with the problem of having to bring home the bacon, developed bipedalism. In this way the first hominids literally walked away from the demographic dilemma.

Lest this sketchy outline appear another caricature, I should say that Lovejoy's attempt to solve the problem of hominid origins by integrating principles of mammalian biology is innovative and stimulating. But like all such attempts, it suffers from a very poor fossil record[22] and, in addition, from a number of questionable assumptions about living hominoids—not just apes but also humans. Certainly the idea that monogamy and the nuclear family are universal human, let alone basic hominid, attributes finds little support from cultural anthropologists (or even modern European historians). Nor is there much support from physical anthropologists for the claim that short birth intervals evolved long ago in hominids.

Perhaps most relevant to my discussion, though, is Lovejoy's claim that the living apes, like their 7-million-year-old Miocene hominoid ancestors, are in some kind of dilemma, this time a demographic one. True, apes are less abundant than modern humans. But so, too, were the australopithecines, as Washburn has emphasized.[23] Without historical data there is no way of knowing whether this represents a dilemma for them (and surely 7 million years is a long time to be in evolutionary crisis). Nor are we in a position to say whether or not the modern human situation is adaptive. Indeed, the overabundance of humans may pose a far greater threat to living apes (and to humans) then do their long birth intervals. The more basic point, however, is that in confronting this new theoretical dilemma, Lovejoy's apes face the same predicament as Osborn and Dart's apes: evolutionary stasis.

And yet there is little evidence for such an assumption. Judging by the fossil record, the living apes have diverged significantly from their Miocene ancestors. Certainly this is true of Sivapithecus and the orangutan, who, as David Pilbeam and others have shown, are probably evolutionarily related.[24] For example, Sivapithecus, with its probably more chimplike limb proportions, may well have spent more time on the ground than do the highly arboreal short-legged, long-armed modern orangutans. Indeed, in some respects, such as features of its dentition (e.g., robust jaws, thick enamel, large cheek teeth), Sivapithecus looks more like a hominid than a modern pongid.

While fossils are shedding light on the modern apes, much insight also comes from comparisons with living species. Here I agree with Washburn that few fossil discoveries have been more important than the discovery of the genetic near identity of humans and chimps. And yet our image of the apes, and of our ape ancestry, remains constrained by old assumptions and archetypes. The myth of the turning point, of the crisis or dilemma, is only one such archetype, though, as I have tried to show, it is certainly one of the most pervasive. Indeed, the whole narrative of human evolution has been prone to such mythological conceptions.

Conclusion

How then do we avoid these biases? To begin with, it is clear from what I have already said that we need to find more fossils. We also need more contextual data—that is, information concerning past climates, habitats, communities, and so on—but we need to collect it independently of our concern for hominids. Only by trying to see the forest (or any other environment) for the hominids will we see what kind of forest there was, if there was one.[25] This in turn means paying more attention to how we see fossils and, in particular, to how we perceive their relationships, in both time and space. Once again, I must confess that what I am saying is not new. Self-reflective paleoanthropologists have been aware for some time now of their theoretical (and ideological) biases and of the limitations of their data. Recognizing that much paleoanthropological reconstruction will remain teleological until more fossils are discovered, many are turning their attention to living systems: attempting to formulate general theoretical principles of morphology, behavior, and ecology rather than to reconstruct the exact nature of specific antecedents.

Misia Landau

Nevertheless, few paleoanthropologists have looked for "the myth of the innocent eye" in their own rhetoric. And yet, as Geertz has observed, "anthropology exists in the book, the article, the lecture, the museum display,"[26] as well as in the field or laboratory. Only by recognizing this fact will paleoanthropologists be free to find new and more workable theories. Only by studying the stories they tell will they tell better—or, in any case, more likely—stories. Still there will be problems. For if we take, with Kermode, "the clock's tick-tock . . . to be a model of what we call a plot, an organization that humanizes time by giving it form," the question arises: can paleoanthropologists use these plots when the interval between tick and tock lasts not a second or a century or even a millennium? Can we—should we—humanize such inhuman amounts of time as geological epochs and eons? The question is, as they say, rhetorical, for the fact remains: we do humanize the past—that is, we impose form on it. And for the moment at least, there appear to be few alternatives to narrative.

Still, seeing the error of our ways can, in the words of Milton, lead "new hope to spring out of despair." If we need more fossils, we also need more stories. We need larger plots and more complicated ones. For the point of my analysis has been to show that in making sense of the past, we have perhaps made too much sense. Bolstered by our simplifying theories and archetypes, we have behaved as though the past were knowable, as though our questions could be answered by fossils when, in truth, they are answered as they are asked: by humans.

"We are not the new theologians," David Pilbeam intoned in a recent essay,[27] and yet he concluded with what he believed at the time to be a Talmudic quotation:

> We do not see things as they are
> We see things as we are.

Having searched in vain for the exact reference, he now believes it came not from the Talmud (as a student told him) but instead from a Chinese fortune cookie. This could be a good omen. For depending on how you regard Chinese fortune cookies (or the Talmud, for that matter), maybe we do have the power after all: if not to see things as they are, then to see, within known limits, how we are.

NOTES

1. Misia Landau, "Human Evolution as Narrative," *American Scientist* 72 (1984): 262–68.

2. Joseph Barrell, "Probable Relations of Climatic Change to the Origin of the Tertiary Ape-Man," *Scientific Monthly* 4 (1917): 23.

3. Frank Kermode, *The Sense of an Ending* (London: Oxford University Press, 1967).

4. Barrell, "Probable Relations," p. 26.

5. Barrell, "Probable Relations," p. 17.

6. Misia Landau, "The Anthropogenic: Paleoanthropological Writing as a Genre of Literature" (Ph.D. dissertation, Yale University, 1981); Misia Landau, David Pilbeam and Alison Richard, "Human Origins a Century After Darwin," *Bioscience* 32 (1982): 507.

7. Charles Darwin, *The Descent of Man* (New York: Modern Library, 1948), p. 444.

8. See Jacques Barzun, *Darwin, Marx, Wagner* (New York: Doubleday, 1958); Stanley Hyman, *the Tangled Bank: Darwin, Marx, Frazer, and Freud as Imaginative Writers* (New York: Atheneum, 1974).

9. Darwin, *Descent*, p. 444.

10. Preadaptation is a common evolutionary concept which holds that structures evolved under one set of circumstances can, given a change of circumstances or minor structural changes, take on quite different functions; that is, it is a concept used to distinguish between present and retrospective significance. In the example given here, our ancestors were preadapted for bipedalism and tool-use by virtue of their small size, which had evolved as an adaptation to life in the trees. As Gould has observed, "the term is unfortunate because it implies a foreknowledge of retrospective significance" (Stephen J. Gould, *Ontogeny and Phylogeny* [Cambridge: Harvard University Press, 1977], p. 434). To avoid these teleological connotations, he and Elizabeth Vrba have proposed an alternative term: "exaptation" (Stephen J. Gould and Elizabeth S. Vrba, "Exaptation—A Missing Term in the Science of Form," *Paleobiology* 8 (1982): 4–15).

11. David Pilbeam, Silliman Lecture, manuscript, 1983, p. 23.

12. The issue here is Lovejoy's proposition that *A. afarensis* was a fully terrestrial, essentially modern, human-type biped. According to Sussman and Stern (and others), many of the fossils attributed to *A. afarensis* show anatomical features associated with arboreal forms of locomotion. See C. Owen Lovejoy, "The Gait of Australopithecus," *Yearbook of Physical Anthropology* 17 (1973): 147–61; R. L. Sussman and J. T. Stern, "The Locomotor Anatomy of *Australopithecus afarensis*," *American Journal of Physical Anthropology* 60 (1983): 279–317.

13. For a recent attempt to avoid the problems of teleology, see P. S. Rodman and Henry McHenry, "Bioenergetics and the Origin of Hominid Bipedalism," *Journal of Human Evolution* 9 (1980): 329–31.

14. Henry Fairfield Osborn, "The Plateau Habitat of the Pro-Dawn Man," *Science* 67 (1928): 570.

15. Henry Fairfield Osborn, "Why Central Asia?" *Natural History* 26 (1926): 263. Although the term "race" can be taken to mean the human species as a whole, Osborn's usage in this passage, as elsewhere, is clearly racist.

16. See Arthur Keith, "Man's Posture: Its Evolution and Disorders," *British Medical Journal* 1 (1923): 451.

17. Raymond A. Dart, "Taungs and Its Significance," *Natural History* 26 (1926): 317.

18. Dart, "Taungs," p. 321.

19. Henry Fairfield Osborn, "Recent Discoveries Relating to the Origin and Antiquity of Man," *Proceeding of the American Philosophical Society* 67 (1927): 384.

20. Metaphorically, apes are seen as "failed experiments" or, in the words of Robinet, "preliminary studies [in] the apprenticeship of Nature in learning to make a man." Arthur O. Lovejoy *The Great Chain of Being* (Cambridge: Harvard University Press, 1964) p. 280. This idea that human evolution is a kind of apprenticeship is especially well developed in the writings of Frederick Wood Jones and G. Elliot Smith. The latter describes the terrestrial realm as "the laboratory in which, for untold ages, Nature was making her great experiments to achieve the transmutation of the base substance of some brutal Ape into the divine form of Man." G. Elliot Smith, *The Evolution of Man* (Oxford: Oxford University Press, 1924), pp. 77–78.

21. C. Owen Lovejoy, "The Origin of Man," *Science* 211 1981): 341–50.

22. Indeed, Lovejoy's theory is untestable, at least paleontologically. As Tim White has observed, "I never seen an estrous fossil." Donald C. Johanson and Maitland A. Edey," How Ape Became Man: Is it a Matter of Sex?" *Science '81* 2:3 (1981): 49.

23. Sherwood L. Washburn, "The Fun of Human Evolution," in R. K. Wetherington, ed., *Colloquium in Anthropology* (Taos, N. Mex. (Fort Burgwin Research Center, 1977), pp. 61–62.

24. David Pilbeam, "New Hominoid Skull Material from the Miocene of Pakistan," *Nature* 295 (1982): 232–34; Steven Ward and David Pilbeam, "Maxillofacial Morphology of Miocene Hominoids from Africa and Indo Pakistan," in Russell L. Ciochon and Richard F. Corruccini, eds., *New Interpretations of Ape and Human Ancestry,* (New York: Plenum, 1982).

25. The problems associated with reconstructing past environments on the basis of fossils have been nicely demonstrated by Nikos Solounias. Looking at Miocene bovids, Solounias finds that unlike modern bovids, who live on savannahs, these fossil forms show anatomical features associated with woodland habitats. This contradicts the widely held belief that fossil bovids show that savannahs spread over much of Eurasia during the Miocene. Solounias's point is that in using fossils to reconstruct past environments, we often recreate the present environments of their modern descendants. Nikos Solounias, "Savannahs in the Miocene," paper presented at the Museum of Comparative Zoology Seminar, Harvard University, April 23, 1982.

26. Clifford Geertz, "Thick Description: Toward an Interpretive Theory of Culture," in *The Interpretation of Cultures* (New York: Basic Books, 1973), p. 16.

27. David Pilbeam, "Major Trends in Human Evolution," in L.-K. Konigson, ed., *Current Argument on Early Man,* (New York: Pergamon, 1980), p. 285.

8

CODIFYING THE SOCIAL

SCIENTIFIC STYLE

THE APA *PUBLICATION MANUAL*

AS A BEHAVIORIST RHETORIC

CHARLES BAZERMAN

The terms "human sciences," "behavioral sciences," "cognitive sciences," and "social sciences" express a shared aspiration to produce statements of knowledge of the kind and authority reputed to come from the natural sciences, statements that seem to rise above rhetoric. Yet scientific discourse embodies rhetorical decisions and raises serious rhetorical issues. Scientific writing is not a single undifferentiated genre, defined by a timeless idea. On the contrary, varieties of scientific writing have developed historically in response to different rhetorical situations, aiming at different rhetorical goals and embodying different assumptions about knowledge, nature, and communication. The form of the experimental report solves a problem—namely, given what we currently believe about science, scientists, the scientific community, the scientific literature, and nature, what kind of statements should we make? To treat scientific style as fixed and epistemologically neutral is rhetorically naive and historically wrong.[1]

In adopting a scientific style of communication, the human sciences neither escape rhetoric nor eliminate the possibility of rhetorical choice. Though many practicing social scientists wish to embrace a single, correct, absolute way of writing science, any model of scientific writing embeds rhetorical assumptions. The explicit examination of these embedded assumptions reasserts our control of choices now determined by tradition, stereotype, and ideology. The forging of a scientific language is a remarkable achievement; but since it is a human accomplishment, it must be constantly reevaluated and remade as the human world changes.

Charles Bazerman

I

To understand the scientific style that emerged in the human sciences over the last century, we need to look closely at experimental psychology. Experimental psychology was the first human science to establish a specialized discourse distinguished from traditional philosophical discourse. Experimental psychology became the model and set the standards for all the psychological specialties that aspired to the status of science. In time it played the same role for sociology, which did not start to develop a predominantly scientific style until the 1920s, and political science, which followed suit in the 1950s. Today the American Psychological Association *Publication Manual* symbolizes and instrumentally realizes the influence and power of the official style.[2]

The official APA style emerged historically at the same time as the behaviorist program began to dominate experimental psychology. Not surprisingly, the style embodies behaviorist assumptions about authors, readers, the subjects investigated, and knowledge itself. The prescribed style grants all the participants exactly the role they should have in a behaviorist universe. To use the rhetoric is to mobilize behaviorist assumptions.

Recent versions of the *Publication Manual*, filled with detailed prescriptions, convey the impression that writing is primarily a matter of applying established rules. The third edition, published in 1983, offers approximately two hundred oversized pages of rules, ranging from the mechanics of spelling and punctuation through substantive issues of content and organization. The important section on "Content and Organization of the Manuscript" focuses almost exclusively on experimental reports, for although it recognizes genres such as review articles and theoretical articles, it comments that "most journal articles published in psychology are reports of empirical studies."

The experimental report is to have specified sections: title, abstract, introduction, method, results, and discussion. Each of the last three sections is to be so titled. Each section must conform to detailed instructions, at times resembling a questionnaire in specificity. In the methods section, for example, one must include separately labeled subsections (usually "subjects," "apparatus," and "procedure"), each reporting specified content. The instructions for describing the experimental subjects indicate the level of prescribed detail:

> Subjects. The subsection on subjects answers three questions:
> Who participated in the study? How many participants were
> there? How were they selected? Give the total number of

participants and the number assigned to each experimental condition. If any participant did not complete the experiment, give the number of participants and the reasons they did not continue.

When humans are the participants, report the procedures for selecting and assigning subjects and the agreements and payments made. Give major demographic characteristics such as general geographic location, type of institutional affiliation and sex and age.[3]

And so on for another two and a half paragraphs.

Few could question, given the collective experience of the discipline, that such information is often important for understanding and evaluating the experimental results. But the assignment of the information to a fixed place in a fixed format lessens the likelihood that researchers will consciously consider the exact significance of such information, whether it and other possible information should be included, and exactly how this information should be placed in the structure of the whole article. The prescribed form of fixed sections with fixed titles creates disjunctions between mandatory sections: the author does not have to establish overt transitions and continuity among the parts. The method section is a totally separate entity from the introduction or results. Although problem, method, and results must correlate at some level, the author escapes the need for transitions to demonstrate the coherence of the enterprise.

The foreword of the *Publication Manual,* well removed from the substantive prescriptions, does contain several disclaimers about linguistic evolution and flexibility. It notes, for example, that

> although [the manual's] style requirements are explicit, it recognizes alternatives to traditional forms and asks authors to balance the use of rules with good judgment. . . . It is a transitional document. It looks at the literature itself to determine forms rather than employing style to contain language.[4]

Yet the introduction to the actual organizational prescriptions takes a hard line:

> Consistency of presentation and format within and across journal articles is an aspect of the scientific publishing tradition that enables authors to present material systematically and enables readers to locate material easily. Finally . . . the traditional structure of the manuscript allows writers to judge the thoroughness, originality, and clarity of their work and to

Charles Bazerman

communicate more easily with other individuals within the same tradition.[5]

In addition to the appeal to tradition—a tradition we will find shorter and more varied than one might guess—his passage urges uniformity on three other grounds: efficiency of reference, evaluative usefulness, and ease of communication. The second reason presupposes that there is one right way to present an experimental report and that wandering from the form is bad science, or at least keeps bad science from being evident. The other two reasons suggest an encyclopedic function for an incremental literature; the concept of incremental encyclopedism will be examined later in this article.

The prescriptiveness evident in the current publication manual has only gradually developed since the first "Instructions in Regard to Preparation of Manuscript" appeared in the February 1929 *Psychological Bulletin*.[6] This original stylesheet is only six and a half pages long. About a page discusses "Subdivision and Articulation of Topics," a third of which is explicitly devoted to experimental articles. Although the authors refer to a "natural order" for the presentation of experiments, internal titles are discouraged: "Necessary headings only should be inserted."[7] Advice is of a general kind: for example, writers should include sufficient detail to allow the reader "to reconstruct and to criticize the experimentation and to compare it with other procedures and results."[8] The committee preparing this set of instructions avoided an authoritative stance, presenting these suggestions for "general guidance" only.

By 1944 the stylesheet, now "The Preparation of Articles for Publication in the Journals of the American Psychological Association," had grown to thirty-two pages.[9] Guidelines for bibliographical reference and the use of tables and graphs had correspondingly increased in length, as did the explanation of the editorial policies of the APA journals. On the structure of the experimental article, however, the stylesheet says little more than the previous edition, although conceding that the form "has now become structured into a fairly developed pattern."[10] Moreover, the stylesheet encourages the use of headings to indicate "the main features of [the article's] framework."[11] The authors offer their advice for the "younger members of the profession, many of whom are writing for publication for the first time."[12] Thus pedagogy allowed prescriptions without committed prescriptiveness.

The 1952 *Publication Manual*, now a sixty-one-page separately bound supplement to the *Psychological Bulletin*, no longer hedges its prescriptive intent: "The purpose of the publication manual is to improve the

quality of the psychological literature in the interest of the entire profession."[13] The manual is the standard. And as a standard it lays out
explicitly just what is demanded. The section on organization lists the
familiar parts of the experimental study, but suggests that headings reflect "the particular requirements of a study," rather than the standard
part titles. Nonetheless, the manual prescribes what should be included within each. For example, the method section "should describe
the design of the research, the logic of relating empirical data to the theoretical propositions, the subjects, the sampling and control devices,
the techniques of measurement, and any apparatus used."[14]

The 1957 and 1967 revisions, although differing in some respects, retain the general length and detail of the 1952 manual.[15] The 1974 edition doubles the length and detail of prescription again, devoting 12
pages of the total 132 to content and organization.[16] The 1983 edition
"clarifies" and "amplifies and refines" this second edition, but adheres
to much of its wording. Notably, to ensure that standards are met on all
levels, this last edition adds a section on grammar.

Two further style changes concerning the summary and reference
formats are worth noting here. In the 1927 stylesheet, the last section of
a paper is defined as a summary entirely distinct from the abstract to be
submitted to *Psychological Abstracts*. The 1944 stylesheet clarifies that
the summary should be a serially numbered list of conclusions. In 1952
the summary, no longer a list, becomes a description of the entire argument, covering "the problem, the results, and the conclusions." This
formal summary could also be used for *Psychological Abstracts*. Beginning in 1967, however, the abstract appears at the start of the published
article, eliminating the final summary.

The prescribed reference format changes from traditional footnotes
in 1927, to cross-references to a numbered bibliography in 1944, to the
current author-date system with a reference list at the end, first prescribed in 1967. These changes help bring the references into the flow
of the discussion as items for conscious attention. Both the dates and
the names of authors now serve as facts in the argument.

II

The evolution of published articles in experimental
psychology reveals the nature of the rhetoric embedded in the *Publication Manual*, for the history of the articles shows the rhetoric in action.[17]
The founding journals of the discipline defined the acceptable range of
writing for the field by the articles they published: *Philosophische Stu-*

dien (hereafter *PS*), founded by Wilhelm Wundt in 1883; the *American Journal of Psychology (AJP)*, founded by G. Stanley Hall in 1887; and the *Psychological Review (PR)*, founded by J. M. Cattell and J. M. Baldwin in 1894. Each began the first issue with an editorial or article discussing the emergence of a new scientific psychology based on experimental results.

Despite these rigorous programmatic statements, the early issues of these journals, particularly the two American ones, contain a wide variety of articles, only some of which could be labeled experimental. The first two volumes of the *AJP* do contain such narrowly experimental studies as "Dermal Sensitiveness to Gradual Pressure Changes," but also contain "A Study of Dreams," "Winter Roosting Colonies of Crows," "Extracts from the Autobiography of a Paranoiac," "The Place for the Study of Language in a Curriculum of Education," "Folk-Lore of the Bahama Negroes," and "On Some Characteristics of Symbolic Logic." Many articles sought to bring empirical data to the philosophical inquiry into the mind. Indeed, the manifesto in the first issue claims a broad audience for the *AJP:* teachers of psychology, anthropologists interested in primitive manifestations of psychological laws, physicians interested in mental and nervous diseases, biologists and physiologists, and anyone else interested in advances in scientific psychology.[18]

Early experimental work measured such quantifiables as perceptual sensitivity and reaction times, but these measurements served only as empirical entry ways into the mysteries of the mind. Although they followed the general structural pattern of experimental reports already established in the natural sciences, the early articles had more the character of philosophical essays: an article in the first issue of the *AJP* by G. Stanley Hall and Yuzero Motora begins with a Greek epigraph from Plato.[19]

The two American journals did not use any internal headings in the articles; consequently, words had to bridge the parts, explaining how the whole inquiry fitted together. In the first volume of *PR*, for example, Hugo Munsterberg presents a series of five "Studies from the Harvard Psychological Laboratory." These studies have no internal divisions, although they clearly follow standard experimental order.[20] Each part grows out of the previous one. The third study, "A Psychometric Investigation of the Psycho-Physic Law," demonstrates this strikingly. The opening theoretical discussion of the psycho-physic law argues that a new kind of measurement is needed. The experimental design then provides the desired measurements. Moreover, each aspect of the experimental method is justified and explained in terms of current knowledge about the psycho-physic law. The specific parameters for measurement refer back to the theoretical problem, and the actual results follow immediately as a response to the specific parameters. Discussion of the consequences of the results for the psycho-physic law follows naturally as part of the thematic continuity of the whole essay.[21]

Articles in the German *PS*, although they frequently use standard section headings, provide careful links among the parts. Often the first paragraph or two of a labeled section considers either general thematic material or the issues raised in the previous section, so that the substance of the section is not directly discussed until it is firmly tied to the total structure of the article.

In these experimental essays, the authors reveal themselves as problem-solving reasoners, figuring out how quantitative experiments might aid understanding of philosophical issues. The discussion of methods plays a crucial role, raising and answering the problem of how one can translate the theoretical problem into concrete empirical results. For example, Munsterberg, in the series mentioned above, repeatedly presents his methods as correcting the failure of previous methods to make proper distinctions. The effort devoted to the presentation of the methods shows clearly that they are a significant part of the intellectual achievement of the work presented in the article. Similarly, the first experimental article in the first issue of *PS* devotes an eight-and-a-half-page methods section to deriving the methods from the nature of the phenomena to be investigated and to evaluating alternative methods.[22]

The early authors believed that psychological phenomena were internal, subjective events and that the measured data were only external indicators of what was going on inside. Trained introspection provided evidence in conjunction with more external quantitative measures. Thus the subjects of the experiments emerge as active characters in the experimental report. Individual experimental subjects, who included trained psychologists, were often identified by name. (Wundt himself was a subject in many experiments performed in his laboratory.) In the experimental report the identification of subjects shows their training and credentials for making accurate introspective judgments. The author of "Experiments in Space Perception," James Hyslop, is himself the experimental subject.[23] Combining psychological knowledge and an unusual ability to use his eyes independently, he devised certain tricks or exercises for himself that help to elucidate principles of perception. The two-part article contains first-person accounts of what he did and what he perceived.

Charles Bazerman

Readers are sometimes treated as quite knowledgeable about the current work, so that much technical background goes unexplained, as, for example, in Hall and Motora's article on dermal sensitivity in the opening issue of *AJP*.[24] Nonetheless, the audience is generally assumed to be concerned primarily with broad issues of psychological understanding. The early articles almost always begin with some issue of general psychological interest and connect the specific study to that issue. In fact, the technical article by Hall and Motora is the one prefaced by the Greek quotation and appears in the issue in which Hall editorially anticipates a broad readership for the journal.[25]

These articles review the literature only sporadically. At most, short summaries present assorted experimental results without establishing definitive findings that lay a stable groundwork for current studies. Frequently articles begin without any specific reference to previous work. In short, the articles give the general impression of a new beginning; they are to be grounded thoroughly in empirical results, as opposed to the implicitly rejected nonempirical earlier work. This is consistent with a philosophical tradition that treats each new approach as a fresh attempt to establish philosophy on its true footing.

Wundt's role in his own journal, which largely published the results of his own laboratory, best reveals the philosophical nature of the endeavor. Wundt, although the founder of the first regular laboratory and frequently called the father of experimental psychology, published no experimental reports in *PS*. Nonetheless, articles by Wundt appeared in the journal at least two or three times a year, and sometimes as often as eight, discussing ideas, methods, and philosophical issues well removed from psychology. These discussions often take the form of reviews or critiques of the work of others, but always have the purpose of explicating fundamental issues. In them Wundt kept the empirical work of the new discipline firmly in philosophical, reasoning focus. Although his students and other followers stayed much closer to the data—and no one else seemed to be granted an equal right to philosophize at length in the pages of the journal—he helped maintain the philosophical thrust of the discourse.

Despite the desire to subordinate the experiments to philosophical inquiry, the experimental data proved too complex and removed from philosophical issues to resolve the problems posed. Typically in the early articles, the continuity of rational discussion breaks down when the results section is reached. The argument bogs down in extensive tables reporting massive amounts of data, frequently raw or subject only to simple aggregating calculations. As in an 1894 study by Joseph

Jastrow in *PR*, the discussion often simply repeats the tabular data with a few low-order statistical generalizations.[26]

Characteristically, no conclusions relative to a substantive problem are drawn, and the ultimate meaning of the data remains murky. Authors often caution against generalizing too quickly on the basis of uncertain results in situations that remain too multi-factored to analyze fully. More decisive results are promised in the future. When substantive conclusions are drawn, the intermediate analysis of the data may be missing, as in one of Munsterberg's studies, which bypasses specific explanations with phrases like, "it is evident," "of course," and "the reason lies evidently in the fact that . . ."[27]

The inability of these massive collections of data to resolve philosophical issues, such as the nature of memory and perception, soon leads to a divorce between philosophical and empirical work.[28] Articles turn to establishing low-level generalizations descriptive of the results. Literature reviews grow longer as the literature itself grows, and there is some attempt to find common denominators or clear patterns of disagreement among the prior studies and to set up the current experiment as a resolution. Methods become standardized and are frequently referred to by eponyms or citations. But the results generally do not resolve substantive issues. Conclusions are often a series of numbered statements, repeating the data. Even where the numbered conclusory statements address the originating question, as in a 1916 article in the *Journal of Experimental Psychology* (hereafter *JEP*), "A Preliminary Study of Tonal Volume," only minimal substantive discussion relates results to the problem.[29] The complex data, both psychophysical and introspective, are left largely to speak for themselves.

Since the true object of inquiry remained internal phenomena, the subject of the experiment remained an important independent actor in the story. Subjects are described to show expertise or particular qualifications for accurate observation. In K. M. Dallenbach's articles throughout the period, for example, subjects are characterized as trained in psychology and familiar with the purposes and methods of the particular experiment under discussion.[30] Introspective accounts provide data and—significantly—possibly interpretations of the measured data. As late as 1930, in a study by S. C. Ferral and K. M. Dallenbach, the introspective accounts of the subjects (who include Dallenbach) are used to guide the analysis of the other results.[31] Another striking example, "An Experimental Study of Fear," is based entirely on introspective accounts of emotional responses to the experimental situation.[32]

Other methods of gaining evidence about the internal processes of humans were also still acceptable. A study of the foster-child fantasy is based on a survey of adolescents rather than on an experiment.[33] An anthropological observation entitled "The Gesture of Affirmation Among the Arabs" is intended to clear up some incorrect and misinterpreted facts used by Wundt.[34] Studies of literary figures based on their works still appeared in *AJP* as late as 1920, when analyses of Charlotte Brontë and Edgar Allan Poe were published.[35]

The author thus remains a problem-solver, trying to gain some understanding of mental processes using empirical data, even though the discussion has now switched from a general philosophical to a more particular descriptive mode. Articles through 1920 still read as continuously reasoned arguments, with internal headings used sporadically and flexibly. Headings, when used, often reflect the specific content of the article and are not typographically prominent.

The implied audience as well remains varied—interested in the workings of the mind, but not necessarily involved in research. Through the 1920s articles still frequently start with familiar problems of everyday experience (such as fear, fantasy, and the sensation of burning heat), and they use a variety of approaches.

III

As behaviorism in its many forms came to dominate psychology between the two world wars, a rhetoric consistent with behaviorist assumptions narrowed rhetorical possibilities and became the basis for the official style reflected in the *Publication Manual*. By "behaviorism" and "behaviorists," I mean the general turn toward behavior and away from mind as the proper subject and data for psychological investigation. Many varieties of explicit behaviorism developed, not just the classic versions of Watson and Skinner. Additionally, many other schools of experimental psychology followed behaviorist procedures, although they did not explicitly espouse behaviorism.

Stephen Toulmin and David Leary associate the dominance of behaviorism and neo-behaviorism with a "cult of empiricism" fostered by an alliance with logical positivism, popular during the same period between the wars. The positivist principles of "physicalism" and "operationalism" legitimated the behaviorist limitations of allowable questions, method, and data. The behaviorist method then could be considered identical to scientific method, excluding other forms of psychological investigation as unscientific.[36] And the behaviorist rhetoric could be identified as the only proper way to write science.

The proper way to write positivist, behaviorist science did not, however, appear immediately on the scene, invented in a burst of self-conscious rhetorical creativity. Instead the style emerged over a number of years as many individuals gradually discovered the form most congenial to their ideas and work. Early works appeared in a variety of styles consistent with the patterns of the past.

Watson, although often identified as the founder of behaviorism, published little behavioristic experimental work. Rather, what is taken as his seminal work, "Psychology as a Behaviorist Views It," is a polemic.[37] It is continuous, persuasive, and aimed at a general audience; it considers a general problem and presents the author and audience as reasoners capable of making intelligent judgments. Furthermore, as editor of *Psychological Review* from 1910 to 1916 and then of the newly founded *Journal of Experimental Psychology* for another ten years, Watson presided over the kinds of articles described in the previous section.[38]

The famous article "Conditioned Emotional Reactions" (1920), which Watson co-authored with Rosalie Raynor, reports one of his few published experimental studies.[39] This unusual article, although different in many respects from both articles that came before and those to come after, still bears more resemblances to the earlier rhetoric than to the later. The study, which describes the conditioning of an infant to fear rats, is told as a coherent story with no real headings or strong divisions to interrupt the flow of argument. The only marked divisions are four questions, labeled with roman numerals, and dated passages from the laboratory notes. The typical structure of introduction, method, results, discussion, is not maintained. Rather, the theory to be demonstrated dominates the organizational pattern, with components of the method and results separated and subordinated to the various questions to be answered.

Thus the authors emerge as reasoners and persuaders, constructing an argument that uses experimental results to persuade the readers of the truth of a general theory. They use the first person throughout in order to present themselves in a number of roles: as conductors of experiments, as holders of certain expectations, as investigators desiring tests of certain questions, as makers of observations, as provers of certain propositions, and as interpreters of results. Furthermore, they present the experimental results in the rather personal form of the lab notes, replete with disjointed phrases and sentence fragments. Even though the notes present the events without reference to internal processes or imputations, rhetorically they serve to show the events through the eyes of the narrator.

The authors also stand well back from the literature, which is presented largely as speculative and unfounded, even Watson's own writing on the subject. This article is, in short, another attempt to begin inquiry into basic matters *de novo*. Here again we see the independent philosopher, impatient with earlier false starts and misguided work. The opening paragraph reviewing the state of the problem is brusque and mildly contemptuous; the next to last paragraph, comparing the authors' conclusions with Freud's, is gratuitously and gleefully nasty, reminiscent of the delightfully vitriolic exchanges of nineteenth-century German philosophers.

Thus the audience is witness to a knock-down intellectual argument and is invited to choose sides, not just between ideas, but between persons: Watson and Freud. The choice rests on the audience's response to a first-person account of a single incident: in essence, a short story. In its narrative simplicity, clarity of argument, and broadness of issue, the article clearly aims at a wide audience. Its vigor of argument assumes that readers can and will make a choice—in favor of Watson.

The subject of Watson's experiment, the infant Albert B., has an immediate presence in the drama of the piece. The detailed description shows how, by virtue of his stability and lack of fear, he is mentally fit for the test to which he will be subjected. He emerges as an individual character in an engaging narrative account of his induced phobia, very much in the tradition of the clinical accounts of the mentally ill that had until recently shared the pages of the journals with experimental reports.

However, two differences set the treatment of Albert apart from the treatment of subjects in previous articles. First, the details of his background establish that his mind is a clean slate, unaffected by special quirks, foreknowledge, or other hindering factors. The subject's identity, in other words, is a sign of the experimenter's control of variables, rather than the subject's special capacity to observe his own reactions. Second, the authors exclude introspection or any other attempt to gain knowledge of the subject's internal processes or sensations. This, of course, is the obvious mark of behaviorism. Yet despite the attempt to turn Albert into an impersonal object of study, the fullness of the narrative produces a certain poignancy. As Albert's phobia grows, the reader sees him become a victim, moved by the manipulations of the experimenter rather than his own volition.

In the period following the publication of this article, the objectification of the subject increases. Author, audience, and literature as well become more objectlike. All the aspects of the drama of the experimental article move into a behaviorist universe. The rhetorical decisions made in the 1920s are elaborated, rigidified, and standardized in subsequent decades. The first APA stylesheet appeared in 1929; the increasing certainty and prescriptive detail of the successive stylesheets confirm the growing influence of the behaviorist style. Articles begin to look like one another, so that we can clearly identify the official style that lies behind the prescriptions of the publication manual.

Only when a community decides that there is one right way can it achieve the confidence and narrowness of detailed prescriptions. In rhetoric, "one right way" implies not only a stability of text, but a stability of rhetorical situation and rhetorical actors, so that there is little room or motive for improvisatory argument.[40] Within a stabilized rhetorical universe, people will want to say similar things to each other under similar conditions for similar purposes. In this context, prescribed forms allow easy and efficient communication without unduly constraining needed flexibility. The behaviorist picture of the world allows that stability and lack of free invention.

The behaviorist world view first makes itself felt, as we have already seen in the article by Watson and Raynor, in characterizations of the experimental subject and the phenomena investigated. Not only do behaviorists categorically eliminate imputations of internal processes and introspective accounts; they no longer consider the external data as indicators of some mental process. The experimental problem switches from one of indicators to one of controls, from getting some hard data on complex individual internal processes to keeping the history of the subject and the environment sufficiently clean. The kind of narrative that Watson provides for Albert B. soon vanishes, for such a narrative grants too much personality to the subject, who is to be reported more as a type exhibiting very specific behaviors in highly controlled circumstances.

The previous tendency toward low-level conclusions that give only aggregate descriptions of the behavior observed is no longer a difficulty—such descriptions are the extent of the enterprise. One looks only for patterns of behavior, not underlying principles or mental operations. The increasing statistical sophistication of experimental articles serves to exhibit and validate patterns of behavior across large numbers of subjects. The results themselves appear in increasingly calculated and patterned ways. Individual behavior disappears in a pattern, displayed in a graph or a table of secondary calculated values, rather than as a raw number. The results sections increasingly begin by describing the display tables and figures. By 1950 statistical talk, describing the statistical methods used and the limits of statistical liability, becomes a standard part of the results section, usually immediately following the presentation of the numerical display.

Instead of a reasoner about the mind, the author is a doer of experiments, maker of calculations, and presenter of results. The author does not need to reason through an intellectual or theoretical problem to justify or design an experiment, nor in most cases does he or she need to identify and take positions on arguments in the literature. To produce new results, the author must identify behavior that has been inadequately described and design an experiment to exhibit it. With the methodological problem reduced to obtaining uncontaminated results, carefulness rather than good reasoning becomes the main characteristic to be displayed in the methods section. The methods section becomes less substantively interesting. Starting about 1930, the section is demoted to small print, where it remains today. Nor are methods customarily covered in summaries or abstracts.

This rhetorical diminution of methods in a science devoted to obtaining experimental results only makes sense when we see that the main rhetorical function of the methods section is not to present news or innovation, or even to help the reader conceptualize the event that produced the results. Its main function is rather to protect the researcher's results by showing that the experiment was done cleanly and correctly. In the articles from sample year 1950 that I examined, this desire to protect the results by constantly demonstrating that one has done things correctly on all counts, from examining the prior literature to using proper statistical methods, becomes obtrusive and accounts for much of the length of the articles. As the conventions for demonstrating proper work become stabilized, through the growing prescriptiveness of the stylesheets and through repeated practice, this competence display is done more rapidly, so that by 1965 these preliminaries take much less space.

Because the methods section no longer serves as an intellectual transition between the problem and the results, the article tends to break into disjointed parts, increasingly labeled by standard headings, as reflected in the successive stylesheets. The results become the core of the article. Discussion often merely sums up the data and is sometimes relegated to small print. Conclusions do little more than repeat confirmation of the descriptive hypotheses.

With the article primarily presenting results, constrained and formatted prescription, authors become followers of rules to gain the reward of acceptance of their results and to avoid the punishment of nonpublication. Accepting this role, they subordinate themselves to the group endeavor of gathering more facts toward an ultimately complete description of behavior—a project of incremental encyclopedism. As behaviorism gradually gained influence, authors began presenting results as ends in themselves, to fill gaps in other results, rather than as potential answers to theoretical questions. In the mid-twenties, introductions rapidly ceased to raise problems and began to give a codified review of the literature, with each item associated with a specific contribution. The experiment to be reported in the article was presented simply as a continuation of the prior work. After a brief period when close analysis of the literature was allowed in small print, disagreements over theory, results, or formulations in the previous literature tended no longer to be discussed. Articles tended to be treated as accumulated facts; literature reviews in the articles tended to lack synthesis, problem-orientation, or interpretation. Edwin Boring, an editor of *AJP,* in a 1930 note attempting to domesticate the Gestalt movement, articulates the principle: "The progress of thought is gradual, and the enunciation of a new crucial principle in science is never more than an event that follows naturally upon its antecedents and leads presently to unforeseen consequents."[41] This communal vision—much narrower than the traditional "shoulders of giants" formulation—diminishes the role of any individual as a thinker.

Several other rhetorical consequences flow from this incrementalism. First, since the function of the article is now to add a descriptive statement to an existing body of such statements, and since the new statement will achieve this goal only if it passes certain tests, strong rhetorical pressure pushes the candidate statement (the hypothesis) near the front of the article. Only then can the reader, in reading the body of the article, judge whether the claim passes the criteria. Thus the descriptive generalization moves from a conclusion to an opening hypothesis that takes on an increasingly central role in the presentation of the experiment.[42] As the main unifying element in the article, the hypothesis often comes to be repeated four or more times in a single article. Similarly, as the abstract switches from a summary of results to the presentation of problem, results, and discussion, the "problem" comes to mean the test of the hypothesis and the "discussion" the confirmation of the hypothesis.

Charles Bazerman

Second, since they were only adding bits to a larger descriptive project, articles decrease in scope and length. The single experiment replaces the series of experiments with minor variations in conditions or procedures. The confirmation of a single descriptive statement replaces the examination of a large phenomenon from a number of angles.

Articles also become shorter with the codification of format and of surrounding knowledge. With a fixed framework of knowledge and communication, one can add one's single additional bit more rapidly. In the selection of articles I examined, the low point in terms of article length was in the mid-1960s. Articles from the same period also show a significant increase in technical vocabulary, indicating a dense, specialized knowledge. Most of the technical terms used earlier (except for statistical ones) are ordinary-language terms given more precise definition—for example, *"stimulus," "condition," "fatigue."* Even such unusual coinages as "retroactive inhibition" are not far removed from ordinary usage. But in the 1965 articles, terms, although originating in common-use vocabulary, take on narrow, concrete meanings that diverge from normal usage. These terms are then used in combination with other such terms. Moreover, key terms are replaced by acronyms or abbreviations. Only those familiar with the technical background can be sure that they know exactly what is being discussed in a phrase like "the effects upon verbal mediation of the delay intervals interpolated between the two acquisition stages of a mediation paradigm or between the second acquisition stage and the test trial."[43]

Third, the *Publication Manual* had adopted a reference style wherein the author and date of a cited work appear as facts or landmarks in the course of the article, visibly demonstrating the incrementalism of the literature. As anyone who has worked with this reference system can attest, it is very convenient for listing and summarizing a series of related findings, but it is awkward for extensive quotation or discussion of another text, and even more awkward for contrasting several texts in detail. The format is not designed for the close consideration of competing ideas and subtle formulations.

Finally, readers are no longer cast in the role of people trying to understand or solve some problem. Rather, they are presumed to be looking for additional bits of knowledge to fit in with their previous bits. They are assumed to be looking for faults because such faults would disqualify the experimental report as a valid increment to the descriptive encyclopedia. The author must display competence to the audience rather than persuade readers of the truth of an idea. If properly demonstrated by a proper experiment, the hypothesis must be accepted by the audience. In an intellectual sense, the audience has little to say about the meaning of an experiment or even about the truth of a hypothesis. Its role, rather, is to judge the propriety of the experimental proof.

Within this rhetorical world, the chaos of intellectual differences is eliminated. Individuals accumulate bits, follow rules, check each other out, and add their bits to an encyclopedia of the behavior of subjects without subjectivity. There is not much room for thinking or venturing here, but much for behaving and adhering to prescriptions. Thus we get to the ever-expanding *Publication Manual*.

IV

Over the last twenty years, another major change in the style of the psychological journals has started to take place, the result of the rising influence of a cognitive psychology based on the computer model. This new approach brings with it a new epistemological and rhetorical universe. It is too soon to give a full account of this new style, nor is it clear how pervasive it will become in the face of the continuing behaviorist rhetoric. One thing is clear: this new style has not yet affected the *Publication Manual* in any significant way. The APA manual still serves basically as a codification of behaviorist rhetoric.

For those social scientists who believe that the behaviorists' positivist program creates an accurate picture of the human world and provides the surest (if not the only) path to knowledge, the prescriptive rhetoric of the *Publication Manual* is precisely the right one. The invention of a way to communicate that is consonant with their beliefs constitutes a major accomplishment. Nonetheless, the realization that behaviorism has not escaped rhetoric, but has merely chosen one rhetoric and excluded alternatives, may temper adherents' certainty about their mode of communication.

For those who have received the rhetoric as a given, the recognition of the implications of the official style reopens the question of how to write. Rhetoric is always sensitive to beliefs about the world. The human sciences are subject to a particularly immediate form of this rhetorical sensitivity, for these sciences create and argue for beliefs about human beings, the inevitable main actors in the drama of communication. If a social science changes our view about the nature of ourselves, we need to change our way of talking to each other. To neglect the implications of our rhetoric is to lose control of what we say.

Charles Bazerman

NOTES

1. See, for example, Charles Bazerman, "Modern Evolution of the Experimental Report in Physics: Spectroscopic Articles in *Physical Review,* 1893–1980," *Social Studies of Science* 14 (1984): 163–96; and idem, "Reporting the Experiment: The Changing Account of Scientific Doings in the *Philosophical Transactions of the Royal Society,* 1665–1800," manuscript, 1983.

2. American Psychological Association, *Publication Manual,* 3d ed. (Washington, D.C.: APA, 1983).

3. Ibid., p. 26.

4. Ibid., p. 18.

5. Ibid., p. 18.

6. Madison Bentley, et al., "Instructions in Regard to Preparation of Manuscript," *Psychological Bulletin* 26 (Feb. 1929): 57-63.

7. Ibid., p. 58.

8. Ibid., p. 59.

9. John Anderson and Willard Valentine, "The Preparation of Articles for Publication in the Journals of the American Psychological Association," *Psychological Bulletin* 41 (1944): 345–76.

10. Ibid., p. 350.

11. Ibid., p. 351.

12. Ibid., p. 345.

13. Council of Editors, *Publication Manual of the American Psychological Association, Psychological Bulletin* 49, pt. 2 (July 1952 supplement): 389–449.

14. Ibid., p. 397.

15. American Psychological Association, *Publication Manual,* rev. ed. (Washington, D.C.: APA, 1957, 1967).

16. American Psychological Association, *Publication Manual,* 2d ed. (Washington, D.C.: APA, 1974).

17. The characterizations that follow are based on analyses of over a hundred articles and examination of several times that number from the chief journals of experimental psychology, clustered in the early period (the last decades of the nineteenth century), the periods of the rise (1916 to 1930) and dominance of behaviorism (1950 and 1965 taken as sample years), and the current period (1980 as a sample year). The selection of articles analyzed and examined is large enough to reveal the major trends, but the dates attributed to the first emergence or dominance of any particular feature are necessarily approximate. Further, any characterizations of large numbers of texts will inevitably obscure differences among texts and may not be accurate for specific features of individual texts; however, as the official behaviorist style emerges, texts become much more uniform. That movement toward prescriptive uniformity forms a central part of the story.

18. G. Stanley Hall, "Editorial Note," *American Journal of Psychology* 1 (1887): 3.

19. G. Stanley Hall and Yuzero Motora, "Dermal Sensitiveness to Gradual Pressure Changes," *American Journal of Psychology* 1 (1887): 72.

20. Hugo Munsterberg, "Studies from the Harvard Psychological Laboratory," *Psychological Review* 1 (1894): 32–60.

21. Hugo Munsterberg, with the assistance of W. T. Bush, "III. A Psychometric Investigation of the Psycho-Physic Law," *Psychological Review* 1 (1894):
45–51.

22. Max Friedrich, "Über die Apperceptionsdauer bei einfachen und
zusammengesetzten Vorstellungen," *Philosophische Studien* 1 (1883): 40–48.

23. James Hyslop, "Experiments in Space Perception," *Psychological Review*
1 (1894): 257–73, 581–601.

24. Hall and Motora, "Dermal Sensitiveness."

25. Hall, "Editorial Note."

26. Joseph Jastrow, "Community and Association of Ideas: A Statistical
Study," *Psychological Review* 1 (1894): 152–58.

27. Munsterberg, with Bush, "A Psychometric Investigation."

28. Indicative of the early divorce between philosophy and psychology is
the changing character of the articles in the English journal *Mind*, founded in
1876 with the stated intention of being the first journal of the new psychology.
The philosophical climate in England, however, did not prove conducive to
the flowering of experimental psychology. Although early volumes contain
glowing reports of the experimental work in Germany (for example, J. Sully,
"Physiological Psychology in Germany," *Mind* 1 [1876]: 20–43), reviews of
experimental work became increasingly critical (for example G. C. Robertson,
"The Physical Basis of Mind," *Mind* 3 [1878]: 23–43; E. W. Scripture, "The
Problem of Psychology," *Mind* 16 [1891]: 305–25). The general complaint
against experimental work was grounded in the mind/body dichotomy; these
philosophers found physical data of no value for understanding issues of
mind. By the turn of the century, discussion of experimental psychology
ended altogether, leaving the journal as a purely philosophic one.

29. G. J. Rich, "A Preliminary Study of Tonal Volume," *Journal of Experimental Psychology* 1 (1916): 13–22.

30. For example, K. M. Dallenbach, "The Measurement of Attention,"
American Journal of Psychology 24 (1913): 465–507; idem, "The Measurement of
Attention in the Field of Cutaneous Sensation," *American Journal of Psychology*
27 (1916): 445–60; and idem, "Attributive vs. Cognitive Clearness," *Journal of
Experimental Psychology* 3 (1920): 183–230.

31. S. C. Ferrall and K. M. Dallenbach, "The Analysis and Synthesis of
Burning Heat," *American Journal of Psychology* 42 (1930): 72–82.

32. Virginia Conklin and Forrest L. Dimmick, "An Experimental Study of
Fear," *American Journal of Psychology* 36 (1925): 96–101.

33. Edmund S. Conklin, "The Foster Child Fantasy," *American Journal of
Psychology* 31 (1920): 59–76.

34. S. S. George, "The Gesture of Affirmation Among the Arabs," *American
Journal of Psychology* 26 (1916): 320–24.

35. Lucile Dooley, "Psychoanalysis of Charlotte Bronte as a Type of the
Woman of Genius," *American Journal of Psychology* 31 (1920): 221–72; and

Charles Bazerman

Lorine Pruette, "A Psychoanalytic Study of Edgar Allan Poe," *American Journal of Psychology* 31 (1920): 370–402.

36. Stephen Toulmin and David Leary, "The Cult of Empiricism and Beyond," in Sigmund Koch and David Leary, eds., *A Century of Psychology as Science: Retrospections and Assessments* (New York: McGraw-Hill, in 1985). Lawrence D. Smith makes a similar point in his "Psychology and Philosophy: Toward a Realignment, 1905–1935," *Journal of the History of the Behavioral Sciences* 17 (1981): 28–37.

37. J. B. Watson, "Psychology as a Behaviorist Views It," *Psychological Review* 20 (1913): 158–77.

38. The *Journal of Experimental Psychology* was founded as an offshoot of the *Psychological Review,* and the two journals shared editorial boards.

39. John B. Watson and Rosalie Raynor, "Conditioned Emotional Reactions," *Journal of Experimental Psychology* 3 (1920): 1–14.

40. For a discussion of the relationship between genre and recurrent social situations and actions, see Carolyn R. Miller, "Genre as Social Action," *Quarterly Journal of Speech* 70 (1984): 151–67.

41. Edwin G. Boring, "The Gestalt Psychology and the Gestalt Movement," *American Journal of Psychology* 42 (1930): 309. He had earlier formulated this principle in "The Problem of Originality in Science," *American Journal of Psychology* 39 (1927): 70–90.

42. The common methodological belief that the formulation of a hypothesis must precede the design of an experiment chronologically in the actual research process may in part derive from this rhetorical order.

43. Margaret Jean Peterson, "Effects of Delay Intervals and Meaningfulness on Verbal Mediating Responses," *Journal of Experimental Psychology* 69 (1965): 60.

9

TURNING PSYCHOLOGY

ON ITSELF

THE RHETORIC OF PSYCHOLOGY

AND THE PSYCHOLOGY

OF RHETORIC

DONAL E. CARLSTON

Psychology may serve as both a target and a tool of rhetorical analysis. As a target, psychology possesses the same dependence on rhetoric that rhetoricians discover in other academic disciplines. Psychological rhetoric is influenced by the prevailing empiricism and logical positivism, which deemphasize the role of rhetoric in attaining knowledge. Yet these philosophies do not reduce the role of rhetoric in psychology—they simply restrict the kinds of arguments used. Examples of psychological rhetoric are provided later in this paper.

More interesting are the contributions of psychology as a tool for examining rhetoric. Psychologists study processes and phenomena that are central to language, stories, persuasion, and other topics of rhetoric and hermeneutics. Such studies can help us to understand the rhetoric of psychology and other disciplines.

Using empirical methods to examine rhetoric may seem unenlightened both to those who celebrate rhetoric as an alternative to empiricism and to those who view empiricism as superior to "mere" rhetoric. But rhetoric and empiricism are both tools in the construction of meaning and knowledge, and neither obviates the need for the other. More often than not, contemporary social scientists use these tools together, though rarely with equal enthusiasm.

Donal E. Carlston

In this essay I simply propose to use a few tools from each set to learn what the field of psychology says about its own practices of rhetoric. It is in this sense that I turn psychology on itself. In doing so, I hope to illuminate both the rhetoric of psychology and the psychology of rhetoric.

For the sake of argument, let me suggest that rhetoric and social psychology interact on three levels, each of which represents a particular claim regarding the role of rhetoric in the human sciences. First, the particular words that social scientists use to describe phenomena and theories influence their thinking and that of others. Second, the theorizing of social scientists is metaphorical storytelling, and many different metaphors can tell the same scientific story. Third, even empirical sciences involve a good deal of argumentation and persuasion: facts rarely speak for themselves, and consequently scientists are required to speak for them. To be sure, these three propositions are highly interdependent: words are the stuff out of which theoretical stories are made, and stories are the grist for persuasive mills. But treating the levels separately allows me to illustrate the ways in which several different areas of psychology relate to rhetoric. For each, I discuss first the psychology of rhetoric and then the rhetoric of psychology.

Semantics

Rhetorical issues at the semantic level were cogently described by the psychoanalyst Ernest G. Schachtel:

> One might well say that the greatest problem of the writer or the poet is the temptation of language. At every step a word beckons, it seems so convenient, so suitable, one has heard or read it so often in a similar context, it sounds so well, it makes the phrase flow so smoothly. If he follows the temptation of this word, he will perhaps describe something that many people recognize at once, that they already know, that follows a familiar pattern; but he will have missed the nuance that distinguishes his experience from others, that makes it his own. If he wants to communicate that elusive nuance which in some way, however small, will be his contribution, a widening or opening of the scope of articulate human experience at some point, he has to fight constantly against the easy flow of words that offer themselves. . . .

> The danger of the schemata of language, and especially of the
> worn currency of conventional language in vogue at the moment
> when the attempt is made to understand and describe an
> experience, is that the person making this attempt will overlook
> the discrepancy between experience and language cliché or that
> he will not be persistent enough in his attempt to eliminate this
> discrepancy. Once the conventional schema has replaced the
> experience in his mind, the significant quality of the experience is
> condemned to oblivion.[1]

The scientific writer, too, may be tempted by terms and phrases that
are convenient and conventional, but not altogether congruent with intended meanings. This problem may be most consequential in the selection of labels to describe recurrent concepts and phenomena. Labels
such as "schema," "emotion," "introspection," or "dissonance" become more than mere words—they become summarizations of theories, histories, issues, and arguments. When such labels are chosen
casually or inaccurately, the "significant quality" of scientific thinking
can be "condemned to oblivion."

Research in social psychology illuminates several facets of this argument. First, Schachtel implies that words force themselves upon us,
and that terms sometimes reflect fortuity or conformity rather than
thoughtful analysis. This argument is consistent with the prevailing
conviction among social cognition researchers that people prefer mental shortcuts to careful and exhaustive analysis.[2] For example, many
theorists[3] now argue that attributions are based on whatever happens
to be salient to people at the moment, not on the careful appraisal of
events suggested by early attribution theories.[4] Herbert Kelman argued years ago that attitudes often reflect conformity to others' views
rather than consideration and internalization of pertinent evidence.[5]
Scientific thinkers are presumably susceptible to this same cognitive
lethargy and conformity in choosing words to express their concepts.

Second, Schachtel suggests that writers' terms shape their own
thoughts (and presumably those of their readers) in ways that modify
perceptions of the thing described. Analogous effects have been demonstrated by cognitive psychologists for more than fifty years. In 1932
L. Carmichael and colleagues demonstrated that descriptive labels accompanying ambiguous pictures distort later reproductions of those
pictures.[6] For example, in attempting to reproduce a picture of two circles connected by a line, subjects who had seen the picture labeled
"eyeglasses" produced drawings that looked more like eyeglasses than

Donal E. Carlston

did subjects who had seen the same picture labeled "dumbbells."
More recently, D. R. Thomas and colleagues demonstrated that color
terms could similarly distort later recognition of ambiguous colors.[7]
Subjects viewed a shade of blue-green and then later tried to identify
color shades that matched it. When the original color was labeled
"blue," subjects incorrectly identified slides that were bluer in color
than the original, and when the original color was labeled "green,"
subjects identified slides that were greener. Other studies suggest
that "stereotypic" labels can influence perceptions of behavior in much
the same way.[8] The labels used to describe scientific phenomena
may similarly alter scientists' perceptions and explanations of those
phenomena.

An imaginative series of studies by Tory Higgins and his colleagues
speaks to both of Schachtel's premises. In one study Higgins, Rholes,
and Jones used a memory experiment to surreptitiously expose subjects to positive or negative terms for personality traits (e.g., "self-con-
fident" or "conceited").[9] Then, as part of an ostensibly separate
experiment, the subjects read ambiguous descriptions of an actor: for
example, "Donald was well aware of his ability to do many things
well." The researchers hypothesized that exposure to the trait labels in
the first experiment would incline subjects to use those labels in interpreting the behavioral descriptions. Consistent with this hypothesis,
subjects' later reproductions of the behaviors, and their overall impressions of the actor, were distorted in the direction of the evaluative
implications of the trait terms they had seen. Subjects exposed to "self-
confident" interpreted Donald's awareness of his own abilities as self-
confidence and formed generally positive impressions of him; those
exposed to "conceited" interpreted that same awareness as conceit,
and formed generally negative impressions.

Of course, scientists seldom label concepts with the first applicable
term that comes to mind. But the terms most recently and frequently in
their thoughts will generally be more salient and thus more available
for use. Studies such as the one just described seem to support
Schachtel's argument that readily available labels can shape thinking
and obscure incongruities between the label and the thing being
described.

The selection of concept labels may also be affected by normative
concerns. That is, scientists may choose labels to conform to the practices or expectations of others in their field. In Schachtel's words, they
may be temped to "describe something that many people recognize at
once, that they already know, that follows a familiar pattern." E. T.
Higgins and W. S. Rholes examined the effects of such labels on the

thinking of the labeler.[10] Subjects received both ambiguous and unambiguous descriptions of a person's behavior and then were asked to summarize this information for a recipient said to like or dislike that person. As expected, subjects chose labels for the ambiguous actions that comported evaluatively with the sentiments ascribed to the recipient. Additionally, they tended to label unambiguous behaviors that agreed with the recipient's feelings, but to ignore unambiguous behaviors inconsistent with those feelings. Most important, communicating these labels altered both the memories and the impressions of the subjects, so that their cognitions become consistent with their labels. Other studies have replicated these effects, which seem likely to occur in a variety of labeling contexts, including scientific endeavors.[11]

My own current research has yet another implication for the effects of concept labeling on scientists. In several preliminary studies, my associates and I found that subjects who are repeatedly induced to use trait labels in summarizing a set of behaviors later have more difficulty recalling those behaviors than subjects who are not so induced. We hypothesize that the labels became cognitive substitutes for the more complex behavioral information and ultimately "preempt" attempts to remember it.[12] The straightforward implication is that the mere act of labeling a phenomenon may "condemn to oblivion" the phenomenal details leading to the label's selection.

Many other psychological studies may be related to these semantic phenomena. For example, J. S. Bruner's seminal paper on construct accessibility describes some of the determinants of labeling.[13] Studies by C. E. Cohen and by J. Zadney and H. B. Gerard demonstrate the effects of labels and interpretations on one's memory for information.[14] Work on conformity processes,[15] groupthink,[16] and anticipatory conformity[17] explores how people shape communications to audiences. The list could be readily extended.

Let us turn briefly from the psychology of rhetoric to the rhetoric of psychology. Although psychologists have their share of concept misnomers, it is unlikely that these simply reflect the salience or conformity phenomena just described. Nonetheless, for whatever reasons, many psychological terms mislead because they are not exactly congruent with the concepts they intend to describe. "Halo effects" may reflect qualities devilish as well as angelic.[18] Harold Kelley's "consensus information" has nothing to do with consent, agreement, or even opinions.[19] "Attributional errors" are not necessarily errors at all but simply incongruities between subjects' attributions and those predicted by some popular theory.[20] The "good subject role" involves conformity to experimental demands, which researchers perceive to be bad for research, not good.[21]

The accuracy of such terms is often impaired by the implications of early theories. "Self-serving bias," for example, denotes a tendency for people to accept credit for successes while denying responsibility for failures. The "self-serving" label implies a self-seeking intent consistent with the first, motivational explanations for such attributions.[22] Yet later research suggests that these kinds of attributions can occur for nonmotivational reasons[23] and that they do not actually serve the subject's self-interest.[24] Nonetheless, researchers persist in terming such attributions "self-serving." The label could lead scientists to adopt motivational assumptions when thinking about such attributions, even though these assumptions appear to be unwarranted.

Normative factors may also influence psychological terminology. The term "introspection" has long been disreputable in the field, mostly because of the behaviorist critique of the structuralist method of "trained introspection."[25] Psychologists continue to ask subjects to introspect but now substitute talk of "self-report measures," "verbal reports,"[26] or "metacognition."[27] to mollify the critics. Only rarely is "introspection" brought out of the closet.[28]

Normative factors also underlie the diversity of terms currently used to describe the cognitive organization of knowledge about other people. The label "stereotype" is standard among researchers in such mainstream areas of social psychology as race relations and attitudes. But "implicit personality theory" is more common among social psychologists who study attribution. And "schema" is preferred by researchers in social cognition, who identify with the experimental traditions of cognitive psychology. Other applicable labels include "expectancy," "prototype," and "script," though these terms are not identical in meaning to the others.

The various terms for "schema" are largely interchangeable, so that a psychologist's choice of one particular term often reflects training or professional identification rather than substantive considerations. Scientists' terms, like their clothes, may be statements about the groups they identify with.

Although these labels for "schema" are denotatively equivalent, they do carry different connotations, reflecting the traditions that spawned them. "Stereotype" implies characterizations that are motivated, inaccurate, and propositional: for example, "psychologists analyze everyone they meet." "Implicit personality theory" projects people as naive, but rational, scientists in the mode of early attribution theories. Rather than propositions, the term connotes spatial or dimensional representations such as those discussed by S. Rosenberg and A. Sedlak.[29] In contrast, "schema" emphasizes basic memory processes rather than naive or motivated theorizing; it evokes images of associative pathways among concepts.[30] Clearly, the surplus meanings of these terms differ in ways that can considerably influence how scientists think about the underlying concept.

Metaphors

A second level of rhetorical analysis characterizes the scientist as a storyteller who weaves existing knowledge into a persuasive metaphor. The role of metaphor in scientific theorizing has been recognized by numerous philosophers of science, including logical positivists such as R. Lachman and E. Nagel.[31] A representative view is that metaphors play an important role in the assimilation and advancement of knowledge, but that their use can be harmful if their limits are not attended to.[32]

Whether the stories that scientists tell are a boon or a bane depends at least partly on how seriously people take the story and whether they can distinguish the story from the reality it describes. This distinction may be difficult for people to make because metaphors can exert a powerful influence on the interpretation, recall, and use of information. Such effects are documented in extensive research on the effects of "schemata" on information processing.[33] Schemata guide the perception and interpretation of events, facilitate the recall of schema-consistent information, bias the recall of ambiguous information, and shape the inferences and conclusions that people draw from available facts. Such processes distort people's knowledge so that it harmonizes with their schemata.

Many studies demonstrate these phenomena. For example, R. C. Anderson and colleagues presented subjects with cleverly ambiguous descriptive paragraphs.[34] One such paragraph could be interpreted as either a rehearsal for a woodwind ensemble or as a card game:

> Every Saturday night, four good friends got together. When Jerry, Mike and Pat arrived, Karen was sitting in her living room writing some notes. She quickly gathered up the cards and stood up to greet her friends at the door. They followed her into the living room but as usual they couldn't agree on exactly what to play. Jerry eventually took a stand and set things up. Finally they began to play. Karen's recorder filled the room with soft and

pleasant music. Early in the evening, Mike noticed Pat's hand and the many diamonds. As the night progressed the tempo of play increased. Finally, a lull in the activities occurred. Taking advantage of this, Jerry pondered the arrangement in front of him. Mike interrupted Jerry's reverie and said, "Let's hear the score." They listened carefully and commented on their performance. When the comments were all heard, exhausted but happy, Karen's friends all went home.[35]

A second paragraph implied either a prison break or a wrestler's attempt to break an opponent's hold. Both paragraphs were given to students in music education and physical education, who were then tested about the readings through multiple-choice questions. Every question had two correct answers, each reflecting a particular interpretation of the story. For example, one question asked what the four people in Karen's room discussed at the end of their gathering. Among the answers were "the sound of their music" and "how well they were playing cards." As predicted, music students gave more answers reflecting a woodwind rehearsal interpretation of the first paragraph, and physical education students gave more answers reflecting a wrestling interpretation of the second. Each group's schemata affected their interpretations of the described facts. In much the same way, different theoretical schemata or metaphors may promote different interpretations of the same scientific phenomenon.

In another study J. Zadney and H. B. Gerard showed subjects a film of two students rummaging through an apartment, touching and moving various items.[36] Beforehand, subjects were told either that the students in the film were waiting for a friend, that they were engaged in a burglary, or that they were hiding drug paraphernalia. After viewing the film, subjects were tested for recall of various depicted activities. As predicted, subjects given a burglary interpretation recalled more activities related to burglary (e.g., looking at a wallet) than did other subjects. Similar research indicates that such schematic biases can occur retroactively, when the interpretive schema is encountered after an event is observed.[37]

Although studies indicate that schemata usually facilitate recall for congruent information, there is some evidence that schemata can facilitate recall for incongruent information instead.[38] Several different explanations have been proposed for this result, but all suggest that information clearly inconsistent with a schema receives additional attention and processing because it is surprising.[39] On the other hand, information that is less clearly inconsistent appears to be interpreted as congruent, and information that is missing altogether is assumed to be entirely consistent.[40]

Again the implications for rhetorical issues are obvious. Scientific metaphors are useful because they can aid interpretation, recall, and generalization of complex facts. But they are also hazardous, because they can obscure alternative interpretations and encourage selective memory, usually for facts that support the accepted metaphor. Such a metaphor may also lead scientists to assume, without evidence, that certain things are true because the metaphor implies that they should be true.

Psychology provides innumerable examples of metaphorical reasoning, from Freud's Oedipal analogy for childhood sexuality to electrical models of human memory.[41] Social psychologists equate resistance to persuasion with medical inoculation,[42] interpersonal relations with economic processes,[43] human memory with laundry bins,[44] behavioral expectations with cartoon strips,[45] impression processes with linear regression,[46] personal space with territoriality,[47] and attribution processes with analysis of variance.[48]

Theorists who use such analogies plainly view them as useful rhetorical tools, and some events seem to justify that belief. For example, Kelley argued that people allocate responsibility for acts by conducting implicit mental analyses of variance.[49] Specifically, he claimed that whether people attribute behaviors to actors or situations depends on the variance in behavior across people, situations, and time. To calculate the effect of actor and situation "factors" from such observations, people use consistency over time as an estimate of "error" or reliability. His metaphor thus equates the attributional efforts of "naive scientists" with those of statisticians.

The analysis of variance (ANOVA) metaphor led to a variety of studies that support its gist while suggesting important qualifications.[50] Kelley himself noted that people usually lack some of the information necessary for a formal analysis of variance and that they therefore use their causal schemata to generate missing data.[51] He also suggested that simple rules such as "discounting" and "augmenting" may be applied in some situations with less effort than that required for a mental analysis of variance. These revisions move the model away from the analytic rationality of early attribution theory to the "mental shortcut" view more popular in social cognition today. The ANOVA model undoubtedly contributed to this shift in orientation by providing a standard against which people's irrationality is apparent. The discrepancies between Kelley's metaphor and the accumulating evidence stimulated research on attributional processes. Although schema research

search indicates that such discrepancies are often overlooked, their recognition in this instance may have been facilitated by the fact that the ANOVA metaphor was just too far-fetched to be taken literally.

In contrast, Leonard Berkowitz described an instance where a theoretical story was so compelling that it produced schematic distortions rather than theoretical progress.[52] He examined how textbooks discuss Schachter's research on communication in small groups. In a 1951 article, Schachter told a compelling "story" suggesting that people initially try to persuade any group member who holds deviant opinions, but give up and quit talking to the deviant if he does not yield to their arguments.[53] Schachter also reported research that supported much of his argument, but provided virtually no evidence of reduced communication toward dogged deviants. Yet, because most authors accepted the validity of Schachter's story, they distorted their textbook accounts of his experimental findings to make them consistent with it. Thus the majority of the texts surveyed indicate that, in Schachter's research, communications to persistent deviants diminished over time. Berkowitz argues that these descriptions evidence the same kinds of schematic biases described earlier.

Argument

The rhetorical nature of semantic and metaphorical practices is often subtle and implicit. But even in empirical work, human sciences also rely on overt argumentation. It occurs behind the scenes, in communications among authors, editors, and reviewers, and in virtually every published paper. Introductory sections try to persuade readers that specific predictions follow logically from general theories, so that a proposed method will shed light on important principles. Discussion sections argue that the findings provide support for the theoretical premises, though perhaps not precisely as predicted. The effectiveness of such arguments determines the acceptance and impact of any published study.

Social psychologists have published literally thousands of studies on persuasion, almost all of them relevant in some way to the persuasive efforts of scientists. For purposes of illustration, I will discuss only two of these, representing rather different approaches. A classic issue in persuasion studies concerns whether it is better to acknowledge and refute arguments contradicting an advocated position (a "two-sided" message) or to ignore their existence altogether (a "one-sided" message). A study by C. I. Hovland, A. A. Lumsdaine, and F. D. Sheffield suggests that when the audience is ignorant about an issue, or is already sympathetic to the position advocated, a "one-sided" argument is more effective.[54] But when the audience is knowledgeable or is antagonistic to the advocated position, a "two-sided" argument works better. By implication, scientific writers can ignore alternative theories and explanations whenever readers are unlikely to think of them. This is presumably most likely when a paper is addressed to a general audience, which is not knowledgeable about the particular domain being discussed, or when the paper's orientation is dominant in the field. From a different perspective, such findings warn readers of scientific papers to distrust the apparent logic of ideas too distant from their own interests or too close to their own point of view.

A second, more contemporary approach to persuasion emphasizes that people can process persuasive information in different ways, depending on such factors as their degree of involvement in an issue. For example, several theorists argue that relatively uninvolved people operate on "automatic pilot," expending little cognitive effort and employing simple rules or "shortcuts" in evaluating the validity of persuasive material. The processing of more involved people is more active and more analytic. Hence uninvolved audiences are more influenced by easily used but logically irrelevant information, such as the status or attractiveness of a communicator, whereas involved audiences are more influenced by the logical validity of arguments.[55] One implication may be that disinterested readers of scientific journals are influenced more by the prestige of writers, and engaged readers by the logic of the writing. More generally, such research suggests that different kinds of arguments affect different kinds of audiences in different ways. This poses a problem for papers like this one that try to persuade readers both inside and outside a specialized discipline.

Although argumentation is found in most scientific articles, it may be most evident in the occasional exchanges that occur between theorists of different persuasions. Recent examples in psychology include R. B. Zajonc and R. S. Lazarus disputing the primacy of affective responses, G. Weary disagreeing with D. T. Miller and M. Ross about the nature of self-serving biases, P. White arguing with R. E. Nisbett and T. D. Wilson about introspection, and my own disagreement with J. Carlopio and colleagues about biases in subject behaviors.[56] Such exchanges emphasize the ambiguity of supposedly objective endeavors such as the collection and interpretation of data. Such ambiguities allow—even necessitate—the practice of scientific argument.

Donal E. Carlston

Conclusions

This essay illustrates the utility of psychology (especially experimental social psychology) as a tool for examining such rhetorical issues as the effects of labels and metaphor on human thought and the persuasiveness of overt argumentation. This research rarely engages rhetorical issues in the specific context of scientific practice, but only a little imagination suffices to show their relevance. Of course, this paper mentions only a small sample of the research domains—let alone the individual studies—that are relevant to the rhetoric of inquiry. Hence the review suggests only a few of the ways in which empirical work may illuminate the psychology of rhetoric.

Psychology also involves the same rhetorical considerations prevalent in other academic disciplines. Therefore, I have touched on the rhetoric of psychology, as well as the psychology of rhetoric. The intertwining of rhetoric and empiricism in this discussion reflects one view of the role of rhetoric in science: empirical efforts complement but do not replace rhetorical practices, and rhetorical analysis illuminates but does not invalidate empirical pursuits. Both rhetorical and empirical methods are tools in the effort to accumulate useful understandings and knowledge.

More to the point, the mutual relevance of psychology and rhetoric identifies an important domain of research largely neglected by psychologists. Just as they study labeling, metaphor, and argumentation in ordinary human subjects, so should they examine such processes in the work of human scientists. The interaction of scientific training and cognitive processes is interesting both in its own right and for its implications regarding the conduct of science. There is no need to extrapolate from general research to scientific contexts when the methods of empiricism can be focused directly on the phenomena of scientific inquiry. In rhetorical terms, this may be the most productive way of turning psychology on itself.

In writing this rhetorical essay, I have come to wonder self-consciously whether I am merely retelling old stories in new terms. Rhetoricians and philosophers of science have already made many of the general points inferred here from psychological research, though not often in the same context or language. This reinforces the recommendation that psychologists might best contribute to understanding the rhetoric of inquiry by studying it more directly and specifically. But it also suggests another, seemingly inevitable, consequence of rhetorical analysis: self-consciousness. After discussing labels, metaphors, and arguments, I find myself terribly aware of the labels, metaphors, and arguments that I am using.

Indeed, rhetoricians of inquiry often suggest that this consciousness of one's own rhetorical practices is as great a benefit of their field as awareness of others' rhetoric. By now it should seem unsurprising that psychologists have empirical data pertaining even to this claim for self-consciousness. Termed "objective self-awareness" by social psychologists, it is said to be an aversive state similar to stage fright. It is significant that self-awareness has been found to make people's thinking less innovative and more conventional.[57] Obviously this finding is inconsistent with the view that rhetorical self-consciousness is both a blessing and a virtue. It therefore raises serious questions about the benefits of turning rhetorical analysis on psychology or any other human science.

But take heart. Earlier sections of this essay summarize cognitive tricks that can be used to dismiss the uncomfortable possibility that rhetorical self-consciousness is stifling rather than enlightening. Strategies might include biased interpretation of the reported results, selective memory, or even overt argumentation. In this instance, these rhetorical strategies might be supplemented with some empirical relief. A recent study suggests that self-awareness leads to a process of continual comparison and self-adjustment, a process that may or may not be aversive, depending on how one fares in comparison with others.[58] Rhetorical self-consciousness may therefore lead scientists to compare their rhetorical practices with those of colleagues in other disciplines, and to make adjustments in the ways they practice science. This should be a satisfying story for rhetoricians of inquiry. But as they embrace it, they might remember the schematic biases that stories can introduce into the thinking of human scientists.

NOTES

1. Ernest G. Schachtel, "On Memory and Childhood Amnesia," *Psychiatry* 10 (1947): 1–26.

2. Cf. Susan T. Fiske and Shelly E. Taylor, *Social Cognition* (Reading, Mass.: Addison-Wesley, 1984); D. Kahneman and A. Tversky, "On the Psychology of Prediction," *Psychological Review* 80 (1973): 237–51; Lee Ross, "The Intuitive Psychologist and His Shortcomings: Distortions in the Attribution Process," in Leonard Berkowitz, ed., *Advances in Experimental Social Psychology,* vol. 10 (New York; Academic Press, 1977), pp. 174–221.

Donal E. Carlston

3. Leslie Z. McArthur, "What Grabs You? The Role of Attention in Impression Formation and Causal Attribution," in E. T. Higgins, C. P. Herman, and M. P. Zanna, eds., *Social Cognition: The Ontario Symposium*, vol. 1 (Hillsdale, N.J.: Erlbaum Associates, 1981), pp. 201–46; Shelley E. Taylor and Susan T. Fiske, "Salience, Attention, and Attribution: Top of the Head Phenomena," in Leonard Berkowitz, ed., *Advances in Experimental Social Psychology*, vol. 11 (New York: Academic Press, 1978), pp. 249–88.

4. E. E. Jones and K. E. Davis, "From Acts to Dispositions: The Attribution Process in Person Perception," in Leonard Berkowitz, ed., *Advances in Experimental Social Psychology*, vol. 2 (New York: Academic Press, 1965), pp. 219–66; H. H. Kelley, "Attribution Theory in Social Psychology," in D. Levine, ed., *Nebraska Symposium on Motivation*, vol. 15 (Lincoln: University of Nebraska Press, 1967), pp. 192–240.

5. Herbert C. Kelman, "Compliance, Identification, and Internalization: Three Processes of Attitude Change," *Journal of Conflict Resolution* 2 (1958): 51–60.

6. L. Carmichael, H. P. Hogan, and A. A. Walter, "An Experimental Study of the Effect of Language on the Reproduction of Visually Perceived Form," *Journal of Experimental Psychology* 15 (1932): 73–86.

7. D. R. Thomas, A. DeCapito Caronite, G. L. LaMonica, and K. Hoving, "Mediated Generalization via Stimulus Labelling: A Replication and Extension," *Journal of Experimental Psychology* 78 (1968): 531–33.

8. S. L. Duncan, "Differential Social Perception and Attribution of Intergroup Violence: Testing the Lower Limits of Stereotyping of Blacks," *Journal of Personality and Social Psychology* 34 (1976): 590–98; E. J. Langer and R. P. Abelson, "A Patient by Any Other Name . . . : Clinician Group Difference in Labeling Bias," *Journal of Consulting and Clinical Psychology* 42 (1974): 4–9; H. A. Sagar and J. W. Schofield, "Racial and Behavioral Cues in Black and White Children's Perceptions of Ambiguously Aggressive Acts," *Journal of Personality and Social Psychology* 39 (1980): 590–98; S. E. Taylor, S. T. Fiske, N. L. Etcoff, and A. J. Ruderman, "Categorical Bases of Person Memory and Stereotyping," *Journal of Personality and Social Psychology* 36 (1978): 778–93.

9. E. T. Higgins, W. S. Rholes, and C. R. Jones, "Category Accessibility and Impression Formation," *Journal of Experimental Social Psychology* 13 (1977): 141–54.

10. E. T. Higgins and W. S. Rholes, "'Saying Is Believing': Effects of Message Modification on Memory and Liking for the Person Described," *Journal of Experimental Social Psychology* 14 (1978): 363–78.

11. M. Manis, S. D. Cornell, and J. C. Moore, "Transmission of Attitude-Relevant Information Through a Communication Chain," *Journal of Personality and Social Psychology* 30 (1974): 81–94; C. Zimmerman and R. A. Bauer, "The Effect of an Audience on What Is Remembered," *Public Opinion Quarterly* 20 (1956): 238–48.

12. See Donal E. Carlston, "The Recall and Use of Traits and Events in Social Inference Processes," *Journal of Experimental Social Psychology* 16 (1980):

303–28; J. D. White and Donal E. Carlston, "The Consequences of Schemata for Attention, Impressions, and Recognition in Complex Social Interactions," *Journal of Personality and Social Psychology* 45 (1983): 538–49.

13. J. S. Bruner, "On Perceptual Readiness," *Psychological Review* 64 (1957): 123–52.

14. Claudia E. Cohen, "Person Categories and Social Perception: Testing Some Boundaries of the Processing Effects of Prior Knowledge," *Journal of Personality and Social Psychology* 40 (1981): 441–52; J. Zadney and H. B. Gerard, "Attributed Intentions and Informational Selectivity," *Journal of Experimental Social Psychology* 10 (1974): 34–52.

15. M. Deutsch and H. Gerard, "A Study of Normative and Informational Social Influences on Social Judgment," *Journal of Abnormal and Social Psychology* 51 (1955): 629–36; Harold H. Kelley, "Two Functions of Reference Groups," in G. E. Swanson, T. M. Newcomb, and E. L. Hartley, eds., *Readings in Social Psychology,* 2d ed. (New York: Holt, Rinehart and Winston, 1952), pp. 410–14.

16. Irving L. Janis, *Victims of Groupthink* (Boston: Houghton Mifflin, 1972).

17. J. Jellison and J. Mills, "Effect of Public Commitment Upon Opinions," *Journal of Experimental Social Psychology* 5 (1969): 340–46.

18. E. Thorndike, "A Constant Error in Psychological Ratings," *Journal of Applied Psychology* 4 (1920): 25–29.

19. Kelley, "Attribution Theory."

20. John H. Harvey and R. P. McGlynn, "Matching Words to Phenomena: The Case of the Fundamental Attribution Error," *Journal of Personality and Social Psychology* 43 (1982): 345–46.

21. S. J. Weber and T. D. Cook, "Subject Effects in Laboratory Research: An Examination of Subject Roles, Demand Characteristics, and Valid Inference," *Psychological Bulletin* 77 (1972): 273–95.

22. N. T. Feather and J. G. Simon, "Attribution of Responsibility and Valence of Outcome in Relation to Initial Confidence and Success and Failure of Self and Other," *Journal of Personality and Social Psychology* 18 (1971): 173–88.

23. D. T. Miller and M. Ross, "Self-Serving Biases in Attribution of Causality: Fact or Fiction?" *Psychological Bulletin* 82 (1975): 213–25.

24. Donal E. Carlston and N. Shovar, "Effects of Performance Attributions on Others' Perceptions of the Attributor," *Journal of Personality and Social Psychology* 44 (1983): 515–25.

25. J. B. Watson, "Psychology as a Behaviorist Views It," *Psychological Review* 20 (1913): 158–77.

26. Richard E. Nisbett and T. D. Wilson, "Telling More Than We Can Know: Verbal Reports on Mental Processes," *Psychological Review* 84 (1977): 231–59.

27. A. L. Brown, "Knowing When, Where, and How to Remember: A Problem of Metacognition," in R. Glaser, ed., *Advances in Instructional Psychology* (Hillsdale, N.J.: Erlbaum Associates, 1978), pp. 77–165.

Donal E. Carlston

28. J. Radford, "Reflections on Introspection," *American Psychologist* (1974): 245–50.

29. Stanley Rosenberg and A. Sedlak, "Structural Representations of Implicit Personality Theory," in Leonard Berkowitz, ed., *Advances in Experimental Social Psychology,* vol. 6 (New York: Academic Press, 1972), pp. 235–97.

30. See J. R. Anderson and G. H. Bower, *Human Associative Memory* (Washington, D.C.: V. H. Winston, 1973); A. M. Collins and E. F. Loftus, "A Spreading Activation Theory of Semantic Processing," *Psychological Review* 82 (1975): 407–28; Robert S. Wyer, Jr., and Donal E. Carlston, *Social Cognition, Inference, and Attribution* (Hillsdale, N.J.: Erlbaum Associates, 1979).

31. R. Lachman, "The Model in Theory Construction," *Psychological Review* 67 (1960): 113–29; E. Nagel, *The Structure of Science* (New York: Harcourt, Brace & World, 1961).

32. Nagel, *Structure of Science.*

33. This literature is reviewed in Fiske and Taylor, *Social Cognition;* Wyer and Carlston, *Social Cognition, Inference, and Attribution.*

34. R. C. Anderson, R. E. Reynolds, D. L. Schallert, and E. T. Goetz, *Frameworks for Comprehending Discourse,* Technical Report no. 12 (Urbana: Laboratory for Cognitive Studies in Education, University of Illinois at Urbana-Champaign, 1976).

35. Ibid., pp. 10–11.

36. Zadny and Gerard, "Attributed Intentions."

37. R. C. Anderson and J. W. Pichert, "Recall of Previously Unrecallable Information Following a Shift in Perspective," *Journal of Verbal Learning and Verbal Behavior* 17 (1978): 1–12; M. Snyder and S. W. Uranowitz, "Reconstructing the Past: Some Cognitive Consequences of Person Perception," *Journal of Personality and Social Psychology* 36 (1978): 941–50.

38. Reid Hastie, "Memory for Behavioral Information That Confirms or Contradicts a Personality Impression," in Reid Hastie et al., *Person Memory: The Cognitive Bases of Social Perception* (Hillsdale, N.J.: Erlbaum Associates, 1980), pp. 155–78.

39. Cf. Donal E. Carlston, "Events, Inferences, and Impression Formation," in Hastie et al., *Person Memory,* pp. 89–120; Reid Hastie, "Schematic Principles in Human Memory," Higgins, Herman, and Zanna, *Social Cognition: The Ontario Symposium,* pp. 39–88; T. K. Srull, "Person Memory: Some Tests of Associative Storage and Retrieval Models," *Journal of Experimental Psychology* 7 (1981): 440–62.

40. M. Minsky, "A Framework for Representing Knowledge," in P. H. Winston, ed., *The Psychology of Computer Vision* (New York: McGraw-Hill, 1975), pp. 211–277; White and Carlston, "Consequences of Schemata."

41. Sigmund Freud, "The Origin and Development of Psychoanalysis," *American Journal of Psychology* 21 (1910): 181–218; Anderson and Bower, *Human Associative Memory.*

42. William J. McGuire and D. Papageorgis, "Effectiveness of Forewarning in Developing Resistance to Persuasion," *Public Opinion Quarterly* 26 (1962): 24–34.

43. John W. Thibaut and Harold H. Kelley, *Interpersonal Relations* (New York: Wiley, 1978).

44. Robert S. Wyer, Jr., and Thomas K. Srull, "The Processing of Social Stimulus Information: A Conceptual Integration," in Hastie et al., *Person Memory*, pp. 227–300.

45. Robert R. Abelson, "Script Processing in Attitude Formation and Decision-Making," in J. S. Carroll and J. W. Payne, eds., *Cognition and Social Behavior* (Hillsdale, N.J.: Erlbaum Associates, 1976).

46. Norman H. Anderson, "Application of a Linear-Serial Model to a Personality Impression Task Using Serial Presentation," *Journal of Personality and Social Psychology* 10 (1968): 354–62.

47. I. Altman, *The Environment and Social Behavior*, (Monterey, Calif.: Brooks/Cole, 1975).

48. Kelley, "Attribution Theory."

49. Ibid.

50. See Fiske and Taylor, *Social Cognition*, pp. 29–35, for a review.

51. Harold H. Kelley, "The Processes of Causal Attribution," *American Psychologist* 28 (1973): 107–28.

52. Leonard Berkowitz, "Reporting an Experiment: A Case Study in Leveling, Sharpening, and Assimilation," *Journal of Experimental Social Psychology* 7 (1971): 237–43.

53. Stanley Schachter, "Deviation, Rejection, and Communication," *Journal of Abnormal and Social Psychology* 46 (1951): 190–207.

54. C. I. Hovland, A. A. Lumsdaine, and F. D. Scheffield, *Experiments on Mass Communication* (Princeton: Princeton University Press, 1949).

55. Shelley Chaiken, "Heuristic Versus Systematic Information Processing and the Use of Source and Message Cues in Persuasion," *Journal of Personality and Social Psychology* 39 (1980): 752–66; R. E. Petty and J. T. Cacioppo, "Issue Involvement Can Increase or Decrease Persuasion by Enhancing Message-Relevant Cognitive Responses," *Journal of Personality and Social Psychology* 37 (1979): 1915–26.

56. Robert B. Zajonc, "Feeling and Thinking: Preferences Need No Inferences," *American Psychologist* 35 (1980): 151–75; R. S. Lazarus, "Thoughts on the Relations Between Emotion and Cognition," *American Psychologist* 37 (1982): 1019–24; Gifford Weary, "Self-Serving Biases in the Attribution Process: A Re-Examination of the Fact or Fiction Question," *Journal of Personality and Social Psychology* 36 (1978): 56–71; Miller and Ross, "Self-Serving Biases"; P. White, "Limitation on Verbal Reports of Internal Events: A Refutation of Nisbett and Wilson and of Bem," *Psychological Review* 87 (1980): 105–12; Nisbett and Wilson, "Telling More Than We Can Know"; J. Carlopio, J. G. Adair, R. C. L. Lindsay, and B. Spinner, "Avoiding Artifact in the Search for Bias: The Importance of Assessing Subjects' Perceptions of the Experiment,"

Donal E. Carlston

Journal of Personality and Social Psychology 44 (1983): 693–701; Donal E. Carlston and Jerry L. Cohen, "A Closer Examination of Subject Roles," *Journal of Personality and Social Psychology* 38 (1980): 857–70; idem, "Avoiding Bias in the Search for Artifact: A Reply to Carlopio, Adair, Lindsay, and Spinner," *Journal of Personality and Social Psychology* 45 (1983): 1225–28.

57. R. A. Wicklund, "Objective Self-Awareness," in Leonard Berkowitz, ed., *Advances in Experimental Social Psychology,* vol. 8 (New York: Academic Press, 1975), pp. 233–75.

58. M. F. Scheier and C. S. Carver, "Cognition, Affect, and Self-Regulation," in M. S. Clark and S. T. Fiske, eds., *Affect and Cognition: The Seventeenth Annual Carnegie Symposium on Cognition* (Hillsdale, N.J.: Erlbaum Associates, 1982), pp. 157–83.

10   AS IF ECONOMISTS AND THEIR

SUBJECT WERE RATIONAL

ARJO KLAMER

The variety and type of remarks about economics that come the way of economists are perplexing. To mention only a few:

A student in economics: "It is as if I were learning a foreign language!"
Another student: "The assumptions are so unrealistic."
A business person: "But they are not talking about real firms!"
A noneconomist giving a speech: "I don't have a Ph.D. in economics, but I think nevertheless that . . ."
A radical: "Economic theory is mere ideology; all it does is provide a rationalization for the capitalist system."
A literary critic: "Where are the people in economic models?"

These reactions speak of frustration, disbelief, and intimidation. Yet economists, especially those in academic circles, do not appear to be perturbed. I propose that we take the general frustration with the discourse of academic economists seriously. Why is it, we need ask ourselves, that the statements of economists often seem to make no sense, or even alienate and offend people?

Questions *about* economics usually lead to discussions on the methodology of economics. We are lured into debates concerning the truth-value of economic theories, their logical structure, the validity of their assumptions, their falsifiability, and so on. The goal appears to be the determination of standards that distinguish true or good theories from false or bad theories.[1]

However, these discussions do not help us out with our question. If we are encouraged by the work of Thomas Kuhn and Richard Rorty, among others, as I am, we might consider them uninteresting, or even futile. The real goal is not to know how we, from an Archimedean position, can design rational criteria of truthfulness; it is instead to comprehend how economists actually argue and how their arguments work.

163

Arjo Klamer

The conception of economics as an art of persuasion appears to be a promising starting point for this inquiry. Just as economists seek a meaningful way to talk about the economy, we face the challenge of talking about what economists do in a meaningful way—that is, using a language and arguments that work. It is my belief that the language of rhetoric and literary criticism is more appropriate to economics than the language of methodology. The central image, suggested by Rorty among others, [2] presents economists as participating in conversations. They argue to persuade each other and, occasionally, to convince non-economists. For that purpose they construct a variety of arguments; use analogies, metaphors, labels; reconstruct intellectual history; and make claims concerning the status of their arguments.

The intention of the rhetorical approach is to render economic discourse transparent—that is, to "see through" the superficial meaning of economists' expressions, to deconstruct them, as some literary critics would say. Whether or not this precipitates challenges to economists' discussions is not immediately clear. Donald McCloskey, whose article "The Rhetoric of Economics" has already had a major impact on the profession, is critical of the ways in which economists talk about what they do, but not of the ways in which they talk about the economy.[3] It is my goal to see through the economic arguments themselves in order to understand the common frustration with these arguments.

The Tribe of Economists

A fruitful entry point for the argument is Clifford Geertz's proposal to think "ethnographically" about the activities of economists.[4] Our vantage point, then, becomes that of an anthropologist: we think of economists as a tribe, and we observe the interactions among the members of that tribe. This perspective produces certain insights. For example, those who aspire to become economists may be said to experience initiation rituals, which take the form of course work, various assignments, tests, the Ph.D. thesis, and much interaction with the people in the tribe. It suggests various other observations as well.

First, an economic model, an empirical test, or anything that is produced by economists is a "cultural artifact": the work of economists has to be understood in the cultural and social context of its production. Second, the culture that makes up the economic tribe is unique; it is distinguished from other cultures through its institutions, its language, its professional code, and so on. Third, in the words of Geertz:

the various disciplines (or disciplinary matrices), humanistic, natural scientific, social scientific alike, that make up the scattered discourse of modern scholarship are more than just intellectual coigns of vantage but are ways of being in the world, to invoke a Heideggerian formula, forms of life, to use a Wittgensteinian, or varieties of noetic experience, to adopt a Jamesian.[5]

Becoming an economist implies more than making a choice for a particular subject; it signifies the adoption of a "cultural frame that defines a great part of one's life."[6] Finally, the main audience for an economist is other economists; in other words, the communication is tribal, or intracultural.

These observations will constitute the points of departure of my argument. I will not elaborate on them here, but I intend the following discussion to add to their significance. One caveat is in order, however. The variety of the economic tribe renders its cohesion questionable. There are, indeed, many types of economists who talk in different ways, often about different issues. I suggest that we overlook much of the variety within the economic tribe for the time being and concentrate on the culture of neo-classical economists, which is the dominant culture among English-speaking members of the discipline. Its rhetoric, concepts, problems, and exercises dominate the textbooks; articles that conform to its norms crowd the prestigious journals. For an understanding of this culture, we will turn to its linguistic expressions. But before pursuing that track, we will first examine how neo-classical economists (from now on I shall delete "neo-classical") perceive the position of their tribe among other tribes.

The Social Science Building

Japanese salarymen, the modern version of the samurai, sing the company song each day before and after their work. College students wear the t-shirts and cheer for the athletes of their college. American citizens stand up on every conceivable occasion to sing the national anthem. In all cases we recognize the celebration of a community: a company, a university, a country. Its purpose appears to be the establishment of an identity that distinguishes the members of the community from outsiders. The quality of the community is extolled; everyone is persuaded that the community is the best of all places. Just like the salarymen and college students, economists have their own tribal song, their own sense of their tribe's superiority.

Arjo Klamer

The building in which I work provides a good analogy. This building is now called the social science building. Originally, it was the physics building, but the physicists moved, very appropriately, to a modernistic structure having some resemblance to the Centre de Pompidou in Paris. The visitor, however, is reminded of their ghost by a stone sign above the entrance proclaiming PHYSICS and showing a calibrating instrument. We, the economists in the building (tribal allegiance compels me to identify myself with them), approve of that; we enjoy the association with physics, as it represents the scientific status we seek. We also like the fact that we occupy the top floor of the building. After all, this corresponds to our belief in the status of economics as queen of the social sciences, a belief that we are sure to convey to our students. The floor below is occupied by sociologists and anthropologists. We do not really know what they do. Once, a couple of years ago, we tried to talk with them, but we got impatient with their asking "What is work?" or "What do you mean by rational behavior?" We had the strong impression that they did not understand our models, and we believed them to be involved in a lot of talk without concrete results. So we have restricted our conversation ever since to relatively innocuous topics like tenure, sports, or academic council.

The bottom floor houses the political scientists. We actually suspect that the "science" in political science conceals a fundamentally nonscientific discipline. It seems to us that apart from the few economists among them, political scientists practice a form of modern history or some kind of sociology. In any case, we do not talk with each other.

To complete the analogy, we economists know where the Chinese department is, since their faculty have their offices in the basement. But most of us do not know how to find the historians, philosophers, psychologists, and linguists. We do, however, frequent the modern science building: not, of course, to talk with the physicists, biologists, and chemists, but to use their computer for our statistical analyses.

Economists have external support for their claim to the top floor. After all, there is a Nobel prize for economics, and not for the social sciences; the president of the United States has a Council of Economic, and not Sociological, Advisors. It is intriguing that their tribal song chooses to celebrate the superior scientific status of economics as a discipline. Economists apparently desire to imitate the natural sciences and hence adhere to the values of quantification, empirical testing, and rigorous formulation, preferably in mathematical symbols, and believe that only economists, among all the social scientists, can live up to these values. Alan Blinder, an eminent economist at Princeton, expresses this desire in explaining his choice of economics as a field of study:

I was interested in applying quantitative, mathematical, and scientific methods to social problems. That only leads to one place for the most part, or it used to [laughter], and that's to economics. Sociology is really very underdeveloped. Anthropology is a whole different thing. I think of that more like history than like a contemporary social science. I'm not sure why sociology is underdeveloped; maybe it's because they haven't been able to quantify things as well as we have. A lot of the things they [the sociologists] deal with are more elusive and harder to get measurements of. And if you don't have mathematics, you don't have science. That may be the reason.[7]

It might be pointed out that this comparison of economics to the natural sciences expresses wishful thinking. If this tribal song is taken literally, it sounds naive and even dogmatic, especially when we take into account the work of people like Thomas Kuhn, Michael Polanyi, Paul Feyerabend, Richard Rorty, and Wayne Booth. But it is not necessary to go through this argument, as McCloskey's "Rhetoric of Economics" has already made an eloquent statement allowing us to see through the scientific claims of economics and perceive the rhetorical dimensions of economic discourse. So, let us now look into how economists express their scientific values in talking about the economy and, especially, about economic behavior.

Economic Agents Are Rational . . .

Undergraduate students often tell me that learning economics is like learning a foreign language because they are asked to use terms that they do not understand. Venturing their first economic essays, they are rebuked for the papers' superficiality and lack of analysis. The students, of course, are only trying to make sense in their own terms. So they discuss incidents and anecdotes as reported in magazines and newspapers. They talk about the loss of confidence in the stock market, the decline of American industry due to mismanagement, or the power of big companies, in the same way that economists like John Kenneth Galbraith, Lester Thurow, and Robert Reich talk about those issues. All this is persuasive to these students, but their professors get out the red pencil.

This tension between students and professors reveals a contrast in intentions. Students seek resemblance; they look for a realistic picture of the economy. Their professors, however, are preoccupied with the art of constructing economic arguments according to the *conventions* of the economic *discipline*. And these coventions are not respected in the writings of Galbraith, Thurow, and Reich, nor are they followed in *Business Week* or the *Wall Street Journal*, all sources that students tend to turn to. Their professors' intention, therefore, is to break students of the journalistic way of thinking used outside the tribe, and to instruct them in the art of economic analysis. The discipline conveys the lesson that one ought to forget about psychology and sociology, so students are told to think in terms of *individual rational behavior*.

Hal Varian begins his reputable microeconomic textbook with the sentence "Microeconomics is concerned with the behavior of *individual* economic units and their interactions."[8] In the next paragraph he tells his reader about the major analytical techniques that will be used in his text—namely, the analysis of optimization and the study of equilibrium. We shall concentrate here on the first technique, which Varian describes as follows:

> The first technique involves the analysis of optimization. We will model the behavior of economic units as optimizing behavior. In doing this we need to specify the *objectives* of the unit and the *constraints* which it faces.
>
> For example, when we model the behavior of firms, we will want to describe the objective as profit maximization and the constraints as technological constraints and market constraints. When we model the behavior of consumers we will describe the objective as utility maximization and the constraints as budget constraints.[9]

This formulation is standard (a nice expression suggesting that economists awakened in the middle of the night can be expected to repeat it), and it is considered by economists to provide a way of answering the question "Why do people do what they do?" Accordingly, the analytical focus is on individual choice, whether that of an individual consumer, worker, or firm, and the fundamental assumption is that any economic choice is rational to the extent that it is consistent with the outcome of the optimization procedure: a rational choice is the optimal choice. Let me give a few examples of the way this assumption is expressed in actual research.

Demand and supply functions, the trademark of economists, seem to make immediate sense: when the price of a good goes up, people tend to buy less and will try to produce more. The economist, however, is not content with this observation and will look for an explanation in terms of individual rational choice. Accordingly, students are taught to "look behind" the demand curve and to see indifference curves, budget constraints, marginal utility, marginal cost, and marginal revenue curves: all concepts that feature in the analysis of individual choice.

Some economists claim that the optimization technique is pertinent to the analysis of any choice, whether it is the choice to buy or invest, or the choice to marry, to commit adultery, or to commit a violent crime. The name of Gary Becker, in particular, is associated with these creative applications. His writings make intriguing reading; for example, in an article entitled "An Economic Analysis of Marital Instability," he writes (with Elizabeth Landes and Robert Michael):

> By assumption, each marital "strategy" produces a known amount of full wealth (i.e., money wealth and value of nonmarket time), and the opportunity set equals the set of full wealths produced by all conceivable marital strategies. The individual ranks all strategies by their full wealth and chooses the highest. Even with certainty, a strategy with marriage, then dissolution, and eventually remarriage might be preferred to all other strategies and would be anticipated at the time of first marriage. Dissolution would be a response perhaps to the growing up of children, or to the diminishing marginal utility from living with the same person, and would be a fully anticipated part of the variation in marital status over the life cycle.[10]

The "micro" theory of individual choice has also made its way into macroeconomics, the study of the economy as a whole. When John Maynard Keynes theorized about total consumption in the thirties, he relied on the psychological insight that people will consume a certain proportion of any additional income they earn, and save the remainder. Such an assumption does not convince many economists nowadays. They want to see an analysis that shows how optimal decisions of *individual* consumers generate the perceived total consumption. To use a famous phrase in contemporary economic discourse, economists are looking for the "microfoundations of macroeconomics."

The importance that can be attached to the "microfoundations" is confirmed by revolutionary events in macroeconomic discourse during the 1970s, when economists saw the possibility of applying the optimization technique to the determination of expectations. This application had always seemed unlikely, as expectations on any future variable are commonly held to be both subjective and volatile. But Robert Lucas, then a young economist at Carnegie-Mellon, saw possibilities in the idea of "rational expectations" conceived by a former Carnegie-Mellon economist, John Muth. Lucas and some other economists solved various technical problems, demonstrating that rational expectations could be built into macroeconomic models to produce many interesting results. The tribe seems to have been converted to their beliefs. No graduate student will get through even preliminary examinations without knowing how rational expectations work. Building a model with rational expectations has become the fashion for people writing doctoral theses in macroeconomics. And the final mark of recognition will probably come in the form of a Nobel prize for Lucas.

Economists are clearly captivated by the idea that economic agents are rational in their decisions. But note that Varian talks of a technique—the optimization technique. This suggests that the assumption of rational economic behavior entails a modeling strategy, or a positive heuristic, to use Lakatos's term. It tells the economists how to model behavior in any conceivable situation, under any constraints. The examples hint at the variety of possibilities of this heuristic: they actually seem infinite. Just as a set of simple rules gives rise to endless creativity and excitement in the game of chess, the rationality assumption provides inexhaustible chances for new and innovative models to stimulate the economic imagination. It engenders numerous puzzles, and has generated interest in all kinds of issues, such as the importance of information and the problem of uncertainty.

The denotation of the rationality assumption as a technique also seems to preclude any discussion of its meaning. Indeed, Varian in his textbook does not bother justifying it in any way; he simply sets to work with it. Such an approach is customary among economists, but I propose that we stop them right at the point at which they formulate their rationality assumption, *before* they get to work with it. For it is at this point that major problems of communication between economists and noneconomists, and even among economists themselves, begin. To understand these problems we need a better understanding of the rationality assumption. We can begin with some questions about economists' assumptions:

An innocent student: What you [the economics professor] are telling me is that people are always selfish, always optimizing profit and something you call utility. Is that realistic?

The economics professor: It makes a lot of sense. Don't we all try to get the best out of life? Think of a nun, for example. You would say that she is altruistic because she prefers to care for others rather than for herself. I would say that she derives utility from caring for others. So she, just like you and me, attempts to maximize her utility. OK? Let's go on then.

A persistent student: But isn't it unrealistic to assume that people are continually solving complicated optimization problems every time they need to make a decision? I don't do that, not when I'm going to buy an ice cream cone, choosing a college education over work, or trying to guess what the price of a personal computer will be next year.

The economics professor: Listen, you and I should be scientific; that is why we are here. You should understand that scientific theories start with abstractions—unrealistic assumptions if you wish. Our primary concern is to develop theories that predict well. The initial realism of our assumptions doesn't matter, so long as they work. We can introduce further refinements when we have a working model, to make it more realistic, if you wish. I suggest you check your reading list for Milton Friedman's *Essays in Positive Economics*[11]—he explains this clearly. For now, let us go on.

An anthropologist (addressing a group of economists): Do you have a theory of consumption?[12]

The economists: Of course we have. We could fill bookshelves with books and articles on the subject.

The anthropologist: But how do you explain, for example, the fact that certain sections of the population have recently begun to grow tomatoes in their back yards?

One economist: Apparently, it is rational for them to do so. Maybe the constraints have changed, such as the price of tomatoes in the supermarket, or maybe people's preferences have changed, now favoring gardening over buying vegetables.

The anthropologist: But that is not a theory of consumption: you don't tell me why people changed their preferences. It could be that people have begun to alter their attitude toward leisure, or it could have to do with changing values—with cultural and social factors.

Economist 1: You may be right, but I don't have much to say about how preferences are formed. In an economic analysis preferences are given and are usually assumed to be constant.

Economist 2: I always get uncomfortable when people begin to talk about values and culture. It doesn't lead to much, especially as those things cannot be measured. And I don't think they make much of a difference.

Arjo Klamer

Some Lessons

The anthropologist exposes the isolationism of the economic tribe. To her question she brings extensive knowledge. Her question, naive as it may have sounded to the economists, is a significant one in conversations among anthropologists, who are presently debating the merits of *substantive* versus *formal* economics. The latter conforms with the traditional approach of economists; the former, propagated by people like Karl Polanyi, holds noneconomic factors accountable for economic phenomena.[13] Economists tend to be unaware of this controversy, as they are unaware of sociological and psychological issues in general; they do not enter the domain of other social scientists. Some economists would acknowledge this isolation as a limitation, but most will use an epistemological argument to justify themselves, suggesting that "noneconomic" factors are unquantifiable and not subject to rigorous analysis. The point is that they do not talk, and generally do not want to and cannot talk, about the issues raised by the anthropologist. They rule the anthropologist out of order: after all, she belongs to another tribe, living a floor below.

The exchange with the two students reveals ambiguities in the "technique" of assuming rational or optimizing behavior. The economist assuages the discomfort of the innocent student by appealing to his common sense. Apparently, the optimization technique is not a mere tool, but also evokes an image of human behavior that is supposed to be understandable. The second student, however, expresses her doubts about how well the tool fits her experience, how well she can understand it. In response the economist presents her with an epistemological argument—or an argument on how one ought to construct a scientific analysis—to put an end to the discussion.

The seeming authority with which he does this is misleading. It presents a façade of resolve and self-confidence, behind which economists express doubt and argue with each other, casting doubt on the technical status of the rationality assumption. However, a good understanding of the tensions and frictions in these discussions is thwarted because of the talk about the "realism" of assumptions.

The unrealistic nature of the rationality assumption has been discussed and criticized by Galbraith and Thurow. Yet these writers, like a score of other critics of neo-classical economists, are considered by the tribe as marginal, unscientific, or at least eclectic. Criticisms expressed among the tribal leadership itself are thus even more intriguing. A Nobel Prize winner, James Tobin, is afraid that rigor in economic analysis is often more valued than relevance. The realism of assumptions is significant, he states, and when speaking of human behavior, he frequently refers to confidence and to animal spirits, even though these notions are incompatible with the optimization technique. Bob Solow, an economist at the Massachusetts Institute of Technology, affirms Tobin's skepticism when he notes that: "One ought not to insist on rationality where rationality becomes so excruciatingly difficult that it is hard to believe that that is how economic agents behave."[14]

These reservations with respect to the rationality assumption (or technique) found symbolic support in the Nobel prize awarded to Herbert Simon, who acquired part of his impressive reputation through developing an alternative notion of rationality that takes into account the *actual* decision-making process. Psychological insights into that process, Simon believes, render the neo-classical assumption of rationality unrealistic.

However, because they target the realism of the rationality assumption, the criticisms are easily intercepted and neutralized by the technicians. Their argument, as captured in the response to the persistent student, seems persuasive. Although realism may be laudable, it is an unattainable ideal. The realist painter cannot paint without abstractions, nor can the economist write without them. Milton Friedman, therefore, appears to be correct when he writes in his controversial essay on "The Methodology of Positive Economics":

> A hypothesis is important if it "explains" much by little, that is, if it abstracts the common and crucial elements from the mass of complex and detailed circumstances surrounding the phenomena to be explained and permits valid predictions on the basis of them alone. To be important, therefore, a hypothesis must be descriptively false in its assumptions; it takes account of, and accounts for, none of the many other attendant circumstances, since its very success shows them to be irrelevant for the phenomena to be explained.[15]

This point of view explains the impatience of economists with students and critics who harp on the unrealistic nature of the rationality assumption. And they are right, in that realism is not the point.

However, the technocrats unjustly bury the issue when they speak of a technique and advocate an instrumentalist position. Realism may not be the point, but a valid issue is brought up in the questions of the students and the anthropologist. That issue concerns the *meaning* and *significance* of the rationality assumption; the question is, "What does it do?" or, more precisely, "What understanding of economic phenomena or even the world at large does its persistent use bring about?" The term "technique" may have connotations of objectivity and meaninglessness, but the innocent student learns that the optimization technique can be understood in plain English and in accordance with a common experience. The assumption of rationality must also be more than a technique if it is so persistently used by economists—even by those who express doubts, such as Tobin and Solow. Why is this?

The simple reason is that the assumption makes a great deal of sense and thus has a wide range of applicability. One can hear it in the humor of economists, who are tickled when someone is able to connect the assumption with an unusual or trivial event—as when an economist talks about preference functions, constraints, and game strategies when a pizza has to be divided (I always find it interesting to observe who cannot laugh at the joke). The assumption makes so much sense that they are not really joking when they write about the rationality of adultery or abortion. Fritz Machlup, an economist who supports the thrust of Friedman's epistemological position, affirms the importance of the commonsense meaning by quoting Alfred Schutz:

> Each term in a scientific model of human action must be
> constructed in such a way that a human act performed within the
> life world by an individual actor in the way indicated by the
> typical construct would be understandable for the actor himself
> as well as for his fellowmen in terms of a common-sense
> interpretation of everyday life. Compliance with this postulate
> warrants the consistency of the constructs of the social scientists
> with the constructs of common-sense experience of the social
> reality.[16]

At this point we can recognize that speaking in terms of individual rationality constitutes a way of being. The rationality assumption, then, is a cultural artifact. Its role becomes transparent when we interpret it as a filter that brings some aspects of the world alive and suppresses others.

The Rationality Assumption as a Sign: Affirmative Images

If someone in an ice cream shop asked, "Can I have a large ice cream cone?" most of us would be surprised if the person took the cone, said, "Thank you," and walked away. Clearly, we interpret the question as a *sign* that signifies a request to exchange money for an ice cream cone. The literal interpretation might make sense to an alien, but to those who "know," it is strange: probably funny, possibly offensive.

The knowledge that allows us to interpret a sign comes from past experiences—in this case the experience that in a shop economic transactions take place, transactions that can be initiated with a friendly question. Such a question, therefore, is to be interpreted within the context of such experiences: the interpretation fills in what the articulated form leaves out.

Because articulated signs are necessarily incomplete, as we cannot say everything in words, there are problems with the proper use and understanding of signs. Let us consider the statement under examination: "Economic agents are rational." Understanding a sign requires knowing how to use it. In the words of Ludwig Wittgenstein: "Try not to think of understanding as a mental process at all—for *that* is the expression which confuses you. But ask yourself, in what sort of case, in what kind of circumstances do we say 'now I know how to go on'?"[17] He suggests that we look at the way an expression is used in the context of what he calls a language game. Knowing how to use the assumption is a matter of knowing the rules of the game. However, these rules cannot normally be articulated: they must be learned through example and practice. Michael Polanyi speaks of the tacit dimension of knowledge, using the example of a bicyclist who knows how to keep her balance but does not think about why she can. This is analogous to economists' view of the rationality assumption as a technique: they know how to use it after extensive practice through problem sets in graduate school, but they do not reflect on why it works. They take most of their language game for granted and do not talk about the context in which the statement that "economic agents are rational" becomes significant.

The student of the rhetoric of economics faces the challenge of speaking about the unspoken, filling in the "missing text" in economic discourse. The context of the rationality assumption is what allows the assumption to work for some and not for others. We can think of that context as a *network* of anecdotes, ideas, beliefs, images, intentions, and desires, all of which are connected to the statement of the rationality of economic agents. The connections are not necessarily tight and logical; they may occur in a process of loose associations or nostalgic emotions. Elements in the network can be dropped without major damage to the significance of the rationality assumption. Thus if the network is extensive, firm believers in the assumption will not easily be persuaded of its flaws. And the particular network relating to

Arjo Klamer

the rationality assumption is very extensive, as the following list of possible connections suggests:

1. An assumption of the rationality of individual behavior conforms with the spirit of the Age of Reason. The belief in the supremacy of reason has been handed down by Greek and Renaissance philosophers, and strengthened by scientific successes. It allows people to overcome superstition and to act upon factors other than intuition, emotion, custom, or prejudice. The dominance of this belief is demonstrated by the difficulty economists have in imagining that agents act irrationally by leaving profit opportunities unexploited, or by not seeking the optimal choice.
2. The analogy between economics and science is extended by several dualities. The split between positive and normative economics, which economists often support, brings out the duality of objective versus subjective, fact and logic versus value and belief, science versus opinion. Accordingly, the choice of goals is a matter of opinion, whereas the study of the means to reach a particular goal is the domain of science, of reason. This split is transposed to attitudes toward economic behavior, to the duality between the subjectivity of preferences and the objectivity of choice. A favorite slogan among economists is "de gustibus non est disputandum"—that is, reason has no application to the determination of tastes or preferences. Hence, economists take as given the preferences of their subjects, and instead focus on the logic of choice: the optimization procedure.
3. The analysis of individual rationality evokes the spirit of individualism: the individual is the center of the world pictured by the economist. Economists want to interpret macro phenomena (like total output and the general price level) as the result of decisions by individual units. This intention accords with the methodological individualism articulated by Hobbes in the seventeenth century: "it is necessary that we know the things that are to be compounded before we can know the whole compound," for "everything is best understood by its constitutive causes."[18]
4. Hobbes is also associated with the notion of self-interest that the rationality assumption entails. It is human nature, he argued, to seek one's self-interest. This perspective appeals to

a majority of economists, whose conversations echo the famous words of Adam Smith, their predecessor:

> It is not from benevolence of the butcher, the brewer, or the baker, that we expect our dinner, but from their regard in their own interest. We address ourselves, not to their humanity but to their self-love, and never talk to them of our own necessities, but of their advantages.[19]

5. Optimization and self-interest are fundamental to the philosophy of utilitarianism, first formulated by Jeremy Bentham. His picture of human beings as pleasure-seekers was translated by economists into the optimization of the *utility* function.
6. The analysis of individual rationality allows economists to focus on economic exchange as the only relevant relationship between individuals. All that matters to economists is the rationality of our choice; they do not address the emotional facets of a relationship, or the influence of traditions, power, or cultural perceptions on relationships. The notion of choice, in turn, implies voluntary action and individual freedom. This connection is eloquently articulated in Milton Friedman's influential *Capitalism and Freedom*.[20]
7. The analysis of rational behavior has strong parallels to the model of the physical sciences in using a mechanistic view of both the individual and the system. Humans calculate their optimal choices using algorithms and equations; the system, too, is characterized by a set of mathematical formulas and symbols. Economists adopt the mathematical forms for rigor, and their passion for methodological individualism finds its source in reductionism and axiomatization, the desire to minimize the number of assumptions from which human actions can be deduced.

It is clear: once we begin to examine the network surrounding the rationality assumption, we are struck by its richness and scope. Apparently, much can be said about these ideas, images, and intentions, which economists tend not to discuss but which nevertheless give meaning to their notion of rational behavior. However, discomfort with this network, or with some of its major elements, is reason enough to resist the implications of the rationality assumption.

Arjo Klamer

Economic Agents Are Rational:
Negative Images

"Where are the people in economic models?" is a question, or an exclamation, often heard outside the world of neo-classical economics. For example, E. F. Schumacher's *Small Is Beautiful* is subtitled "Economics as If People Mattered." Herbert Simon attempts to model the *actual*, rather than the "ideal," decision-making process. Radical economists talk about people as social beings living in a alienating and divided society. In all these expressions we recognize protest against the network of beliefs that constitutes the neo-classical way of being. Although each protestor has individual reasons for rejecting "Rational Economic Man," a common motivation is that our reason, to use Henri Bergson's words, "feels less at ease in a world where it no longer finds, as in a mirror, its own image."[21] We cannot recognize ourselves in the neo-classical version of human beings.

The rejection can be better understood when we consider the metaphorical aspect of the statement that "economic agents are rational in the sense that they optimize their objective functions under a set of relevant constraints." According to Aristotle, "metaphor consists in giving a thing a name that belongs to something else; the transference being either from genus to species, or from species to species, or on the grounds of analogy."[22] But using a metaphor is not a simple matter of name switching. Colin Turbayne points out that "the use of metaphor involves the pretense that something is the case when it is not."[23] That pretense, however, can be ignored by the user or not understood by the audience; this appears to be the case with the metaphor of the Rational Economic Man. Perhaps many neo-classical economists take it literally; certainly their critics assume that they do. Turbayne would say that they are "being used by the metaphor," taking it too far in their attempt to validate it.

But the metaphor is not entirely "dead," as Turbayne would say. Partly in reaction to the critics, some neo-classical economists are invoking Milton Friedman's phrase—"as-if assumptions"—to defend it. They are saying that their models present agents *as if* the agents were robots that optimize objective functions under certain constraints. The "as if" idiom is the idiom of the analogy. Milton Friedman and many other economists use it to dispel the criticisms, but they misunderstand the role of the analogy or metaphor.

Max Black's interaction view suggests that this unusual combination of human beings and robots produces new insights and new meaning for both components. Economists see the computer programs that guide the robot's behavior as a model for representing human behavior. We have discussed the analytical value of the analogy, but Black points out that the analogy (he actually discusses the metaphor, but there is no significant difference) also works as a filter: the negative correspondence between human beings and robots is suppressed. The analogy, he argues "*organizes* our view of man."[24] A good analogy or metaphor, therefore, produces an "attitude shift," and it is the attitude shift required by the robot analogy that its critics resist. To them, the meaning of the analogy is unappealing because the negative correspondence between human beings and robots is simply too important. Let us, in light of these perspectives, review some of their criticisms.

The so-called Austrian economists agree in many ways with neo-classical economists: they place the individual in the center of the universe, believe in individual rationality, and focus on exchange relationships. But they dislike the mechanistic metaphor. It negates, they argue, the creativity of human beings, and the uncertainty under which decisions are made. For similar reasons, business people are generally repelled by the way economists talk about their behavior. They too have in their network of beliefs the romantic image of the heroic individual as depicted in the American Dream.

Incidentally, the Austrians' criticism brings out the irony of the use of the mechanistic metaphor in neo-classical discourse. The romantic belief in the freedom of choice, and thus the free individual, coincides with the positing of a rather uninteresting if not tragic human being who is predictable and acts like a programmed robot.

Those who ask, "Where are the people?" on the other hand, may have difficulties with the metaphorical human beings in neo-classical discourse as well as the network that surrounds it. To them, the filter of the metaphor removes the psychological *and* sociological complexity of each individual, projecting a one-dimensional, solipsistic, characterless "unity" with no social bonds. People questioning the pessimistic image of the Rational Economic Man are dissatisfied with the dominance of self-interest, as if people were solely preoccupied with their own interest, motivated only by monetary gain! These critics probably like the saying of Rabbi Hillel: "If I am not for myself, who will be for me? If I am only for myself, what am I?"

Radical critics find in the notion of rationality an attempt to justify the capitalist system that they seek to change. They concur with John

Maynard Keynes, who noted in a little-known work that the utilitarian ideas

> accorded with the practical notions of conservatives and of lawyers. They furnished a satisfactory intellectual foundation to the rights of property and to the liberty of the individual in possession to do what he liked with himself and with his own. This was one of the contributions of the eighteenth century to the air we still breathe.[25]

The filter works, from the radical perspective, in favor of those who seek control through technology and bureaucratic institutions. Moreover, it suppresses the class structure of capitalist society and rules out the understanding of conflictual relationships.

Philosophically minded critics, for their part, have trouble with the highly problematic utilitarian philosophy and with the misleading dualities implied by the neo-classical notion of rationality. Their reaction points to another ironic twist in neo-classical discourse: the will to find certainty in objective reason results in the relinquishing of the extensive terrain of values, ethics, and preferences to subjective and nonrational factors.

More generally, critics may object to the style of argument that the robot analogy entails. Many are uncomfortable with the use of mathematical symbols, and there is no definitive reason why a conversation on economic issues should require the rigor of mathematics. Moreover, a critic could point out that a predilection for mathematical models filters out factors not easily formalized and quantified, factors that may nevertheless be significant. We may recall the economist's reluctance to entertain the anthropologist's proposal of considering attitude shifts or changes in cultural perceptions.

All critics of neo-classical discourse have in common the desire to speak in different terms, using different analogies, on economic issues. The Austrians want to emphasize the creative individual; Schumacher speaks of the cooperative individual and searches for ways to talk about the quality of economic life; radicals feature social beings, connected through class relationships, and seek analogies that shift the focus from economic exchange to the workplace. Each of these ways of talking represents an alternative network, distinctively different from that of neo-classical economics.

"So What?"

Whatever else the perception of the metaphorical quality of economic discourse does, it certainly confronts us with the difficulties and confusion of the discursive process. How do I respond to someone who does not find my building analogy appropriate, because it ignores the fact that economists have the disadvantage of having to climb two flights of stairs? I might call attention to the existence of an elevator in the building, but once the discussion takes this direction, the metaphor goes off the track. Such discussions exemplify the exasperating process of persuasion.

This same process takes place in discussions of metaphors in neo-classical discourse. As a matter of fact, most criticism of the neo-classical rationality assumption is a criticism of what the metaphor does. We recognize Kuhn's notion of incommensurability in the problems of communication between neo-classical economists and their critics. The interactions so far have not been fruitful. Neo-classical economists do not see what the fuss is about and maintain that rationality is only a technique, and a very successful one at that. Their critics keep arguing that the assumption does not signify much or, more important, has a meaning they cannot accept.

Neo-classical economists have the advantage of "cultural hegemony" in the economic tribe and consequently can exert considerable social and institutional pressure to bring about in their students the attitude shift required for acceptance of neo-classical metaphors. Admittedly, the Rational Economic Man strikes a responsive chord among certain groups, especially in American society: I have always been surprised by the facility with which my American students accept the image of self-interested and greedy individuals, in contrast to European students' revolts against such an image. But most students have great difficulties with the form, the mathematics, in which the assumption is articulated.

Neo-classical economists protect their hegemony by placing themselves on the top floor of the social science building: they claim scientific status for their theories, display confidence by pointing out their past successes and promising developments of their analogies, and ignore alternative discussions. Criticisms of their arguments have as much impact as rain on a duck's back.

This essay constitutes an attempt to "see through" the way in which economists argue. My intentions go beyond those of McCloskey. We agree that those who desire to reflect on economic discourse might change their choice of literature: instead of reading Carl Hempel, Karl Popper, and Imre Lakatos, as economic methodologists tend to do, they might turn for illumination to the works of Richard Rorty, Kenneth Burke, Wayne Booth, and the like. This reading could make economists more modest in their pretensions concerning economics as a discipline and more uncomfortable with economics as an intellectual discourse.

An examination of the rhetorical dimensions of economic discourse illuminates not only the attractions of the neo-classical way of speaking, but also the reasons for discomfort, if not outright frustration, with it. The economic metaphors produce a perspective on our world that can be unacceptable to economic actors. Consequently, students are not being silly when they doubt the meaningfulness of neo-classical economics. Business people and workers are unfairly ruled out of order when they say that they cannot recognize themselves in the economic models of their behavior. Other social scientists have reasons to resist economic imperialism and to cherish their sociological and historical methods, even though these methods may violate the rules of mathematical language games. The point is to turn discussions on economic subjects into interesting exchanges: conversations that are meaningful. Talk based on the pretense that everyone is rational may simply not be that interesting.

NOTES

I wish to thank Michael Grimaud, Suzanne Jackson, and Laura Nader for comments on an earlier draft of this paper.

1. See, e.g., Mark Blaug, *The Methodology of Economics* (Cambridge: Cambridge University Press, 1980); Lawrence A. Boland, *The Foundations of Economic Method* (London: George Allen & Unwin, 1982); Bruce Caldwell, *Beyond Positivism: Economic Methodology in the Twentieth Century* (London: George Allen & Unwin, 1982).

2. Richard Rorty, *Philosophy and the Mirror of Nature* (Princeton: Princeton University Press, 1979).

3. Donald McCloskey, "The Rhetoric of Economics," *Journal of Economic Literature* 21 (1983): 481–517.

4. Clifford Geertz, *Local Knowledge* (New York: Basic Books, 1983).

5. Ibid., p. 155.

6. Ibid.

7. Arjo Klamer, *Conversations with Economists* (Totowa, N.J.: Rowman, 1983), pp. 151–52.

8. Hal Varian, *Microeconomic Analysis*, 2d ed. (New York: W. W. Norton, 1978), p. 1.

9. Ibid.

10. Gary S. Becker, Elizabeth M. Landes, and Robert T. Michael, "An Economic Analysis of Marital Instability," *Journal of Political Economy* 85 (1977): 1143.

11. Milton Friedman, *Essays in Positive Economics* (Chicago: University of Chicago Press, 1953).

12. This exchange is a stylized representation of an actual exchange between a group of economists and Laura Nader, an anthropologist.

13. See, for example, Harold K. Schneider, *Economic Man* (New York: Free Press, 1974).

14. Klamer, *Conversations*, p. 190.

15. Friedman, *Essays*, p. 14.

16. Alfred Schutz, quoted in Fritz Machlup, *Methodology of Economics and Other Social Sciences* (New York: Academic Press, 1978), p. 153.

17. Ludwig Wittgenstein, *Philosophical Investigations*, section 154, trans. G. E. M. Anscombe, 3d ed. (New York: Macmillan, 1973), p. 61.

18. *The English Works of Thomas Hobbes*, ed. Sir William Molesworth (London: John Bonn, 1966), I: 67.

19. Adam Smith, *The Wealth of Nations*, ed. R. H. Campbell, A. S. Skinner, and W. B. Todd (Oxford: Clarendon Press, 1976), pp. 26–27.

20. Milton Friedman, *Capitalism and Freedom* (Chicago: University of Chicago Press, 1962).

21. Henri Bergson, *The Creative Mind* (New York: Wisdom Library, 1946).

22. Aristotle, *Poetic*, xx, 5–10, 1457b.)

23. Colin Turbayne, *The Myth of Metaphor* (New Haven: Yale University Press, 1962), p. 13.

24. Max Black, *Models and Metaphors* (Ithaca: Cornell University Press, 1962).

25. John Maynard Keynes, *Laissez-faire and Communism* (New York: New Republic, Inc., 1926), p. 7.

11 REASON AS RHETORICAL

ON RELATIONS AMONG

EPISTEMOLOGY, DISCOURSE,

AND PRACTICE

RICHARD HARVEY BROWN

In some times and places persons become aware of their own reasoning activity and so are able to study the workings of reason as an autonomous process. In such studies, called epistemology, three basic views have appeared in the West.[1] The dominant modern view sees reason essentially as calculation, as in Bacon, Descartes, Hobbes, or Karl Popper: "When a man *reasoneth*, he does nothing else but conceive a sum total, from *addition* of parcels; or conceive a remainder, from subtraction of one sum from another. . . . reason, in this sense, is nothing but *reckoning*, that is, adding and subtracting."[2] A second view sees reason as interpretation of natural laws and their application to specific instances and actions. Aquinas, Locke, Kant, and Leo Strauss stand in this tradition. As Kant said, "Everything in nature works according *to the conception* of laws, that is, according to principle. . . . The deduction of actions from principles requires *reason*."[3] In the third perspective, as in the work of Plato, Hegel, Alfred North Whitehead, or Jürgen Habermas, reason is a transcendental creativity, an agency or activity that shapes or informs the world but stands above or outside it.

In this paper I try to subordinate the first and second concepts of reason and to decenter and reformulate the third. That is, following Diesing,[4] I wish to show how the interpretation of natural laws and calculation are but two possible forms of reasoning, each appropriate to different social orders. Moreover, I argue that the conception of reason

184

as creative can embrace the two other conceptions if this creativity is seen not as transcendental and idealist, but as a practical and social construction of meaning and order through discourse. In sum, I advance a conception of reason as rhetorical.

Viewing reason as rhetorical has two advantages. First, as a heuristic, it facilitates the study of social and political organization as a human product. When one sees reason purely as mathematical, technical, or economic calculation (the first perspective), one tends to conceive of human reason as an attribute purely of individuals, either the system-designer herself, or the persons who seek to act morally or to optimize utiles within a pregiven set of norms or scarcities. Conversely, when one views reason purely in terms of natural law and freedom (the second perspective), one tends to reify social systems into cybernetic processes or transcendental principles. In contrast to both these views, the conception of reason as a creative intersubjective practice tends to overcome the dualism of subject versus object, and to encourage an understanding of both society and individuals as emergent from social interactions.

A second advantage of the conception of reason as social creativity is that it invites an appreciation of alternative types of rationality, each with its own social form and *telos*. Such an appreciation includes a reflective awareness of the interests presupposed in one's own reasoning, as well as in that of others. This implies, in turn, the concomitant virtues of tolerance for the limitations in other people's ways of thought, as well as responsibility for the consequences of one's own cognitive choices. In sum, this conception of reason is both humanistic and critical even while affirming the relative validity of science within its proper domain.

Vico: Reason as Poetic

The last great spokesman for the view that knowledge emerges from civic discourse was Vico, who complained in the eighteenth century that prudential wisdom in politics was being replaced by the scientific rationalism of such scholars as Galileo, Descartes, and Hobbes:

> The imprudent *scholars*, who go directly from the universally true to the singular, rupture the interconnection of life. The *wise men*, however, who attain the eternal truth by the uneven and insecure paths of practice, make a detour, as it is not possible to attain this

by a direct road; and the thoughts which *these* conceive promise
to remain useful for a long time, at least insofar as nature
permits.[5]

Vico argued that this practical or prudential wisdom was created
through language. In Vico's time it was still possible to distinguish
three major views of language: nominalism, humanism, and logo-
mysticism. Nominalists followed Occam in separating language from
reality, and cognition from sensation. This division gave rise eventually to the two dominant aspects of positive theories of science and of
language: rationalism and empiricism in philosophy of science, and
syntax and semantics in linguistics. By contrast, the renaissance humanists stressed pragmatics and rhetoric, the practical wisdom of situated interactions and speech. By grounding knowledge in the
prudence and common sense of speech, however, the humanists were
vulnerable to criticisms based on theoretical knowledge of mathematics
and natural science. To resist the challenge of abstract analysis, humanists derived support from Cicero, who had asserted the natural priority
of the "art of discovery" *(ratio inveniendi),* rooted in everyday knowledge, over the procedure of logical-empirical demonstration *(ratio iudi-
candi).* Moreover, the Renaissance rhetoricans also drank from the
Platonic and biblical springs of logo-mysticism. Given the mystical
powers of the word, language was seen neither as a neutral tool nor as
casual usage, but instead as the medium of a transcendental act of communication. "Conceived as *kerygma* or disclosure of meaning, language
participated in the ongoing and unfinished creation of the world. The
alliance between humanism and logos-speculation reached its climactic
expression in Vico's conception of a transcendental or universal 'philology,' a theory of the human authorship of the world through
language."[6]

Vico argued that ordinary language provides the pretheoretical basis
and forms that are presupposed in every scientific analysis. But Vico's
insights into the practical situational and interactional aspects of language and knowledge were drowned in the rising tide of positivism.
The differences in emphasis between Descartes's rationalism and
Bacon's empiricism, or between Leibniz's *vérités de raison* and *vérités de
fait,* were overcome by the emerging concept of truth as a correlation of
logical rigor and the empirical content of statements. Instead of persuading the judgment of persons through argument, reason was seen
as a cognitive coercion through irrefutable logical and empirical proofs.
Seen from Vico's rhetorical perspective, however, human language is
not a mere conveyor or distorter of knowledge but its very medium and

constitution. Truth is unavoidably linguistic, since logical rigor is a product of syntactic correctness and empirical content is a function of semantic propriety.

In addition to syntactics and semantics, there is a third dimension of language—pragmatics. Pragmatics deals with language as performance, as a practical activity much like communal artisanry and crafts. For Vico, as for the ancients, all three of these dimensions of language—syntactics, semantics, and pragmatics—were part of rhetoric. Rhetoric seeks to establish reason as a moral political practice, a communal speech activity, a pragmatics, even while preserving the syntactics of logical analysis and the semantics of empirical interpretations.

Sociology of Knowledge and Sociology of Science

That rational discourse creates and is engendered by a social order is of course a principal finding and assumption of sociology of knowledge. Most sociologists, however, have adhered to the positivists' refusal of self-reflection, with the result that sociology of science (that is, of positive science) has been separated from sociology of knowledge. Sociologists of science study everything social about science except its claims to truth. Sociologists of knowledge treat all other forms of cognition as ideology. This segregation is perfectly consistent with the positivist distinction between the social processes by which knowledge might be gained and the logical or empirical validity of the results of such processes. In this view, discovery may be nonrational, psychological rather than cognitive. Verification (or falsification) of what is discovered, however, is seen as logical and objective, and as the feature that distinguishes science from ideology. In this spirit von Schelting criticized the "nonsense . . . that factual origins and social factors . . . in any way affect the value of ideas and conceptions thus originated, and especially the theoretic achievements."[7] Similarly, Speier said, "The validity of a judgment does not depend upon its genesis."[8]

This is an inadequate view of science. It disregards the constructed, rhetorical nature of data, evidence, and falsification themselves,[9] and it denies that the *canons* for judging the "value of ideas" or "theoretic achievements" are themselves dependent on social factors and interests. That is, Speier's (and other such) assertions assume a positivist epistemology that is itself inconsistent and that provides no basis for understanding the historical origins and social bases of the positivist conception of truth itself. Absolute judgments of truth claims are dubious even within a given canon of validity, since the interpretation and application of such canons are inevitably symbolic acts intended to persuade an audience according to some interest.[10] In addition, such canons themselves exist in social and historical contexts. Canons of validity, and epistemologies generally, are legitimations of belief. As such, they are rhetorical in nature. Logical criteria of validity are not unitary. There are numerous forms of thought (e.g., teleology, determinism), and numerous criteria of adequacy (e.g., cogency, repeatability), the use and acceptability of which are highly variable in different times and places. In sum, the formulation, acceptance, and rejection of the criteria of truth themselves are open to cultural influence and therefore sociological investigation. In segregating sociology of knowledge from sociology of science, however, positivists have declared that whatever validity depends upon, it cannot be examined as rhetorical.[11] Instead of investigating the genesis and legitimation of scientific beliefs empirically and sociologically, therefore, most researchers have either reduced these questions to ones of personal psychology or vaporized them into universal rules and logic.

The Historicity of Reason

The relative, rhetorical, socially constructed character of reason is highlighted when different forms of rationality are examined in comparative and historical perspective. The leisured civic existence of the dominant class in Greece, for example, accounts in part for their use of social-aesthetic criteria of truth. For these elites *epistēmē* was apodictic knowledge gained through aesthetic dialogal reflection on the regularities of nature. Such knowledge was not thought possible for practical political affairs, since the latter do not show the consistencies or regularities of occurrence that are the precondition for scientific investigation (Aristotle, *Physics,* II:viii; *Metaphysics,* XI:viii). Instead, the cognitive capacity of political thought is *phronēsis,* or in Cicero *prudentia,* a prudent judgment of particular cases. The classical conception of the *polis* is consistent with this view of political reason as prudence. The political community was an end in itself, the realization of human nature as that of a *zōon politikon.* Similarly, politics was meant to cultivate character in the struggle for the good life. Politics thus was an extension of ethics and pedagogy and, unlike modern positive rationality, had nothing to do with management or technique.

By contrast, the theocratic epistemology of the medieval period was influenced by, and helped to maintain, the hierarchically centralized position of the clerical elite, with its transnational political and intellectual power.[12] The high development of moral and theological reasoning was generated by and expressed in a society that conceived of itself as a divine and moral order. Prudential judgment still was seen as the proper form of political reason, but the classical focus on civic liberty and justice shifted to civic order and peace. In the Greek *polis* order ideally was realized through the direction of law and administration by citizens. For Thomas Aquinas, however, the proper order *(ordo)* is no longer that of the freedom of citizens, but that of *pax*, of tranquility and peace. As the scope of government expanded, an interest in its quality diminished. The *ordo civitatis* now included labor, the family, and other domains that for Greeks had been outside the sphere of politics. Simultaneously, the emphasis shifted from self-direction by citizens to the power of the state, from *polis* to police.[13]

These concepts of reason and politics continued in various forms until the early modern period, when, through the work of Machiavelli, Hobbes, and others, there began to emerge a science *of* politics.[14] In this new science, technical requirements of survival were divorced from moral obligations in politics. Reason became value-neutral and instrumental. As Machiavelli put it, "The sole aim of the Prince must be to secure his life and his power. All means which he employs toward this end will be justified. . . . A Prince [is] often forced, in order to preserve his Princedom, to act in opposition to god, faith, charity, humanity, and religion."[15] Thomas More, substituting "everyone" for Machiavelli's "Prince," wrote that "everyone knows that however prosperous the republic may be, he will starve of hunger if he does not make some private provision for himself. And so he is forced to believe that he ought to take account of himself rather than the people, that is, others."[16] With a similar focus on survival, Hobbes used Galilean mechanics and Cartesian logic to argue that absolute state power is the only barrier against a life that is nasty, brutish, and short. Seeing citizens' freedoms solely in terms of the monarch's supremacy, Hobbes identified freedom with the private individual, saw reason as instrumental calculation, and reconstituted the public sphere as that of the total power of the state.

Luther, and later Kant, accepted these terms of discourse by clearly segregating the inward freedom and rationality of the individual from the rational administrative legality that governed his external conduct. The state was no longer seen as the arena for the public pursuit of virtue. Mechanism and determinism replaced organism and teleology;

Richard Harvey Brown

scientific technical rationality was harnessed to serve the amoral *raison d'état;* and values, or the natural ends of man, were banished from rational public discourse.

This conception of reason and its relation to politics continues today. In modern capitalist as well as communist states, the calculated rationality of "survival" dominates in practice as well as in theories of such rational practice. In contemporary positivist approaches to planning and governance, for example, scientific calculation is thought to be the only possible form of applied reason. Any method of societal direction that exceeds available scientific knowledge, as Karl Popper said, "simply does not exist: it is impossible," because it violates the principles of scientific method.[17]

The application of science to society takes the form of technical-economic rationality.[18] Most theorists of social planning agree with Popper in assuming that technical-economic rationality is the whole of applied rational thought, and so they exclude nontechnical or non-economic processes as unreason. Ludwig von Mises, for example, asserted, "The economic principle is the fundamental principle of all rational action, and not just a particular feature of a certain kind of rational action. . . . All rational action is therefore an act of economizing."[19]

This is a radically modern formulation. From ancient Greece to the Renaissance, "scientific theory" was thought to concern universal or at least highly regular phenomena and so could not be "applied" to the vagaries of practical affairs. Instead, "applied reason" was seen as prudential rather than instrumental, a process of reflection on the "good life" and an interpretation of possible actions in light of this ideal.

This is to say that economizing is appropriate only for a given range of problems, chiefly those involving scarcities between comparable utiles. Such problems are properly called "economic." What is more interesting for an analysis of reason as rhetorical, however, is the process by which circumstances come to be represented as "economic problems" in the first place. One of the preconditions for economizing is that different ends are seen as comparable alternatives. The universalization of economizing therefore requires in practice the elimination of cultural barriers to the comparability of ends. An American woman, for example, may experience a choice between sending her parents to a nursing home or keeping them with her. In such a choice, some cost-benefit calculation certainly would play a role. For a Hindu woman, however, there are cultural barriers to the occurrence of a parallel situation, and if one somehow did arise, it would not be experienced as a matter of choice, much less an economic choice. Similarly, it is not

culturally permitted for an American male to calculate the value of sexual pleasure with his wife in comparison with his pleasure in pigs or
other gifts, but such an economic calculation is possible for a
Trobriander. These cultural limits are not experienced *as* cultural by
members, of course, but are apprehended as absolute canons of decency, unquestionable duties, and the like.

Such cultural definitions and practices limit the application of instrumental rationality; yet the universalization of economizing presupposes an abolition of such boundaries. This is made clear by Swift's
economic solution to the problem of famine and overpopulation: eat
the babies. Positive reason cannot explain why this is not an adequate
solution, since it can only calculate the efficiency of means toward comparable ends, not assess the rationality of the ends themselves or the
cultural acceptability of the means. Jeremy Bentham, writing with neither the irony of the eighteenth century nor the cybernetic mystifica-
tion of the twentieth, expressed matter-of-factly the attitude satirized
by Swift. "Money," said Bentham, "is . . . the measure of . . . pleasure.
It is the same between pain and pain; as also between pain and pleasure. . . . If we would understand one another, we must make use of
some common measure. The only common measure [that] the nature
of things affords is money. . . . Those who are not satisfied with the
accuracy of this instrument must find out some other that shall be more
accurate, or bid adieu to politics and morals."[20]

Of course it was Bentham himself who sought to say goodbye to
morals and politics by reducing them to economic comparability and
commodity exchange. In the century since he wrote, this philosophic
vision has been realized in a world in which virtually all things, including people, can be used as means and subjected to calculations of efficiency. This is a world of commodities. Commodities are not things as
such, but things understood in their comparable aspect, in terms of
their value as means for getting something else—as items for exchange
rather than for use. Commodities therefore presuppose a cash market,
or some functional equivalent thereof, since without it goods would remain incomparable, like apples and oranges with no *price* to express
their exchange value. Without commodity consciousness and a market
mechanism, there is no "rational" or "objective" basis for comparing
and choosing.

Economizing not only assumes *comparability of ends;* it also presupposes *commonality of means.* That is, it requires that the use of particular
means be culturally permitted for a plurality of ends. Work rules imposed by unions in factories often are "irrational" in just this sense,
since they impose limits on the use of the means (human labor) for al-

ternative ends. For example, if hod-carriers are not permitted to lay bricks or bricklayers not permitted to hang drywall, this will likely inhibit the most economical use of manpower through the most efficient assignment of tasks.[21]

Since commodities are neutral, the more that labor or anything else is turned into a commodity, the more it can be used purely as a means. The definition of things as commodities increases with the development of a market economy, and with this more and more "means" become available to people in their daily lives. Actions formerly taken on the basis of tradition or as though by instinct become "allocation decisions" in which means are allocated to alternative ends. Hence people come to think of decisions in terms of means and ends; they come to take as common sense what for Weber was only a heuristic model: that all practical rationality is a calculation of means and ends.[22]

This conception of applied rationality is not only rhetorical but also ideological. Any form of applied rationality (that is, decision making) can be thought appropriate only when conditions obtain that present the sorts of problems that this type of decision procedure can successfully address. By treating economizing as the *only* form of applied rationality, most modern theories of decision making presuppose as natural and universal the historically specific preconditions for its own success. By positing the historical and contingent as eternal and absolute, positivistic rationality assumes, but does not account for, the cultural division of means from ends, the definition of things as commodities, and the social world of markets, all of which are required for technical-economic calculus. Such theories of reason thereby deny the legitimacy of other forms of thought. They function as ideologies that justify the cash nexus, commodity consciousness, and instrumental calculation as natural, normal, inevitable, or just.

Garfinkel: Reason as Discursive Practice

In addition to comparative historical analyses, another step toward a sociology of reason as rhetorical has been taken by ethnomethodologists such as Harold Garfinkel and Aaron Cicourel, who have revealed what might be called the nonrational nature of rational conduct. By looking beyond the question-begging assumptions of functionalists (and beneath the analytic heuristics of Weberians), ethnomethodologists have shown that reason itself is composed of what ordinary folk would call nonrational activities. By unmasking rationality as itself a social, rhetorical construction, Garfinkel and others demystify the positivist mystique.

In theoretical as well as detailed observational studies, ethnomethodologists have demonstrated how social actors employ rationality retrospectively to account for actions that, from a rationalistic point of view, were chaotic and stumbling when performed. For example, in "Some Rules of Correct Decision That Jurors Respect,"[23] Garfinkel describes in detail the talk, bargaining, and muddling that go on in jury discussions, and how rules, rather than guiding this process, emerge from it. At first the jurors do not quite know what they are doing, but as their sentiments take shape through the contesting of various viewpoints, they begin to invoke rules of evidence and rationality to justify positions they have taken or are in the process of forming. The rational justification of their decisions crystallizes at about the time the decisions do, or in many cases even afterward, when a summary is being prepared for presentation to the court. Thus Garfinkel shows us that rationality does not instruct us as to what action to take, nor is it a property inherent in conduct or in the social system as such. Instead, rationality emerges in discursive interaction and then is used retrospectively to legitimize what has already taken place or is being enacted.

Ironically, our interpretation of Garfinkel's studies reveals their affinity with the neo-Marxist critique of instrumental reason. Max Horkheimer and Theodor Adorno, to name but two such theorists, have argued that means-ends rationality has provided an instrument as well as a rationale for technocratic domination.[24] For example, just as rationality can provide a rhetoric for legitimizing past conduct (as in Garfinkel's microsociology), so it can be employed as a *prospective* rhetoric for closing off unwanted alternatives and advancing one's own agenda. Moreover, by focusing discourse on the efficiency of alternative means, instrumental reason displaces attention from the appropriateness of pregiven ends and the class interests that they serve.

A principal use of rationality as a prospective rhetoric is the planning done by firms, agencies, and nations. The organizational plan, for example, can be seen not as a set of instructions for what actually will take place, but rather as a rhetorical intervention to build constituency, to define the limits of "responsible opinion," and in general to impose the planners' or managers' definition of reality upon discourse and conduct within and around the organization. That is, just as statements made by jurors must be susceptible to rationalization in terms of the emergent rules of evidence, so public talk about what goes on within

Richard Harvey Brown

organizations must be couched in terms of how it rationally serves (the directorate's statement of) the organization's nature, purpose, and goals.

This rhetorical function of rationality appears inevitable. For example, even if the organizational plan is taken seriously as a set of instructions for future action, it is readily reinterpretable as a vocabulary for covering the difficulties that will unfold as attempts are made to follow it. That is, in actual practice the plan of action produces problems, the responses to which are reconceptualized as the "solution" or achievement of the organization's "goals." According to Garfinkel, this upside-down process is in fact what rationality is all about. A good example of this is the work of coroners, who must classify bodies as dead by "accident," "criminal intent," "suicide," or "natural causes." According to coroners' instructions, the number of definitions they may use for dead bodies is limited. However, corpses do not come already labeled. The coroners' instructions are thus in effect instructions on how to generate a set of difficulties in naming, the solution of which will constitute the production of the instruction's goals. Coroners, in doing their duty, find convenient but nonrational mechanisms for solving the problem of fitting recalcitrant cadavers into the limited categories of an organizational agenda. Again, such "postmortem" efforts to restate a chaotic process in terms of some formal structure are the stuff of which rational action is constituted.[25]

Thus rationality, rather than being a guiding rule of individual or social life, turns out to be an achievement—a symbolic product that is constructed through speech and actions that in themselves are nonrational. We could even say that this dichotomy between rationality and nonrationality is itself ultimately unfounded, emerging mainly from the legitimacy in our culture of "rational," and the illegitimacy of "nonrational," conduct. Precisely because this particular hierarchy of legitimacy prevails in the modern West, Westerners tend to legitimize their activities by accounting for them in terms of rationalistic vocabularies of motive. At the level of micro processes, however, the dichotomy between rational and nonrational conduct breaks down completely, suggesting that these forms of activity have the same basic components.

Such a radical critique also suggests a means of radically reformulating our sociological understanding of reason. Rather than seeing reason solely as a conscious calculus of individuals or an unconscious casuistry of systems, we may now focus on persons and groups as engaged in continuing processes of constructing "rationality."

Conclusion

All these observations support a view of reason as a civic rhetorical practice, for all of them illuminate the ongoing creativity of members within a social-linguistic system. Reason exists through discourse. For Marxists as well as ethnomethodologists, reason is a practical human activity, a dialectic of form and performance. Social structures canalize rational thought; reasoning creates and recreates social structures. Economic reasoning issues into a market system; legal reasoning engenders a world of law; moral discourse creates a moral order. The reverse, of course, is also true. Reason is the child of the order it creates.[26] It is not a matter of transcendent reason working upon the world, but of persons creating ordered worlds through rational processes, worlds that embody reason in their structured properties and thus serve as guides and contexts for further creative human reason. For example, modern economies are orders that embody multifarious decisions of marginal utility, a form of reasoning that is itself possible because markets exist that permit the comparability of various raw materials and end products. Similarly, a legal order embodies the multifarious decisions of judges past, thereby providing algorithms of tradition as well as a context of creativity for judges present. A legal order can develop only through the continuous, historical application of jurisprudential reasoning to cases. Jurisprudence is a public practice, a collective civic reasoning about the law.[27] As Garfinkel noted, participants in particular cases or transactions may focus only on validating a privilege or making a deal. But the rules of evidence or calculations of efficiency that they invoke to justify their claims are those of the legal or commercial orders, just as these orders exist in and are continually reconstituted through such invocations and usages.

In sum, the conception of reason as rhetorical, as social-linguistic creativity, abolishes absolute divisions between means and ends, between subjectivity and objectivity, between social planning and personal praxis. Instead, abstract individual reasoning and concrete social order are *both* seen as emergent from practical intersubjective symbolic action, two moments in the same dialectic, each engendering the other.

NOTES

1. Such classifications are useful when heuristic rather than conclusionary. This one is intended to distinguish the special properties of a rhetorical view

Richard Harvey Brown

of reason. This is close to what Gonzalo Munevar calls the "performance" theory of knowledge (*Radical Knowledge: A Philosophical Inquiry Into the Nature and Limits of Science* [Indianapolis: Hackett, 1981]), and what Imre Lakatos terms a "revolutionary activist" theory of knowledge ("Falsification and the Methodology of Scientific Research Programmes," in Imre Lakatos and Alan Musgrave, eds., *Criticism and the Growth of Knowledge* [New York and London: Cambridge University Press, 1970]).

2. Thomas Hobbes, *The Leviathan* (New York: Random House, 1939), p. 143.

3. Immanuel Kant, *Fundamental Principles of the Metaphysic of Morals*, trans. Thomas K. Abbott (Chicago: Regnery, 1949), p. 30.

4. Paul Diesing, *Reason in Society: Five Types of Decisions and Their Social Conditions* (Westport, Conn.: Greenwood Press, 1962); *Science and Ideology in the Policy Sciences* (New York: Aldine, 1982).

5. Giambattista Vico, *On the Study Methods of Our Time*, trans. Elio Gianturco (Indianapolis: Bobbs-Merrill, 1965), p. 34.

6. Fred Dallmayr, *Beyond Dogma and Despair: Toward a Critical Phenomenology of Politics* (Notre Dame, Ind.: University of Notre Dame Press, 1981), p. 153; see Karl-Otto Apel, "Die Idee der Sprache in der Tradition des Humanismus von Dante bis Vico," *Archiv für Begriffsgeschichte*, 8 (1963): 20, 29, 83, 141.

7. Alexander von Schelting, review of Karl Mannheim, *Ideologie und Utopie*, *American Sociological Review* 1 (1936): 674.

8. Hans Speier, review of Ernst Grünwald, *Das Problem einer Soziologie des Wissens*, *American Sociological Review* 1 (1936): 682; see Robert K. Merton, "The Sociology of Knowledge," in *Social Theory and Social Structure* (New York: Free Press, 1957), p. 456–88.

9. See Richard Harvey Brown, *A Poetic for Sociology: Towards a Logic of Discovery for the Human Sciences* (London and New York: Cambridge University Press, 1977); Kenneth Burke, *Permanence and Change: An Anatomy of Purpose* (Berkeley: University of California Press, 1984); Paul Feyerabend, *Against Method: Outline of an Anarchistic Theory of Knowledge* (London: Verso, 1978); Ernest Gellner, *Legitimation of Belief* (London: Cambridge University Press, 1974).

10. Bruno Latour and Steve Woolgar, *Laboratory Life: The Social Construction of Scientific Facts* (Beverly Hills: Sage, 1979); Hilary Rose and Steven Rose, eds., *Ideology of/in the Natural Sciences* (Cambridge, Mass.: Schenkman, 1979).

11. C. Wright Mills, *Power, Politics, and People* (London and New York: Oxford University Press, 1963), pp. 457–58.

12. Ibid., p. 455.

13. Jürgen Habermas, *Theory and Practice* (Boston: Beacon Press, 1974).

14. Alasdair MacIntyre, *After Utopia* (Notre Dame: Ind.: University of Notre Dame Press, 1981); Eric Voegelin, *The New Science of Politics: An Introduction* (Chicago: University of Chicago Press, 1952).

15. Niccolò Machiavelli, *The Prince*, trans. Hill Thompson (New York: Limited Editions Club, 1954), p. 130.

16. Thomas More, *Utopia*, trans. Peter K. Marshall (New York: Washington Square, 1965), p. 124.

17. Karl Popper, *Conjectures and Refutations* (London: Routledge & Kegan Paul, 1969), p. 69.

18. Technical rationality means the efficient achievement of a single goal. It is thus a subset of *economic* rationality, which is the maximum achievement of a plurality of goals. In technical rationality the end is given and the means may be varied. In economic rationality there may be variance or "trade-offs" between both the ends and the means.

19. Ludwig von Mises, *Epistemological Problems of Economics* (Princeton: Van Nostrand, 1960), p. 148.

20. Quoted in W. C. Mitchell, "Bentham's Felicific Calculus," *Political Science Quarterly* 33 (1918): 161.

21. The same may be said of the "irrational" requirements for credentials and licensing by guilds such as those of lawyers and morticians. The sociology of professions in general can be understood as an unmasking of economistic rationality as a rhetoric intended to legitimate professional privilege. Randall Collins's *The Credential Society* (New York: Academic Press, 1979) is an example of such ironic translation of economist rhetorics of motives back into political ones.

22. Diesing, *Reason in Society*, p. 36; Talcott Parsons, *The Structure of Social Action* (New York: McGraw-Hill, 1937), p. xiii.

23. Harold Garfinkel, *Studies in Ethnomethodology* (Englewood Cliffs, N.J.: Prentice-Hall, 1967), pp. 104–55.

24. Max Horkheimer, *The Eclipse of Reason* (New York: Seabury Press, 1974); Max Horkheimer, "Traditional and Critical Theory," in *Critical Theory: Selected Essays*, trans. Matthew J. O'Connell (New York: Herder and Herder, 1972), pp. 188–243.

25. Jack D. Douglas, *The Social Meaning of Suicide* (Princeton: Princeton University Press, 1967), pp. 186–88.

26. Burke, *Permanence and Change;* Diesing, *Reason in Society*, p. 243.

27. Diesing, *Reason in Society*.

12 STORIES OF SCIENCE

AND POLITICS

SOME RHETORICS OF

POLITICAL RESEARCH

JOHN S. NELSON

How would political science change were it to take rhetoric seriously? What would happen to its conception and practice of science? What would change about its conception and study of politics? Implicit in these questions, of course, is a thesis: that political science does not now take rhetoric seriously. Here I want to defend this thesis and explore a collective answer to these questions.

Along the way, I propose to spin some stories of science and politics, especially in the recent past. Individually, most of these tales are too familiar to political scientists, at least, to need extensive evidence. Moreover, the detail possible in a single essay could not persuade doubters from any discipline of the basic veracity of the particular stories told here. We do not, accordingly, devote much effort to supporting the stories. We concentrate instead on eliciting their collective implications. Related analytically and argumentatively, as we tell them here, these stories suggest a common moral: *rhetoric is crucial for any good conception, conduct, and content of political science*. To say why, the tales together imply, is to tell what rhetoric of inquiry can do for political science—and the other way around. I begin with the perplexing story of science as politics in the discipline of political science.

Science as Politics

It is often observed—and not only by scholars—that academic politics must be among the most fierce, complex, and inclusive. ("Petty" is another favorite adjective in this context, but here I hope to show how it is not entirely apt.) Is there anywhere a scholar of any kind—let alone a political scientist—who can attend to the least part of everyday affairs in the academy without discerning that politics is important in scholarship? Many novels have been written on the subject. (It is even rumored that one or two of the authors have been political scientists.) And I have heard on several campuses the folkloric opinion that political scientists rise in academic administration and prosper in institutional influence more than their modest numbers would explain, precisely because the enterprise of academics is so thoroughly political.

I do not, however, have in mind only the politics of administration and self-interest. Instead, I intend all the many kinds of politics that together permeate the entire academy, but with special emphasis on the politics of ideas and inquiry. How can political scientists, in particular, deal daily in the business of fields, subfields, conferences, disciplines, editors, panels, review boards, and professional associations without witnessing manifold phenomena of politics—in virtually every sense of the word? And this is before we even get around to life with departments, deans, universities, trustees, foundations, and the like. Nor should we forget that most early and enduring of political relationships in the academy—between teachers and students.

The evidence suggests that political scientists, like other scholars, do in fact notice large parts of academic politics, although their appreciation might slant unduly toward the kinds dominated by interest coalitions. The main evidence is that political scientists, like other scholars, do indeed practice various sorts of politics, in virtually every aspect of their academic activities, and often with a vengeance that shows their concerns to be truly serious. Another source of evidence is the cocktail conversation at professional meetings, where the major mode of talk addresses little else. ("Gossip" is my word, sometimes unjustly pejorative, for this peculiarly precious type of political intelligence about personal relationships.) A similar kind of data comes from the hallway, lounge, and luncheon dialogues among political scientists at home. And still another brand of evidence involves the practical counseling that professors give graduate students as part of their informal but crucial socialization to the discipline. On all these occasions and others,

John S. Nelson

the contents of professional lore, calculation, and even seemingly idle chatter testify persuasively to a recognition by political scientists that political science is a political enterprise.

The simple fact, though, is that political scientists seldom acknowledge academic politics in their research. The discipline predicates none of its scholarly structures and functions on a sophisticated appreciation of their politics. Neither does the discipline study the academy as an important domain of politics. So it should come as no surprise that the discipline fails to explore inquiry and epistemology as significant modes of politics. The discipline's ideals of inquiry concede no legitimate place to politics in the scholar's pursuit or defense of truth, save whatever denatured politics of democracy and authority might remain in vague images of a free marketplace of ideas somehow reconciled to hierarchies of expertise. Consistent with the partial realism peculiar to their discipline, political scientists assume that politics must be alien or even hostile to scientific truth.[1]

As a political scientist interested in the diverse politics of everyday life, I have long wondered why my colleagues disdain to study their central subject in some of its most accessible and familiar occurrences.[2] For related reasons, I have also pondered how my colleagues can feel comfortable acting on principles of human inquiry plainly inconsistent with so many of their discipline's conclusions about human action.[3] As a philosopher of inquiry, political and otherwise, I have been struck by the failure of epistemologists and other scholars to acknowledge the presence—if not the propriety—of politics in collective inquiries of every kind.[4] A few historians and sociologists of science follow a few political themes as minor parts of their work, but altogether even their attention to the politics of inquiry remains scattered and unsophisticated. Perhaps only that self-proclaimed anarchist of epistemology, Paul Feyerabend, has addressed the politics of research in any detail.[5] And with friends like that, one needs more friends—fast!

I can expose the tie that binds these perplexities through a single question: why does the discipline of political science display so little interest in the political institutions and processes of research, at least in political science? The short answer is: because of the discipline's conception of science. Yet I pose the first question less for its own sake than because it leads to a second: why should political scientists study the politics of inquiry? This time the answer is more complicated but still easy to summarize: because such study will improve our understandings of politics and of inquiry in ways that will enable us to improve our practices of both. But that prompts a third question: precisely how should we practice the politics of inquiry in order to enrich substantive research into all types and domains of politics?

As it happens, pursuing such a sequence of questions over the last decade has brought me to a possible answer to the third, key question. We should practice the politics of inquiry as a dimension of the rhetoric of inquiry. Stated so simply, of course, this answer can only provoke further questions. First, why emphasize rhetoric, which we seldom take seriously, especially in contexts of science? Second, even if scientists should respect rhetoric more, why tie it particularly to politics? And third, how can the special ties of rhetoric to politics and science enable rhetoric of inquiry to enhance substantive research throughout political science?

To answer these last three questions is to explain why political scientists should do rhetoric of inquiry as a regular part of their substantive research, and that is my main purpose here. To answer the latter questions is also to answer most of the former, however, so let me consider (1) the sources and consequences of the failure by most political scientists to take rhetoric seriously; (2) the ways rhetoric should figure in science; (3) the ways it should configure political science; and (4) the advantages to political scientists of the resulting rhetoric of inquiry.

Why Not Rhetoric?

My second story is the sad tale of a gradual turn against rhetoric. Parts of the full story appear elsewhere in this volume, and I try to avoid repeating too much of it here. But unlike the other tellings, mine emphasizes relatively recent events; and it focuses, of course, on political science.

Ubiquity breeds undue familiarity, which gets things taken for granted. What renders neglect for the politics of inquiry so astonishing in one light thus makes it more comprehensible in another. Surely the main recent source of neglect, however, is the family of late-modern epistemologies that dominated the Anglo-American academy until the last quarter of the twentieth century. Such logic of inquiry, as I term it, left no room for politics in true science. It conceived science as a rigorously impersonal system of observation and inference not only governed but also legitimated by formal rules of procedure. It regarded the rules as dictated by a structure common to all situations of inquiry.[6] Thus philosophers could deduce the rules from universal properties of the human relationship to reality, or they could induce the rules from

John S. Nelson

successful practices of research. Either way, the abstracted essence of science as the rational and disinterested pursuit of truth contradicted the general view of politics as the partisan and often irrational pursuit of power. That many proponents of these contrasting conceptions of science and politics had reason to see science as the epitome of success and politics as the focus of failure put passion into their opposition.[7]

The received view of science, as some philosophers call it, influenced one after another of the political movements in political science that pledged to make the discipline more scientific.[8] Often under the banner of behavioralism, leaders of the discipline rededicated themselves to replace old methods (normative, selective, speculative) and objects (mentalities, ideologies, institutions) with new methods (empirical, systematic, deductive) and objects (behaviors, conditions, individuals). They invoked the received view of science because it promised to cumulate findings into predictive theories and nonpartisan expertise— that is, precisely because it promised to keep science free of politics. The behavioralists' terms for comprehending and conducting science departed somewhat from the received view, partly because the rhetorics of political movements cannot achieve axiomatic consistency and partly because the behavioralists needed to accomplish research as well as talk about it. Moreover, behavioralist practices of research often departed radically from behavioralist rhetoric, let alone the received view, partly because the movement grew as much from a new technology as from a new philosophy of research and again because the behavioralists actually did substantive research.[9] Even so, the general conception of science recited by behavioralists and such partial successors as rational-choice theorists emphasizes the maximum possible exclusion of politics from practices of research.

For the same reasons that the received view seeks to exclude politics from science, it tries also to denigrate or ignore rhetorics in research. By rhetorics, I mean less the hollow, decorative, or manipulative talk opposed by the received view (and its precursors as far back as Plato) than the substantive, expressive, and persuasive talk needed for communication among humans. The received view and its kin in political science attempt to pretend, while never beginning to show, that inquiry can be conducted exclusively in some neutral language of formal logic. (This is one reason to call it logic of inquiry.) Although major parts of that aspiration long ago collapsed, in epistemology as well as political science, its former advocates and their successors have been slow to acknowledge the implication that rhetoric must play a legitimate role in collective inquiry of any kind.[10]

In political science, residues of behavioralism augment these directly philosophical sources of resistance to taking rhetoric seriously. To conceive politics as the externally observable motions of individual bodies is to leave little room for rhetoric as persuasive communication. In a limited sense of research priorities, at least, the old dictum of action theory is right: causes chase out reasons. Rhetoric depends on notions of reason, action, decision, evaluation, and the like that seem inconsistent or superfluous for sciences of stimulus and response, behavioral conditioning, determination by causes of economy or biology, and so on. Such behavioral or causal sciences as these do not, of course, seem the least consistent with the senses of reason and decision crucial to logic of inquiry. This puts behavioralists in the embarrassing position of preaching (though not necessarily practicing?) a kind of science inconceivable by their epistemic convictions. They respond by ignoring both the inconsistencies and the obvious presence of rhetorics (and politics) in their research. Paying little attention to rhetorics in politics, they feel little pressure from the substance of their research to take rhetorics more seriously in matters of science.

The case for a more rhetorical (and political) epistemology begins with the manifest inadequacy of recent logic of inquiry. It suits the actual practice of political science no better than it accords with the realities of human action evident in practices of politics. Logic of political inquiry seldom extends beyond changing abstract principles of philosophy into very general rules for political inquiry. The focus falls on logical forms or issues of description, explanation, prediction, and testing, for logic of political inquiry has almost nothing to say about specific subjects of political research or particular problems in political science. It offers few implications for detailed methods of political inquiry because it borrows from a family of epistemologies too abstract to give daily guidance for substantive studies of politics. (Again, that is why behavioralism in political science cannot be reduced to logical positivisms and empiricisms in philosophy, notwithstanding the many ties between them.)

Part of the trouble is that logic of inquiry encourages seriously misleading conceptions of inquiry. But in practice, that matters much less than one might imagine. For the larger problem is that such epistemology stays too abstract to connect in any solid, reliable way with specific studies of politics. Thus logic of inquiry may have less chance to pervert political science than critics usually assume. Of late, in fact, most fields of the discipline have developed in virtual isolation from any avowed, substantive theory of inquiry. As a result, their research

John S. Nelson

designs, methods, and theories have suffered various—sometimes chronic—defects.[11]

By contrast, epistemology done as part of inquiry appreciates that apt principles of research do not necessarily (or usually) come before actual practices of research. Few useful principles of epistemology are so general that they span wide varieties of disciplines. Instead they come from specific programs of scholarship, through internal criticism and comparison with other projects. They are principles that express and direct the basic impulses, procedures, and perspectives of study. Lacking substantive theories of inquiry, recent political inquiry has lacked precisely these principles of study.[12]

The mistake of most logic of inquiry has been to strive for fundamental separation from the contexts of concrete inquiry. This leaves even the questions—not to mention the answers—of such logics largely beside the point of scientific researches in particular fields. In this sense, much logic of inquiry has become caught up in pseudoquestions. The few scientists who attend much to them have been badly misled about priorities and techniques. Like their philosophical colleagues, they founder on abstract problems that have no useful answers at the levels posed.[13]

Epistemologies should encourage and enable scholars to criticize their own moves in method and theory. This need not rule out all divisions of labor between substantive scholarship and philosophy of inquiry, but it should produce much greater interaction than is prompted by logic of inquiry. Epistemology must stay in intimate touch with the substance of particular inquiries, and scholarship must engage in epistemology pertinent to those inquiries.

Although logic of inquiry fails this test, so does most of the criticism thus far against it. Even self-proclaimed contextualists tend to stay as abstract as the logicians.[14] Forays into specific instances of research must be the minimum requirement; but if they remain mere examples for an otherwise abstracted epistemology, then the main need will go unmet. The challenge is to do epistemology as a continuing part of inquiry, and this cannot be accomplished by philosophizing from above the details. (A saving grace of the imperial style intrinsic to logic of inquiry is the vagueness of its dictates.) The needed reconstructions of research must be conducted from within particular programs of research. Would-be epistemologists must know the substantive specifics of research, almost as well as the researchers.

It is equally important to avoid the mirror mistake. Just as logic of inquiry seldom condescends to the specifics of theory, method, and evidence, so political science seldom rises to the self-criticism of epistemic reflection. Political scientists do criticize one another's research, to be sure, but the scrutiny within particular projects of inquiry seldom reaches the major and sometimes misguided commitments that generate those projects.[15] Nor do current criticisms benefit enough from careful comparisons among projects and fields of inquiry.[16] Political scientists scarcely have the language—let alone the information—for adequate criticism of their own researches. Finding little help in previous philosophies of inquiry, the average student of politics has learned to steer clear of such airy domains when trying to get on with everyday research.[17]

That course offers some advantages but still more disadvantages. One result in political science is the breakdown in communication between the social-scientific and humanistic wings of the discipline.[18] Another is the alienation of many kinds of political theory from political practice.[19] A third is the inability of political theories to comprehend and direct everyday research in several important parts of the discipline.[20] A fourth is the irrelevance to actual politics of the little epistemology that political scientists do perform.[21] And a fifth is the gap between theories of political inquiry and practices of political science— the problem at the center of this essay. None of these troubles stems solely from the paucity of immanent epistemology in political science, but each owes much to it. My tale of what to do about these troubles is the story of science as rhetoric. It features a brief account of the hero of this volume: rhetoric of (political) inquiry.

Science as Rhetoric

A better course by far is to make rhetoric of inquiry an ordinary part of political science. Rhetoric of inquiry concerns the interaction of communication and inquiry. It studies the reasoning of scholars in research communities—not to distill some single model of Reason, Logic, or Method, but to improve many styles of scholarship. It rejects the notion that a single and autonomous set of rules for inquiry can stand apart from actual practices. Working from within projects of research, it seeks to give them greater awareness of their assumptions and operations. Working across fields of inquiry, it tries to put them into better communication with one another. Inside and outside the academy, it endeavors to learn how reason is rhetorical and how recognition of this should alter inquiry.[22]

Rhetoric of inquiry intends to help scholars improve the rhetoric— and therefore the content, as well as the reception—of their research.

John S. Nelson

To do this, it must play down generalized methodologies and play up specific situations of scholarship. In the language of Stephen Toulmin, rhetoric of inquiry must resist supposedly universal rules of inference in order to make room for the warrants and backings of particular arguments.[23] Thus it takes into account the roles of various audiences for research: exploring how backings are shared, the extent to which warrants are accepted, and why. It appreciates the figurative and mythic dimensions of inquiry: examining how tropes are deployed, where stories are implicit, and to what effect. And it accommodates studies of the many shared but often unarticulated features of human communication in scholarship.[24]

Rhetoric studies the nature of communication in general. Traditionally, however, it does this through detailed study of the origins, media, messages, styles, results, and potential improvements in particular communications. Rhetoric of inquiry could be said to expand or refocus these concerns to include the interaction of communication with inquiry. By contrast with logic of inquiry, however, rhetoric of inquiry notes in detail how substantive inquiries depart from externally dictated norms, so that scholars legitimately invoke different reasons persuasive in different contexts. Accordingly, it studies academic reasoning by analyzing the rhetoric of actual arguments among scholars. The aim is to reveal the rhetorical structures of good argument, in order to show how standards for good reasoning operate. These structures include the use of linguistic conventions to designate meaning and significance, the creation and application of standards for good reasoning, the invocation of symbols and more explicit comparisons to other entities or contexts, the projection of audiences, the reliance on tropes, and other devices of rhetoric.

Early responses to work on rhetoric of inquiry suggest that three largely philosophical problems stand in the way of better appreciation and practice of rhetoric. Produced by modern epistemology, the first obstacle is the persistent inclination to oppose rhetoric and rationality. When this is done, rhetoric of inquiry provokes accusations of radical relativism, where any argument is no more and no less acceptable than any other because there remain no standards for distinguishing them.

Consequently the first philosophical task for rhetoricians of inquiry is to explain how rhetoric is reasonable and how reason is rhetorical. In general terms, this involves arguments that rhetoric legitimates good standards of persuasion and that (at best) logic of inquiry can do no better than rhetoric.[25] Yet these general arguments are not enough, and they require augmentation within particular disciplines. Perhaps the primary way to accomplish this in political science is to show that cases of good argumentation depart from the rules of rationality recognized by logic of inquiry but accord with the principles of persuasion promoted by rhetoric of inquiry. As long as political scientists still divide argumentation into three compartments for epistemological, theoretical, and practical issues, the rhetorical analysis ought to include cases of all three kinds.[26]

The second problem arises from some solutions to the first. The charge of relativism is that rhetoric lets anything go in argumentation. The charge of conventionalism is that rhetoric favors conservative arguments, simply because they accept the conventions of the status quo. The rhetorical critique of foundational and transcendental grounds of Rationality leaves all standards conventional. The fear is that the only effective standards would be the ones already established, so that inquiry informed by rhetoric would become unable to criticize and improve existing practices—whether of inquiry or politics.

A second philosophical task for the rhetorician, therefore, is to show that this accusation depends on a dichotomy between the conventional and the natural (rational, foundational, transcendental) that makes poor sense in general and especially in contexts of argumentation important for political scientists.[27] Or to put the challenge more positively, the rhetorician needs to show how sets of conventions usually contain—or can readily generate and defend—reasonable criteria for self-criticism.[28] If a particular audience is more impressed by the conservative force of hegemonic conventions, as were the many critics of behavioralism who alleged its intrinsic conservatism, then the rhetorician may rejoin that such occurrences of conservatism under logic of inquiry eliminate any comparative disadvantage of conventionalism claimed against rhetoric. For a more positive argument, the rhetorician may examine the instances noted earlier of self-criticism by political scientists. Flawed though they may be in other respects, such cases make categorical accusations of conservatism highly implausible.

The third problem is a recurrent disinclination to consider rhetoric as actually practiced. The result is that rhetoric *within* inquiry slides into clichés which can neither report nor improve the real conduct of research. Similarly, rhetoric *about* inquiry slips into ignorance of the subjects and decisions of research, encouraging empty or misleading methodologies.

Here there is no useful philosophical response beyond recognizing the difficulty as a call to practice rhetoric of inquiry—in these cases, presumably, within political science. Then the rhetorician can locate the slippage between clichés and actual conditions, adjusting arguments to the contexts at hand. From there, the rhetorician who still

John S. Nelson

needs to argue for rhetoric of inquiry as well as practice it can proceed
to detail how those contexts are constructed through rhetoric. In fact,
the single best strategy for answering all three objections is simply to
do rhetoric of inquiry as much and as well as possible, particularly in
political science.[29] The recognition that rhetoric is a necessary and valuable aspect of already legitimate inquiries should dispel the specters
of radical relativism and uncritical conservatism, while keeping rhetoric a part of research. Such demonstrations will establish how sound
inquiry occurs apart from—and even in defiance of—official logics and
methods that have lost touch with research or never established contact
in the first place.

Success in addressing these three problems should underscore the
advantage of rhetoric over logic in contributing to the substance of research in various disciplines. In this respect, the distinctive feature of
rhetoric is its reluctance to separate epistemic concerns from theoretical questions, categories, and methods. Likewise, it resists dividing
matters of theory from practical limits, tactics, and performances.
Rhetorical analysis can comprehend modern dichotomies between
theory and practice; but in treating them as particular rhetorics, it displays their considerable disadvantages in many circumstances. Rhetoric strives insistently to span subject and object, epistemology and
ontology, audience and action, academy and polity. It encourages a
kind of practice theory meant to keep inquiries aware of the contexts of
events without sacrificing the capacity to criticize their conventions.[30]

This feature of rhetoric accounts for its ability to become a species of
immanent but comparative epistemology. It stems from practical questions of inquiry, informs its answers with awareness of other practices,
but stays dedicated to pursuing practical questions. As epistemic, rhetoric remains insistently substantive. It arises within as well as about
particular researches, so that addressing issues in rhetoric of inquiry
becomes addressing issues in substantive research.[31]

Political scientists should note that this same feature identifies a special kinship of rhetoric with politics as the set of practices meant to comprehend and manage other practices.[32] Politics has been conceived this
way throughout most of the modern world. Even though this special
tie between rhetoric and politics holds for most of the cultures prominent in the studies of political scientists, the discipline attends to it only
erratically. Taking rhetoric seriously for the substance of political science would develop several promising projects to the point where major parts of the discipline could be said to conceive politics as rhetoric.
To suggest how, I offer a story of politics as rhetoric—one with many a
turn to the plot.

Politics as Rhetoric

Many cultures have made politics in some sense prominent enough to qualify for special responsibility in coordinating their other sets of practices. In the West, we usually credit the ancient Greeks and Romans with generating politics in this special sense.[33] This is worth noting because the same Greeks and Romans invented and developed rhetoric—specifically for their politics. The Greek sophists who initiated the discipline intended rhetoric as a systematic study of politics. The Roman rhetoricians who articulated the discipline resisted the antirhetorical teachings of Greek philosophers enough to articulate rhetoric as their science of conduct in civic affairs. For the most part, later rhetoricians augmented—rather than repudiated—the specifically political concerns of rhetoric.[34] As the first science of politics, accordingly, rhetoric was and continues to be a pointedly practical one.

The special tie between politics and rhetoric is evident in the admittedly partial but provocative definition of politics as rhetoric. One instance is David V. J. Bell's treatment of politics as talk:

> Politics is talk. An oversimplification, of course, but one that ultimately lies closer to the truth than definitions like [Harold Lasswell's] "who gets what, when, how." "Getting" can be an intensely private affair; talk (ordinarily) involves others. Not by accident does the term Parliament stem from the French *parler*, to speak. But politics is more than "a government of talk," because government itself is too restrictive. Much non- or even anti-governmental talk is political nonetheless. Is all talk political? Perhaps. To the extent that talk *affects* others (and most talk does), it has by definition assumed political overtones. For politics must be concerned in the widest sense with how people affect each other. A suitable reformulation might be, *politics: who talks to whom, when, how.*[35]

As Bell argues, talk is seldom idle: rhetoric intends to affect people, and it does—though not always as intended. This puts the definition of politics as talk or rhetoric at the heart of political science, for this is tantamount to defining rhetoric as persuasion. Political scientists often define themselves as students of power, and they often define power as persuasion (rather than sheer force, coercion, or violence). Of course, this essay relies for the most part on defining rhetoric as the science of argumentation, insisting that argumentation should be conceived as contextual persuasion rather than formal proof or abstract demonstration.

John S. Nelson

The disciplinary study of politics as power as persuasion has probably advanced farthest in the field of international relations, where the attention to processes of power has been the most intense and sustained. Nonetheless, the relationship of politics to rhetoric is especially intimate in the domestic politics of America and other representative democracies. Constitutionally and often practically, the major processes, institutions, and issues of representational politics are communicational. To ask about the legitimacy of governors, laws, and policies in a representational polity is largely to ask how well it communicates public opinion to public officials, how well the officials communicate public needs to citizens, and how well the citizens communicate among themselves about public problems. To concentrate research on elections, campaigning, mass media, and political socialization is to concede—however implicitly or ineffectually—the centrality of rhetoric to representational politics, at least. Some of these subjects prove important for other types of polities as well, and many of the topics that emerge for nonrepresentational regimes also reek of rhetoric: mobilization, propaganda, political symbols, suppression of dissent, and so on.

Despite the special importance of rhetoric to politics, neither the history nor the advantages of treating politics as rhetoric are much evident today in political science. The tale of how this came to pass is substantially the same as the story of how rhetoric became discredited as subversive or superfluous in philosophy and science.[36] But two unusual twists deserve special attention.

The first departure from form occurred well into the modern age. After its heyday among the Renaissance humanists, rhetoric declined dramatically in reputation and attention as a result of relentless hostility from the modern epistemology pioneered by Descartes. But rhetoric fared far better among students of politics than among contributors to other branches of inquiry. Presumably, this is because the substantive tie between politics and rhetoric remained so great that theorists of politics could not easily overcome it. Even from materialist and behaviorist foundations, for instance, Hobbes produced a political philosophy that made proper naming one of its main concerns. Not until the nineteenth century, in fact, did teachers stop training students in rhetoric as a crucial element of their education in civic virtue.

Whatever the reasons, however, modern theorists of politics continued to study and write about rhetoric long after assaults by modern epistemologists had reduced its credibility to a new low. Thus the Scottish Enlightenment that inspired a founding philosophy for American politics was mainly the work of men well aware of the close connection between rhetoric and politics.[37] Even Adam Smith wrote lectures on rhetoric (though not particularly good ones). The engines of modernization devastated respect for rhetoric elsewhere but diminished it only slowly in political theory.

When disciplines of the social sciences started to form toward the end of the nineteenth century, though, political science gradually began to catch up with other renouncers of rhetoric. As already described, the turn away from rhetoric culminated among political scientists in the behavioral revolution following the Second World War. Their neglect of rhetoric in science accompanied inattention to rhetoric in politics. The more political scientists avoided categories of mentation, ideology, and institutions, the less reason or resources they had for appreciating the political importance of rhetoric.

That development provides a second twist to the story of rhetoric in the study of politics. In the 1960s and 1970s, behavioralists consolidated their dominance of political science, not only in one field of research after another, but especially in the discipline's structure of governance. At the same time that behavioralism managed at long last to obscure the significance of rhetoric for politics, other disciplines in the academy were beginning to consolidate scattered efforts into the groundwork for a new renaissance in rhetoric.[38] Thus political science missed an important opportunity to help itself and other disciplines by hastening the revival of rhetoric through contributing sophisticated accounts of the special connection between rhetoric and politics. Political scientists spurned rhetoric epistemically, as already explained, but they also turned away from rhetoric both methodologically and substantively.

Methodologically, behavioralists increasingly sought general correlations between measures of initial conditions (treated as stimuli) and subsequent conditions (regarded as responses). Thus they slid gradually toward conceiving the challenge of political inquiry as securing strong enough correlations to warrant classifying the subsequent conditions as consequent ones, supporting claims of causation. They gave less and less attention to interactions and processes detailed enough to sustain persuasive or provocative stories about how initial conditions became consequent ones.

As a result, even their inferences of causation began to suffer from making multivariate analyses in grab-bag models. These "explain" occurrences by displaying degrees of correlation among lots of variables. But what such largely correlational models seldom attempt or support is a step-by-step account of how the states specified by the independent variables become the conditions specified by the dependent vari-

212

John S. Nelson

ables. For two decades or more, in major parts of political science, issues of interaction and process either vanished altogether or appeared only in forms so skimpy that they could not hope to comprehend the convolutions that make many kinds of politics (and rhetoric) notorious. Not even the statistical mechanics of causal path analysis can do much for a discipline's study of processes when its few informal stories no longer express complicated narratives and its main research questions no longer address processual complexities. As a texture of intricate strategies, tactics, interactions, and processes, rhetoric escapes ready or adequate comprehension through behavioralist modes of analysis seldom able or intended to specify processes in detail.

Substantively, behavioralists typically consigned questions of political rhetoric to computer mechanics of content analysis or the surpassing subtleties—and unscientific inferences—of the humanities. The early crudities of computer analysis of content (now impressively overcome in some quarters, largely outside political science) soon led to its desertion by the discipline. No doubt the very willingness of a few "traditional" or "normative" theorists of politics to continue to take rhetoric seriously reinforced the inclination of the discipline's self-proclaimed scientists to stay away from rhetorical issues in politics. But even the "nonscientific" theorists tended to turn their attention elsewhere: some to modes of analytical philosophy at best implicitly rhetorical, some to styles of liberalism and marxism either uninterested in rhetoric or openly hostile to it, and others to defensive preoccupations with epistemology leading, as already recorded, away from rhetoric. In substance, behavioralism produced numerous studies of voting, coalitions, and attitudes. All these subjects could accommodate rhetorical dimensions, all are in fact rife with them, but behavioralists studied none of them in extensively rhetorical terms.

By the 1970s game theory and rational-choice theory were no longer new to political science. But they became increasingly popular among political scientists, primarily as attempts to take seriously the official but neglected commitment of behavioralism to make the discipline scientific by producing axiomatic or deductive theories of politics. From the start, both branches of formal theory had shown considerable interest in political processes; and with greater attention, they began to display considerable sophistication in comprehending interactive processes in particular. Both had also, unsurprisingly, shown more concern and skill for rhetorical issues about politics—especially questions about strategies and incentives. The rhetorical advantages of game theory emerge, for example, in its treatment of deterrence; and those of rational-choice theory appear somewhat in its account of voting and even more in its concern for agendas.

Neither game theory nor rational-choice theory yet goes far toward appreciating politics as rhetoric, however, because neither yet accommodates a sophisticated notion of persuasion. The starkly constraining assumptions that provide the analytical power of such formal theories become their main obstacles to comprehending the complications of political persuasion. For instance, rhetorical moves to alter preferences or transform situations are commonplace and important in politics but must elude theories predicated on given preferences and situations. A founding father of rational-choice theory has recently proposed a new field for addressing these problems, which he concedes to lie beyond the bounds of such formal theory. William Riker distinguishes rhetoric from his new field, which he calls "heresthetics."[39] Rhetoricians anytime, anywhere, would recognize and approve this as rhetoric.[40] But most rhetoricians would wonder what the separation of heresthetics from rational-choice theory would cost in rhetorical ability to understand interactions between the two fields, both encompassed by rhetoric as a discipline.

As far as behavioralism is concerned, though, the main effect of these recent developments in the direction of greater appreciation of rhetorical politics is simply to highlight the poverty of behavioralist attention to politics as rhetoric. In method and substance, political science as a behaviorally dominated discipline has tended to short-circuit issues of rhetoric, transforming them into correlations of characteristics and conditions or into issues of stimulus and response. The full-circuit studies needed to trace intact processes of political communication have seldom arisen; and when they have surfaced in the work of a few political scientists, disciplinary colleagues have done little to take advantage of such initiatives. Harold Lasswell's interest in propaganda and political language has been transubstantiated into surveys of political attitudes and public opinion that develop his commitment to behavioral science at the cost of his concern for issues of political communication and rhetoric.[41] Karl Deutsch's prolegomenon to cybernetic studies of political communication has been lauded but largely shelved until studies in artificial intelligence and cognitive psychology made it newly relevant, also in the 1980s.[42] Murray Edelman's rhetorically oriented research on political symbolism has been read widely, praised highly, but pursued infrequently by others until the 1980s.[43] Even the field of political communication formed mostly outside the mainstreams of political science, as an interdisciplinary study, though participation by political scientists has become common since the field began to burgeon late in the 1970s.[44]

For the current cause of politics as rhetoric, however, the most important aspect of each case may be the concluding qualification. In the last ten years, as rhetoric of inquiry has begun to crystallize from many projects of rhetoric in other disciplines, political science has begun to return to rhetorical issues. This positions political science to gain from rhetoric of inquiry a rhetorical sophistication that reaches throughout the discipline's conceptions, studies, and practices of both science and politics. But it also enables political science to endow rhetoric of inquiry with a political sophistication that it often lacks otherwise, since scholars from other disciplines have been no more inclined than political scientists to appreciate the politics of inquiry. Together, these themes generate a set of stories about rhetorics of political research.

Rhetorics of Political Research

A major lesson from rhetoric of inquiry for political science is that many recent projects in the social sciences and humanities share data, methods, and modes of analysis. Despite the legacy of behavioralism, political scientists have the resources and motivation to learn this lesson well. The increased commonality between social sciences and humanities comes as a considerable surprise to veterans of old disputes between scientific and literary cultures. They remember well how each social science promised to supplant humanistic styles of inquiry into its subjects. For some contributors to the behavioral revolution in political science, the new conversations among traditionally humanistic and avowedly scientific projects might appear astonishing and, in some cases, even distressing. But the newly evident convergence does not reflect reduced dedication of social scientists to rigorous observation and testable theories of human behavior. Instead, it expresses an unanticipated tendency for scientific techniques to develop greater range and complexity in tandem with diverse methods still distinctive of the humanities. Hence many research programs in political science reveal intricate interrelationships among approaches previously segregated as scientific and humanistic.

This is more than a matter of preserving humanistic concerns in the traditionally humanistic field of political theory. For one thing, its projects of conceptual and institutional analysis, political ethics, epistemology, history, and imagination are slowly diffusing throughout the rest of the discipline—as theoretical projects in other fields interact more explicitly with those central to political theory as a field. For another, humanistic methods increasingly prove complementary to scientific techniques as students of politics argue through the meanings of their research. This surfaces in the two faces now presented by several fields of the discipline: judicial behavior and public law, comparative politics and area studies, international relations and peace research, political socialization and political education. It shows in the aim of policy analysis to meld empirical and normative studies. It appears in the proclivity of formal theories to elicit normative treatments of federalism, historical studies of parties, rhetorical analyses of movements such as environmentalism, and other humanistic inquiries.

One implication of the surprising interpenetration of political science and various humanities is that political scientists do far more humanistic research than they have recognized. For rhetoric of inquiry, this raises fascinating issues about disparities between official rhetorics of research and actual practices or unofficial rhetorics of research. For political science, this also poses the intriguing possibility that resources available for research have gone unnoticed. These include humanistic disciplines with fields relevant substantively or methodologically to various projects in political science. The underused resources also include funding agencies interested in the sorts of humanistic studies in fact conducted by political scientists who nonetheless neglect the humanistic contents and techniques of their own research.

But the main resource neglected by political science and celebrated by rhetoric of inquiry is the capacity for persuasive argument. As an internal need of the discipline, an ability to argue skillfully is the collective faculty for thinking well about problems of inquiry. As an external need of the discipline, it is the facility for learning from other projects and for teaching them what political scientists have discovered. As attention to the quality of argument in research, rhetoric of inquiry is a movement toward self-scrutiny and -improvement on the part of all disciplines.

Political science can contribute centrally to this movement, for several reasons. First is the special tie between politics and rhetoric. As already remarked, the first form of political science simply was the discipline of rhetoric, and their close connection has held in substance ever since. Speech, persuasion, deception, symbols, and other aspects of rhetoric are too important to politics for the tie to lapse or even loosen to any great degree. The same is true of the place of political processes and settings in the study of communication.

John S. Nelson

A second resource of political science stems from the need for rhetoric of inquiry to comprehend academic disciplines as political systems. Expertise in the study of such political systems can help to give epistemology a sophisticated appreciation of the politics in the operations of scholarship. This ranges from governmental policy for education and research to everyday politics of professions and university departments. Revivals of rhetoric outside political science have often missed how political epistemology should be. The result has been lots of loose talk about scholarly communities and scientific revolutions that seldom signals enough knowledge or care about politics for developing a detailed politics of inquiry. Political scientists should be able to contribute immensely to this neglected dimension in rhetoric of inquiry.

Since rhetoric of inquiry tends to see the social sciences and humanities as interdependent or interpenetrating projects, it can learn a great deal from fields that overtly combine scientific and humanistic modes of study. Thus a third resource of political science for rhetoric of inquiry is the discipline's rich mixtures of arguments, data, and techniques drawn from diverse humanities and social sciences. Its continuing questions of action, authority, community, law, legitimacy, and representation span the humanities and social sciences. Moreover, many of its major programs of research combine methods of the humanities and social sciences.

Examples abound. Formal modelers seek to reproduce processes of voting and legislation identified independently through humanistically thick descriptions of decision making by voters and legislatures. Organization theorists mesh data from surveys and social observation with depth interviews, archival research, and symbolic interpretations of work environments. Policy analysts inform normative evaluation with statistical studies of policy needs, effects, and processes. Students of public opinion and political ideology increasingly combine survey research and cognitive science with literary interpretation of texts and rhetorical analysis of communication, reasoning, and symbolism. Archival research on foreign policy interacts with computer simulations of decision processes. Analyses of aggregate data about refugees, trade, and flows of information reshape traditionally humanistic studies of human rights, distributive justice, and free speech. Comparative investigators of voting, regulation, and parties in various countries carry on a dialogue with conceptual analysts of authority, democracy, government, power, and rights. Such interactions of diverse issues, methods, and kinds of data make political science a natural laboratory for rhetoric of inquiry.

The capacity of several projects in political science to address the problems of philosophy now confronting rhetoric of inquiry can count as a fourth resource of the discipline. The study of political reasoning and belief systems has started to get beyond simple oppositions between rationality and its utter absence. Increasingly, political scientists investigate the diverse rationalities reflected in distinct sets of beliefs, concepts, and symbols—that is to say, represented in different rhetorics. Political research on tolerance carries similar implications for attempts to privilege any single perspective as an exclusive standard of rationality. Relatedly, studies of political culture and socialization identify many aspects of political thinking which can be divorced from specific occasions of learning only at the cost of accurate understanding of their character and contents. This could lead toward better appreciation of the political culture and socialization of political scientists and other scholars. It could also increase recognition of their many processes of inquiry within real situations of research. In addition, the discipline's canons of ancient and recent classics surely comprise the richest tradition of rhetoric in all the social sciences.

The study and practice of rhetoric are so deeply related that neither can be pursued without the other. Rhetoric comprehends not only what is communicated but the conditions, processes, effects, improvements, and comparative character of communications. Through rhetoric of inquiry, we can teach ourselves how to make these connections benefit our research. In recognizing how science is rhetorical, we can recover for political science a neglected capacity to improve its argument and therefore its inquiry. In recognizing how rhetoric is political, we can recover for every human science a neglected appreciation of politics and therefore political inquiry.

My stories of science and politics are at an end. As I said at the beginning, these tales together have several morals—and now they can be told. To reconsider science as politics can overcome the modern reluctance to take seriously the fact that disciplines of inquiry are interactions of humans. To recognize rhetoric as epistemic can counter the Western inclination to dismiss or condemn rhetoric as style rather than substance. To recreate science as rhetoric can correct the modern gaps between epistemology, theory, and practice. To regard rhetoric as politics can renew the ancient project of rhetoric as a political science. And to reconceive politics as rhetoric can provoke the substantial improvement of political science in its current forms. But the main lesson is that these possibilities are coming true: the political scientists already exploring rhetoric, and the others who will soon join them, give the discipline a good chance to enhance its many rhetorics of research.

NOTES

1. See J. Peter Euben, "Political Science and Political Silence," in Philip Green and Sanford Levinson, eds., *Power and Community* (New York: Random House, 1969), pp. 3–58.

2. See John S. Nelson, "Political Argument in Political Science: A Meditation on Disappointments of Political Theory," paper for the Annual Meeting of the American Political Science Association, Chicago, 1983.

3. See John S. Nelson, "Doing Rhetoric of Political Inquiry: Approaches, Opportunities, and Priorities," paper for the Annual Meeting of the Midwest Political Science Association, Chicago, 1986.

4. See John S. Nelson, "Political Foundations for Rhetoric of Inquiry," paper for Temple University's Seventh Annual Conference on Discourse Analysis: Case Studies in the Rhetoric of the Human Sciences, Philadelphia, 1986.

5. See Paul K. Feyerabend, *Against Method* (Atlantic Highlands, N.J.: Humanities Press, 1975).

6. See Gerard Radnitzky, *Contemporary Schools of Metascience* (Chicago: Henry Regnery, 1973); Frederick Suppe, ed., *The Structure of Scientific Theories* (Urbana: University of Illinois Press, 1973).

7. Allan Janik and Stephen Toulmin, *Wittgenstein's Vienna* (New York: Simon and Schuster, 1973).

8. See John G. Gunnell, *Philosophy, Science, and Political Inquiry* (Morristown, N.J.: General Learning Press, 1975); *Political Theory* (Cambridge, Mass.: Winthrop, 1979); *Between Philosophy and Politics* (Amherst: University of Massachusetts Press, 1986). Also see David M. Ricci, *The Tragedy of Political Science* (New Haven: Yale University Press, 1984).

9. See John C. Wahlke, "Pre-Behavioralism in Political Science," *American Political Science Review* 73 (1979): 9–31; John S. Nelson, "Accidents, Laws, and Philosophic Flaws," *Comparative Politics* 7 (1975): 435–57; Nelson, "The Ideological Connection, I–II," *Theory and Society* 4 (1977): 421–48 and 573–90.

10. See John S. Nelson and Allan Megill, "Rhetoric of Inquiry: Projects and Prospects," *Quarterly Journal of Speech* 72 (1986): 20–37.

11. See John S. Nelson, "Education for Politics," in John S. Nelson, ed., *What Should Political Theory Be Now?* (Albany: State University of New York Press, 1983), pp. 413–78; William H. Panning, "What Does It Take to Have a Theory? Principles in Political Science," ibid., pp. 479–511.

12. See Ira L. Strauber and John S. Nelson, "Epistemology in Political Theory," paper for the University of Iowa Faculty Rhetoric Seminar, Iowa City, 1983.

13. See Gunnell, *Philosophy, Science, and Political Inquiry*.

14. See John S. Nelson, "Once More on Kuhn," *Political Methodology* 1 (1974): 73–104; Ira L. Strauber, "Politics and Values in a World Without Criteria," in John S. Nelson, ed., *Tradition, Interpretation, and Science* (Albany: State University of New York Press, 1986), pp. 257–80; Nelson, "Destroying Political

Theory in Order to Save It," ibid., pp. 281–318; John G. Gunnell, "Annals of Political Theory," ibid., pp. 319–66.

15. See Charles Helm, "Party Identification and Perceptual Screening," *Political Methodology* 4 (1977): 289–312; Helm, "Party Identification as a Perceptual Screen," *Polity* 12 (1979): 110–28; Nelson, "The Ideological Connection."

16. See Nelson, "Education of Politics."

17. To find exceptions, though, we need look no farther than our colleagues G. R. Boynton ("Linking Problem Definition and Research Activities," in Judith A. Gillespie and Dina A. Zinnes, eds., *Missing Elements in Political Inquiry* [Beverly Hills, Calif.: Sage, 1982], pp. 43–60; "On Getting from Here to There," in Elinor Ostrom, ed., *Strategies of Political Inquiry* [Beverly Hills, Calif.: Sage, 1982], pp. 29–68) and Benjamin A. Most and Harvey Starr, ("International Relations Theory, Foreign Policy Substitutability, and 'Nice' Laws," *World Politics* 36 [1984]: 383–406; "Getting Started on Political Research," paper for the Annual Meeting of the Midwest Political Science Association, Chicago, 1986). That they are by no means alone in their departments—let alone their discipline—can encourage us to expect still more immanent epistemology from political scientists.

18. See John S. Nelson, "Natures and Futures for Political Theory," in Nelson, *What Should Political Theory Be Now?* pp. 3–24; Richard Ashcraft, "One Step Backward, Two Steps Forward," ibid., pp. 515–48; Robert Booth Fowler, "Does Political Theory Have a Future?" ibid., pp. 549–80.

19. See John G. Gunnell, "Encounters of a Third Kind," *American Journal of Political Science* 25 (1981): 440–61; "In Search of the Political Object," in Nelson, *What Should Political Theory Be Now?* pp. 25–52; "Political Theory," in Ada W. Finifter, ed., *Political Science* (Washington, D.C.: American Political Science Association, 1983), pp. 3–45.

20. See Nelson, "Education for Politics"; "Political Argument in Political Science."

21. See Paul F. Kress, "Against Epistemology," *Journal of Politics* 41 (1979): 526–42.

22. See John S. Nelson, Allan Megill, and Donald N. McCloskey, "Rhetoric of Inquiry," in this volume; Donald N. McCloskey, *The Rhetoric of Economics* (Madison: University of Wisconsin Press, 1985).

23. See Stephen Toumin, *The Uses of Argument* (Cambridge: Cambridge University Press, 1964).

24. See John S. Nelson, "Seven Rhetorics of Inquiry," in this volume.

25. For the first half of this general argument, see Douglas N. Walton, *Arguer's Position* (Westport, Conn.: Greenwood Press, 1985). For the second half, see Feyerabend, *Against Method*.

26. Nelson's "Destroying Political Theory in Order to Save It" demonstrates the rhetoricity of some epistemological argumentation in political science. The rhetoricity of theoretical argumentation in the discipline is shown by Nelson's meditation on "Political Science as Political Argument." Ira L.

John S. Nelson

Strauber has written a number of essays that display the rhetoricity of good argumentation in practical politics, including "Political Philosophy and Political Action," in Nelson, *What Should Political Theory Be Now?* pp. 55–74; "Transforming Political Rights Into Legal Ones," *Polity* 16 (1983): 72–95.

27. See Stanley Cavell, *The Claim of Reason* (New York: Oxford University Press, 1979), esp. pp. 20–28 and 86–125.

28. See Strauber and Nelson, "Epistemology in Political Theory."

29. In this volume, the chapters by Jean Elshtain, Charles Anderson, and Michael Shapiro exemplify rhetorical analysis in the practice of political inquiry.

30. See John S. Nelson, "Practice Theory," paper for the Annual Meeting of the Midwest Political Science Association, Chicago, 1985.

31. See Nelson, "Natures and Futures for Political Theory," pp. 4–8.

32. Compare the notion of politics as the category of totality: see ibid., pp. 11 and 17–18.

33. See Hannah Arendt, *The Human Condition* (Garden City, N.Y.: Doubleday, 1958), pp. 9–69; idem, *Between Past and Future*, enlarged ed. (New York: Viking Press, 1968), pp. 91–171; Sheldon S. Wolin, *Politics and Vision* (Boston: Little, Brown, 1960), pp. 28–68; John G. Gunnell, *Political Philosophy and Time* (Middletown, Conn.: Wesleyan University Press, 1968), esp. pp. 3–16.

34. See John S. Nelson, "Political Theory as Political Rhetoric," in Nelson, *What Should Political Theory Be Now?* pp. 169–240; Michael C. Leff, "Modern Sophistic and the Unity of Rhetoric," in this volume.

35. David V. J. Bell, *Power, Influence, and Authority* (New York: Oxford University Press, 1975), p. 10.

36. See Nelson and Megill, "Rhetoric of Inquiry," pp. 20–24.

37. See Garry Wills, *Inventing America* (New York: Random House, 1978).

38. See Nelson and Megill, "Rhetoric of Inquiry," pp. 24–28 and esp. 28–32.

39. See William H. Riker, *Manipulatory Politics* (New Haven: Yale University Press, 1986).

40. See Nelson, "Political Argument in Political Science."

41. See Harold Lasswell, *Psychopathology and Politics* (New York: Viking Press, 1930); idem, *Politics: Who Gets What, When, How* (New York: World, 1936); idem, *Power and Personality* (New York: Viking Press, 1948); Harold Lasswell and Abraham Kaplan, *Power and Society* (New Haven: Yale University Press, 1950).

42. See Karl W. Deutsch, *The Nerves of Government* (New York: Free Press, 1963; 2d ed., 1966).

43. See Murray Edelman, *The Symbolic Uses of Politics* (Urbana: University of Illinois Press, 1967); *Politics as Symbolic Action* (Chicago: Markham, 1971); *Political Language* (New York; Academic Press, 1977).

44. See Dan D. Nimmo and Keith R. Sanders, eds., *Handbook of Political Communication* (Beverly Hills, Calif.: Sage, 1981); Keith R. Sanders, Dan D. Nimmo, and Lynda Lee Kaid, eds., *Political Communication Yearbook 1984* (Carbondale: Southern Illinois University Press, 1985).

13 THE RHETORIC OF HISTORY

ALLAN MEGILL

DONALD N. McCLOSKEY

The rhetoric of history is concerned with the tropes, arguments, and other devices of language used to write history and to persuade audiences. Fustel de Coulanges once interrupted applause for a lecture: "Do not applaud me. It is the voice of history that speaks through me."[1] Cunning fox, he knew well that the applause would redouble. Denying as Descartes did the human and rhetorical character of one's performance is commonly an effective rhetoric. The rhetoric of history deserves more than this.

A small but suggestive literature on the rhetoric of history exists now, including works by J. H. Hexter, Paul Veyne, Hayden White, Richard Vann, Lionel Gossman, Stephen Bann, and Hans Kellner.[2] It is a promising beginning, though some of it identifies rhetoric too closely with the pleasing and seductive arts of fiction—with tropes (often called "literary" devices), with narrative, with the multiple meanings of poetry. The rhetoric to which we here appeal includes these but more: it is the full art of persuasion. It is the "rhetoric" of olden times, of Aristotle and Quintilian. It is an art of doing things with words that many since the seventeenth century have held in low esteem, though using it daily.[3] A work of history, we argue, does not derive chiefly from solitary illumination in the archives. It is a writing, an attempt at persuasion. Histories can be read as orations.

There is much to be learned from such a reading. Social scientists and philosophers might learn how ineradicable is the context of persuasion—so different from the "context of justification" in which they claim to work. Paul Rabinow and William M. Sullivan note that "as long as there has been a social science, the expectation has been that it would turn from its humanistic infancy to the maturity of hard science, thereby leaving behind its dependence on value, judgment, and individual insight."[4] History has been insulated from such expectations, perhaps because of its rhetorical ancestry in the Renaissance. It has not set aside its interpretive and public dimension. The social sciences were born of a Cartesian philosophy that proclaimed its hostility to rhetoric: Descartes, Locke, and Kant saw rhetoric as a deceiver. Such philosophy gives allegiance rather to Method, seen as rhetoric-free. The social sciences have had recourse to a methodological rigorism, insisting that one Method alone has legitimacy and that Science is no mere argument before the Athenian Assembly.

On the Resistance to Rhetoric of History

The writing of history is rhetorical—that is, argumentative, using at its best all the devices of language and fact and logic to sustain an argument. "Rhetoric" is not confined to falsehoods. Trying to write history unrhetorically is like trying to tell a joke unverbally. "The rhetoric of history," it should be noted, has the same maddening ambiguity as "history" itself, being either the events of Bull Run or the account of the events; it can be either the metaphor of a river of retreating Union troops or an account of the use of metaphors in Allan Nevins's account of the retreat—or it can be the rhetoric of the event itself, if the roar of retreating troops is argument.[5]

Historians will resist the notion that their writing is "rhetorical." Few want to be caught in company with so nasty a word. Since the decline of classical civilization, rhetoric has acquired a bad name, worsened by abuses in the age of Goebbels and J. Walter Thompson. In the popular sense rhetoric comes from the mouths of bad politicians ("heated rhetoric") or from our enemies ("mere rhetoric"). Yet, to repeat (for it bears repetition), the word has an older, wider, and more useful definition, embodied in the present volume, namely, the art and science of argument.

Some historians do not think of themselves as arguing anything or persuading anybody. History, they believe, is merely "written up," as scientists like to say about their lab reports. The issues are settled in the archives and are at the writing desk merely reported. Only philosophers and other questionable folk are constrained to persuade. Historians "study," then tell it like it is—history being so much more *solid* than philosophy will ever be.

The metaphor of going to the solid facts and looking at them is powerful in our culture, embodied, for example, in the objectivist rhetoric of the scientific paper since Newton.[6] In historiography it takes the form of what might be called "archivism." By this we mean the tendency of the historian to think that the most important relation is not

with the readers, the times, or the questions but with the archives—
with what the historian misleadingly calls "the sources" of history.

The sources of a historian's work are to be found almost every place
except the archives. Problems in the present impel the writing of history. The problems that arise in the conversation of historians owe their
life to the wider world. Does "entrepreneurial decline" account for England's falling economically behind Germany and the United States in
the late nineteenth and early twentieth centuries?[7] What effect did
Wesleyanism have on the politics of the British working class?[8] Was
there really a "Jacksonian democracy" in early nineteenth-century
America?[9] What is the relationship between Protestant sectarianism
and wealth accumulation?[10] Though scholastic-sounding to nonhistorians, these are not questions only of the schools. And still more
obviously public are the immense literatures generated by World Wars
I and II. Recently, the women's movement has generated an entire new
field.[11]

Yet archivism maintains its grip. The mythology of the profession
supports it. The legend says that Leopold von Ranke's achievement
was the examination of hitherto unexamined archives, on the basis of
which he wrote history *wie es eigentlich gewesen*.[12] It is forgotten that
Ranke's main documentary "source," the reports *(relazioni)* that Vene-
tian ambassadors wrote home, were connected accounts—not, as one
might assume, disconnected collections of "objective facts" known
with certitude.[13] The *relazioni* were "always already" rhetorical. Had
this not been the case Ranke could not have made use of them. In the
shadow of positivism and scientism, though, historiography came to
be seen as a matter of gathering discrete, disconnected facts, and then
in a separate operation inducing to generalizations.[14]

In the way of myths the Rankean one is based on experiences that
historians frequently have. There *is* a romance in the quest through
British Museum Add. MSS or the Archives Nationales *manuscrits fran-
çais*. Historians do experience a spiritual movement from archival dust
to the glinty fact. The apprentice is particularly susceptible to the romance, which is easier to teach than the muddy complexities of writing
and talking to other historians. The archive missed is the commonest
explanation of the book unfinished, as though the main work of the
historian were squirrelish nut-gathering.

On Rhetoric in History

It is notable that historians have written rhetorically
with little accounting for their rhetoric. In 1968 J. H. Hexter observed:

> Rhetoric is ordinarily deemed icing on the cake of history, but our investigation indicates that it is mixed right into the batter. It affects not merely the outward appearance of history, its delightfulness and seemliness, but its inward character, its essential function—its capacity to convey knowledge of the past as it actually was.[15]

Since then historians have not much heeded Hexter's call that they "subject historiography . . . to an investigation far broader and far more intense" than they have done in the past. This is not to say that considerations of the rhetoric of history do not exist; for, as we have noted, they do. It is to say that the bulk of attention to historiography has focused on different issues.

There is one full-scale analysis of historical rhetoric, Hayden White's widely noticed *Metahistory* (1973). White does not mention Hexter's earlier call for a rhetoric of history, which oversight suggests that a general conversation had not yet developed. Dealing with a different aspect of rhetoric than does Hexter, White seeks to provide an analysis of "the deep structure of the historical imagination."[16] He tries to trace the ways that historians constitute historical facts back to their "deep" styles of writing history. As John Nelson and others have pointed out, White does not make good on this promise.[17] Nonetheless, *Metahistory* remains an important work, for it focuses attention on the tropal, stylistic aspects of historiography, seeing how these interact with the arguments and politics of writing history. It teaches sensitivity to the fact that *what* is said, in historical "sources" or in historians' accounts, can be fully grasped only if we attend to *how* it is said.

White's contribution is mainly to the *study* of historical rhetoric. In Paul Veyne's *Writing History* (1971; English translation 1984), the practical dimension of rhetoric is prominent, as suggested by the French title of the work, *Comment on écrit l'histoire*.[18] Veyne is alert to the difficulties that historians confront in the course of their work and shrewd in his account of how those difficulties are actually overcome. Perhaps because he is a classical historian and thus works in a field notorious for the fragmentary character of its documentation, he is acutely conscious of the extent to which history deals in uncertainties. Where Fustel de Coulanges was a historical Cartesian, Veyne is an anti-Cartesian. His approach is not to claim certainty but to admit uncertainty: thus he suggests that instead of titling a chapter "The Rural History of Rome," we might better title it "What We Know of the Rural History of Rome."[19] This (and other things) suggest a sympathetic relation to rhetoric, for the rhetorical tradition has always traded in uncertainty. Yet, remarkably, Veyne does not mention the rhetorical tradition: perhaps he thought it too obvious to mention. Nor does he mention Hexter's earlier essay. Until recently, Veyne's book was itself unmentioned in the English-reading world. The *disjecta membra* of historical rhetoric lay strewn about, the body unassembled.

A rhetorical criticism could be of use to history, just as the best literary criticism enriches and improves literature. Criticism is accounting, a giving of accounts. The writing could use such criticism, helpfully modest. The intervention of philosophers, usually hostile to the very notion of rhetoric, has mostly been unhelpful criticism. The logical empiricists (Hempel, for instance) narrowed what historians do in order to make it analyzable by their favored methods.[20] The work of some more recent philosophers has been broader, more willing to understand that history is not some imagined social physics. One notes for instance Danto's examination of *Narration and Knowledge* and Ankersmit's *Narrative Logic*.[21] But even these works have paid little notice to rhetoric.

An example of what can go wrong in the absence of the rhetorical tradition is the compilation of *Historians' Fallacies* (1970) by the historian David Hackett Fischer. This learned book, filled with pregnant examples, takes as "fallacious" many supporting arguments in works of history. A piece of storytelling or an apt metaphor or an argument from probabilities does not match a proper syllogism and is tagged "fallacious." The tagging satisfies a philosophical urge, but it does not generate a helpful account of human reasonings, even by recent philosophical standards.[22] Irving Copi, in the fifth edition of his elementary text on formal logic, praises Fischer's zeal in rooting out no less than 112 fallacious heresies in the arguments historians actually use.[23] It does not occur to him that he and Fischer repeatedly commit the "fallacies" they attack—a reflexive criticism rhetoricians would not miss. The very use of the word is a *fallax ad indignationem*, that is, name-calling; and it is a *petitio principii*, for it assumes the conclusion that arguments identified as "fallacies" are to be set aside.

On Style as Voice

Twenty years ago Hayden White characterized history as "perhaps the conservative discipline par excellence," suggesting that it combined "late-nineteenth-century social science" (Freud, Weber, et al.) with "mid-nineteenth-century art" (Scott, Thackeray, et al.).[24] At about the same time in literary criticism, Scholes and Kellogg were deploring the tendency of critics to apply "the standards of nineteenth-century realism" to all fiction of whatever period.[25] Literary criticism today no longer exhibits this tendency, but among historians the hold of nineteenth-century literary convention is strong.

In particular, many historians remain unconsciously wedded to the historiographical equivalent of mainstream nineteenth-century narrative fiction.[26] Most nineteenth-century novelists strove to create an impression of omniscience, of continuity, of unbroken flow. The "voice" of professional historians has traditionally been a variant of this novelistic voice. Novelists have an easier time claiming omniscience than do historians. Historians have their often fragmentary "sources" to contend with. Yet the style exerts pressure to produce a whole and continuous story, sustaining the impression of omniscience, leaping over evidential voids.

The voice of continuity is not the only conceivable one. In modernist and postmodernist literature from Joyce onward the role of the authoritative narrator is rejected. There are occasions where historians, too, ought to reject it. Much better is Veyne's notion of the "incomplete nature of history": "from one page to the next the historian changes tense without warning, according to the tempo of his sources; . . . every history book is in this sense a fabric of incoherences, and it cannot be anything else."[27]

The old ways are not obsolete, but would be more persuasive if they were self-conscious. Consider, for example, the vista of Samuel Eliot Morison's two-volume *European Discovery of America* (1971, 1974).[28] Morison's work is written in the expansive style of late nineteenth-century American historiography; he tells us that his mode of presentation is based on Justin Winsor's *Narrative and Critical History of America* (1884–89). The narrative is ample and personal; it introduces his own travels and takes account of the uncertainties in the evidence. Its style is studied as to author, subject, and audience.

For some historiographic problems a new style might be appropriate. Carlo Ginzburg's *The Cheese and the Worms: The Cosmos of a Sixteenth-Century Miller* (1976; English translation 1980) is one of the most interesting and widely discussed works of history of the last decade.[29] Ginzburg examines the encounter between Menocchio—the miller of his title—and the Inquisition, seeking to reconstruct his world view. Ginzburg had at his disposal inquisitorial records (fashionable now after long neglect), which give a detailed account of Menocchio's encounter with the authorities. But beyond the actual encounter the documentary evidence is lacking, and the world of the sixteenth century is far from our own. How is he to tell Menocchio's story?

The book is written not in long, flowing, omnisciently narrated chapters rising smoothly to a climax, as in Ranke, Parkman, and other masters of nineteenth-century historiography, but in short, numbered sections, which in the table of contents are assigned descriptive titles. The format encourages the back-and-forth movement of Ginzburg's intellect. It accords with the fragmentary nature of much of his evidence. By distancing himself from the telling of a continuous story, he also distances himself from the temptation to fill in gaps more enthusiastically than his evidence allows. At the same time he becomes free to speculate where speculation is called for, knowing that the speculation can be marked off. He is able to shuttle between Menocchio's testimony and other evidence that illuminates its meaning. He can more easily bring into play the different voices in the story—Menocchio, his friends and neighbors, the inquisitors. Perhaps most important, the format makes it easier for him to modulate his own voice. Sometimes it is the earnest historical researcher who speaks and sometimes the committed intellectual; sometimes the tone of irony is uppermost, sometimes that of compassion. Ginzburg refuses to filter his message through the ready-made model of style that most historians take as given. His is the analytical prose of Marx and his successors, given suppleness and changeability by resources derived from newer traditions, from writers like Queneau and Calvino.

There are contrary approaches to style. At least since G. M. Trevelyan's "Clio: A Muse" (1903), there have been laments that the growing scientization of history robs it of a wide public and ignores its literary dimension. Such appeals to the importance of "arrangement, composition, and style" sharply distinguish the presentation of history from research and reflection. Trevelyan holds that history has three "functions" or operations: the scientific, the imaginative, and the literary. We have heard this before. Historians first accumulate facts and sift evidence. Then they make guesses and generalizations. Only at the close do they exercise "the *literary* function, the exposition of the results of science and imagination in a form that will attract and educate our fellow-countrymen."[30]

Those who go beyond Trevelyan's premise that style is a matter of presentation alone sometimes step into other traps. Peter Gay, in *Style in History* (1974), does not think that style is mere icing on the cake of historiography.[31] But he confines his treatment of "style in history" to four historians of previous centuries—Gibbon, Ranke, Macaulay, and Burckhardt. The implication, clearly unintended, is that "style in history" is a category applicable to an earlier stage in the evolution of his-

Allan Megill and Donald N. McCloskey

toriography but not to serious professional historiography today. Interest in such a subject is made to seem retrograde.

Another trap is to identify the rhetoric of history with evocative, ambiguous, "literary" expression: the multiple meanings of poetry, as we have said. J. H. Hexter comes close to doing this in praising historians for using imprecise language having "a rich aura of connotation," sacrificing "exactness" for "evocative force."[32] He distinguishes, too, between study of "the structure of historiography" (which he identifies as the particular concern of rhetoric) and study of "the nature of data, evidence, and inference in works of history" (which he says has so far been the "central preoccupation" of historians).[33] Separation of rhetoric from data, evidence, and inference is a mistake, for persuasion in history cannot take place without these. Hexter here seems under the influence of a literary view of rhetoric and an idealized view of logic and science.

Historians are not in the business of producing literary artifacts that stand isolated from the world. They do produce literary artifacts, but in doing so they also produce arguments intended to persuade particular audiences of the truth of particular statements. A rhetorical criticism of history would by-pass the audience-free excesses of the New Criticism in literary studies. A history that is more than solipsistic has occasion to speak, and in speaking is rhetorical. On emerging from the archive the historian cannot say everything. Rhetoric supplies the standards of inclusion and exclusion. Is this fact or connection *telling*? Does it *persuade*? Does the audience *want* it?

On Argument

One way of addressing the speech of historians is by the detailed disassembly of tropes. We have in mind here not the deep tropes of consciousness and prefiguration that White seeks to expose but surface tropes of language and argument, intended to seduce and persuade. Consider Robert W. Fogel's "cliometric" classic, *Railroads and American Economic Growth* (1964).[34] Self-consciously scientific, *Railroads* is also rhetorical even in its most quantitative and trivial details. In setting his argument Fogel uses nearly twenty classically recognized figures of speech in barely two pages.[35] The classical names of the figures show the rhetoric. One sees a house—really sees it—only when equipped with the carpenter's vocabulary of soffit and quoin and gable.

The whole of Fogel's argument is the piling up of arguments on one point *(diallage)*, the point being that what matters to the question of whether railroads had a significant impact on American economic growth is how good the possible substitutes were—the rivers and canals and carts that would have carried corn and passengers had the railroad not been invented.

Within the *diallage* he repeatedly concedes a smaller point to achieve a larger *(paramologia)*: "If the axiom of [the railroads'] indispensability merely asserted [X] . . . there would be no reason to question it." "Although the evidence demonstrating that the eruption of a boom psychology . . . is considerable . . ." "Even the demonstration that railroads produced effects that were both unique and important . . ." The concession is part of his most characteristic rhetorical figure, by which he says, in effect, "Even if I concede to my opponents such-and-such a point, my argument wins." The figure is lawyerly—and mathematical and Socratic: it is the *elenchos* that so annoyed Socratic Athens. It is far removed from the apparently unargumentative tone of narrative.

Repeatedly, he draws attention to what he claims is the important aspect of a case. Thus he emphasizes the importance of substitutes for railroads by the repetition of a word or phrase at the beginning of successive sentences *(anaphora)*: "The crucial aspect. . . . The crucial aspect. . . ." These two expressions of the same idea are repeated for effect: *commoratio*. Each of the two sentences contains a strongly parallel structure, balancing the phrases in the first sentence *(isocolon)*, leaving out phrases in the second *(ellipsis,* as this sentence left out the second occurrence of "sentence").

The beginning of the paragraph that follows repeats the point again; the second sentence repeats still again: four repetitions of the point in different words *(tautologia)*, bordering on *pleonasm*. It is the main point of the book, and one difficult for much of Fogel's implied audience to grasp. If any point warranted emphasis, this one—a fortiori—did. The subsequent paragraphs draw attention to the central point by attacking its alternatives—that is to say, by attacking various alternative definitions of what it might mean for railroads to have been "indispensable": the figure is *apophasis*, the orderly rejection of all the alternatives except one.

Repeatedly in these two pages Fogel disparages opposing arguments *(diasyrmus)*, a technique so obviously forensic that most historians use it gingerly. Repeatedly he notes the absence of decisive evidence. He makes an appeal to the ideally modernist historian-scientist, who does not take an umbrella without a scientifically certified prediction of light rain. The "evidence" so often mentioned is quantitative. The figure *(quantitas)* is therefore a modern one, little used in the nonquantitative civilization that thought most carefully about the means of persuasion.

Allan Megill and Donald N. McCloskey

A derivative of the modern enthusiasm for properly quantitative evidence is the following figure: "no evidence has been supplied. . . . And it is doubtful such evidence can be supplied" (note the parallel construction). This is one of the common *topoi* of modern intellectual life, carrying conviction nowadays among all who pretend to intellectuality.

The most important of Fogel's rich array of common topics with his argument from lower or upper bounds. The book consists of an attempt to find the least upper bound on the benefit from railroads. If the upper bound is small, then a fortiori the true effect is small. He draws on the argument here and throughout the book, biasing the case against himself.

Fogel's use of this particular figure led many graduate students to take up careers of under- and overestimating things. In such matters the usual rhetoric of history (and of economics, though less prominently displayed) demands "accuracy." An estimate of the population of fifth-century Athens must be "accurate"; a description of the American economy as competitive is to be judged for "accuracy." Any physicist would attest that the word is meaningless without bounds on the error, and any literary critic would attest that the accuracy necessary to an argument depends on the conversational context. There is no absolute sense of "accuracy."

Heavy use of the common topics will inspire a charge of "mere rhetoric," such as Fogel faced for his trouble. But he also uses topics special to a particular field. The example at the end of page 11 is known among engineers and scientists as "simulation" (a Fogelian favorite, occurring repeatedly throughout the book), one of the special topics in economics and other quantitative subjects. These carry conviction only among experts. The use of special topics characteristically inspires commendations for eschewing mere rhetoric, the rhetoric disappearing from view behind the mask of the economic or historical Scientist. But Science is not an alternative to rhetoric: science, whether economic or historical, must be rhetorical to achieve its end.

On Audience

Since rhetoric aims at persuasion, it directs attention to audience, as logic does not. Fogel would seem to require two implied readers, both close to contradictions in terms: the Historically Interested Economist and the Economically Sophisticated Historian. Fields under dispute between two methods, as American economic history was during the 1960s, cannot have one reader. Yet much writing,

Fogel's included, presupposes one alone, able to appreciate every nuanced remark about fixed capital-output ratios or the wisdom of the Joint Traffic Association, *Proceedings of the Board of Managers,* 1896. At the time Fogel wrote there were few actual readers who could take on the role of his ideal implied reader.

Fogel created an implied reader more definite than merely a generalized historical economist. His reader is an earnest fellow, much impressed by Science, in love with figures and the bottom line, a little stubborn in his convictions but open to argument and patient with its details. Such an implied reader is less attractive than the one more commonly addressed in successful academic prose. A book written about the same time on about the same subject by another economist and historian, Albert Fishlow, had less impact.[36] It created an implied reader who was more distant and disengaged, one sensitive to ironies, amused by verbal rotundities, impatient with close economic argument but very patient indeed with narrative indirection—something like the implied reader of the best history.

The relation between argument and implied audience can be illustrated again by comparing William L. Shirer's immensely popular *The Rise and Fall of the Third Reich* (1960) with Karl Dietrich Bracher's *The German Dictatorship* (1969; English translation 1970).[37] The two works deal with the "same" topic—namely, the history of the Third Reich—but in their styles and narrative strategies differ radically. Shirer's account is characterized by its simplicity and immediacy. He reduces the rise and fall of Nazi Germany to the story of Hitler and a few of his henchmen. Shirer was on the scene during much of the Third Reich and he does not hesitate to introduce himself into the book, referring to his own thoughts and experiences. The word "narrate" is especially appropriate (it is never out of place in history) considering the single plot line and audible voice of the storyteller that mark the book.

Bracher's *German Dictatorship* is different. Bracher seeks to understand "the multiplicity of conditions and causes, the multicausal nature of historico-political processes."[38] At once the reader knows that the voice is academic. Bracher rejects single-tracked formulas; he rejects narrative itself, so far as it is distinguished by "the presence of a story and a story-teller."[39] The straight-line narrative rhetoric of Shirer, in which event A leads to event B to event C and so on, gives way to an analytical rhetoric, in which the historian deliberates.

Professional historians commonly reject Shirer's work out of hand, as bad history. Bracher is subtle, distanced, self-critical; Shirer is attuned to immediate answers and is disinclined to search further. Shirer notes in his foreword: "I have tried to be severely objective, letting the facts speak for

Allan Megill and Donald N. McCloskey

themselves and noting the source for each."[40] But facts never speak for themselves; it is always historians who speak for them. Moreover, *The Rise and Fall* depends for much of its force on an appeal to its readers' preconceptions about the Third Reich. It allowed its readers to retain those preconceptions, building on wartime stereotypes. Thus in a certain sense readers of *The Rise and Fall* learned nothing from it. Yet it was not simply because it appealed to preconceptions that the book became a worldwide bestseller. For all his historiographic limitations, Shirer is a superb storyteller. To what extent is it possible to write history as accessibly as Shirer does while retaining the analytical sophistication found in Bracher? The question is forced by a rhetoric of history.

The quality of works of history is dependent on the quality of the audiences available to them. A Shirer-type audience is willing to listen to a long story but is resistant to ideas that it finds unfamiliar; a Bracher-type audience is willing to live with complexity (indeed, demands it, even when it is not there) and can learn something from it. The quality of the audiences is to a large degree dependent on what the historian is willing to make of them. To assume a pedestrian audience is to get one. Some assumed audiences are great of soul; some are not, regardless of the author's quality. Shakespeare wrote for groundlings too.

The matter of audience is often missed. Geoffrey Elton, to take a relevant example, gives an account of historical scholarship in which audience is an afterthought. The historian is alone with History, seeing her plain. He immerses himself in "the sources"—ideally in *all* the sources. From his knowledge of this evidence he comes to know the "right" questions to ask of it. The questions do not come from the historian's present, for this would go against "the first principle of historical understanding, namely that the past must be studied in its own right, for its own sake, and on its own terms." No need to argue—just look, or study; and when the studying is done, the historian "turns to write up his findings."[41]

On Professional and Amateur Rhetorics of History

One of the most striking developments in the historiography of the last twenty or thirty years—a development that an exclusively literary conception of rhetoric might overlook—has been the marked rise in the rigor of the evidential demands that historians make upon their colleagues. In other words, standards have arisen: Fogel, and "cliometric" history in general, is one manifestation among many. Confident generalizations that in 1960 might have passed muster are likely now to be greeted with suspicion. Professional historians now recognize, more clearly than they once did, that the judgments they make are often quantitative and are properly subject to quantitative test. As a result, many shibboleths have been demolished.[42] W. O. Aydelotte speaks for a large community when he points out the uncertainties of historical inference and suggests that historians "may have more to gain not by extending our generalizations but by restricting them, by pursuing limited (and quantitative) generalizations on which we have some prospect of reaching tenable ground."[43]

With the rise in evidential standards a growing split has developed between professional historians and the wider public. A work of history that satisfies the wider public is unlikely to satisfy a professional audience; and only a few works that satisfy a professional audience manage to have a wider appeal. In other words, divergent historiographic audiences now exist. Journalistic historians retain an epistemological naiveté and a predilection for focusing on heroes and villains; they also retain a wide audience. Professional historians question their evidence and increasingly refuse to let the prominent men of an age stand for the age as a whole; their audience is small.

Still, some of the most interesting presentday historians try to combine audiences, articulating a rhetoric capable of working with both. The trick is to appeal to the nonprofessional reader while still living up to the epistemological and subject-matter expectations of professional historians. The trick is not easily done. It requires compromise; it also demands something of audiences. But it is worth the attempt.

The Cheese and the Worms again provides an example. The book, Ginzburg tells us, "is intended to be a story as well as a piece of historical writing. . . . it is addressed to the general reader as well as to the specialist. . . . I hope that both will recognize in this episode an unnoticed but extraordinary fragment of a reality, half obliterated, which implicitly poses a series of questions for our own culture and for us."[44] Notice Ginzburg's various cross-cuttings: history, but also story; addressed to specialists, but also to general readers; presenting a fragment, but the fragment of a (half-obliterated) totality.

Or consider Natalie Davis's *The Return of Martin Guerre*, the story of an impostor in sixteenth-century France. (Early modern European historiography seems rich in innovative work—in part, one suspects, because of the imaginative demands of bad evidence.) Here is the opening of the work:

Allan Megill and Donald N. McCloskey

> "Femme bonne qui a mauvais mary, a bien souvent le coeur
> marry" (A good wife with a bad husband often has a sorry heart).
> "Amour peut moult, argent peut tout" (love may do much, but
> money more). These are some of the sayings by which peasants
> characterized marriage in sixteenth-century France. Historians
> have been learning more and more about rural families from
> marriage contracts and testaments, from parish records of births
> and deaths, and from accounts of courtship rituals and charivaris.
> But we still know rather little about peasants' hopes and feelings;
> the ways in which they experienced the relation between
> husband and wife, parent and child; the ways in which they
> experienced the constraints and possibilities in their lives. We
> often think of peasants as not having had much in the way of
> choices, but is this in fact true? Did individual villagers ever try to
> fashion their lives in unusual and unexpected ways?
>
> But how do historians discover such things about anyone in
> the past? We look at letters and diaries, autobiographies,
> memoirs, family histories.[45]

Davis's rhetoric is intriguing in its complexity, arising from her attempt
to speak across disciplinary divisions. She seeks to address as broad an
audience as she can manage, including people who know nothing
about history or about how historians work.

Note the directness of Davis's beginning, with proverbs quoted first
and then identified. How better to capture the attention of an audience
than by using so elemental a literary form? (By providing translations
she signals the kind of audience she hopes to have.) Having spoken
with the voice of popular wisdom she shifts direction, and tells the audience about how historians operate ("Historians have been learning . . ."). In part this is a statement of required information, for the
audience is quite ignorant of what historians do in general and of what
they have been learning recently. But it is also a claim to authority: historians have been learning more and more, and I am one of these sav-
ants. Yet to claim that everything important is already known is to
exclude the possibility that the work now being presented has anything original to say. Thus Davis shifts to something that historians are
not well informed about—namely, the inner life of peasants, culminat-
ing in what is obviously (perhaps too obviously) a "rhetorical" question: Did peasants have choices? Finally, in an attempt to educate her
audience, she turns to a discussion of historical "sources" in general
and her own in particular.

The seams in the text are evident, its intentions clearly telegraphed. Such a beginning is not subtle. Ideally, perhaps, one would want a text that works simultaneously on different levels, speaking one way to an unsophisticated and another way to a sophisticated audience. Yet for all that, it is a beginning (and a book) that works well. It speaks a common, not a technical, language. It evokes problems of universal dimension. It informs its readers of two things: of the historian's effort to understand the past, and of the past in question. Its visible architecture is a sign of the difficulty of speaking of such a distant past to an audience initially both ignorant and indifferent. Yet if the writing of history is to be an enterprise worth pursuing the effort to assemble an audience must be made.

Conclusion

How then is history to create worthy audiences? The question is not much addressed. This is unsurprising, for professional historiography is a creation of the historical century par excellence, the nineteenth. The historian of 1870 already had his audience. But when historicism lost its hold early in this century so too did an important argument for the historical project in general.[46] Historians have seen their difficulties as lying in epistemology narrowly construed and have neglected problems of style, genre, figure, and audience. Especially because the increasing sophistication of the discipline creates barriers for nonhistorians, these problems are more compelling than before. What point would there be in a humanistic or social scientific discipline unable to speak beyond its own boundaries? Such a discipline would lose contact with the important problems that can alone justify it.

The need is not to abandon the epistemological standards. These too are part of the discipline and of its conversation. They mark out a successful attempt to make history, like science, cumulative. Yet at the same time they create an obstacle. History that tries to do without rhetoric loses its contact with the wider conversation of humankind. Rhetoric is not exhausted by imitation of certain nineteenth-century models. Other models, early and late, are ready for use.

NOTES

1. Quoted in G. P. Gooch, *History and Historians in the Nineteenth Century* (London: Longmans, Green, 1913), p. 212.

2. J. H. Hexter, "The Rhetoric of History," in Hexter, *Doing History* (Bloomington: Indiana University Press, 1971), pp. 15–76, first published as "Historiography: The Rhetoric of History," in David L. Sills, ed., *International Encyclopedia of the Social Sciences* (New York: Crowell, Collier and Macmillan, 1968), 6:368–94; Paul Veyne, *Writing History: Essay on Epistemology,* trans. Mina Moore-Rinvolucri (Middletown, Conn.: Wesleyan University Press, 1984); Hayden White, *Metahistory: The Historical Imagination in Nineteenth-Century Europe* (Baltimore: Johns Hopkins University Press, 1973); Richard Vann, "The Rhetoric of Social History," *Journal of Social History* 10 (1975): 221–36; Lionel Gossman, "The Go-Between: Jules Michelet, 1798–1874," *Modern Language Notes* 89 (1974): 503–41; Gossman, "Augustin Theory and Liberal Historiography," *History and Theory, Beiheft* 15 (1976): 3–83; Stephen Bann, *The Clothing of Clio: A Study of the Representation of History in Nineteenth-Century Britain and France* (Cambridge: Cambridge University Press, 1984); Hans Kellner, "Disorderly Conduct: Braudel's Mediterranean Satire," *History and Theory* 18 (1979): 197–222. Nancy S. Struever provides a compendious review of much recent work relevant to the rhetoric of history in her "Historical Discourse," in Teun A. van Dijk, ed., *Handbook of Discourse Analysis,* vol. 1: *Disciplines of Discourse* (London: Academic Press, 1985), pp. 249–71.

3. On the marginality of rhetoric, see Robert Hariman, "Status, Marginality, and Rhetorical Theory," *Quarterly Journal of Speech* 72 (1986): 38–54; on the most recent of its revivals, see John S. Nelson and Allan Megill, "The Rhetoric of Inquiry: Projects and Prospects," *Quarterly Journal of Speech* 72 (1986): 20–37.

4. Paul Rabinow and William M. Sullivan, "The Interpretive Turn: Emergence of an Approach," in Rabinow and Sullivan, eds., *Interpretive Social Science: A Reader* (Berkeley and Los Angeles: University of California Press, 1979), p. 1.

5. Allan Nevins, *The War for the Union,* vol. 1: *The Improvised War, 1861–1862* (New York: Scribner's 1959), p. 219.

6. See Charles Bazerman's essay in this volume, and his *Shaping Written Knowledge: Essays in the Growth, Form, Function and Implications of the Scientific Article* (Madison: University of Wisconsin Press, 1988).

7. See Donald N. McCloskey, ed., *Essays on a Mature Economy: Britain After 1840* (Princeton: Princeton University Press, 1971).

8. Edward P. Thompson, *The Making of the English Working Class* (New York: Knopf, 1963).

9. Lee Benson, *The Concept of Jacksonian Democracy: New York as a Test Case* (Princeton: Princeton University Press, 1961).

10. The starting point for historians' discussion is Max Weber, *The Protestant Ethic and the Spirit of Capitalism,* trans. Talcott Parsons, with a foreword by R. H. Tawney (New York: Scribner, 1930 [orig. 1904–5]). For one attempt to test the "Weber thesis," see W. D. Rubinstein, *Men of Property: The Very Wealthy in Britain Since the Industrial Revolution* (New Brunswick, N.J.: Rutgers University Press, 1981), pp. 145–75.

11. See issue on "Women's History Today," *American Historical Review* 89 (1984): 593–732.

12. Bann, *The Clothing of Clio*, pp. 1–14, is one of several writers who have pointed out that Ranke's role is more complicated than the legend suggests.

13. As Leonard Krieger notes in *Ranke: The Meaning of History* (Chicago: University of Chicago Press, 1977), p. 117.

14. On the positivist distortion of Ranke, which was particularly evident in America, see Georg G. Iggers, "The Image of Ranke in American and German Historical Thought," *History and Theory* 2 (1962): 17–40. The *summum* of late nineteenth-century positivist historical methodology is Charles Langlois and Charles Seignobos, *Introduction to the Study of History*, trans. G. G. Berry (New York: Henry Holt, 1904 [orig. 1898]).

15. Hexter, "The Rhetoric of History," p. 68.

16. White, *Metahistory*, p. ix.

17. John S. Nelson, review of *Metahistory, History and Theory* 14 (1975): 75.

18. It is unfortunate that a book as important as Veyne's has been so badly translated into English. Readers able to do so may wish to consult the original, *Comment on écrit l'histoire: Essai d'épistémologie* (Paris: Seuil, 1971).

19. Veyne, *Writing History*, p. 16.

20. Carl G. Hempel, "The Function of General Laws in History" (1942), reprinted in Patrick Gardiner, ed., *Theories of History* (New York: Free Press, 1959), pp. 344–56.

21. Arthur C. Danto, *Narration and Knowledge* (including the integral text of *Analytical Philosophy of History*) (New York: Columbia University Press, 1985); F. R. Ankersmit, *Narrative Logic: A Semantic Analysis of the Historian's Language* (The Hague: Nijhoff, 1983).

22. David Hackett Fischer, *Historians' Fallacies: Toward a Logic of Historical Thought* (New York: Harper & Row, 1970). To be sure, Fischer is frequently acute in his observations on the limitations of particular historical arguments. The fault lies in their classification as "fallacies," defined by an idealized logic unrelated to field. The first work that Fischer cites in *Historians' Fallacies* is Stephen Toulmin, *The Uses of Argument* (Cambridge: Cambridge University Press, 1958). Fischer cites Toulmin favorably but does not understand Toulmin's argument. See also Douglas N. Walton, *Arguer's Position: A Pragmatic Study of Ad Hominem Attack, Criticism, Refutation, and Fallacy* (Westport, Conn.: Greenwood, 1985).

23. Irving Copi, *Introduction to Logic*, 5th ed. (New York: Macmillan, 1978), p. 87.

24. Hayden White, "The Burden of History," *History and Theory* 5 (1966): 112, 127, reprinted in White, *Tropics of Discourse: Essays in Cultural Criticism* (Baltimore: Johns Hopkins University Press, 1978), pp. 28, 43.

25. Robert Scholes and Robert Kellogg, *The Nature of Narrative* (Oxford: Oxford University Press, 1966), pp. 5–6.

26. As Dominick LaCapra points out in "History and the Novel," in LaCapra, *History and Criticism* (Ithaca: Cornell University Press, 1985), pp. 115–34.

Allan Megill and Donald N. McCloskey

27. Veyne, *Writing History*, p. 16.

28. Samuel Eliot Morison, *The European Discovery of America* (New York: Oxford University Press, 1971, 1974).

29. Carlo Ginzburg, *The Cheese and the Worms: The Cosmos of a Sixteenth-Century Miller*, trans. John and Anne Tedeschi (Baltimore: Johns Hopkins University Press, 1980).

30. George Macaulay Trevelyan, "Clio: A Muse," in *Clio, A Muse, and Other Essays Literary and Pedestrian* (London: Longmans, Green, 1913), pp. 30–31.

31. Peter Gay, *Style in History* (New York: Basic Books, 1974), pp. 188–89.

32. Hexter, "The Rhetoric of History," pp. 18–19.

33. Ibid., p. 16.

34. Robert W. Fogel, *Railroads and American Economic Growth: Essays in Econometric History* (Baltimore: Johns Hopkins University Press, 1964).

35. We here analyze pp. 10–11, the two most important pages in the book.

36. Albert Fishlow, *American Railroads and the Transformation of the Ante-Bellum Economy* (Cambridge: Harvard University Press, 1965).

37. William L. Shirer, *The Rise and Fall of the Third Reich: A History of Nazi Germany* (New York: Simon & Schuster, 1960); Karl Dietrich Bracher, *The German Dictatorship: The Origins, Structure, and Effects of National Socialism*, trans. Jean Steinberg, with an introduction by Peter Gay (New York: Praeger, 1970).

38. Bracher, *The German Dictatorship*, p. xii.

39. Scholes and Kellogg, *The Nature of Narrative*, p. 4. To be sure, there is a wider sense of narrative, exemplified in Cicero's assertion that "the *narrative* is an exposition of events that have occurred or are supposed to have occurred"; see *De Inventione*, I:xix: 27, in Cicero, *De Inventione, De Optimo Genere Oratorum, Topica*, trans. H. M. Hubbell (Cambridge: Harvard University Press, 1949). On this reading, *all* history is narrative history.

40. Shirer, *The Rise and Fall of the Third Reich*, p. xii.

41. G. R. Elton, *The Practice of History* (New York: Crowell, 1967), pp. 66, 19, 65, 177. To be fair, despite the wrong-headed epistemology, Elton's book contains much good sense.

42. For some examples, see William O. Aydelotte, *Quantification in History* (Reading, Mass.: Addison-Wesley, 1971), pp. 42–44.

43. See Aydelotte, "The Problem of Historical Generalization," in *Quantification in History*, pp. 81–82.

44. Ginzburg, *The Cheese and the Worms*, preface to the English edition, p. xii.

45. Natalie Zemon Davis, *The Return of Martin Guerre* (Cambridge: Harvard University Press, 1983), p. 1.

46. Maurice Mandelbaum, *History, Man, and Reason: A Study in Nineteenth-Century Thought* (Baltimore: Johns Hopkins University Press, 1971), pp. 41–138, 369–370.

14 ON THE WEAKNESS

OF LANGUAGE IN THE

HUMAN SCIENCES

GERALD L. BRUNS

What is the status of discourse in the human sciences?
This is (roughly) what Wilhelm Dilthey wanted to know when he asked
about the foundations of the *Geisteswissenschaften*. For Dilthey the question was whether the human sciences could be made to measure up to
the natural sciences in objective validity: the road to validity, he said,
"must pass through the objectivity of scientific knowledge."[1] Our
present intellectual situation would require us to rewrite Dilthey's
question in a number of significant ways. For one thing, it is no longer
clear that there exists, for any discipline, whether humanist or scientific, anything like a "road to validity" in Dilthey's sense of epistemological justification. For another (but perhaps this is the same
thing), there is the question of language, which Dilthey had no opportunity to address. How we address it depends on the account of language that we would give. My opinion is that on this point we have
only two options—that is, we must choose between two traditions of
giving an account of language. The one is the tradition of Gottlob
Frege, the other that of Martin Heidegger. These two traditions seem to
me incommensurable with one another in the sense that there is no
way an account of anything in the one tradition could be translated into
the other's language,[2] but it appears that both are informed by comparable (or, anyhow, parallel) insights into what Plato, in the *Seventh
Letter,* called "the weakness of the *logos*" (342 E 4: "*ton logon asthenēs*").
This weakness shows itself above all in the tendency of whatever we
put into words to get away from us and to throw what is said into question—but, of course, how we characterize this weakness (what we say
about it) will depend on whether we are Fregeans or Heideggerians.

239

Gerald L. Bruns

The point is that the view one has of the human sciences, and whether, or in what sense, they are worth anything at all (which is what Dilthey worried about), will depend on how one settles Plato's question about the *logos*. In this paper I want to show a way of settling it.

The tradition of Frege is the tradition of Bertrand Russell, the early Ludwig Wittgenstein, Alfred Tarski, and Rudolf Carnap. One way to characterize this tradition is to say that the accounts that it gives of language are not of any language anyone actually speaks, because (so Frege thought) no coherent account of any natural language can be given. One's accounts have to be of a language formalized by mathematical reasoning.[3] The great drama of this tradition has been the way in which it has struggled not just with the weakness of language, but with its contempt for this weakness ("contempt" is not too strong a word).[4] Thus one could say, as Richard Rorty says, that this tradition has in fact produced an assortment of antithetical movements—in the work of the later Wittgenstein and in ordinary-language philosophy, for example, and also in the work of Willard Quine, Wilfred Sellars, Donald Davidson, and Hilary Putnam, for whom an account of language must entail an account of its use, where "uses" means the linguistic behavior of human beings.[5] "What is it," Davidson wonders, "for words to mean what they do?"[6] This seems different from the old positivist line about pseudo-statements. However, it is not clear that an answer to Davidson's question—a theory of meaning, say, or (as Davidson would prefer) a theory of truth—can be arrived at for a language that has not been formalized or regimented or "gerrymandered" to produce a transparent picture of its workings. J. L. Austin, rather more a philologist than a logician, thought that one could simply study how people talk and be done with it, but no one seems to think this any more. How one addresses Davidson's question (whether one addresses it at all) apparently depends on exactly where one stands with respect to two discernible poles in current analytic thinking: whether, for example, one stands with Michael Dummett, who wants to uphold the rigor of the original Fregean view that what matters (perhaps *all* that matters) is the logical form of language, not its social reality (i.e., the behavior of those who use it); or whether, on the other hand, one sides with Rorty, who presses linguistic behaviorism as far as it will go, which is as far as saying that an account of language, much less a theory of meaning (or of truth), is not anything we really need—call it simply one of the things people who are good at making arguments like to argue about.[7]

What I want to do in this paper, however, is to address the question of the discourse of the human sciences from the standpoint of the Heideggerian tradition. It does not appear that analytic philosophy, in any of its forms and ingredients, can find the human sciences anything but trivial to discuss. Either one follows the hard Fregean line of Dummett, which is that the discourse of the human sciences is "just talk," and that philosophy's job is to correct such talk (or to show it up for what it is), or one follows the soft line of Rorty, which is that it is a bit silly to be talking about the human sciences at all, since there is no intelligible distinction to be drawn between the sciences and the humanities—our university disciplines are only so many heterogeneous styles (or traditions) of educated conversation. If you look for a middle ground between the logicism of Dummett and the behaviorism of Rorty, you get something like Hilary Putnam's *Meaning and the Moral Sciences*, which is very much at home when it takes up the familiar topics of analytic philosophy (Tarski's "truth theory," Quine's "indeterminacy thesis"), but which sounds very strange when it introduces, for example, the hermeneutical concept of *verstehen* that comes down to us from Friedrich Schleiermacher, Dilthey, and Hans-Georg Gadamer (a concept that historically has been made central to any discussion of what goes on in the human sciences). What Putnam makes of *verstehen* ("putting oneself in someone else's place") has very little to do with the way in which this notion has been discussed in hermeneutics.[8] It turns out that Putnam's concern is with the controversial appropriation of this idea by the social sciences (which is largely what Putnam means by the "moral sciences"), with their endless worry over whether they engage in scientific explanation (as opposed to "empathetic" understanding, which is what the social sciences mean by *verstehen*). It is not easy for me to imagine what Putnam would make of the human sciences, with their preoccupation with history and stances toward all that comes down to us from the past (poetry, philosophy, the law—not to mention physics, economics, social theory, and so on). It appears that among Putnam's people this question is either trivial or too complicated to be formulated in any interesting way.[9]

From the standpoint of the Heideggerian tradition, the question of the weakness of the *logos* was stated most forcefully by Nietzsche. "What is usually called language," Nietzsche said, "is actually all figuration."[10] How are we to take this statement? One way is to follow the thinking of Jacques Derrida and Paul de Man, who represent Heidegger's Nietzschean side, and for whom all that comes down to us from the past (but chiefly philosophy) has to be understood in the light of its gross ignorance of its own metaphoricality. What I would like to do, however, is to follow (starting from Heidegger) a line of thinking different from this deconstructive one, although, from an analytic point of view, the difference will almost certainly seem obscure. My point is that the question of the discourse of the human sciences requires us to come to terms with metaphor. In the end I want to mention the law (understood hermeneutically rather than analytically) as an example of a discourse that has come to such terms, but in order to get to this point I will have to work in some detail through two texts—Heidegger's account in section 32 of *Being and Time* of the "as-structure" of interpretation, and Gadamer's account, in his Plato essays, of Plato's notion of dialectic. This notion of dialectic is, I believe, a good way of coming to terms with the logical scandal of the "as-structure"—that is, the logical scandal of understanding and interpretation, or (what amounts to the same thing) "the weakness of the *logos*," which is just the idea, in Gadamer's words, that "the whole basis of language and speaking, the very thing which makes it possible, is ambiguity or metaphor."[11] But what can this mean if it does not mean what Nietzsche (or Derrida and de Man) thought it meant?

It seems to me that in order to determine the sense of this question, one has to approach metaphor hermeneutically rather than analytically—that is, in terms of how something is to be taken rather than in terms of its formal properties.[12] Let me try to clarify this by referring to section 32 of *Being and Time,* where Heidegger says that "interpretation is grounded existentially in understanding; the latter does not arise from the former. Nor is interpretation the acquiring of information about what is understood; it is rather the working-out of possibilities projected in understanding."[13] This is a crucial text because it is here that hermeneutics (and, one could add, the whole of the human sciences) is said to take its ontological turn away from Dilthey's project for a logical grounding of *verstehen*. Interpretation, Heidegger says, is not a methodological production of understanding; rather, it makes what is already understood explicit. Now, in order to say what this means, Heidegger introduces his notion of the "as-structure" of interpretation:

> All preparing, putting to rights, repairing, improving, rounding-out, are accomplished in the following way: we take apart in its "in-order-to" that which is circumspectively ready-to-hand, and we concern ourselves with it in accordance with what becomes visible through this process. That which has been circumspectively taken apart with regard to its "in-order-to," and taken apart as such—that which is *explicitly* understood—has the structure of *something as something*. The circumspective question as to what this particular thing that is ready-to-hand may be, receives the circumspectively interpretive answer that it is for such and such a purpose [*es ist zum* . . .]. If we tell what it is for [des Wozu], we are not simply designating something; but that

which is designated is understood *as* that *as* which we are to take the thing in question [das Genannte ist verstanden *als* das, *als* welches das in Frage stehende zu nehmen ist]. That which is disclosed in understanding—that which is understood—is already accessible in such a way that its 'as which' can be made to stand out explicitly. The 'as' makes up the structure of the explicitness of something that is understood. It constitutes the interpretation. [*SZ*, pp. 148–49; *BT*, p. 189]

The point here is that our relationship to our world, our being in it, is already hermeneutical in the sense that our world is not something strange which we are required to grasp conceptually as an object in order to make sense of it; it is a familiar world that for the most part does not require a second thought from us. In Dilthey's words, "We are at home everywhere in this historical and understood world."[14] For Heidegger, this means that we know how to get on, in a practical way, with everything around us—that is, with what is "ready-to-hand." "Circumspection" is the word Heidegger uses to characterize the special kind of sight by which we take what is ready-to-hand in the practical way that we do—that is, we do not intuit what is ready-to-hand as any sort of object; rather we take it in terms of its "in-order-to," or in terms of what it is for, or (more fundamentally still) just in terms of what it is doing there in the situation in which we find ourselves. (We know what it is doing there, and we are not surprised by it; no special account of it has to be given.) Heidegger speaks of the "equipmental" kind of being possessed by what is ready-to-hand—the example that frequently turns up in *Being and Time* is that of the hammer—but by this he does not mean that we live in a world of tools, but only that our relationship to our world is one of practical concern rather than one of theoretical interest.

Now, what I would like to know specifically is this: what is the meaning of this "as" that Heidegger emphasizes so strongly when he says that "that which is *explicitly* understood"—that is, that which is interpreted—"has the *structure of something as something*"? My opinion is that what Heidegger means is that the structure of interpretation *(Auslegung)* is figural rather than, say, intentional. The "working-out of possibilities projected in understanding" is the working-out of how something is taken, or figured, in the situation in which it is at hand; it is the explication of a question implicit in concrete circumstances as to how something is to be addressed or received or, as Heidegger says, "articulated." What sort of articulation is this? That which lies at hand is never simply grasped in the purity of its self-possession; it is never simply (or before everything else) designated *as such*. Indeed, elsewhere (in the elaboration of the notions of earth and world, for example) Heidegger will say that what anything is as such always closes itself up before every effort that we make to penetrate into it and to grasp it as an object in itself.[15] In the everyday world of practical concern, however, what lies at hand reposes not in itself but *as something:* "that which is designated," Heidegger says, "is understood *as* that *as* which we are to take the thing in question." That which is understood is not just something *there;* it is there *as something*, where the "as" means "in terms of." The "as" is a term of figuration or transference or metaphor whereby something is taken as something other than just its brute self. Heidegger calls this the "hermeneutical 'as,'" and sometimes also the "existential-hermeneutical 'as'" (*SZ*, p. 158; *BT*, p. 201). It is that by which something is taken circumspectively in terms of its situation, rather than that which is grasped "intuitively," "intentionally," or "thematically" as an object.

The upshot of what Heidegger says here is that we are not (as Dilthey, for example, thought) in a realm of consciousness; rather, we are in a realm of language. The linguistic turn in Heidegger's thinking can be located here in section 32 of *Being and Time*, not the so-called later writings on poetry, thinking, and saying. Let me try to clarify this by making the following points.

The first is that the "as" already structures our perception of the world, even before anything is remarked in the form of a statement. "In dealing with what is environmentally ready-to-hand by interpreting it circumspectively," Heidegger says, "we 'see' it as a table, a door, a carriage, a bridge. . . . Any mere pre-predicative seeing of the ready-to-hand is, in itself, something which already understands and interprets. . . . In the mere encountering of something, it is understood in terms of a totality of involvements; and such seeing hides itself in the explicitness of the assignment-relations (of the 'in-order-to') which belong to that totality" (*SZ*, p. 149; *BT*, p. 189). The "as," in other words, is primordial—that is, ontologically prior to intuition—notwithstanding the whole history of ontology since the Greeks to the contrary (cf. *SZ*, p. 358; *BT*, p. 410). "When we have to do with anything," Heidegger says, "the mere seeing of Things which are closest to us bears in itself the structure of interpretation, and in so primordial a manner that just to grasp something *free*, so to speak, *of the 'as,'* requires a certain readjustment. When we merely stare at something, our just-having-it-there-before-us lies before us *as a failure to understand it any more*. This grasping which is free of the 'as,' is a privation of the kind of seeing in which one *merely* understands. It is not more primordial than that kind of seeing, but is derived from it" (*SZ*, p. 149; *BT*, p. 190).[16] We will come back to this mere staring, or this failure to understand, in a moment.

The second point is that there will always be a plurality of interpretations with respect to our understanding of anything. Intelligibility is always plural rather than singular in the sense that understanding can be made explicit in an indefinite number of ways; or, to put it another way, understanding cannot be brought to a halt in the form of a fixed and final interpretation. The "as" means that the structure of interpretation is open, not closed; that is, it reaches out, as Heidegger likes to say, into "a totality of involvements," and it is with respect to this totality that the question always remains open as to how anything, in any situation, is to be taken. This is, of course, a notorious problem. The logical scandal of understanding has always been the difficulty of fixing it in order to make it unambiguous—that is, *free* of the "as," or free of the "totality of involvements" in which anything is encountered. (Later I will refer to the law as an example of this.) "In interpretation," Heidegger says, "we do not, so to speak, throw a 'signification' [*Bedeutung*] over some naked thing which is present-at-hand, we do not stick a value on it; but when something within-the-world is encountered as such, the thing in question already has an involvement [*Bewandtnis*] which is disclosed in our understanding of the world, and this involvement is one which gets laid out by the interpretation" (*SZ*, p. 150; *BT*, pp. 190–91). The thing in question is never just its brute self because it is never just *by itself*; its being is not just a presence-at-hand for our inspection but is *always situated*, always temporal and historical, always ready-to-hand with respect to something going on—or, indeed, with respect to many things: it is implicated in our being-in-the-world, and this is what interpretation tries to make explicit. To take something *as* something, that is, to interpret it, means to understand it in its being—that is, with respect to, or in terms of, the situation in which we find ourselves with it.

This is perhaps why, following Gadamer, we should think of understanding in terms of the situations in which it goes on rather than in terms of the entities with which it is concerned, because understanding is always of situations rather than simply of objects isolated by our subjective gaze. For Gadamer, at any rate, situations are primary: to understand means to enter into or to be in a situation in a certain way. It is not just a grasping of something. It is an affair of being rather than of consciousness.[17]

This is also why such logical notions as sign, reference, intention, and meaning (as correspondence to an object) are inadequate to describe the structure of interpretation. These notions are all object-oriented—that is, they presuppose the Cartesian-Kantian axis of subject and object. For Heidegger, they belong to the realm of assertion *(Aussage)*, which is the theme of section 33 of *Being and Time*, and which is characterized as "a derivative mode of interpretation" (*SZ*, p. 153; *BT*, p. 195). Here is the "readjustment" that Heidegger spoke of (*SZ*, p. 149; *BT*, p. 190), which allows us to grasp something "free of the 'as,'" and to resolve ambiguities and eradicate double meanings in the interest of logical purity or univocalness. Most people will recognize this "readjustment" as the beginning of philosophy (philosophy as the logically rigorous science of sciences). The assertion, Heidegger says, is a "modification" of the "as-structure" of interpretation: "When an assertion has given a definite character to something present-at-hand, it says something about it *as* a 'what'; and this 'what' is drawn *from that* which is present-at-hand as such" (*SZ*, p. 158; *BT*, p. 200). The assertion allows us to take something unambiguously by suppressing the structure of *something as something:* "In its function of appropriating what is understood," Heidegger says, "the 'as' no longer reaches out into a totality of involvements. As regards its possibilities for Articulating reference-relations, it has been cut off from that significance which, as such, constitutes environmentality. The 'as' gets pushed back into the uniform plane of that which is merely present-at-hand. It dwindles to the structure of just letting one see what is present-at-hand, and letting one see it in a definite way." Here at last we are able just to *stare* at something, that is, to take it *as such* (as something simply present)—as if this were the goal of experience! As Heidegger says, "This levelling of the primordial 'as' of circumspective concern to the 'as' with which presence-at-hand is given a definite character [an *as such*] is the specialty of assertion. Only so does it obtain the possibility of exhibiting something in such a way that we just look at it" (*SZ*, p. 158; *BT*, pp. 200–201).

What is it, however, to have something before us so that we just look at it? I have already quoted Heidegger to this effect: "When we merely stare at something, our just-having-it-there-before-us lies before us *as a failure to understand it any more*. This grasping which is free of the 'as,' is a privation of the kind of seeing in which one merely understands" (*SZ*, p. 149; *BT*, p. 190). To understand things is to be at home among them. Assertion is alienating. To be sure, in assertion we are not exactly "free of the 'as.'" It is rather that the "as" in *as such* is no longer, strictly speaking, hermeneutical (the "as" of something *as* something); it is now, Heidegger says, *apophantic*— that is, predicative, objectifying, conceptual, methodical—such that we can now take the thing in question as if it were no longer in question; that is, we can now take it in the form of a categorical statement (always taking it the same way). Heidegger's point is that this specifying of anything categorically as a "what" is, after all, just another way of taking it. The difference is that the apophantic "as" marks the transition from a circumspective concern for things (being at home among them) to a theoretical interest in them (bringing them under inspection or analysis); or, as Heidegger says, it marks "the genesis of theoretical behaviour" as against the practical behavior that makes up our everyday being-in-the-world (*SZ*, p. 360; *BT*, p. 412). Here things as such begin to take priority over the situations in which we find ourselves among them. And here we have the beginnings of our analytic and scientific attitudes—and also, one must point out, our aesthetic attitude as well.

This matter of the aesthetic attitude is worth a second thought. In his essay on "The Origin of the Work of Art," Heidegger remarks that museums are no place for works of art, since they can only exhibit them as such: that is, as deprived of their being, or in such a way that we just look at them. This is interesting because it suggests that the great work of art may well leave us, as we say, spellbound or dumbfounded—at a loss for words (beyond interpretation)—not just by virtue of any intrinsic power that it may have to hold us in thrall, but because of the place we have set aside for it, or because we have set it aside and fixed its interest for us in such a singular or single-minded way: hence, "our just-having-it-there-before-us lies before us *as a failure to understand it any more*." Our only recourse in this event is to adopt apophantic attitudes toward the work—that is, to become experts at just looking at it (connoisseurs), or proficient at showing how it works or how it is made (figuring it as a system, for example, in order to describe it in terms of its structural features, or in terms that always remain the same—as in grammar). In this way we try to recuperate the loss of understanding by means of technical knowledge or know-how. No wonder that the question of what it is to understand a work of art is one of the most difficult of all hermeneutical questions and one that is frequently repressed or converted into a matter of cultivation, taste, or sensitivity to experience. Anyhow, there is no doubt that Heidegger wants to overcome the view, basic to aesthetics since Kant, that the work of art belongs to a luminous realm of its own, or that it is simply not part of everyday being-in-the-world but is rather a liberation from everydayness. Heidegger would thus be radically opposed to Roman Ingarden, for example, and would have sided with William Carlos Williams, who said that a poem can be made out of anything—out of whatever lies at hand—as against Northrop Frye, who said that a poem can only be made out of other poems.[18] Heidegger situates the work of

Gerald L. Bruns

art within the horizon of our circumspective concern rather than before our subjective gaze. For him, the work of art is worldly: it opens up a world or gathers a world around itself, and it is in terms of the environmentality of such a world—its character as our dwelling-place—that the work is understandable. Connoisseurship means simply taking up one's place among museum pieces.

However, I want to turn this line of thinking back to Heidegger's conception of the structure of interpretation and what it can tell us about the discourse of the human sciences. The point I wish to make is that, from the standpoint of literary study, there is nothing really very strange about Heidegger's conception, and certainly nothing very scandalous. I have already characterized the hermeneutical "as" in terms of the rhetorical concept of figuration or metaphor whereby something is taken in terms of (or "as") something other than just its brute self. The "as" is not a figure of likeness or analogy in which something already taken as something is specified further as something resembling it. The term "metaphor" is being used here in its original (and metaphorical) sense of transferring the strange into the familiar in order to make sense of it, where the alternative to such transference is not anything literal or proper (something in itself) but, on the contrary, nothing at all (no "sense" of any sort). To take something in terms of its own brute self just does not make any sense; it is not to take it at all—it is not to understand it. It is, as Heidegger says, just to stare at it (blankly, as if in bewilderment). The very notion of a "brute self" is in this respect a clear example of catachresis, which is itself a species of metaphor (naming the unnamable). The notion of brute self, like that of brute fact, is an empty one—one of the empty dogmas of empiricism.

Another way to think about this is by way of the hermeneutical concept of allegory. To take something *as* something, and not just as something given as such, is to allegorize it. I mean that what Heidegger calls the "as-structure" of interpretation is nothing more or less than the traditional structure of allegory, which has always meant the taking of what cannot be taken by itself as something other, that is, as something "as which" it can be sensibly taken—as opposed to that "as which" it makes no sense at all. It is easier to see the essentially allegorical structure of interpretation if we think in terms of the understanding of texts rather than simply in terms of equipmental kinds of being like the hammer or the shoes of a peasant. "Allegory" here is to be taken in its antique rather than in its romantic and modern sense. It does not mean the personification of ideas but refers rather to the interplay between a text and the intellectual framework in which the understanding of the text goes on. Allegory here means that the reading of a text (that is, the study of it) is never simply a "grasping" of what is said or never simply a decipherment; it is always a *reading-as*—that is, a taking of what is said in a way that makes sense. "Grasping" is a metaphor that allows us to think that what we do when we read is like knowing something rather than construing it. What is said, however, can never be unequivocally determined in itself ("grasped" as such) but always presupposes something not said, something unspoken, something embedded in the situation in which the reading or study of the text occurs.

This is, in effect, what Heidegger means in his famous paragraphs in section 32 on the "fore-structure" of understanding. These paragraphs are of interest here for the way in which Heidegger puts his hammer aside in favor of the example of textual interpretation in order to make the point that when taking something *as* something, what this something is to be taken as is something that is already in place. "In every case," he says, "interpretation is grounded in *something we have in advance*"—in a *fore-having*, a *fore-sight*, and a *fore-conception* (*SZ*, p. 150; *BT*, p. 191). The frequently quoted statement is this one: "An interpretation is never a presuppositionless apprehending of something presented to us. If, when one is engaged in a particular concrete kind of interpretation, in the sense of exact textual Interpretation, one likes to appeal [*beruft*] to what 'stands there,' then one finds that what 'stands there' in the first instance is nothing other than the obvious undiscussed assumption [*Vormeinung*] of the person who does the interpreting" (*SZ*, p. 150; *BT*, pp. 191–92). What Heidegger wishes to show here is the "existential-ontological connection" between the "as-structure" of interpretation and the "fore-structure" of understanding. The two structures are, as it happens, the same, owing to the historicality of the "as." To take something as something is to take it as situated—that is, in terms of the situation in which it comes down to us and in which we find ourselves with it.

Or, in other words, the understanding of anything is always embedded in history. Thus when Philo of Alexandria, for example, in the first century B.C.E., takes the biblical story of Cain and Abel as a text of moral philosophy—as the story of the conflict between the two elemental principles of life or conduct, self-love versus the love of God—the "as" of his interpretation specifies an implicit understanding of it that the intellectual framework of Hellenism makes possible. Notice that the text is not replaced by Philo's reading of it. The text tells its story as it always does, but it always does so within a situation of understanding. The "as" opens us onto the environmentality of the understanding of the text. Philo's hermeneutical practice is, of course, the locus classicus of allegorical interpretation, and our habit is to regard

Gerald L. Bruns

such practice as misreading plain and simple, but on reflection it is hard to see how we can be right. Heidegger helps us to see, in any case, that modern practice—what he calls "exact textual Interpretation," or the sort of exegesis that philology or literary criticism performs—is no less allegorical than Philo's. When we take the biblical story of Cain and Abel "objectively" (as we say) as an ancient document to be read according to the rules of historical criticism, or in terms of any of the categories of modern textual scholarship, the "as" according to which we construe the text is no less historically situated than Philo's. It is an illusion to believe that our way of reading gives us an objectivity and a truth that Philo's does not. We take the text within the intellectual framework of currently practiced criticism, as when we construe the Cain and Abel story form-critically as, for example, a crime-and-punishment tale, one of a sequence of such tales recurring throughout the text of Genesis. As Gadamer tried to show in *Truth and Method*, a given interpretation of a text never occurs by itself, as if in some pure logical space, but is always part of a specific, finite, historical tradition of doing such a thing, so that every construction that is placed upon a text, even one that claims validity on the basis of the rules of historical criticism, is part of a vast structure of prior determinations. To make sense of a text is always to make sense of it in terms of such a structure. This is what is meant when it is said that allegory is not one method of interpretation among others—not a methodological production of understanding—but the structure of interpretation as such.[19]

The example of allegory provides a dramatic way of confronting the problem of the weakness of the *logos*. The modern reader, in any event, does not need to be reminded of the logical weakness of allegory. Indeed, the romantic and modern contempt for allegory seems to me to go hand in hand with the analytic contempt for language: both derive from what Timothy Reiss has called "the discourse of modernism," which he characterizes as "an 'analytico-referential' class of discourse" that became during the Enlightenment "the single *dominant* structure and the necessary form taken by thought, by knowledge, by cultural and social practices of all kinds."[20] In such a discourse the hermeneutical "as" is a scandal. To put it plainly, the "as" is what makes the hermeneutical circle circular: the "as" closes the circle and makes it what it is—it fills the logical "gap" between past and present, between tradition and appropriation, between what is handed down and its application in unforeseen situations, between what is said and what is understood. Yet Heidegger's line of thinking makes it difficult to feel the force of this scandal. As he says near the end of section 32, "The assimilation of understanding and interpretation to a definite ideal of knowledge is not the issue here. Such an ideal is itself only a subspecies of understanding—a subspecies which has strayed into the legitimate task of grasping the present-at-hand in its essential unintelligibility [*Unverständlichkeit*].[21] If the basic conditions which make interpretation possible are to be fulfilled, this must rather be done by not failing to recognize beforehand the essential conditions under which it can be performed. What is decisive is not to get out of the circle but to come into it in the right way" (*SZ*, p. 153; *BT*, pp. 194–95). The "as" cannot be accommodated within a hermeneutical theory that tries to describe understanding according to an epistemological model of perceptual or intentional consciousness, or according to the structure of a correspondence between subject and object. It is not that the "as" stands in the way of a coincidence of what is said with the understanding of it; on the contrary, it is that the "as" is the condition in which the understanding of what is said occurs. It is what is always in place when there is understanding. The "as" is productive rather than destructive. The notion of grasping what is said free of the "as"—of understanding as the simple reproduction of what is said—is an empty one.

Gadamer has made the productivity of the "as" a major theme of his hermeneutical reflections, not only in *Truth and Method*, with its famous words on the differential character of understanding—"It is enough to say that we understand in a different way if we understand at all" (*WM*, p. 280; *TM*, p. 264)—but also as part of his attempt to describe the dialectical structure of human thinking and discourse as such. I am referring here particularly to Gadamer's Plato essays, in which he addresses directly Plato's question concerning the weakness of the *logos*. Gadamer puts Plato's question this way: why is it that in speaking we are unable to compel anyone to understand anything? "Why does the possibility of compelling someone to understand in the way mathematics can, for example, not exist for philosophy?"[22] Why is it that in any use of language—even in our most systematic constructions—what is said always remains open to question or to second thoughts or to reversals of meaning that leave us in bewilderment? The short answer is that in everything that we say there is an element of indeterminacy that prevents us from specifying things exactly and once for all. But what does this mean? Gadamer shows that, for Plato, this indeterminacy does not merely repose in the words that we use; that is, it is not just the waywardness or ambiguity of signs, the incommensurability of words and things, that opens up our discourse in this way and makes what we say subject to constant revision. Indeterminacy invades even the great classificatory structures that we build in our attempt to overcome the ambiguity of signs by means of conceptual definition and methodical

Gerald L. Bruns

progress toward irrefutable conclusions. As Gadamer says, "The inter-weaving of the highest genera in the *Sophist* and, even more, the dialec-tical exercise which the young Socrates is put through by the elder Parmenides lead only to the *negative* insight that it is not possible to de-fine an isolated idea purely by itself, and that [the] very interweaving of ideas militates against the positive conception of a precise and un-equivocal pyramid of ideas [*die positive Vorstellung einer, eindeutigen Be-griffspyramide*]" (*DS*, p. 22; *DD*, p. 110). For Plato, as Gadamer reads him, the essential weakness of the *logos* is the weakness of conceptual predication; it is what Heidegger referred to as the eternal dependence of the apophantic "as" of assertion on the hermeneutical "as" of every-day understanding and interpretation in which things always have to be construed in respect to particular situations.

The long answer to the problem of indeterminacy, however, is that indeterminacy is not a problem. On the contrary, it is a basic compo-nent and even a basic resource of thinking and discourse: without it there would be no discourse at all. This is what Gadamer wants to ar-gue. His view is that for Plato dialectic is not a method for constructing "a precise and unequivocal pyramid of ideas." It is not (as it became for Hegel) a "method of systematic, universal development of all deter-minations of thought" (*DS*, p. 5; *DD*, p. 93). Rather, dialectic is rooted in the interdependence of the One and the Many—or, more precisely, in the interdependence of the One and what Aristotle, expounding Plato in the *Metaphysics*, called the indeterminate "dyad" (987 B 26). Gadamer sees an analogy between the theory of the generation of numbers and the discursive disposition of ideas in human thinking: both are endless and inconclusive rather than systematic and definite. In an essay on Plato's "unwritten" teaching, Gadamer (connecting Heidegger and Plato on the theme of historicality or finitude) says that this inconclusiveness results "from the nature of human knowing, which, as human, is incapable of comprehending the entire order of being and ideas *uno intuitu*. Instead it is capable of uncovering only lim-ited ordered sequences as it goes through the ideas one by one and must then relinquish these sequences again to a whole without inter-nal differentiation. . . . Although each number is definite, counting goes on indefinitely 'into infinity,' and [this] fact implies the equal in-volvement in counting of both the dyas and the hen" (*PUD*, p. 27; *DD*, p. 151). Similarly, there is an equal involvement in all thinking and dis-course of the One and the Many, Sameness and Difference, Being and Not-Being. "It is my contention," Gadamer says, "that Plato's concern is not with achieving a unified system of dihairetical generation [*dihairetischer Erzeugung*] but only with the fact that the principles of the

One and the Two are able to generate the series of all numbers—*just as they make all discourse possible"* ("PUD," p. 28; *DD*, p. 152).

It is this last remark that I would like to emphasize here: the principles of the One and the indeterminate Two "make all discourse [*Rede*] possible." This remark is, in one sense, deconstructive; that is, it implies the impossibility of systematic discourse or the ordering of ideas into a permanent and logically justifiable structure. It implies the impossibility of giving an account of anything that would stand up under questioning for all time. Hence Plato's point about "the weakness of the *logos*." Gadamer's point, however, is that discourse is dialectical rather than, as Derrida would say, a-logical and undecidable. To be sure, discourse is not a linear, constructive, progressive, and conclusive movement—here Gadamer and Derrida would be in agreement—but neither would it be enough to describe it formally as an infinite series of reinscriptions within a system of differences (or, in other words, as a purely grammatical operation). For Gadamer, it is a movement back and forth again and again over the same ground (topic or subject) between the One and the Many, determinacy and indeterminacy, something-as-such and something-as-something. "Plato's doctrine of ideas," Gadamer says, "turns out to be a general theory of relationship from which it can be convincingly deduced that dialectic is always unending and infinite. Underlying this theory would be the fact that the *logos* always requires that one idea be 'there' together with another. Insight into one idea per se does not yet constitute knowledge. [The *logos*, pace Derrida, is not logocentric.] Only when the idea is 'alluded' to in respect to another does it display itself *as* something" (*PUD*, p. 28; *DD*, p. 152). And here Gadamer refers us explicitly to Heidegger's "hermeneutic 'as'" and what he calls its "constitutive significance":

> Departing from Aristotle's analysis of the structure of
> predication, we can say that we can make a statement about a
> thing in different respects—even categorically different respects.
> As a consequence of the point of view chosen, any particular
> assertion singles something out from that about which it is made,
> and in making the assertion it "raises" the particular thing into
> our awareness. Only as a relationship thus "raised" into our
> consciousness is the relationship actually "there," i.e., placed in
> the openness and obviousness of what is present in our believing
> and our knowing. (*PUD*, p. 28; *DD*, p. 152)

Or, in other words, following Heidegger rather than Aristotle, assertion is fundamentally interpretive; that is, it is the taking of something in a certain respect, and not just in one respect but in one sense or another, *as* something and again *as* something in a categorically different respect—and so on to no finite term.

For Gadamer, this negative inconclusiveness is simply the openness of the dialectical process, which results, he says, "from the multiplicity of respects in which a thing may be interpreted in language" [*der Mannigfaltigkeit sprachlicher Auslegungshinsichten*] (*DS*, p. 23; *DD*, p. 111). Gadamer is thinking here of what Aristotle says about the productivity of the dyad: "[Plato's] making the other entity besides the One a dyad was due to the belief that numbers, except those which were prime, could be neatly produced out of the dyad as out of some plastic material" (*Metaphysics*, 987 B 34–38). The indeterminacy of the Two is productive. Similarly, the productivity of the dialectic lies in the endless saying of things (about whatever is in question) that indeterminacy at once requires and makes possible. In this regard Gadamer asks us to remember the first hypothesis in Plato's *Parmenides:*

> There that multiplicity [of respects] was not a burdensome ambiguity [*Vieldeutigkeit*] to be eliminated but an entirety of interrelated aspects of meaning [*ein Ganzes in sich zusammenhängender Bedeutungshinsichten*] which articulate a field of knowing [*Sachereich*]. The multiple valences of meaning which separate from one another in speaking about things contain a productive ambiguity, one pursued, as we know, not only by the academy but also by Aristotle with all his analytic genius. The productivity of this dialectic is the positive side of the ineradicable weakness from which the procedure of conceptual determination suffers. That ever contemporary encounter [*alternde Widerfahrnis*] with the logoi of which Plato speaks [*Philebus* 15 D 9–10] is found here in its most extreme form. It is displayed here as the experience which we have when the conventional meaning of single words gets away from us. But Plato knows full well that this source of all *aporia* is also the source of *euporia* which we achieve in discourse. He who does not want the one will have to do without the other. An unequivocal, precise coordination of the sign world with the world of facts, i.e., of the world of which we are the master with the world which we seek to master by ordering it with signs, is not language. The whole basis of language and speaking, the very thing which makes it possible, is ambiguity or "metaphor," as the grammar and rhetoric of a later time will call it. (*DS*, pp. 23–24; *DD*, p. 111)

What Gadamer says here will seem strange only if we continue to hold exclusively to the perspective of language as a system of taxonomic differences or as a system of designations and rules for the making of propositions, because for Gadamer language is always escaping system and rule—always getting away from us: "We speak," he says in *Truth and Method*, "and the word goes beyond us to consequences and ends which we had not, perhaps, conceived of" (*TM*, p. 497). However, this open indeterminacy is not, therefore, a disruption of reason; rather, it is an emancipation of reason from what has already been decided and fixed upon or what is already in force without regard to what time may turn up. It is an openness of reason to new sources of understanding—an openness of logic to history. Only in this emancipation from what is fixed is insight possible.

As Gadamer says, this openness can be characterized rhetorically by means of the concept of metaphor, where metaphor is not a trope of likeness but the trope of tropes, the figure of figuration—that is, the turning of one thing into another that enables us to interpret it endlessly in a "multiplicity of respects," now as this, now as that, without ever exhausting our inventory of things to say. Gadamer's own preference, however, is to characterize this openness by appealing to the figure of the question and specifically to the interplay of *aporia* and *euporia*, bewilderment and insight, in Socratic questioning.

Socratic questioning, Gadamer says, never simply deposits us at an impasse. In *Truth and Method*, for example, Gadamer speaks of "the logical structure of openness" (*WM*, p. 344; *TM*, p. 325) that belongs to the nature of experience insofar as experience is not simply inductive but (as in the Socratic dialogues) an experience of the negation, reversal, or supercession of what is in place and accepted as such. "Every experience worthy of the name," Gadamer says, "runs counter to our expectation" (*WM*, p. 338; *TM*, p. 319). However, this is the negativity of the opening and not just the negativity of the Chinese Wall at which everything must come to a stop: "The recognition that an object [*die Sache*] is not as we first thought," Gadamer says, "obviously involves the question of whether it was this or that. The openness that is part of experience is, from a logical point of view, precisely an openness of being this or that. It has the structure of a question" (*WM*, p. 344; *TM*, p. 325). To pose a question of something is not just a way of unmooring it and setting it adrift (not just a way of getting rid of it); it is to restore it to the domain of understanding where it is once more open to interpretation and once more in a position to be taken, one way or another, in respect to something. It is, so to speak, reconnected to something at issue, or to what Gadamer calls "the sense of the question." "To ask a question," Gadamer says:

> means to bring into the open. The openness of what is in question [*des Gefragten*] consists in the fact that the answer is not settled. It must still be undetermined [*noch in der Schwebe sein*], in order that a decisive answer can be given. The revelation of the questionability of what is questioned [that is, its ability to be taken as this or that or in a different sense] constitutes the sense of the question. The object [*die Gefragte*] has to be brought into this state of indeterminacy, so that there is an equilibrium pro and contra. The sense of every question is realised in passing through this state of indeterminacy in which it becomes an open question. (*WM*, p. 345; *TM*, pp. 326–27)

The question, like Heidegger's "as-structure"—like Platonic dialectic and like metaphor and ambiguity—is structured as an interplay of determinacy and indeterminacy, or as a structure of plural (or, as Gadamer would say, open) signification. Insight, or what Gadamer calls "the sudden idea" *(Einfall)*, has this same structure. It is rooted in the *aporia*—that is, in the negativity of experience that has been analyzed so vividly in deconstruction. "Insight [*Einsicht*] is more than the knowledge of this or that situation," Gadamer says. "It always involves an escape from something that had deceived us and held us captive" (*WM*, p. 338; *TM*, pp. 319–20). Insight is never simply intuition; it is an unexpected turn in thinking produced by the recognition of difference, otherness, duplicity, the plurality of sense or the metaphoricality of what had been taken as definite. Insight in this respect is always deconstructive. What distinguishes Gadamer from Derrida and de Man, however, is that Gadamer never loses sight of what is in question. Whereas deconstruction always has its eye on a mental state (undecidability, for example, or freedom from deception), Gadamer's eye is always on *die Sache* or *die Gefragte*—that is, always on the subject at issue, or that which calls for understanding. Deconstruction turns the negativity of experience into a method—a "hermeneutics of suspicion" by which we try to free ourselves from whatever comes down to us from the past or by which we try to escape our own historicality. By contrast, the opening of which Gadamer speaks is never simply the methodical emancipation from mental bondage; it is an opening into what is in question. It is how understanding occurs—whatever the case. "The real nature of a sudden idea [*Einfall*]," Gadamer says, "is perhaps less the sudden realisation of the solution to a problem than the sudden realisation of the question that advances into the openness and thus makes an answer possible. Every sudden idea has the structure of a question" (*WM*, p. 348; *TM*, p. 329). Insight does not mean that we now know how something is to be taken care of or dispensed with; it means that now we understand what is at issue and how we may proceed. As Wittgenstein would say, it means that now we can go on.

When Gadamer speaks of "the hermeneutical priority of the question" (*WM*, p. 344; *TM*, p. 325), he means that we understand something only when we are able to hold it in question. That which is taken as settled and fixed is not understood; that is, it is just not understandable in its own terms but has to be restored to the qestioning that gives it its sense. Here we can begin to see what Gadamer means when he says that "the logic of the human sciences . . . is the logic of the question" (*WM*, p. 352; *TM*, p. 333). That is, the logic of the human sciences is dialectical rather than propositional. It consists in keeping open what propositional thinking tries to close up; it makes it possible to understand things in their historicality, that is, in their temporal being. The understanding of things in their historicality has always been the task of the human sciences.

A perfect example of the meaning of this task is to be found in legal understanding. It is well known that the meaning of a law can never be fixed as if it were a grammatical or logical rule, because it always has to be forceful or binding in relation to a particular state of affairs in which some question needs to be decided.[23] The law is perhaps the most fruitful example we have of what is meant by tradition—and also of what is meant by a human science.[24] The law comes down to us from the past, not, however, as so many museum pieces that have to be referred back to their original state in order to be understood, but as a language that is appropriated anew at every moment of its history. As a language the law is not a fixed system but an ongoing discourse structured as a dialectic of text and history—that is, a movement back and forth between a traditional text and the situation in which we are called upon to decide something.[25] As I have said elsewhere in this connection, "The law will be that by which we understand our present situation, even as our situation will throw its light upon the law or help us to understand the law more fully, or in a way that will enable the law to remain forceful instead of lapsing into a merely documentary existence."[26]

I began by asking about the status of discourse in the human sciences, particularly with respect to the logical weakness of language—its metaphoricality and historicality. I have come round to the example of the law as a discourse that depends upon metaphoricality and historicality for its existence. It seems to me that here we have a way of rewriting Dilthey's question about the foundations of the human sciences, for now it is clear that it more closely resembles a question about what it is for a law to be just than one about the justification of propositions, beliefs, claims to truth, or intellectual disciplines. My point, at any rate, would be that if we wish to understand the human sciences, we ought to reflect, not on physics or mathematics or analytic philosophy of language, but on the law, because the law is exemplary for the discourse of the human sciences in view of its openness to new situations and to the multiple interpretation that history demands. In this respect the discourse of the human sciences is not just a discourse that we perform but one in which we stand as within a jurisdiction or a horizon of being. The temporal openness of this discourse, so far from being a logical defect, is rather its strength, since it is what enables us to make our way in the world, providing us with the ability to speak exactly in a historical rather than simply in a logical sense—enabling us to respond exactly to unheard-of situations. Otherwise we would be like the written word about which Socrates complains in the *Phaedrus*, always repeating the same thing, never understanding what we say (274 D 1–7).

Indeed, Plato understood the paradoxical aspect of the "weakness of the *logos*" very well, although this is a side of his thinking that professional philosophers sometimes seem anxious to repress. In the *Philebus*, for example, Socrates distinguishes between two sorts of understanding [*epistēmē*], "one turning its eyes towards transitory things, the other towards things which neither come into being nor pass away, but are the same and immutable forever" (61 D 12–E 1: Loeb trans.). A distinction of this sort is frequently taken to be foundational for philosophy and to be the prototype of the historical distinction between the natural and the human sciences, or between logic and history, or between mathematics and metaphor. What does not often get noticed is the hermeneutical turn that Socrates gives to this distinction in the *Philebus*:

> SOCRATES: Let us assume, then, a man who possesses wisdom about the nature of justice itself, and reason in accordance with his wisdom, and has the same kind of knowledge of all other things.
>
> PROTARCHUS: Agreed.
>
> SOCRATES: Now will this man have sufficient knowledge, if he is master of the theory of the divine circle and sphere, but is ignorant of our human sphere and human circles, even when he

uses these and other kinds of rules or patterns in building houses?

PROTARCHUS: We call that a ridiculous state of intellect, Socrates, which is concerned only with divine knowledge.

SOCRATES: What? Do you mean to say that the uncertain and the impure art of the false rule and circle is to be put in our mixture?

PROTARCHUS: Yes, that is inevitable, if any man is ever to find his own way home. (62 A 2–B 8)

Or, in other words, the good life—in fact, the very possibility of living at all—requires that we loosen up what is logically fixed. Wisdom purified of temporality is just no wisdom at all.

NOTES

1. Wilhelm Dilthey, "The Construction of the Historical World in the Human Studies," in *Selected Writings,* trans. H. P. Rickman (Cambridge: Cambridge University Press, 1976), p. 183.

2. See, however, Ernst Tugendhat, *Traditional and Analytical Philosophy: Lectures on the Philosophy of Language,* trans. P. A. Gorner (Cambridge: Cambridge University Press, 1982), which tries to raise a theory of meaning on the basis of an analysis of the predicative sentence—and which is dedicated to the memory of Martin Heidegger. Tugendhat says: "I became convinced that Heidegger's question about the understanding of 'Being' can only acquire a concrete and realizable meaning within the framework of a language-analytical philosophy. Although there is hardly any mention of Heidegger in these lectures I owe to him the specific mode of access with which I approach the problems of analytical philosophy" (p. x).

3. The classic text here is Alfred Tarski's "The Concept of Truth in Formalized Languages" (1931), in which formalized languages are "roughly characterized as artificially constructed languages in which the sense of every expression is unambiguously determined by its form." See Tarski, *Logic, Semantics, Metamathematics,* trans. J. H. Woodger (Oxford: Clarendon Press, 1956), pp. 165–66.

4. See Michael Dummett, "Frege's Distinction Between Sense and Reference," in *Truth and Other Enigmas* (Cambridge: Harvard University Press, 1978), p. 116: "Frege was the founder both of modern logic and of modern philosophy of language. The use of the latter phrase, in connection with him, has an odd ring, since he frequently expressed a contempt for language; he did so because, on his pen, 'language' meant 'natural language,' and he believed that natural languages are very faulty instruments for the expression of thought. Not only are surface appearances, in sentences of natural language,

Gerald L. Bruns

grossly misleading, but, according to Frege, natural languages are incoherent in the sense that no complete systematic account of the use of the sentences of such a language could be framed."

5. Rorty calls this "epistemological behaviorism," or "what society lets us say," in *Philosophy and the Mirror of Nature* (Princeton: Princeton University Press, 1979), pp. 173–82. See Rorty's account of the antipositivist turn in analytic thinking in "Philosophy in America Today," in *Consequences of Pragmatism* (Minneapolis: University of Minnesota Press, 1982), pp. 211–30. The return of positivism is represented by Michael Dummett, who argues that it is not the theory of knowledge which is foundational for philosophy (and all intellectual disciplines) but rather the theory of meaning. See Dummett, *Frege: Philosophy of Language*, 2d ed. (Cambridge: Harvard University Press, 1981), p. 669.

6. Donald Davidson, *Inquiries Into Truth and Interpretation* (Oxford: Clarendon Press, 1984), p. xiii. For Davidson, a theory of how words mean, or a theory of truth, must contain, or be accompanied by, a theory of interpretation, which is what he means by an account of how speakers (and listeners) behave—what they believe on given occasions of utterance, and so on. See "Thought and Talk," in *Truth and Interpretation*, pp. 155–70.

7. The question of whether theories of meaning or truth can be adapted to natural languages is discussed by Dummett, "What Is a Theory of Meaning? (II)," in Gareth Evans and John McDowell, eds., *Truth and Meaning: Essays in Semantics* (Oxford: Clarendon Press, 1976), p. 68; and Davidson, "Radical Interpretation," in *Truth and Interpretation*, pp. 132–33. See also Michael Dummett, "The Social Character of Meaning," in *Truth and Other Enigmas*, esp. pp. 424–26, in which he makes the argument that Frege's disregard of the social reality of language was a mistake but not one that amounted to very much. See also Dummett, *Truth and Other Enigmas*, p. xii: "I began my philosophical career thinking of myself as a follower of Wittgenstein; and, although I should no longer have claimed this in 1960, it helped to inoculate me against the influence of Austin; although he was himself unquestionably a clever man, I always thought that the effect of his work on others was largely harmful, and therefore regretted the nearly absolute domination that for a time he exercised over Oxford philosophy." In much the same spirit many in analytic philosophy now write ordinary-language philosophy off as a position without adherents, but Stanley Cavell maintains a strong allegience to Austin—although less as a linguistic philosopher than as a "philosopher of the ordinary." Cavell gives an autobiographical reflection on this point in "Politics as Opposed to What?" in W. J. T. Mitchell, ed., *The Politics of Interpretation* (Chicago: University of Chicago Press, 1983), pp. 181–202. See Rorty, "Philosophy in America Today," pp. 218–23.

8. Hilary Putnam, *Meaning and the Moral Sciences* (Boston, London, and Henley: Routledge & Kegan Paul, 1978), pp. 74–75. Dilthey, of course, thought of *verstehen* as *Nacherleben* or *Nachbildung*, not as *Einfühlung*. See *Selected Writings*, pp. 226–27.

9. See Michael Dummett, "The Reality of the Past," in *Truth and Other Enigmas*, pp. 358–74.

10. Carole Blair, trans., "Nietzsche's Lecture Notes on Rhetoric," *Philosophy and Rhetoric* 16 (1983): 108.

11. Hans-Georg Gadamer, "Dialektik und Sophistik im siebenten platonischen Brief," *Heidelberger Akademie der Wissenschaften: Philosophisch-Historische Klasse* 2 (1964): 23–24, hereafter cited as *DS*; "Dialectic and Sophism in Plato's Seventh Letter," in *Dialogue and Dialectic: Eight Hermeneutical Studies on Plato*, trans. P. Christopher Smith (New Haven: Yale University Press, 1980), p. 111, hereafter cited as *DD*.

12. As Paul Ricoeur says, "a metaphor does not exist by itself, but [only] in and through an interpretation": *Interpretation Theory: Discourse and the Surplus of Meaning* (Fort Worth: Texas Christian University Press, 1976), p. 50. A metaphor is a false statement that one reads in such a way as to make it true. See Donald Davidson, "What Metaphors Mean," in *Inquiries Into Truth and Interpretation*, pp. 245–64. If I understand him correctly, Davidson argues that an analytic theory of metaphor is impossible, since you cannot tell a metaphor by its form.

13. *Sein und Zeit* (Tübingen: Max Niemeyer, 1960), p. 148, hereafter cited as *SZ*; *Being and Time*, trans. John Macquarrie and Edward Robinson (New York: Harper & Row, 1962), pp. 188–89, hereafter cited as *BT*.

14. *Selected Writings*, p. 191.

15. For example, in "The Origin of the Work of Art," in Heidegger, *Poetry, Language, Thought*, trans. Albert Hofstadter (New York: Harper & Row, 1971), pp. 17–81.

16. One could compare this with Wittgenstein's famous duck-rabbit remarks in *Philosophical Investigations* (where seeing is always "seeing-as"), but in fact the apt comparison would be with Nietzsche's idea that perception itself is metaphorical. See Lawrence Hinman, "Nietzsche, Metaphor, and Truth," in *Philosophy and Phenomenological Research* 43 (1982–83): 184–85. The point is that Heidegger's conception of the "as-structure" of interpretation, like Nietzsche's notion of metaphor, puts any sort of empiricism—including Wittgenstein's—out of the question.

17. *Wahrheit und Methode* (Tübingen: J. C. B. Mohr, 1960), pp. 284–90, hereafter cited as *WM*; *Truth and Method*, trans. and ed. Garrett Barden and John Cumming (New York: Seabury Press, 1975), pp. 267–74, hereafter cited as *TM*.

18. See Williams, *Kora in Hell: Improvisations*, in his *Imaginations*, ed. Webster Schott (New York: New Directions, 1970), p. 70; and Frye, *Anatomy of Criticism* (Princeton: Princeton University Press, 1957), p. 97.

19. I have made this argument about allegory at greater length in "The Problem of Figuration in Antiquity," in Gary Shapiro and Alan Sica, eds., *Hermeneutics: Questions and Prospects* (Amherst: University of Massachusetts Press, 1984), pp. 147–64. There is a similar argument by Fredric Jameson in *The Political Unconscious: Narrative as a Socially Symbolic Act* (Ithaca: Cornell

Gerald L. Bruns

University Press, 1980), pp. 17–102. Allegory, properly understood, is not a repression of what a text says but an opening up of reading to the claims that a text makes, in contrast to a documentary form of reading, which puts the claims of a text aside as part of its own claim to be an "objective" and "true" reading. Allegory presupposes a dialogical rather than a subject-object relationship with a text.

20. Timothy J. Reiss, *The Discourse of Modernism* (Ithaca: Cornell University Press, 1982), p. 23

21. Cf. *SZ*, p. 149; *BT*, p. 90: "When we merely stare at something, our just-having-it-there-before-us lies before us *as a failure to understand it any more.*" The "present-at-hand in its essential unintelligibility" is that which we seek to grasp "free of the 'as,'" as when we take a theoretical interest in something in contrast to our being-with it in our everyday practical concerns.

22. *DS*, p. 18; *DD*, p. 99; references below will also be to Gadamer, "Platons ungeschriebene Dialectik," in *Heidelberger Akademie der Wissenschaften: Philosophisch-Historische Klasse* 2 (1968): 9–30, hereafter cited as *PUD;* and to "Plato's Unwritten Dialectic," in *DD*, pp. 124–55.

23. See, for example, Ronald Dworkin, "The Model of Rules," and also "Hard Cases," in *Taking Rights Seriously* (Cambridge: Harvard University Press, 1977), pp. 14–45, 81–130.

24. Edward H. Levi, *An Introduction to Legal Reasoning* (Chicago: University of Chicago Press, 1949), p. 6: "It is only folklore which holds that a statute if clearly written can be completely unambiguous and applied as intended to a specific case. Fortunately or otherwise, ambiguity is inevitable in both statute and constitution as well as with case law." A related topic is the problem of "legal fictions." See Lon Fuller's celebrated essays on this subject in *Legal Fictions* (Stanford, Calif.: Stanford University Press, 1967), esp. pp. 93–138: "Is Fiction an Indispensable Instrument of Human Thinking?"

25. H. L. A. Hart, *The Concept of Law* (Oxford: Clarendon Press, 1961), p. 125.

26. "Law as Hermeneutics: A Response to Ronald Dworkin," in Mitchell, *The Politics of Interpretation*, p. 317. See James Boyd White's valuable essay, "Constituting a Culture of Argument: The Possibilities of American Law," in *When Words Lose Their Meaning: Constitutions and Reconstitutions of Language, Character, and Community* (Chicago: University of Chicago Press, 1984), pp. 231–74. Both Dworkin and White try to loosen up the analytical conception of legal discourse by taking recourse to the analogy of law and literature. This analogy, however, seems to me to block a hermeneutical conception of the law, since it constrains one to approach the law from the standpoint of one who writes rather than from the standpoint of one who understands.

15 LITERARY INTERPRETATION

AND THE RHETORIC OF THE

HUMAN SCIENCES

PAUL HERNADI

Anyone who makes a living by taking literature seriously has good reason to applaud the current interest in the rhetoric of the human sciences. That interest evinces not only the revival of the ancient art—or is it the oldest human science?—of rhetoric. It also signals a growing awareness of the literary dimension of all speech and writing. When human scientists begin to reflect on the master metaphors of their texts, the literary critic can welcome them as fellow students of figurative language. When they discover the role of plausible storytelling at various stages of their inquiry, the literary critic can feel reinforced in his or her concern for narrative structure. And when they recognize that their disciplines evolve in the institutional settings of conversation, the literary critic can rejoice in seeing concepts of dramatic interaction applied to what often masquerades as an unsituated, disembodied use of words.

Some academic planners will no doubt continue to regard the familiar triad of freshman or sophomore English courses on poetry, fiction, and drama as a device to prevent undergraduates from overcrowding the computer center and to keep literary scholars off the welfare roles. But from the vantage point of a volume like this one, things look different. Human scientists investigating the rhetoric of their own fields may regard poetry, fiction, and drama classes as pedagogically essential laboratories where thought experiments are being performed on three basic features of verbal communication: polysemous language, narrative worldmaking, and interpersonal dialogue. On such a view, even the recent expansion of the traditional literary curriculum seems eminently justified. Why not study proverbs and aphorisms, essays, sermons, and manifestos, biographies, autobiographies, philosophical dialogues, and the Bible *as literature*? If placed in the context of poetry, fiction, and drama, such works of assertive discourse can serve very well indeed to highlight semantic overdetermination, stipulative referentiality, and situated occurrence as irreducible aspects of all speech and writing.[1]

Nothing would seem more natural for professors of literature than to embrace this kind of definition of their field of teaching and research. No more need to apologize for the multiple sense of what poetry says, the imaginative reference of what fiction speaks about, or the relativistically perspectival image that the structure of dramatic dialogue projects of human motivation and action. And certainly no need to defend literature against the ever-recurring charges against it as vague (if not purposefully equivocating) discourse engaged in escapist, vicarious wish fulfillment (if not calculated deception) through inauthentic roleplaying (if not premeditated self-effacement with ulterior motives). After all, if all discourse, including the language of the human sciences, turns out to be situationally conditioned figurative storytelling, those traditional charges against imaginative literature appear to have missed their target.

This is not the place to rehearse the history of the attacks on literature and of the defensive counterattacks by (to name three) Aristotle against Plato's *Republic,* Sir Philip Sidney against the Puritans, and Percy Bysshe Shelley against protoscientistic utilitarianism.[2] Suffice it to say that a latter-day proponent of the Perfect State, Revealed Truth, or Technological Progress may at any time "retarget" the missiles so as to threaten, rather than poetry, fiction, and drama, the human sciences themselves *as* poetry, fiction, and drama: deplorable instances of what they appear to imply all discourse is—namely, referentially vacuous verbal roleplaying. It may thus be well to insist, by way of reappropriating some insights from earlier defenses of literature, on the indispensable cultural significance of poetic, imaginative, and performative discourse.[3] My present purpose is different, however. In this essay, I will try to shed light on the rhetoric of the human sciences from the point of view of literary interpretation.

Let me start by making a simple distinction between rhetoric and hermeneutics as complementary approaches to human communication. Whereas the prime domain of rhetoric is expression, hermeneutics focuses on comprehension. It ought to go without saying that verbal expression and its comprehension—speaking and writing on the one hand, listening and reading on the other—are very different activities. Yet two facts seem to militate against clear thinking on the subject. One is that no product of spoken or written expression can function as a means of communication unless it is comprehended as such. The other is that the (always mental) process of comprehension becomes available for public inspection only when it has been transformed into a new (audible or visible) product of expression. Thus we tend to speak and even think about T. S. Eliot's "reading" of *Hamlet*, for example, when in fact we mean to speak or think about our reading of one of his writings about the play. What gets lost in this terminological muddle is not only the rhetorical dimension of all expressed comprehension—just how the circumstances of a verbal formulation and its intended audience influence the way in which mental acts of comprehension will be expressed. More important still, we risk losing sight completely of the less obvious difference between Eliot's actual reading of a particular passage of the play and his subsequent thinking about that reading experience with a view to clarifying, whether for himself or an intended audience, what he has read and how. Someday in the perhaps not too distant future, the difference between the mental acts involved in verbally triggered comprehension, deliberate interpretation, and verbal expression may become observable through the analysis of brain waves. For the time being, however, we forego the best chance we have of recognizing, through informed introspection, the interplay of hermeneutic and rhetorical activities in the internal dialogue of deliberate interpretation if we fail to distinguish between purely hermeneutic comprehension and purely rhetorical expression.

As the rhetorical art—or is it the second oldest human science?—of interpretation, systematic hermeneutics has evolved to guide precisely that passage from initially private comprehension to eventually public expression. One becomes aware of the need for such an art or science when the road toward spontaneous comprehension is suddenly blocked. In the absence of such mental roadblocks, we tend to be no more conscious of our interpretive activity than cats or birds can be supposed to realize that they engage in the instinctual "rhetoric" and "hermeneutics" underlying their courtship behavior. Yet all comprehension, and especially the comprehension of spoken or written words, involves a great deal of interpretation. When we assume that we can do without deliberate rhetorical-hermeneutic activity, we have only taken for granted a particular line of interpretation that has been or could have been based on our initial comprehension of a set of verbal or nonverbal signs.[4]

This is most often the case with inferential interpretation, rudimentary instances of which also occur in the animal kingdom. Take the hunter's interpretation of a footprint or of a large black cloud as indicating that a deer has crossed his path or that a storm is coming. His inter-

Paul Hernadi

pretation is based on the assumption of a factual connection between an unintended nonverbal sign and what that sign means as a clue for past or future events. In literary and other kinds of textual interpretation, the drawing of inferences on the basis of clues cannot even begin without some familiarity with the linguistic conventions that enable us to comprehend a set of verbal signs as a communicated message. To the extent that we possess a "native" or near-native command of a particular language, we will express and comprehend messages couched in that language quasi-spontaneously—as if the cultural potential of its code has become what used to be called our "second nature." But I cannot interpret the recurrence of a stylistic feature in a Japanese text as a clue that was factually conditioned, for example, by its author's repressed Oedipal feelings or ill-disguised petty bourgeois ideology if I have not learned the linguistic conventions of Japanese. Whatever "seeped into" a text from the factual infrastructure of its natural or social context must thus be inferred from the text after it has been comprehended as a coded cultural product of verbal expression.

Some "seepage" of this kind occurs in virtually every discourse. Therefore, our inferential detection of factual connections, however hypothetical, between a text and its historical context can usefully supplement our no less hypothetical, convention-based decoding of the author's verbalized "message." The same statement applies to oral utterances in an even more obvious way: their verbal appeal to our comprehension is typically accompanied by a set of clues (e.g., accent, intonation, gestures) to the speaker's background, motivation, and personality. In certain instances, however, our interpretation of message and seepage elicits a strong sense of the interpreted expression's existential relevance to our own decisions and actions. Such relevance is attributed by theological and by legal hermeneutics to sacred scriptures and to decrees of human law. In the interpretive theory and practice of those disciplines, it has long been recognized that the more or less accurate discovery of the communicative intentions and historical situation of the people who wrote, for instance, the Bible or the United States Constitution does not exhaust the meaning of either text for a person who aspires to live in accordance with it. He or she must also learn what a text of this kind, emerging from the past yet perceived to be still valid, means here and now.

Literary hermeneutics likewise confronts past texts with a strong claim of present validity on responsive readers.[5] Literary interpreters must thus go beyond explicating linguistically coded messages and explaining historically conditioned seepage. They also need to explore in what sense (if any) they feel directly addressed by works like the *Odys-*

sey, Hamlet, or *Madame Bovary* as versions of the imperative *Du musst dein Leben ändern* ("You must change your life").[6] That imperative is attributed in Rilke's famous sonnet about an "Archaic Torso of Apollo" to a partially preserved sculpted image, and we may generalize the poet's message as follows: all art requires the onlooker's active imaginative participation for the comprehension of its *ad personam* existential meaning. As is the case with the suggestively incomplete torso in the Rilke poem, the literary work's present appeal to us does not reside in the extant decodable message—that truncated product of an act of expression which is now largely divorced from the concrete intentionality of its original occurrence. Nor does it reside in the perhaps reconstructable but certainly past, "dated" set of factual circumstances that can be said to have occasioned the expressive act. Rather, it emerges from the imaginative interaction between text and reader. This is why literary hermeneutics cannot be based exclusively on the Saussurean model of the verbal sign as the unity of the signifier and the signified in the precoded system of a particular *langue*—the sum total of phonological, lexical, and grammatical conventions of a given language at a given stage of its historical development.[7] And this is also why the critic's hermeneutic endeavor must both include and transcend the inferential interpretation of the decoded message as a set of factually determined clues on which to base the discovery of historically conditioned seepage.

Interpretation in general and literary interpretation in particular are concerned with profoundly situated acts of comprehension. To invoke another term from Ferdinand de Saussure's posthumously published *Course in General Linguistics,* systematic hermeneutics is or should be the study of the historically situated reception of historically situated *paroles,* and those verbal products of oral or written expression carry potential meaning in the three combinable modes of signification distinguished by Charles Sanders Peirce as the symbolic, the indexical, and the iconic.[8] As a set of Peircean symbols, the literary work conveys an authorial message on the basis of codified *conventional association* between signifier and signified. As a set of Peircean indexes, it points to biographical or culture-specific seepage (e.g., repressed desires or ideological distortions) on the basis of inferred *factual connection* between indicator and indicated. And as a Peircean icon or set of icons, it projects the image of a desirable or undesirable world that, on the basis of *perceived similarity* or pronounced dissimilarity to the reader's own world, brings about or reinforces the reader's commitment to affirm or else to change the latter.

Paul Hernadi

Peirce realized, of course, that the symbolic or conventionally coded, indexical or factually conditioned, and iconic or similarity-based modes of signification usually interact, with one serving as *primus inter pares*. From the point of view of literary hermeneutics, his remarks about why "the iconic character is the prevailing one" in algebraic formulas are particularly illuminating: "For a great distinguishing property of the icon is that by the direct observation of it *other truths concerning its object* can be discovered than those which suffice to determine its construction. Thus, by means of two photographs a map can be drawn, etc. . . . . This *capacity of revealing unexpected truth* is precisely that wherein the utility of algebraical formulae consists."[9] I submit that literature's "capacity of revealing unexpected truth" to the minds of successive generations of interpreters relies on the ability of great works to acquire new meaning in the iconic dimension of their signification. As quasi-algebraic formulas of human experience, they present ever new imperatives by asking and answering ever new questions in the historically changing world of their readers.

To be sure, our comprehension of a literary work (just like our comprehension of any other text or utterance) need not reach the articulate stage of an explicitly verbalized interpretation. The explication of what we take to be the work's authorial message, the explanation of what strikes us in the work as historically conditioned seepage, and the exploration of what we experience as the mimetic image evoked by the work may remain in the realm of unexpressed mental events. Yet even our unexpressed, rhetorical-hermeneutic acts of mental explication, explanation, and exploration have much in common with three types of usually public interpretation. I am thinking of the interpretive activities of (1) translators who attempt to *reproduce* or at least approximate a verbal message in a different language; (2) medical diagnosticians or criminal investigators who attempt to *infer* from what they consider symptoms or clues to the underlying facts of either health or disease, of either guilt or innocence; and (3) performers who attempt to *enact* a role (e.g., Hamlet) through existential participation in its mimetic potential. The three analogies seem to me to apply whether or not we go public with our interpretations: we "explicate" the work by *standing under* the linguistic code governing it as symbolically conveyed message; we "explain" the work by *standing over,* and looking with the bird's eye view of historical hindsight at, the circumstances that have conditioned it and are indexically signified by it as factual seepage; and we "explore" the work by *standing in for* the "mode of being in the world,"[10] that it iconically projects as an image of our own potential existence. It is clear, however, that our private interpretive acts of under-standing, over-standing, and standing-in-for the work—those incipient attempts at reproductive translation, inferential detection, and existential enactment—tend to become one-sided and even idiosyncratic unless they are tested against each other and especially against other people's explications, explanations, and explorations.[11] This is why public acts of interpretation are required for the literary tradition to remain a living force in historically changing culture.

Some proponents of empathetic explication, inferential explanation, and participatory exploration slight or even oppose what they perceive as illegitimate rivals to their favored line of hermeneutic inquiry. They tell us that the main or proper objective of the critical reader is, respectively, to "reconstruct" the author's communicative intention, to "deconstruct" the text's symptomatic façade, or to "construct" a personally or socially relevant reappropriation of the work in question.[12] It seems to me, however, that great works of literature cannot exert their full impact unless their capacity of signifying as Peircean symbols, indexes, *and* icons is continually heeded. Indeed, our best moments of private comprehension tend to integrate silent acts of under-standing, over-standing, and standing-in-for into a single response to the work as message, seepage, and image. In the public dialogue of critical readers, too, it is essential to promote interaction between differently oriented theories and practices of interpretation lest the history of literary reception degenerate into random clashes of blindfolded intellectual armies doing battle in the night of willful ignorance.

How does all this, including my last pluralistic exhortation to fellow interpreters of literature, apply to the theory and practice of the human sciences? Were it not for my awareness of the figurative aspect of all discourse, I would say: literally. There is no reason why human scientists should not attempt to explicate, explain, and explore all instances of human speech and writing as message, seepage, and image. It is true that most texts and utterances that they study, as well as most texts and utterances in which they express their findings, do not invite and reward the sustained rhetorical-hermeneutic attention that readers and critics of different outlooks and generations have been affording to the works of, say, Sophocles, Cervantes, and Emily Dickinson. We cannot predict, for example, how long certain jokes and the Marxist or Freudian studies of popular culture investigating them will interest us in the three modes of their symbolic, indexical, and iconic signification. But literary works, too, move in and out of the textual canon, which, much like the body of legal documents considered valid for the continuing process of jurisprudence, represents a culture's or subculture's selection of items for continued interpretive elaboration. It seems to me,

Paul Hernadi

therefore, that every text and every utterance deserves to be treated, at least initially and hypothetically, as if it did invite and might reward sustained attention. Only in that way will it be treated as the kind of thing it is: a semantically overdetermined, historically situated project of imaginative worldmaking.[13] Admittedly, not all human scientists or all literary critics are equally inclined and able to interpret symbolically, indexically, and iconically. They should, I think, nonetheless be aware of what they are doing and why in the full context of alternative rhetorical-hermeneutic options.[14]

Among other things, such awareness may serve to remind us that our own texts and utterances, too, will be comprehended not only as conventionally symbolized messages. People who *understand* our verbal expressions also *overstand* them—how unkind!—as unintended indexes of factual seepage; and they also *stand in for* our words—how gratifying!—as their appropriated means of discovering some "unexpected truth" about the iconically imaged "object" of our discourse. With the exclamatory asides of my last sentence I am sure to have alerted you to the circumstance that the rhetoric of this essay privileges, however slightly, the third members of the respective triads: message, seepage, image; explication, explanation, exploration; translation, inference, enactment; understanding, overstanding, standing in for; and so forth. I must confess that there are times when I indeed feel that the hermeneutic spiral winds its way to ever higher—or is it deeper?—levels of comprehension with special stress in the rhythm of its progress on that third phase which is, in a certain sense, both the first and the last: the phase of iconic disclosure through the listener's or reader's existential participation in a comprehended verbal expression. Don't I always "begin" by appropriating meaning according to my own image of the world, and go through the motions of attributing whatever suits that image to authorial message and to factual seepage so that I may "end" (tentatively at least, until the next turning of the spiral from exploration to explication) by reappropriating what is essentially the same meaning in a more complex fashion but once again according to my own, now enriched, image of the world? Or, to express the primacy of the same iconic phase of interpretation in a less subjectivistic register than the one that I have just used (and that has been favored by some recent American reader-response critics): don't I experience the existential interaction between the author's past and my present in and through our shared history when I explore, with present hindsight into the explained factual conditions of the explicated past text, what it means *now* that he or she meant this or that *then*? On such a view, which is indebted to Hans-Georg Gadamer, the interpretive fusion of past and present—those separately very "imperfect" tenses—yields a meaning that has emerged in my comprehension of another person's meaning *as ours*.[15] The tense of "has emerged" is, of course, designated by grammarians as present perfect, and one might be tempted to see each genuine act of comprehension as the com-prehending, a grasping together, of different times and persons by turning past author and present reader (a ''he was'' or ''she was'' and an ''I am'') into the hermeneutically perfect presence of what "we have become."

Yes, I was occasionally tempted and will surely be tempted again to triangulate the hermeneutic spiral into the explicatory thesis of *understanding* and the explanatory antithesis of *overstanding* with *standing in for* as the crowning exploratory synthesis. But my pluralistic guardian angel keeps warning me against the grave monistic consequences of the sin of prideful sublation or *Aufhebung*—the synthesizing attempt at simultaneously "canceling," "preserving," and "raising to a higher plane" the thereby subordinated positions held by other people. With angelic assistance against Hegel's self-styled Absolute Spirit, we should be able to hold fast to a resolutely pluralistic theory of comprehension modeled after Peirce's coordinating typology of preponderantly symbolic, indexical, and iconic signs. And if further support is needed against the evil spirit's offer of the forbidden fruit of synthesis as privileged access to the one and only truth, there is always that trusty breviary: Kenneth Burke's discussion of the "four master tropes" in a somewhat enigmatic but most thought-provoking appendix to *A Grammar of Motives*.[16] Burke examines the role of metaphor, metonymy, synecdoche, and irony "in the discovery and description of 'the truth'." He suggests that the four tropes "shade into one another," as do their " 'literal' or 'realistic' applications"—perspective, reduction, representation, and dialectic. Looking beyond the often contradictory definitions provided by dictionaries and textbooks of rhetoric, Burke characterizes the four tropes and the analogous conceptual operations as follows: metaphor or perspective "is a device for seeing something *in terms of* something else"; metonymy or reduction tends "to convey some incorporeal or intangible state in terms of the corporeal or tangible"; synecdoche or representation implies, especially in the prototypical case of microcosmic representation of the whole by one of its parts, "an integral relationship, a relationship of convertibility," between two terms; and irony or dialectic "arises when one tries, by the interaction of terms upon one another, to produce a *development* which uses all the terms." If I correctly relate Burke's concepts to mine, he encourages us to see metaphor or explicatory perspective, metonymy or explanatory reduction, and synecdoche or exploratory microcosmic

Paul Hernadi

representation as impartially coordinated figures of thought. In their attempt to discover and describe "the truth," each keeps circling along one of three equidistant trajectories around the center of unmediated comprehension and literal expression. Why the center itself must be defined negatively as that which human modes of comprehension and expression will never occupy is intimated by the fourth master trope, which, humble and humbling shadow of the other three, may show but cannot tell: dialectical reversal or irony.[17]

NOTES

1. I attempt to interrelate the lyric, narrative, dramatic, and thematic principles of literary microstructure in *Beyond Genre: New Directions in Literary Classification* (Ithaca: Cornell University Press, 1972), p. 156–70.

2. See Aristotle's *Poetics* (about 330 B.C.), Sidney's *Apologie for Poetrie* (1583), and Shelley's *Defense of Poetry* (1821). Helpful introductory commentaries about the particular context of each can be found in such anthologies as Hazard Adams, ed., *Critical Theory Since Plato* (New York: Harcourt Brace Jovanovich, 1971).

3. Good arguments for seeing literary works as particularly salient illustrations of the poetic or self-referential, imaginative or worldmaking, and performative or worldchanging capacity of all speech and writing may be found in, based on, or derived from (respectively) Roman Jakobson, "Linguistics and Poetics," in Thomas A. Sebeok, ed., *Style in Language* (Cambridge, Mass: MIT Press, 1960), pp. 350–77; Northrop Frye, *Anatomy of Criticism* (Princeton: Princeton University Press, 1957), esp. pp. 326–54; and J. L. Austin, *How to Do Things with Words*, ed. J. O. Urmson and Maria Sbisà, 2d ed. (Cambridge: Harvard University Press, 1975), esp. pp. 133–47.

4. The ubiquity of interpretation does not mean, of course, that the explicit interpretation of individual works must be the chief concern of critics dealing with literature or the other arts. It seems to me, however, that Susan Sontag and Jonathan Culler polemically understate the importance of rhetorical-hermeneutic activity, without which the alternative critical projects favored by them—Sontag's "erotics of art" and Culler's theoretical or historical poetics— would not be conceivable at all. Cf. Susan Sontag, *Against Interpretation and Other Essays* (New York: Laurel, 1969), pp. 13–23 and Jonathan Culler, "Beyond Interpretation: The Prospects of Contemporary Criticism," *Comparative Literature* 28 (1976): 244–56, a revised version of which is reprinted as the programmatic opening piece of Culler's *The Pursuit of Signs: Semiotics, Literature, Deconstruction* (Ithaca: Cornell University Press, 1981), pp. 3–17.

5. The close affinity between literary hermeneutics and its legal and theological counterparts has been stressed by Hans-Georg Gadamer in *Truth and*

Method, trans. Garrett Barden and John Cumming (New York: Seabury Press, 1975), esp. pp. 289–305, and elsewhere.

6. Rainer Maria Rilke, "Archaischer Torso Apollos." See Walter Kaufmann, ed. and trans., *Twenty German Poets: A Bilingual Collection* (New York: Random House, 1962), pp. 220–23.

7. Ferdinand de Saussure, *Course in General Linguistics,* ed. Charles Bally and Albert Sechehaye, trans. and annotated by Roy Harris (London: Duckworth, 1983), esp. pp. 36 and 66–67, as well as pp. xi–xvi of translator's introduction.

8. *The Philosophy of Peirce: Selected Writings,* ed. Justus Buchler (New York: Harcourt, Brace, 1940), pp. 98–119. It should be noted that most of the pertinent selections under the heading "Logic as Semiotic: The Theory of Signs" have been published posthumously. Peirce shares with a number of other heroes of modern and postmodern literary theory the fate of having become influential on the basis of hard-to-interpret writings that were not intended for publication in the versions that we know. In addition to the works by Aristotle, Sidney, Shelley, Austin, and Saussure cited above, some seminal texts by Hegel, Marx, Nietzsche, Husserl, and Wittgenstein come to mind. I know of no comprehensive treatment of the hermeneutic and rhetorical problems involved with the editorial and subsequent interpretation of posthumously discovered manuscripts—a fascinating area of much-needed inquiry. Some pertinent issues have been raised from the technical point of view of the editing of literary works (whether previously published or unpublished) by G. Thomas Tanselle, "Textual Scholarship," in Joseph Gibaldi, ed., *Introduction to Scholarship in the Modern Languages and Literatures* (New York: Modern Languages Association, 1981), pp. 29–52.

9. *The Philosophy of Peirce,* pp. 105–6, italics added. It is important to realize that Peirce, while insisting on the inescapable mediation by the "sign" between the "object" and the (usually mental) "interpretant," presupposes the existence of a (not necessarily physical) object in all instances of signification. By contrast, Saussure is generally assumed to have restricted the semiological study of the sign to its two aspects (roughly corresponding to Peirce's "sign" and "interpretant") as "signifer" and "signified" and to have possibly denied the existence of any object being referred to. On the basis of the following quotation from Saussure's *Course,* p. 14, I rather suspect that his customary silence about linguistic reference should be attributed to his methodological stress on the study of *langue* (language as system) rather than *parole* (individual speech act or utterance). Having attempted his first definition of those two kinds of manifestations of *langage* (language in general), Saussure adds: "It should be noted that we have defined things [*choses*], not words [*mots*]. . . . Consequently the distinctions established are not affected by the fact that certain ambiguous terms have no exact equivalents in other languages [*d'une langue à l'autre*]." Cf. also the French text, *Cours de linguistique générale,* 4th ed. (Paris: Payot, 1949), p. 31. It seems to me that according to Saussure, his *parole* of defining *langue* and *parole* is a referential speech act: it speaks about certain

"things" *(choses)* rather than "concepts" *(signifiés)*. In a similar vein, Peter Strawson, "On Referring," *Mind* 59 (1950): 320–44, argued that we grasp the reference of a verbal expression in addition to its nonreferential meaning or sense only if we know what use is being made of the expression in a particular instance of speech or writing. Cf. my "Literary Theory," in Gibaldi, *Introduction to Scholarship,* pp. 98–115, esp. pp. 104–5.

10. Paul Ricoeur, *Interpretation Theory: Discourse and the Surplus of Meaning* (Fort Worth: Texas Christian University Press, 1976), esp. p. 94.

11. My respective sources for the two puns ("under-standing" versus "over-standing") are E. D. Hirsch, *Validity in Interpretation* (New Haven: Yale University Press, 1967), p. 143, and Wayne C. Booth, *Critical Understanding: The Powers and Limits of Pluralism* (Chicago: University of Chicago Press, 1979), pp. 235 and passim. Hirsch makes the following distinction: "one understands meaning; one judges significance. In the first instance, one submits to another—literally, one stands under him. In the second, one acts independently—by one's own authority—like a judge." Booth means by "overstanding" the occasionally justified "imposition" of the reader's questions or values on a text: "I will no more accede to all the demands of *Mein Kampf* or *Justine* than to the demands of the con-man's text when it insistently rules out the question 'Are you lying?'" (p. 242). Neither critic seems to allow for the performer's posture of participatory standing-in-for as a third alternative or, better yet, as a third interactive phase of any profound comprehension.

12. Each of the following recent statements illustrates one of the three (more or less exclusionary) theoretical dispositions. P. D. Juhl, *Interpretation: An Essay in the Philosophy of Literary Criticism* (Princeton: Princeton University Press, 1980), p. 15: "any (and only) evidence of the author's intention is *ipso facto* evidence of the meaning of the work." Pierre Macherey, *A Theory of Literary Production,* trans. Geoffrey Wall (London: Routledge & Kegan Paul, 1978), pp. 78–80: "the work is not *created* by an intention (objective or subjective); it is *produced* under determinate conditions. . . . To explain the work is to show that, contrary to appearances, it is not independent, but bears in its material substance the imprint of a determinate absence which is also the principle of its identity." Norman N. Holland, "Re-Covering 'The Purloined Letter': Reading as a Personal Transaction," in Susan R. Suleiman and Inge Crosman, eds., *The Reader in the Text: Essays on Audience and Interpretation,* (Princeton: Princeton University Press, 1980), p. 370: "We each read differently. . . . Instead of subtracting readings so as to narrow them down or cancel some . . . , let us use human differences to add response to response, to multiply possibilities, and to enrich the whole experience." There are, of course, many other versions of privileging a single interpretive orientation. Rather than toward the actual author, convention-based explication is often geared toward a "speaker," "voice," "persona," or the text's implied or postulated author. The respective followers of Marx, Nietzsche, and Freud in turn engage in inferential explanation with widely different objectives and results. Proposals for

participatory exploration also range from those favoring the private and impressionistic through those invoking the hermeneutic habits of presently existing interpretive communities to those presupposing the Gadamerian "fusion of horizons"—the reader's merging into the historical tradition from which the present meaning of past texts emerges. (See Gadamer, *Truth and Method*, esp. pp. 267–78.)

13. Cf. Nelson Goodman, *Ways of Worldmaking* (Indianapolis: Hackett, 1978).

14. Each of those options—the explication of texts as communicative signals, their explanation as informative symptoms, and the exploration of our experiencing their appeal to us as existential imperatives—relies on just one of what I elsewhere called the three axioms of critical interpretation: authors communicate; texts conceal; readings disclose. Needless to say, any formulated explication, explanation, or exploration of what has been communicated, concealed, or disclosed is subject to further explication, explanation, and exploration by subsequent listeners or readers. This is why neither the hermeneutic circle of reciprocally illuminating textual parts and wholes, nor the hermeneutic shuttle oscillating between a better and better understood text and a better and better understanding individual reader, is an adequate spatial metaphor for the increasing penetration of critical comprehension. The ongoing transpersonal interaction between words and minds should rather be described as a hermeneutic spiral: cultural progress through repeated recourse to the reconstructive explication, deconstructive explanation, and constructively participatory exploration of authorial signals, textual symptoms, and experienced disclosures. See my introduction to Paul Hernadi, ed., *What Is Criticism?* (Bloomington: Indiana University Press, 1981), pp. xiv–xv.

15. See nn. 5 and 12 above.

16. Kenneth Burke, *A Grammar of Motives*, 3d ed. (Berkeley: University of California Press, 1969), pp. 503–17.

17. The question arises how irony, under such description, avoids turning into the one and only Master Trope—if not, indeed, into the supposedly direct, nontropological expression and comprehension of the truth about all figures of speech and thought. The charge implied by that question is analogous to the charge of self-serving inconsistency that can be leveled against all versions of relativism and historicism that ignore their own relative nature and historical contingency. And here is my answer to the question: as soon as the ironic principle of dialectic reversal begins to masquerade as a stable, privileged means of expression and comprehension, it becomes defenselessly vulnerable to its own "internal fatality" (Burke, *Grammar of Motives*, p. 517), so that, to use a currently fashionable term, it deconstructs itself.

THE RHETORIC OF

THEOLOGICAL ARGUMENT

DAVID E. KLEMM

In this essay, I examine the rhetoric of theological argument as it is carried out in departments of religious studies in contemporary secular universities. By "theology," I mean academic theology, not just any discourse that purports to speak about God. Spontaneous expressions about God, no matter how significant they may be to particular religious communities, are not theological. Theological discourse is always the outcome of critical reflection both on what it means to speak about God and how such claims may be considered true.[1] Moreover, theology so defined is genuinely philosophical and requires no special religious commitment on the part of its practitioners. Theology in this sense belongs to the human sciences.

The primary audience of theology is the university community, and it is primarily answerable to the standards of that community. This means that "confessional" modes of discourse are not appropriate for theological studies. Confessional theology begins from divine revelation recorded in scripture, dogmatic formulations, or creedal confessions taken as unrevisable and authoritative principles. It then proceeds both to unfold the content of belief for a religious community that adheres to the starting point and to criticize discourse that is not consistent with it. Confessional theology thus operates as citation and elaboration of religious principle. Such a mode of operation violates the standards of critical reflection in the human sciences. These standards minimally include commitment to critical inquiry into evidence for purposes of testing the truth of one's assertions.[2] The starting point of confessional theology, however, cannot withstand such scrutiny. When the only test is to recite the revealed scripture, creed, or other source of the confession, those people who do not find the truth of the confession self-evident will judge that the test begs the question.

The division between university and seminary tends to create a lag between the emergence of theological discourse and its reception by

276

religious groups. And it contributes to the persistence of the purely confessional mode of discourse in some seminaries, for such persistence would be less likely were seminaries more closely connected to universities. Ultimately, the institutional division contributes to the separation of religious discourse and the discourse of inquiry.[3] Seminaries and religious groups are by no means altogether insulated from theology, however. Theological discourse is addressed beyond the university to the religious communities, especially insofar as the specific religious traditions and their systems of myth, ritual, and traditional discourse come up for theological inquiry.

Finally, theology speaks to society at large as a bearer of certain fundamental values crucial to the Western spiritual heritage. In this role, theology both deciphers and articulates society's pressing questions concerning its own destiny. Has existence any ultimate meaning? Is courage, faith, or a fundamental trust possible given the negativities of existence? In short, is God a reality? These questions abide after the traditional answers have been confronted by the radical criticisms of Marx, Freud, Nietzsche, and others. Theology must identify how such questions are actually being posed today under transformed conditions. And theology reflects on the answers and interprets the symbols that traditional religions, and the secular culture in its religious dimension, provide for them.[4]

In what follows, I shall reflect on two issues basic to theology. First, when contemporary theologians argue on behalf of the reality of God, how do they picture God? What, in other words, is the fundamental metaphor of God's being that they invoke in making theological arguments? Second, what specific form do these arguments take? In raising these questions, I refer to the tradition of contemporary Protestant thought. This tradition has exerted profound influence on Roman Catholic and Jewish thought in the twentieth century and has been instrumental in the emergence of academic theology.

I

[God] is the wholly non-rational and "other," the being of sheer mystery and marvel.
—Rudolf Otto[5]

The arguments for the existence of God neither are arguments nor are they proof of the existence of God. They are expres-

> *sions of the* question *of God which is implied in human finitude.*
> —Paul Tillich[6]

Much has been said and written about the disunity and fragmentation of theology in our day. But in spite of apparent plurality, a discernible unity and common ground, rarely addressed as such but routinely trodden in theological writing, can be articulated. That unity is found in the leading metaphor of God in contemporary theology: God as the breaking-in of "otherness" to human existence.

Individual theological programs part ways when layers of description are added to this fundamental metaphor. Accounts of otherness vary. So do interpretations of how the breaking-in occurs. Likewise, views of the human existence where this breaking-in takes place are different. But however various the theological schemata may be, they are overwhelmingly governed by this metaphor.

The breaking-in of otherness has not always been the central theological metaphor for God. It does not characterize nineteenth-century theology, which was dominated by the great systems of German idealism. These systems figured God as the Absolute, as the complete identity of thinking and being. The nineteenth-century metaphor of God as absolute knowledge lacked the element of "breaking-in." The human activity of reflexive thinking was itself the reflecting surface or mirror of the being of God. In the twentieth century, by contrast, no human activity on its own reflects the being of God. Instead, human activity is merely the place where the breaking-in of what is wholly other occurs.

Nor did earlier types of theology find their unity in such a metaphor. In Enlightenment theology, the central image was the deistic watchmaker or divine mechanic, outside the natural world but occasionally intervening in it. Such a figure can hardly be called "wholly other." Lutheran theology figured God as the accusing Judge, whose condemnation is paradoxically turned into forgiveness through His doubling as the persuasive advocate for the accused. Here, perhaps, we have the closest approximation to the twentieth-century metaphor. The forgiving Yes was, after all, wholly other than what could be expected. But there is an important difference: for Luther, the breaking-in of God signaled the end of guilt and condemnation; in twentieth-century theology, it signals the end of meaninglessness. Finally, the metaphysical theology dominant at least from Augustine to Aquinas and Bonaventure pictured God as intelligible supreme being, the heavenly Lord of creation. Here, human intellectual and volitional activities display (though imperfectly) the divine life, which is therefore not "wholly other."

World War I fractured the sense of continuity between human existence and the being of God. Since the publication of Rudolf Otto's *The Idea of the Holy* (1917), the metaphor of the breaking-in has been pervasive and persuasive in theological discussion. What implications does this metaphor have for theological thinking and its audiences?

At first glance, any discussion of the methodology of twentieth-century theology appears to open a vista of sheer confusion. Transcendental methods, the phenomenology of religious experience, the hermeneutics of text and existence, anthropological and archaeological studies, psychoanalytic methods, critique of ideologies, structuralism, and deconstruction are all to be found. Underlying them all, however, is one fundamental approach: contemporary theology is most basically *hermeneutical* in its methodology.

By this I mean that in seeking to confront God, contemporary theologians employ methods that are historical, temporal, and interpretive. They generally acknowledge that their descriptions of the what, where, and how of the theological object are interpretations. These will evoke new interpretations if they have any meaning and truth to them. The hermeneutical character of theological method is related directly to contemporary theology's metaphor of God, for this metaphor figures God as a sign to be interpreted and not as a self-sufficient object or an absolute synthesis. Hence the need for hermeneutics—that is, theoretical inquiry into the task of rendering explicit what is understood in a sign.

The unity of contemporary theological thinking may further be seen not only in its common hermeneutic character, but also in its configuration of speaker and audience. In employing the breaking-in metaphor, theologians speak in universal terms and address an audience that is never denominational only. Because the metaphor specifies neither a conceptual content nor any particular image of deity, it projects the speaker beyond the immediate audience to the universal community of theological discourse.[7] One consequence of this is that current theological language stands beyond the division of individuals into theistic and atheistic camps. Both sides of that now obsolete division are encompassed by it.

The focal argument of contemporary theology justifies the meaning and truth of the claim that "God is." Paradoxically, it takes the form of an argument that is not an argument. In saying this, I am not dabbling in linguistic sleight of hand. Theologians *do* argue. They make claims for which they produce data, warrants, and backings.[8] Their arguments are sometimes convincing and even powerful, or so I would say.

David E. Klemm

But given the very nature of the theological object, the otherness that may or may not break into a situation, the argument that "God is" seems necessarily to pertain to the nonarguable.

There appears to be a contradiction, in other words, between the subject matter of theology and argumentation as such. Consider William J. Brandt's remark in *The Rhetoric of Argumentation* that "the writer of argumentation always stands, with the reader, outside the subject under consideration."[9] This structural feature of argumentation, and of critical thought generally, is necessarily violated whenever some "I" speaks or argues about God. For whatever one means by God, the word itself suggests the ultimate dimension of reality, the ground and power of being itself. Hence there can be no standpoint that is external to God. The same insight prompted Rudolf Bultmann, among others, to conclude that "it is not legitimate to speak about God in general statements, in universal truths which are valid without reference to the concrete, existential position of the speaker."[10] I must *bespeak* God, but I cannot *speak about* God.

This means that theological argumentation cannot be carried out in the form of the theistic argument for the existence of a supreme being. If what we mean by God is the ground and power of being itself, no object or being, not even a "supreme being," can be God. Arguments can be made, however, that demonstrate how it is possible for individuals to say with certainty and not as a matter of probability that "God is." Such arguments do not make an assertion about some being. Instead, they seek to show the possibility of an event of disclosure—namely, the breaking-in of otherness.

Suppose that "God is" is shown to be utterable with conviction on the grounds that the appearance of otherness in a human world is possible. If this is so, it follows that when we argue that "God is," we argue with regard to the possibility of God appearing as what is not God but a "sign of" God. What breaks in as God is not, strictly speaking, God. What breaks in must be the appearance, symbol, or manifestation of God—hence God in its otherness as word or language. Consequently, in current theology, the most basic statement made about God is that "God is God as word." God breaks in as otherness in word. Notice the significant ambiguity in the phrase "the otherness of God." What breaks in is God, who is wholly other than what we can understand on the basis of our familiar world. But God breaks in as what is other than God. What breaks in is word, the otherness of God, which is also the medium of our thinking and being and hence in some sense familiar, albeit normally hidden or forgotten.

Any argument that claims that "God is" presents data, warrants the move from the data to the claim, and backs the warrant. In form at least, this is a theological argument. But because God's being is to be other than God, theological arguments attempt to affirm the being of what is other than itself while being itself. How can one argue for the systematically elusive? God as the wholly other must stand outside argumentation or be falsified by it. In consequence, the truth of theological argumentation must reside in the possibility of the argument undercutting itself as argument, even as it retains its standing as argument. Theological arguments affirm that "God is" by arguing against the possibility of a logically sound argument for the existence of God. This is what I mean in saying that a theological argument is an argument that is not an argument.

To elucidate this characterization of the rhetoric of twentieth-century theology, let me attempt a close reading of a representative theological argument found in Gerhard Ebeling's important essay "Existence Between God and God." The theme of this essay pertains directly to the focal theological argument that "God is." Thus the subtitle of the essay is "A Contribution to the Question about the Existence of God."[11] Two levels of Ebeling's contribution are relevant to our purposes, and to them I shall add a third.

At the first level (considered in section II below), the essay interprets the type of cosmological argument for the existence of God found in the *Summa Theologica* of Thomas Aquinas. At this first, literal level of meaning, Ebeling takes the argument at face value and criticizes it as such. The criticism claims that the proofs come to nothing. But this does not end matters, for the negation of the literal argument signals a second level of meaning. On the second level (considered in section III below), Ebeling interprets the argument as a metaphor or model for new meaning. When we read his interpretation of Aquinas, moreover, a third level appears. At the third level (considered in section IV below), Ebeling's interpretation of Aquinas's argument may itself be interpreted as an argument both about the being of God figured as the breaking-in of otherness and about theological argumentation as such.

II

The existence of God may be proven in five ways.
—Thomas Aquinas[12]

David E. Klemm

> *The arguments [for the existence of God] are a failure insofar*
> *as they claim to be arguments.*
> —Paul Tillich[13]

Ebeling cites various reasons why Aquinas's five ways to prove the existence of God fail as arguments. First, the metaphysical form of natural theology loses the *mystery* of God. Metaphysical propositions make claims that are universal and necessary and that are about existent things. In natural theology, the topic is the existence and essence of God. In the *Summa Theologica*, for example, Aquinas's procedure is to ascertain first that God exists, then to determine the essence of God by inquiring into the manner of God's existence, and finally to discuss the concordance of these concepts with scripture.[14] But when God is cast into metaphysical propositions, the mystery of the otherness of God is lost. God's being as the breaking-in of word is eclipsed behind neutral descriptions that are *about* God as *ens realissimum*, a supreme being. Indeed, natural theology describes a very special being, one whose essence is to be; but in such descriptions the reality is lost of the God who remains hidden even in manifestation.

Second, the metaphysical approach abstracts from the lived, historical situation of real human beings. Today, the argument for the existence of God must silence our questioning about a ground of courage or meaning. How, we ask, is faith possible? The "I" who questions is situated within the distress concerning the finitude of existence. When the fragility of human existence is focal, and the negativities of existence threaten us with meaninglessness, a metaphysical theology of the essence of God in His majesty is not able to address the situation. The transfer of attention from existence to a transcendent world cannot present us, in the twentieth century, with the reality of the ultimate ground of courage from which we may draw the insight and strength to accept anxiety. The problem is that metaphysical argument refers us to a timeless sphere apart from the historically situated and freely deciding self. A hermeneutical theology of the unveiling of God as empowering word within human fragility, however, speaks directly to our situation.

In sum, Ebeling contends that the metaphysical arguments for a supreme being create an obliviousness to the mystery of God and to the "mineness" (*Jemeinigkeit*) of the self. Metaphysics reduces God to a metaphysical principle or banishes God to the otherworldly, whereas "God must come to language as that which encompasses the contradictions in existence."[15] And metaphysics displaces the deciding self with the neutralized observer, forgetting that "that on which your heart depends and relies, that is authentically your God."[16] Thus Ebeling interprets these arguments as showing a deeper level of meaning—one in accord with the image of God as the breaking-in of otherness.

Not everyone is convinced, however, that the Thomistic arguments for the existence of God must fail as arguments. And since Ebeling does not so much argue against Aquinas as oppose him on rhetorical grounds by presenting a more compelling image, let me analyze one of Aquinas's arguments. Here is the text of the "first and more manifest way" of proving the existence of God—the argument from motion:

> It is certain, and evident to our senses, that in the world some things are in motion. Now whatever is moved is moved by another for nothing can be moved except it is in potentiality to that towards which it is moved; whereas a thing moves inasmuch as it is in act. For motion is nothing else than the reduction of something from potentiality to actuality. But nothing can be reduced from potentiality to actuality, except by something in a state of actuality. Thus that which is actually hot, as fire, makes wood, which is potentially hot, to be actually hot, and thereby moves and changes it. Now it is not possible that the same thing should be at once in actuality and potentiality in the same respect, but only in different respects. For what is actually hot cannot simultaneously be potentially hot; but it is simultaneously potentially cold. It is therefore impossible that in the same respect and in the same way a thing should be both mover and moved, i.e., that it should move itself. Therefore, whatever is moved must be moved by another. If that by which it is moved be itself moved, then this also must needs be moved by another, and that by another again. But this cannot go on to infinity, because then there would be no first mover, and, consequently, no other mover, seeing that subsequent movers move only inasmuch as they are moved by the first mover; as the staff moves only because it is moved by the hand. Therefore it is necessary to arrive at a first mover, moved by no other; and this everyone understands to be God.[17]

There are three significant steps to this argument. First, Aquinas claims that every moved thing is moved by another. The data from which he starts are our evident experiences of things in motion. The warrant for the movement from data to claim is the definition of motion as the reduction of something from potentiality to act, coupled with the recognition that the actualization of something requires the existence of something already actual in that sense. Together, these rule out the possibility that something might move itself. The backing for the warrant is provided in the form of an example: for wood, which is potentially hot, to become actually hot, something already actually hot must ignite it.

Second, Aquinas claims that there must be a first mover. The data here are the elements of the series of moved things and movers. The warrant for the claim involves the inconceivability of an infinite series of movers. If there were an infinite series of movers, nothing could have started anything else moving, and there would be no motion; hence we must think of some first mover. The backing for the warrant is the necessity of inferring a first mover in order to avoid denying the evidence of our senses.

Third, Aquinas claims that the first mover is God. At first glance this move appears to be altogether unwarranted. The warrant, however, is found in a distinct and further part of the argument. Aquinas contends that the necessary being whose existence has been established is incomprehensible in its essence but that some of its attributes may be derived from the inferred first mover. These are perfections traditionally associated with God: unity, eternality, infinite goodness, freedom, and omnipotence.

What about this argument? It has met with divided reaction through the centuries, and it still evokes both defense and attack. But certain standard objections to the argument will probably prevent it from ever gaining the high ground over its detractors.

Like the other Thomistic versions of the cosmological argument, the proof from motion begins by reasoning about experientially verified facts. The proof proceeds by reference to the principle of sufficient reason (PSR)—an a priori principle: "If a certain causal activity is now going on which results in something being in a process of change, there must be an explanation of the fact that the causal activity is now going on."[18] Criticisms of the argument focus on the standing of the PSR and on its application.

Consider the first step of the argument: the assertion that every moved thing is moved by another. The PSR demands an explanation for the fact of motion. The explanation is provided in the rule that actualization requires as a cause something already actual in the relevant respect. But this rule cannot provide a general explanation, for there are many instances of one body moving another (for example, by gravitational attraction) without itself being in motion. And apart from any specific explanations, why should we assume that the PSR is true? Does not the adoption of the PSR overlook the possibility that change might be a "brute fact" without explanation?[19]

The second step of the argument—from the series of moved things to the claim that there is a first mover—again raises the question of the truth of the PSR. The PSR has us look for a first mover, unmoved by any other, to explain the series of moved entities. Admittedly the argument is very subtle here. For if we are dealing with a series of essentially ordered or per se causes, we must think of a first in the series in order to explain the fact of the series. But how do we know that there must be an explanation? What about the possibility of a brute fact that the series is so?

If the PSR purports to tell us a necessary truth about reality, it is highly questionable. If it more modestly claims the status of a presupposition of reason, we can deceive ourselves in applying it to reality. Reality need not conform to a truth necessary for reason. And in an argument for the existence of God, the possibility for error is highest. Here the search for a cause for contingent states of affairs is carried beyond the sensible world, the only place where it is applicable, to the metaphysical. But it is not necessary to think that the necessity of thinking of a first and unmoved mover entails an existent metaphysical entity.[20]

In this connection Kant wrote that "unconditioned necessity, which we so indispensably require as the last bearer of all things, is for human reason the veritable abyss."[21] Reason is obliged to assume something necessary as a condition of the existent in general, but it cannot think of any particular thing as in itself necessary. Reason is placed under the claim to seek the unconditioned ground of reality, but it is forbidden to treat anything in particular as that reality. The concept of a supreme being may in some sense be a necessary concept, yet its objective reality can be neither proved nor disproved.[22]

The literal sense of the cosmological argument ends up in an unresolvable dialectic between the assertions "God is" and "That one is not God." Ebeling interprets this tension as a sign of the powerlessness of metaphysical theology. He sees this powerlessness as opening us to the breaking-in of God as word-event. In short, he understands the failure of the literal sense of the argument in much the same way as Ricoeur understands the overturning of the literal sense of a metaphor: a significant contradiction between terms of interpretations in the literal sense discloses a new field of meaning. As Ricoeur puts it, this contradiction "imposes a sort of twist on the words, an extension of meaning thanks to which we can make sense where a literal interpretation would be literally nonsensical."[23]

When Aquinas's argument is read as metaphor, the contradictions in the literal sense point "backward" and "forward." They point backward to the central symbol of God the Lord. It sets the original context for the intelligibility of the argument but no longer supports the argument for current readers. The contradictions point forward to a new interpretation of the argument sustained by the current image of God. I shall describe the backward reference in the remainder of this section. In the next section I shall discuss Ebeling's interpretation of the projective reference of the argument read as metaphor.

To determine how the Thomistic cosmological argument points back to the metaphor of God as Lord, Ebeling places the argument in the context of Aquinas's whole theological system. It falls within the initial section on the doctrine of God, which stands at the beginning of natural theology. The theological system as a whole includes both natural theology and revealed theology. The latter follows in subject matter the main narrative line of the Bible from the creation, through Jesus Christ, to final things. Revealed theology is, in fact, "a stylized salvation history."[24] The translation into general concepts of the representations of God in narrative, poetry, law, prophecy, gospel, and so on was not an innovation of the theological tradition. That process begins already in biblical texts. However, the placement of a doctrine of the timeless essence of God at the beginning of the system, prior to creation and apart from God's appearance in history, definitely is the product of the theological tradition. What is the meaning of the location of this metaphysical doctrine of God?

For Ebeling, the placement of the doctrine of God carries hermeneutical significance. The encounter between metaphysical and biblical language was focal in this doctrine, which integrates the natural experience of the world and the befalling of revelation by showing how each is possible only through God. The metaphysical doctrine of God served the hermeneutical function of establishing the preunderstanding that is necessary for the comprehension of revelation. It offered a conceptual and neutral way of grasping that and what God is, before explication of God's free acts.[25]

Articulation of a metaphysical doctrine of God does not remove the word "God" from its home in narrative and religious contexts, however. The notion of God as supreme being is the conceptual rendering of the biblical metaphor of God as Lord of Creation because it depicts God as absolutely independent of the world, as the creator of time before all time, as the ruler and monarch of history. Indeed, the unquestioned background for the reception of the Thomistic argument is the metaphor of God as Lord. When the natural theologian brackets out the biblical narrative to construct a doctrine of God, that image is not excluded. The self-evident image of God as Lord lends power to the proof for a supreme being.

How do we know that the metaphor of God as Lord has affective power in the Thomistic argument? Ebeling finds a clue in Aquinas's procedure of first asserting the existence of God, then discussing the essence of God, and finally turning to scripture. Ebeling argues that it is odd to begin with the existence claim because one cannot question whether something exists without already having a preliminary understanding of what it is. And indeed, the necessary preunderstanding is provided by the traditional ways of speaking about God in the Bible, creed, and liturgy. Granted, biblical discourse and religious language bring the word "God" into play under many different and sometimes contradictory representations and concepts, but the leading metaphor is that of heavenly Lord.[26]

Edward Farley, in his recent deconstruction of theological reflection, shows how the metaphor of God as Lord (or King) supports the very project of metaphysical theology. The Bible, narrative home of the metaphor, depicts how God offers salvation to humans through His own acts. It follows from the metaphor of lordship that if God wills salvation through Torah and Gospel not only for the generations of Moses and Jesus but for all subsequent generations, an ongoing line of representatives is required. Each representative must be identified with God's will. The sequence of representatives leads from certain founding events, to a canon of writings, to doctrinal formulations, to dogmatic theology. Patriarchs, prophets, exile, incarnation, apostolic witness, scriptural canon, and doctrinal formulations all occur as "God's teleological disposal of history," with each taking on the status of God's very own communication and wisdom. Platonic and Aristotelian philosophy added the conceptual means by which to call dogmatic content "true" in the "classical Hellenistic sense of an ahistorical immutable essence," inerrant like the Scripture, God's own truth about God.[27]

The metaphor of God as Lord is dying in current theology, except where it is taken as an instance of breaking-in. Many reasons could be cited for its collapse. One is that the metaphor seems, in its triumphalism, to be undermined by the overwhelming presence of evil in such events as the Holocaust and Hiroshima. A second reason is that the picture of the finite world clarified by the image of the infinite supreme being standing over against creation is defunct. Thus the image of lordship no longer clarifies anything. For Aquinas the temporal-spatial world was bounded by the infinite being of God. Nonetheless, the

David E. Klemm

proof rests on the assumption of a single continuous structure of reality, which permits a passage without break from the finite to the infinite, the sensible to the supra-sensible. Recent thought no longer supposes that there is a causal nexus leading from this world into another one. Hence under new conditions of thought, a different image of the being of God has worked its way into theological argument.

III

Human existence also involves, seemingly first and foremost, the effort, either crude or subtle, to lay hold of unveiled, immediate reality, to plan and dominate, possess and enjoy, press on and break records. But this effort to lay hold of naked immediacy misses reality unless it is bridled through our being grasped by that which can only be a matter of hearing and waiting, and thus is a matter of word.
—Gerhard Ebeling[28]

Ebeling's treatment of Aquinas's argument does not end with an erasure of the argument as argument. On the contrary, the contradictions in the argument provide him with hints for reinterpretation. Ebeling is convinced that the classical tradition of dogmatic thought is able to make a contribution to an authentic understanding of God in this historically stamped situation. His claim is that the argument indicates not that God is the unmoved mover or the necessary existence in a world of contingency, but that speaking of God provides or donates something that is necessary to human existence in its disruptedness.

The contradiction that projects this second meaning arises between the ontological assumption of Aquinas's procedure in constructing the doctrine of God and the being of God which he describes. Aquinas's procedure is first to argue for the existence of God and then to discuss the manner of existence in order to know the essence of God. Ebeling does not say that Aquinas's procedure is illegitimate or that it covertly does something other than he intended. Rather, Ebeling suggests that the procedure strikes us as odd and signifies a second meaning. What sense does it make to speak abstractly about the existence of God when the simplicity of God means that God is beyond the ontological split between essence and existence? Aquinas's procedure depends on this split. And yet his argument is about God, whose essence is to exist. Since the distinction between the essence and the existence of God is determinative for the procedure of the doctrine of God, the procedure appears to contradict the being of God that it discusses.

The possibility for interpretation opened up by the contradiction is that the demonstration records a word-event: an experience with the depth of language.[29] Separating the discussion of the existence of God from that of the essence of God points to a possibility that proof is limited to the human situation of finitude, in which existence is distinct from any timeless essence. Each of Aquinas's five proofs originates in the experience of being struck by something. They arise from experiencing how things can be called into question. All belief and unbelief, all talk about and around God, proceed from this experience.

By interpreting the steps of the argument as a movement in human existence, Ebeling contends that he draws closer to the intention of the argument even while breaking down its literal claims. The proof from motion projects the inbreaking of God to human reality. To show this requires that I elaborate on Ebeling's interpretation of the three steps of Aquinas's argument.

In the first step, Aquinas claims that every moved thing is moved by another. Ebeling interprets this step as a model or paradigm of an elementary experience of being-in-the-world. In our fundamental encounter with entities, we are summoned to question what is beyond those entities by virtue of what is lacking in them. Entities point beyond themselves to other entities, which likewise refer beyond themselves. The worldliness of the world shows itself in how everything is connected with everything else. Furthermore, worldly existence is characterized by its questionability, its openness to question. Worldly experience is open to questions of the meaning of being-in-the-world, and this for at least two reasons. First, because all worldly entities are interdependent, each is permeated with nonbeing. Every existing thing is a "being together of being and nonbeing that is worthy of being questioned."[30] Second, because each thing points beyond itself to other things in sequence, our experience of the world is eminently temporal. To be in the world is to temporalize the interconnectedness of things at hand. Finitude and temporality raise the question of the meaning of worldly being.

To what does worldliness, the interdependence of entities, point? Ebeling does not raise that precise question, but speaks only about openness-to-question of human existence. The classic text evoked by his analysis is Heidegger's discussion of the worldliness of the world in *Being and Time*.[31] Heidegger attempted to interpret human existence, or being-in-the-world, as a sign that points out the meaning of the various modes of being. He hoped thereby to formulate that meaning in a clear concept. Heidegger's unsuccessful attempt to complete *Being and Time* led him to see that the leading meaning of human being-in-the-world is a sign that cannot be interpreted: "The sign remains without interpretation."[32] Worldly experience is openness in pointing beyond itself. But what it points out is nothing—just more pointing. According to Heidegger, the nothingness pointed to by human openness is not merely nothing. By virtue of the mood or fundamental attunement to the whole of reality that accompanies human openness, nothingness actually becomes a positive given for experience. For Heidegger, mood or attunement is not mere emotionality but is a genuine mode of experience. The mood associated with the openness to the questionability of the world expressed in the first step of the argument is dread or *Angst*.[33]

In the second step, Aquinas claims that there must be a first mover, a final term to stop the infinite regress, for it is impossible to proceed to infinity. Ebeling interprets Aquinas's logical leap here as the expression of a movement in existence. Something happens that overcomes the nothingness to which our openness to the questionability of the world exposes us. Somehow the infinite appears within existence, and this appearance negates the restless tracing of interconnections in the world.[34] In other words, Ebeling appeals to an event in which something befalls me that does not remove the worldliness of human existence but enables me to suffer and accept it. In this donative word-event, I am given the courage that overcomes dread. The breaking-in of such a power of being or presence of meaning does not do away with the openness of human finitude but grants the ability to temporalize my activities authentically, to actualize my greatest possibilities, and to take responsibility for my future.

We can understand Ebeling's existential interpretation with reference to language. Since language is the medium of thinking and being, ontological structures of language as such reflect possibilities of being as such. Basic experiences with language mirror and record basic understandings of the meaning of being.[35] In the first step of Aquinas's argument, the linguistic experience that corresponds to recognition of the interconnectedness of worldly being is that of the interconnectedness of words. Words as mere vocables refer endlessly to more words. The interconnectedness of words in a dictionary, where each word is defined by the other words, suggests something about the anonymity of language as a system. The structure of interconnectedness of words cannot be the whole of language; for unless language is open to what is other than language, we would have nothing to talk about. Words point to their groundedness in the Word, or depth of language, which is the openness of language to being.

In the second step, where a first mover is inferred, there is also a corresponding linguistic possibility. The restless movement through the interconnectedness of words is brought to a halt only when the vocables somehow manifest to us language's infinite power of articulating meaning. As Heidegger puts it, such a grant of language would disclose the essential possibility of human existence.[36] For Ebeling, the breaking-in of word enables the projection of an authentic future and thus imparts the possibility of becoming who I truly am. This occurs when words manifest the infinite power of word to which I am answerable as a user of language. Ebeling writes, "Man in his linguisticality is not master of himself. . . . He lives from the power of a word that is not his own, and at the same time he thirsts after the power of a word that likewise cannot be his own."[37] The breaking-in of Word is the existential meaning of the inference of a first mover. Word breaks in as what is other than words but gives and sustains them—and through them, a meaningful world.

In the third step, Aquinas claims that the first mover is identical with God. Ebeling interprets this not as the conclusion of a procedure of demonstration but as a movement that one must execute for oneself: the leap into the language of faith. What Aquinas sees as first mover, the metaphysical counterpart to the image of heavenly Lord, Ebeling conceives as the breaking into existence of the depth of language or Word. But both are willing to invoke "God" as a word at this point.

Why does Ebeling use "God" in connection with the word-event? Let me answer by indicating how a current interpretation of the Thomistic argument for the existence of God carries with it an implicit argument for the existential possibility of such an event of breaking-in. In effect, this could be a new argument for the claim that "God is," built around the metaphor of breaking-in. It too would then be an argument that is self-consciously not an argument, because its success depends on its own overturning.

IV

> We cannot speak of otherness, or of its ground, its final ground, without speaking of God. By speaking of God we speak of the finality of otherness, of an otherness that will ever be other than itself.
> —Thomas J. J. Altizer[38]

The hermeneutical tradition in contemporary theology implicitly offers its own argument for the claim "God is." The

David E. Klemm

argument appears to have two parts. First, the claim is made that we do have experiences with word-events. From time to time, words cease to be tools for communication and signification and become the medium of the self-presentation of language. In these instances "language speaks," to use Heidegger's phrase. In such events, we are so drawn up, as auditors or readers, into the subject matter of what is said that the subject matter is actualized or performed in the hearing or reading.[39] The warrant for this claim is that language is the means not only for grasping reality through significant expression but also for the reception of reality. Language is the medium of both human thinking and experiencing. The same language that enables us to point to the world also enables the world to show itself. At the limit of such responding through language is the presentation of my most authentic being in relation to the whole of being through words spoken to or read by me.[40] In this stage of the argument, an analysis of the nature of language must be offered to show that such a word-event is genuinely possible; and instances must be offered to show that linquistic events of appropriation actually happen.

Second, the argument identifies the word-event with the appearance of God. When "language speaks" so as to make me true in relation to the whole of being and to donate my authentic future, then "God is."[41] The warrant for such identification is that experience of the word-event is experience of sheer otherness breaking-in to the openness of human existence. As the medium of being, language makes the absent present and the present absent. It manifests otherness, and what is meant by "God" is sheer otherness. Ordinarily, our experience is marked by the split that defines finitude: a finite self stands over against a finite object or another self. Language is the medium of the interaction of self and other. But in the word-event, the split in experience is overcome even as it is preserved. This means that the event of disclosure draws the "I" into itself and incorporates that "I" into a higher subjectivity—the subjectivity of the word-event—even as the "I" retains awareness of its identity as a location of being. The experience of the transcendence of finitude within finitude is the experience of what is wholly other than finitude. It is the breaking-in of otherness, and God is that otherness.

But this too must be an argument that is not an argument. If it in any way pretends to be an argument from experience to the existence of a deity, it must necessarily fail as an argument. Any argument to a deity from religious experience defeats itself because it adjudicates the question whether God exists on the basis of a criterion that it claims to possess, thus elevating the criterion above the divine.[42] The very application of the criterion eliminates the trace of the divine sought in experience. Contingent on meeting a criterion, the divine loses its divine standing.

The problem resides in an ineluctable conflict between reflection and religious experience. Of any particular claim for religious experience, reflection necessarily must judge that God was not the object of experience. This applies to the crucial claim of the argument that the word-event is an appearance of God. It means that although we may argue that word-events can and do happen and that they are appearances of God, we may not say that any particular event in language or any particular texts are truly word-events and thus sacred events or texts.

What does this imply for the possibility of truth in theology? In the shift from traditional dogmatic theology to hermeneutical theology, have we exchanged the aim of truth for the aim of developing new meanings of unknowable truth? In other words, does the shift from the traditional theological system (ruled by the metaphor of the Lord) to recent theological thought (ruled by the metaphor of otherness) entail surrendering truth as correspondence between assertion and reality? Does it require adopting a weaker form of truth as disclosure of new meaning? Does the change in the rhetoric of theological argument from assertions about reality to interpretations of word-events imply that academic theology has, by its denial of metaphysics, cut itself off from the only possible support for a nonconfessional theology? Is theology reduced to confession by this move? All of these questions arise from differences between the traditional rationality of the theological system and the kind of rationality to which hermeneutical theology appeals.

Walter R. Fisher draws a helpful distinction between traditional and narrative rationality.[43] The former is at work in Aquinas; the latter, in Ebeling. Traditional rationality operates within what Fisher calls the rational world paradigm of human communication. In part it presupposes that humans are essentially rational beings, that argument is the paradigmatic mode of human decision making and communication, and that the world is a set of logical problems for which solutions are possible in principle. The functional principle of traditional rationality is deliberation. On the other hand, narrative rationality operates within what Fisher calls the narrative paradigm of communication. It presupposes that humans are essentially storytellers, that presentation of "good reasons" is the paradigmatic mode of human decision making and communication, and that good reasons take many forms in different situations and genres. In essence, the world is a set of stories

David E. Klemm

among which we must choose in order to make sense of life. The functional principle of narrative rationality is identification with the characters and events of the stories that make up our world.

The shift from metaphysical theology to hermeneutical theology entails a shift from traditional rationality to narrative rationality. Still, hermeneutic theologians do not abandon traditional rationality but supplement and relativize it. The radicality of the shift can easily be overemphasized. It is, after all, a shift of emphasis within rationality, not a movement away from rationality. In both cases, good reasons are sought for decisions, although the two paradigms differ on how good reasons are produced. Traditional rationality produces them through objectified knowledge of the subject-matter. Narrative rationality locates good reasons by understanding and critically appropriating the norms that are immanent in the modes of existence portrayed and lived out in myth, history, biography, culture, and character. Both seek truth as correspondence between what is asserted and what is actual.

The shift from metaphysical theology to hermeneutical theology does not represent a surrender of the aims of academic theology. Two reasons prevent hermeneutical theology from collapsing into confessional theology. First, a theology focused on word-event is not restricted to recitation and elaboration of religious texts. It appeals both to texts that convey a word-event and to the mode of existence that the texts project. It thus submits to general criteria of textual coherence and to correspondence of textual meaning with independently derived descriptions of authentic human being. Second, the new metaphor of the breaking-in of otherness carries a hidden resource for testing the truth of word-events by the canon of traditional rationality: formal correspondence between assertions and their referents. The hidden resource is the self-negating element in the image of otherness: otherness is other even than itself.

If we ask whether any particular word-event recorded in a text is an appearance of God, the following minimal criteria apply. The word-event must impress someone or some community as a manifestation of God. It does so by presenting the power of language, the otherness of God. The problem with this experiential criterion is that there is inevitably someone else or some other community that is not so impressed. But if the image or metaphor that presents the power of the word also denies on its own that it is divine, then the word-event may be determined to be true. If reflection, operating within traditional rationality, asks whether a word-event is the appearance of God, it inevitably answers "no." This answer agrees with the outsider and the word-event itself. A living symbol of God that denies that it is a symbol of God breaks out of the disclosive truth of narrative rationality and merges with the truth of traditional rationality.[44]

The possibility of interpreting instances of the self-negating symbol of God enables hermeneutical theology to argue that "God is," even though no symbol or word or event literally is God. The argument may legitimately be employed because it leads us not to the metaphysical claim that "God exists," or even its denial, but to the truth that embraces them both: God is God as what is not God but the event of coming-to-oneself through word.[45] This formulation preserves the unity and mystery of God while affirming a potential plurality of witnesses to God's appearances. Moreover, it rules out claims that restrict those appearances.

NOTES

1. Schubert Ogden, "Theology and Religious Studies: Their Difference and the Difference It Makes," *Journal of the American Academy of Religion* 46 (1978): 3–15.

2. Edward Farley, *Ecclesial Reflection: An Anatomy of Theological Method* (Philadelphia: Fortress Press, 1982), pp. 172–83.

3. In contrast to the situation in the United States, in Germany theological faculties for the education of clergy, designated as Catholic or Protestant, are found within the public universities. Confessional theology takes place in the public arena of the university. This leads to a higher academic standard among church theologians and to a smaller gap between church and educated public.

4. On the threefold audience of theology—university, religious community, and society—see David Tracy, *The Analogical Imagination* (New York: Crossroad, 1981), pp. 3–31.

5. Rudolf Otto, *The Idea of the Holy,* trans. John W. Harvey (Oxford: Oxford University Press, 1923, 1959), p. 193.

6. Paul Tillich, *Systematic Theology,* Vol. *1* (Chicago: University of Chicago Press, 1951), p. 205.

7. Chaim Perelman and Lucie Olbrechts-Tyteca, *The New Rhetoric: A Treatise on Argumentation,* trans. Wilkinson and Purcell Weaver (Notre Dame, Ind.: Notre Dame University Press, 1969), pp. 31–35.

8. I follow here the well-known analysis of argument in Stephen Toulmin, *The Uses of Argument* (Cambridge: Cambridge University Press, 1958), especially pp. 94–145.

9. William J. Brandt, *The Rhetoric of Argumentation* (New York: Bobbs-Merrill, 1970), p. 51.

10. Rudolf Bultmann, "What Does It Mean to Speak of God?" in his *Faith and Understanding,* ed. Robert Funk, trans. Louise N. Smith (New York: Harper & Row, 1969), 1: 53.

David E. Klemm

11. Gerhard Ebeling, "Existenz zwischen Gott und Gott," *Zeitschrift für Theologie und Kirche* 62 (1965): 86–113.

12. *Introduction to Saint Thomas Aquinas: Summa Theologica, Summa Contra Gentiles,* ed. Anton C. Pegis (New York: Modern Library, 1948), p. 25.

13. Tillich, *Systematic Theology,* Vol. 1, p. 204.

14. Aquinas, *Summa Theologica,* Q. 3, p. 28.

15. Ebeling, "Existenz zwischen Gott und Gott," p. 88 (my translation).

16. Ibid. Ebeling quotes Luther here.

17. Aquinas, *Summa Theologica,* p. 25.

18. See William L. Rowe, *The Cosmological Argument* (Princeton: Princeton University Press, 1975), pp. 1–114, for a discussion of the reliance of the proof on the principle of sufficient reason, especially pp. 32–39. The quotation is from p. 38.

19. Ibid., pp. 15–17.

20. Immanuel Kant, *Critique of Pure Reason,* trans. Norman Kemp Smith (New York: St. Martin's Press, 1965), p. 511 (A610/B638). See also Robert P. Scharlemann, *The Being of God: Experience and Truth in Theology* (New York: Seabury Press, 1981), pp. 5–6.

21. Kant, *Critique of Pure Reason,* p. 513 (A616/B644).

22. Ibid., p. 531 (A642/B670).

23. Paul Ricoeur, *Interpretation Theory: Discourse and the Surplus of Meaning* (Fort Worth: Texas Christian University Press, 1976), p. 50.

24. Ebeling, "Existenz zwischen Gott und Gott," p. 91.

25. Ibid.

26. Ibid., p. 96.

27. Farley, *Ecclesial Reflection,* pp. 94–95.

28. Gerhard Ebeling, *God and Word,* trans. James W. Leitch (Philadelphia: Fortress Press, 1966), p. 23.

29. Ebeling, "Existenz zwischen Gott und Gott," pp. 97–100.

30. Ibid., p. 98.

31. Martin Heidegger, *Being and Time,* trans. John Macquarrie and Edward Robinson (New York: Harper & Row, 1962), sections 14–18, pp. 91–114.

32. Martin Heidegger, "Was heisst Denken?" in *Vorträge und Aufsätze* (Pfullingen- Günther Neske, 1954), p. 136.

33. Martin Heidegger, "What Is Metaphysics?" trans. David Farrell Krell, in Heidegger, *Basic Writings,* ed. David Farrell Krell (New York: Harper & Row, 1977), pp. 91–112.

34. Ebeling, "Existenz zwischen Gott und Gott," p. 99.

35. See David E. Klemm, *The Hermeneutical Theory of Paul Ricoeur: A Constructive Analysis* (Lewisburg, Pa.: Bucknell University Press, 1983), p. 146.

36. Martin Heidegger, *On the Way to Language,* trans. Peter D. Hertz (New York: Harper & Row, 1971), p. 72.

37. Ebeling, *God and Word,* p. 29.

38. Thomas J. J. Altizer, *The Self-Embodiment of God* (New York: Harper & Row, 1977), p. 31.

39. Martin Heidegger, "Language" in *Poetry, Language, Thought*, trans. Albert Hofstadter (New York: Harper & Row, 1971), pp. 187–210. See also Hans-Georg Gadamer, *Truth and Method*, trans. and ed. Garrett Barden and John Cumming (New York: Seabury Press, 1975), pp. 431–47.

40. Thus words spoken to me may enable me or empower me to become myself when I receive them from another. Robert P. Scharlemann cites as examples "Good morning" or "Cheer up," which in certain situations may actually give a person courage that was beyond his or her grasp prior to hearing the words. See "Being Open and Thinking Theologically," *Journal of the American Academy of Religion* 48 (1981): 118.

41. Ebeling, *God and Word*, p. 38.

42. Scharlemann, *The Being of God*, pp. 62–63, 94–95.

43. Walter R. Fisher, "Narration as a Human Communication Paradigm," *Communications Monographs* 51 (1984): 1–22, esp. pp. 4–9.

44. For further discussion of this topic see Paul Tillich, *The Dynamics of Faith* (New York: Harper & Row, 1957), pp. 95–98. See also Scharlemann, *The Being of God*, pp. 177–83.

45. See Scharlemann, *The Being of God*, pp. 153–83, for a full discussion of "God is God as word."

17 RHETORIC AND LAW

THE ARTS OF CULTURAL AND

COMMUNAL LIFE

JAMES BOYD WHITE

In this paper I wish to make a general suggestion about the relation between law and rhetoric, which I can summarize this way: that law is most usefully seen not, as it normally is by academics and philosophers, as a system of rules, but as a branch of rhetoric; and that rhetoric, of which law is a species, is most usefully seen not, as it normally is, either as a failed science or as the art of persuasion, but as the central art by which community and culture are established, maintained, and transformed. On this view rhetoric is continuous with law and like it has justice as its ultimate subject. I will develop the more general position at some length, for it is in a sense a precondition to what I suggest about the nature and structure of legal rhetoric.

I

When I say that we might regard law as a branch of rhetoric, I may seem to say only the obvious. Who ever could have thought it was anything else? The ancient rhetorician Gorgias (in Plato's dialogue of that name) defined rhetoric as the art of persuading the people about matters of justice and injustice in the public places of the state, and one could hardly imagine a more compendious statement of the art of the lawyer than that. A modern law school is, among other things, a school in those arts of persuasion about justice that are peculiar to, and peculiarly effective in, our legal culture. And the commitment of the rhetorician to the cause of his client presents him, in the ancient and the modern world alike, with serious (and similar) prob-

298

lems of intellectual and personal integrity. What do people think law is if it is not rhetoric, and why do they think so?

The answer lies I think in two traditions, one old, the other new. The older (primarily Judaic and Christian) tradition saw the law as a set of authoritative commands, entitled to respect partly from their antiquity, partly from their concordance with the law of nature and of God. On this view law is not rhetoric but authority. The newer tradition is that of institutional sociology, the object of which is to describe and analyze the structure and function of various social institutions, so far as possible from the point of view of "value-free" social science. These institutions may of course have certain kinds of political authority internal to the culture in which they can be found, but they are normally not seen as sources of true moral authority, as law once was. With the apparent death of the first tradition in most Western European (but not Islamic!) countries, we are left with the second, and tend to view law as a system of institutionally established and managed rules. As this conception has worked itself out in practice, it has led to a kind of substantive neutrality or emptiness that makes it natural once again to see a connection between modern law and ancient rhetoric, and to face—as Plato did in the *Gorgias*—the great question of what talk about justice can mean in a world as relativistic, adversarial, competitive, and uncertain as ours is and theirs was.

For these reasons the law is at present usually spoken of (by academics at least) as if it were a body of more or less determinate rules, or rules and principles, that are more or less perfectly intelligible to the trained reader. Law is in this sense objectified and made a structure. The question "What is law?" is answered by defining what its rules are, or by analyzing the kinds of rules that characterize it. The law is thus abstracted and conceptualized: H. L. A. Hart's major book on jurisprudence was appropriately entitled *The Concept of Law*. Sophisticated analysis of law from this point of view distinguishes among various kinds of legal rules and different sets or subsets of legal rules: substantive rules from procedural or remedial rules, or primary rules from secondary rules, or legal rules from more general principles.

This idea of law and legal science fits with, and is perhaps derived from, the contemporary conception of our public political world as a set of bureaucratic entities, which can be defined in Weberian terms as rationalized institutions functioning according to ends-means rationality. These institutions are defined by their goals, purposes, or aims, which they achieve more or less perfectly as they are structured and managed more or less well.

James Boyd White

In this way the government, of which the law is a part (and in fact the entire bureaucratic system, private as well as public), tends to be regarded, especially by lawyers, managers, and other policymakers, as a machine acting on the rest of the world; the rest of the world is in turn reduced to the object upon which the machine acts. Actors outside the bureaucratic world are made the objects of manipulation through a series of incentives or disincentives. Actors within the legal-bureaucratic structure are either reduced to "will-servers" (who regard their obligation as being to obey the will of a political superior), or they are "choice-makers" (who are in a position of political superiority, charged with the responsibility of making choices, usually thought of as "policy choices," that affect the lives of others). The choices themselves are likewise objectified: the items of choice are broken out of the flux of experience and the context of life so that they can be talked about in the bureaucratic-legal mode. This commits the system to what is thought to be measurable, especially to what is measurable in material ways; to short-term goals; and to a process of thought by calculation. The premises of cost-benefit analysis are integral to the bureaucracy as we normally imagine it. Whatever cannot be talked about in these bureaucratic ways is simply not talked about. Of course all systems of discourse have domains and boundaries, principles of exclusion and inclusion; but this kind of bureaucratic talk is unselfconscious about what it excludes. The world it sees is its whole world.

Law then becomes reducible to two features: policy choices and techniques of their implementation. Our questions are, "What do we want?" and "How do we get it?" In this way the conception of law as a set of rules merges with the conception of law as a set of institutions and processes. The overriding metaphor is that of the machine; the overriding value is that of efficiency, conceived of as the attainment of certain ends with the smallest possible costs.[1]

This is a necessarily crude sketch of certain ways in which law is commonly thought of. Later in this essay I shall propose a different way of conceiving of law, which I think can be both more true to its actual nature as practiced and more valuable to us as critics.

II

I turn now to what is usually meant by "rhetoric." This term is in greater flux, and what I say must be somewhat less dogmatic. But it is my impression that rhetoric is at present usually talked about in either of two modes. The first of these is by comparison with science.

The main claim of science is that it contributes to knowledge by inform-
ing us of what is knowable in the sense that it can be demonstrated.
This is true both of deductive sciences, which estabish propositions by
demonstrating their entailment in certain premises, and of inductive
sciences, which establish, but with less certainty, propositions that can
be regarded as the most complete and economical accounts of the evidence available to us, and hence as presumptively true. From this point
of view rhetoric is thought of as what we do when science doesn't
work. Instead of dealing with what is "known," it deals with what is
probably the case. Thus in Aristotle the enthymeme is defined as a syllogism based upon propositions that are not themselves true but probable. Rhetoric is the art of establishing the probable by arguing from
our sense of the probable. It is always open to replacement by science
when the truth or falsity of what is now merely probable is finally
established.

The other heading under which rhetoric is frequently discussed is
explicitly pejorative: rhetoric is defined as the ignoble art of persuasion.
As I suggested above, this tradition has a history at least as old as the
Platonic dialogues, in which rhetoric is attacked as a false art;[2] and it is
as contemporary as the standard modern condemnations of propaganda in government and of advertising as practiced by the wizards of
Madison Avenue. To the extent that law is today regarded as a kind of
rhetoric, these two traditions establish the terms of analysis. In the
courtroom the truth is never known, and each of the lawyers tries to
persuade the jury not of the truth, but that his (or her) view is more
probable than the other one or that the other side's case has not attained
some requisite degree of probability. In doing so each employs untrust-
worthy arts of persuasion by which he seeks to make his own case,
even if it is the weaker one, appear the stronger. Rhetoric, in short, is
thought of either as a second-rate way of dealing with facts that cannot
really be properly known or as a way of dealing with people instrumentally or manipulatively, in an attempt to get them to do something you
want them to do.

The tendency to think of rhetoric as failed science is especially
powerful in the present age, in which such determined attempts have
been made to elevate, or to reduce, virtually every discipline to the status of true science. The idea of science as perfect knowledge has of
course been recently subjected to considerable criticism, both internal
and external. It is now a commonplace that scientific creativity is imaginative, almost poetic; that scientific knowledge is only presumptive,
not certain; and that science is a culture that transforms itself by principles that are not themselves scientific. Yet the effort to make the lan-

guage and conventions of science the ruling model of our age, our popular religion, lives on in the language and expectations of others, especially of those who are in fact not true scientists. Much of economic discourse, for example, is deformed by the false claims of the discipline to the status of perfect science, which leads to the embarrassing situation in which economic speakers representing different political attitudes couch their differences in scientific terms, each claiming that the other is no true economist. This not only confuses the observer but renders the field of economics less intelligible than it should be, even to its participants, and it reduces important political differences, which might be the topic of real conversation, to the status of primary assumptions.

III

In this essay I shall propose a somewhat different way of conceiving of law, and indeed of governmental processes generally: not as a bureaucratic but as a rhetorical process. In doing this I will also be suggesting a way to think about rhetoric as well, especially about that "constitutive" rhetoric of which law can I think be seen as a species.

I want to start by thinking of law not as an objective reality in an imagined social world, not as a part of a constructed cosmology, but from the point of view of those who actually engage in its processes, as something we do and something we teach. This is a way of looking at law as an activity, and specifically as a rhetorical activity.

In particular I want to direct attention to three aspects of the lawyer's work. The first is the fact that, like any rhetorician, the lawyer must always start by speaking the language of his or her audience, whatever it may be. This is just a version of the general truth that to persuade anyone you must in the first instance speak a language he or she regards as valid and intelligible. If you are a lawyer this means that you must speak either the technical language of the law—the rules, cases, statutes, maxims, and so forth that constitute the domain of your professional talk—or, if you are speaking to jurors or clients or the public at large, some version of the ordinary English of your time and place and culture. Law is in this sense always culture-specific. It always starts with an external, empirically discoverable set of cultural resources into which it is an intervention.

This suggests that one (somewhat circular) definition of the law might be as the particular set of resources made available by a culture for speech and argument on those occasions, and by those speakers, we think of as legal. These resources include rules, statutes, and judicial opinions, of course, but much more as well: maxims, general understandings, conventional wisdom, and all the other resources, technical and nontechnical, that a lawyer might use in defining his or her position and urging another to accept it.[3] To define "the law" in this way, as a set of resources for thought and argument, is an application of Aristotle's traditional definition of rhetoric, for the law in this sense is one set of those "means of persuasion" which he said it is the art of rhetoric to discover.

In the law (and I believe elsewhere as well) these means of persuasion can be described with some degree of accuracy and completeness, so that most lawyers would agree that such-and-such a case or statute or principle is relevant, and another is not. But the agreement is always imperfect: one lawyer will see an analogy that another will deny, for example. And when attention shifts to the value or weight that different parts of the material should have, disagreement becomes widespread and deep. Ultimately the identity, the meaning, and the authority of the materials are always arguable, always uncertain. There is a sense in which the materials can be regarded in the first instance as objective, external to the self; but they are always remade in argument. Their discovery is an empirical process; their reformulation and use an inventive or creative one.

This suggests that the lawyer's work has a second essential element, the creative process to which I have just alluded. For in speaking the language of the law the lawyer must always be ready to try to change it: to add or to drop a distinction, to admit a new voice, to claim a new source of authority, and so on. One's performance is in this sense always argumentative, not only about the result one seeks to obtain but also about the version of the legal discourse that one uses—that one creates—in one's speech and writing. That is, the lawyer is always saying not only, "Here is how this case should be decided," but also "Here—in this language—is the way this case and similar cases should be talked about. The language I am speaking is the proper language of justice in our culture." The legal speaker always acts upon the language that he or she uses; in this sense legal rhetoric is always argumentatively constitutive of the language it employs.

The third aspect of legal rhetoric is what might be called its ethical or communal character, or its socially constitutive nature. Every time one speaks as a lawyer, one establishes for the moment a character—an ethical identity, or what the Greeks called an *ethos*—for oneself, for one's audience, and for those one talks about, and proposes a relationship among them. The lawyer's speech is thus always implicitly argumentative not only about the result—how should the case be decided?—and the language—in what terms should it be defined and talked about?—but about the rhetorical community of which one is at that moment a part. One is always establishing in performance a response to the question "What kind of community should we who are talking the language of the law establish with each other, with our clients, and with the rest of the world? What kind of conversation should the law constitute, should constitute the law?"

Each of the three aspects of the lawyer's rhetorical life can be analyzed and criticized: the discourse he is given by his culture to speak; his argumentative reconstitution of it; and his implicitly argmentative constitution of a rhetorical community in his text. The study of this process—of constitutive rhetoric—is the study of the ways we constitute ourselves as individuals, as communities, and as cultures, whenever we speak. To put this another way, the fact that the law may be understood as a comprehensibly organized method of argument, or what I call a rhetoric, means that it is at once a social activity—a way of acting with others—and a cultural activity, a way of acting with a certain set of materials found in the culture. It is always communal, both in the sense that it always takes place in a social context, and in the sense that it is always constitutive of the community by which it works. The law is an art of persuasion that creates the objects of its persuasion, for it constitutes both the community and the culture it commends.

This means that the process of law is at once creative and educative. Those who use this language are perpetually learning what can and cannot be said, what can and cannot be done with it, as they try—and fail or succeed—to reach new formulations of their positions. It also means that both the identity of the speakers and their wants are in perpetual transformation. If this is right, the law cannot be a technique, as the bureaucratic model assumes, by which "we" get what we "want," for both "we" and our "wants" are constantly remade in the rhetorical process. The idea of the legal actor as one who is either making policy choices himself (or herself) or obeying the choices made by others is inadequate, for he is a participant in the perpetual remaking of the language and culture that determines who he is and who we are. In this way we might come to see the law less as a bureaucracy or a set of rules than as a community of speakers of a certain kind: as a culture of argument, perpetually remade by its participants.

IV

All this flows from the fact that the law is what I have called culture-specific, that is, that it always takes place in a cultural context into which it is always an intervention. But it is in a similar way socially specific: it always takes place in a particular social context, into which it is also an intervention. By this I mean nothing grand but simply that the lawyer responds to the felt needs of others, who come to him or her for assistance with an actual difficulty or problem. These felt needs may of course be partly the product of the law itself, and the very "intervention" of the law can create new possibilities for meaning, for motive, and for aspiration. From this point of view the law can be seen, as it is experienced, not as an independent system of meaning, but as a way of talking about real events and actual people in the world. At its heart it is a way of telling a story about what has happened in the world and claiming a meaning for it by writing an ending to it. The lawyer is repeatedly saying, or imagining himself or herself saying: "Here is 'what happened'; here is 'what it means'; and here is 'why it means what I claim.'" The process is at heart a narrative one because there cannot be a legal case without a real story about real people actually located in time and space and culture. Some actual person must go to a lawyer with an account of the experience upon which he or she wants the law to act, and that account will always be a narrative.

The client's narrative is not simply accepted by the lawyer but subjected to questioning and elaboration, as the lawyer sees first one set of legal relevances, then another. In the formal legal process that story is then retold, over and over, by the lawyer and by the client and by others, in developing and competing versions, until by judgment or agreement an authoritative version is achieved. (Think of the way that, in Sophocles' *Philoctetes*, Neoptolemus recasts Philoctetes' story, with a different beginning and a different sense of causation, to give it a different meaning and to make a different ending seem possible, indeed inevitable and right.)[4] This story will in the first instance be told in the language of its actors. That is where the law begins; in a sense this is also where it ends, for its object is to provide an ending to that story that will work in the world. And since the story both begins and ends in ordinary language and experience, the heart of the law is the process of translation by which it must work, from ordinary language to legal language and back again.

The language that the lawyer uses and remakes is a language of meaning in the fullest sense. It is a language in which our perceptions

James Boyd White

of the natural universe are constructed and related, in which our values and motives are defined, in which our methods of reasoning are elaborated and enacted; and it gives us our terms for constructing a social universe by defining roles and actors and by establishing expectations as to the propriety of speech and conduct. Law always operates through speakers located in particular times and places speaking to actual audiences about real people. Its language is continuous with ordinary language: it always operates by narrative; it is not conceptual in its structure; it is perpetually reaffirmed or rejected in a social process; and it contains a system of internal translation by which it can reach a range of hearers. All these things mark it as a literary and rhetorical system.

V

What I have said means something, I think, about what we can mean by "rhetoric" as well. What I have been describing is not merely an art of estimating probabilities or an art of persuasion, but an art of constituting culture and community. It is of rhetoric so understood that I think we can see the law as a branch.

Let me approach what I mean about rhetoric with a primitive example, meant to suggest that what I call "constitutive rhetoric" is actually the set of practices that most fully distinguish human beings from other animals. Imagine a bear, fishing for salmon in a river of the great Northwest. What is he doing? Fishing we say. Now imagine a man fishing in the same river for the same fish. What is he doing? Fishing, we say; but this time the answer has a different meaning and a new dimension, for it is now a question, as it was not before, what the fishing means to the actor himself. If a person does it, it has a meaning of a kind it cannot otherwise have. Today the meaning may well be that of sentimental escape to the wilderness by one sportily clad in his L. L. Bean outfit, demonstrating his place in a certain social class; but once—for a Native American, say—it might have been a religious meaning.

Whenever two people fish (or hunt, or anything else) they necessarily share the question of the meaning of what they do. Their views may differ, and their differences may reach the meaning of their relationship as well as that of their common activity. There is, for example, the question of dominance or equality: is one person following the other, or are they in some sense together? Do their views of the meaning of what they do coincide, and if so how do they know? Or is there tension or disharmony between them, and if so what is to be done about that? How long will the terms upon which they are proceeding remain stable? The establishment of comprehensible relations and shared meanings, the making of the kind of community that enables people to say "we" about what they do and to claim consistent meanings for it—all this at the deepest level involves persuasion as well as education, and is the province of what I call constitutive rhetoric.

Let me expand my example a bit. Think of the kind of opposition that begins the *Iliad*, the opposition between two male human beings quarreling over a female. From one point of view this is just like two other male mammals doing the same thing, say two male bears or dogs. But from another point of view there is a completely new dimension added to the dispute: the question of what it means, from each point of view including that of the woman. It is from such a dispute, and from the claims of competing meanings for the events involved, that arose both the Trojan War (at least in Greek myth) and, from our point of view much more importantly, the *Iliad* itself. Agamemnon and Achilles are engaged in a struggle. At some level the struggle is an animal one, with will opposed to will. It is also a human struggle, a struggle over what ought to be done, and why, and this is a struggle over meaning: what it means for Agamemnon to be deprived of a prize, or of this woman, or for Achilles to be deprived of a prize, or of this woman. At moments in this poem attention is directed to what it means from the point of view of the woman herself, as in the cases of Andromache, Helen, and at one moment Briseis herself.

Once the quarrel has begun, and Achilles has separated himself from the other Achaeans, the question shifts to what *that* means, and, as time goes on, to how the quarrel might be made up. "Making up" a quarrel is a process in which the parties gradually, and often with great difficulty, come to share a common language for the description of their common past, present, and future, including an agreement as to what will be passed over in silence. In this process they reestablish themselves as a community with a culture of their own. In the *Iliad*, Agamemnon's attempts to make up the quarrel fail; community between them is never reestablished, even when Achilles returns to the battle, because that is done for a different reason, the death of Patroclus.

Or think of another great literary moment, the beginning of *Paradise Lost*, when Satan and the other rebellious angels try to establish a community of their own in Hell, based upon a new language of value and meaning. Their incredible attempts at self-creation and self-assertion have won them the admiration of many readers, from Shelley onwards; some even see Satan as the unacknowledged hero of the poem. ("The mind is its own place, and in itself / Can make a Heav'n of Hell, a Hell of

James Boyd White

Heav'n.") But the poem shows that no community can be built upon the language that they use, a language of selfishness and hatred—a language that in fact made a "Hell of Heav'n"—even by figures with such enormous capacities of imagination and will as Milton represents the angels to be. Compare with this the efforts of the participants at our own Constitutional Convention in the summer of 1787, who were also trying to find or make a language, and a set of relations, upon which a new community could be made, a new life proceed. Their arguments can be read as the gradual attempt to make a language of shared factual assumptions, shared values, shared senses of what need be said and what need not—of what could be said ambiguously, of what they could not resolve at all—resulting in a text that they could offer to others as the terms on which a new community might begin its tentative life.

What kind of community shall it be? How will it work? In what language shall it be formed? These are the great questions of rhetorical analysis. It always has justice and ethics—and politics, in the best sense of that term—as its ultimate subjects.

The domain of constitutive rhetoric as I think of it thus includes *all* language activity that goes into the constitution of actual human cultures and communities. Even the kind of persuasion Plato called dialectic, in which the speaker is himself willing, even eager, to be refuted, is in this sense a form of rhetoric, for it is the establishment of community and culture in language.

VI

Like law, rhetoric invents, and like law it invents not out of nothing but out of something. It always starts in a particular place among particular people. There is always one speaker addressing others in a particular situation about concerns that are real and important to somebody, and always speaking a particular language. Rhetoric always takes place with given materials. One cannot idealize rhetoric and say: Here is how it should go on in general. As Aristotle saw—for his *Rhetoric* is for the most part a map of claims that are persuasive in his Greek world—rhetoric is always specific to its material. There is not an Archimedean point from which rhetoric can be viewed or practiced.

This means that the rhetorician—that is, each of us when we speak to persuade or to establish community in other ways—must accept the double fact that there are real and important differences between cultures and that one is in substantial part the product of one's own culture. The rhetorician, like the lawyer, is thus engaged in a process of meaning-making and community-building of which he or she is in part the subject. To do this requires him or her to face and to accept the condition of radical uncertainty in which we live: uncertainty as to the meaning of words, uncertainty as to their effect on others, uncertainty even as to our own motivations. The knowledge out of which the rhetorician ultimately functions will thus be not scientific or theoretical but practical, experiential, the sense that one knows how to do things with language and with others. This is in fact our earliest social and intellectual knowledge, the knowledge we acquire as we first begin to move and act in our social universe and learn to speak and understand. It is the knowledge by which language and social relations are made.

The rhetorician thus begins not with the imagined individual in imagined isolation, as political philosophers who think in terms of a social contract do, and not with the self isolated from all of its experience except that of cogitation, as metaphysicians in the Cartesian tradition do, but where Wittgenstein tells us to begin, with our abilities of language, gesture, and meaning. This knowledge is itself not reducible to rules, nor subject to expression in rules, though many analysts wish it were; rather it is the knowledge by which we learn to manage, evade, disappoint, surprise, and please each other, as we understand the expectations that others bring to what we say. This knowledge is not provable in the scientific sense, nor is it logically rigorous. For these reasons it is unsettling to the modern scientific and academic mind. But we cannot go beyond it, and it is a mistake to try. In this fluid world without turf or ground we cannot walk, but we can swim. And we need not be afraid to do this—to engage in the rhetorical process of life—notwithstanding our radical uncertainties, for all of us already know how to do it. By attending to our own experience, and that of others, we can learn to do it better if we try.

VII

What would be the effects of thinking of law in this rhetorical way? If, as I think, it is more true to the experience of those engaged in the activity of law than the standard conceptual accounts, it should in the first place lead to richer and more accurate teaching and practice of law and to a greater sense of control over what we do. Law might come to be seen as something that lawyers themselves make all the time, whenever they act as lawyers, not as something that is made by a political sovereign. From this point of view the law can be seen as the culture that we remake whenever we speak as lawyers. To look at law this way is to direct one's attention to places that it perhaps normally does not rest: to the way in which we create new meanings, new possibilities for meaning, in what we say; to the way our literature can be regarded as a literature of value and motive and sentiment; to the way in which our enterprise is a radically ethical one, by which self and community are perpetually reconstituted; and to the limits that our nature or our culture, our circumstances and our imagination, place on our powers to remake our languages and communities in new forms.

To see law this way may also lead to a different way of reading and writing it. As I suggest above, the United States Constitution can be regarded as a rhetorical text: as establishing a set of speakers, roles, topics, and occasions for speech.[5] So understood, many of its ambiguities and uncertainties become more comprehensible; we can see it as attempting to establish a conversation of a certain kind, and its ambiguities as ways of at once defining and leaving open the topics of the conversation. Similarly, a statute can be read not merely as a set of orders or directions or commands, but also as establishing a set of topics, a set of terms in which those topics can be discussed, and some general directions as to the process of thought and argument by which the statute is to be applied. To see the statute as a way of starting a conversation of a certain kind on a certain set of subjects might well assist both one's reading and one's writing of the form. Similarly, the judicial opinion, often thought to be the paradigmatic form of legal expression, might be far more accurately and richly understood if it were seen not as a bureaucratic expression of ends-means rationality but as a statement by an individual mind or a group of individual minds exercising their responsibility to decide a case as well as they can and to determine what it shall mean in the language of culture. All this is necessarily to define the lawyer's own work as far less manipulative, selfish, or goal-oriented than the usual models, and as far more creative, communal, and intellectually challenging.

From the point of view of the nonlawyer, this way of regarding law as rhetoric invites a certain kind of reading and of criticism, for it invites you to test the law in part by asking whether your own story, or the story of another in whom you have an interest, is properly told by these speakers, in a proper language. The basic premise of the hearing is that two stories will be told in opposition or competition and a choice made between them. It is the role of the jury to insist upon the ultimate translatability of law into the common language of the culture. You are entitled to have your story told in your language (or translated into it), or the law is failing. To ask, what place is there for me in this language, this text, this story, and to feel that you have a right to an answer, is a very different way of evaluating law from thinking of it as a mechanism for distributing social goods. The central idea is not that of goods, but of voices and relations: what voices does the law allow to be heard, what relations does it establish among them? With what voice, or voices does the law itself speak? These are the questions with which rhetorical criticism would begin.

As I suggested above we can also see that the current habit of regarding law as the instrument by which "we" effectuate "our policies" and get what "we want" is wholly inadequate. It is the true nature of law to constitute a "we" and to establish a conversation by which that "we" can determine what our "wants" are and should be. Our motives and values are not on this view to be taken as exogenous to the system (as they are taken to be exogenous to an economic system) but are in fact its subject. The law should take as its most central question what kind of community we should be, with what values, motives, and aims; it is a process by which we make ourselves by making our language.

This means that one question constantly before us as lawyers is what kind of culture we shall have, as well as what kind of community we shall be. What shall be our language of approval and disapproval, praise and blame, admiration and contempt? What shall be the terms by which we identify and refine—by which we create—our motives and combine them into coherent wholes? This way of conceiving of law invites us to include in our zone of attention and field of discourse what others, operating under present suppositions, cut out, including both the uncertainty of life and the fact that we, and our resources, are constantly remade by our own collective activities. The pressure of bureaucratic discourse is always to think in terms of ends and means; in practice ends-means rationality is likely to undergo a reversal by which only those things can count as ends for which means of a certain kind exist. This often results in a reduction of the human to the material and the measurable—as though a good or just society were a function of the rate of individual consumption, not a community of a certain sort, a set of shared relations, attitudes, and meanings. To view law as rhetoric might enable us to attend to the spiritual or meaningful side of our collective life.[6]

Such a conception of law as I describe would lead to a rather different method of teaching it as well. It would at first require a rather old-fashioned training in the intellectual practices that are the things that lawyers do, from reading cases to drafting statutes and contracts. The rhetorician must always start with the materials of his or her language and culture, and we should continue to train our students to understand these materials, their resources and limits, and to learn to put them to work in the activities of narrative and analysis and argument that make up their professional lives.

But these activities would not merely be learned as crafts to be performed as efficiently as possible; they would be contrasted with other ways of doing similar things, both from ordinary life and from other disciplines. Learning how to argue in the law about the meaning of rules, or of fairness, or of blaming, can be informed by attending to the ways in which we already know how to do these things, in ordinary life, and by learning how they are done elsewhere. One focus would accordingly be upon the connection between legal language and ordinary language, legal life and ordinary life, as rhetoric connects them. Another focus would be upon other formal intellectual practices, in an interdisciplinary curriculum rather different from current models: not law *and* sociology or history or economics or literature, but law *as* each of these things. What kind of sociology or history or anthropology are we implicitly practicing in this legal rule, in that legal action or argument, in this judicial opinion? What can be said for and against our implied choices?

But the largest difference would be a shift in the conception of the triadic relation between the student, the teacher, and the subject. The law we teach would not be regarded as a set of institutions that "we" manipulate either to achieve "our policies," as governors, nor "our interests," as lawyers, but rather as a language and a community—a world, made partly by others and partly by ourselves, in which we and others shall live, and which will be tested less by its distributive effects than by the resources of meaning it creates and the community it constitutes: who we become to ourselves and to one another when we converse.[7] And our central question would become how to understand and to judge those things.

VIII

By this kind of conjunction with the law, rhetoric itself can perhaps be seen in a somewhat different light. No longer a substitute for science when science does not work, it can be seen as a science itself, at least in the eighteenth-century meaning of that term as an organized form of knowledge. It is the knowledge of who we make ourselves, as individuals and as communities, in the ways we speak to each other. Rhetorical knowledge is allied with artistic knowledge in that it is tacitly creative and acknowledges both its limits and the conditions of uncertainty under which it functions. Rhetorical analysis provides a way of addressing the central questions of collective existence in an organized and consistent, but not rule-bound, way. It directs our attention to the most significant questions of shared existence, which are wholly outside the self-determined bounds of science. Justice and ethics are its natural subject, art its natural method.

Rhetoric may also provide a set of questions and attitudes that will enable us to move from one academic and social field to another and in doing so to unite them. For at least tentative judgments of the kind rhetoric calls for can be made about the work of experts—in history say or psychology—without one's having to be an expert in the professional sense oneself. Not that one has not always something to learn—of course one has—but one can never know everything and ought not be barred from making important observations and judgments of one kind by a want of competence at making others. We can say a lot about the kind of history written by Gibbon, for example—about the sort of community he establishes with us, about his language of value and judgment—without being able to make professional judgments about his use of certain inscriptions as evidence on a certain point.

Rhetoric in the highly expanded sense in which I speak of it might even become the central discipline for which we have been looking for so long—which "science" has proven not to be—by which the others can be defined and organized and judged. One reason rhetoric might be able to perform this role is its continuity with ordinary discourse and hence with real communities, real values, and real politics. It is at least contiguous to a ground that is common to us all. Rhetoric must deal with ordinary language because it is the art of speaking to people who already have a language, and it is their language you must speak to reach and to persuade them. This is the sense in which, as I suggested above, rhetoric is always culture-specific. You must take the language you are given and work with that.

One result of this affirmation of ordinary language is that it provides a ground for challenge and change, a place to stand from which to reformulate any more specialized language. It establishes a kind of structural openness. Another result is that it confirms our right and capacity to say what we think is really good about what is good in our world and what is really terrible about what is terrible. Rhetorical analysis invites us to talk about our conceptions of ourselves as individuals and as communities, and to define our values in living rather than conceptual ways. For example, consider what is good about America: our present public rhetoric seems to assume that what is good about it is its material productivity. But that is often wasteful, self-destructive, and ugly. I think what is really good about this country is its fundamental culture

James Boyd White

of self-government, independence, and generosity. These facts are all too often obscured or denied by the ways in which we habitually talk about our government and law.

How does rhetoric enable us to talk about these matters? It does so by giving us a set of very simple but fundamental questions to ask when someone speaks either to us or on our behalf, or when we ourselves speak. These questions focus on the three aspects of the lawyer's rhetorical situation I identified above.

1. *The inherited language.* What is the language or culture with which this speaker works? How does it represent natural and social facts, constitute human motives and values, and define those persuasive motions of the mind that we call reason? What does it leave out or deny? What does it overspecify? What is its actual or imagined relation to other systems of discourse?

2. *The art of the text.* How, by what art and with what effect, is this language remade by this speaker in this written or oral text? Is the text internally coherent, and if so by what standards of coherence? Is it externally coherent (that is, does it establish intelligible relations with its background), and if so, by what standards of coherence? How, that is, does this text reconstitute its discourse?

3. *The rhetorical community.* What kind of person is speaking here, and to what kind of person does he or she speak? What kind of response does this text invite, or permit? What place is there for me, and for others, in the universe defined by this discourse, in the community created by this text? What world does it assume, what world does it create?

Such questions may enable us to approach a set of texts as they are actually made, in widely varying cultures, languages, and human relations, and to establish connections among them across their contexts, above or behind their particularities. To ask them is of course not to answer them: but it may direct our attention to the proper place for thought to begin and suggest, by implication, appropriate modes of inquiry and judgment.

IX

Consider, for example, the criticism of judicial opinions. It is common, and in a sense perfectly natural, for judicial critics to direct their attention primarily to the legal results reached by a particular court or judge. This kind of criticism argues the merits of the questions presented and resolved. You might thus criticize a judge, or a court, for being in your view insufficiently sensitive to the importance of free speech or to the rights of states to govern their own affairs; or you might argue that his (or her) method of statutory or constitutional interpretation, or his treatment of precedent, is unsatisfactory. In either case you can expect your argument to be met by others. The resulting conversations—let us call them political and professional—are important branches of judicial criticism. But there is I think another even more fundamental branch of judicial criticism, in which attention is focused less on results or methods than on a special kind of judicial ethics that is in large measure a matter of voice.

Of course one may properly argue against the results of particular cases and, more deeply, against a judge's institutional or political premises, and one may properly criticize technique as well. But any judge brings a set of basic values and orientations to his or her work and it is hard to fault someone for having a different set from one's own. The law is meant to be a way in which people can live together in spite of their differences. Our most important concern is accordingly less with the original preferences and attitudes a judge brings to the bench than with what he or she does with them; here we can imagine ourselves greatly admiring the work of a justice with whose substantive predispositions we disagreed, and having contempt for one who largely shared our own social and political attitudes. This is partly a matter of meeting what can be called professional standards—treating precedent in an appropriate way and knowing how, and how not, to use legislative history, for example. But what we admire cannot be reduced to such skills. The deepest judicial excellence is an excellence of attitude and character.

The ideal would be a judge who put his (or her) fundamental attitudes and methods to the test of sincere engagement with arguments the other way. We could ask, does this judge see the case before him as the occasion for printing out an ideology, for displaying technical skill, or as presenting a real difficulty, calling for real thought? The ideal judge would show that he had listened to the side he voted against and that he had felt the pull of the arguments both ways. The law that was made that way would comprise two opposing voices, those of the parties, in a work made by another, by the judge who had listened to both and had faced the conflict between them in an honest way. In this sense the judge's most important work is the definition of his own voice, the character he makes for himself as he works through a case.

James Boyd White

Or take an example from substantive law: in evaluating the law that regulates the relations between police officials and citizens (which in our system is largely the law of the Fourth and Fifth Amendments to the Constitution), I think the important question to be asked is not whether it is "pro-police" or "pro-suspect" in result, nor even how it will work as a system of incentives and deterrents, but what room it makes for the officer and the citizen each to say what reasonably can be said, from his or her point of view, about the transaction—the street frisk, the airport search, the barroom arrest—that they share. Here too the central concern is with voices: whether the voice of the judge leaves room for the voices of the parties.[8]

X

The practice and teaching of rhetoric is by its nature self-reflective, for the questions that one learns to ask of others can be asked of oneself as well. We have asked, for example, what kind of community and culture a speaker or writer makes when he or she engages in a particular kind of intellectual analysis, say cost-benefit analysis. Those communities and cultures, performed and tentatively offered to the world, can be analyzed and judged. But the same question can be asked of what we ourselves say and what we think. What kind of community do we make in our own writing and our own speech, what language of meaning do we create? What is the voice with which we speak? These are the first and hardest questions, and they can be asked of this essay and of all of our expressions to each other. Whenever we speak or write, we should be prepared to ask ourselves what kind of community and culture we make, what kind of meaning they shall have.[9]

NOTES

Portions of this chapter have previously appeared in the University of Chicago Law Review (Summer 1985) and in James Boyd White, *Heracles' Bow: Essays on the Rhetoric and Poetics of the Law* (Madison: University of Wisconsin Press, 1985).

I am grateful for helpful comments by Pete Becker, Lee Bollinger, Bruce Gronbeck, Terrance Sandalow, Joseph Vining, and Christina Whitman.

1. This bureaucratic language is very deep in our ordinary culture as well: think of a conversation at a curriculum committee meeting where someone

says, "Let us first state our educational goals and then determine how we can arrive at them." That is a dreadful way to talk about teaching, yet it is dominant in our world, and once the conversation has begun on those terms it is almost impossible to deflect it to address any true educational concerns.

2. "The Ethics of Argument: Plato's *Gorgias* and the Modern Lawyer," 50 *University of Chicago Law Review* 849–95 (1983): an analysis of Plato's attack on rhetoric, and a defense, against that attack, of the rhetorical practices of modern law.

3. In light of the current view of law as a set of rules, it is worth stressing that while much legal argument naturally takes the form of interpreting rules, or redefining them, and while some rules are of course superior in authority to others, the material as a whole is not structured as a set of rules with a hierarchical or other order, nor is it reducible to a set of rules. The rule is often the subject as well as the source of argument; its form and content and relation to other rules are in principle arguable. The best way to understand what a rule is, as it works in the legal world, is to think of it not as a command that is obeyed or disobeyed but as a topic of thought and argument—as one of many resources brought to bear by the lawyer and others both to define a question and to establish a way to approach it.

4. See James Boyd White, "Heracles' Bow: Persuasion and Community in Sophocles' *Philoctetes*," in *Heracles' Bow: Essays on the Rhetoric and Poetics of the Law* (Madison: University of Wisconsin Press, 1985), pp. 3–27.

5. For a fuller statement of the "rhetorical" view of the Constitution outlined here, see my *When Words Lose Their Meaning* (Chicago: University of Chicago Press, 1984), chap. 9.

6. As one example of what I mean by the difference between the material and the meaningful, consider the question of the invasion of privacy by officials. One way to try to compare different regimes would be to inquire how frequently, for example, police officers stopped individuals on the street, asked for their identification, and subjected them to pat-downs or searches. That would be a material mode of determining "how much" privacy existed in a particular culture. It could in principle be determined statistically. But far more important than that is the meaning of the described activities of the officers both to them and to the citizens. There are circumstances, war being the most obvious, in which almost everyone would agree that this kind of policing was important and valuable, and citizens by and large not feel that their privacy was invaded, because they would feel that the officer was acting as their fellow worker in a common enterprise.

7. I do not mean that distributive effects are irrelevant but that the context in which they are relevant, and from which they derive their meaning, is social and ethical. What does it mean about us that power and wealth are divided this way, or that? Or, more precisely—since power and wealth are at bottom social and cultural—what does it mean about us that we create these powers, these wealths, in this way? Without a social and ethical context, one

James Boyd White

has after all nothing but brute material, which has of itself no meaning at all, as wealth, power, or symbol.

8. For further analysis of what I call the rhetoric of the Fourth Amendment, which regulates and in part constitutes the relation between citizen and official in our culture, see my articles, "The Fourth Amendment as a Way of Talking About People: A Study of the *Robinson* and *Matlock* Cases," 1974 *Supreme Court Review* 165–232, and "Forgotten Arguments in the 'Exclusionary Rule' Debate," 81 *Michigan Law Review* 1273–84 (1983).

9. Another book that sees law as a way of making meaning in an uncertain world by reasoning through progressive analogies is Edward H. Levi's seminal *An Introduction to Legal Reasoning* (Chicago: University of Chicago Press, 1949). For a general view of rhetoric rather similar to my own, see Ernesto Grassi, *Rhetoric as Philosophy: The Humanist Tradition* (University Park: Pennsylvania State University Press, 1980).

18 FEMINIST POLITICAL

RHETORIC AND

WOMEN'S STUDIES

JEAN BETHKE ELSHTAIN

Women's studies is a highly charged activity, a field of inquiry with explicit connections to a political movement and to the rhetoric of that movement. The nexus between women's studies as an academic enterprise and feminist political rhetoric is clear in a way that most links between academic disciplines and a broader social field are not. At present, women's studies is a rather large magnet drawing scholars from diverse disciplines into an effort characterized, and celebrated, as interdisciplinary. Under the broad umbrella of women's studies one finds a lively, at times contentious, world of competing epistemologies, ideologies, narrative styles, and ethical and political commitments. Women's studies, at this point, crosses the spectrum of academic disciplines and methodologies.[1] Encompassing a diversity of perspectives is the ideal (however imperfectly realized) of the enterprise.

The rhetoric of feminist politics, however, shares with ideologies in general a "will to truth" that quashes ambiguity and squeezes out diversity. The central focus of this paper is the complex and wary relationship between women's studies scholarship and criticism and grand feminist rhetorical strategies. Women's studies seeks to legitimize concern with women within established disciplines and as a field of inquiry in its own right. Feminist political rhetoric aims to provide the ideological glue for sustained political identity and action. This sets the stage for the unfolding of a complex scenario in which feminist political rhetoric and aims, on the one hand, and the scholarly claims and accomplishments of women's studies, on the other, give rise to another politics: politics among writers to determine which rhetorics, forms of discourse, and narratives will take precedence over the long haul.

Jean Bethke Elshtain

"Any cultural description," writes James Clifford, "is an ensemble of ancedotes, narratives, interpretations, typical events and characters, allegories, partial arguments—in short, a complex rhetorical performance."[2] The critic who interjects herself into this complex performance—who becomes one rhetor among others—by that act confirms the importance of the narrative voice, of what is communicated and how.

I shall focus on feminist political rhetoric by taking the measure of two strongly teleological accounts that invite closure. The narratives in question create taut frameworks—lock-step sexual scripts. If one works within these frameworks, one poses questions in ways that compel too easy and too universal conclusions. I share Iris Marion Young's conviction that relentless repetition of a short menu of metaphors stifles energetic and diverse discourse. Locutions that may at first enable us to see the world in new and startling ways (for example, "the personal is political"), as "they become worn, too familiar to be visible," go on to "assume a constraining power."[3]

Feminist political rhetoricians have problematized received categories and understandings. This essay aims at a similar defamiliarization with reference to their own, by now familiar, constructions. The deconstructive portions of the essay set the stage for my defense of a more open narrative form. This latter alternative acknowledges uncertainties and ambiguities. I will, in short, be pointing to two narratives that close out space for ongoing, lively scholarship and criticism in order to distinguish these from an open-textured discursive universe that enables women's studies scholars to live with and within fructifying, desimplifying complexities. Confronted by the necessity of embracing vast quantities of work in a single short essay, I shall take up one general theme—the question of *difference*—zeroing in on the way difference is treated in grand political rhetorics and my preferred heterodox alternative. The problem of difference has long bedeviled feminism and currently provides women's studies with an inexhaustible terrain for research and analysis. I shall sketch the alternatives briefly as ideal types before going on to take up each approach in depth, showing as I do overlap and complexity within types.

First, there is the narrative of *sex neutrality*. This form of feminist political rhetoric begins with the presumption that real or presumed sex differences are imposed upon generic human material from birth. Neonates are ungendered, and the social imposition of gender literally engenders maleness, femaleness, and what counts as masculinity and femininity in any and all cultures. The contemporary political vision of sex equality that flows from the presumption of sex neutrality is one in which equality is, or requires, some form of homogeneity, with men and women becoming interchangeable social actors playing out identical *roles*. In other words, the fact that one is a biological male or biological female can and should cease to be a central and defining feature of personal or social identity and need no longer form the basis for either individual narrative or collective political and social history.

Second, there is the narrative of *sex polarity*. This narrative starts with the presumption that the sexes are radically divided and that they must and should remain so. If this separatism is given an ontological base, the sexes are construed as "separate species"; the world is viewed in potently dualist terms; and politically "separatist" strategies follow. A softer version of the sex polarity argument subsumes bi-polarity into a series of strong epistemological claims.

Third, there is *sex complementarity*. This narrative is less prominently featured in feminist political rhetoric but more visible in women's studies scholarship, particularly feminist literary criticism and cultural anthropology. The starting presumption is that gender differences and embodiment matter—though how much and to what ends is culturally diverse and philosophically contestable. In addition, relations between the sexes present a complex mosaic, tell a story of contextualized complementarities. "Complementarity" is perhaps not the most felicitous term to characterize this more fluid narrative possibility—a position that flourishes, remember, only to the extent that the sex neutrality and polarity postures are exposed and critiqued in their uncompromising form. The term may conjure up, at least initially, images of happy male and female peas in some harmonious cultural pod. It may suggest an unwarranted consensus, and this is not what I have in mind. Complementarities can be antagonistic and conflicted and do not preclude dominance by one sex over the other. On the other hand, complementarity neither presumes nor requires, as the other positions seem to do, a terribly abstract vision of male and female social actors that ignores the body altogether, on the one hand, or constrains women within pregiven ontological forms having a biological base, on the other.[4]

Both the sex neutrality and the sex polarity positions push strongly toward, or are derived from, the foundational presumption of an "original position."[5] Each privileges Archimedean points from which the analyst may survey culture and history, past and present. Each gives "gender" *preeminent* force on all levels of social reality, from individual identity up to and including the structures of modern nation-states, frequently forgetting that human beings are not reducible to gendered categories. The sex complementarity alternative promises and achieves greater complexity by deflating the teleological and rhetorical certainties that follow from such presumptions. It offers, instead, a discourse within which theory can paint its gray in gray, creating a backdrop for unexpected splotches of color and unanticipated ruptures of form. Having (perhaps prematurely) indicated where I wind up, I propose in what follows to unpack how I got there.

Sex Neutrality: The Androgynous Claim

The sex neutrality story, in its prototypical form, begins thus: In the beginning man made oppression. Oppression requires an object, a subject to subjugate, and she was there. The narrative requires a pregiven female "self" that is then denied self-status by pregiven males driven by a collective *intention* to tyrannize. Thus women became the first oppressed class. All subsequent oppression—that of class, race, the "third world"—is modeled on this original fall. But woman's oppression alone is pan-cultural and universal, coterminous with history itself.[6] Women are variously constituted through this discourse as a "sex-class," a "sex-caste," or a permanent "fourth world" that antedates "third world" oppression. "We find it self-evident," begins one early tract, "that women are a colonized group who have never—*anywhere*—been allowed self-determination."[7]

The male sex-class imposes a damaging and defective *role* on women. Although male motivation for women's oppression is variously construed, the male was able to defeat women handily because women's "unfortunate sexual anatomy" (a Sartrianism repeated by Simone de Beauvoir) set them up as the "victim of the species," relegated to *nature*, which the men "transcended," thus beginning the story of *culture*. Culture is and has always been *patriarchal*. Culture, therefore, is the grand target of reproof and ultimate regeneration in this narrative.

The story continues: women to this day are prisoners of gender, caught in the snare of a systemic *sex-gender system*. This system dictates social roles, purposes, and norms. It inhibits, punishes, and devalues women, while enabling, rewarding, and valorizing men. Generic human, the "biological raw material," goes in, and gendered "social products" come out.[8] This system is operative in all societies, for "all sex-gender systems have been male dominated," and hence driven to assign social gender at birth "on the basis of genitalia."[9] Women are consigned to the sphere of *reproduction*, or unfree nature; men are assigned to the world of *production*, or are free to seize their freedom. The dominant male is constituted variously as a true agent, a layer down of the Law (of the Father), and a transcendent being-for-himself who occupies the productive sphere of history making, the superordinate arena of social existence.

Now, this is a powerful story indeed. It features an archetypal account of origins as an initial point of departure and a constant point of reference; it sets up a readily identifiable political target—culture itself—as a focus for attack; it affords a broad historicizing sweep that gathers all differences of culture, past and present, into a single bin; it claims to account for the "rock bottom" to which all societies conform; it revolves around potent dualisms, including nature/culture, oppressor/oppressed, free/bound, powerful/powerless, reason/emotion, that serve doubly as universal categories for analysis and as political rhetoric. Whether in this paradigmatic form or in softer versions, the narrative inspires political and discursive challenges to received social arrangements by problematizing all aspects of human existence around questions of male and female relations and by reopening in new ways some old debates: nature versus nurture, cultural determinism versus free will, and so on. Several acknowledged classics of modern feminism—from J. S. Mill's nineteenth-century essay *The Subjection of Women* to Simone de Beauvoir's seminal *The Second Sex*—belong within this genre.

But the explanations that flow from, and reinforce, the deep structure of the narrative grant to the feminist rhetor a too smooth sailing from starting premise to inexorable conclusion. A supple narrative clears a space for the introduction of subplots, new characters, story revisions, perhaps even rewrites. A narrative of closure *begins* from a culmination couched in the form of a query. The point of the narration structured by the query can only be to reaffirm the conclusion imbedded in the query in the first place. Thus: How, or why, did the universal story of women's oppression begin? What holds this oppression in place in all cultures? What can be done to undo it? The truth of women's universal subordination is self-evident, and it is the *truth* of that truth which requires a feminist original position, offers the promise of an Archimedean point, and, in practice, tends to affirm a picture of human life that yields devaluations of women in history and in "traditional" (non-Western, peasant) cultures in the present.

Some important questions do not get asked, for they cannot be posed *inside* the larger picture of the human condition to which sex neutrality commits its interlocutors. These include: why ask why in a certain way? That is, what does one search for when one searches for origins, embracing a discourse that promises the answer or the "key" to the riddle? How and why are we justified in claiming that we understand a past age and that this past can be conveyed in and through the

rhetorical usage of a later time—our own? How and why are we justified in overriding the self-understandings of prior epochs, and other
cultures or individuals and groups within our own culture, if these self-
understandings do not mesh with our rhetorical requirements? By
now, hundreds of books, essays, and tracts are available that subscribe,
implicitly if not self-consciously, to the teleological narrative of sex neutrality in one or another of its variants. The variations draw on important features of the discourse in its ideal typical form. For example: an
analyst may choose not to commit herself to the radical feminist analysis that the first oppression was man over woman in a direct, unmediated sense but then go on to embrace other central tenets of the sex
neutrality myth. I shall sketch the way various narratives unfold by
drawing on several of the strongest and most influential texts only.

If the genre in its modern form has an ur-narrative, it is Beauvoir's
The Second Sex.[10] Her argument begins from a Sartrian ontology that
cleaves the world into twains: nature/culture, in-itself/for-itself, deter-
mined/free, bad faith/good faith. Civilization is a male project, and
men are its essential actors; women (though free in the noumenal
sense) lie outside civilization, in nature, stuck in the Sartrian practico-
inert. By now we all know this story. Beauvoir and the many who follow her lead begin with a universalistic set of premises that add up to
an overdetermined yet simple model of oppression. These premises offer an unambiguous linkage between dualistic pairs: nature is to
culture as woman is to man as oppressed is to oppressor, the latter
being powerful by definition, the former powerless. Further, commitment to the narrative invites the conviction that all societies can be
modeled along dualistic lines, with women everywhere devalued,
men everywhere in ascendance.[11]

For example: inserting her anthropological arguments explicitly inside Beauvoir's narrative, Sherry B. Ortner begins her seminal piece,
"Is Female to Male as Nature Is to Culture?" with a conclusion: cultural
differences are reducible in the first and last instance to the "universal
fact" of women's subordination.[12] More troubled by how to explain
cultural diversity than Beauvoir, but committed at the outset to the thesis of universal female oppression, Ortner adopts a stratigraphic metaphor. All societies have layers, and once the analyst reaches the
bottom, or basic layer, she excavates the foundation of reality. The presumption is that Culture (and cultures) have a rock-bottom level from
which all else emerges. This first or primary level is "the universal devaluation of women." With women's devaluation given, all that remains is to puzzle further over how this came about and what can be
done to undo it. All the other features of a society—its economic ar-

rangements, its language, its history, its political and social institutions—are reduced to "local variables" of the culture. If one adopts such a presumption as the basis of one's research, one's scholarly mission will be to seek out evidence of that primary level, affirming thereby the deep structure of one's meta-narrative and reinforcing the political strategies it secretes.

Hardening of the categories is unavoidable. For example: Juliet Mitchell, in her bold *Psychoanalysis and Feminism,* declared the Law of the Father (patriarchy) to be "culture itself," with women universally subject to, and subjugated by, this law even into the interstices of "the Unconscious." Mitchell not only presumes that she can advance lawlike claims about *every* culture without describing in detail *any* culture; she is compelled by the force of her narrative to *interpret* all points of contact between women and men, no matter what they may appear to be and no matter how the subjects themselves may understand these matters, as instances of the working out of "the universal culture" of female subordination.[13] Within the rationalism to which the sex neutrality narrative commits its advocates, women will be "free" only when "nature" is *aufgehoben*—both her own "nature" (the species victimization of which de Beauvoir writes) and Nature, those features of human existence, those aspects of the natural surround, not yet brought under rational will or shaped to its specifications. This is the direction in which analysts who are daughters of Beauvoir must move; she closes off other paths. The key—the narrative promises a key—is to transcend the bodily, the unfree, the unthought, the lower (and female) level. Women, too, Beauvoir insists, can enter the world of transcendence—they can remake themselves through an act of will, the possibility for controlling nature being at hand.

In addition to the versions of the sex neutrality tale indebted to de Beauvoir or to the structuralist forms noted above, there is a variant of the narrative that shares its teleological impetus and general picture of human possibility. I refer to analyses that begin from behavioral psychology or from those modes of psychoanalysis most compatible with a conditioning model. The rhetorical picture of human life to which such analysts—currently exerting strong influence inside American academic feminism—commit themselves is one of relentless and total (or nearly so) conditioning under the sway of a sex-gender system. The implicit theory of human nature is familiar: *tabula rasa.* We are raw materials that become social products. That we come out "gendered" means that a system of controls and reinforcements can consistently produce conventional results. In a piece that helped to set the framework for narratives in this mode, Gayle Rubin writes that "a systematic social apparatus . . . takes up females as raw materials and fashions domesticated women as products."[14] We perforce require a new sex-gender system to create "androgynous" or "symmetrical" human beings.

Going in as generic human, no longer assigned more or less arbitrarily to a gender category, we will come out stamped with the imprint of sex neutrality and infused with a combination of "the positive capacities" of each gender "but without the destructive extremes" gendered identity now requires.[15] By resocializing away from sexed identities, we can erase "men" and "women," eliminate any biological need for sex to be associated with procreation at any time or for anyone, eradicate all sex-based role differentiation, and, at last, "transcend sexual gender."[16]

The urge to assimilate is powerfully clear in these formulations: we must rub all the rough edges off human material. The aim is a world in which the sexes can play infinitely interchangeable *roles*. Interestingly, the idea of a social role is of relatively recent vintage, entering sociological discourse in the 1930s. Nobody talked about "sex roles" before World War II. Yet the applicability of this concept is presumed by sex neutralists to be universal and transhistorical. The language of "role" serves this narrative well because of its externalized and instrumental features—deploying sex-role rhetoric means that the analyst can veer away from sharper and deeper questions of human identity.

What does the narrative promise, and what does it require? We are once again promised transcendence—from what is regarded as the prison of gendered identities—and in thus transcending we will also overthrow the systematic denial of our authentic selves by the oppression of the sex-gender system. Despite its deterministic model of the conditioned human, the deeper ontology of the narrative portrays the self as a robust unity, now fractured by faulty and exploitative social forms. Ultimately, patriarchal culture having been deconstructed, human beings will no longer be reared in ways that guarantee a psychology of sex oppression, and hence will no longer "need" to coerce or manipulate others. This is the way the story ends; indeed, this is how it *must* end, given the motor of teleological necessity that drives it. Finally, the sex neutrality narrative is too thin to sustain *over time* a rich rhetoric and to prompt complex inquiries. The profusion of recent and important works in social history, anthropology, epistemology, literary criticism, and myth outstrips the constraints of the perspective, an important development that I note in my discussion of sex complementarity below.

Sex Polarity: Manichean Moments

The original Manichees severed the world in dualistic fashion between a Kingdom of Light, from which sprang the soul, and a Kingdom of Darkness, the realm of the body. I use the term here as shorthand for an essentially dualistic feminist political rhetoric dominated by an ontology that, in the strong statement of this position, divides the sexes into something akin to separate species. What is the attraction and strength of this narrative? Through what rhetorical usages and narrative strategies does sex polarity discourse invite closure? The "manichean moment," with its suggested metaphysic of spirit versus matter and good versus evil, offers clues to the deep structure of the discourse. The critical interpreter is driven by the rhetoric of strong sex polarists to what they take to be the "root of the matter"—sexuality. Specifically, they are driven to male sexuality, to which authentic female sexuality offers a contrast model. The central concerns of narratives in this mode are sex and violence.

There are antecedents for today's politics and rhetoric of sex polarity in nineteenth- and early twentieth-century feminism. Though it is by no means the whole story, one important feature of this discourse was a vision of sexual hygiene, for male lust was seen as a destructive force requiring taming and domestication. Important feminist thinkers and publicists extolled the broader virtues of healthy and rational sexuality as an essential part of a wider platform of social planning and equilibrium. Male "indulgences, appetites, and vices," in the words of Elizabeth Cady Stanton, at the midpoint in a long and various career that saw her embracing a variety of not always harmonizable rhetorics, subverted, if unchecked and unrationalized, any hope for progress, harmony, and scientific reconstruction of social life.[17]

Suffragist political rhetoric of the sort that Aileen Kraditor has called "arguments from expediency" resounds with claims that women—at least white and native-born women—formed the "large proportion of patriotism, temperance, morality, religion" and as such would, once enfranchised, transform and purify politics itself.[18] Women are "more exalted than the men" because "their moral feelings and political instincts" are "not so much affected by selfishness, or business, or party consideration."[19] Rather than denying or deflecting the insistence on the part of male antisuffragists that women were too "pure" for political life, many leading feminists accepted the appellation and turned it to their own purposes. Thus sexuality entered political discourse and rhetoric within the literary and ideological constraints of the sex polarity narrative.[20]

Although discourses never precisely repeat themselves, there is a mythic, archetypal quality to the sex polarity narrative that helps to give it its compelling power. In common with the sex neutrality narrative, sex polarists tell a tale of the historic subjugation of the female, though she is located more as history's universal victim than as its prototypical oppressed class. This subjugation, in some versions, represents the male defeat of an age of matriarchy: all of "patriarchal history," therefore, is stained with the shame of its origins. The narrative presumes powerful universals. The key is *patriarchy*—a category deployed variously to describe and to explain history and every culture known to or within it.

The remorselessness of male victimization of the female—her enthrallment to his will and design—in turn enthralls the reader, tapping the deeply rooted Western narrative form of goodness enchained. Thus the rhetoric of radical feminist separatism on the matter of destructive versus positive forms of sexual expression has at its disposal the deep structure of the strong narrative. An unmediated conduit is presupposed between the patriarchal, repressive family and the heterosexual male's "normal" violence—up to and including militarism, wars, nuclear technology, despoliation of nature, advertising, pornography: all are construed as the predictable, inevitable outgrowths of unchained masculinism.[21] The politics of pornography and antiwar protest are two current concerns that afford evidence of the impossibly heavy burden placed on "female virtues" in challenging military masculinism, on the one hand, or in eradicating the breeding ground of masculinist culture in what is construed as one of its prototypical bastions, on the other. The latter choice of battlefields fills out the story, for pornography is taken to be the graphic public representation of private relations between men and women: it mirrors reality, and the mirror must be shattered. What Catharine Stimpson has called a "vulgar theory of mimesis" comes into play as feminist antipornographers argue for an identity between the "representational" and the "real."[22]

I cannot present in detail the massive literature of the current sexual manicheanism.[23] Essential for the purpose of this essay is the centrality of universal dichotomies of victim/victimizer, innocent/guilty, pure/tainted, in the sex polarity narrative, doubling as metaphor and metonymy and helping to set an agenda both for feminist politics and—certainly this is one aim—for women's studies. There is little room for ambiguity in this highly charged discourse. Those certain of hard and fast truths and the politically "correct" actions they inspire correctly see theories and rhetorics of complexity, contradiction, irony, and paradox as corrosive of totalized ideological commitment. They recognize that more open narrative possibilities are thorns in the sides of would-be actors, for they complicate the political as well as the discursive universe.

A rhetoric that requires as its original position a picture of woman as ur-victim is additionally troubling, particularly as a basis for women's studies scholarship. This is a question I have addressed before, but it is worth one more pass. In an important 1973 essay in the *Monist*, Abigail Rosenthal wrote of the "masks" through which discourse speaks and how such masks may enable the interlocutor to raise important questions but, finally, send her into a self-defeating rhetorical roundelay because her chosen "mask" signifies a narration of closure. One mask identified by Rosenthal is the "mask of purity," the presumption that the victim speaks in a pure voice.[24] In order to sustain the mask of purity, and feelings of victimization, rhetoric must bear a heavier and heavier burden of rage. In addition, the mask offers a license to evade the ways in which definitions of "victimization" are also means to coerce or control—but these cannot be acknowledged.[25]

Patricia Meyer Spacks, for example, in an essay on the contributions of feminist criticism, warns that "the discovery of victimization can have disastrous intellectual consequences. It produces . . . one note criticism. Readers newly aware of the injustices perpetrated on one sex find evidence of such injustice everywhere—and, sometimes, *only* evidence of this sort. They discover over and over, in language, structure, and theme, testimony to women's victimization." The upshot, Spacks concludes, is almost invariably a shrill, monotonous rhetoric caught in the self-confirming cycle of its own story. Similarly, Stimpson warns that genderizing too zealously, whether in language or in stories of human culture, casting all into binary oppositions of male and female forms, "is another reconstitution of an older pattern: a dualistic model of human activity that denies the dazzle, the dappledness of life."[26] It is to exemplary, even dazzling alternatives to such rigidified rhetoric and ideology that I next turn.

Sex Complementarity: Staying Alive

As I indicated above, I wish that there were a more apt tag than *sex complementarity* for this alternative narrative form, for I do not mean to paint a picture of harmony between the sexes. Complementarities can be, and often are, antagonistic and conflicted. The point is to put men and women into the same story, but in a supple way at odds with the static oppositions featured in closed narratives. The markers of a narration of closure, remember, are: (1) a search for some "original position" from which history has proceeded, with its beginning determining its forward movement; (2) a clearly identified, universally construed object of critique (for example: patriarchal culture) that gives the political agenda supported by the narrative its form and meaning; (3) an explicit or implied universal subject; (4) a dehistoricizing sweep that deflects from cultural particularities in a search for the "root" of all ways of life; (5) a defined end-point, whether in the overthrow of patriarchy or the creation of a benign sex-gender system that will resocialize human beings in some wholly new way; (6) finally, an Archimedean point that offers the feminist analyst claims of epistemological privilege. Having discussed the first five of these criteria above, I shall turn to the final point—the question of "speaker's privilege."

All scholars find the prospect of a privileged epistemic ground seductive. Those laboring in the vineyard of women's studies are no exception. The problem of "point of view" is central to debates within and between feminist thinkers. I shall take up this debate through the work of two anthropologists, both critics of claims to epistemological privilege inside their own discipline. (Of course, this example by no means exhausts the issue, which is being fought out in all disciplines.) Assessing the contention of a group of feminist anthropologists that, as members of a "universal category," they are "somehow . . . free from bias," Marilyn Strathern notes the self-confirming nature of their claims. The argument is that one validates one's anthropology by taking up, and speaking from, the "women's point of view," under the presumption that a woman has a "specific, non-replicable insight" into any given culture that is unavailable to a male researcher.

The self-consciously female (feminist) point of view, the argument goes, is not subject to the charges of bias that can be justly leveled against a male point of view. Moreover, an identity is said to exist between "the author and subject of study," a "naturally grounded" congruity. The result is a position of privilege that enables the feminist anthropologist to dismiss male knowledge claims or interpretations. It also lets her derail challenges from female anthropologists who disagree on the ground that "some" women who have experienced western patriarchy but fail to "see" through the double-consciousness that their femaleness/feminism affords them are instead double-blinded. Similarly, Judith Shapiro questions the claim that a double standard in anthropology is legitimate for assessing "male bias" on the one hand and a privileged female "double consciousness" on the other.[27]

Sex complementarity narratives offer no privileged standpoint, presuming instead that all points of view are partial and incomplete. Hermeneutical dilemmas cannot be evaded. Though knowledge and understanding may, in some interesting ways, be embodied—and this might help to explain why men and women, at least some of the time and to culturally specific ends and purposes, experience the world in different ways—no embodied being, male or female, has access to "the whole" or anything like "the totality." One is free, therefore, to explore differences without presuming the superiority of a gendered narrative that closes out alternate or contesting interpretations. Not being hobbled in advance by the conceptual chains of gender as prison, the critic is open to the intimations and possibilities of gender as prism.

Encumbered with culture and history, the analyst not only acknowledges but creates narrative space through her choice of metaphor and her understanding of ontology or being. Unlike the abstract, overdetermined subjects of sex neutralists and polarists, the subjects who populate her world of complex complementarities are engaged in social relations in diverse settings. Although gender may be determinative to some ends and purposes, it also matters whether one is American or Russian, an urban Catholic or a rural Baptist. But one cannot explore these other markers of identity, or describe them "thickly," if one begins by presuming that one's ethnic heritage, one's religion, one's community ties, the books one reads, the movies one goes to, the candidate one votes for, the dreams one has, are a more or less trivial icing on the real cake of gender. Notes Stimpson: "Because of the legitimate pressure of such groups as black feminists, feminist critics are now more apt to remember that every woman is more than a woman. She belongs, as well, to a class, a race, a nation, a family, a tribe, a time, a place."[28]

Because the sex complementarity narrative does not invite the analyst to claim either universality or exclusivity, she is free to draw upon particular features of the closed narratives whose overall structure and rhetoric she has rejected. For example, the sex neutrality position reminds her to be vigilant concerning the ways in which social life constructs sexuality, intimacy, education, leisure, and so on: things do not "just happen." And she is especially on the lookout for those pervasive images and expectations that push and pummel women this way or that to ends and in interests they have no hand in formulating. From the sex polarity narrative, she takes a concern with the violent face that intimacy may present and with the aggressive forms that the social construction of masculine identity makes more available to all men—

Jean Bethke Elshtain

though she acknowledges that some men are more immersed in that identity or susceptible to its claims than others. A social narrative, if it is to open up vistas rather than pull down the blinds, must afford supple, not mechanistic, ways of looking at power, authority, equality, freedom, the public, the private, family, meaning, intentionality, decency, and so on.

For example: we have learned from anthropologists that the world is untidy, yet narratives of sex neutrality and sex polarity require neatness, order, and clear lines of power and control. Peggy Reeves Sanday, author of *Male Dominance, Female Power*, offers a particularly interesting example of growth. Sanday began her work from the closed presumption that women were universally subordinate, men dominant. She expected that her analysis of over 150 ethnographies would offer proof along such lines. To her initial consternation, her evidence challenged her theory. Not only was it not the case that men were the universal, culture-creating, dominant sex; there were many societies in which women wielded or had wielded great authority and power. "This realization," she writes, "meant I had to switch my theoretical stance midstream and become at least semiliterate in symbolic anthropology."[29] Her salient point is that the abstractness of global approaches and presumptions blinds the observer to potent symbolic markers of male and female identity, power, and authority. Sanday, Karen Sacks, and others suggest that a pronounced inability on the part of Western anthropologists, including feminists, to "see" patterns of authority and power in traditional societies may derive from our persistent statist bias, from our tendency to conflate difference with inequality, and, more recently, from an ideological compulsion to read into cultures not-our-own rhetorical convictions about some universal male/female relation.[30] These writers deconstruct the constitutive criteria of the sex neutrality and polarity positions and open up space for consideration of more complex possibilities.

A second example—and the best way to take the measure of the sex complementarity narrative is through exemplary texts—is to be found in the fluid variety now evident in the field of social history. Social historians offer one rich account after another demonstrating transformations in family life that are incompatible with the presumption of a universal, patriarchal form and showing that preindustrial family life was laced through and through with complex sex complementarity in home and community. A fascinating addition to this growing list is Martine Segalen, *Love and Power in the Peasant Family*. Segalen notes in her introduction that to explore the texture of peasant life, one must first confront the reigning dogma on the rural family. In her words, the notion that the rural family "was 'patriarchal', that the authority of the husband over the wife was absolute, and the wife's subordination universally accepted, that old cliché is alive and well. Whether they are seen as the good old days, a model for resolving the crisis of contemporary society, or whether such an attitude is rejected—as in feminist pronouncements—there remains a persistent belief in the absolute authority of the husband over the wife, and, more generally, in the domination of the female group by the male group."[31] By asking why such rigidified attitudes persist, Segalen clears the space for exploring the meaning of the "wealth of symbol" in rural discourse (folklore, proverbs, architecture) and dealing with the "content of matrimonial life; relationships of labour and authority; the relationship between the couple, and between the couple and the village community."[32] The world that emerges from her pages is one of complementarities, which differ from region to region and decade to decade.[33]

The sex complementarity narrative acknowledges the forcefulness of this burgeoning scholarship and affords a loose-fitting discursive frame that helps to focus and interpret diverse material. This narrative presumes a world of dynamic sociality rather than static Hobbesianism or structural-functionalism. If we think of male and female relations exclusively along the lines of the "oppression" model—on individual or social levels—we promote a hollow picture of social life and possibility. No long-term relationship stays the same. What are the patterns of ebb and flow in the forms of complementarity and the shifting patterns of authority, control, and so on? Although the narrative has room for clashes and challenges—these, too, often have a dynamic complementarity—it does turn the perspectival lens toward complex reciprocities and shifting balances of power. The narrative has no predetermined end, no prewritten script, leaving room for social participants to engage in at least some improvisation, for individual and social narratives are not presumed to be precisely homologous.

Take, for example, Marina Warner's *Joan of Arc*. Her Joan is "an individual in history and real time" but simultaneously "the protagonist of a famous story in the timeless dimension of myth, and the way that story has come to be told tells yet another story, one about our concept of the heroic, the good and the pure."[34] In a work that is more a genealogy than a history, Warner constructs Joan's history and the competing histories of that history (Joan's "afterlife") in a provocative way because she is uninterested in playing out a predetermined line (e.g., Joan as the female victim of masculinist power, or Joan as a feminist precursor determined to break "gender roles"). Alert to the danger of prefabrication, Warner notes in her prologue that in writing female biography, "it is easy to revert unconsciously to known stereotypes."[35] Instead, Warner offers textual space for Joan and her accusers in Joan's time, and those who have used her legend subsequently, to speak to us.

We are reminded of the distance that separates her time from ours because Warner alerts us to transformations in understandings of "the self" by delineating the terms of Joan's self-identity, showing the ways in which she valorized or shook off the markers of both maleness and femaleness. Those markers did not constitute, as the sex polarists and neutralists would have it, some hard cleavage along gendered lines but were more densely located—in competing understandings of embodiment, of the equality of souls despite differences in physical form, in lists of the virtues. Warner writes: "In European languages, the use of the feminine to embody different aspects of goodness is . . . remarkable, and the phenomenon was seized on, in most cases probably unconsciously, by numerous women in Christian history."[36] But it was seized on in such a way that reversals were possible—for example, the association of a queen like Elizabeth with glorious "martial" virtues. The complexity of it all is the point, highlighting the many questions the sex complementarity narrative enables the interlocutor to ask, since all the answers have not been provided in advance by the trajectory of a closed story.[37]

Similarly, Natalie Zemon Davis, in an essay on men, women, and the problem of collective violence, argues that the opposition presumed by sex polarists between "life-givers" and "life-takers" was not so clear-cut if one looks carefully at "the historical record of the late Middle Ages and the early modern period."[38] She sketches the numerous competing and compelling notions of manhood available in early modern Europe, from warrior to absolute pacifist, and notes the "nuanced" reflections about male violence available in contrast to the "simplistic terms" that tended to dominate discourse on women and violence—though there were "multiple ideals for sexual behavior" for both sexes.[39] The distinguishing characteristic of Davis's discussion is its desimplifying quality, whereas the overriding feature of narrations of closure is the radically oversimplified story they tell.

As a final example, Kristin Luker's *Abortion and the Politics of Motherhood* offers desimplifying discourse and open-textured analysis as an ideal for women's studies.[40] Feminist positions on the abortion debate hardened long ago. Within the sex polarity and neutrality narratives, abortion becomes both a woman's absolute (or nearly so) right and a weapon in the sex war. The presumption is that men have used women's "reproductive capacity" to keep women in their place. It follows that abortion is necessary for liberation or freedom as defined in these accounts. The writer who raises questions about the moral dimensions of abortion in a complex way, or veers from the orthodox position, is located as a reactionary or worse.[41] But Luker's study, involving in-depth interviews with pro-choice and pro-life activists, shows that matters are not so simple. She lets both sides—primarily women—develop their world views and self-understandings. We come to appreciate—as we cannot if there is a simple contrast of right and wrong or pro and anti—the deeper philosophic presumptions that animate activists on both sides of this highly charged debate. We see dimensions of the abortion controversy that are glossed over or denied in feminist rhetoric, particularly its class features and the question of the cultural hegemony of the upper middle and knowledge classes to which most feminists belong. Luker exemplifies scholarship that is engaged, truly aroused by and involved in its subject, but not blinded by the determination to rank ideological conviction over scholarly curiosity or what Hannah Arendt called the life of the mind.

Feisty Kent, King Lear's combative man, proclaims to a fellow with whom he is engaged in a fracas, "I shall teach you differences." But lessons learned at the end of a Kent's clenched fist, or at the end of a narrative that in answering everything may spark nothing, are valuable largely in a negative sense. If we would learn and teach differences, we must have a discourse and a rhetoric, a language of description and interpretation, sinewy and playful enough to take us into the heart of that which we would understand. We require narrations that help us to tell the story of the embodied, the concrete, the spheres of practical reason, the cross-purposes, overlappings, confusions, paradoxes, inconsistencies, intentions, fears, and hopes of everyday life in diverse settings.[42] This means that we cannot hope to bring all of life under one overarching narration; we cannot pin reality down with a few premises and put it on display as part of a still life.

This means, as well, that we must be circumspect about importing narratives and rhetorics from one arena, in which they help to constitute and shape the reality of a particular activity in a delimited sphere, and make them do double-duty in a sphere animated by very different concerns, populated by a different cast of characters whose ends may diverge dramatically from those whose actions the narrative described originally. For example: the by now commonplace deployment of the rhetoric of "reproduction" as the chosen characterization for human procreation in feminist ideology distorts what it purports to describe by presuming that human birth from the body of a woman and the care of a vulnerable infant are essentially functional activities that mimic the instrumentalism of production. But this courts absurdity, albeit of the functionalist sort: it requires that we construe an activity that is embodied, emotional, particular, singular, and irreplaceable with an activity that is (in modern labor) mechanical, detached, shorn of deep meaning, generic, and infinitely replaceable. One could multiply the examples of distortion that result when econometric discourse, game theory, or some other abstract analytic device is brought into the kitchen, boudoir, shopping center, or playing field.

Even as we are alert, in Wittgenstein's wry phrase, to language "gone on holiday," we must also steer clear of language gone wild, of narratives that turn rhetoric loose upon past and present to rampage at will. The sex neutrality and sex polarity narratives begin with the presumption that those in possession of the story-line, who "know" the basic plot and characters, have unlimited access to past and present. They presume, and their discourse constitutes, an omniscient subject: a self or *the* Self, who looks uncannily like our-selves. In this narrative, the Self is wound up, given its marching orders, and sent stalking backward in time, forward into the future, or sideways into all other societies. When the Self reports back, it speaks in our categories, reaffirms our narrative, and legitimates our judgments. The de-simplifying discourse I have sketched through example offers no such handy entity, for we understand that the self itself is a contested concept, fabricated variously in and through history.

I began this essay by pointing to the complex connection between women's studies and feminist politics. I suggested that the claims and aims of the two were not identical and might, at times, be at odds. Others share the same concern, and I shall conclude on a note of ambiguity, with reflections from Judith Shapiro and Catharine Stimpson that take up the matter from two distinct, yet not antagonistic, points of view. Acknowledging the "energy" that feminist political concerns generated for women's studies, Shapiro now believes that the time has come for women's studies to loosen the tie between its endeavors and the political rhetoric and ideological claims of feminism. "The danger," she writes, "in too close an association between scholarship and social reformism is not only in the limits it places on intellectual inquiry, but also in the implication that our activities as social, moral, and political beings are dependent on what we are able to discover in our scientific research. Loosening the tie would have liberating consequences . . . for anthropological investigation and for feminism as a social movement."[43] Stimpson, however, does not want the wedge between feminism and feminist criticism driven so far. She writes that feminist critics "must hold fast to the feminist principles" underlying their criticism.

"Feminist criticism began, in part, as an anatomy of the pain that the pressures of history had imprinted on women, as a passion to erase that pain, and as a hope, often inadequately expressed, to ally that passion with other progressive political energies. At their shrewdest, feminist critics also know that such activities must not mask a fantastic desire to regain a human paradise. To long for perpetual bliss is to behave like a consumer whose Visa accounts are never rendered, whose masters never charge."[44] Between Shapiro's voice of caution and Stimpson's voice of passionate, yet dis-illusioned insistence, lies the narrative ground occupied by women's studies at its best.

NOTES

1. Elizabeth Langland and Walter Gove, eds., *A Feminist Perspective in the Academy: The Difference It Makes* (Chicago: University of Chicago Press, 1981), covers literature, criticism, theater and related arts, religious studies, American history, political science, economics, anthropology, psychology, and sociology.

2. James Clifford, "The Other Side of Paradise," *Times Literary Supplement,* May 13, 1983, p. 476.

3. Iris Marion Young, "Is There a Women's World? Some Reflections on the Struggle for Our Bodies," in "The Second Sex-Thirty Years Later: A Commemorative Conference on Feminist Theory," (New York: Institute for the Humanities, 1979), p. 44.

4. My argument does not turn on the claim that all feminist writers are aware of the underlying ontological presumptions and epistemological commitments that animate their discourse.

5. Neither the sex neutrality nor the sex polarity position corresponds in a tidy way to political divisions between radical, liberal, Marxist, and socialist feminisms; members of each of these political identifications may share some or all of these potent rhetorics.

6. Women's oppression is given as a starting point, but often not unpacked conceptually. A situation of oppression requires that one group of agents enslave, dominate, or pacify some other group. Lurking in the model of oppression is a strong presumption of malicious intent, for oppression is purposive, not simply the effluence of inchoate flailings or haphazard accidents.

7. Barbara Burris, "The Fourth World Manifesto," *Notes from the Third Year: Women's Liberation* (New York: n.p., 1971), p. 1.

8. The quoted material is drawn from Gayle Rubin, "The Traffic in Women: Notes on a 'Political Economy' of Sex," in Rayna R. Reiter, ed., *Toward an Anthropology of Women* (New York: Monthly Review Press, 1975), p. 165, and Nancy Chodorow, *The Reproduction of Mothering* (Berkeley: University of California Press, 1978), p. 9.

Jean Bethke Elshtain

9. Kathleen E. Grady, "Androgyny Reconsidered," in Juanita H. Williams, ed., *Psychology of Women: Selected Readings* (New York: W. W. Norton, 1979), p. 174.

10. Simone de Beauvoir, *The Second Sex*, trans. H. M. Parshley (New York: Bantam Books, 1978).

11. A lucid critique of "the promiscuous overuse of nature-culture rhetoric," tracing its emergence in modern form to the Enlightenment, where one first finds sustained arguments that women embody the antinomy to Reason, may be found in L. J. Jordanova's essay, "Natural Facts: A Historical Perspective on Science and Sexuality," in Carol P. MacCormack and Marilyn Strathern, eds., *Nature, Culture and Gender* (Cambridge: Cambridge University Press, 1980), pp. 42–69.

12. Ortner's essay helped to inaugurate a flood of discourse on the nature/culture theme. See especially Michelle Rosaldo and Louise Lamphere, eds., *Woman, Culture and Society* (Stanford, Calif.: Stanford University Press, 1974), pp. 67–87. Shulamith Firestone, *The Dialectic of Sex* (New York: Bantam Books, 1972), expresses her clear indebtedness to Beauvoir as she takes the argument to its *reductio ad absurdum*. I critique Firestone at length in *Public Man, Private Woman: Women in Social and Political Thought* (Princeton: Princeton University Press, 1981), pp. 204–28.

13. Juliet Mitchell, *Psychoanalysis and Feminism* (New York: Pantheon, 1971). This is a bold book because Mitchell offers a sustained defense of Freud, identified as a central villain by many feminist writers. Eleanor Burke Leacock, "The Changing Family and Lévi-Strauss, or Whatever Happened to Fathers?" *Social Research* 44 (1977): 235–59, offers a critique of the urge to universalize abstractly about cultures.

14. Gayle Rubin, "The Traffic in Women," p. 158.

15. Chodorow, *The Reproduction of Mothering*, p. 218.

16. See, for example, Ann Ferguson, "Androgyny as an Ideal for Human Development," in Mary Vetterling-Braggin, Frederick A. Elliston, and Jane English, eds., *Feminism and Philosophy* (Totowa, N.J.: Littlefield, Adam, 1977), pp. 62–63. The androgyny literature is enormous at this point, having been inaugurated in its current form by essays that date from the early 1970s.

17. Elizabeth Cady Stanton, "Speech to the American Equal Rights Association," *Revolution*, May 13, 1869. The liveliest critical treatment of the link between feminism, moral reform movements like temperance, and "scientific" social and biological engineering is William Leach, *True Love and Perfect Union: The Feminist Reform of Sex and Society* (New York: Basic Books, 1980).

18. Cited from Ida Husted Harper, ed., *History of Woman Suffrage*, Vol. 5 (New York: J. J. Little and Ives, 1922), p. 77. See also Aileen Kraditor, *The Ideas of the Woman Suffrage Movement, 1890–1920* (Garden City, N.Y.: Doubleday Anchor Books, 1971).

19. From Elizabeth Cady Stanton, Susan B. Anthony, and Matilda Joslyn Gage, eds., *History of Woman Suffrage*, Vol. 2 (Rochester: Charles Mann, 1891), p. 17.

20. For a critique of the narrative see Emma Goldman, *The Traffic in Women and Other Essays in Feminism* (New York: Times Change Press, 1970). Goldman acerbically condemned the suffragist as "essentially a purist . . . naturally bigoted and relentless in her effort to make others as good as she thinks they ought to be." Although Goldman's indictment of suffragist discourse in general is too harsh, she shows great insight in zeroing in on this feature.

21. For one of the liveliest recent examples of the genre by one of its most prolific and best-known spokeswomen, see Mary Daly, *Pure Lust* (Boston: Beacon Press, 1984).

22. Catharine Stimpson, "Feminism and Feminist Criticism," *Massachusetts Review* 24 (1983): 282. For a political discussion of this issue, see Jean Bethke Elshtain, "The New Porn Wars," *New Republic*, June 25, 1984, pp. 15–20.

23. For a more complete critical analysis, with bibliographical references, see my discussion in chapter 5 of *Public Man, Private Woman*, esp. pp. 204–28.

24. Abigail Rosenthal, "Feminism Without Contradictions, "*Monist* 51 (1973): 29.

25. See, for example, Helen Moglen's discussion of this theme in *Charlotte Brontë: The Self Conceived* (New York: W. W. Norton, 1976), and Anne Douglas's *The Feminization of American Culture* (New York: Avon, 1977). Douglas is critiqued by Mary Kelley, *Private Woman, Public Stage: Literary Domesticity in Nineteenth-Century America* (New York: Oxford University Press, 1984).

26. Spacks, "The Difference It Makes," in Langland and Gove, *A Feminist Perspective in the Academy*, pp. 7–24; quoted material is from Stimpson, "Feminism and Feminist Criticism," p. 287.

27. Marilyn Strathern, "Culture in a Netbag: The Manufacture of a Sub-discipline in Anthropology," *Man* 16 (1981): 665–88; and Judith Shapiro, "Anthropology and the Study of Gender," in Langland and Gove, *A Feminist Perspective in the Academy*, pp. 110–29.

28. Stimpson, "Feminism and Feminist Criticism," p. 276.

29. Peggy Reeves Sanday, *Male Dominance, Female Power* (Cambridge: Cambridge University Press, 1981), p. xvi.

30. Karen Sacks, "State Bias and Women's Status," *American Anthropologist* 78 (1976): 565–69.

31. Martine Segalen, *Love and Power in the Peasant Family*, trans. Sarah Matthews (Chicago: University of Chicago Press, 1983), pp. 1–2.

32. Ibid., p. 7.

33. Forerunners whose work in social history countered theses of universal female subordination include Mary Beard's classic *Woman as Force in History* (New York: Collier, 1972. [orig. 1948]), and Eileen Power's pioneering *Medieval Women* (New York: Collier Books, 1972). See also Power, "The Position of Women," in C. G. Crump and E. F. Jacob, *The Legacy of the Middle Ages* (Oxford: Clarendon Press, 1926), pp. 401–33.

34. Marina Warner, *Joan of Arc: The Image of Female Heroism* (New York: Vintage Books, 1982), p. 7.

35. Ibid., p. 9.

36. Ibid., p. 229.

37. Warner explicitly positions herself against "feminists who wish to abolish the grammatical differences" of gender classification in language, arguing that this would result in a "primitive and monolithic language with lesser flexibility, less accuracy and less capacity to express distinctions." Ibid., p. 228.

38. "Men, Women, and Violence: Some Reflections on Equality," *Smith Alumnae Quarterly,* April 1972, pp. 12–15.

39. Ibid., p. 15.

40. Kristin Luker, *Abortion and the Politics of Motherhood* (Berkeley: University of California Press, 1984).

41. See, for example, the ideological rigidifications in Judith Stacey, "The New Conservative Feminism," *Feminist Studies* 9 (1983): 560–83.

42. See, for example, Clifford Geertz, *The Interpretation of Cultures* (New York: Basic Books, 1973). Another example: Carlo Ginzburg, *The Cheese and the Worms: The Cosmos of a Sixteenth-Century Miller* (New York: Penguin Books, 1982).

43. Shapiro, "Anthropology and the Study of Gender," p. 126.

44. Stimpson, "Feminism and Feminist Criticism," pp. 287–88.

19 THE HUMAN SCIENCES AND

THE LIBERAL POLITY IN

RHETORICAL RELATIONSHIP

CHARLES W. ANDERSON

The rhetorics of science and politics have always been interdependent and mutually reinforcing. We have long appealed to conceptions of universal order in grounding political arguments. At a subtler level, the premises of political order may help to underwrite the "common sense" of the science of an age. A commercial civilization no doubt feels more at home with a dynamic representation of the universe than does a feudal one.

Furthermore, science and politics have long been used as metaphors for one another. Thus for many ancient civilizations, the order of nature was interpreted through political analogies. The gods of Homer, the Norsemen, and the Mesopotamian river civilizations met in parliaments or councils, and natural events were ascribed to political motives and interactions. Greek philosophy taught, conversely, that politics was properly regarded as a counterpart of natural order: for Plato, as a reflection of noncontingent forms; for Aristotle, as a phenomenon that could be understood, as could a biological organism, by inquiring into its essential principles of development and its final purposes. To the mind of the Middle Ages, the anchoring point in a world of contingency and flux was the will of God, known through faith and reason. A hierarchical view of natural order, derived from Aristotle, both legitimated and was reflected in the institutions of medieval society.

The impulse to seek foundations for political thought in the dominant scientific ethos is, of course, particularly apparent in the intellectual development of the West in the modern age. The preeminence of physics and mathematics as the indicated modes of scientific reason in the world of Descartes and Newton led to a politics and economics of

341

Charles W. Anderson

laws of force and motion, natural equilibria, checks and balances. Metaphors of politics were physical and mechanical, reflecting a clocklike universe. In the nineteenth century, the "discovery of time," the new achievements in archeology, geology, and biology, led to political theories that were organic, historicist, and evolutionary in temper.

Classic liberalism sought the authority of classic science. What seems most remarkable, then, about the pragmatic temper of our own time (a term I shall use loosely, but I think accurately, to describe certain preeminent trends both in the philosophy of science and in political thought) is the tendency of images of science and politics to be mutually reinforcing and for each to serve as a justification for the other. Thus John Dewey regarded the state as analogous to an ideal scientific society, engaged in an ongoing experimental search for coherent solutions to public problems. But in doing so, Dewey was drawing on Charles Sanders Peirce's notion of science as a "community of inquiry," an image itself taken from the vocabulary of politics and heavily weighted with political implications.[1] It does not seem at all surprising that contemporary philosophers of science, parties to a discourse itself broadly influenced by philosophic pragmatism, should speak so often of scientific ideologies and revolutions, of methodological anarchism, of gatekeepers and guardians, procedural norms and constitutive principles.

Recently, Thomas Spragens proposed an interpretation of liberal politics based on Stephen Toulmin's conception of a "rational enterprise" in science. Like liberal politics, the "rational pursuit of knowledge" requires collective institutions, norms of procedure, and submission to appropriate restraint. Yet science, like liberal politics, rests ultimately on the legitimacy of the free mind and requires institutions that permit and encourage criticism and dissent. If science proceeds through discussion aimed at the adaptation and refinement of concepts to solve scientific problems, politics might be understood analogously as the progressive refinement and adaptation of institutions and practices to solve public problems. Although there are obvious differences between science and politics—the pursuit of truth is not quite the same thing as the pursuit of public purpose, and science permits a certain suspension of judgment, which politics does not—Spragens contends that the idea of the reason-giving rational enterprise far better suits the spirit of liberal politics than the ideal of immutable rational principles, positive models of preference aggregation, or the "muddling through" of interest group brokerage.[2]

There is a pleasing symmetry about such an argument, and I believe it strikes chords that resonate distantly in the Western mind. If our ideals of science and politics support one another, if each can be interpreted in the light of the other, then perhaps our efforts are in fact coherent.

Herein, I want to explore some of the implications of this idea of discourse in science and politics. I will be particularly interested in the role that certain classic principles of liberal political thought might play in providing a conception of method for reasoned argument in both realms. I shall also want to examine how pragmatism's presumption of intellectual pluralism—the idea that theoretical and cognitive frameworks are multiple and potentially incompatible—bears upon such a conception of practical reason. Let me suggest briefly why I place particular emphasis on these themes.

Classic liberalism did provide a system of rules and principles for adjudicating among the diverse interests, undertakings, and conceptions of the good that arise within a larger ordered community. The logic of argument is highly structured and systematic in form. The presumption lies with the rights of individuals to free expression, association, and action, which are represented institutionally through the ideal of contractual voluntarism and related marketlike arrangements. The burden then falls to those who would adjudge the worth or merit of the "practices" that emerge spontaneously in the pluralist order to demonstrate a "public interest" in them, to give good reasons for their suppression or control or, alternatively, their protection or promotion through exceptional public measures. The warrants that might be offered in support of such contention include presumed flaws in the contractual nexus, various forms of market failure, considerations of the social efficiency of a practice, or various overriding commonwealth interests and concerns for the provision of legitimate public goods. Such argument, it must be stressed, either can address the probable harm to individual rights or general interests inherent in various projects and undertakings or can speak to a public interest in their potential promotion, diffusion, or universalization—as in the public support given to such initially pluralist projects as education, science, social insurance, trade unions, and the like.

Now I think this conception of the logic of reasoned argument applies as much to a pragmatic conception of discourse as it does to a more classic ideal of liberalism. The fundamental adjustment that must be made is to see the basic liberal standards of right and public interest as applying not so much to individual actions as to pluralist "collective endeavors," which I shall normally describe as "projects" or "practices" in politics and "programs" in the scientific realm.

Nonetheless, given pragmatism's sensitivity to multiple and conflicting frameworks of interpretation, I think the status of such rational principles is somewhat different in classical reason and in pragmatic discourse. In classical liberal reason, such standards are often presumed to provide axiomatic tests of the worth of a statement. Thus one vindicates an argument by appeal to principles of individual right or aggregate social utility. However, pragmatic liberalism is very much aware that the foundation principles of liberalism can be weighted and ordered in many different ways and that they are subject to varying interpretations. Thus argument in pragmatic discourse is not only *from* principles but *about* principles, concerned with the implications of their use in defining the character of problems and situations, and with the consequences of investing them with meanings that will be used as precedents for judging future situations. My view would be that in pragmatic discourse, such liberal standards as contractual voluntarism and social efficiency are less elements in a logic of justification, and more artifacts of social criticism, "ideals of natural order," again to borrow a phrase from Toulmin, which point to paradoxes and puzzles, anomalies and problems in our established ways of doing things, and to which the political community may respond adaptively and proximately, through the adjustment or reconstruction of established institutions and practices.

The remainder of this essay will be devoted to working out some of the implications of these propositions. Let me sketch the general line of argument briefly. I begin by suggesting that pragmatism, in science and politics, is less an effort to repudiate classical criteria of reason than to qualify them, to make them attainable, so that these enterprises do not delegitimate themselves by virtue of the very rigor of their standards. I go on to discuss some of the implications of rationalism and rational criticism in science and politics.

I next turn to the problem that I believe is peculiar to pragmatism— that of evaluating ongoing collective undertakings in the light of standards of individual right and public interest. Since pragmatism cannot prejudge such undertakings, but must evaluate them only after the experiment that they represent has matured, it is fated to have to come to terms with dominant institutions and orthodoxies. Since such "going concerns" have presumptive standing in pragmatic thought, both as successful adaptations and valued pluralist solidarities, yet are always subject to legitimate criticism in the light of ideal liberal criteria, they create an occasion for deliberate judgment that is unique to pragmatism.

I go on to outline a conception of discourse that I believe accounts for, if it does not fully resolve, this problem of "theory" and "practice" in pragmatic thought. I shall conclude with a brief discussion of the role of the human sciences in a political discourse organized along these lines.

The Pragmatic Qualification of Classic Rationalism in Its Own Best Interest

Both liberal politics and science avow the primacy of the skeptical intellect—the principle that no persons are obligated to a conception of truth or social good unless, in the full light of reason and evidence, they can, in effect, "do no other." For both liberalism and science, as for Protestant Christianity, this must be the ultimate expression of man's "essential freedom" and such a methodological imperative the only safe protection against tyranny over the human mind and conscience. In both politics and science, then, the burden should lie always with the proponent of a proposition about the nature of the case or the desirable policy. And the ultimate criterion of acceptability—that no rational doubt or disinterested criticism could be raised against the mooted contention—implies unanimity as the final test of common commitment, in the realm of either truth or public action. Descartes, Luther, Rousseau, and James Buchanan have at least this much in common.

It is the failure of science to produce a "mirror of nature," like that of liberal politics to produce unique principles of social order, that seems to exonerate the individual from a responsibility to reason in the classic sense and opens the door to relativism, subjectivism, and perhaps the program of the "new rhetoric." However, the failure of absolute criteria also sets up an argument among those who would preserve the historic enterprises of science and liberal politics. This argument becomes the project of pragmatic reason: a "crisis" for those who do not wish it well and a "problem" for those who would work within it. Much of the effort of contemporary philosophy of science and of political theory seeks to specify a conception of method that would be *attainable* within a pragmatic conception of the powers of human reason.

This broad argument on appropriate criteria and the rules of scientific and political discourse is complex, and one simplifies it at some peril. The following is merely meant to suggest some parallel "meta-principles" of discourse that have been proposed for science and politics:

Charles W. Anderson

1. Idealist conceptions of method

    In science, strict adherence to Cartesian principles of rational proof or irrefutable demonstration

    In politics, the continuing search for rationally compelling criteria that culminate in some unanimity principle, as in contemporary contractarian and consent theories

2. Experimentalist theories

    In science, the doctrine that the appropriate test of a theory is its capacity to illuminate a problem identified by the shared paradigm of a community of inquiry and to yield repeatable observations according to universal principles of experimental observation

    In politics, the broad pragmatic theme that social projects and policies are appraised according to their ability to resolve a problem identified by the public philosophy of a community and to yield results consistent with the principles of that community in a variety of contexts and situations

3. Economizing theories

    In science, the view that available theories are compared to find that which provides the most parsimonious and elegant solution to a problem of inquiry

    In politics, the utilitarian precept that human projects and policies should be compared to find that which yields the greatest net social utility

4. Contractarian or rhetorical conceptions of method

    In science, the effort to reveal the contingency of all rules of rational method and the view that warranted assertion rests on persuasive force within a shared framework of understanding

    In politics, the evocation of a regime of contractual markets, or of perfect pluralism, as an ideal of social order. The warrant for a social project or policy is the principle of affiliation and its acceptance by a number sufficient to make it socially tenable.

We cannot interpret either our science or our politics as a passage through historic epochs, each represented by one of these models of appropriate procedure, a persistent relativizing process in which step by step we have retreated from the rigidities of classic rationalism and concurred in the adoption of more proximate and attainable canons of inquiry. Rather, we experience argument, in each realm, as more of a composite and cumulative process in which older doctrines are not repudiated but retained as part of a repertoire of possibilities. Thus, in science, Cartesian and Humean standards are invoked alongside more recent formulations of the point and purpose of scientific inquiry. In politics, Lockean precepts are not displaced by a later utilitarianism and pragmatism, but all of these elements intermingle in law, policy, and public debate. Such eclecticism is no doubt the despair of sterner folk who would keep their doctrines in better order. However, it is this very eclecticism that makes pragmatism necessary and possible. A variety of tests of warranted assertion come into play, and it is necessary to adjudicate among them in the interest of collective action. The principles of classic reason represent a source of legitimate claims in both science and politics. More than enough practicing scientists affirm the ultimate truth-value of their guiding theories and the power of their methods to reveal, progressively, the actual order of nature. In politics, large segments of the population would avow the basic Lockean principles as revelations of natural reason and regard all deviations from them as expediential corruptions of liberal practice. At the very least, these are "social facts" with which pragmatic analysis must contend. But, in a stronger sense, the claims of classic reason have standing in the discourse of science as in that of politics. For the classic principles continue to define the problematic situations—the anomalies that lead to the reconsideration of theoretical frameworks within science and within institutions and practices in politics.

Rationalism

Rationalism, as an appeal to absolute criteria of proof, may have lost its grip on the Western mind. But there is another sense in which rationalism, as a constitutive principle of human institutions, remains a value to be reckoned with in pragmatic thought.

This sense of rationalism has similar connotations in science and politics. The object is to reduce the personal, idiosyncratic, whimsical, and arbitrary to orderly system. The scientist is to subsume personal observations under impersonal, universal laws. The policymaker is to justify action by subsuming decisions under general principles of rightful authority. The function of science is to render nature comprehensible, and, to that extent, predictable and routine. The function of politics is to design institutions that will render human performance knowable, orderly, repetitive, and, in that sense, predictable and routine. The justification for this search for order and system would seem to rest ultimately on a certain conception of human freedom. As Friedrich

Charles W. Anderson

Hayek expresses it, the purpose of law (and here we may, analogously, think of scientific law as well) is to create a stable, comprehensible framework within which people may design life plans with some assurance of their success.[3]

The virtue of rationally designed laws, airline networks, telephone systems, motel chains, and physical principles is that they will work as they are expected to when one calls on them. Rationality implies efficiency, to speak in economic terms. People assume instrumental control over their affairs; life becomes a matter of mastery rather than drift, to borrow from the legacy of pragmatic thought.

Such rational enterprises, or communities of good practice, represent reliable and disciplined ways of knowing and acting within the larger society. It is not only the pluralism of the market but the pluralism of the self-governing guild that gives such entities their valued status within the polity. They provide a background of relative stability—an infrastructure of settled meaning and dependable process—within the general atmosphere of transitoriness, flux, and change that characterizes the liberal polity. The human sciences, religious bodies, and professional associations are all rational enterprises in this sense. Furthermore, such entities are an important source of organic solidarity in contemporary societies. The brotherhoods of pilots and firefighters, geophysicists, doctors, and architects, cutting across the lines of formal organizational affiliation, are probably more important in giving the individual a sense of meaning and purpose, a conception of virtue and of place in the larger social order, than are the loyalties of region, ethnicity, or class.

Pragmatic thought has always assigned an important place to the rational enterprises that arise autonomously within the larger social order. Their disciplines of method and rules of good practice are the result of an evolutionary and cumulative process of trial and error, exploration and experimentation, and purposive internal self-criticism. Pragmatism has always identified rationality as much with the emergence of such collective undertakings as with the very different sense of rationality entailed by the logic of self-interested market choice.

Scientific and political argument arises normally out of challenges to established orthodoxy. Such criticism comes easily, for workaday experience is inevitably a rough approximation of ideals and a seasoned accommodation with exigency. However, if pragmatic discourse is to be truly deliberative, a conscientious weighing of alternatives, the case must always be made for the going concern. Established practice must find a systematic protagonist. And when the practitioners cannot make the rationality of their undertaking explicit (for, as Michael Oakeshott and Michael Polanyi have noted, practice as art and style is frequently inarticulate),[4] it may be the task of the detached analyst or scholar to interpret the implicit rationality of a human project. Thus Karl Popper, Stephen Toulmin, and Imre Lakatos may try to show the sense in which programs of inquiry are rational though they may not conform to the received ideals of science.[5] Similarly, the "functionalist" social analyst may try to interpret social practices as forms of rule-governed activity, to understand their meaning for those who participate in them, though the "good reasons for a practice" may not be readily apparent to those who are not parties to it, or to those who would seek to understand it only in terms of the categories of classic rationality.

In pragmatic argument it is always necessary to hear the case for the prevailing orthodoxy. However, this is but one element in the discourse of the human sciences as of the liberal polity, and not the whole of it. Pragmatism, presuming that all rational frameworks are contingent, must perennially keep the door open to contemplation of alternative images of reality and conceptions of good practice. It is always suspicious of what Veblen called the "trained incapacity" of the practitioner, the tendency to extend an approach to inquiry or practice beyond its proper sphere or to invoke the authority of the guild to discredit novel alternative conceptions of rational performance. Furthermore, pragmatism must be open to the appraisal of such pluralistic collective undertakings in the light of values that pertain to the integrity of the overriding activities of science and liberal politics itself. Thus a variety of parts must be played, a number of forms of argument must be represented, if pragmatic discourse is to be coherent, balanced, and undistorted.

Rational Criticism

Donald McCloskey, in his perceptive study of the rhetoric of economics, quotes approvingly Einstein's remark that "whoever undertakes to set himself up as a judge in the field of truth and knowledge is shipwrecked by the laughter of the Gods," and goes on to say that "the methodologist fancies himself the judge of the practitioner. His proper business, though, is an anarchistic one, resisting the rigidity and pretension of rules."[6]

It is interesting to examine the implications of this rhetorical conception of method. In the absence of standards, preference becomes the test of value. Science is seen as persuasive argument, and the success of a research program is tested by its ability to win adherents in the marketplace of ideas. The rule is that of *caveat emptor*. The community of science assumes no collective responsibility for its product.

However, I would think that the activity of criticism must have a place in any idea of reasoned discourse. In criticism, we evaluate the worth and merit of actions and projects and support such judgments by appealing to general principles of propriety and good practice that should apply to *any* undertaking in a given realm of activity. Such rational criticism is always public-regarding in character and at least implicitly legislative in intent.

To be sure, such reasoned criticism has little place in marketlike arrangements, and one can, it would seem, think of science as well as trade in goods and services in these terms. Such "discourse" as takes place in markets is largely a matter of purveyors making a case for their products. In the process, they may knock the competition, but such criticism is incidental, not essential. Consumers need give no reasons for their choices. They may say that they *like* Kant better than Hegel, much as they might prefer Pontiacs to Toyotas. Or they may say—as, significantly, they frequently do—that they find a certain theoretical scheme "interesting," "stimulating," or "provocative," appealing to what are, in essence, hedonistic norms.

It would seem that we are only obliged to give reasons for our judgments or appeal to relevant standards when we are recommending, or justifying, an authoritative choice made on behalf of a community. In this sense reasoned discourse is essentially political in form, for the essence of politics is deliberation on common commitments concerning the promotion or control of the undertakings and activities, the projects and programs, that arise within a community.

Criticism has always been assumed to be essential to science as it is to politics. The purpose of scientific criticism may be the progressive correction and development of research programs, but it is also a form of quality control. As the social critic asks whether a social practice is compatible with individual rights or the public interest, so the scientific critic asks whether a given approach to inquiry can be certified to produce reliable knowledge. And in doing this, the scientific critic must, of necessity, invoke some rules of appropriate method, just as the political critic must ground judgment in some principles of rightful order.

Critical argument is a necessary ingredient in political or scientific discourse. Yet the case of the critic is not necessarily definitive or compelling. The standards invoked by the critic may themselves be contentious and subject to deliberative appraisal. Or, as we have noted, the rational ideals of politics and science may be too demanding, tending to discredit established projects without suggesting possible alternatives. In pragmatic deliberation, the case from rational principles is to be weighed against that for the going concern, in order to find a satisfactory accommodation of these rival claims.

Pluralism and the Functions of Criticism

Criticism, of course, does not take place in a vacuum. We can only sensibly evaluate concrete opportunities for expression and action. It is the common conviction of science and liberal politics that one cannot anticipate all human initiatives, nor ought one to try to do so. Appraisal then, ideally, is reactive, a judgment passed on the worth of an act, idea, or enterprise that has already been realized in the life of a community.

In the first instance, science and politics are committed to the widest, most diverse freedom of expression and action compatible with minimal requirements of orderly endeavor. Thus science, ideally, must admit into its discourse the broadest range of conjecture and hypothesis and permit the development of rival schools of thought. Similarly, pluralist liberalism, at the outset, would endorse the emergence of a broad range of collective undertakings: forms of enterprise and association, systems of belief, action, and purposive solidarity. The common, and pragmatic, presumption of both scientific and liberal pluralist thought is that the merit of a project cannot fairly be judged until its implications are actually understood and experienced as a going concern. The thousand flowers must actually bloom—they cannot be nipped in the bud; and for one hundred schools to contend, personal vision must grow, through affiliation and systematization, until it reaches institutionalized form. The pragmatic imagination has little faith in a priori value judgments. But it does believe that such judgments can be made a posteriori, in the light of experience with a theoretical enterprise or social undertaking.

The greater problems of pragmatic deliberation and judgment arise, then, not so much in relation to individual thought and action as institutionalized thought and action. It is not so much Descartes as Cartesianism, not so much the private entrepreneur as the role of the modern business corporation, that creates dilemmas of evaluation and policy.

The issues are very much the same in science and politics. The first is power, potential or actual. The second is effective and efficient per-

Charles W. Anderson

formance, for, in a pluralist system, important social functions are, in effect, delegated to autonomous institutions within the larger community.

Power has both an external and an internal aspect. The first is generally characterized, in the language of liberal political economy, as the problem of market failure. The dominance of an organization, or set of organizations, in any realm of activity poses a presumptive problem of public concern, as does the ability of an enterprise to impose the costs of its activity on those who are not parties to it, or on the community at large.[7]

The internal aspect of power has to do with the rights of individuals within organizations. In pluralist society, autonomous organizations take on a political character: they assume functions of governance, structuring what are, in effect, systems of law and right, penalty and reward, that are imposed on their members. It is incumbent on the liberal polity to examine the authority structures that emerge within pluralist organization, to appraise their compatibility with overriding conceptions of individual right and due process of law.[8]

The related problem in science is that of orthodoxy. When a mode of inquiry or a methodological commitment becomes dominant in an academic discipline, a question arises in some respects parallel to that of market failure in liberal thought. The issue is, strictly speaking, a political one and concerns the ability of the guardians of established knowledge to impose their conception of the truth on members of the community of inquiry or on society at large.

Nonetheless, in dealing with institutionalized undertakings, as pragmatic liberalism and science must, and in evaluating them against a background faith in autonomous individual reason, as liberalism and science must, the questions of the warrants of orthodoxy inevitably arise. At some point in the discourse of both science and politics, the burden of proof subtly changes. At the outset, the presumption is strongly in favor of minimally constrained thought and action, expressed in incipient patterns of collective endeavor. But as individual initiative passes into organized enterprise, the burden would seem to fall more on the protagonists of the going concerns, who must demonstrate that their undertakings are in fact rightful within an order that requires, ideally, that every social institution reflect the revealed expression of individual will in the presence of alternatives.

This creates a delicate problem of social appraisal. What indeed can be said on behalf of a successful enterprise when it is charged that its very existence distorts individual choice and inhibits alternative modes of expression? There are those, like Michel Foucault, who see intimations of domination in every widespread cultural artifact. It would seem necessary to make careful distinctions between the rational enterprises—the scientific paradigms, technologies, and institutions—that become stable parts of the social fabric primarily because they work well and those that represent some conspiracy to exclude competition. It is also necessary to recognize a democratic society's right to universalize and enforce certain privileged establishments—of law, education, technology and the like—simply to create a common, predictable background for life. Yet so long as liberal society retains its base referent of the open market, or the pragmatic continuing experiment, the legitimacy of such privileged establishments can be no more than tentative. They are to be defended on the basis of practical considerations of manifest workability and sustained successful performance, for they are always vaguely suspect when measured against the regulative ideals of the liberal order.

The question of power concerns the legitimacy of the pluralist enterprises that arise in an open society or an open community of inquiry. The performance of these entities is also a proper subject of collective evaluation and deliberation. In the polity, this is the issue of rational efficiency. In science, it is that of reliable knowledge. We have already remarked on the close affinity between these criteria, the common responsibility for quality control, or predictable performance well fitted to the "ends in view," in both realms of action.

It is often said that the liberal state is purely procedural and impartial among human goods or ends, so long as there is a broad latitude for self-regarding market choice. Yet in the highly organized pluralist state, we can, and we do, make evaluative judgments about the complex "delivery systems" that have emerged, historically, to perform crucial social functions. Thus we collectively debate the "rationality" (in the broadest sense) of our transport and energy systems, our established practices for getting housing, medical care, education, personal security, and legal justice to people. We no longer presume that such matters are satisfactorily resolved by experts or professionals or the automatic mechanisms of the market. There is a collective interest in the economy, efficiency, "fittedness to purpose," and distributive equity of such arrangements. The critical appraisal of such systems has become an essential element in political discourse.

By the same token, the scientific communities have a collective interest in the projects and programs undertaken in their name. It will not suffice to say simply that a diversity of approaches to the study of economics, or physics, or mathematics should be encouraged. That, as I have suggested, is a necessary preliminary aspect of the endeavor, but it is not the whole of it. Once diverse approaches to inquiry have become established, it is necessary to make discriminating judgments among and between them. Somehow, collectively, a curriculum will be established and an agenda set. To say that the disciplines should simply practice mutual toleration, permitting practitioners to do whatever they want to do, seems, to the wary outsider, little more than the self-protective and self-satisfied corruption of the guild. The members of a scientific community would seem to have a collective responsibility for the quality of their product. It is the counterpart of their right of autonomy, and it implies the application of general and clear criteria of scholarly excellence and reliable knowledge. That in turn presumes an ongoing deliberation on the nature of the appropriate criteria.

The difficulty with the pragmatic, pluralistic approach, in either science or politics, is that once projects have developed far enough for us to assess their consequences, they may be very difficult to reverse. Established enterprises have momentum and support, and people have come to rely on them. In some sense, they work in practice. The task of the critic, who would point out anomaly and paradox, the failures of such practices to meet formal norms of rationality, is always difficult. Although the audience may concur that the critic is "right in principle," they may hesitate to act on the critic's judgment, given the patent workability of the going concern. Institutions must fail in fairly remarkable ways for such criticisms to be heeded and acted upon.

Of course, rational criticism, in either science or politics, can take a variety of forms. It can be either revolutionary or reformist in temper. The legacy of liberalism and science celebrates those heroic moments in which the "clear light of reason" discredited powerful orthodoxies. However, there is a gentler, Aristotelian form of criticism, in which established practice is accepted as having inherent value, but is subject to reconsideration in the light of critical analysis and reflection. That form of criticism seems more congenial to the pragmatic temper, and it may be the only way that pragmatism can deal with its inherent dilemma.

Discourse

Today one hears much of "discourse" as a central ideal of inquiry in science, politics, and philosophy. Yet the idea of discourse has a variety of connotations and is used by contemporary writers to evoke very different images of desirable patterns of communication. At the very least, I imagine, it could be said that discourse is to be opposed, on the one hand, to collective judgments reached merely through the aggregation of preference, without deliberation or discussion—the method taught by utilitarian economics—and, on the other, to "demonstration," in which the worth of statements is tested by explicit criteria and rules of method. To me, "discourse" connotes an orderly, structured, and extended exchange of ideas, in which both assertions and prospective tests of the worth of assertion are deliberated. In this sense, the idea of discourse would be associated with a pluralist and pragmatist conception of truth and the common good. Appeal, ultimately, is to the community of inquirers, as Peirce and Dewey described it.

However, I think it is possible to say something more about the nature of discourse, about its content, structure, and method. Specifically, I think it is possible to identify certain forms of argument that are essential to deliberation in science or politics, certain roles that must be performed if the exercise is to succeed. If any of these elements is missing, the process of discourse would seem to be biased and incomplete. Discourse to me implies advocacy, explanation, criticism, and, in the end, deliberative judgment, and each of these I associate with a distinctive position, or point of view, in the processes of science and politics.

The task of advocacy is that of the proponent of a new undertaking, a project or policy in the realm of human affairs, a conjecture or research program in science. The problem of advocacy is to give good reasons for the novel undertaking, to show that it is worthy of affiliation and support. I shall call this the position of the entrepreneur, one who, as Bertrand de Jouvenal puts it, "attempts to enlist the support of other wills" in a common endeavor.[9] The entrepreneur represents the pluralist element in thought, the possibility of alternative, more promising, conceptual schemes in science, of "better ways of doing things" in some area of social activity. A fundamental premise of pragmatism is that the door must always be open for entrepreneurs to make their case and promote their projects in the forums of science and politics, provided they meet requirements of contractual probity and orderly endeavor.

Explanation is the task of those I shall call the trustees of the going concern. Their rhetorical problem is to explicate the rationale of prevailing practice, defending the orthodox scientific vision or the existing institutional fabric of society, its systems and practices, organic solidarities, customs, habits, and traditions. Whereas the spirit of the entrepreneur is like that of the Sorcerer's Apprentice, constantly creative and iconoclastic, seeking novelty and transformation, the deliberations of trusteeship run more to considerations of duty and obligation, prudence and responsibility, a mature understanding of valued continuities and traditions.

It is often assumed that it is the reformer who bears the burden of proof. Yet given liberalism's commitment to persistent skepticism and its celebration of those who contend with and overthrow entrenched orders, it is frequently those who would speak for established ways of doing things who suffer systematic disadvantage in argument. The "conventional wisdom" is often presented in such a way as to serve as a straw man for criticism. For reasons we have noted, the practitioner is often inarticulate about the rational justification of a craft. Thus the burden of trusteeship is often that of restating and reinterpreting the inherent logic of custom, putting "old wine in new bottles," showing the wisdom of precedent in meeting new situations, or pointing up the ways in which ancient truths can illuminate current perplexities.

The function of the critic is to judge projects and programs in the light of principles. To associate rational standards, and the rules of method, with the tasks of criticism may seem puzzling. Methodology is supposed to guide inquiry in science, as rational principles are supposed to provide the basis for decision in politics.

My own view is that such rational rules of procedure are not problem-solving but problem-creating in character. The rules of methodology do not enable us to "prove" a scientific contention. Cost-benefit analysis does not culminate, logically, in a "solution" to a public problem, but rather in a statement of trade-offs among values. However, the ideals of rational procedure constitute a legitimate source of claims against practice, a standing case in scientific as in political argument, and the agenda for public policy, like the agenda of scientific inquiry, arises always out of such critical assertion. Such claims have privileged standing in the discourse of science and politics. They cannot be ignored or dismissed as "beside the point." However, such claims are not definitive or compelling. Rather, they require a deliberate weighing of the values inherent in practice against the foundational ideals of the liberal and scientific enterprises.

The reason for this is that rational ideals are always radical in character. Thus all institutions and practices in liberal society are to be regarded as forms of voluntary association, resting on willful consent and contract. To meet this test, it must be shown that the parties to a project or practice are equals in all significant respects. Any disparities of power or opportunity, of information or access, raise questions about the legitimacy of the undertaking. Yet in the real world, all markets fail in some respect, and intimations of dominance are always present.

Similarly, the simple test of economic efficiency can be a ground of social criticism that calls into question the initiatives of entrepreneurs and the prudential counsel of trustees. In the utilitarian formulation, the measure of all practices is their contribution to aggregate social utility. Thus if a way can be shown to perform a function more economically, prevailing practice is properly regarded as socially wasteful. It is a question of opportunity costs. To deploy resources for one purpose is to forego their use for others. The economic analyst stands in constant judgment of the prevailing order. Yet the relentless quest for social efficiency is hardly a perfect counsel of statecraft. The issue for deliberate judgment is when to apply this norm to the reconstruction of practice and when to relax it in recognition of other important attributes of existing institutions.

In the end, the object of deliberative discourse is to decide "what to do" in the light of the diverse considerations developed in argument. The object of such pragmatic analysis is to find possibilities for common endeavor that somehow reconcile diverse contentions. The mode of analysis may be meliorative, incrementalist, experimental, or synthetic in character. However, the pragmatic analyst is not simply a neutral adjudicator but very much a party to the argument. From the diverse materials of discourse, some will be selected for emphasis, others relegated to "background." Such deliberative judgment is, as Polanyi asserts, a matter of personal knowledge, or as Lakatos would have it, a question of decision. In the end, it is an act of commitment. But usually it is a negotiation between theory and practice. For it is in the nature of rational criticism that no entrepreneurial project and no existing institutions can quite be certified as fulfilling the inherent standards of the larger enterprise. The problematic situation arises out of recognition that the available repertoire of techniques for "doing things" does not quite measure up in the light of widely held norms and values. The task of pragmatic deliberation, then, is to adjust practice to value, or value to practice.

There are, I think, four distinct kinds of argument that must be represented, four kinds of roles that must be performed, if practical deliberation is to be considered and complete. Each is partial and imperfect when considered in isolation from the rest, though each is believed, in some systems of thought, to be the distinctive and unique path of right reason and method.

Thus, the entrepreneur focuses on projects and the means to their attainment. For the methodological anarchist, this is sufficient. All that is required is initiative and the search for support by other wills in a free

Charles W. Anderson

market of ideas or actions. Yet the very idea of discourse, in liberalism or science, presupposes collective reflection on the merits of the universe of alternatives available to the community.

The trustee focuses on practices, on the inherent legitimacy and rationale of established institutions. For the conservative, this is sufficient, for the only possible foundation of judgment is custom, tradition, and usage. Yet liberalism and science both presume that it is possible to reflect critically on the adequacy and legitimacy of practice.

The critic focuses on principles and presumes that all judgment must culminate in an appeal to standards that are general, clear, and can be endorsed consistently. However, such categoric judgments generally fail to provide a compelling conception of remedy, or a clear and unique rule of choice among available initiatives and opportunities.

The pragmatist focuses on problems, which are, in Dewey's definition, precisely those occasions of judgment that arise out of conflicting evaluations of existing patterns of activity. Yet for the meliorative discourse characteristic of pragmatism to emerge, there must be something to meliorate. And that emerges precisely from the claims and contentions of those who play other roles of advocacy in the deliberative process. Thus none of the modes of reason is sufficient in itself. All are requisite to the process of reasoned discourse.

I do not mean to imply that these four positions are mutually exclusive. Obviously, the considerations representative of each intertwine, either in our deliberations with ourselves or in discussion with others. However, I do think that at the outset of inquiry, one of these will represent a predominant cognitive focus for the individual. We will start from a conception of a project, a sense of obligation to an ongoing institution or activity, from certain ideals or principles, or from a desire to play the role of mediator or pragmatic problem-solver. The function of discourse, then, is to broaden our sense of the considerations relevant to choice. And the idea of discourse opens the possibility that, in the end, we may be led to "change our minds." The trustee may "discover" that the institution he or she felt committed to defending was inherently inequitable, and become the champion of reform "on principle." The pragmatic mediator may become the enthusiast of some novel undertaking. In a closed system of inquiry, the solution to a problem is always inherent in the premises. In open systems of thought, it should always be possible to end up somewhere other than where one began. It is this possibility of "changing one's mind"—that mysterious capacity of individuals and groups to end up in a position they could not have anticipated before reflective consultation—that makes reasoned discourse a process quite different from rational method.

The Human Sciences and the Liberal Polity

Science and liberalism have always had a close—some might say a symbiotic—relationship. What, then, should be said of the role of the scientist in the liberal polity? This topic has been long and heatedly debated. Weber attempted to distinguish between the vocations of science and politics. The pragmatists, with their enthusiasm for "social therapy" and "social experimentation," made much of the relationship, but perhaps no more than the philosophic tradition of the Enlightenment or activist Marxism. Today the so-called policy sciences continue to debate the efficacy and propriety of "speaking truth to power." The place of the expert in a democracy has been the subject of many volumes.

My own view is that the human sciences do not play a differentiated role in the discourse of liberal politics but that the scientist can and has played each of the parts that seem essential to political deliberation and decision. They may be innovators and entrepreneurs, as in the work of the Progressive economists who helped contrive the basic programs of the American welfare state. They may be the interpreters of the implicit rationality of tradition. One thinks of the anthropologists who explored the rationality of the peasant as well as the organization theorists who explicated the nonclassic rationality of people in organizations.

It is conventional for the scholar to assume the role of social critic, measuring established institutions against fundamental ideals. In fact, many of the more notable social science "discoveries" of the twentieth century are precisely of this type: that the corporation may not act, and thus be justified, by the logic of the market; that the American voter does not decide on the basis of calculated self-interest; that group competition will not culminate in a harmonious equilibrium of interests. Departure from such hypothetical "ideals of nature" signals a significant problem for empirical inquiry but also a normative issue in the life of the polity.

Finally, the scientist may adopt the persona of the pragmatic analyst, taking the role of a surrogate policymaker, recommending contrivances that may lead us out of quandaries of theory and practice. The general support given by both conservative and liberal political econo-

Charles W. Anderson

mists to the idea of a negative income tax as a solution to the problem of welfare reform may represent an activity of this type.

It is the natural inclination and perhaps the peculiar social function of the scholar to "think otherwise" about matters. As Albert Hirschman has suggested, we already know so much about the social world that for a social science discovery to be significant for us, it must be counterintuitive and somewhat unexpected.[10] This suggests that the social scientist, in particular, serves the polity as *agent provocateur*.

However, when the role of "thinking otherwise" is taken seriously as part of political deliberation, it seems clear that the goal is not simply social criticism, as I have defined it, but the restoration of positive balance to the terms of discourse. At any time, on any subject, the roles we have specified as essential to reasoned consideration of an issue tend toward a kind of natural disequilibrium. Momentum flows with the spirit of novelty, innovation, and entrepreneurship; or defense of established and customary ways; or principled criticism of prevailing practices; or the practical resolution of immediate issues. Our rhetoric is always swept up in one or another of these enthusiasms. Such imbalance can mark an age or a transient consideration of a particular issue. In either event the specialized task of the autonomous scholar would seem to be to stand for the neglected but essential considerations that must be entertained if discourse is to be truly deliberative.

In effect, then, the scholar "unbalances" discourse in the interest of a larger, more reflective balance. Thus in an age of criticism, when all social norms and values are questioned and reduced to relativism, it may be the time to reexplore tradition, seeking, once more, the underlying meaning and coherence of a civilization. At a more immediate and practical level, when all are sure that an existing social policy is in urgent need of reform, the analyst who would "unsettle" the argument will explore the historic rationale for that policy—why it was thought a good idea in the first place—or the inherent rationale of prevailing practice. (One thinks of Jane Jacobs making the case for the spontaneous, organic order of the city against the planners' vision of the city-as-system.)

Conversely, when everything seems most settled, when society fails to question custom and routine, the inquiring mind seeks novelty and unexpected possibilities. This is the classic, Enlightenment view—the intellect set against unquestioned orthodoxy—but it is, in fact, only one of the possible forms of timely dissent. There is, indeed, a third possibility suggested by our notion of the modes of discourse. For when a people is unsettled, when everything is chaotic and up in the air, it may be the time to be merely practical. The scholar dissents from uncertainty by seeking proximate solutions, workable institutions. (The Progressive reformers perhaps played this role in an intellectual climate where many felt that democratic capitalism was either unchangeable or doomed.)

This is not a vision that will appeal to those who see the task of science and scholarship as putting an end to argument through the discovery of rationally unassailable principles or empirically validated truths about the nature and destiny of man. The object, as Richard Rorty suggests, may be simply that of keeping the conversation going.[11] Nonetheless, my main point has been that there may be more *method* to all of this than the more radical pragmatists suggest. My purpose, then, has been to play the role of prescriptive methodologist in an argument where that role is highly suspect and, in an exercise that folds back upon itself, to suggest the need for greater rigor and a greater concern for the legitimate claims of rationality in the rhetoric of rhetoric itself.

NOTES

1. John Dewey, *The Public and Its Problems,* 2d ed. (Chicago: Swallow Press, 1954 [orig. 1927]), esp. pp. 144–219. On Peirce, see esp. "Consequences of Four Incapacities" and "Grounds of Validity of the Laws of Logic," in Arthur Burks, Charles Hartshorne, and Paul Weiss, eds., *Collected Papers of Charles Sanders Peirce,* 2d ed., vol. 5 (Cambridge: Cambridge University Press, 1960), pp. 318–57.

2. Thomas A. Spragens, Jr., *The Irony of Liberal Reason* (Chicago: University of Chicago Press, 1981), pp. 357–95.

3. Friedrich A. Hayek, *The Constitution of Liberty* (Chicago: University of Chicago Press, 1960), pp. 156–59.

4. Michael Oakeshott, "Rationalism in Politics," in *Rationalism in Politics and Other Essays* (New York: Methuen, 1962), pp. 10–11; Michael Polanyi, *Personal Knowledge* (New York: Harper, 1964), pp. 49–65.

5. Karl Popper, *The Logic of Scientific Discovery* (New York: Harper, 1959); Stephen Toulmin, *Human Understanding I* (Princeton: Princeton University Press, 1972); Imre Lakatos, *The Methodology of Scientific Research Programmes* (New York: Cambridge University Press, 1978).

6. Donald N. McCloskey, "The Rhetoric of Economics," *Journal of Economic Literature* 21 (1983): 490.

7. On the idea of market failure generally, see Duncan MacRae, Jr., *The Social Function of Social Science* (New Haven: Yale University Press, 1976), pp. 162ff.

8. On the internal aspect of power generally, see Sanford Lakoff, *Private Government* (Glenview, Ill.: Scott, Foresman, 1973).

Charles W. Anderson

9. Bertrand de Jouvenal, *Sovereignty* (Chicago: University of Chicago Press, 1959), p. 17.

10. Albert O. Hirschman, "Morality and the Social Sciences," in *Essays in Trespassing: Economics to Politics and Beyond* (New York: Cambridge University Press, 1981), pp. 297–98.

11. Richard Rorty, *Philosophy and the Mirror of Nature* (Princeton: Princeton University Press, 1979), pp. 389–94.

20 THE RHETORIC OF

SOCIAL SCIENCE

THE POLITICAL RESPONSIBILITIES

OF THE SCHOLAR

MICHAEL J. SHAPIRO

The dominant approach to responsibility within the enterprise of social science operates with more or less the same understanding that animates issues of responsibility in everyday life. The prevailing assumption in both domains is that ethical or moral notions, prescriptions that give marching orders to persons in various roles, belong to a separate domain of discourse. The view is that there is a nonethical language whose function is to describe and explain situations and events. If, for some reason, someone operating within this view is asked to evaluate the "findings" of a social science research product for purposes of making policy recommendations, the request is taken as an invitation to use ethical language to evaluate products emerging from reasoning within a nonethical ("empirical") language.

Consider, for example, the title of an address given at a recent medical ethics conference: "Can Medical Ethics Keep Pace with Technology?" Embedded in this question is the assumption that ethical discourse is an autonomous domain of evaluation. Doubtless, the question presumes that medical practice increasingly involves the use of "high-technology equipment"—most notably, perhaps, artificial organs—and that because medical discourse is intrinsically ethically neutral (because it is "scientific"), even when its traditional human "objects" are increasingly the sites for creative intervention, it is necessary to upgrade the exogenous ethical discourse to cover "new issues"—for example, the invasion of the domains of other supposed "creators."

Michael J. Shapiro

If we reject this view of ethical discourse, we recognize that medical speech, like any form of practice, is shot through with value commitments and notions of responsibility. More specifically, medical discourse has played a role in *creating* what we understand as "the human body," not by virtue of the implantation of "artificial organs," but by the implantation of various codes that constitute much of our understanding of who or what "we" are. The body that modern medicine has helped to create is a body understood not as a "thing" to be scientifically described but as a site for the constitution of identities that facilitate the functioning of existing structures of power and authority. Just as the discourse of social work has participated in creating the "multiple-problem family" and the discourse of educational psychology has participated in creating "dimensions of intelligence"—both of which are identities related to authoritative processes of social regulation—so medicine has participated in the proliferation of subjects and objects related to processes of regulation.

For example, under the rubric of what he calls "the perverse implantation," Michel Foucault has shown how medicine helped to create a code that identifies various "sexual perversions." This "implantation" imagery conveys Foucault's theme of the relationship of power to sex as the enforcement of a garrulousness about sex that allows for the monitoring of conduct in a society increasingly interested in having conduct measured, predicted, and regulated, rather than a repression or silencing. "The implantation of perversions is an instrument-effect: it is through the isolation, intensification, and consolidation of peripheral sexualities that the relation of power to sex and pleasure branched out and multiplied, measured the body, and penetrated modes of conduct."[1]

Medicine has *always* constituted the complex, socially implicated phenomena it addresses because, like all practices, it operates within the understandings that govern the social formation of which it is a part. The question about ethics keeping pace with modern technology is thus epistemologically naive, for the level of "technology" is but one aspect of the social formation that helps to *create* our ethics, our notions of value and responsibility. Ethics cannot help but keep pace with technology when it is part of the same process of formation.

This naïveté, which afflicts both the epistemology of everyday life (and thus the self-understanding within which social inquiry is received) and the practice of inquiry itself, is tied to a disabling view of language. Within the domains of both everyday life and social inquiry, understandings relating what is to be done, or who ought to be the privileged agents for doing it, to what is presumed to be "the situation" are beguiled by the idea that there can be a neutral language of social inquiry and understanding, that language can function as a transparent medium linking our thoughts to the world of objects.

This is not the place to elaborate on all the intellectual developments that have impeached the philosophical foundations of what I have called the "disabling view of discourse." What are especially relevant for purposes of this discussion are the critiques of the "primacy of epistemology." These attacks on the position that knowledge consists in a relationship between things and cognizing subjects who apprehend them have called into question attempts to found certainty of understanding on "objective facts" or referents of statements (naturalism and empiricism) or on the universal attributes of the self (idealism).[2]

The impeachment of these foundational approaches to knowledge has set the stage for productive alternatives, new approaches to discourse that emphasize the way that various discursive practices constitute kinds of objects and kinds of selves. Within such a notion of language, one in which we regard the things and selves of which we speak as products of the codes governing speech and writing practices, our orientation to the value of statements must shift. Rather than treating statements as propositions to be regarded as "true" or "false," based on the fidelity of their representation, we can consider them on the basis of their allocation of enablements. Foucault has suggested a way to treat statements within this latter frame of analysis:

> To analyze a discursive formation is to weigh the "value" of statements, a value that is not defined by their truth, that is not gauged by a secret content but which characterizes their place, their capacity for circulation and exchange, their possibility of transformation, not only in the economy of discourse, but more generally in the administration of scarce resources.[3]

Foucault underscores the manifestly political implications of this frame of analysis for statements when he goes on to characterize discourse as an "asset" that both "poses the question of power" and becomes an object in a "political struggle."[4] These latter notions of power and struggle inform Foucault's more recent investigations, to which I refer below.

"Discourse," which is any systematic or disciplined way of constituting subjects, objects, and relationships within a linguistic practice, is an increasingly recognizable conception in Anglo-American social science circles as Continental perspectives find their way into the talk of splinter groups of the various social science disciplines. But more important than its increasing legitimacy are its implications for analysis, for, among other things, it provides grounds for rethinking

Michael J. Shapiro

the role of the social scientist. This is because a concern with discourse implies a view of language that, in breaking with the orthodoxy conferred by empiricist philosophy of social science, legitimates the knowledge-relevance of disciplines like literary criticism, which focus on productive mechanisms—the style of utterances and statements. Moreover, once the social scientist becomes aware that analysis is a form of discursive deployment—in other words, that the expressions involved in the analysis are a form of writing—*how* to write becomes a problem (for the social science genre is seen as entangled with the literary genre). This "blurring of genres," as Clifford Geertz has called it, has a salutary effect inasmuch as it alerts us to the way that standard disciplinary practices have made us obtuse to the political content sequestered in the subjects, objects, and relationships we have inherited within both our ordinary and our disciplinary ways of speaking and writing.[5]

If we are to remain alert to the valuation enacted in the supposedly neutral or norm-free discourses of social science analysis, we need to look at these discourses within the framework of a genre that is conscious of the relationship between linguistic mechanisms—for example, the grammatical, rhetorical, and narrative structures of a discourse—and "reality." Various contemporary versions of literary theory have helped to create such a genre, which has, as I shall show below with a specific example, both epistemic and political significance. This is because literature, as understood by various modern literary critics and philosophers of literature, involves (in Regine Robin's words) "a critical questioning outside the establishment." To effect this questioning, it is oriented so as to "produce a confusion of genres, or writings, and of disciplines, to penetrate surreptitiously into the utmost gaps and interstices of the dominant discourses."[6] If this is the case, the introduction of such a literary consciousness can serve both to show the way that writing in other genres produces ideological/political meanings and to encourage social scientists to undertake forms of analysis that avoid the uncritical valorization of the realities created by dominant, "official" modes of discourse.

Writers of what is often called the "poststructuralist" persuasion have been especially prominent in emphasizing this failing of unreflective genres of writing. Christian Metz's remark about the writings of certain unreflective film critics is to the point here: "Discourse about the cinema is too often part of the institution, whereas it should be studying it and believes or pretends that it is doing so. It is . . . its third machine after the one that manufactures the films, and the one that consumes them, the one that vaunts them, that valorizes the product. . . . writings on films become another form of cinematic advertising and at the same time a linguistic appendage of the institution itself."[7]

A literary approach to political phenomena is not entirely new. Well before the arrival of the politically oriented analyses of the poststructuralist thinkers, the literary theorist Kenneth Burke carried out an analysis of *Mein Kampf* in which rhetorical mechanisms were both the object and vehicles of the writing. Characterizing most of the reviewers of Hitler's text as "vandals," he declared that "there are other ways of burning books than on the pyre—and the favorite method of the hasty reviewer is to deprive himself and his reader by inattention."[8] The attention that Burke pays is to Hitler's writing, showing how "the testament of a man who swung a great people into his wake" develops its appeal by evoking rhetorical structures that already belong to widely shared discursive practices. In Burke's analysis, *Mein Kampf*'s deeper level of argumentation reveals itself as textual; it emerges as the appropriation of theological discourse ("Church thought" in Burke's terms), which provides a ready-made script for connecting economic ills to the issue of personality and the idea of personal responsibility. This creates the rhetorical legitimation for scapegoating "inferior races."

It is not necessary, however, to select a violent polemic to show how the argumentation and appeal of a "text" (in the broadest sense) derives in part from its figurative structure. For example, attitudes toward nuclear energy in the United States are, to a significant extent, a function of the discursive frame that competes successfully for public attention. Obviously the outcome of this competition is largely determined by control over the mass media. In the case of this issue, media coverage has disproportionately conveyed the discursive frameworks promoted by national leaders. Without going into an extended analysis, it should be evident that the selling of nuclear energy has been effected primarily through the use of the venerable strategic code. Within such a mode of thinking/speaking—a mode that places the United States in a hostile, competitive environment in which any failure to maintain autonomy is read as a "threat to survival"—nuclear energy becomes a "necessity for survival" rather than simply a source of power to be evaluated on the basis of cost effectiveness, environmental hazards, or any of a variety of other frames of reference.

But "frames of reference" is too loose a conception to use in understanding the ideological impact of discourses impinging on the public policy domain. When we bracket out cognitive structure or the distribution of beliefs and values as an explanation of attitudes toward "public issues" and events, and emphasize instead the structure of the message-conveying discourses, we are well advised to heed the *way* that discourses constitute objects and events by using a genre of interpretation that is sensitive to the details of a discourse—the grammatical and rhetorical tropes and narrative structures that create values, attitudes, and motives *in* the discourse. When we employ a literary perspective on discourse, it becomes evident that even what appear to be primarily denotative or descriptive accounts harbor mythologies, stories whose details and overall structures are designed to motivate conduct that accords with the authority and power that the mythologies defend and legitimate.

Poststructuralism, or, as it is sometimes called, "textualism," has distinguished itself by its contribution to the argument that the literary genre has important epistemic and political significance. Influenced by Saussurean linguistics, with its emphasis on the "sign," an element in an intralinguistic system of relationships that produce objects and events ("signifieds"), poststructuralists pursue a level of human relationships that remains obscure to those who treat linguistic elements as symbols or referents that refer to some aspect of "reality."

This is not the place to review the variety of poststructuralist analyses. The emphasis, particularly in the deconstructive orientation practiced by Jacques Derrida and Paul de Man, has been to show how texts harbor something that eludes their authors, and how the rhetorical movements of the text carry commitments that exceed and even contradict whatever demonstration a writer might intend to make. Exemplary of this kind of demonstration is de Man's deconstructive critique of the theories of understanding of Locke, Condillac, and Kant. Locke, for example, constructed his approach to understanding within a primarily semantic view of language, arguing that good language serves as a conduit between ideas—the "simple," extralinguistic elements of thought—and "things." Locke combined this view with a general suspicion of language, which, he thought, interposes itself between ideas and things. This mistrust of language led Locke to be especially distrustful of figures of speech, which he regarded as mere adornment that could further impede our clear understanding of things. De Man demonstrates that Locke's text belies his explicit argument. Noting that Locke should be read, "not in terms of explicit statements . . . but in terms of the rhetorical motions of his own text," de Man shows how Locke's argument against tropes is made with the use of them.[9]

For example, Locke's conception of the "idea," which he regarded as a "simple" (extralinguistic) element in understanding, turns out to be a metaphor coming from the Greek *eide*, meaning "light." Ironically, Locke used "light" as one of his examples, saying that we understand light when we have the idea of it. Given de Man's discovery of the met-aphoricity of "idea," Locke's statement can be translated such that "to understand the idea of light" becomes "to light the light of light." De Man provides similar deconstructions of Condillac and Kant, showing how their texts too undermine their attempts to build models of under-standing based on the avoidance of figural language.

Yet although the deconstructive critiques have gone a long way to-ward producing a pedagogy for unraveling texts, if a literary analysis is to yield significant results for social and political thinking, one needs more of a political frame of understanding than has come out of such studies. It is one thing to note that there are ideological commitments woven into the texture of a text and quite another to venture a charac-terization of them by showing how, specifically, prevailing discursive practices represent the deployment of power and authority.

It is precisely this that Foucault has done in his readings of the histor-ical development of various disciplinary practices. His emphasis has been on the subject-objects scripted by various disciplinary agencies (including the human sciences), for he has seen this scripting as the constitution of identities that create what he calls "docile bodies" amen-able to the workings of entrenched structures of power and domina-tion. His analysis of the collective identity, the "population," provides a telling example:

> One of the great innovations in the techniques of power in the eighteenth century was the emergence of the "population" as an economic and political problem: population as wealth, population as manpower or labor capacity, population balanced between its own growth and the resources it commanded. Governments perceived that they were not simply dealing with subjects, or even with a "people," but with a "population."[10]

Characteristically, rather than following the familiar form of analysis of empirically oriented social science, which would look for referents of the term "population," Foucault analyzes the development of "popula-tion" as a discursive phenomenon, as a thing brought into speech by the workings of power.

The problem now is to move from a poststructuralist mode of analy-sis in general and a Foucauldian mode of politicized understanding in particular to a way of construing the responsibility of the social scien-tist. Let us first pay attention to *how* Foucault politicizes, to what it is in his style that provokes a political consciousness and problematizes what, within other styles, comes through as natural or unproblematic. Then we can consider an issue area—in this case it will be the area of "criminal" investigation and sentencing—and examine the role of the social scientist within a Foucauldian problematic.

Foucault's politicizing style relates to the analysis of the literary genre offered above. Foucault's approach to a subject-matter, apart from the genealogical analytic with which he focuses on the historical production of subjects of disciplinary knowledge, is to speak imperti-nently. *His* style produces (to recall Robin's words) "a confusion of gen-res, of writings, and of disciplines"; it penetrates "surreptitiously into the utmost gaps and interstices of the dominant discourses." Put dif-ferently, Foucault challenges conventional notions of pertinence by writing in a figural language that opposes the figuration found in pre-vailing discursive practices. For the ordinary and thus tranquilizing imagery of pedagogical and socialization language, he substitutes a jar-ring imagery, organized around the metaphor of the body. For exam-ple, his references (quoted above) to the "implantation of perversions" and to the way in which power relations have "penetrated modes of conduct" lead us to see human identities not as natural phenomena but as products of power-related practices. With this style of writing, in short, Foucault reveals the existence of forms of power that never di-rectly pose as such. His writing seeks to disinherit the power and au-thority bequeathed by prevailing ways of speaking. This disinheriting is carried out by showing how "subjects"—the individual and collec-tive identities of persons—are delivered by discourses that purport in-nocently to describe and explain phenomena.

Having treated the dimension of politicization through style, we can move to the analysis of the specific issue area. Here the focus is on two recent studies by James Q. Wilson, one on criminal investigation and the other on the efficacy of punishment. Written in a conventional pub-lic policy–public administration style, both studies can be shown to yield a different kind of interpretation when read within a politicized, literary perspective. The first one, *The Investigators*, loses its ideological innocence when we pay attention not to the statement of motives (in which Wilson declares himself to be innocent of partisan or polemical purpose) but, in de Man's terms, to "the rhetorical motions of [the] text." When we do this we find that what Wilson has created is, in gen-eral, a legitimating pamphlet for the existing power structure and, specifically, an apology for the Federal Bureau of Investigation (FBI) and the Drug Enforcement Administration.[11]

This legitimation/apology consists primarily in Wilson's uncritical ac-ceptance of the prevailing discourse of "criminal investigation." He de-scribes and analyzes the two investigative agencies using the language that they use to describe themselves and their adversaries. He invites us to visit a world of subject-objects called "investigators," "informants," "extremists," and "drug traffickers," and he describes their conduct in language that we ordinarily associate with the genre of business or administrative job performance evaluation. There is thus a "radical entanglement"[12] between the genre in which Wilson writes and the practice of investigative agencies. This implies an obvious failure, on Wilson's part, to politicize the field he works. For example, a "drug trafficker," for Wilson, is one so identified by investigative agencies. Large pharmaceutical companies, whom some would want to recruit into this category, receive no mention. In short, Wilson does not approach the language of investigative conduct from the point of view of the historical processes that have resulted in the proliferation of various "criminal" identities. He treats criminal roles as if they were self-selected, rather than as nominations that emerge from complex, power-related processes.

Let us provide a contrast by dealing with penalties for "criminal behavior," for example, not as natural or appropriate responses to acts that are clear violations of right conduct, but rather as discursive strategies that, in effect, constitute the acts for which they are applied as deterrents. Doing this, we politicize the problem of crime rather than being complicit in structures of domination producing what is to be a "crime." Foucault's approach to penalties exemplifies this politicized contrast:

> Penalty would . . . appear to be a way of handling illegalities, of laying down the limits of tolerance, of giving free reign to some, of putting pressure on others, of excluding a particular section, of making another useful, of neutralizing certain individuals and of profiting from others. In short, penalty does not simply "check" illegalities; it differentiates them, it provides them with a general "economy" and, if one can speak of justice, it is not only because the law itself in the way of applying it serves the interest of a class, it is also because the differential administration of illegalities through the mediation of penalty forms part of those mechanisms of domination.[13]

Rather than stepping outside the discourse of the administration of criminal investigation and opposing it with a politicized understanding—in which one sees the role assignments for criminal and non-criminal conduct as part of the mechanisms of domination—Wilson's genre of writing provides a grammar of absolution. He nominates the task as the appropriate initiator of action, arguing that a properly administered investigative agency would allow the "task" to determine the behavior of the investigator. The grammatical role of the task still sounds relatively innocent, but what do we have if we treat the "task" at the level of its metaphoricity? If we recall de Man's style of deconstruction, it can be shown how this rhetorical commitment in Wilson's text undermines his explicit political motive, a recommendation that the "task" replace the prevailing top-down model for running investigative agencies.

If we regard a "task" not simply as a thing to be done (a "job" or performance) but as something that has meaning within a context of organized exigencies, we see it in a more revealing interpretive context. It turns out that its meaning within an organizational context is close to its linguistic origins, for "task" is a metaphor deriving from *taxo, taxare*, Latin for "a fixed payment to a king or feudal superior."[14] Clearly, then, a task determines conduct only because it implies an organizational hierarchy and the duties associated with it. In performing a "task," one is deferring either to an individual or to an institutionalized collectivity in authority. Wilson's political program is thus vacuous, inasmuch as "top-down administration," for which he would substitute the "task," is simply reintroduced, more subtly, in a management-by-task model.

It should be noted that there is nothing unusual about the studies of James Q. Wilson, except, perhaps, the skill with which he structures and consummates his inquiries into the administration of public policy. Almost any contemporary public policy analyst could be selected for this kind of deconstructive criticism and subjected to a politicized literary reading. If we put ourselves in the place of analysts like Wilson and assume that the clientele for our investigation, apart from the readers of social science, is the police, FBI, or any similar agency, we can bracket out the politicizing aspect of the social science vocation and wonder with them about "efficiency" questions—for example, such issues as why various agencies do not do well what they are supposed to do. What I am questioning, however, is whether we *should* be in such a place. This issue gets more complex when we imagine another readership, the public at large instead of the administrators in investigative agencies. This brings us to the second of Wilson's studies, one in which he tells us all how we should think about crime.

In "Thinking About Crime," Professor Wilson not only purveys an ideological posture disguised in the scientific code but also denounces what he calls the "radical critics of America." He claims that these critics might be right about the need for changes in our criminal justice system, but that "to the extent that they propose anything but *angry rhetoric*, they would have us yearning for the good old days when our crime rate may have been higher but our freedom was intact" (italics added).[15]

Wilson's insinuation that the only possible radical criticism of American institutions would substitute some form of rigid political control for our supposedly benign market system is belied by the existence of nations with a high rate of employment, a low crime rate, a low level of inequality, *and* the "freedom" of which he speaks. But this part of his claim is less interesting for present purposes than his remark about rhetoric. Wilson does not sound angry, but there is a rhetorical dimension to his language, and if there is a characterization appropriate to the rhetorical content and force of the writing in "Thinking About Crime," I would again choose to call it apologetic. Wilson's apology belongs to a typical and fairly sophisticated genre of apology for inequality in America, and it emerges, as before, in the "rhetorical motions of the text," displaying itself in a variety of ways.

One of the most immediately apparent features of the text is the omnipresence of the science code. The language that comprises this code contains the terms familiar to scientific experimentation. For example, "findings" are reported in the language of probability, and in the quantitatively oriented terms of weighing, measuring, and so on. There is a discussion of the "probability of imprisonment for drug dealers," and he speaks of "hard to measure factors" and "hard to observe" persons. And once the evidence is "weighed," the public policy options that Wilson adduces are all entertained within the same weighing and balancing metaphors, making his conclusions appear logical rather than polemical:

> All this means that it is difficult but not impossible to achieve desired deterrent effects through changes in the law. To obtain these effects, society must walk a narrow line—the penalties must be sufficiently great to offset, at the margin, the benefits of the illegal act, but not so great as to generate in the criminal justice system resistance to their prompt imposition.[16]

The political obtuseness of this kind of analysis has already been discussed above in connecton with *The Investigators*. Unlike Foucault, who sees penalties as responsible for the *creation* of subordinated subjects, Wilson takes these subjects—for example, the "drug dealer"—for granted and neglects the processes wherein persons and activities are assigned criminal identities. The weighing and balancing figures of speech, which appear both in the scientific code and in the code of policy calculation, presume that there *are* unproblematic "things" to be weighed and measured. But there is a political process involved in creating the objects of the kind of penal science immanent in Wilson's thinking. To recover this political process, one needs to think of the social codes aiding and abetting an analysis whose explicit linguistic vehicle is the scientific code. As Heidegger put it, "science always encounters only what its kind of representation has admitted beforehand as an object possible for science."[17] What Wilson's neglect of this "beforehand" amounts to is a political insensitivity, a failure to examine what his various ways of speaking deliver.

In addition to the scientific code, which is Wilson's primary analytic device, are the rhetorical commitments that arrive along with the code of individualism running through his discussion. Marxists, structuralists, and, in fact, theorists of almost every interpretive stripe have long recognized that a focus on the actions or attributes of persons blinds us to the structures or wholes within which attributes of individual persons, their actions, and the things they contemplate have meaning. For example, as I have pointed out elsewhere, to describe an individual as "disabled" is to exonerate disabling social structures, whose performance demands create the meaning context within which disabled identities are produced.[18] Lurking in *any* attribute of an individual is a disguised social formation or structure, but the language within which Wilson analyzes crime and punishment is almost totally nonstructural. He presents an individual decision-making model in which a "criminal" is construed as one who has chosen between making an honest living and a life of crime. Crime statistics then become simply the sum of individual choices on the life-of-crime side of the selection process.

The bias in this kind of thinking is very much like the one we encounter in individualistic approaches to explaining inequality. Unless we realize that, for example, "owning capital" is a disguised relationship among individuals (a realization that requires structural-level figures of speech), such that X's poor position is understood to be related to Y's favorable position in the economic system, we are left with only individual-level explanations (e.g., poor motivation or bad luck) for the differences in income levels.[19] Similarly, the absence of structural imagery in Wilson's discussion of crime leaves him with no explanatory or interpretive resources when his individual-level model yields puzzling conclusions. Failing to understand that structural language can provide a meaning context or interpretive frame for understanding both the way persons end up in criminal role assignments and, more important, how such assignments develop (Foucault's major focus), Wilson is forced back into the naive empiricist use of the scientific code. In one of the few places where he refers to the notion of structure, or, as he puts it, "economic conditions," he dismisses the issues that might arise, noting that such conditions are "hard to measure." Given such a jejune methodological and political imagination, coupled with the absence of articulate views of structure and process, it is not surprising to find this amusing statement: "Perhaps if ex-offenders had more money, especially during the crucial few months after their release, they would not need to steal in order to support themselves."[20] But "having money" is similar to "owning capital"; it is a disguised relationship. Mr. X can "have money" only to the extent that something else happens in the totality of relations within which he functions.

Wilson's failure to think about crime is thus represented in the grammatical and rhetorical commitments in his text. Grammatically speaking, he lacks verbs and overuses nouns—for example, he wonders about how to treat "criminals" but fails to wonder about how things become criminalized. Rhetorically speaking, he relies too much on the scientific code, which harbors the metaphors of measurement (weighing, balancing, observing, etc.), and the individualism code with its metonymic commitment to representing persons in terms of their "criminal" attributes.

Let us go back to what prompted my decision to give Wilson's essay on crime and punishment some attention. It will suffice to note that, unlike the "radical critics of America" to whom he refers, Wilson does not give us *angry* rhetoric, but he does give us rhetoric. His insensitivity to the polemical dimensions of rhetoric in general, through his almost exclusive reliance on the code of science and his reification of the identities of persons (the "drug dealers," etc.) and their acts ("drug dealing"), renders him politically insensitive. What he does is *fail* to think of crime inasmuch as he fails to produce a pedagogy, a way of thinking/speaking that reveals how and why modern society has created the reality implicit in the everyday language (and the public policy analysis language) of crime and punishment.

With this analysis as background, how can we arrive at a view of the responsibility of social scientists? To provide a context for this issue, it is useful to review the idea of responsibility that I evoked at the beginning of this essay. The prevailing notion of the responsibility of social scientists is that they should speak in a way that can be understood by the lay public or, in special cases, by persons in roles that consume the expertise of social scientists. This common wisdom also has it that social scientists should avoid ethically charged language in the "descriptive" or explanatory part of their presentation. This is sometimes construed, as it is by Wilson, as a matter of presenting the "evidence" (evidence that has emerged from social scientific investigations) in relatively nontechnical language, and *then* evaluating the alternative policy options in light of that evidence. But descriptions of evidence contain evaluations. Figures of speech, and rhetorical and grammatical structures of discourse, are not simply extra means of expression used to represent thoughts. What is thought is produced by the figuration of the text. For example, the employment of an individualistic discourse allocates responsibility for crime to persons whose conduct has been criminalized. Such a discourse is part of what Foucault calls the "mechanisms of domination," for it speaks in the language of the administration of penalties. Social scientists who speak in the ordinary way, which is familiar to policymakers and the public at large, are letting the prevailing power structure play ventriloquist. When social scientists let the existing structure of domination speak through their mouths, the alternative policy responses proferred for meeting the "situation" are predetermined by the interests that constitute "the situation" to begin with.

Social science, then, is necessarily a polemical practice. Once we recognize that its value, the resources it lends, and the kinds of persons it presumes and creates come about through its rhetorical and grammatical strategies, we are in a position to rethink the relationship it has with its clientele. In one respect, the social science vocation is the same within this productive approach to discourse as it is in the representational approach: it is supposed to provide *analysis*. But the kind of analysis is different. Rather than accepting and reifying the subjects, objects, and surface relationships deployed by the languages of public policy and of everyday life, it makes available the practices that have produced the referents of that language. Ordinary, empiricist social science is best understood in terms of the metaphor of administration. To the extent that it seeks to explain "things," it is administering knowledge—namely, the "knowledge" built into the existing social formation—rather than creating or questioning it. A social science that treats as "conventional" the subjects and objects with which we consort— that is, treats them as human products rather than as naturally occurring phenomena—is more analogous to psychoanalysis as an interpretive paradigm than to empirical, causal explanation, for psychoanalysis is an interpretive approach that is suspicious of "things" and thus inquires into the practices responsible for their formation. Such a social science would therefore swap such things as "crimes" (e.g., "stealing entertainment," a newly proposed crime consisting of using a video cassette recorder to tape a film shown on television) for the process by which various interests (e.g., those of the film industry) have produced this new kind of "crime." Imagine the folly of wondering whether aspects of "temperament and family experience" (to quote Wilson's speculations about what leads people to be "offenders") contribute to the likelihood of using a video cassette recorder.

Psychoanalysis as a practice is similarly directed toward overcoming fetishes, making the psychic processes that result in various "personal identity problems" available to the subject so that the subject can see his or her complicity in the creation of the objects available to consciousness. However, the psychoanalytic practice is only *analogous* to what I am suggesting as appropriate to the social science vocation. As a concrete practice, psychoanalysis, like any discipline, operates in behalf of various interests. A politically sensitive social science would ask of psychoanalysis just how and why the subjects and objects *it* creates emerge as objects of knowledge. Psychoanalysis, like any discipline concerned with knowledge about humans, has helped to create a kind of human subject. To analyze psychoanalysis is thus not simply to adopt its discourse uncritically. A good example of someone who did this is the "Wolf-Man," one of Freud's most famous cases.

As a result of his experience with Freud, the Wolf-Man became a subject who, in Foucault's terms, was adept at "telling the truth about himself."[21] In the Wolf-Man's case, this was a matter of learning to tell psychoanalytic truths. In his memoirs, written long after his experience in psychoanalysis, one can hear psychoanalysis speaking through him. For example, recalling a decision he made to visit a Professor Kraepelin, he asks, "But could not this decision have been also a belated reaction to my father's death and an unconscious desire to find a substitute for him?"[22] The Wolf-Man had no illusions about the source of his interpretive orientation, for just six lines later he notes, "It is of course only now that these possibilities come to my mind, since in those days I knew nothing of psychoanalysis and could therefore not make any such attempt at interpretation."[23] Whatever one might say about the value of the Wolf-Man's telling the truth about himself in psychoanalytic terms, by the time he wrote his memoirs, his possession of a psychoanalytic self made him a subject of power. Of course he possessed other kinds of subjectivities as well, understanding himself within the prevailing political, economic, and administrative discourses of his day. He was thus constituted as a subject across a number of power relations. What psychoanalysis did for the Wolf-Man was perhaps to help him recover the mechanisms through which he had constructed an unwanted personal repertoire of acts and responses; it did not give him an analytic purchase on the historical processes that constituted him as a *social* subject.

Michael J. Shapiro

Within a Foucauldian account of what is involved in self-understanding, the role of the social scientist is not to promote a particular disciplinary discourse, psychoanalytic or otherwise, but rather to provide ways of speaking (and therefore of thinking) that make it possible to resist power—ways of speaking with grammatical and rhetorical structures that constitute a challenge to existing, institutionalized discursive practices. Through analysis, then, we reveal the process by which power makes us what we are, the way it creates multiple-subjects that are collective (the "population") or individual (the self-suspecting Wolf-Man). Through writing, the social scientist makes resistance possible by creating genres that are antagonistic—for example, describing the "helping professions" in political language or using literary language to evaluate conventional political language. Foucault has summed up this aspect of resistance: "Maybe the target nowadays is not to discover who we are but to refuse who we are. We have to imagine and to build up what we could be to get rid of this political 'double bind,' which is the simultaneous individualization and totalization of modern power structures."[24]

Finally, although my emphasis has been on the Foucauldian encouragement of resistance and refusal, there is another side to the discursive production of social science. This is the side of facilitation. Once we reject an empiricist model of truth as correspondence between statement and reality, we see the criterion of truth not only as the operation of power (for "domination" and "subjugation" do not exhaust the processes involved in human relations), but also as negotiation, the creative activity of persons involved in conversation. From the point of view of *this* process, the role of the social sciences becomes one of helping to find discursive strategies (including the use of the "scientific" code) for keeping conversations alive, for creating interpretive frames and enacting inquiries that provide more coherence with existing values, that help to enable collective action, and that offer mechanisms for transaction across disciplinary and institutional boundaries. But it is important to avoid naiveté about "facilitation" and always to wonder if help or facilitation is another kind of power representing itself as something else. It is important, in short, to keep one's ears attuned to the Foucauldian snicker and thus to be ready to challenge *any* statement by asking about its place in the economy of power relations.

NOTES

1. Michel Foucault, *The History of Sexuality,* trans. Robert Hurley (New York: Pantheon, 1978), p. 48.

2. See, for example, Richard Rorty, *Philosophy and the Mirror of Nature* (Princeton: Princeton University Press, 1979).

3. Michel Foucault, *The Archeology of Knowledge,* trans. A. M. Sheridan Smith (New York: Pantheon, 1972), p. 120.

4. Ibid.

5. Clifford Geertz, "Blurred Genres: The Refiguration of Social Thought," *American Scholar* 49 (1980): 165–79.

6. Regine Robin, "Toward Fiction as Oblique Discourse," *Yale French Studies* 59 (1980): 230–42.

7. Christian Metz, *Psychoanalysis and Cinema: The Imaginary Signifier,* trans. Celia Britton, Annwyl Williams, Ben Brewster, and Alfred Guzzetti (London: Macmillan, 1983), p. 14.

8. Kenneth Burke, "The Rhetoric of Hitler's 'Battle,'" *Southern Review* 5 (1939–40): 1–39.

9. Paul de Man, "The Epistemology of Metaphor," in Sheldon Sachs, ed., *On Metaphor* (Chicago: University of Chicago Press, 1978), pp. 11–28.

10. Michel Foucault, *The History of Sexuality,* p. 25.

11. This analysis of Wilson's *The Investigators* (New York: Basic Books, 1978) is developed at greater length in my "Literary Production as a Politicizing Practice," *Political Theory* 12 (1984): 387–422, and in Michael J. Shapiro, ed., *Language and Politics* (Oxford: Basil Blackwell, 1984), pp. 215–53.

12. This expression is used by D. A. Miller in his analysis of the way nineteenth-century novels support, by virtue of their narrative structures, the functions of the policing authorities. He speaks of a "radical entanglement between the nature of the novel and the practice of the police." See "The Novel and the Police," in *Glyph 8* (Baltimore: Johns Hopkins University Press, 1981), pp. 127–47.

13. Michel Foucault, *Discipline and Punish: The Birth of the Prison,* trans. Alan Sheridan (New York: Pantheon, 1977), p. 272.

14. *The Shorter Oxford English Dictionary on Historical Principles* (Oxford: Clarendon Press, 1933), s.v. "task."

15. James Q. Wilson, "Thinking About Crime," *Atlantic Monthly,* September 1983, pp. 86–87.

16. Ibid., p. 79.

17. Martin Heidegger, "The Thing," in *Poetry, Language, Thought,* trans. Albert Hofstadter (New York: Harper & Row, 1971), p. 170.

18. See my *Language and Political Understanding* (New Haven: Yale University Press, 1981), chap. 7.

19. These observations are based in part on points made by Alan Garfinkel, *Forms of Explanation* (New Haven: Yale University Press, 1981), p. 85.

20. Wilson, "Thinking About Crime," p. 82.

Michael J. Shapiro

21. Michel Foucault, "Structuralism and Post-Structuralism: An Interview with Michel Foucault," *Telos* 55 (Spring 1983): 207.

22. Muriel Gardiner, ed., *The Wolf-Man by the Wolf-Man* (New York: Basic Books, 1971), p. 69.

23. Ibid., pp. 69-70.

24. Michel Foucault, "Afterword: The Subject and Power," in Hubert L. Dryfus and Paul Rabinow, *Michel Foucault: Beyond Stucturalism and Hermeneutics* (Chicago: University of Chicago Press, 1982), p. 216.

21

WHAT ARE NICE FOLKS LIKE

YOU DOING IN A PLACE

LIKE THIS?

SOME ENTAILMENTS OF

TREATING KNOWLEDGE

CLAIMS RHETORICALLY

MICHAEL CALVIN McGEE

JOHN R. LYNE

Until very recently, it seemed to be the wrong century to devote serious intellectual labor to the study of rhetoric. In fourth-century Rome, rhetoricians might have aspired to the position of a Themistius, Imperial Professor of Rhetoric, person in charge of educating future Emperors, purveyor of the cultural ideals of the Empire, and guardian of a respectable intellectual tradition that stretched back even before the Golden Age of Greece. For most of the past three centuries, however, rhetoricians have been banished to the margin of reputable intellectual activity. The suppression of rhetoric was accomplished, in part, by such unargued sneers as the figure that describes it as "The Harlot of the Arts" and the Italian maxim that asserts that "facts are masculine and words are feminine." In sexist Western traditions, the smokescreen of alleged male superiority makes such denigration seem plausible: it comes out that rhetoricians are really practicing seduction, that they are indifferent to truth and virtue, and that they are therefore willing to sell their expertise to advertising agencies, politicians, or any other powerful interest outside the cloisters of the academy. Rhetoric, in a word, was *patronized*. That is, relations of power were figured from what was assumed to be a natural order of male dominance, a patriarchy. Cultural stereotypes of femininity were used to suggest that rhetoric had a place to stay. "Bad rhetoric," like the "bad girl" of sexist mythology, plays loose with allegedly objective facts, making mere opinion seem a formidable opponent of scientific truth. "Good rhetoric," like the virtuous wife of sexist mythology, was quietly confined to the so-called service course (figurative equivalent of bedroom and kitchen) where freshmen are supposed to learn the fundamental communicative skills that prepare them for exciting, truly important work in more substantive disciplines. The clear presumption, of course, was that rhetoric is naturally bad, that "keeping it in its place" within the university's power structure requires constant vigilance lest other academics be tempted by the seductress and inflicted with creeping relativism.

The irony of this volume, and the Iowa symposium from which it stems, is that representatives of nearly all the human sciences come now to the place their intellectual forebears defined as a bordello to find a conception of discourse powerful enough to help them throw off the yoke of an unwanted academic orthodoxy. There is occasion for rhetoricians to celebrate the rhetorical turn in contemporary letters, for the academic community at large seems willing now to acknowledge that the way scholars argue among themselves may in part determine what will be counted as an increment of the "knowledge" they are supposed to produce and preserve. But there is also good reason for students of rhetoric to be cautious, perhaps even suspicious, of this new movement. The art of rhetoric has always focused on the discourse of marketplace and forum, where the material power of contending factions holds more sway than academic notions of dispassionate and disinterested reason. When respectable academics come to rhetoric's abode, have they really abandoned their old faith in the mythical value-freedom of academic discourse? Or do they entertain a hope of transforming rhetoric into a practice that pious ex-positivists can embrace in good conscience while they continue to devalue the passions and logics of the political economy?

The Difficulty of Being Positive

The rhetorical turn seems motivated theoretically by reaction against a hegemonic movement in twentieth-century philosophy. Though originally little more than a vision of one day finding a single, certain basis for what we know, "academic positivism" came to be a formulary orthodoxy in American social science. As Kenneth Burke suggests, a simplistic dialectic was created in the declaration that true knowledge can be achieved only by pursuing the scientific method; all else was primitive magic.[1] The quest for certainty prompted the transformation of many academic pursuits: "politics," for example, became "political science" and "moral philosophy" became instead "social science." This state of affairs alarmed those academics whose work could not be scientific—artists, literati, rhetoricians, metaphysicians, and most historians. Nervous plaints from such quarters helped mask the fact that the rhetoric of the positivist movement never quite produced the projected unity. Positivism was kept alive more in the minds of opponents than in the daily practice of scientists, becoming in the end more epithet than signifier, more the ghost of horrified imaginations than a coherent body of thought.

This is not to say that positivism was entirely the child of threatened imaginations. Rather, it simply did not exist as a unique and coherent philosophical position after the breakup of the Vienna Circle. Its chief influence consisted in an attitude toward the ideal relationship of the fields of knowledge, and for this attitude we will use a less specific (and less dated) term, "scientism." The story of scientism is at once cold, calculating, and romantic. The greatest miseries of humanity have been caused by irrational belief in magic, religion, and other intellectually indefensible rubbish. Reason, understood as virtually equivalent to scientific method, can save humanity. Science is universal in the sense that the logic of its inquiry is the same in any domain where knowledge is possible. The universal objective of inquiry is explanation and prediction. An event is explained by showing that it occurred as the result of laws, rules, or principles of nature and society; and knowledge of laws, rules, conditions, and so on makes prediction possible. Inquiry is "value-free" or "value-neutral"; it strives to be as objective as possible, showing how to change circumstances to produce results, but never recommending that one particular policy be selected. *Scientists* may offer value judgments, but *science* is mute on the problem of decision, for no "ought" claim can be derived from knowledge of facts. No claim will be acknowledged as fact until it has been verified by observation, and no proposition will be treated seriously even in theory unless it is possible to envision the conditions of its verification.[2]

As Chaim Perelman and Lucie Olbrechts-Tyteca suggest, the notion that inquiry must be "value-free" apparently puts moral questions and

Michael Calvin McGee and John R. Lyne

problems of decision making beyond the pale of this kind of knowledge. Yet as philosophers of law, Perelman and Olbrechts-Tyteca realize that they cannot give themselves up to definitions of reason, logic, and knowledge that exclude or fail to account for the moral dimension of human existence: "Must we draw from this evolution of logic, and from the very real advances it has made, the conclusion that reason is entirely incompetent in those areas which elude calculation and that, where neither experiment nor logical deduction is in a position to furnish the solution of a problem, we can but abandon ourselves to irrational forces, instincts, suggestion, or even violence?"[3] No academic should pay such costly, ultimately irrational tribute to scientism. But what paths of argument lead to a conception of *rhetoric* as an alternative to this powerfully entrenched prejudice? Four routes lead to four different "rhetorics of inquiry."

The first, exemplified by Perelman and Olbrechts-Tyteca, supposes that moral knowledge is a different *kind* of knowledge. The difficulty is that what has been identified as *the* scientific method is *inappropriately applied* when scholars attempt to describe for themselves the logics and passions of public life. The principle at stake in this line of thinking is the alleged universality of method in science. Such "scientific" criteria as accuracy, clarity, and precision are thought to be necessary in making moral judgments; but if scholars are bound by the definitions of these criteria in vogue in scientism, they are damned from the start to be imprecise at best on moral questions, and perhaps incompetent to address them at all. A new method is needed, which is to say, in the case of Perelman and Olbrechts-Tyteca, a "new rhetoric," presented as a theory of argumentation and based on the principle of adherence. In this argument, rhetoric of inquiry becomes a technical apparatus, an engine for producing a distinctive kind of knowledge. This is a palliative conception in that rhetoric is portrayed as a stopgap for one of the deficiencies of scientism.

A second route to rhetoric of inquiry suggests that the very idea of method is an inappropriate description of the unification of knowledge. On this view, claims for method advanced since the Renaissance have been much inflated suggestions that we have been able to cure smallpox and predict election results and fly to the moon *because* of our disciplined adherence to a particular method. In fact, this argument suggests, advances in knowledge must be explained by a complex of factors, including such things as technological capacity to publish knowledge (increasing the number of those working to create knowledge); the development of universities (producing a climate and fund of resources conducive to the creation of knowledge); and the need for knowledge in the political economy at large (creating a market and a demand for the production of knowledge previously unknown). The story of the rapid growth of knowledge might best focus on the development of what Alvin Gouldner has called a "culture of critical discourse":

> The culture of critical discourse (CCD) is an historically evolved set of rules, a grammar of discourse, which (1) is concerned to *justify* its assertions, but (2) whose *mode* of justification does not proceed by invoking authorities, and (3) prefers to elicit the *voluntary* consent of those addressed solely on the basis of arguments adduced. CCD is centered on a specific speech act: justification. It is a culture of discourse in which there is nothing that speakers will on principle refuse to discuss or make problematic; indeed, they are even willing to talk about the value of talk itself and its possible inferiority to silence or to practice.[4]

In this argument, the unification of knowledge is presented as a social fact (not, as in scientism, a desirable goal); and it is accomplished by virtue of *dissemination* (not by the uniformity of factors involved in its production). Rhetoric of inquiry becomes a mode of communication, specifically of justification, among those who trade in knowledge as merchants in commodities. The problem of knowledge production is not a question of method, but one of manufacture within a "knowledge industry." That is, the truth and usefulness of knowledge are determined in its appeal as it is addressed to the scholarly community; nothing intrinsic to knowledge (such as the mode of its creation) is relevant to the interesting problem of its truth or importance. With regard to the hegemony of scientism, Gouldner portrays a revolutionary, subversive rhetoric that others have described as epistemic,[5] as a "rationale of the informative and suasory in discourse" that simultaneously constitutes and justifies what will count as knowledge.[6]

A third route to rhetoric of inquiry lies in the political implications of the apparent oxymoron "knowledge industry." The word "knowledge" is quite properly associated in common language with "scholarship," the "academy," and "academics." Each of these terms conjures up a vision of medieval life, a time when scholars interested more in truth than in power were sequestered from the secular world so that they might concentrate on studies of life and nature with the same asceticism they manifested in cloistered prayer. In contrast, the word "industry" is associated with the secular world, with the routine of everyday life in the political economy. Linking the two terms calls attention not only to the fact that knowledge production is now big business,

Michael Calvin McGee and John R. Lyne

but also to the misleading dichotomy between the academic and the secular. A modern state simply cannot survive without a knowledge industry. In consequence, the sanctity of the academy is violated by the infusion of vast sums of money to fund an agenda of research set by business and government; further, the power of wealth and of public office is made dependent upon the technical expertise found in universities.[7]

From this perspective, the unification of knowledge has less to do with the reliablity of facts or the persuasiveness of truth claims in an academic community than with the appropriation and integration of expert opinion within the political economy, the functional unity of theory and praxis. Some writers object in principle to the intimate connection of power and knowledge. So, for example, Michel Foucault wants to expose and disrupt what he views as an inseparable integration more accurately represented by the single term "power/knowledge."[8] For Foucault and other postmodern writers, studies of a rhetoric of inquiry should be a kind of cultural or social criticism focused on the problem of domination. That is, rhetoric is viewed as an instrument of power used to clothe political polemics in scholarly garb, making it difficult to see where truth has been shaped and pruned to serve the interests of the prevailing social and political hegemony.

Other writers see much the same sort of rhetoric, but characterize the relation between academics and the general public very differently. They do not object in principle to integrated power/knowledge, arguing instead that such integration is natural and necessary. In this vision, academics are related to the public as technical advisers to decision-makers. The difficulty lies not with scholarly manipulations, but with the incompetence of the public. That is, the technical experts of the academy, portrayed as fundamentally disinterested in the projects of political factions, are said already to have sufficient communicative skill to give clear advice; the public, however, is said to be deficient in the skills needed to interpret expert advice and to act wisely in response to it. "The essential need," John Dewey wrote, "is the improvement of the methods and conditions of debate, discussion, and persuasion. That is *the* problem of the public."[9] In this view, the integration of power/knowledge is a prerequisite to successful democracy. Whether one thinks of such integration as inherently problematic (with Foucault et al.), or as the hope of civilizing the undereducated masses (with Dewey et al.), rhetoric of inquiry is said to be remedial, a cure for dangerous discourse practices developed to disseminate or to interpret the truth claims that will constitute knowledge in the public arena.

A fourth route to the rhetoric of inquiry, the one closest to our own view of the matter, arises in the need to negotiate competing knowledge claims. The first three lines of argument foresee a unity of inquiry of some sort, whether provided by a number of methods (each appropriate to a peculiar domain of knowledge), by solidarity in the academic community, or by carefully contrived integration of knowledge and action. In each case, the unity of inquiry is a regulative ideal, the vision of a yet-to-be-realized state of affairs. On the fourth view, by contrast, knowledge presents itself, both to scholars and to lay people, as fragmented, partial, and controversial. This need not be a problem if, as is usual in the academy, there is the luxury of not having to decide which of two or more truth claims to authenticate. Indeed, the ability to suspend judgment has produced the genre of prose called "theory," where competing claims can be presented *ad infinitum* as if they were true. When situations present an exigency, however, competing knowledge claims must be settled; knowledge needs less to be unified than negotiated, using the requirements of the moment as criteria for *deciding* what will be regarded as fact.[10]

Exigencies sufficient to force a negotiation of competing truth claims may arise in academic communities as part of the natural evolutionary process of science,[11] in response to interfield or interdisciplinary competition for the material resources of knowledge production, or simply as the consequence of interfield debates among those who study similar problems from widely diverse perspectives.[12] The more common and pressing problems, however, arise in practice, as members of the academic community are asked to give advice in the public interest on contingent matters that require immediate action. Voters, for example, are asked to judge such matters as the construction of nuclear power plants and find the experts serving up very different accounts of the facts, depending on their political or economic alignments, or simply on their different methods. In legal practice, juries are asked to mete out awards and punishments on the advice of a bewildering parade of hired experts, each telling a different story—experts who are not their peers, and who unhappily have been selected because they support the predetermined position of the defense or the prosecution.

Two orders of understanding claims clash in distinct ways in such situations. Obviously, there is the need to sort and evaluate conflicting testimony on the matter at issue (more of that in a moment); but more significantly, there is the need to negotiate competing claims proceeding from two different domains of human rationality. Ordinary people who make up juries and the voting polity "narrativize" or "dramatize" exigent situations. That is, they look for stories that put alleged facts into a narrative sequence that can be judged more and less probable as an account of what happened or what might happen. Facts and testimony are valued and devalued more because of the way they fit together in cultural narratives than because of their representational accuracy or the method used to generate them within the stories of scientism.[13] By contrast, the experts who offer advice do so on the basis of reasoning conventions used in the academy, usually the rules of scientism and the discourse practices of the culture of critical discourse. As we suggested earlier, scientism is built in part on the desire to brand as irrational most of the reasoning one finds in the decision making of juries and polities.[14] Indeed, Alasdair MacIntyre suggests that scientism has proceeded so far that "we have—very largely, if not entirely— lost our comprehension, both theoretical and practical, of morality."[15] In an impressive monograph on the Three Mile Island crisis, for example, Thomas Farrell and Thomas Goodnight compare the two kinds of reasoning and knowledge we have been discussing. They call the grammar and rhetoric of scientism "technical reasoning," suggesting that the press, government, and industry have come to expect a particular kind of discourse from the expert, and to employ it themselves in controversies they formerly would have perceived as governed by the rules and conventions of "social reason." An analysis of the public discourse generated in response to a near-meltdown at the Three Mile Island nuclear facility led them to conclude that technical reasoning was so incompetent that it nearly caused the serious nuclear accident that so many people fear.[16]

In this argument rhetoric of inquiry arises in an attempt to make wise and prudent choices from among competing truth claims in exigent situations. It is a managerial rhetoric, concerned neither with recuperating truth (now subordinated to discourses of power), nor with the reeducation of the public to a level of competence Dewey might find satisfactory. It is also a strategic rhetoric, concerned neither with subverting scientism by changing the grounds of the unity of knowledge from scientific method to communicative competence, nor with creating a new rhetoric as a palliative to cure ills in the scientific method. This version of rhetoric of inquiry attempts to deal with knowledge claims as they are presented and not as they are idealized. Two domains of reason (the technical and the social) are portrayed as opposed and irreducible one to the other.[17] The object of rhetoric of inquiry is to test knowledge claims proceeding from these two domains of reason against the moral and material requirements of exigent circumstances to determine what should be treated as fact. It is a very standard, traditional rhetoric of "adjusting ideas to people and people to ideas."[18]

The Dialectic of Rhetoric and Antirhetoric

We prefer this last route to rhetoric of inquiry because it exposes and features a dialectical tension that is only implicit elsewhere. Other arguments lose the issue because they make it appear that rhetoric is setting itself against the rigor and reliability of a practice that results in the largesse of technology. Rhetoric in fact values scientistic discourse, if only because the scientific method is a powerful and persuasive form of argument. But it is neither the only nor the most persuasive argument in all situations. The impulse to say that there is one reliable way to argue in all circumstances, in effect to confine knowledge in the fantasy of rational certainty, is not unique to scientism: such a dream is, as Herbert Marcuse suggests, "the original concern of Western thought and the origin of its logic."[19] More specifically, Richard Rorty argues that commitment to rational certainty as the regulative ideal of philosophy can easily be traced to Plato.[20] Though his ideas ultimately found a home in the sequestered halls of the academy, Plato's interests were social and political. He wanted a cure for what he saw as an epidemic of perverse modes of thought.[21] The illness was rhetoric, the art of the sophists, and the cure was Plato's version of philosophy, replete with its commitment to the principle of rational certainty. The issue we are discussing can thus be raised in a different light: with regard to rational process, scientism is not "positive" at all. It is an antirhetoric, a negation. The dialectic that undergirds the turn to rhetoric in contemporary letters lies in an opposition between passionate and prejudiced social reason (traditionally associated with the rhetoric of marketplace and forum) and an antirhetoric of cool, comfortably neutral technical reason (associated in the public mind with computing machines and sterile laboratories).

The dialectic of rhetoric and antirhetoric is best explored from the perspective of ordinary people who are constrained to rely on the advice of experts. This reliance is not a comfortable one. If the general public appears convinced that experts must play an important role in the political economy, it does not want them to control it. Experts, as the sentiment is crystallized rhetorically, should be "on tap, but not on top." The public's impression that judgment should be informed by, but not bound by, "authority" is reinforced by the use of experts in such forums as the court of law. When half a dozen well-qualified psychiatrists pronounce a person insane, only to be countered by a dozen others who pronounce the same person sane, the limits of "expertise" are manifest. The laity, seeing famous psychiatrists assert opposite positions on fundamental questions, must know that more than a difference in technical competence is involved. The narrative conventions of their culture teach them that they are witnessing the embeddedness of technical questions in larger frameworks where intellectual commitments and political agendas (among other things) dictate how technical questions will be framed and answered. What the academic thinks of as commitment to a theory is perhaps not unlike the commitment a defense attorney gives a client: each seeks advantageous use of authority for a purpose. And this works because audiences are willing to reciprocate. Both general and scholarly audiences defer to (other) experts who are cognitive authorities in order to lay claim to their knowledge.[22] Yet this kind of authority rarely entitles one to take action, for in between knowing (in an intellectually warranted way) and doing lies a sea of such "confounding variables" as trust and power, the engines of rhetoric.[23]

RHETORIC

Aristotle's description of the "art of discovering the available means of persuasion" is both a historically prominent account of rhetoric and a primer on understanding and manipulating those who claim authority by virtue of custom, status, experience, or knowledge.[24] Though rhetoricians throughout the tradition talk about science as formal argument, the art of persuasion Aristotle professed was not intended to have a place within the sciences.[25] For Aristotle, rational philosopher though he was, rhetoric had no necessary connection to the truth. He does nod faintly in the direction of conscience in the claim that, all things being equal, truth will have an advantage over falsehood in rhetorical combat. But the problem for rhetoric, its *raison d'être* within the Aristotelian architectonic, was *adherence*, not truth. How does one gain the confidence and support of audiences who possess the power of judgment in each of the various public forums? This problem does not take care of itself, as proponents of scientism often suppose, once advocates clearly understand "what is the case," if only because most advocacy is not truth-regarding in the first place—sophists through all ages, from Athens to Madison Avenue, have practiced techniques that produce adherence independently of truth seeking. But even in those cases where rhetoric *is* truth-regarding, it cannot merely preserve the result of inquiry, for the logic of dicovery may be dysfunctional as a rationale in public justification before different audiences. Arguments that produce solidarity in a scientific community are thus "technical and filled with jargon" when compared with the "greatly over-simplified, popularized versions" of "the same facts" that funding agencies, Congressional bodies, journalists, or the lay public find convincing.[26] In the end, scientific discourse is so much pruned and shaped by the requirements of its dissemination that what identifies it as scientific is that it was produced by a scientist. Its internal characteristics, the type and style of its proofs, are covariant with the expectation of the audience whose adherence is being sought.[27]

There is one strong affinity between scientism and Aristotelian rhetoric: like the scientific method for scientists, rhetoric for Aristotle was a morally neutral instrument. It might give expression equally to truth or superstition or whatever else is necessary in the quest for a favorable judgment. To whatever end rhetoric was used, it would be judged by the quality of its proofs. In the Aristotelian scheme, acceptable proofs fall under the headings of *ethos* (the credibility of the speaker), *pathos* (the psychological condition of the audience), and *logos* (the apparent rationality of the argument itself). Perhaps foremost among these resources was *ethos:* the moral quality of rhetoric depended ultimately on the moral fiber of rhetoricians.[28]

The function of rhetoric, however, is not to provide acceptable proofs, but to induce decisions and judgments, to move from the relevant facts to some action or disposition regarding them. A successful application of rhetoric therefore supposes authority of a sort that can support and justify action. Credible experts, on the rhetorical model of authority, *must facilitate the act of judgment*—that is, they must speak that language of knowledge which translates easily into the language of action and promotes a fusion of the two. Thus we should not be surprised to discover that we do not know how to translate the "findings" of a scientific study into meaningful action, when, as Burke observes, we have exorcised the very principle of meaningful action from the vocabulary of the social sciences.[29] For better or for worse, and usually for both, authority on the rhetorical model moves cognition in some tendentious way. More than merely privileging the truth, rhetoric must *make its claims come true;* it urges judgment-for-a-purpose, and it is this very capacity that makes it authoritative. Rhetorical authority is obliged to pay special attention to the continuity of belief and habit within the community addressed; to recognize and play upon the persistence of "what people think"; to respect common knowledge, not as a matter of etiquette, but as the price of effectiveness; and to comport with common sense, even while defining or redefining it.

ANTIRHETORIC

As we have suggested, the central motif in Western philosophy and science (the securing of knowledge by reliable means and methods) poses a different model of authority, usually antithetical to the rhetorical model. With reference to its origins in antirhetoric, we call this the Platonic model of authority. The function of Platonic authority is not to gain adherents, but to authenticate claims to knowledge in such a way that the agreement of others is irrelevant, tangential, or supplementary to one's own confidence in the claim. There is wide variation in the *location* of authority: some see it in a rationally introspective individual, others in empirically verifiable facts, in authoritative texts, and, especially since Descartes, in finding and applying the right method.[30] However defined, authority on the Platonic model is established in its production or revelation of that sort of truth which can exist, in principle, independently of human will. The question of the function or application of knowledge is simply irrelevant to the problem of securing confidence in its truth.

There is thus no easy movement between the language of knowledge and the language of action within the framework of antirhetoric. Academics are urged not to confound *is*'s and *ought*'s, not to let their moral principles, political ideologies, and religious faith "corrupt their science." Language is carefully chosen to dispel any hint of prejudice—some might say that even mind disappears in locutions that substitute "observation" for "interpretation," "report" for "argument," or "findings" for "inference/conclusion." Scientific findings, in fact, often take on the special glow of truth *just because* they are "counterintuitive," unsupported by popular or academic prejudices. Authority here is a means of getting at the truth rather than the connection of truth with any purpose that audiences may share with speakers. Authority on the Platonic antirhetorical model must try to do no more than reflect the truth-producing capacity of a method while eschewing the manipulative potentials of *ethos* and *pathos*.

The criteria most often respected as epistemically authoritative are those that are fixed independently of an audience and remain unbending in the face of "common knowledge" and "common sense." By toeing the straight and narrow line of independent standards, it is assumed that progressively revealed truths will replace every ignorant superstition (including, usually, religious belief—in nearly all its formulations, scientism stops barely shy of being officially atheistic). The fact that newly revealed truths might not gain broad adherence is essentially irrelevant; that is, the *effectiveness* of knowledge would be interesting only in the context of a sociology of belief. Thus the distinction between rhetoric and philosophy is often drawn in terms of the difference between mere belief and real knowledge, which the received view parses as "justified true belief." The philosophy that supports scientism puts the emphasis on justification and truth conditions, with the creation of belief usually cast off as psychological (or sociological) dirty work to be conducted elsewhere. Introducing the complexities of an audience orientation at the bar of inquiry would threaten this picture of the unity of science and endanger its control over credentials. Such a portrait depends, of course, on the clearly impossible notion that knowledge is a thing that can be separated from how it enters human judgment and action.

THE DIALECTICAL TENSION

The historical tension between rhetorical and Platonic models of authority is frequently represented as one between two mutually exclusive approaches to the manufacture of belief.[31] Yet there is a sense in which antirhetoric's appeal to objective knowledge and its accompanying denunciation of rhetoric is one of the most effective rhetorical strategies available. No one was a greater master of the strategy than Plato. In our time, masters of the rhetoric of science command the most formidable rhetorical *ethos*. Theirs is the chaste rhetoric that pretends not to be rhetorical.[32] Expert testimony in a legislative hearing, in interviews with the press, and in trial proceedings typically parades the rhetoric of objectivity even while playing the attitudes of the designated audience like so many keys of a piano. The intense conviction of testifying experts that they are not acting rhetorically casts an aura of authenticity over their performance. This is not to say that such rhetoric is deceptive, for in these settings expertise is functioning just as it should, largely *because* testifying experts are ignorant of their own artifice. That is, they appear sincerely convinced by methodological rigor of the truth (and the limits) of their testimony; they believe that decision-makers can be persuaded by the same arguments (limited by the same qualified statistical probabilities). In fact, decision-makers listen with care to "the story" experts tell, searching for anomalies in "the big picture," for "the bottom line" that statistical probability conceals, and ultimately for the markers of sincerity, good will, and trustworthiness. Ironically, experts who try to inform with reason wind up *being yielded*

Michael Calvin McGee and John R. Lyne

to in an act of obeisance to power reserved in former ages for kings, priests, magicians, and wizards. As a rule, decision-makers who yield neither understand nor care about the rational procedure underlying expert advice; for them, the only proof is in the eating; and except on the most vital questions, there is always time to hang an errant expert out to dry.

The evident contradiction in antirhetoric invites a "dialectical" description of the tension between rhetorical and Platonic models of authority. As Anthony Giddens suggests, however, we must be conscious of unproductive understandings of "contradiction."[33] When opposed alternatives appear to be mutually exclusive so that one must be rejected as the other is chosen, the relationship is not truly dialectical, for the opposites do not create a unity of understanding in their opposition.[34] So, for example, proponents of the rhetorical model have reacted negatively to antirhetoric because it devalues commitments that are warranted more by cultural conventions and traditions than by observation and experiment. If the situation is perceived as one of forced choice between the alternatives, the result is complete rejection of Platonic authority—which in praxis translates as more or less intolerant anti-intellectualism.[35] When proponents of scientism react in like fashion to the seeming irrationality of rhetorical authority, the result is usually some sort of quixotic flailing at the most deep-seated, cherished, and rhetorically entrenched beliefs of society. So, for example, the eminent physicist Arthur Kantrowitz's 1976 proposal that a Court of Science be created stood against the right of trial by jury of peers, an Anglo-American commitment more ancient than the English aristocracy. Understood within the rhetoric of scientism, it was a sensible idea: the Court of Science was to serve the function of rendering judgment on disputed technical questions. Thus, for instance, the court might rule on whether cyclamates could cause cancer in human beings. Having heard the best scientific evidence from the most qualified experts, the court would pass judgment on the relevant questions of fact. Politically constituted decision-making bodies could then act in confidence that the best-qualified minds had settled the troublesome, mysterious, technical questions. But an entailment of making experts into magistrates is reduction of the capacity for public judgment. Though the idea was widely debated, it died a timely death wherever it appeared in public: no public body was willing to trade liberty for informed expertise.[36]

Properly considered, the dialectical tension between rhetorical and Platonic models of authority is not simply between two rival approaches, in which case one might expect to cheer the victory of one over the other. Rather, each term for authority is conditioned by the co-presence of the other. The opposition is not to be eliminated as the result of verbal combat, nor transcended as the consequence of logical gymnastics, but *managed* to promote a productive integration of power/knowledge. Should the Platonic model be viewed as triumphing over the rhetorical (as progressive science was said to triumph over primitive magic), the presence of rhetoric is ideologically repressed in the scholar's professional self-conception; clearly rhetorical arguments aimed at persuasion are confused with "simple, clear statements" that "merely inform." Conversely, should the rhetorical attitude be lauded as ascendant or triumphant, the technological complexities of postindustrial society are dangerously oversimplified. Clearly warranted auguries (of nuclear annihilation, for example) are in the first case mixed up with the "hard sell" techniques of persuasion that everyone is taught to dismiss out of hand; in the other case, panic sets in as every tale of doom comes to sound like scientific prediction. The trick is thus to think of rhetorical and Platonic models of authority as *a unity of opposites*.

In theory, the "unity of opposites" may sound too mysterious, too much like the Christian riddle of the Trinity. But, in practice, such unity is already achieved by the requirement that testifying experts serve both epistemic and rhetorical needs. Witnesses are put in a situation that perpetually deconstructs the two "rival" categories of authority and demonstrates that the very attempt to make them function antithetically is itself a rhetorical stance: the more experts hold themselves "above" rhetorical manipulation, the more they consolidate the power of their *ethos* and even the trust that permits them to speak authoritatively at some remove from their actual technical competence. So people defer to a Margaret Mead or a Carl Sagan or a Noam Chomsky on the assumption that their technical virtuosity is somehow generalizable.[37] In Greek rhetorical theory, it would be said that such celebrity scientists are accorded the honor, privilege, and deference owed to the *phronimos*, the person of integrity, experience, and knowledge. This combination of qualities partook of two modes of knowing: *epistēmē* (identified here with the Platonic model of authority) and *doxa* (identified here with a rhetorical model of authority). The product, however, was as distinctive as any finished recipe from its ingredients: *phronēsis* was a unity of opposites, a "practical wisdom" more respectful of faith and power than *epistēmē*, more stable and reliable than *doxa*.[38] In Roman rhetoric, the vision of the *phronimos* came to be a cultural ideal, expressed as the *vir bonus* doctrine: a good citizen is "a good man speaking well" in public on important issues of the day.[39] If

Hans-Georg Gadamer is right, the greatest loss in humanity's four-century love affair with scientism is *phronēsis*: "knowledge" has come to mean but a part of what must be included in the dialectic that constitutes practical wisdom.[40]

If the vision of knowledge as wisdom needs to be recovered, and if we understand *phronēsis* to be a product of managing the dialectical tension between Platonic and rhetorical conceptions of authority, the obvious response to scientism is to revalue the rhetorical. Such recovery is well under way even now. Richard Rorty is a prominent figure among those who roil the waters by appealing to "conversations" rather than "demonstrations," to "vocabularies" instead of "reality" in describing the development of knowledge. The sciences do not get closer or farther from reality, Rorty has argued, nor do they make progress toward truth. If the technical terminology of Galileo was more productive than that of Aristotle, then it was because he had found a more successful way of talking, not a truer mirror of nature.[41] Reading the likes of Rorty, Paul Feyerabend, Mary Hesse, and other philosophers who have become advocates of science-as-social-practice promotes a sense of liberation; and it comports so well with the old prejudices of humanists throughout the academy that it is tempting to make an open-throttled rush to proclaim the rhetorical as the framework now best suited for unifying the academy. The problem is deciding what "rhetoric" shall mean, for if academics jump at too easy an answer, the resultant practice might end up mimicking, in a transfigured way, the very pretensions of scientism that have proved impossible to realize. As positivism held forth a picture of a unifying perspective—a consistent and ideally integrative array of methods—an equally "methodized" idea of rhetoric will ultimately commit equally consequential errors.

The Methodization of Rhetoric: Trading One Piety for Another?

We began by alluding to the patriarchal depiction of rhetoric as "the harlot of the arts," and so we might end by returning to that imagery. Within the human sciences, an attitude toward knowledge has emerged that anticipates release from an unhappy marriage to method. Rhetoric is now attractive to scholars in disciplines traditionally dominated by antirhetoric. Many of these writers feel no strain of contradiction in their dalliance, for they entertain the naive hope of saving the harlot from sins only academics see as sinful. Every shave-ling wants to find the harlot's heart of gold, not really for the harlot's sake, but to vindicate his own uncertain commitment to decent society: people need only extend their working *logics* to account for those politi-cal and economic exigencies that dictate "being rhetorical"; and mov-ing from forum to academy, from bordello to bedroom, will make rhetoric amenable to the best plans and intentions of methodical, aca-demic minds. One or another "new rhetoric," the artificial separation of a "rhetoric of inquiry" from other, less noble applications, or the re-cently proliferating descriptions of "practical reasoning" might provide a new set of rules by which rhetoric could be made to play a respectable game, complementary to the highest standards of rationality.

But what ultimate frustrations can be expected if rhetoric is to be em-braced with such an attitude? If scholars' aspirations are the same as they were when scientism was embraced (if, that is, the goal of dalliance is to make the world over in an ideal image of what knowl-edge should be), it will become clear that the problems of marriage lie neither with wife nor harlot, but with professors who fetishize cer-tainty, solidarity, and other visions of purity. Some writers—certainly Jürgen Habermas and perhaps Rorty—envision a kind of rhetoric that has never existed and in all probability cannot exist. For Habermas, it would occur in an "ideal speech situation," a condition under which such things as differential power relations and the lack of truthfulness and cooperation would not "distort" the allegedly intrinsic power of persuasion. Nothing would overshadow the force of the better argu-ment.[42] For Rorty, rhetoric would arise in polite conversation, schol-arly talk governed by unspoken elitist codes of public behavior rather than by rule of reason or conventions of method. If politeness could induce compromise of self-interest and cultural prejudices, if the ideal speech situation were skillfully fabricated, some standard would of course be set, against which the shortcoming of a real rhetorical inter-action could be assessed. Even as ideals, however, both concepts are flawed, for little would remain in so airy and bloodless a world to make us take any argument seriously (even in the sciences, where, as Feyera-bend concluded, "arguments without an attitude achieve nothing").[43]

Ironically, envisioning speech (or "conversation") situations as their own ultimate context invites the nightmare of Plato's and Descartes's impossible world where speech can be depersonalized, taken out of history, and considered free from social or cultural differentiations.[44] The feasibility of such a dream is less troublesome than its pure dys-function, perhaps its wickedness, in a world that increasingly requires expertise. Power/Knowledge is an indivisible unity in a postindustrial

Michael Calvin McGee and John R. Lyne

world, a single term split asunder only at peril. To think the interests of the political economy and the interests of scholars apart, and then to idealize the interests of scholars, leads to the very gulf between technical and social reasoning that can produce the confused statistical morality of Three Mile Island. Academics tend to have much faith in the rectitude of their own vocabularies and standards of thought, disdaining to play the game of nonacademic traditions. If the rhetorical turn becomes merely an academic version of a social movement, wherein scholars claim rhetoric as *their* project, *their* intellectual cause, and not the fully interactive social process that it is, one academic piety will have been traded for another, to no clear end and with little expectation of profit.

The problem is to understand the ways in which knowledge can become embedded in broader or overlapping communities, how it can be woven into a social fabric where the life of the intellect is but one determinant of the weave. Not all reasonable processes obey a single principle (much less *our* chosen principle) of rationality.[45] Hence there is no single basis upon which all rational persons must be persuaded to accept claims on their belief, because there are diverse and competing ways of taking account of arguments. Arguments are in fact but a special case of rhetorical tactics in general (subtler forms of manipulation sometimes being far more effective), and the assumption that they will be key determinants of serious knowledge claims is unwarranted. Modeling knowledge in the image of scientific expertise (thus subordinating "common sense" to abstract theories taken on trust by the public) may be both an intellectual trap and a public disservice. Feyerabend is thus led to a kind of "anarchism," to rejection of *enforced* Platonic authority in favor of something more pragmatic. On this point, Rorty and a host of postmodernists seem in near agreement. Does it then follow that scholars should give up the very idea of authority? Must one now think of *rhetorical authority* as "anarchic," irreducible to a common standard?

The failure of authority on the Platonic model in no way signals the failure of authority on the rhetorical model; the search for a rhetorical common ground is not equivalent to the search for an epistemological foundation. Academic discourse enjoys something of a privilege in being (relatively) disengaged inquiry, somewhat sheltered from direct external pressures. The rhetorical side of the knowledge production problem is more an integrative question—that is, one of making social knowledge "count" in social contexts.[46] Rhetoric works upon recurrent and embedded conditions that do not change in the same ways that academic practices or intellectual fashions may change. If one thinks of rhetoric without a common ground, as a "free play" of the mind, it is reduced to sophistry (or poetics); and if one thinks of it as grounded in the advances it supports, it is reduced to Platonic epistemology. Profit in the rhetorical turn can be imagined only if one thinks of rhetoric as culturally grounded: it is measured by its effect, by the degree to which it creates conditions for the persuasion of an audience whose stake in the inquiries is manifest. This urges detailed attention to the conditions under which relevant publics may be addressed so as to promote the application of knowledge in action generally, with as much force outside the academy as in it. It is not enough, therefore, to appeal to some abstract notion of gentle persuasion as a principle funding the rhetoric of inquiry, as that falsely presupposes that persuasiveness per se exists and will work its way over any rational mind confronted with it.

In the space of public discussion, there are *presumptions* that constrain discourses and largely determine how they can function, and these are not usually manifest *within* the discussion. They are rather "structuring absences" that achieve or prevent efficacy for our talk. Consider, for example, a series of propositions that one might frame in consequence of understanding the "common sense" behind the political practice of American voters:

1. Personal qualities in politics are and ought to be more important than the technical competence of reasoned discourse.
2. Justification is important, not as a criterion of selection from among possible policies, but as evidence that political leaders have themselves considered all options before acting.
3. Though governments ought to act so as to respect the rights of individual citizens, social order must be maintained.
4. Though people are free to disagree about meanings and applications in particular circumstances, the basic values of liberalism are beyond criticism—people should, on principle, permanently refuse to discuss systemic alternatives to the Anglo-American political order.
5. Ideological values are, and should remain, so equivocal that their meaning must be negotiated in every critical circumstance of usage.
6. Good political speech should be grounded in traditional societal authority, constructed so that the exercise of governmental power is kept implicit in what seems to be reasoned discourse.

Michael Calvin McGee and John R. Lyne

Each of these propositions characterizes Anglo-American political rhetoric now and for the last three hundred years. And they are collectively, if not individually, at odds with the regulative ideals of the academy. The political culture, in other words, and the culture of critical discourse stand in stark contrast to one another. If we are truly willing to imagine and to construct a dialogue between rhetoric and anti-rhetoric, presumptions such as those just enumerated need to be taken seriously, and their power understood. This power is not adequately depicted, we believe, by the metaphor of conversation, which carries with it an implication that one might simply withdraw from talk that fails to meet one's expectations of it—that one might simply find a more compatible clique at the intellectual cocktail party (as it were) who will latch onto the language game one wishes to play. Such imagery is not far off the mark as a description of much academic discourse,[47] but it does not serve to underscore the responsibility we in the human sciences have to each other and to a broader public.[48] If academics "image" themselves in such a way as to make it easy freely to select pleasing interlocutors, they will have resigned themselves to the charge that what they do is *merely* talk, and they will have cut themselves off in yet another way from the broader audience that willy-nilly conceives of scholars as "the experts."

In sum, rhetoric must operate in the context of pervasive power structures, normative commitments, and practical needs; and the rhetoric of the human sciences should take note of that as its starting point. The problem is not finding with Michel Foucault that power/knowledge is a unity, and hoping that unmasking this connection is a liberation from power and passion. Rather, the human sciences should be seeking ways of managing the inevitable integration of power/knowledge within discourses that give life direction. This is what it must mean to treat knowledge claims rhetorically, if rhetoric is not to slide into sophistry, on the one hand, or become a new mode of academic self-perpetuation on the other.

NOTES

1. Kenneth Burke, *A Rhetoric of Motives* (New York: Prentice-Hall, 1950), pp. 40–46.

2. See Fred R. Dallmayr and Thomas A. McCarthy, *Understanding and Social Inquiry* (Notre Dame, Ind.: University of Notre Dame Press, 1977), p. 2, for a listing in propositional form of the principles included in this story. For more detailed and more favorable characterization, see the collection of seminal

essays in A. J. Ayer, ed., *Logical Positivism* (New York: Free Press, 1959). For a similar discussion of the principles as they apply directly to the theory and practice of discourse, see Richard Rorty, ed., *The Linguistic Turn: Recent Essays in Philosophical Method* (Chicago: University of Chicago Press, 1967).

3. Chaim Perelman and Lucie Olbrechts-Tyteca, *The New Rhetoric: A Treatise on Argumentation*, trans. John Wilkinson and Purcell Weaver (Notre Dame, Ind.: University of Notre Dame Press, 1969), pp. 2–3.

4. Alvin W. Gouldner, *The Future of Intellectuals and the Rise of the New Class* (New York: Seabury Press, 1979), p. 28.

5. See Robert L. Scott, "On Viewing Rhetoric as Epistemic," *Central States Speech Journal* 18 (1967): 9–17; and "On Viewing Rhetoric as Epistemic: Ten Years Later," *Central States Speech Journal* 27 (1976): 258–66.

6. Cf. Donald C. Bryant, "Rhetoric: Its Functions and Its Scope," *Quarterly Journal of Speech* 39 (1953): 401–24; Donald C. Bryant, *The Rhetorical Dimensions of Criticism* (Baton Rouge: Louisiana State University Press, 1973), pp. 3–23.

7. R. J. Brym, *Intellectuals and Politics* (London: Allen & Unwin, 1980), pp. 35–69; Seymour M. Lipset and Asoke Basu, "The Roles of the Intellectual and Political Roles," in Aleksander Gella, ed., *The Intelligentsia and the Intellectuals* (Beverly Hills, Calif.: Sage, 1976); Roderick Martin, *The Sociology of Power* (London: Routledge & Kegan Paul, 1977), pp. 144–60; Maurice Zeitlin, "Corporate Ownership and Control: The Large Corporations and the Capitalist Class," *American Journal of Sociology* 70 (1974) 1073–119.

8. See Michel Foucault, *Power/Knowledge*, ed. Colin Gordon, trans. Colin Gordon, Leo Marshall, John Mepham, and Kate Soper (New York: Pantheon Books, 1980), pp. 109–33; Noam Chomsky, *American Power and the New Mandarins* (New York: Pantheon Books, 1969).

9. John Dewey, *The Public and Its Problems*, 2d ed. (Chicago: Swallow Press, 1954 [orig. 1927]), pp. 208–9. See also Walter Lippmann, *Public Opinion*, reprint ed. (New York: Free Press, 1965 [orig. 1922]), pp. 233–62; Richard Sennett, *The Fall of Public Man* (New York: Random House, 1974), pp. 294–336.

10. See Lloyd F. Bitzer, "The Rhetorical Situation," *Philosophy and Rhetoric* 1 (1968): 1–14; Richard M. Weaver, *The Ethics of Rhetoric* (Chicago: Henry Regnery, 1953), pp. 55–84.

11. See Stephen Toulmin, *Human Understanding: The Collective Use and Evolution of Concepts* (Princeton: Princeton University Press, 1972), pp. 478–503; Thomas S. Kuhn, *The Structure of Scientific Revolutions*, 2d ed. (Chicago: University of Chicago Press, 1970), pp. 66–91.

12. See Calvin O. Schrag, "The Idea of the University and the Communication of Knowledge in a Technological Era," in Michael J. Hyde, ed., *Communication, Philosophy, and the Technological Age* (Tuscaloosa: University of Alabama Press, 1982), pp. 98–113; Charles Arthur Willard, *Argumentation and the Social Grounds of Knowledge* (Tuscaloosa: University of Alabama Press, 1983), pp. 134–44.

13. See W. Lance Bennett, "Storytelling in Criminal Trials: A Model of Social Judgment," *Quarterly Journal of Speech* 64 (1978): 1–22; Walter R. Fisher,

Michael Calvin McGee and John R. Lyne

"Public Moral Argument: The Nuclear Controversy," and Bruce E. Gronbeck, "Storytelling as a Mode of Moral Argument: A Response to Professor Fisher," both in David Zarefsky, Malcolm O. Sillars, and Jack Rhodes, eds., *Argumentation in Transition: Proceedings of the Third Summer Conference on Argumentation* (Annandale, Va.: Speech Communication Association, 1983), pp. 441–70: Hugh Dalziel Duncan, *Symbols in Society* (New York: Oxford University Press, 1968), pp. 112–13.

14. See Bertrand Russell, *The Scientific Outlook,* reprinted. (New York: W. W. Norton, 1962 [orig. 1931]), pp. 203–69.

15. Alasdair MacIntyre, *After Virtue: A Study in Moral Theory* (Notre Dame, Ind.: University of Notre Dame Press, 1981), p. 2.

16. Thomas B. Farrell and G. Thomas Goodnight, "Accidental Rhetoric: The Root Metaphors of Three Mile Island," *Communication Monographs* 48 (1981): 273.

17. This is not to say that one cannot *imagine* a way to collapse the social into the technical, but that such theorizing is *merely imagination,* that the attempt to create a single version of logic or method, appropriate to all exercises of human reason, has been a failure. Though success in such an enterprise is still possible in principle, it seems better to work with what presents itself in practice—namely, a dialectic of horse sense and book learning, common knowledge and expert opinion.

18. Bryant, "Functions and Scope," p. 411. Though this subject was approached by participants in the Iowa Symposium as if it were new and revolutionary, rhetoric of inquiry is, as Bryant points out, at least as old as Roman theories of invention.

19. Herbert Marcuse, *One-Dimensional Man: Studies in the Ideology of Advanced Industrial Society* (Boston: Beacon Press, 1964), p. 123.

20. Richard Rorty, *Philosophy and the Mirror of Nature* (Princeton: Princeton University Press, 1979), pp. 156–64.

21. See Alvin Gouldner, *Enter Plato* (New York: Basic Books, 1965), pp. 327–42; Jacques Derrida, *Dissemination,* trans. Barbara Johnson (Chicago: University of Chicago Press, 1981), pp. 63–171; Everett Lee Hunt, "Plato and Aristotle on Rhetoric and Rhetoricians," in *Studies in Rhetoric and Public Speaking in Honor of James Albert Winans* (New York: Century, 1925), pp. 3–60.

22. S. P. Stich and R. W. Nisbett, "Justification and the Psychology of Human Reasoning," *Philosophy of Science* 47 (1980): 198–99, point to the general inattention in epistemological literature to cognitive authorities.

23. See Niklas Luhmann, *Trust and Power,* trans. Giovanni Poggi (New York: John Wiley & Sons, 1979), pp. 109–18.

24. Interpretations of Aristotle's rhetoric underpin many contemporary explorations of what should count as knowledge in postscientistic theories of academic practice. Contrast, for example, Gadamer's evolving appropriation of what he characterizes as "Aristotelian" rhetoric with emerging "material rhetorics": Hans-Georg Gadamer, "On the Scope and Function of Hermeneutical Reflection (1967)," trans. G. B. Hess and R. E. Palmer, in David

E. Linge, ed., *Philosophical Hermeneutics* (Berkeley, Calif.: University of California Press, 1976), pp. 19–24; Hans-Georg Gadamer, *Reason in the Age of Science*, trans. Frederick G. Lawrence (Cambridge, Mass.: MIT Press, 1981), pp. 69–87; and Michael Calvin McGee, "A Materialist's Conception of Rhetoric," in Ray E. McKerrow, ed., *Explorations in Rhetoric: Studies in Honor of Douglas Ehninger* (Glenview, Ill.: Scott, Foresman, 1982), pp. 23–48.

25. See, e.g., Paul Newell Campbell, "The *Personae* of Scientific Discourse," *Quarterly Journal of Speech* 61 (1975): 391–405; Walter B. Weimer, "Science as a Rational Transaction: Toward a Non-Justificational Conception of Rhetoric," *Philosophy and Rhetoric* 10 (1977): 1–29; Michael A. Overington, "The Scientific Community as Audience: Toward a Rhetorical Analysis of Science," *Philosophy and Rhetoric* 10 (1977): 143–64. James L. Kinneavy has argued that extension of the Aristotelian schema into science is illicit, on the grounds that it "implies that the same sort of conviction is achieved in science and information and exploration as in strictly persuasive work" (*A Theory of Discourse: The Aims of Discourse* [Englewood Cliffs, N.J.: Prentice-Hall, 1971], p. 217). Our concern is not with the kind of conviction that may be achieved in scientific discourse, but with the functions it serves.

26. See, e.g., Michael Altimore, "The Rhetoric of Scientific Controversy: Recombinant DNA," manuscript, University of Iowa, 1982; Michael Altimore, "The Social Construction of a Scientific Controversy: Comments on Press Coverage of the Recombinant DNA Debate," *Science, Techology, and Human Values* 7 (1982): 24–31; Allan Mazur, *The Dynamics of Technological Controversy* (Washington, D.C.: Communications Press, 1981); John Lyne, "Ways of Going Public: The Projection of Expertise in the Sociobiology Controversy," in David Zarefsky, Malcolm Sillars, and Jack Rhodes, (eds., *Argument in Transition* (Annandale, Va.: Speech Communication Association, 1983), pp. 400–415.

27. This condition is no doubt an invitation to the devious, but there is nothing inherently devious about thinking that (even) truth needs the help of rhetoric. Philosophers from Plato to Peirce have conceded that it does, although philosophy has often maintained its self-respect by disdaining the rhetorical (with a fervency that begs for deconstruction, as Derrida has shown). See Jacques Derrida, "The White Mythology: Metaphor in the Text of Philosophy," *New Literary History* 6 (1974): 7–74.

28. Aristotle writes: "It is not true, as some writers on the art maintain, that the probity of the speaker contributes nothing to his persuasiveness; on the contrary, we might almost affirm that his character [*ethos*] is the most potent of all the means of persuasion" (*Rhetoric*, I:ii:10–15, 1356a). What seemed to count most in Aristotle's view was that an audience finally be swayed by the perception that a speaker was competent, wise, and trustworthy.

29. See Kenneth Burke's discussion of "Scope and Reduction" in *A Grammar of Motives* (New York: Prentice-Hall, 1945), pp. 59–126. Later Burke speaks of a "Hamletic" strategy of delaying embarrassing decisions in appeals to the need for more research. "In keeping with the nature of their specialties,

Michael Calvin McGee and John R. Lyne

[scientists] can gather more data and still more, to aid us in the making of wise decisions. And when the matter has been documented beyond a doubt, they may go on and document it beyond the shadow of a doubt. Assuredly, there will be something for them to do as long as the subsidies last; for no decision in the world's history was ever made on the basis of all the 'necessary facts,' nor ever will be" (p. 247).

30. An incisive history of the search for rational authority since the seventeenth century appears in William W. Bartley, III, *The Retreat to Commitment* (New York: Knopf, 1962), pp. 110ff. We should note that there are other antirhetorical stances besides the appeal to rational justification. Irrationalism, for instance, is equally antirhetorical, but falls outside the scope of the present discussion.

31. See Samuel Ijsseling, *Rhetoric and Philosophy in Conflict: An Historical Survey* (Boston: Kluwer Academic Press, 1976); Brian Vickers, "Territorial Disputes: Philosophy *versus* Rhetoric," in Brian Vickers, ed. *Rhetoric Re-Valued* (Binghampton, N.Y.: Center for Medieval and Early Renaissance Studies, 1982), pp. 247–66.

32. A classic study of the hidden rhetoric of positivistic social science is Richard Weaver, "The Rhetoric of Social Science," in *The Ethics of Rhetoric* (Chicago: Henry Regnery, 1953), pp. 186–210.

33. Anthony Giddens, *Central Problems in Social Theory: Action, Structure and Contradiction in Social Analysis* (Berkeley: University of California Press, 1979), pp. 131–64: idem, *A Contemporary Critique of Historical Materialism* (Berkeley: University of California Press, 1981), pp. 230–39.

34. See Everett Lee Hunt, "Dialectic: A Neglected Method of Argument," *Quarterly Journal of Speech* 7 (1921): 221–32. See also Hans-Georg Gadamer, *Dialogue and Dialectic: Eight Hermeneutical Studies on Plato*, trans. P. Christopher Smith (New Haven: Yale University Press, 1980); idem, *Hegel's Dialectic: Five Hermeneutical Studies*, trans. P. Christopher Smith (New Haven: Yale University Press, 1976).

35. See Richard Hofstadter, *Anti-Intellectualism in American Life*, reprint ed. (New York: Knopf, 1966 [orig. 1962]).

36. See Task Force of the Presidential Advisory Group on Anticipated Advances in Science and Technology, "The Science Court Experiment: An Interim Report," *Science* 193 (1976): 653–56. Most of the actual debate took place within the culture of critical discourse. That the wicked proposal was taken so seriously is evidence of the widespread hegemony of scientism. The Presidential Task Force had based its recommendation on a geometer's conception of the ideal alignment of competence and authority: "The Court of Science is directed at reducing the extension of authority beyond competence, which was Pascal's definition of tyranny" (p. 653). Objections raised against the court, ironically, were often on grounds that the perceived authority of such a court would likely extend beyond its competence. See Nancy Ellen Abrams and R. Stephen Berry, "Mediation: A Better Alternative to Science Courts," *Bulletin of the Atomic Scientists*, April 1977, pp. 50–53. Among advo-

cates of the Court of Science, there was some awareness of the tension between rhetorical and technical dimensions of authority, although this was simplistically characterized in terms of the harlot's "improper advances." Allan Mazur, for example, worried that "a particularly persuasive adversary might sway [seduce?] the judges more by his oratory than by his evidence, just as a successful trial lawyer can win a jury to his side more by appeals to sympathy than to logic." "Disputes Between Experts," *Minerva* 11 (1973): 262.

37. In fact, of course, technical competence and rhetorical efficacy do not closely correlate. R. Gordon Shepherd, for examples, says that in covering the issue of the safety of marijuana smoking, the media relied principally on "celebrity" scientists rather than those who had done actual research in the area—with the full cooperation of the celebrity scientists, of course. See "Selectivity of Sources: Reporting the Marijuana Controversy," *Journal of Communication* 31 (1981): 128–37.

38. See Lois S. Self, "Rhetoric and *Phronesis:* The Aristotelian Ideal," *Philosophy and Rhetoric* 12 (1979): 130–45; Hans-Georg Gadamer, *Truth and Method,* trans. and ed. Garrett Barden and John Cumming (New York: Crossroad, 1982), pp. 278–305; Richard J. Bernstein, "From Hermeneutics to *Praxis,*" *Review of Metaphysics* 35 (1982): 823–45.

39. See Prentice A. Meador, Jr., "Quintilian's *vir bonus,*" *Western Journal of Speech Communication* 34 (1970): 162–69; George Kennedy, *The Art of Rhetoric in the Roman World* (Princeton: Princeton University Press, 1972), pp. 496–514; Donald Lemen Clark, *Rhetoric in Greco-Roman Education* (New York: Columbia University Press, 1957), pp. 178–212.

40. See Hans-Georg Gadamer, "Hermeneutics and Social Science," *Cultural Hermeneutics* 2 (1975): 307–16; Gadamer, *Reason in the Age of Science,* pp. 1–20, 69–87.

41. Richard Rorty, "Relativism," Howison Lecture, University of California at Berkeley, January 31, 1983.

42. For the critique of Habermas' conception from the perspective of rhetorical theory, see Thomas B. Farrell, "The Ideality of Meaning in Argument: A Revision of Habermas," in George Ziegelmueller and Jack Rhodes, eds., *Dimensions of Argument: Proceedings of the Summer Conference on Argumentation* (Annandale, Va.: Speech Communication Association—American Forensic Association, 1981), pp. 905–22.

43. Paul K. Feyerabend, *Science in a Free Society* (London: NLB Verso Editions, 1978), p. 61.

44. There is considerable irony in associating Rorty at all with such a tendency, since this "dream" is the object of much polemical attack on his part. We only wish to point out that one rhetorical implication of "seeing *conversation* as the ultimate context within which knowledge is to be understood" (Rorty, *Mirror of Nature,* p. 389) may be to *isolate* talk from other social practices. What gives the academy its significance in the political economy is that its mysterious talk has positive consequences, in growing and useful technologies, in "hard data" that decision-makers can use to fool themselves and

Michael Calvin McGee and John R. Lyne

the public into thinking that elements of ideology are irrelevant in formulating policy. If academics claim no more than "conversational solidarity" as their product, an open invitation has been extended to political anti-intellectualism.

45. On the contrast between abstract versions of rationality and concrete reasonableness, see Chaim Perelman, "The Rational and the Reasonable," in Theodore F. Geraets, ed., *Rationality Today* (Ottawa: University of Ottawa Press, 1979), pp. 212–19.

46. Anthony Giddens speaks of the need to account for the practical knowledge that enables members of a society chronically to reproduce the structures of that society; we believe his account of "structuration" is, in the main, consistent with the view taken here. See *Central Problems in Social Theory.*

47. See Robert Hariman, "The *Professional* Scholar?" paper presented at the Seminar on Continental Philosophy and the American Rhetorical Tradition, Speech Communication Association, Washington, D.C., November 1983.

48. Rorty's imagery of the polite conversation, in which voices are held in dialogue more by civility than by common purpose, permits little more generalization than the claim that discourses will be judged according to prevailing social practices, and that they require the absence of heavy-handed external influences, conjured imagistically as "the police" (*Mirror of Nature,* pp. 357–94). This modest bow to the relevance of social conditions seriously underestimates the pervasive structuring influences of social power—influences that shape a discourse without actually entering it. Contrast the Rorty "police" metaphor with José Ortega y Gasset, *Man and People,* trans. Willard R. Trask (New York: W. W. Norton, 1957), pp. 171–221.

22 SEVEN RHETORICS OF INQUIRY

A PROVOCATION

JOHN S. NELSON

The eye's plain version is a thing apart,
the Vulgate of experience. Of this,
A few words, an and yet, and yet, and yet—[1]

Modern epistemology legitimates little more than the plain motion of bodies seen by an eye always distant. It turns them into literal signs that report or process facts to inform behavior, and it avoids figural symbols that narrate or dramatize truths to perform action. Thus it celebrates *logos* and pursues logic of inquiry to the virtual exclusion of other dimensions and domains of knowing. For the same reasons, it denigrates *mythos* and eschews rhetoric of inquiry as the virtual opposite of rational principles and products of learning.

The respectable grounds of modern research are logics, linguistics, mathematics, and statistics. Modernists take them to promise the certain foundations of science required for progress against tradition, emotion, nature, and strife. Yet modern sciences and philosophies have begun to lead beyond themselves. Darwin's account of natural selection, Einstein's theory of relativity, Heisenberg's principle of uncertainty, Gödel's limit on formalization, Quine's critique of empiricism, Kuhn's history of scientific revolutions: a century and more of such developments are moving us toward a new knowledge of reality. Coupled with changes of culture, economy, environment, and polity, these and related initiatives are slowly unsettling the modern academy. They have even started to transform the social sciences and logic of inquiry—among the latest, if not the last, citadels of modernism. As we recognize how grounds of inquiry must slip and shift, we replace modern aspirations to transcendental criteria of methodology and rationality with postmodern explorations in limited standards of persuasion and reason.

John S. Nelson

Enter rhetoric of inquiry. As postmodern epistemology, it replaces logic of inquiry by pluralizing, incorporating, and contextualizing modern grounds of research—not by eliminating them. But what does this mean? What, concretely, is rhetoric of inquiry? The volume at hand is an early answer, yet its very profusion of specifics may reassert the question on another level. To read the preceding essays as exercises in rhetoric of inquiry is to wonder what joins their diverse arguments about major issues of study in many fields. How are the essays all experiments in rhetoric of inquiry? The authors pursue strikingly different senses and strategies of rhetoric. They address immensely various subjects and situations. They encourage sharply separate questions and urge highly disparate conclusions. Where do they converge on a common field? What problematics do they share? And why?

More than aversion to modern epistemology, these and other essays in the rhetoric of the human sciences share a concern for aesthetics, dialectics, ethics, politics, and other postmodern grounds of inquiry. They recognize that logics, linguistics, mathematics, and statistics must figure importantly in good research and argument. But they insist that such modern grounds must acknowledge limits and origins as never before. They realize that modern grounds cannot meet modern demands for certainty and should not always try to satisfy modern cravings for generality. They appreciate that postmodern grounds tend to constitute modern ones, as much as or more than the other way around. Often as not, aesthetics and dialectics produce logics and statistics, while ethics and politics govern the use of linguistics and mathematics. Thus the essays here reach for archeologies, genealogies, hermeneutics, semiotics, and other recent inventions to supplant, correct, or augment modern epistemics. Disagreements among these approaches should not obscure their common dedication to improve not only the conception but also the conduct of the human sciences. Nor should specific disputes occlude their commitment to put all academic inquiry on better terms with public affairs.[2]

Rhetoric of inquiry anticipates these advantages for all fields of inquiry, but especially for the humanities and social sciences. Speaking generally, the gains would probably be greatest in the social sciences because they are the disciplines most affected by misleading logics of inquiry and most perplexed by questions of application in public affairs. The arts and academized professions such as law, business, medicine, and engineering have been less impeded by attention to formalist philosophies of inquiry. They also have been less troubled by problems of authority or expertise in practice—the arts, presumably, because they claim so little, and the professions because they enjoy so much.

But these fields, too, would benefit considerably from turning toward the alternate grounds of research recommended by rhetoric of inquiry. Even the physical, biological, and logical sciences (such as mathematics, statistics, linguistics, and artificial intelligence) could manage to learn from more attention to the rhetoric of inquiry. For reasons of economy in exposition and credibility in argument, though, let me follow this volume's focus on the human sciences—where I perceive the most to be at stake and where I make my academic home.[3]

Negative arguments for rhetoric of inquiry explain how academic arrogance and practical incompetence have come to characterize modern epistemology and its application in academic studies of human affairs. Positive arguments show how rhetoric of inquiry can improve current and future research. In my judgment, the foregoing essays advance both sorts of arguments in ways at once persuasive and provocative. As a result, however, they raise all the more urgently the question of what they have in common. If the answer is rhetoric of inquiry, then they ask all the more pointedly what it is. And if the further response is that it studies and practices postmodern grounds of research, then the question becomes what they are and how they cohere in curing ills of modern epistemology. Thus I argue that the previous essays identify at least seven grounds of postmodern research and that these seven coalesce into a discrete set of epistemics that it is reasonable to call *rhetoric of inquiry*. What may seem initially to be seven separate grounds of research converge as seven rhetorics of inquiry—so that postmodern poetics, tropics, topics, dialectics, hermeneutics, ethics, and politics of inquiry display their interdependence under the rubric of rhetoric.

Unitary talk about rhetoric of inquiry allows summary references to all postmodern grounds of research, and it provides polemical reminders of their convergence. Still, my argument depends as much on distinguishing as on conjoining the seven (or more) dimensions of rhetoric in research. For I contend also that the first five dimensions privilege the last two. Thus the poetics, tropics, topics, dialectics, and hermeneutics of research encourage us to emphasize the ethics and politics of inquiry. This confutes many (though not all) aspects of modernism in the self-conception of scholars, and it contravenes some (but far from all) practices in recent research. The ethics and politics of inquiry carry out the rhetorical concern for standards and strategies of study, and they also confirm the rhetorical commitment to better research and better relations with the wider society.[4]

In part, therefore, my argument is also a plea to rethink relations between the academy and the polity. In particular it is a program to put the postmodern multiversity into more direct and responsible contact with

ethics and politics.[5] In some respects it is a proposal to ethicize and politicize the human sciences. But mostly it is a recommendation to improve
how the human sciences are already ethicized and politicized.

To detail this argument would require myriad qualifications and refinements now omitted for the sake of brevity and clarity. Somewhat in
the style of Richard Rorty, the full argument would inventory defects in
the philosophy of inquiry—tracing each to antirhetorical premises
about the places and properties of logics, linguistics, mathematics, statistics, and other modern foundations for research.[6] After the fashions
of Michael Leff, Richard Brown, and Gerald Bruns, it would study the
history of hostility between rhetoric and philosophy, with special attention to the tandem development of analytical philosophy and the
social sciences.[7] It would produce accounts, akin to that of Philip Davis
and Reuben Hersh, of how modern foundations prove rhetorical. It
would also explore how ignoring this has led social scientists, especially, to rely on such poor practices of inquiry as the uncritical use of
mathematics and statistics to slip past troubles entailed by defective
philosophical rhetorics.[8]

The argument would also tie many achievements and failures of the
recent sciences of humanity to various rhetorical principles, processes,
and projects. In the volume at hand, this concern is evident in the essays by John Campbell, Donal Carlston, David Klemm, and me.[9] In
modes comparable to those used by Charles Bazerman and Arjo
Klamer, the argument would identify differences among fields of inquiry as contrasts of rhetorical strategy.[10] It would explore public implications of academic discourse—as do Charles Anderson, Jean
Elshtain, John Lyne, Michael McGee, and Michael Shapiro. Like Misia
Landau, Renato Rosaldo, and James White, the argument would emphasize ways to improve current rhetorics. And like Paul Hernadi,
Donald McCloskey, and Allan Megill, it would distinguish competing
rhetorics, comparing their advantages and disadvantages across diverse contexts of inquiry.[11]

Even then, the argument would barely have begun. A single essay
cannot hope to provide a general justification for the primacy of rhetoric in the study and practice of inquiry. Nor can it expect to specify
even the main reasons for construing rhetoric in at least seven related
ways—not to mention the major implications of emphasizing the ethics
and politics of inquiry over other rhetorical dimensions of research. In
fact, almost any rhetoric would imply that such tasks are beyond the
capacity of a single scholar—let alone a single essay.

Since this essay is bound to be more provocative than argumentative,
I pursue its aims as much through poetry as prose. Poetics of inquiry is

no more limited to exploring what poets have written about learning than rhetoric of inquiry is restricted to applying what rhetoricians have said about research. Even so, poets are probably at least as profound as the rest of us in the study and practice of inquiry. In particular, therefore, this essay relies amply on the poetry of Wallace Stevens, arguably a giant among recent students of inquiry. As Stevens said, "The great well of Poetry is not other poetry but prose: reality. However, it requires a poet to perceive the poetry in reality."[12] His poetic words show acutely how the conditions and needs of research now return us to poetics and other rhetorics of inquiry, and they state well the ambition of philosophy and science as favored forms of modern inquiry. More skillfully still, his poetic lines imply the pure paradox of this aspiration: it would reflect to transcend reflection, speak to pass beyond speech, and banish poetry to produce "the poem of pure reality, untouched by trope or deviation."[13]

Accordingly I deploy the poetry of Stevens to evoke connections, themes, and theses that the essay needs to acknowledge but cannot detail. For related reasons, I let the previous essays provide much of my evidence. I rely also on the reflexivity of rhetoric, which inevitably tends to make every essay on rhetoric of inquiry into a small demonstration of the various rhetorics evident in research. To sketch seven senses of rhetoric is a good way to say what rhetoric of inquiry is, what it can become, and why. First, though, let me say a little more about what rhetoric of inquiry is not, by contrasting it to modern logic of inquiry.

Logics

The plainness of plain things is savagery,
As: the last plainness of a man who has fought
Against illusion and was, in a great grinding

Of growling teeth, and falls at night, snuffed out
By the obese opiates of sleep. Plain men in plain towns
Are not precise about the appeasement they need.

From the time when philosophy repudiated poetry and rhetoric in order to pursue ideals of pure rationality, the relationship of epistemology to the rest of human endeavor has become ever more troubled. As specific sciences and other distinct fields of substantive inquiry have formed, the field of philosophy has constricted. Professional philosophy has become increasingly abstract, especially in its treatment of inquiry. Seeking olympian heights and alchemic depths, too much of it grows distant from substantive disciplines, everyday understandings, and actual issues in research. It slips toward preoccupation with uncontextual epistemology, universal valuation, and other metatheoretical inquires.[14]

Thus has philosophy come increasingly to comprehend itself as the study of the roots of knowledge, as the authoritative assessment of first principles, as the rational reconstruction of argumentative and imaginative forms, or as the systematic critique of presuppositions. In the conceptions of rationality which dominate current philosophy can be seen much the same commitment—lately strengthened, if anything—that led Plato and Aristotle to subordinate poetry and rhetoric to philosophy and dialectic. The distinctive concerns of the poets and sophists—whether ancient or modern—remain peripheral to recent philosophy. Indeed, they become compatible with modern epistemology only insofar as they turn out to be capable of analysis in terms of philosophical commitments to proof rather than persuasion, literality rather than figurality, science rather than myth, and reason rather than emotion or imagination. Whereas most poetics and rhetorics would realign or undermine these sorts of oppositions, most modern philosophies have reinforced and extended them.[15]

Not only have theories and controversies of rationality become the heart as well as the head of recent philosophy, but abstraction from substantive discourse is turning the study of rationality ever more back upon itself. Philosophical epistemology is losing contact with the substantive inquiry that it purports to "reconstruct," seeking first (or instead) to shore up its own resources of rationality. Without philosophical ideas of inquiry that are inspired either explicitly or implicitly by models from formal logic, the relevance of recent epistemologies to actual research is left in limbo. And when rhetorics are recognized to constitute logics, as much or more than the other way around, then modern philosophy finds that its epistemic foundations lose their reliability as well as their priority.

In defense of modern philosophy, I must add that both its formalisms and its epistemological obsessions only echo concerns and commitments that resonate throughout modern culture.[16] Stevens himself was well aware of the needs and dangers behind the generally self-reflective and specifically epistemic temper of the times. In fact, the lines quoted here from Stevens suggest that our penchant for abstraction and our fascination with form are well embodied within his poetry—a paradox of some significance.

Still, Stevens insisted on something that late-modern philosophies of science too readily forget: the acute, often ironical reflection and self-scrutiny now surfeit in society as well as philosophy were meant to serve, not themselves primarily, but what Stevens summoned as "a new knowledge of reality."[17] The purpose of our philosophies may be to root out, seek out, or reconcile uncertainties, yet we must resist temptations to retreat from reality just as strenuously as we must reject tendencies to embrace it uncritically and unimaginatively. The idolizations of reality counseled by Stevens's arch enemies, the "rigid realists,"[18] stay less in tune with changing realities than his "blue guitar" of postmodern poetry. It "becomes the place of things as they are" precisely because "things as they are / are changed upon the blue guitar."[19]

Recent rhetoricians have argued, and the foregoing essays testify, that rhetoric is epistemic.[20] If so, then rhetoric—rather than logic or some equivalent—should form the grounds of postmodern epistemology. Recognizing this is a step toward saving epistemology and philosophy of inquiry from their confusion and sterility in much of the twentieth century. Here the claim concerns the general enterprise of rhetoric rather than any particular rhetoric of inquiry, and the preceding essays suggest that a variety of rhetorics can generate insights into our inquiries.

The declaration that rhetoric is epistemic might be construed as a call to replace philosophy of science with rhetoric of inquiry. The ancient and, in some cases, continuing hostility of philosophers toward rhetoric would encourage that interpretation. Yet the more specific opponent is logic of inquiry, in the singular and relentlessly abstracting style that loses the reality and substance of research. Indeed, renewed recognition that rhetoric is epistemic owes much to the work of some recent philosophers. For present purposes, therefore, a better interpretation would be that a logic of inquiry already pluralizing itself should be complemented by diverse rhetorics of inquiry. Or we might also say that modern epistemology and philosophy of science should yield to postmodern philosophies of inquiry that accept and, in some cases, even celebrate rhetoric.

The new philosophies of inquiry must situate themselves in actual contexts of research. They must explore the twilight zone between abstracted logics and detailed arguments. Rather than deduce general rules for all research, they must produce particular comparisons of inquiries that might learn from one another. Rather than transform substantive issues into philosophical questions, they must reform philosophical analysis into substantive argument. Rather than remain a discipline apart, they must become a part of all other disciplines.

Forgetting how logics are artifacts of rhetorics, even the latest of modern epistemologies end in perplexity. At best, they generate ironies born of the modern quest for a scientific rationality that could be disembodied, unemotional, noncontextual, and apolitical—but still could comprehend human beings. One irony of recent logical positivisms and empiricisms is that their modern realism tends to produce unrealistic accounts of research, a major theme in most of the preceding essays. This is especially evident in the numerous myths of Scientific Method still propagated through logics of inquiry—another irony in light of the modern intention to demarcate and propagate the features that separate science (in the singular) from myth, speculation, and other forms of selective perception.[21]

If sciences are conceived as kinds of inquiry that lead humans reliably toward truths, then sciences must make substantive arguments for their specific claims. Historians of science show repeatedly that scientists seldom—if ever—settle significant controversies through appeals to formal logics that the disputants agree are to govern their decisions. As a discipline of argument, rhetoric shows repeatedly that no fixed set of utterly formal tests for adequate argumentation can decide well—if at all—in many conflicts over substantive claims. The search for strictly formal criteria for the existence of science—let alone purely formal rules for the conduct of science—is bound to fail unless all sciences prove to have essentially one substance: a grandly unified content grasped by some omniscient being.

Rhetoric of inquiry neither wants nor needs to banish logic of inquiry; instead the challenge is to pluralize it. Once we accept with Willard Quine and others that interdependence of form and content is a formal, analytical necessity, we have reason to accept sciences in the plural. Then when we reconstruct scientific logics without reducing them to a single form, we will remain entangled in their diverse, substantive particulars. We will realize that we are outlining aspects of their arguments—of their rhetorics. We will remember that, even within a single science, the logics must remain plural as long as the discipline avoids monism and dogmatism. And we will recognize that it is not mere poetry to regard those logics as only some of the poetic forms properly apparent in rational inquiry.

Poetics

Inescapable romance, inescapable choice
Of dreams, disillusion as the last illusion,
Reality as a thing seen by the mind,

Not that which is but that which is apprehended,
A mirror, a lake of reflections in a room,
A glassy ocean lying at the door,

A great town hanging pendent in a shade,
An enormous nation happy in a style,
Everything as unreal as real can be,

In the inexquisite eye. Why, then, inquire
Who has divided the world, what entrepreneur?

If logics of inquiry outline structures of argumentation, then poetics of inquiry locate origins of explanation. Construed broadly, poetics of inquiry would include explicit tropes of research as well as the implicit styles that could be said to create them. To identify distinct rhetorics of inquiry, however, it is useful to save studies of the details and effects of explicit figures for the separate category of tropics. Then poetics of inquiry confine themselves to comprehending how specific figures of research arise, reproduce, and decline. Tropics of inquiry address overt or patent characters (economic man), images (equilibria), models (free markets), statistics (significance tests), and other figures of research. Poetics of inquiry assess covert assumptions and latent figures to discern how they contribute to forming the particular, readily apparent tropes that configure reasoning and communication.

Construed narrowly, poetics explore the beginnings of experience and the (re)sources of expression.[22] Poetics generate and appreciate the *pre*suppositions and *pre*figurations of language or thought. Poetics of inquiry do the same for research. Prefigurations are the ordinarily inarticulate figures that influence the typically articulate ones. They arise and are known through extended discourses of language, bodies of literature, and fields of research. Single texts are seldom enough to warrant inferences from foreground tropes to background figures. To separate surfaces from depths usually requires comparing many related appearances. Yet poetically potent texts evoke their backgrounds almost before their foregrounds can be grasped in detail. Thus do the exemplars that precipitate Thomas Kuhn's scientific revolutions create conviction for their early converts, even before the new paradigms can produce enough specifics to achieve persuasion through the presentation of detailed alternatives.

Moved to reflect on the current proliferation of books about the poetics of various human activities and sciences, Anatole Broyard proposes that it might express recent disillusionment with the modernist ideal of science.

"We've come to realize that much of science—especially social science—is only debased poetry, a mixture of metaphors, images and ambitious language." He muses that "the passion for poetics sounds like a welcoming of feelings, especially irrational ones"; and he invokes T. S. Eliot's test of genuine poetry, which "can communicate before it is understood."[23] In addressing this property of poetry, poetics become at least anticipations of the previously unspecified, often explorations of the seemingly ineffable, and sometimes communications of the formerly inexpressible. Directed toward research, these facilities make poetics of inquiry into studies of the elements, influences, or processes of imagination and inspiration that modernist logics of inquiry would consign to the supposedly ineluctable or insignificant context of discovery.

Comparison across many texts and contexts is the hallmark of five postmodern theorists of inquiry notable for practicing poetics in this strict sense. Interest in "collective representations" led Owen Barfield to distinguish "figuration" (as their initial apprehension) from subsequent "alpha-thinking" (as cognition about them) and "beta-thinking" (as reflection on their nature). The notion of figuration as perception prior to cognition led him in turn to portray the study of meaning as "poetic diction."[24] Exploration of "tacit knowledge" spurred Michael Polanyi to a "post-critical" theory of "personal knowedge" that encompasses scientific and other kinds of inquiry.[25] Stephen Pepper's analysis of "root metaphors" and "world hypotheses" attempts to explicate diffuse structures of evaluation and judgment that shape human experience.[26] In distinguishing Metaphor, Metonymy, Synecdoche, and Irony as the "four master tropes," Kenneth Burke tries to explain the sources and uses of more specific figures of speech and action.[27] Hayden White's scheme of *Metahistory* coordinates the categories of Pepper and Burke with basic figures from Northrop Frye and Karl Mannheim to reveal the "prefiguration of the phenomenal field" addressed by contrasting works of history.[28]

Such theories differ in their specific purposes as well as their particular dynamics of perception and inspiration. Yet they unite as poetics of inquiry in a common concern for the origins of knowledge and intellectual commitment. Moreover, as White discerns, a shared interest in prefiguration—in the coordinating figures behind, beneath, or within the manifest figures—inclines their poetical patterns to be complementary or reinforcing. Of the several essays in this volume that touch on issues of prefiguration, surely Hernadi's argument about understanding, overstanding, and standing-in-for most directly addresses rhetoric of inquiry at this level of poetics.

From Aristotle to the present, poetics have also included theories of genre, narrative, and drama. These may be construed as theories of prefiguration because they explicate the basic conventions or deep structures of various kinds of texts. Such theories try to account for the constraints, choices, and effects of particular texts and kinds of texts, especially in interplay with one another. By noting changes in the *Publication Manual* of the American Psychological Association, Bazerman traces alterations in the discipline's genre of the research report, and from them he infers changes in the presuppositions of American psychological research. By showing how paleoanthropology depends on implicit and often implausible stories, Landau impels her colleagues to become more critical about their suppressed narratives, and she may help them to create more sophisticated plots. Much the same could be said of the argument that I make for attending to stories and tropes in political science, or of the case that Elshtain advances for augmenting the main paradigms of rhetoric for research in women's studies.

If a poetic produces and comprehends presuppositions and prefigurations, a rhetoric could be said to select and develop them for purposes of action. Then poetic is the domain of expression and communication, whereas rhetoric is the realm of persuasion and motivation. Yet the two interact so much, especially in improving inquiry, that each usually calls forth or even becomes the other. To understand and evaluate meanings adequately, poetics of inquiry recurrently find themselves exploring implications for persuasion and motivation. Likewise, to comprehend and assess arguments thoroughly, rhetorics of inquiry repeatedly find themselves investigating dynamics of expression and communication. Swayed by Burke, in fact, many theorists of literature and communication long ago assimilated poetic to rhetoric, and vice versa. The two share an insistence on respect for myth, emotion, and imagination as integral to human understanding. Rather than renounce literality, logicality, or rationality, poetics and rhetorics merge in pluralizing and situating these modes of analysis within wider webs of capacities and commitments. The same goes for tropics as the study of explicit figures of language and argument.

Tropics

Reality is the beginning not the end,
Naked Alpha, not the hierophant Omega,
Of dense investiture, with luminous vassals.

. . . .
But that's the difference: in the end and the way
To the end. Alpha continues to begin.
Omega is refreshed at every end.

Tropics of inquiry study the explicit figures of language and argument in research. If modern epistemology tends to ignore implicit figures, genres, and stories in research, it typically scorns explicit tropes—dismissing figuration as mere ornamentation or obfuscation. It stipulates (but never demonstrates) that all figures of speech can be translated into literal language without any loss or alteration of meaning. It insists that cogent metaphors, metonymies, oxymorons, hyperboles, ironies, synecdoches, and all other tropes can be transliterated completely. They may provide colorful language or convenient abbreviations, but they contribute nothing lasting or essential to research. Modern language need retain no vagueness or ambiguity. Logics, mathematics, statistics, and other formal languages become the grounds of modern inquiry because they seem to promise media that stay transparent and precise enough to literalize anything worth saying about the world. Seeking utter specificity in all statements, such literalism would reduce all figural language to straightforward prose.

To be sure, literalism and modern epistemology are themselves textures of tropes—most evoking clarity of vision, as Stevens suggested. But their troubles run deeper than surface inconsistency. Such opponents of literalism as Max Black have produced many persuasive arguments that transliteration without loss of meaning is impossible in principle.[29] Worse, modern sciences turn out to rely heavily and irreducibly on patent tropes, especially metaphors.[30] And if that were not scandalous enough, modern epistemologists are beginning to concede that variance in the meaning of key terms shared by competing theories is virtually inevitable. Yet this implies that literality is tacitly plural and that even the most modern of literalities may be regarded as relatively stable (or stale?) networks of figures.[31]

Accordingly, tropics of inquiry consider investigators' descriptions, explanations, and theories as sets of tropes. As figures of language, these tools and products of inquiry evoke the directions, conditions, aporias, and repressions that structure inquiry—and provoke deconstructivists to ply their trade. In this volume, McCloskey and Megill trod the constructive path, exploring figures of speech among historians to ascertain how they conceive issues and persuade readers. By contrast, Shapiro romps through a deconstruction of unacknowledged tropes in the political science of James Q. Wilson, revealing tropal subtexts that contradict and indict the surface positions. Both approaches show how lively attention to figures of language should inform the study and practice of inquiry in the human sciences.

Beyond tropes of language, however, there are also tropes of argument; and they prove just as crucial to rhetorics of inquiry. Since Aristotle, tropes of argument have often been mistaken for elliptical arguments—omitting steps that could be supplied or condensing ones that could be specified, were the details needed enough to repay the effort. But this is just another version of literalism, for it assumes that anything and everything meritorious or meaningful in an argument can be stated fully in transparent prose—subject only to limits of time, material, and talent. Like figures of speech, figures of inference instead comprise irreducible expressions essential to argumentation and inquiry. Taking human limits of time, material, and talent seriously enough to internalize them, argumentative tropes seek necessary economies of reason in a world of scarcity. They cannot be transliterated without loss or alteration of reasoning.

Where modern epistemology sees grounds and methods of inference, postmodern epistemology often recognizes tropes of argument. They include turning information into statistical data, translating explanations into formal languages, representing relationships as models, transforming assumptions into ideal types, conducting experiments through intellection, selecting evidence through sampling principles, defining variables by anecdotes, and so on through a variety of figures apparent in recent research. Sometimes we identify fields by their distinctive tropes of argument: economics by its model of economic man, sociology by its ideal type of society, psychology by its statistics of significance. Still, figures of inference originated in one field are soon borrowed by others, aptly or not.

However necessary, tropes of argument remain subject to abuse, and they can suffer all the fallacies noted by logicians as well as the infelicities identified by rhetoricians. Thus diehard literalists condemn argumentative figures for tending to conceal missteps that cost far more than tropes can save by economizing on a few sound steps. Perhaps the best response to that danger lies in staying sensitive to potential abuses while continuing to acknowledge the argumentative need for tropes. Even so, the modest contextualism implicit in reasoning by tropes cautions against categorical proscription of specific fallacies, which occasionally turn out to be defensible inferences.[32] Moreover, fallacies often call forth tropes of argument as responses to recurrent challenges to reasoning. For example, compositional and ecological fallacies loom so large in the social sciences because social scientists repeatedly need to reason from aggregate to individual characteristics or from parts to wholes. Through principles, statistics, ideal types, and other tropes of arguments, social scientists try to forge links strong enough to support inferences across such levels of analysis. A different kind of example might be the pathetic fallacy often criticized by students of literature but usually taken by authors as a task to be negotiated with literary skill.

Fallacies and infelicities are not the only troubles that beset figures of argument. The human sciences suffer at least three main abuses of inferential tropes that twist them into tokens, detours, and traps of argument. By defining these abuses in principle, I advance them as three further tropes of argument. (Consequently tokens, detours, and traps—like the related tropes of fallacies and infelicities—can occasionally serve inquiry well in odd contexts; but here we need not detail that complication.) Working to recognize and counter these abuses is a major way for rhetorics of inquiry to improve the conduct and content of everyday inquiry in substantive disciplines.

When tropes replace—rather than accomplish—argument, they function merely as tokens. In my experience, this typically happens when a particular trope becomes so familiar to researchers that they cease to consider its proper purposes and limits. Then invoking a statistic, following an exemplar, citing a principle, or telling an anecdote that has been used well many times before in similar situations can substitute for an argument rather than providing one. It can stop—rather than stimulate—the critical production of reasons. As White suggests in this volume, rule-analysis often slips from a trope to a token of legal argumentation. Klamer identifies tokens of argument in economics, and the "rhetorical mathematics" excoriated by Davis and Hersh could surely count as tokens of inference in social science. Tropes become tokens when they suppress argument instead of creating it.

Tropes become detours when they deflect argument into irrelevancies. Done intentionally, the purpose is often to secure undue advantage in argument. Yet I suspect that the human sciences suffer detours less from outright manipulation than from gradual misdirection of argument. In political science, for instance, the appeal to epistemology has become a prominent trope of argument. For some substantive issues of political study, it is indispensable as well as economical.[33] For many uses, however, the trope becomes a detour from issues important to political science—let alone politics: scholars become engrossed in epistemic issues that may have been irrelevant to politics even in the beginning and that in any event lead relentlessly away from political questions rather than rejoining them.[34] Often the human sciences invoke foundational principles from philosophy as argumentative tropes to certify a position or defend a method, only to become caught in a morass of modern epistemology instead of pursuing substantive concerns. McGee and Lyne are right to caution in this volume against allowing rhetoric of inquiry to turn into a similar detour, but we should note also the intimation here by Campbell that Darwin became bogged down in an attempt to avoid acknowledging the postpositivist principles of his biology. One way or another, figures of inference sometimes contort into detours of argument.

We need argumentative tropes to cope with the openness demanded by inquiry. They constrain and direct reasoning enough to make needed connections—sometimes anticipated, sometimes surprising—without foreclosing the criticism or further inference that might overturn present conclusions. Even tropes can become traps of argument, however, because their constraint and direction are no less real for acknowledging limits. When a field favors only a few figures of argument, insufficient for addressing its subjects, then it becomes trapped by its tropes.[35] Traps are especially hard to recognize from within, since their victims mistake the exclusion of competing perspectives and evidence for the absence of anomalies that would call their research into question. Shapiro's portrait of political science might imply that it suffers from an insufficiency of argumentative—as well as linguistic—tropes. Another vivid instance in this volume of rhetorical attacks on inferential traps is Rosaldo's case for a reversal of inferential figures in anthropology: turning the discipline's tropes of estrangement back on anthropologists in order to spring them from a recurrent trap of argument in ethnography.

Topics

> The objects tingle and the spectator moves
> With the objects. But the spectator also moves
> With lesser things, with things exteriorized
>
> Out of rigid realists. It is as if
> Men turning into things, as comedy,
> Stood, dressed in antic symbols, to display
>
> The truth about themselves, having lost, as things,
> That power to conceal they had as men,

Just as issues of prefiguration lead easily into questions of figuration, reflections about how (or how not) to deploy tropes

John S. Nelson

quickly become considerations of the strategies and tactics of argumentation. Since Aristotle, to investigate the differences among and uses of common lines of argument has been to study the topics of argument (or *topoi*, for short and to retain the Greek plural—the equivalent of replacing "tropics" with *tropoi*). Shall we argue by defining terms, analyzing opposites, creating correlatives, building part by part to the whole, noting possible motives, citing consequences, or developing contradictions? To assess the advantages or disadvantages of these and like techniques in research is to pursue topics of inquiry. Even today, when people discuss rhetoric without intending to disparage the referent, they usually mean matters of topics; and surely these must remain central to rhetoric of inquiry.[36]

Despite recent preoccupations with method, such specifically rhetorical issues about strategies and tactics seldom receive the attention that they deserve in the human sciences. Viewing methods as machines that secure impersonal conclusions, modernist scholars debate the suitability of different lines of analysis only in terms of their ability to satisfy the (methodo)logical standards supplied by disciplinary conventions or the epistemological rules supposed to stand behind them. By contrast, topics treat methods as paths that produce personal persuasions. Topics concern not only techniques of argument about the objects of study but also modes of relationship among the students, the objects, and the further audiences for the inquiry. Whereas modernist methods express general rules of inference, topics emphasize the needs of particular speakers to persuade particular audiences of particular claims—while remaining open to counterargument and cooperative discussion. As a result, the strategies and tactics addressed by postmodern topics of inquiry range far beyond the crimped domain of modern methodologies.

An obvious example is topical attention to the rhetorical ethos or credibility of speakers—their standing in relationship to their messages and audiences. If the book at hand were to address scholars throughout the human sciences by parading before them only professional rhetoricians, its rhetorical analysis might be more sophisticated in places, but its ethos of special interest would probably leave the book largely unread. Or if read, its ethos of ill-reputed outsiders (from rhetoric) preaching to respected insiders (from the fields addressed) about how to conduct the latter's business would likely make the message incredible. When diverse but highly reputed insiders attempt some of the same arguments, however, their cases carry far greater conviction.

Such rhetorical considerations receive little attention and less legitimacy from modernist methods in the human sciences, even though they repeatedly find rhetorical considerations to be immensely important in human affairs. While Bazerman shows in these pages how modern psychology preempts topical choices in journal writing, Carlston explains how the resulting research testifies time and again to their inescapable significance in virtually all human endeavor. Of course, Carlston's is not the only chapter here to suggest immense commonalities of subject matter between the dimensions of rhetoric and the disciplines of human science. In different ways, Bruns and White each establish convergence between rhetoric and law, Anderson analyzes politics in rhetorical terms, Rosaldo hints at a distinctively rhetorical conception of culture, and Klemm does the same for theology. These substantive ties should help to keep rhetoric of inquiry from becoming a detour of argument for the human sciences.

Dialectics

We keep coming back and coming back
To the real: to the hotel instead of the hymns
That fall upon it out of the wind. We seek

The poem of pure reality, untouched
By trope or deviation, straight to the word,
Straight to the transfixing object, to the object

At the exactest point at which it is itself,
Transfixing by being purely what it is,
A view of new Haven, say, through the certain eye,

The eye made clear of uncertainty, with the sight
Of simple seeing, without reflection. We seek
Nothing beyond reality. Within it,

Everything, the spirit's alchemicana
Included, the spirit that goes roundabout
And through included, not merely the visible,

The solid, but the movable, the moment,
The coming on of feasts and the habits of saints,
The pattern of the heavens and high, night air.

Capacities of justification, comparison, and reflection help rhetoric of inquiry to resist becoming a trap for the human sciences. Together these are its dimension of dialectics: its tools for criticism. Dialectics of inquiry not only examine but also conduct these activities in research. By justifying, comparing, and reflecting on research, this dimension in rhetoric of inquiry intends to make individual researchers and their communities self-critical in ways that will enhance their facilities for self-improvement. Among the arguments for rhetoric of inquiry made in most of the preceding chapters, this may be the most important.

Descartes, Hobbes, and other early modern foes of Aristotle turned his exaltation of dialectic into an insistence that some disembodied or even transcendental dialectic must reign supreme over the human and contextual concerns of rhetoric. Otherwise humans could never attain rationality or truth. Postmodern epistemology rejects the possibility that dialectic could escape or dominate rhetoric; and as Leff relates in a prior chapter, it challenges the Western legacy of Plato's attack on sophistic.[37] By deconstructing the antirhetorical dialectics of classical, medieval, and modern epistemologies, it reveals them to be rhetorics that sacrifice reflexivity to remain unaware of their own rhetorical limits. Thus it creates room for rhetoric of inquiry to return dialectic to contexts of rational persuasion, as Bruns may be read to argue earlier in the book.

Justification involves reasons and warrants. Reasons justify claims or judgments, and warrants justify reasons. Why accept Brown's thesis here that reason is rhetorical? Inspect the reasons provided by his survey of sociological theories and entertain other reasons, for and against his claims. What warrants those reasons? Consider their mutual consistency, their congruence with relevant evidence and other theories, their responses to probable objections. Do their tropes and topics persuade? Do their assumptions, methods, and interpretations make good sense? In the human sciences, reasons and warrants are the most familiar tests of argumentation—in principle, at any rate.

Within rhetoric, dialectic must abandon transcendental pretensions to total specification and inspection of reasons, let alone warrants. Navigating particular contexts of argumentation, dialecticians need the other resources of rhetoric to address the limitations of their situations. Lacking absolute criteria for rationality, dialecticians must mount sophisticated comparisons of occurrences and contexts.[38] These comparisons reveal the properties of reasoning through various kinds of stories, tropes, topics, and other resources of rhetoric. They highlight aspects of each situation of inquiry significant for its arguments. The comparisons also identify relevant evidence, counterarguments, and alternatives to any particular complex of reasons and warrants. These comparisons resemble the ones made among student papers by a new teacher who wants to generate just standards for grading. As an exercise in comparison, the essay at hand seeks to learn from related projects, especially in this volume. By example as well as argument, they suggest that immanent dialectics require comparisons across contexts to refine capacities to reason and warrant arguments in any particular inquiry.

Bringing the comparisons home to our own projects is the act of reflection. Stevens's poetry shares with nineteenth-century philosophies from Hegel and Marx to Kierkegaard and Nietzsche the conviction that modern epistemology suffers most through its failures of reflection. Their postmodern dialectics intend to restore capacities of reflection to our inquiries and other activities, and their means usually revolve around resurrecting rhetorical consciousness.[39] The other dimensions of rhetoric contextualize modern dialectics. Beyond the third (often deterministic or millennarian) moment of modern dialectics, encompassing rhetorics add a fourth (deconstructive) moment: thesis (position), antithesis (negation), synthesis (negation of the negation), and now also self-analysis (reflection).[40] In fact, postmodern dialectics typically present themselves as immanent yet self-critical rationalities that enable humans to comprehend surrounding conditions and amend them for the better.[41] Informed by other dimensions of rhetoric, this is precisely what dialectics of justification, comparison, and reflection in inquiry can become.

Hermeneutics

The poem is the cry of its occasion,
Part of the res itself and not about it.
The poet speaks the poem as it is,

Not as it was: part of the reverberation
Of a windy night as it is, when the marble statues
Are like newspapers blown by the wind.

Pursued apart from rhetoric, reflection in the West has sought to reach beyond self-criticism and -improvement to immutable foundations of being or knowing. These are to provide certain assumptions and methods crucial for warranting warrants, rationalizing reasons, and any other paradoxical operations necessary for our epistemic or moral welfare. Rhetorical reflection reaches assumptions and methods, even when they are regarded as substantive and procedural foundations, but it recognizes that they change through further inquiries and activities of other kinds. It considers them accordingly as conventions, though it treats conventions less as polar opposites of anything natural or inevitable than as diverse practical conceptions of how to relate to whatever might prove enduring in human experience.[42] Of late, our main name for the rhetorical study of conventions is hermeneutics.

We usually define hermeneutics as studies of texts or textuality; but the central categories of texts, contexts, and pretexts may cover vast sets of human objects and activities—encompassing anything conventional.[43] Thus hermeneutics can address how to recognize or compare assumptions and methods in diverse practices. More generally, hermeneutics can explain how to learn and create conventions, how to choose and use them, how to conserve or replace them, how to assess them from within or without, and how to suit them to diverse circumstances or changing occasions.

Consequently, dialectics of inquiry call forth hermeneutics of inquiry to extend rhetorical reflection beyond established paradigms and settled conditions of research. This agrees with Rorty's notion of hermeneutics as the study of abnormal or unfamiliar discourse:

> Abnormal discourse is what happens when someone joins in the discourse who is ignorant of these conventions or who sets them aside. . . . The product of abnormal discourse can be anything from nonsense to intellectual revolution, and there is no discipline devoted to the study of the unpredictable, or of "creativity." But hermeneutics is the study of an abnormal discourse from the point of view of some normal discourse—the attempt to make some sense of what is going on at a stage where we are still too unsure about it to describe it, and thereby to begin an epistemological account of it.[44]

Rorty argues accordingly that "we will be epistemological where we understand perfectly well what is happening but want to codify it in order to extend, or strengthen, or teach, or 'ground' it. We must be hermeneutical where we do not understand what is happening but are honest enough to admit it."[45]

Although Rorty sometimes writes as though foundations were impossible, so that quests for them must prove futile and pernicious, he and other hermeneuticists might better be taken to glimpse how foundations are communal, so that quests for them must prove ethical and political. Assumptions, methods, and other elements of rhetoric can and do found inquiries (and other activities). These foundations can never transcend human limitations—epistemic, temporal, or otherwise. To recognize that we cannot know our limitations for all circumstances simply completes the famous circle of hermeneutics by appreciating our foundations as our limits, conventional and therefore changeable though they must ultimately be.

As studies of interpretation, hermeneutics can come to terms with the ways in which successful foundations generate activities, conventions, and institutions stable and resourceful enough to earn notice as practices. Foundations are the favored pretexts that lead us to produce the texts of our lives in the contexts of our times. Practices that endure and expand within slowly changing limits become traditions that conserve themselves through the continual criticism that we call interpretation. Good traditions grow through time by "augmentation," as Hannah Arendt termed it, sustaining their authority by interpreting their texts for new contexts and pretexts.[46] As all hermeneutics should know, these interpretations are their traditions: if practices are frameworks of convention, then traditions are textures of interpretation.

Most essays in this volume could be interpreted as showing the relevance of such hermeneutics to particular practices and traditions of inquiry, but those by Rorty, Bruns, Hernadi, White, and Anderson provide especially detailed and encompassing arguments to this effect. By giving us ways to study our studies as rhetorical practices and traditions, hermeneutics of inquiry can enable and enhance the dialectics of justification, comparison, and reflection in research. By emphasizing interpretive communities, however, hermeneutics must also raise issues about the ethics and politics of research. These questions concern struggles over standards, procedures, and other institutions of inquiry. They seldom receive sustained attention in hermeneutics, where the focus is instead on how human activities are conventional. Much as dialectics of research must summon hermeneutics, so must hermeneutics of inquiry elicit ethics and politics.

Ethics

> *This endlessly elaborating poem*
> *Displays the theory of poetry,*
> *As the life of poetry. A more severe,*
>
> *More harassing master would extemporize*
> *Subtler, more urgent proof that the theory*
> *Of poetry is the theory of life,*

Textbooks on method in the social sciences usually cover ethics of inquiry with a brief concluding chapter on the rights of human subjects in research—addressing issues such as confidentiality, deception, harm, and privacy. They seldom acknowledge the manifold temptations to fraud, perhaps because modern methods and institutions of science are supposed to prevent all but occasional cases that will swiftly be detected and set aright.[47] They neglect issues of ownership, profit, and proper uses of research. They fail to contemplate the possibility that whole schools or disciplines could become subtly corrupted. But worst, they do not even recognize that the procedures and standards of disciplines are constructs of ethics.

Ethics stem from *ethos*. This was the ancient Greek name for rhetorical standing in a community precisely because it also meant—as it does still today—the atmosphere or spirit of the community, especially in particular situations. Rhetorical credibility is an ethical construct because it is an artifact of the relationships that compose communities as lasting fabrics of communication. Ethics of inquiry no more encompass only the treatment of research subjects than the procedures and standards of communities address only the standing of speakers. (But if we construe the last term broadly, then we might insist that the ethics of inquiry include the procedures and standards for relations among all those who are in any way subject to or subjects within research communities: the students, the studied, the support staff, and the bystanders affected as well.)

At the level of individuals, ethics of inquiry should pluralize yet pursue the classical ideal of the excellent rhetor: the good human who argues well. This rebuts the usual accusation that rhetoric teaches amoral skills soon put to immoral manipulations. But it provokes in turn the dismissive (not to mention sexist) remark that rhetoric of inquiry merely enjoins the researcher to become a good scholar and a gentleman, too. More than a few rhetoricians of inquiry might plead guilty as charged, but all should reply in part with questions about the qualities of scholarship encouraged by other codes of conduct in research.

At the level of institutions, ethics of inquiry should recognize every project of research as a political community, whether actual or potential. Rhetoric of inquiry needs ethics of research in the most inclusive sense so that it can resist the hermeneutical tilt toward conventionalisms that accept current procedures and standards simply because they exist. The individualism and transcendentalism of modern moralities incline them to promise continual scrutiny of conduct but to deliver institutionalized methods that soon cease to criticize themselves. To contest such relativism or conservatism, though, the need is not to debate them in the abstract. Instead it is to examine daily activities and continuing institutions. Too often they fail to meet their own standards through sheer inattention or cynicism, and then ethics of inquiry can call attention to possible needs for refining the standards and rededicating researchers to them. When departures become legion, however, ethics of inquiry must reassess the standards and processes of the community in question—and perhaps also of related communities. Then ethics of inquiry should become politics of inquiry, returning rhetoric to its beginning as a specifically political science.

Politics

The barrenness that appears is an exposing.
It is not part of what is absent, a halt
For farewells, a sad hanging on for remembrances.

It is a coming on and a coming forth.

When the foundations, the basic standards and procedures, of a research enterprise come into question, we confront the political contours and contents of the research community. Perceiving the constitutive rules of any community as subject to human decision is apt to horrify some members, elate others, and subdue still more. As a discipline, rhetoric arose under precisely such conditions. The sophists created rhetoric as a science of political action in situations ranging from tyranny to anarchy, progress to decline, and stability to upheaval. Ever attentive to constitutional and institutional circumstances, rhetoric seeks to turn our talk toward ways to improve the situations at hand. In this sense, rhetorics are politics.[48]

The textbooks on method in social science that diminish ethics of research do the same to politics of inquiry. Typically they limit political issues of scholarship to questions of government financing, secrecy, and abuses of knowledge. For other times and places, the particulars may differ, but for us politics of inquiry would address the actions and organizations involved in founding disciplines, instituting their daily standards and procedures, maintaining their boundaries, regulating their relations with one another and with other kinds of communities, initiating their members, establishing their priorities, and deciding how to manage their other concerns. As indicated by the introduction to this volume, recent treatments of inquiry often make loose comparisons between politics and researches. But politics of inquiry would develop such comparisons in the detail needed to improve the actual governance of particular researches.

From casual observation of state activities, let alone from personal experience of academic endeavors, we know far more about government and politics than the few generalizations about revolutions and communities that so far exhaust the political insights of postmodern epistemology. As a discipline, rhetoric thrives on realism about ourselves and our situations because it teaches us to inventory all our resources and use them well. Fearful that the epistemic implications of acknowledging the ethics and politics of inquiry would turn research into anarchy, modern epistemology revalued our talents for ethics and politics, turning them into the least recognized and utilized of our resources for knowledge. But with modern epistemology in disarray, and the time for rhetoric of inquiry at hand, surely the hour has come round at last for politics of inquiry as well.

Epistemics

It is not in the premise that reality
Is a solid. It may be a shade that traverses
A dust, a force that traverses a shade.

If rhetoric is epistemic, then rhetoric of inquiry involves at least these seven dimensions of postmodern epistemology. Contributions to rhetoric of inquiry are as diverse as rhetoric—and the needs of the human sciences. Each dimension is at once an activity to study in many fields, a distinct area of research, a significant activity within research, and a perspective on inquiry as an activity. Examined in detail, each nonetheless coheres as a dimension of rhetoric, leading into the others and joining with them to form a cogent approach to inquiry. Rhetoric of inquiry *is* rhetoric as epistemic, in the many ways now much needed by the human sciences. Its purpose is to let these many concerns of rhetoric provoke us to better inquiry.

NOTES

1. All epigraphs are from Wallace Stevens, "An Ordinary Evening in New Haven," *The Collected Poems of Wallace Stevens* (New York: Knopf, 1975), pp. 465–89. All this essay's poetry by Stevens is reprinted from that volume with

the publisher's permission. Let me also acknowledge invaluable help from the University of Iowa Rhetoric Seminar. There this essay succeeded so much as a provocation that I must not only thank the participants but emphasize the usual caution that responsibility for the text is mine alone.

2. See Michael Calvin McGee and John S. Nelson, "Narrative Reason in Public Argument," *Journal of Communication* 35: 4 (1985): 139–55, esp. 151–55.

3. By "human sciences," I mean mainly the humanities and social sciences. They may be individuated by institutionalized disciplines: history, language, literature, philosophy, speech, and so on as humanities; anthropology, communication, economics, geography, linguistics, political science, psychology, sociology, and the like as social sciences. Or they may be differentiated by paradigms and research programs to offer a cross-cutting conception of the human sciences in postmodern multiversities. Either way, the human sciences currently share more interests with the arts and professions than with the physical and biological sciences. Whether the evident drive of the human sciences toward more concern for the logical sciences will alter these relationships remains to be seen.

4. Nelson and McGee, "Narrative Reason in Public Argument," pp. 139–46.

5. "Postmodern multiversity" is meant to evoke the institutions and ethos of higher education in advanced industrial and politically pluralistic societies of the last half of the twentieth century. It fits the United States best, but it also suits higher academies in other countries. "Postmodern" and "modern," along with the related isms, receive strikingly different usages in various disciplines. Wallace Stevens, for example, is usually treated by literary critics as a "modernist," rather than the "postmodernist" label he could earn in my field of political theory. In essays on recent political theory, I detail and defend a special sense of "postmodern" as pertaining to political and social conditions in the last century and a half: "Political Theory as Political Rhetoric," in John S. Nelson, ed., *What Should Political Theory Be Now?* (Albany: State University of New York Press, 1983), pp. 169–240; "Stands in Politics," *Journal of Politics* 46 (1984): "Irony and Autonomy," in John S. Nelson, ed., *Tradition, Interpretation, and Science* (Albany: State University of New York Press, 1986), pp. 1–20. "Multiversity" is Clark Kerr's concept, advanced in *The Uses of the University* (New York: Harper and Row, 1963); "What We Might Learn from the Climacteric," *Daedalus* 104 (Winter 19759: 1–7. It underscores the diversity of projects that comprise institutions of higher education and research in the postmodern period. It also questions whether those projects cohere well enough to support more than undermine one another.

6. See Nelson, "Political Theory as Political Rhetoric," esp. pp. 171–204; Nelson and Allan Megill, "Rhetoric of Inquiry: Projects and Prospects," *Quarterly Journal of Speech* 72 1986): 20–37; Donald N. McCloskey, *The Rhetoric of Economics* (Madison: University of Wisconsin Press, 1985), esp. pp. 3–112.

7. On the antagonism between philosophy and rhetoric, see Chaim Perelman and Lucie Olbrechts-Tyteca, *The New Rhetoric*, trans. John Wilkinson and Purcell Weaver (Notre Dame, Ind.: University of Notre Dame Press,

John S. Nelson

1969); Paul Ricoeur, *The Rule of Metaphor,* trans. Robert Czerny, (Toronto: University of Toronto Press, 1977); Ernesto Grassi, "Can Rhetoric Provide a New Basis for Philosophizing? The Humanist Tradition, I and II," *Philosophy and Rhetoric* 11 (1978): 1–18 and 75–97. On the interdependence of analytical philosophy and the social sciences see Richard J. Bernstein, *Praxis and Action* (Philadelphia: University of Pennsylvania Press, 1971); idem, *The Restructuring of Social and Political Theory* (Philadelphia: University of Pennsylvania Press, 1976); idem, *Beyond Objectivism and Relativism* (Philadelphia: University of Pennsylvania Press, 1983).

8. See John S. Nelson, "Models, Statistics, and Other Tropes of Politics," in David Zarefsky, Malcolm O. Sillars, and Jack Rhodes, eds., *Argument in Transition* (Annandale, Va.: Speech Communication Association, 1983), pp. 213–29; McCloskey, *The Rhetoric of Economics,* pp. 138–73.

9. See Peter L. Berger and Thomas Luckmann, *The Social Construction of Reality* (Garden City, N.Y.: Doubleday, 1970); Richard H. Brown, *A Poetics for Sociology* (New York: Cambridge University Press, 1977); Clifford Geertz, *Local Knowledge* (New York: Basic Books, 1983); McCloskey, *The Rhetoric of Economics,* pp. 69–137.

10. See John S. Nelson, "Meaning and Measurement Across Paradigms," paper for the Annual Meeting of the American Political Science Association, Washington, D.C., 1977; Nelson, "Political Theory as Political Rhetoric," pp. 214–34.

11. See William T. Bluhm, *Theories of the Political System* (Englewood Cliffs, N.J.: Prentice-Hall, 1965; 2d ed., 1971).

12. Wallace Stevens, quoted in Robert Pinsky, "This Supreme Magician," *New York Times Book Review,* June 1, 1980, pp. 13 and 32–3, on p. 33.

13. Stevens, "An Ordinary Evening in New Haven," p. 471.

14. See Paul K. Feyerabend, *Against Method* (Atlantic Highlands, N.J.: Humanities Press, 1975); John G. Gunnell, *Philosophy, Science, and Political Inquiry* (Morristown, N.J.: General Learning Press, 1975); idem, *Between Philosophy and Politics* (Amherst: University of Massachusetts Press, 1986); Richard Rorty, *Philosophy and the Mirror of Nature* (Princeton, N.J.: Princeton University Press, 1979).

15. See Nelson, "Political Theory as Political Rhetoric," pp. 169–204.

16. See Annie Dillard, *Living by Fiction* (New York: Harper and Row, 1982).

17. Wallace Stevens, "Not Ideas About the Thing but the Thing Itself," p. 534.

18. Stevens, "An Ordinary Evening in New Haven," p. 470.

19. Wallace Stevens, "The Man with the Blue Guitar," pp. 165–84, on pp. 168 and 165.

20. See Robert L. Scott, "On Viewing Rhetoric as Epistemic," *Central States Speech Journal* 18 (1967): 9–16; Scott, "On Viewing Rhetoric as Epistemic: Ten Years Later," *Central States Speech Journal* 27 (1976): 257–66; Paul N. Campbell, "Poetic-Rhetorical, Philosophical, and Scientific Discourse," *Philosophy and Rhetoric* 6 (1973): 1–29; Michael C. Leff, "In Search of Ariadne's Thread: A

Review of the Recent Literature on Rhetorical Theory," *Central States Speech Journal* 29 (1978): 73–91.

21. See John S. Nelson, "Destroying Political Theory in Order to Save It," in Nelson, *Tradition, Interpretation, and Science*, pp. 281–318.

22. See Edward Said, *Beginnings* (New York: Basic Books, 1975).

23. Anatole Broyard, "Sadder Music and Stronger Poetics," *New York Times Book Review*, April 27, 1986, pp. 14–5, on p. 15.

24. See Owen Barfield: *Poetic Diction* (Middletown, Conn.: Wesleyan University Press, 1928; 3d ed., 1973); *Saving the Appearances* (New York: Harcourt, Brace and World, n.d.).

25. See Michael Polanyi: *Personal Knowledge* (New York: Harper and Row, 1958; 2d ed., 1964); *The Study of Man* (Chicago: University of Chicago Press, 1959); *Beyond Nihilism* (Cambridge: Cambridge University Press, 1960); *Science, Faith, and Society* (Chicago: University of Chicago Press, 1964); *The Tacit Dimension* (Garden City, N.Y.: Doubleday, 1966); *Knowing and Being*, ed. Marjorie Grene (Chicago: University of Chicago Press, 1969).

26. See Stephen Pepper, *World Hypotheses* (Berkeley: University of California Press, 1942).

27. See Kenneth Burke: *A Grammar of Motives* (Berkeley: University of California Press, 1945); *A Rhetoric of Motives* (Berkeley: University of California Press, 1950); *The Rhetoric of Religion* (Berkeley: University of California Press, 1961); *Language as Symbolic Action* (Berkeley: University of California Press, 1966); *The Philosophy of Literary Form* (Berkeley: University of California Press, (1941; 3d ed., 1973).

28. See Hayden White: *Metahistory* (Baltimore: Johns Hopkins University Press, 1973); *Tropics of Discourse* (Baltimore: Johns Hopkins University Press, 1978). Also see John S. Nelson: "Review Essay," *History and Theory* 14: 1 (1975): 74–91; "Tropal History and the Social Sciences," *History and Theory* 19: 4 (1980): 80–101.

29. See Max Black, *Models and Metaphors* (Ithaca, N.Y.: Cornell University Press, 1962).

30. See Mary B. Hesse, *Models and Analogies in Science* (Notre Dame, Ind.: University of Notre Dame Press, 1966); Earl R. MacCormac, *Metaphor and Myth in Science and Religion* (Durham, N.C.: Duke University Press, 1976); Nelson, "Meaning and Measurement Across Paradigms."

31. See Paul K. Feyerabend, *Against Method* (Atlantic Highlands, N.J.: Humanities Press, 1975); Nelson, "Meaning and Measurement Across Paradigms."

32. See Douglas N. Walton, *Arguer's Position* (Westport, Conn.: Greenwood Press, 1985).

33. See John S. Nelson: "Accidents, Laws, and Philosophic Flaws," *Comparative Politics* 7 (1975): 435–57; "The Ideological Connection, I–II," *Theory and Society* 4 (1977): 421–48 and 573–90; "Education for Politics," in Nelson, *What Should Political Theory Be Now?* pp. 413–78.

34. See Paul F. Kress, "Against Epistemology: Apostate Musings," *Journal of Politics* 41/42 (1979): 526–42; Gunnell, *Between Philosophy and Politics*.

35. See Nelson, "Models, Statistics, and Other Tropes of Politics," pp. 222–25; Gabriel Stolzenberg, "Can an Inquiry Into the Foundations of Mathematics Tell Us Anything Interesting About Mind?" in George A. Miller and Elizabeth Lenneberg, eds., *Psychology and Biology of Language and Thought* (New York: Academic Press, 1978), pp. 221–69; Robert M. Pirsig, *Zen and the Art of Motorcycle Maintenance* (New York: Bantam Books, 1974), pp. 298–318.

36. See Nancy S. Struever, "Topics in History," *History and Theory* 19: 4 (1980): 66–79.

37. Also see Nelson, "Political Theory as Political Rhetoric," pp. 171–204.

38. See Nelson, "Education for Politics," pp. 473–78.

39. See White, *Metahistory*, pp. 81–425; Paul de Man, *Allegories of Reading* (New Haven: Yale University Press, 1979), pp. 79–131.

40. See John S. Nelson, "Ironic Politics" (Ph.D. diss., University of North Carolina, Chapel Hill, 1977), esp. pp. 232–317; "Political Theory as Political Rhetoric," pp. 184ff.

41. See Karel Kosik, *Dialectics of the Concrete*, trans. Karel Kovanda and James Schmidt (Boston: D. Reidel, 1976); Ben Agger, "Dialectical Sensibility, I–II," *Canadian Journal of Political and Social Theory* 1 (1977): 1–30 and 47–57. Also see David Bloor, "The Dialectics of Metaphor," *Inquiry* 14 (1971): 430–44; Paolo Valesio, *Novantiqua* (Bloomington: Indiana University Press, 1980), pp. 61–144.

42. See Stanley Cavell, *The Claim of Reason* (New York: Oxford University Press, 1978), pp. 86–125.

43. See Paul Ricoeur, "The Model of the Text: Meaningful Action Considered as a Text," *Social Research* 38 (1971): 529–62; *Interpretation Theory* (Fort Worth: Texas Christian University Press, 1976).

44. Rorty, *Philosophy and the Mirror of Nature*, pp. 320–1.

45. Ibid., p. 321.

46. See Hannah Arendt, *On Revolution* (New York: Viking Press, 1963), pp. 179–215.

47. See William Broad and Nicholas Wade, *Betrayers of the Truth* (New York: Simon and Schuster, 1982).

48. See Nelson, "Political Theory as Political Rhetoric," pp. 204–40.

INDEX

INDEX

Academia, 166. *See also* Politics, academic

Action theory, 203

Adherence, 390

Adorno, Theodor, 194

Advocacy, 355

Agreement, 24; unforced, 42, 46, 48, 49

Allegory: hermeneutical concept of, 248–51

Altizer, Thomas J. J., 291

Anderson, Charles W., 410, 423, 427

Anderson, R. C., 151–52

Angluin, Dana, 60

Ankersmit, F. R.: his *Narrative Logic*, 225

Anthropologic writing: on death, 96–103; preserving differences in, 107*n*3; language in, 109*n*12; Misia Landau, 123*n*6. *See also* Ethnography, rhetoric of

Anthropology, 331, 332, 336. *See also* Geertz, Clifford

Antipositivism, 260*n*5

Antirhetoric, 392–93

Aquinas, Thomas: his *Summa Theologica*, 281–93 *passim*; Gerhard Ebeling on Aquinas' argument on *Summa Theologica*, 281–94 *passim*

Archivism, 222–23

Arendt, Hannah, 335, 427

Argument, 207–8; theory of, 14; of human scientists, 22; standards of verification, 24; in math, 67; in psychological studies, 154–55; as contextual persuasion, 209; rhetoricity in political science argument, 219–20*n*26; in history, 228–30, 232–33; kinds of in practical pragmatic deliberation, 357–58

Aristarchus, mentioned, 69

Aristotle, 5, 111, 178, 301, 308, 341, 412, 424; his *Rhetoric*, 5, 308; against Plato's *Republic*, 264; his rhetoric, 303, 390–91. *See also* Criticism, Aristotelian

Attributional incongruities, 149

Audience, 132, 134–36, 139, 140, 155, 207, 230–32; importance of, 15; adaptation to, 20; Cicero, 20; of specialists for discourse, 30; intended,

61, 67–68; claimed for APA publications, 130; shaping communication to, 149; intended for *The Return of Martin Guerre*, 234–35; and speaker configuration, 279; of theology, 295*n*4

Augustine, 278

Austin, J. L., 240, 260*n*7

Authority: Platonic model of, 392

Aydelotte, W. O., 233

Bacon, Frances: his *Advancement of Learning*, 71; inductivism, 72, 75, 77, 83–84

Barber, Bernard, 13

Barfield, Owen, 416

Barlow, Nora: and Darwin's notebooks, 73–74

Barrell, Joseph, 112, 113, 114–15, 119

Bazerman, Charles, 75, 412, 417, 423

Beauvoir, Simone de. *See* De Beauvoir, Simone

Becker, Gary, 169

Behaviorism: assumptions, 126; alliances, 135–37; world view, 137; in political science, 202; departure from received view, 202–3; practitioners, 203; critics of, 207; and political science, 211–12

Bell, Daniel V. J.: politics as talk, 209

Bentham, Jeremy, 177, 191

Berger, Peter: with Thomas Luckmann, *The Social Construction of Reality*, 13

Bergson, Henri, 178

Berkowitz, Leonard, 154

Black, Max, 13, 21, 178, 418

Blinder, Alan, 166

Booth, Wayne: his *Now Don't Try to Reason with Me*, 14; good reasons, 14; his *Modern Dogma and the Rhetoric of Assent*, 14, 181

Boring, Edwin, 139

Bracher, Karl Dietrich: his *The German Dictatorship*, 231–32

Brewster, David: his review of Comte's *Philosophie Positive*, 78

Brooks, John Landon, 84*n*5

Brown, Richard H., 410, 424

CONTRIBUTORS

Charles W. Anderson
Department of Political Science
University of Wisconsin–Madison

Charles Bazerman
Department of Literature,
Communication, and Culture
Georgia Institute of Technology

Richard Harvey Brown
Department of Sociology
University of Maryland, College Park

Gerald L. Bruns
Department of English
University of Notre Dame

John A. Campbell
Department of Communication
University of Washington

Donal E. Carlston
Psychology Sciences
Purdue University

Philip J. Davis
Department of Mathematics
Brown University

Jean Bethke Elshtain
Department of Political Science
Vanderbilt University

Paul Hernadi
Departments of English and
Comparative Literature
University of California–Santa Barbara

Reuben Hersh
Mathematics and Statistics
University of New Mexico

Arjo Klamer
Department of Economics
George Washington University

David E. Klemm
School of Religion
University of Iowa

Misia Landau
Department of Anthropology
Boston University

Michael C. Leff
Department of Communication Studies
Northwestern University

John Lyne
Department of Communication Studies
University of Iowa

Donald N. McCloskey
Departments of Economics and History
University of Iowa

Michael Calvin McGee
Department of Communication Studies
University of Iowa

Allan Megill
Corcoran Department of History
University of Virginia

John S. Nelson
Department of Political Science
University of Iowa

Richard Rorty
University Professor of Humanities
University of Virginia

Renato Rosaldo
Department of Anthropology
Stanford University

Michael J. Shapiro
Department of Political Science
University of Hawaii

James Boyd White
Law, English, and Classics
University of Michigan

Rhetoric of the Human Sciences

John Lyne, Donald N. McCloskey, and John S. Nelson
General Editors
